CJ Lim

INHABITABLE INFRASTRUCTURES:
Science fiction or urban future?

Routledge
Taylor & Francis Group
NEW YORK AND LONDON

INHABITABLE INFRASTRUCTURES:
Science fiction or urban future?

In Memory of Zaha Hadid

First published 2017
by Routledge
711 Third Avenue, New York, NY 10017

and by Routledge
2 Park Square, Milton Park, Abingdon, Oxon, OX14 4RN

Routledge is an imprint of the Taylor & Francis Group, an informa business

© 2017 CJ Lim / Studio 8 Architects

The right of CJ Lim to be identified as author of this work has been asserted by him in accordance with sections 77 and 78 of the Copyright, Designs and Patents Act 1988.

All rights reserved. No part of this book may be reprinted or reproduced or utilised in any form or by any electronic, mechanical, or other means, now known or hereafter invented, including photocopying and recording, or in any information storage or retrieval system, without permission in writing from the publishers.

Trademark notice: Product or corporate names may be trademarks or registered trademarks, and are used only for identification and explanation without intent to infringe.

British Library Cataloguing-in-Publication Data
A catalogue record for this book is available from the British Library

Library of Congress Cataloging-in-Publication Data
Names: Lim, C. J., author.
Title: Inhabitable infrastructures : science fiction or urban future / CJ Lim.
Description: New York, NY : Routledge, 2017. | Includes index.
Identifiers: LCCN 2017011238| ISBN 9781138119666 (hardback) | ISBN 9781138119673 (pbk.)
Subjects: LCSH: Sustainable urban development. | City planning--Environmental aspects. | City planning--Climatic factors. | Cities and towns--Forecasting.
Classification: LCC HT241 .L55 2017 | DDC 307.1/216--dc23
LC record available at https://lccn.loc.gov/2017011238

ISBN: 978-1-138-11966-6 (hbk)
ISBN: 978-1-138-11967-3 (pbk)
ISBN: 978-1-315-65220-7 (ebk)

Typeset in DIN
by Studio 8 Architects

Publisher's Note: This book has been prepared from camera-ready copy provided by the author.

Printed in the United Kingdom
by Henry Ling Limited

Contents

Preface — 7

Climate Change and the City — 9

Science Fiction: The imagination sourcebook — 19

Science Fiction or Urban Future? — 47

The City as a Collection of Infrastructures — 61

To Protect — 79

urban future i — London Is Flooding? — 107
urban future ii — Swine Under the Sheltering Skies — 131
urban future iii — The City of Frozen Spires — 151

To Provide — 165

urban future iv — Twenty Thousand Fish Above the Sea — 193
urban future v — The City of a Thousand Lakes — 211
urban future vi — The Forest: An infrastructure for urban resilience — 227
urban future vii — Perfection — 237

To Participate — 251

urban future viii — Corporate Republic: The search for utopia — 279

Research and Reproduction Credits — 298

Index — 300

6

Preface

Climate change is a reality. Changes in solar irradiance and other natural factors, together with human activities such as the conversion of land and the burning of fossil fuel, have severely affected the environment. Increases in global temperature have caused sea levels to rise at an accelerating pace, changing patterns and quantities of precipitation, and the probable expansion of subtropical deserts. According to the United Nations Intergovernmental Panel on Climate Change (IPCC), the greatest threat from climate change is the profound manner in which it could impact upon every aspect of our lives, from community security to foreign policy. Local to global impact assessments, efforts toward risk management and adaptation of cities for climate change are continuing.

However, a relatively unstudied area is that of climate change-related design and planning opportunities beyond single-use adaptation. The sustainability discourse of the built environment has to date centered around meeting the energy demands of a rapidly expanding urban population through the design of discrete low-energy buildings. 'Inhabitable Infrastructures' focuses instead on the potential of large-scale interventions that address the fundamental human requirements to protect, to provide and to participate. The book culminates in the creation of innovative multi-use infrastructures and integrated self-sustaining support systems that meet the challenges posed through climate change and overpopulation, and the reciprocal benefits of simultaneously addressing the threat and shaping cities.

The stimulus for the multi-use infrastructures derives from postulated scenarios and processes gleaned from science fiction (SF) and futurology as well as the current body of scientific knowledge regarding changing environmental impacts on cities. SF is interdisciplinary by nature, aggregates the past and present, and evaluates both lay opinions and professional strategies in an attempt to develop foresight and to map possible futures. While SF has found its way into the mainstream having been adopted by defense departments and food technology industries, it is treated with wariness in respect to architecture and planning, leading to pejorative accusations of utopianism. This has not always been the case – Ebenezer Howard's garden city, for example, was inspired by the utopian tract, 'Looking Backward: 2000–1887', written by the American lawyer, Edward Bellamy. The third biggest seller of all time when published in 1888, Bellamy's novel immediately spawned a political mass movement and several communities adopting its ideals. Letchworth Garden City and Welwyn Garden City in the UK, founded on Howard's concentric plan of open space, parkland and radial boulevards that carefully integrated housing, agriculture and industry, remain two recognized realizations of utopia in existence.

Eight locations – London, Nuuk, Copenhagen, Malé, Gaochun, Maribor, Melbourne, and the equator – have been identified as case studies to establish hypotheses and strategies for the employment of new forms, to provide a functional range of economic, cultural, social and political factors, and to represent regions facing climate change of different degrees of severity. The speculative and polemic visions of urban futures, whether or not they are realized, are reflections of the society in which they are imagined and have a powerful influence on the public consciousness. They aspire to transform socio-economic relations, reassure community security, and ultimately promote a new paradigm for urban living. JG Ballard has written that the psychological realm of SF is most valuable in its predictive function, and in projecting emotions into the future.

8

Climate Change and the City

'Cities are particularly vulnerable in that they are immobile. As such, infrastructure, the historic sense of place, and rootedness of residents are critical attributes of cites. These strengths of place can, however, become liabilities if the local ecosystems are unable to adapt to the climate-induced changes. Climate change poses serious threats to urban infrastructure, quality of life, and entire urban systems. Not only poor countries, but also rich ones will increasingly be affected by anomalous climate events and trends.'
— The World Bank, 'Cities and Climate Change', 2010

According to the UN Habitat Global Report of Human Settlement 2011, there could be as many as 200 million climate change-displaced people by 2050.[1] Today, more than half of the world's population is now living in urban centers, and this is anticipated to increase to two-thirds within the next few decades. Of those numbers, half the population again lives within 60 kilometers of the sea, as three-quarters of all large cities are located on the coast.[2] The UN estimates that there are 3,351 cities in low elevation coastal zones around the world; many of these cities also happen to be in developing regions.[3] By 2070, the population at risk from sea flooding could rise to 150 million people.[4] For the communities, global climate change is a threat to survival; in particular, rising temperatures and changing patterns of precipitation are affecting the availability of food (including crops and livestock) and potable water, leading to more hunger, increased volatility in food prices, and heightened regional tensions, affecting international stability and security. An increased frequency of extreme weather events adversely affects human health, disrupts the flow of natural resources and commodities, and threatens global infrastructure.

Mombasa, with over 700,000 inhabitants, is Kenya's second largest city. The largest seaport in East Africa, it serves Kenya and many landlocked countries and the north of Tanzania. The city faces both direct and indirect consequences of climate change, from droughts and strong cyclones to the severe annual flooding which has continued to plague the city, often with loss of life. The floods in October 2006 were particularly serious, affecting some 60,000 people in the city and the wider province. In addition, around 17% of Mombasa's area could be submerged by a sea level rise of 0.3 meters, with a larger area rendered uninhabitable or unusable for agriculture because of water logging and salt stress.[5] Sea level rise and frequent flooding have also caused the spread of climate-sensitive diseases such as cholera, affecting large numbers of communities in densely populated areas of the city. Frequent drought has lead to severe drinking water shortage and exacerbated food insecurity and malnutrition, especially among poor communities. The impacts of climate change pose serious threats to lives and livelihoods.

facing page: The Maldives, a series of low-lying archipelagos, is the flattest and lowest country in the world.

1. UN Human Settlements Programme (UN-Habitat), 'The Impacts of Climate Change Upon Urban Areas', Earthscan, London, 2011, p.85

2. Urban Environment Unit, 'Cities and Coastal Areas', United Nations Environment Programme (UNEP), 2005 [http://www.unep.org/urban_environment/issues/coastal_zones.asp], retrieved 25 March 2015

3. International Strategy for Disaster Reduction, 'World Disaster Reduction Campaign 2010-11', United Nations, 2010 [http://www.unisdr.org/files/14030_FAQscampaignpresskit.pdf], retrieved 25 March 2015

4. RJ Nicholls & S Hanson, 'Ranking of the World's Cities Most Exposed to Coastal Flooding Today and in the Future', OECD Environment Working Paper no.1, 2007 [https://www.oecd.org/env/cc/39721444.pdf], retrieved 25 March 2015

5. C Awuor, VA Orindi & AO Adwera, 'Climate Change and Coastal Cities: The case of Mombasa, Kenya', International Institute for Environment and Development (IIED), Sage Publications, vol.20, no.1, April 2008

The context for cities in developing nations is dramatically different from developed countries. Here, the challenges of adaptation to climate change mirror the deficiencies of current systems for accommodating rapid urbanization, including ineffective land use, inappropriate and poorly implemented regulatory systems, poor disaster resistance of the housing stock, ineffective infrastructure planning and funding, and poorly functioning cities.

Cities of the developed nations are better positioned to deal with the effects of global warming. They benefit from more resources, well-established practices, and much stronger governance systems. For these cities, notwithstanding the enormous costs involved, adaptation is largely a matter of incorporating new data, technology, and practices into existing planning processes, investments, and regulations.

Denmark has a coastline of more than 7,300 kilometers in length, although Copenhagen city itself is not highly vulnerable to coastal flooding today due to its high standards of defense.[6] It is not yet clear how climate change will influence the characteristics of extra-tropical cyclones; while the events could be less frequent, there could be a larger number of more intense storms. Precipitation in Copenhagen is expected to increase by 30–40% by 2100, while water levels around the city are likely to rise by 33 to 61 centimeters over the next decade.[7]

Cities have profound impact on climate change and efforts to mitigate its effects. The International Energy Agency estimated in its most recent survey that urban areas are responsible for 71% of global energy-related carbon emissions, and this percentage will grow as urbanization trends continue.[8] Copenhagen has set itself the ambitious target of becoming, by 2025, the world's first CO_2 neutral capital. The city has already lowered its environmental impact by cutting CO_2 emissions by more than 20% over the last 10 years, and ensuring 30% of its energy supply comes from carbon-neutral sources.[9] The city opts strongly for the creation of pocket parks, i.e. small green spaces which help cool the city on hot days and absorb rain on wet days. Copenhagen is making a substantial investment in wind turbine projects, which will allow citizens to invest in green energy and, by using biomass, the energy from power stations will be CO_2 neutral. There is equally a focus on the next generation to be climate-aware citizens and have the benefit of eco-infrastructures. However, most of the world's largest cities are in developing nations and have difficulty achieving global standards for clean air and other healthy environmental qualities.

The urban form of most cities has grown through piecemeal planning, development, and control under multiple, independent decision-making units which rarely consider environmental spillovers beyond their area of control to be of any concern. Apart from reducing greenhouse gas emissions, the reshaping of 21st century cities with multi-use infrastructures can innovate various means to increase surface reflectivity, lower the heat island effect, and vary impacts on water and energy consumption by introducing a new suite of sustainability trade-offs. Gordon McGranahan, Deborah Balk and Bridget Anderson, for example, have written of the effect of climate change on coastal settlements, analyzing how these settlements are changing in light of the self-reinforcing and cumulative nature of urban development and the difficulties inherent in shifting the direction of population movement.[10]

Global sea level rise projections by the Intergovernmental Panel on Climate Change (IPCC) for the 21st century vary from 20 centimeters to more than a meter. In the last century, sea levels rose by an average of 18 centimeters.[11] Rising sea levels can inundate low-lying areas, increase the rate of shoreline erosion, cause loss of coastal wetlands and saltwater intrusion, raise water tables and increase the likelihood of flooding. The combined effects of sea level rise and other climate-related factors such as storm surges could result in rapid and significant coastal changes. In addition, coasts are changing significantly for a range of other reasons such as sediment starvation and human-induced subsidence, driven by the rapidly growing population, developmental activities and urbanization. One of the major issues in most coastal countries is the continuing development pressures on coastal areas despite the existing and growing risk of flooding and damage from storm surges and wave actions.

According to the World Bank, 'Maldives Environmental Management Project' estimated 248,000 tons of solid waste was generated in the Maldives in 2007 and this figure is predicted to rise by 30% to 324,000 tons over the next five years. In addition, around 510 tons of medical waste is produced in the Maldives each year.[12] This uncontrolled disposal is a threat to the coastal, marine and coral reef ecosystems and a blemish on the pristine landscape. Poor solid waste management remains the most visible threat to the reefs; this is a grave concern because the coral reefs around the Maldives stand as the first line of defense against storms and sea level rise. At the same time the islands themselves, although in a very minute way, are a net contributor to their climate change issues; virtually all of their energy needs are provided by imported fossil fuels. Given the Least Developed Country (LDC) status of the Maldives and its small scientific and research resources, global expertise would be welcome in the development of viable sustainable solutions.

The IPCC has encouraged cities to simultaneously consider other potential impacts that climate change could have: temperature and precipitation change along with extreme weather events including droughts, flash floods, heatwaves, and wildfires are all projected to become more frequent and more intense. By 2100, global-mean temperature is predicted to rise between two and six degrees Celsius.[13] This is obviously dependent upon how global emissions are controlled; temperature rises at the lower end of these ranges can create droughts, subsequent food shortages, water scarcity, facilitate the spread of disease, and hasten the melting of the ice sheets endangering coastal regions with the subsequent sea level rise. For some regions, there will be increased flooding risk and damage to land as it is predicted that, globally, precipitation will increase. However, some areas including coastal areas will experience substantially decreased precipitation, which will lead to high levels of drought.

Investment in sustainable infrastructure often needs sunken investments, has low/medium returns, and requires a long-term investment horizon. The global tightening of credit may further discourage decision-makers and investments in green programs. The Stern Review on the Economics of Climate Change stressed that 'the benefits of strong, early action on climate change outweigh the costs'.[14]

Asia accounts for two-thirds of the world's urban population and almost three-quarters of that population live in the low elevation coastal zones, which are located less than 10 meters above sea level. The Tianjin-based National Marine Data and Information Service (NMDIS) reported that by 2050, the sea level at the Yangtze River Delta would have risen 20 to 60 centimeters.[15] The International Institute of Environment and Development (IIED) and China's State Oceanic Administration named the city of Shanghai as one of the most vulnerable, but Chinese planners are slow in reacting. Higher sea levels and sinking land

6. U Agerskov & MP Bisgaard, 'Denmark in Figures', Statistics Denmark, 2015 [http://www.dst.dk/Site/Dst/Udgivelser/GetPubFile.aspx?id=19006&sid=denmark2015], retrieved 18 March 2015

7. Environment Eco-innovation Action Plan, 'Copenhagen Plans Adaptation for Climate Change', European Commission, 2010 [https://ec.europa.eu/environment/ecoap/about-eco-innovation/policies-matters/denmark/480_en], retrieved 18 March 2015

8. C Rosenzweig, W Solecki, SA Hammer & Shagun Mehrotra, 'Cities Lead The Way in Climate Change Action', Nature, Macmillan Publishers, December 2010, vol.467, pp.909–911

9. Environment Eco-innovation Action Plan, 'Copenhagen Plans Adaptation for Climate Change', European Commission, 2010 [https://ec.europa.eu/environment/ecoap/about-eco-innovation/policies-matters/denmark/480_en], retrieved 19 March 2015

10. G McGranahan, D Balk & B Anderson, 'The Rising Tide: Assessing the risks of climate change and human settlements in low-elevation coastal zones' in 'Adapting Cities to Climate Change', J Bicknell, D Dodman & D Satterthwaite (eds.), Earthscan, London, 2009, pp.51–72

11. JA Church, R Nicholls, JE Hay & V Gornitz, 'Ice and Sea-level Change' in 'Global Outlook for Ice and Snow', United Nations Environment Programme (UNEP), 2007, chapter 6C, p.158 [http://www.unep.org/geo/geo_ice/PDF/GEO_C6_C_LowRes.pdf], retrieved 19 March 2015

12. The World Bank, 'Climate Change in the Maldives', 2010 [http://www.worldbank.org/en/news/feature/2010/04/06/climate-change-in-the-maldives], retrieved 18 March 2015

13. H Riebeek, 'How Much More Will Earth Warm?', NASA Earth Observatory, 2010 [http://earthobservatory.nasa.gov/Features/GlobalWarming/printall.php], retrieved 27 March 2015

caused by dropping water table levels complicate Shanghai's already difficult task of providing safe water supplies to its 20 million people due to salt water leaching into its aquifer. The pumping of groundwater has been exacerbated by the city's rapid urban development. The sea is steadily advancing on Shanghai, tainting its freshwater supplies as it turns coastal land and groundwater salty, slowing drainage of the area's heavily polluted flood basin and eating away at the precious delta soils that form the city's foundations. As China's financial center, Shanghai has committed to constructing billions of dollars worth of new infrastructure.

Climate change could become a sufficiently strong catalyst to bring several stakeholders and programs together within receptive cities. The World Bank and its key stakeholders, such as UNEP, UN-HABITAT and Cities Alliance, urge all agencies and businesses working on cities to use a common suite of urban metabolism indicators, such as the Global City Indicators Facility (GCIF), Greenhouse Gas Emissions Standards, Energy Sector Management Assistance Program, Urbanization Review, Eco2 Cities: Ecological Cities as Economic Cities, Cap/Trade Program, and City-Wide Carbon Finance Methodology.[16] There is also a sizeable and growing body of scientific literature on climate scenarios, both specific impact and mitigation options for urban areas. Data on predicted sea level rise, local-regional precipitation, extreme weather incidence, and warming become core factors in setting design and planning strategies. Evaluation of overall climate change should extend to the analysis of the combined impacts on urban ecosystem/landscape function, and demands on water and energy consumption.

Just as cities are crucial to global environmental mitigation efforts, they also have important roles to play in both ensuring that current infrastructure assets are protected from long-term and acute affects, and developing revolutionary new infrastructure systems fit for changing climate conditions. The effects of climate change on infrastructures are not limited to changes of weather, but include changes in behavior, demographics, population growth and economic environment. Globally, governments are now acknowledging that climate change will pose serious future security questions. Security issues of food, water and shelter provide the potential for multiple co-benefits to cities in limiting future climate change, reducing the urban heat island effect, managing waste and energy consumption, and also improving physical and social wellbeing.

By understanding the urgency of climate change as a 'security' issue, we need to recognize the importance of revolutionizing and innovating new multi-use infrastructure systems and programs; adapting to climate change is not just a matter of managing risk. No longer should the issue of climate change be considered solely in the realms of scientific policy, but as an issue that is multidisciplinary – the professions of the built environment including architects, planners and engineers have a crucial role to play. Like many scientific policies, the strongest design visions and planning policies will simultaneously address problems in multiple domains and functions, to become constructs for the practice of everyday life and transformation of the urban environments. Innovative responses and a holistic understanding of urban infrastructure design and security in cities can enhance the resilience of nations regardless of the severity of climate change impacts.

'Engrave ideas onto naked walls and build in fantasy without regard for technical difficulties. To have the gift of imagination is more important than all technology, which always adapts itself to man's creative will.'
– Walter Gropius, 'Arbeitsratfur Kunst Berlin', 1919

Gropius went on to predict that the future architect would make 'gardens out of desert' and 'pile up wonders to the sky'.[17] Scientific research groups are looking into the technical possibilities of artificial islands to address environmental issues. There are a few engineers and architects who are working on similar projects for climatic refugees such as the Belgian designer Vincent Callebaut, who has proposed the 'Lilipad' (2008), a 500,000-square-meter floating ecopolis consisting of three marinas and three mountains with a centrally located artificial lagoon. Although not design-based research, Mark Jackson and Veronica della Dora at the School of Geographical Sciences of Bristol University have also carried out studies on the social and cultural significance of artificial islands as signifiers of global progress.[18]

Atmospheric water harvesting, another potential science fiction (SF) trope that has appeared in novels such as Frank Herbert's 'Dune' (1966), has been identified as a viable mechanism for securing fresh water where rainfall is scarce. Implemented in small rural communities in arid and semi-arid regions by agencies such as Fogquest in Canada, fogwater harvesting uses mesh screens to capture fog droplets that feed via gravity into a supply network. An assessment has been carried out by Sean Graham Furey at Cranfield University, and the potential for upscaling the technology is considerable.[19]

Grimshaw Architects, designers of the Eden Centre in Cornwall, have proposed a more technologically advanced solution for atmospheric water harvesting for Santa Catalina Isthmus, a narrow stretch of land on the coast of Las Palmas in Grand Canaria. The three-kilometer long promenade with a theatre and botanic garden is cooled and irrigated by natural means, converting seawater into clean drinking water with minimum energy expenditure. A series of tall, vertical evaporation 'gills' are positioned to face towards the sea and the incoming coastal breeze. Warm seawater, taken from close to the surface, is pumped so that it trickles down these units. As the seawater evaporates, salt is left behind and clean, moist air passes through until it encounters a series of cold vertical pipes on which clean water condenses. In an effort to reproduce a closed-loop system, Grimshaw has developed an indoor tropical rainforest designed to sit on an existing landfill site. For most of the year, solar systems on the glazed roof will provide heat to maintain the hothouse. During the colder months additional heating comes from landfill biomass. The building is flanked by a number of large vertical vessels into which biodegradable waste, originally intended for the landfill, will be deposited. As the waste breaks down in these large composting units, it reaches temperatures of up to 75 degrees Celsius, heating the indoor garden. The infrastructure will not only be carbon-neutral but will also generate income by providing waste disposal services, earning up to £7 million a year by acting as a substitute for a landfill site, and as a restorative closed-loop, the resulting compost can be sold for agricultural use.[20]

The same architects are designing the 'Croton Water Treatment Plant' (2018) in New York, 32 acres of underground city infrastructure with public space above. Water informs the site planning and building design strategies – stormwater and groundwater will be collected and redistributed through a system of landscape interventions and site subtractions. Through the use of bio-swales and runnels, the water will be directed to collection ponds and filtering locations. All surface water will flow naturally, led by gravity without the use of pumps, pipes or valves. The collection ponds, or 'moats', also serve as a security boundary necessary to protect plants, eliminating the need for unsightly fencing.

14. N Stern, '2006 Stern Review on the Economics of Climate Change', HM Treasury, London, 2006, p.i

15. H Zou & C Wu, 'Rising Sea Levels Trigger Fear Over Shanghai's Future', Regional News, China Daily, 4 September 2007

16. D Hoornweg et al., 'Cities and Climate Change: An urgent agenda', The International Bank for Reconstruction and Development and The World Bank, Urban Development Series Knowledge Papers, December 2010, vol.10 [http://siteresources.worldbank.org/INTUWM/Resources/340232-1205330656272/CitiesandClimateChange.pdf], retrieved 25 March 2015

17. U Conrads (ed), M Bullock (trans), 'Programs and Manifestoes on the 20th Century Architecture', The MIT Press, Cambridge, Massachusetts, 1970, pp.46–47

18. M Jackson & V della Dora, 'Dreams So Big Only The Sea Can Hold Them: Man-made islands as anxious spaces, cultural icons, and travelling visions', Environment and Planning A, 2009, vol.41, pp.2086–2104

19. JSG Furey, 'Fogwater Harvesting for Community Water Supply', Silsoe College, Cranfield University, 1998

20. Technology Quarterly: Q3, 'Borrowing From Nature', The Economist, 2007 [http://www.economist.com/node/9719013], retrieved 25 March 2015

With respect to food and permaculture waste management systems that take advantage of synergies between farming and urban settlements, there have been a number of interesting theoretical models, most notably from Dr. Mae-Wan Ho, geneticist and director of the Institute of Science in Society.[21] Ho has been developing the 'Dream Farm 2', a model of an integrated, 'zero-emission', 'zero-waste' farm that maximizes the use of renewable energies and turns waste into food and energy resources. An implementation and extension of George Chan's Integrated Food and Waste Management System (IFWMS), Ho likens the farm to an organism, ready to grow and develop, to build up structures in a balanced way and perpetuate them. The closed cycle creates a stable, autonomous structure that is self-renewing and self-sufficient.

Key to the process is a zero-entropy or zero-waste directive that must be adhered to as far as possible. The human body tends towards this ideal, explaining why we age relatively slowly and do not spontaneously decompose. The Dream Farm becomes more productive as more life cycles are incorporated, with increasing amounts of energy and standing biomass stored within the system. Echoing the lessons of crop rotation, researchers have rediscovered that productivity and biodiversity are happy bedfellows in a sustainable system, with different life cycles reciprocally retaining and circulating energy for the whole system.

The integration of agriculture into urban environments at infrastructure scale is still in its infancy, both in terms of design and implementation. Dickson Despommier, professor at Columbia University, has developed physical proposals that can be incorporated into urban centers. The 'Vertical Farm Project' employs multi-storey indoor environments, resulting in the sustainable production of a safe and varied food supply (year-round crop production), and the eventual repair of ecosystems that have been sacrificed for horizontal farming.[22] The benefits of a hermetic environment for crop cultivation are substantial – external natural processes as confounding elements in the production of food can be eliminated since crops will be grown indoors under carefully selected and well-monitored conditions, ensuring an optimal growth rate for each species of plant and animal year round. However, such technologies may not be appropriate for economically deprived areas.

Following China's era of 'opening up' to the outside world that began in 1978, Shunde has taken advantage of its cultural position and geographical proximity to Hong Kong, Macau and Taiwan to develop into a major manufacturing center from traditional agricultural origins and was designated as a pilot city for the comprehensive reform of Guangdong in the 1990s. Studio 8 Architects proposed a large-scale waterfront infrastructure, for 11 square kilometers at Dongyi Wan East in Shunde for a public-private partnership. The scheme comprised an amphibious landscape bordering the DeSheng River, providing recreational and urban agriculture resources to a new residential quarter of approximately five square kilometers.[23]

The waterfront site lies three meters below the perimeter road that separates the main development from the DeSheng River and is subject to annual flooding. Although the floods are relatively predictable, arriving during the summer monsoon period, the waterfront is unsuitable for conventional development. This condition, however, frees up welcome opportunities for creating an innovative hybrid landscape of marina, artificial beach, cultivated land and wetland wildlife reserve. The Pearl River Delta is a vast alluvial plain containing possibly the highest density of intersecting rivers in the world, and is one of the most fertile regions in China. The climate is ideal for growing crops. By establishing the majority of the low-lying plain as agricultural land, the floods are transformed from a nuisance and potential catastrophe into a benefit by using the soil recharged with nutrients from alluvial deposits. Additionally, the floodplains support rich

climate change and the city

biodiversity – the river water supplies an instant rush of nutrients in the form of decomposing organic matter on which microorganisms flourish. The microorganisms in turn attract a sequence of predators on the food chain ruled by migratory birds such as winter swans and cranes that reward human study.

Dongyi Wan East represents a new functional hybridized infrastructure, previously considered unoccupiable. The development is sustainable, taking advantage of natural flood cycles to grow produce for the local populace. Spatially, the multi-use infrastructure is created through human occupation and a plethora of recreational spaces encourages social interaction. It is flexible and inclusive, with the allocation of multiple functions on the same space depending on the season. Industrial growth in the region has in the past eroded and damaged vital wetlands in pursuit of economic expansion, a process that needs urgent reversal to renew and clean the country's watercourses and to preserve natural wildlife habitats. Dongyi Wan East provides a model for coexistence with natural systems that benefits the community as well as the environment.

Dealing with climate change is an integral part of city planning and management which protect local quality of life, provide basic services, and assess city performance alongside community expectations. Adapting existing and implementing new multi-use infrastructure in response to climate change within urban environments raise questions over legacy or lock-in effects, economy, urban land use, governance, and environmental co-benefits to be gained in the reconfiguration of cities. The design and planning infrastructures should afford innovative systems beyond efficient adaptation and palliative reaction. Climate change offers opportunities for imaginative and innovative interventions and can become a new lens through which cities are forced to review priorities and established dogma.

following pages: The MOSE (Modulo Sperimentale Elettromeccanico), a series of large sophisticated flood barriers, can be automatically raised to isolate the Venetian lagoon from the rising Adriatic Sea.

21. MW Ho, 'Dream Farm 2 – Story So Far', Institute of Science in Society (ISIS), 2006 [http://www.i-sis.org.uk/DreamFarm2.php], retrieved 25 March 2015

22. D Despommier, 'The Vertical Farm: Reducing the impact of agriculture on ecosystem functions and services', Columbia University [http://agritecture.com/post/77701004861/the-vertical-farm-reducing-the-impact-of], retrieved 23 March 2015

23. CJ Lim & E Liu, 'Smartcities and Eco-warriors', Routledge, Oxford, 2010, pp.162–169

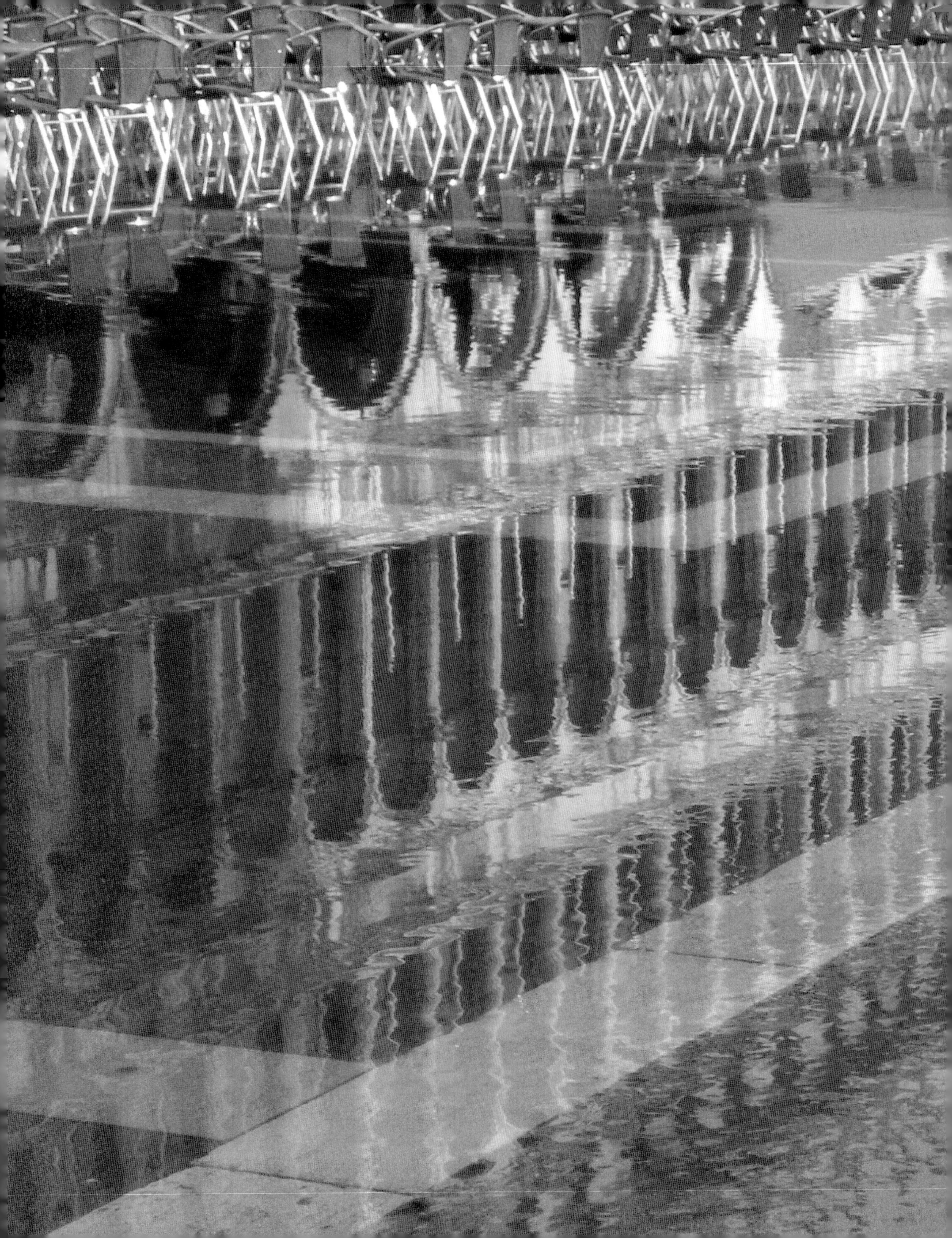

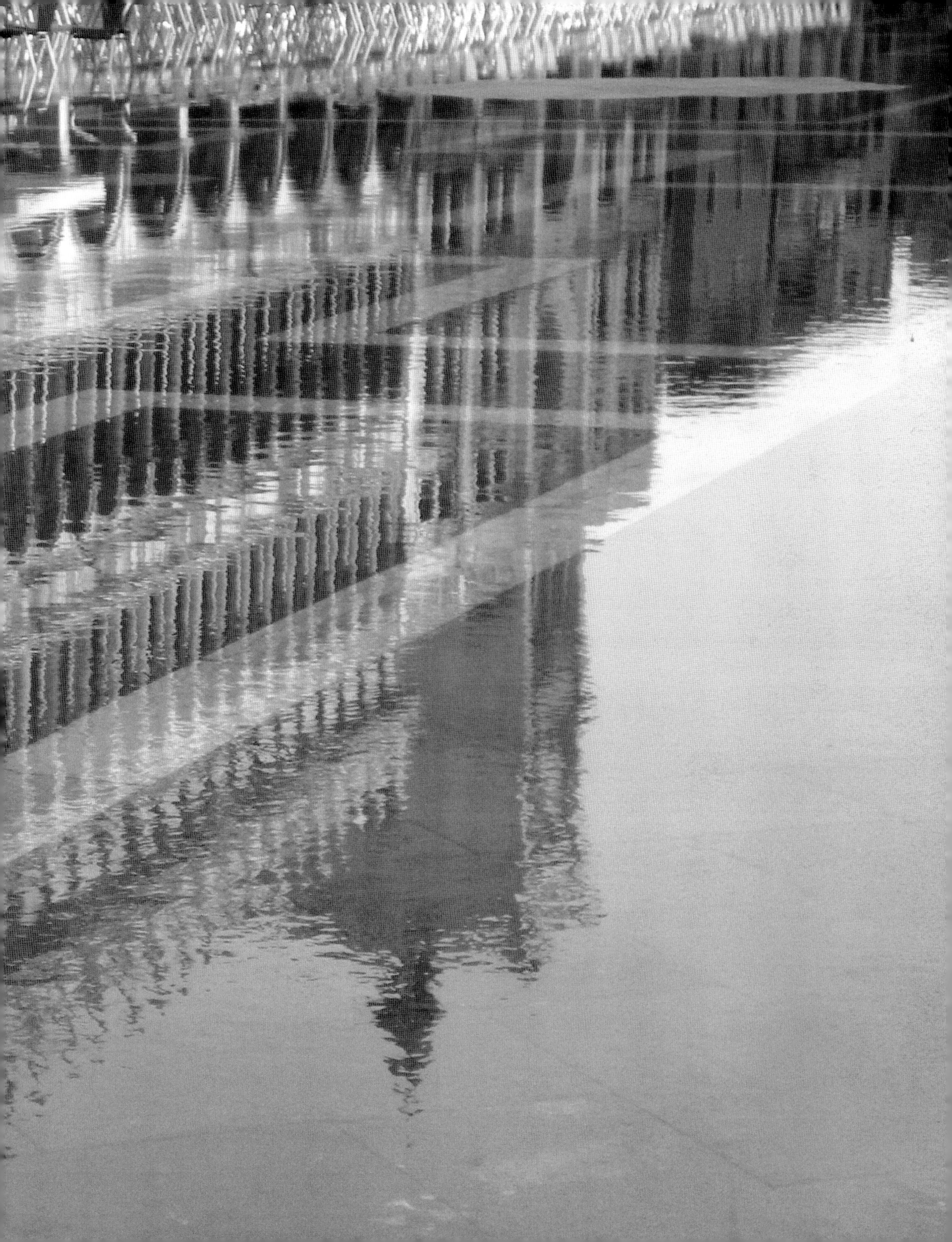

18

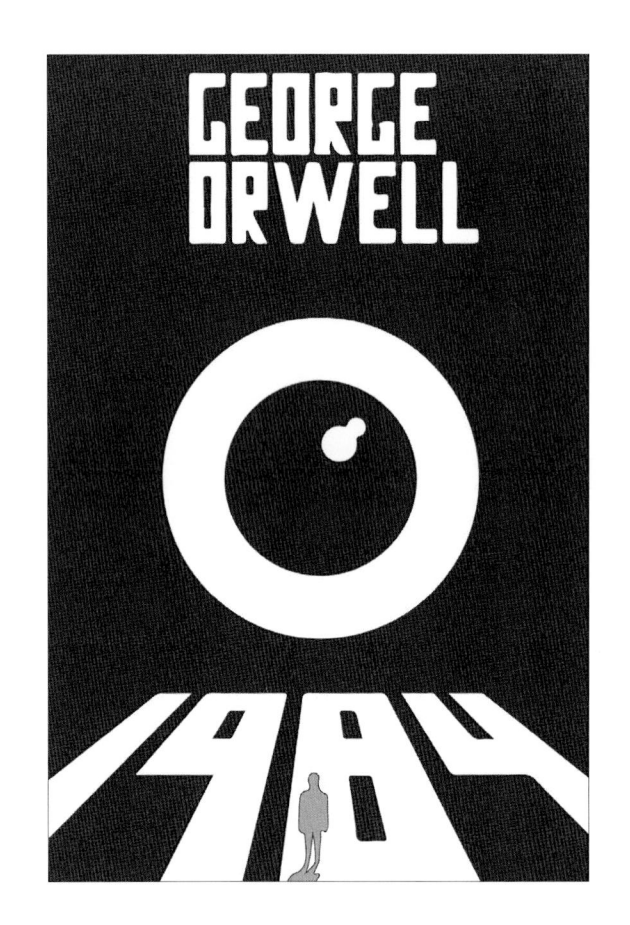

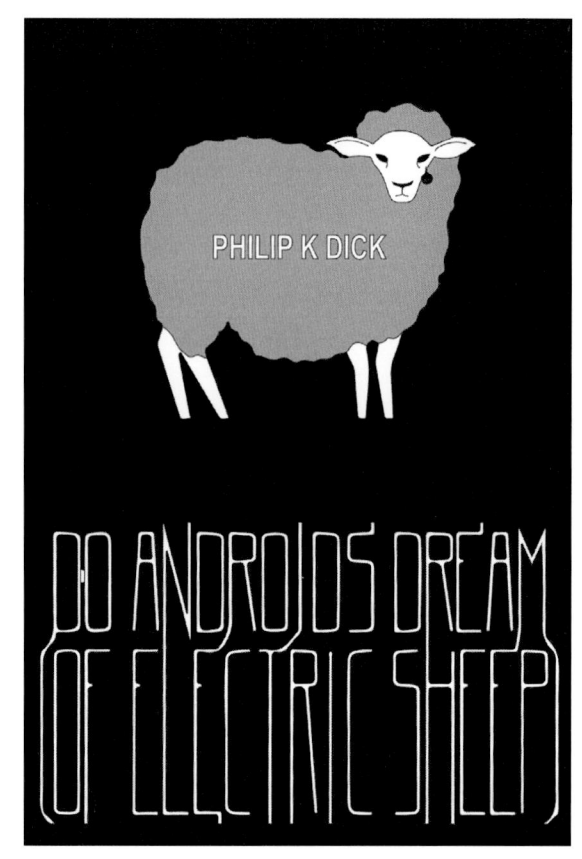

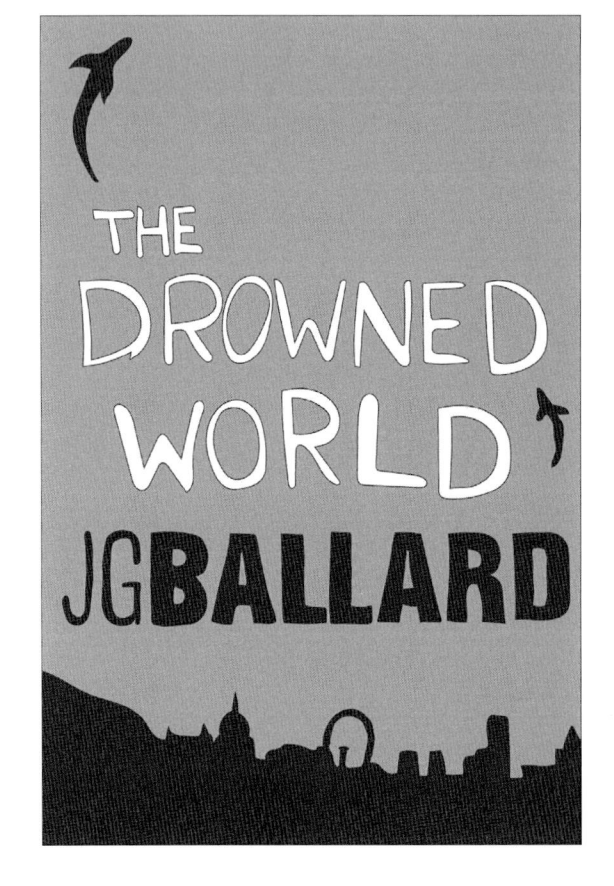

Science Fiction: The imagination sourcebook

'Everything is becoming science fiction. From the margins of an almost invisible literature has sprung the intact reality of the 20th century. What the writers of modern science fiction invent today, you and I will do tomorrow... The future is a better key to the present than the past.'
— JG Ballard, 'Fictions of Every Kind', 1971

Science fiction (SF) is prophetic, often predicting future visions that are never possible, as much as critiquing the past and present. The scenarios of retro futures and dystopian worlds utilize megacities to cite the context of a crammed earth abundant with human life. Literature and films tend to apply a polemic viewpoint, before unfolding stories of the humane throughout those worlds with the intention of questioning the nature of humanity. The SF genre might have been better described as 'speculative fiction', and need not have anything to do with 'science' at all. Instead, it is more concerned with the general principles of life and associated imagined consequences. The medium of fiction allows us to speculate as a response to a phenomena or a scientific discovery. When science gave us the first glimmers of its possibilities, there was a huge rise in fiction concerning space exploration, interplanetary travel, and extra-terrestrial life.

Imaginative SF often predates modern technology and cities, and is much more than the narrow pop-culture definition given to stories about spaceships and intergalactic battles. Key proponents of the genre have taken seeds of real-world concerns and grown whole environments from them. In 'Nineteen Eighty Four' (1949), George Orwell examines the utopic ideals of a society and reveals fear of authoritarianism as the main antagonist — a world where scientific resources can be used for all manner of reasons including the detection of thought crime. Unlike many examples of the genre, which retreated to dealing with the supernatural or made-up science, Orwell's writing exaggerates notions of surveillance, brainwashing, and total control over human actions. The work is allegorical, where future scenarios act as backdrops to conventional storylines that could easily be interchanged with, for instance, an American Spaghetti Western.

Application of SF to architecture and cities may not seem immediately obvious when dealing with prevalent issues of the day since, in many cases, it offers very little in the way of tangible immediate solutions. However, its fundamental qualities of imagining futures, both 'good' and 'bad', may well give us extremely pertinent insight into the consequences of our actions, or even provide us with the unexpected and possibly indispensable returns for taking a leap of faith.

facing page: According to Iain Banks, 'science fiction is trying to find alternative ways of looking at realities'.

A cursory inspection of the innovative concepts and issues raised in SF reveals the legitimacy and prophetic qualities of speculative writing. Perhaps one of the most celebrated works of futurology by a SF author was Arthur C Clarke's prediction of a network of satellites in geostationary orbits. The idea of satellites had been floated before, but Clarke was the first to see the possibilities for their use as relays for broadcasting and communications. In 1945, Clarke presented his ideas in 'Extra-Terrestrial Relays' – the essay was not SF but a speculation in which Clarke examined radio-relay systems, rockets and the London Television Service, and offered up an imaginative proposal 17 years before the launch of pioneering communications satellite Telstar 1.[1]

Slowly, notions derived from SF are gaining traction in academic circles – the University of Pennsylvania hosted a convention in 2013, looking at how spaces (both built and un-built) in SF texts and films help shape the relationships between humans, other living beings and their shared environments. The basic argument is that depictions of the future, that may include, but move beyond, dystopias, offer us ways to reinvent ourselves, and especially our perspectives on new environments.

The fundamental necessities of our survival and civilization have always remained the same: protection, provision of food and water, and certain community or societal participation. Each of these key themes is dealt with across the genres of SF, presenting us with projected insights and critiques of our current actions by their utopian or dystopian consequences.

SF authors speculate to conquer new territories of spatial possibilities and contribute to the cultural imagination. HG Wells pushed boundaries and launched into the skies, ventured into the oceans and burrowed into the center of the earth. JG Ballard gave us dark landscapes of dystopian desolation, and bleak squalor in colossal concrete. Ursula le Guin brings the concerns of environmentalism together with fantasy, alternate histories and multi-planetary human civilization. China Miéville, who often describes his work as 'weird fiction', takes on almost every genre of literature providing mind-bending and surreal imaginary worlds occupying liminal spaces of SF and fantasy genres, while William Gibson conjures noir cities and the extra dimensions of 'cyberspace'. Philip K Dick's works have defined a generation of SF cinema as well as literature – 'Minority Report' (2002) is based on a short story of the same title, 'We Can Remember It for You Wholesale' (1966) was the foundation for 'Total Recall' (1990), and the striking spectacle of 'Blade Runner' (1982) grew from 'Do Androids Dream of Electric Sheep?'. Connie Willis introduces us to the sociology of time travel in 'Fire Watch' (1983), 'Doomsday Book' (1993) and industries of digital manipulation in 'Remake' (1996). Based on his short story 'The Sentinel' (1951), Arthur C Clark in collaboration with Stanley Kubrick produced the haunting extra-terrestrial 'Monolith' in '2001: A Space Odyssey', and launched networks of orbital infrastructures.

TO PROTECT
'Every generation must build its own city. This constant renewal of the architectonic environment will contribute to the victory of Futurism which has already been affirmed... and for which we fight without respite against traditionalist cowardice.'
– Antonio Sant'Elia, 'Manifesto of Futurist Architecture', 1914

Scales of SF Shelter

Protection implies shelter and safety. With the task of protecting the escalating population predicted for the real world, we might draw inspiration from the large-scale architecture and multi-use inhabitable infrastructures required in the often-harsh and dense environmental conditions in SF. The integration of shelter into infrastructures is common in SF, especially in scenarios of scarcity and mega-density. Vast numbers of giant infrastructures have been brought into existence by the demands of compact living conditions. Global industrial, scientific and medical revolutions have extended our lives, population and the complexity of our needs and networks. The scale of our infrastructure is based on radical approaches to survival.

The physical scale of infrastructures in SF is often employed as a literary device, usually to enlarge the scope of the imagination and the intensity of the scenario. In many cases, large overwhelming infrastructures are used not to generate a sense of wonder or achievement, but instead to make the reader feel small, or threatened. The very first line of Aldous Huxley's 'A Brave New World' (1931) is 'A squat grey building of only thirty-four stories'. The immediate effect of the sentence is to paint a bleak image: architecturally 'squat' sounds awkward, 'grey' sounds austere, and 'only thirty-four stories' immediately conjures huge towering structures in the surroundings.

Small – In 'The Truman Show' (1998), Andrew Niccol scripted the main protagonist into the synthetic coastal 'home' of Seahaven, a giant set built under an arcology-type dome. Truman is oblivious of an outside world and is the unsuspecting star of a 30-year reality television show. He has been secretly filmed his whole life by thousands of hidden cameras, 24 hours a day, seven days a week, interacting only with actors, and falling in love with Lauren (an extra, called Sylvia in the real world).

Big – The tower in JG Ballard's 'High-Rise' (1975) is a self-contained city with schools, shops, and swimming pools interspersed amongst residential floors. The floor on which individuals reside is demarcated by class demographics, with the rich (naturally) at the top.

Really Big – Fritz Lang's 'Metropolis' (1927), presents a vast city of towering skyscrapers and multi-level streets in the sky. The film's visionary renderings of both modernity and the power of progress captured the public's imagination at that time. The wealthy occupied the pleasure gardens in the clouds, whereas deep down below ground, the city is a dark pit of clamouring, relentless and powerful machineries. Workers march in and out of drudgery akin to slavery with conditions unseen by the world above.

At around the same time that Fritz Lang was working on his epoch-making film, the architect Hugh Ferriss illustrated his ambitious aspirations of early American Modernism – three distinct chapters of 'The Metropolis of Tomorrow' (1929). Part One: 'Cities of Today' is a poetically rendered and lovingly explored portrait of American buildings and cityscapes, including the great monuments of New York City. In Part Two: 'Projected Trends', Ferriss critically distils the architectural essence of the time, romantically describing and delineating 'The Lure of the City', 'Pedestrians Over Wheel-Traffic', 'Churches Aloft', 'Apartments on Bridges', and 'Hanging Gardens' among others, as well as speculating

1. M Ashley, 'Out of This World: Science Fiction but not as you know it', The British Library, London, 2011, p.27

22

science fiction: the imagination sourcebook

the use of materials, construction technique and future technology. For Part Three: 'An Imaginary Metropolis', industry, politics, religion and power are scrutinized and re-formed as compositional elements within the charcoal utopia of Ferriss.[2] Visionary SF architects and planners have implanted in us the possibility of the future mega-city; the cities are getting denser and more complex day by day. The age of the skyscraper is still running its course and in many parts of the world, and they are getting taller and greater in quantity every day. While Ferriss' illustrations promise 'the ultimate embodiment, in structural form, of certain human values', each drawing has a dark side to its underlying reality, delineated in the gloomy color palette of a polluted and uncertain future city.

Small or Big? – In Charlie Kaufman's 'Synecdoche, New York' (2008), theatre director Caden Cotard spirals into psychological mania and builds a New York inside a warehouse, inside a bigger New York inside a bigger warehouse, ad infinitum. The play set reaches devastating scale and complexity, with actors recreating the lives of director and crew; it becomes a play within a play, within a play, ad infinitum.

Castles in the Sky

There are a number of recurring spatial tropes in SF. One such trope is the artificial island, a meme that has appeared in stories ranging from 'Gulliver's Travels' to the Bible, and to the millionaire enclave of Jules Verne's 'L'Île à hélice'. Hovering above the ground or floating on water, the infrastructure epitomizes the overcoming of nature and a utopian superiority over the worlds below.

Jonathan Swift's 'Gulliver's Travels' (1726) features a maneuverable floating island with an adamantine base in the sky, 'Laputa'. Occupied by mad scientists who often brought terrible destructions to the world below, the magnetically levitated aeronautic mechanism is 'exactly circular, its diameter over about four miles and a half, and consequently contains 10,000 acres. It is a 300-yards thick. The declivity of the upper surface, is the natural cause why all the dews and rains, which fall upon the island, are conveyed in small rivulets towards the middle, where they are emptied into four large basins, each of about half a mile in circuit.'[3] The 'Castle in the Sky' is last seen floating in orbit, with a guardian robot tending the vast 'tree of life' in the garden in Hayao Miyazaki's 1986 version of the same story.

Douglas Trumbull's 'Silent Running' (1972) features a large space freighter in orbit, also with the last remaining specimens of plant life from earth protected in large geodesic domes. With an initial intention of one day reforesting the home planet, the botanists work to study and secure the preservation of the all-but-extinct species. When the mission is called off, the protagonists jettison the domes into space, along with the robots programmed to care for the plants, rather than have them destroyed as ordered.

God was enraged with the human population and their sinful, violent and corrupt habits in 'Noah's Ark', Genesis 6-9. The prophet Noah received instruction to build a giant sea-faring infrastructure in the desert, filled it with all the animal species on earth, and was tasked to protect them from the coming flood. Noah completes the impossible feat with help from his family and divine assistance. In contrast, the floating construct of 'Waterworld' (1995) is far less of a utopian ark. Set in a post-apocalyptic future where polar icecaps have melted and the land surface of the earth is almost entirely submerged, the

facing page: The floating landscapes of Pandora in James Cameron's 'Avatar' (2009)

2. H Ferriss, 'The Metropolis of Tomorrow', Princeton Architectural Press, Princeton, 1986

3. J Swift, 'Gulliver's Travels', Jones & Company, London, 1826, chapter 3, p.22

protagonists struggle against starvation and pirates known as 'Smokers'. In place of aeronautic islands, plant life is cultivated in valuable dirt on artificial atolls built from recycled and reclaimed scrap materials from the old-world.

In the real world, there are many innovative vernacular examples of artificial floating infrastructures – the reed-bed constructs of Lake Titicaca, and Makoko, the fascinating slum neighborhood of Lagos. With one of the largest urban populations in the world, Lagos is a powerhouse in Nigeria's booming economy, driven in part by one of Africa's busiest ports. With large economic draw comes a large population, and in developing countries it almost always materializes as informal slum settlements. The journalist Tolu Ogunlesi, noted that the 19th century fishing slum Makoko looks serene – 'wooden shacks stand on stilts, as boats glide across the still water. Close-up, though, it throbs with the kind of energy that marks Lagos out and has made it a darling of urban theorists. Makoko shares with Lagos the exceptional situational inventiveness that makes the entire city tick.'[4]

The kind of urban theorists that Ogunlesi is referring to may include the architect Kunlé Adeyemi, whose practice NLÉ Works completed the seminal floating school in collaboration with the Makoko Waterfront Community in 2013. Despite the nature of informal settlements being by definition fragile and ultimately at the mercy of lawmakers, this floating infrastructure was a beacon of hope that made an emphatic political statement to maintain the 'innovative' settlement in the face of demolition by the state. The architect also has a follow-up urban design proposal to develop a much greater expanse of the lagoon as 'the impact of rapid urbanization and economic growth of cities in Africa is now common knowledge, yet it cannot be overemphasized. Particularly in coastal African cities that now experience significant increases in sea levels, rainfall and flooding... Makoko Floating School is a prototype floating structure, as a pilot project, its main aim is to generate a sustainable, ecological, alternative building system and urban water culture for the teeming population of Africa's coastal regions.'[5]

With naval engineers, architects who have explored state-of-the-art artificial island designs in recent years include the Shimizu Corporation, who have developed designs for circular islands, three kilometers in diameter, centered around a kilometer-high tower surrounded by farms and businesses. In the proposed location of the equatorial region, sunlight for energy is plentiful and typhoon impact is limited. Perhaps even more pioneering, the German architect Wolf Hilbertz has experimented with electro-deposition to design a self-assembling city from the sea called Autopia Ampere. Using photovoltaic energy, a low current passed through a mesh of wire armatures will accrete sea-based minerals to coalesce into walls of calcium carbonate, mimicking natural shell formation. In 1994, Renzo Piano's Kansai became the first airport to be constructed on an entirely artificial island, and in the 21st century, the Nakheel Corporation has developed the Dubai Palm Island Projects, featuring man-made landmasses surrounded by hemispherical reefs.

In developing nations, artificial islands have occurred serendipitously; for example, as a by-product of the Tucurui Hydropower Complex in Brazil with undesirable consequences: 'A number of displaced people, estimated to be 3,700, colonized the myriad of islands that were formed by the hilltops when the reservoir was formed. There was no infrastructure on these islands and the lack of tenure was a disincentive for further improvements. In the summer, the only water source available was the reservoir, even for drinking. The lack of sanitary infrastructure, clean drinking water and the use of smudge pots to ward off mosquitoes rendered them vulnerable to diseases such as malaria, diarrhoea and respiratory problems. In addition, these dwellers were harassed by the former owners of these lands and by loggers.'[6]

While the artificial island of SF has become a reality, its design development as an infrastructural strategy has become ever more urgent. In the wake of the Copenhagen Climate Change Conference, Pacific nations including Tuvalu and Kiribati, which are rapidly losing landmass due to erosion, are seeking global funding for the creation of floating islands to avoid forced migration and thus to protect over eight million people.

Futurism and the Inhabitable Machines

Manufacturing machines in the industrial world are infrastructural in scale. It is no surprise that Japan has traditionally been seen as the spiritual home of futurism; their car industry is renowned for precision, quality and for its armies of robotic workers. In fact, each vehicle is a sophisticated machine in its own right, and many factories are mechanical inhabitable infrastructures. The evocative photography of Edward Burtynsky and his film 'Manufactured Landscapes' (2006) featured endless repetitive horizons and showed the interchangeability of the human work force and its machine counterparts. It is especially moving to draw pictorial comparisons between the robotic assembly lines and the way new cities are manufactured in China. In the modern age, Le Corbusier stated that the house is 'a machine for living in'[7] and high-tech architects have since articulated building forms with service ducts and mechanical equipment. The Centre Georges Pompidou in Paris and the Lloyds Building in London reveal to the public that modern buildings are, in fact, colossal inhabitable machines.

A visit to a construction site would reveal the extent to which all of our buildings are wired, ducted and plumbed. Networks of cables envelope the inhabited volumes of houses and workplaces, while countless electrical switches hide behind walls and under floors. In 'Invisible Cities' (1972), Italo Calvino imagined a city entirely of pipes and plumbing: 'whether Armilla is like this because it is unfinished or because it has been demolished, I do not know. It has no walls, no ceilings, no floors: it has nothing that makes it seem a city except the water pipes that rise vertically where the houses should be and spread out horizontally where the floors should be: a forest of pipes that end in taps, showers, spouts, overflows...'[8] In South Africa, when planning new zones for informal settlements and slum development, the government practically builds Armilla – sewerage systems and toilet blocks are set-out on a grid as are points for electricity and water. The whole formal backbone of the new city is established to enable new inhabitants to add pretty much whatever they can afford. The hope lies with the very spirit of invention that can be found with the inhabitants, and their ability to adapt, rebuild and re-imagine their environment. For slums to offer social solutions for mega-density in cities, they are required to develop complex and intelligent infrastructures, both hard and soft.

Terry Gilliam, Tom Stoppard and Charles McKeown conceived an absurdly bureaucratic society in the dystopian satirical SF 'Brazil' (1985). The full reliance on procedural rules and archaic machines to process data presents a risk to society. As highlighted in the film, when a fly jammed the printer, the read-out printed 'Archibald Buttle' instead of 'Archibald Tuttle', the wrong man is incarcerated and has a fatal ending for being a suspected terrorist. The architectural backdrop to the world is tangled with mechanical service pipes, cables and ductwork, austere surfaces and vast amounts of tightly crammed repetitive storage and office space.

4. T Ogunlesi, 'Inside Makoko: Danger and ingenuity in the world's biggest floating slum', Guardian Lagos Week, The Guardian, 23 February 2016

5. NLÉ Works, 'Lagos Water Communities Project: Lagos, Nigeria 2012' [http://www.nleworks.com/case/lagos-water-communities-project/], retrieved 12 March 2016

6. EL La Rovere & FE Mendes, 'Tucuruí Hydropower Complex Brazil', The World Commission on Dams, 2000

7. L Corbusier, J Goodman (trans.), 'Toward An Architecture', The Getty Research Institute, Los Angeles, 2007, p.151

8. I Calvino, 'Thin Cities 3' in 'Invisible Cities', Vintage, London, 1997, p.49

'Slartibartfast', in Douglas Adams' 'Hitchhiker's Guide to the Galaxy' (1978), belongs to the Magrathean race and is an architect of planets. He designed Earth Mk. I and II, and the Fjords on the coast of Norway, originally devised the Blueprint of Earth, the Magrathean super computer 'Deep Thought', who found 'The Answer to the Ultimate Question of Life, The Universe, and Everything', but was unable to establish the question. Living beings are incorporated into the planet-shaped computational matrix infrastructure; effectively the whole of earth is a computer. SF blockbusters including 'Tron' (1982) and 'The Matrix' (1999) rely on the internal space of the computer to provide a platform for a variety of participation, a game as well as an illusion of reality respectively. The key part of the idea is the notion of 'space'. William Gibson created an astonishing critical vision for 'Neuromancer' (1984), and coined the phrase 'cyberspace' that is now widely used for the realm of information networks, internet and the inhabitation of virtual realities. His definition of cyberspace is 'a consensual hallucination experienced daily by billions of legitimate operators, in every nation, by children being taught mathematical concepts. A graphic representation of data abstracted from the banks of every computer in the human system. Unthinkable complexity. Lines of light ranged in the non-space of the mind, clusters and constellations of data. Like city lights, receding.'[9]

Speculative Futures – The Problems of the Unimagined
Few cities have achieved the potential of their modernist dreams or at least consequences of their shortcomings, while many visions of the future are left unfulfilled. Today, in the world of architecture and urban planning, utopian ideals are met either with incredulous admiration or lofty condescension (sometimes both), and an overview of professional periodicals of the past decade reveals a marked shift away from fantastic speculative propositions in favor of constructed reality. The floating, walking and flying propositions of Buckminster Fuller, Archigram, the Metabolists et al. have all but floated, walked or flown away. This is not so much due to narrow-mindedness on the part of our current crop of designers, but more a sign of the times. The power of speculation of the 1950s and 1960s was brought down by the tumult of global fear of starvation, poverty and endless wars. JG Ballard reflected, 'I would sum up my fear about the future in one word: boring. And that's my one fear: that everything has happened; nothing exciting or new or interesting is ever going to happen again ... the future is just going to be a vast, conforming suburb of the soul.'[10]

Just as SF can only be a doppelgänger for the present, urban visions are chained to the presiding zeitgeist; only in the aftermath of great upheaval such as World War I would a scrupulously practical man like Walter Gropius call for future architects to build wonders in desert and sky without regard for technical difficulties. Following World War II, Kenzo Tange and the Metabolist Movement recognized the ashes and devastation as an opportunity to rebuild not just buildings but cities, and even ideology and lifestyle. Tange's evaluation of architects at that moment was that they 'tend to depreciate themselves, to regard themselves as no more than ordinary citizens without the power to reform the future. I feel however, that we architects have a special duty and mission (to contribute) to the socio-cultural development of architecture and urban planning.'[11]

In the book 'Project Japan, Metabolism Talks' (2011), Rem Koolhaas and Hans-Ulrich Obrist reminded us of the influential visions of the Metabolists 'from the capsule to artificial ground, from modular growth to group form, floating cities to the joint core and forest-like megastructures; they created a host of new concepts, and new territories – on the land, on the sea, in the air – on which to build them.'[12] Across the globe, the Metabolists' visions included Tange and Kenji Ekuan's 'City for Pilgrims' (1974), a collapsible lightweight temporary city for those on Hajj in Mecca, and the floating megastructures archipelago of Kiyonori Kikutake's 'Marine City' (1958) where once an artificial housing or industrial island reaches redundancy, it can be dragged away and sunk. The Yamanashi and Shizuoka Broadcasting and Press Centres (1966/1967) have a machine-like modular design that captures the essence of heroic infrastructures within the scale of an individual building. The architecture presents the expression of an incomplete state, always ready for future growth and spatial reconfiguration, or to make connections to other buildings in the network.

The building in Shizuoka has an un-built counterpart in Arata Isozaki's 'Clusters in the Air' (1962). For the Metabolists, cities are not just 'on' the ground, they can forge artificial grounds of their own and float on the sea or in the sky. 'The Nakagin Capsule Tower' (1972) by Kisho Kurokawa is perhaps the movement's most emblematic structure. The prefabricated housing modules are bolted to a reinforced concrete central services and circulation core; the individual 'capsules' are detachable and replaceable. The building is a precursor to the high-tech style and modern prefabrication; the capsules of the Lloyds of London (1986) by Richard Rogers bear striking resemblance to those created by Kurokawa, as does the entire system of attaching replaceable parts to a primary structure.

The intensity of the vision of Tange et al. was showcased to the world at the 1970 World Expo in Osaka. Japan presented a great number of modular and structurally daring pavilions and towers, but it was the main public space 'The Festival Plaza' which provided the quintessential 'Metabolist' moment. The big roof of the plaza is effectively an inhabitable infrastructure, a hovering space frame that houses a number of plug-in capsules, including one designed by Archigram. Koolhaas and Obrist suggested that the major precedents for the Expo's 'Big Roof', and occasionally for the Metabolists in general, are works of unrealized western projects; they cited Konrad Wachsmann's aircraft hangar, Yona Friedman's 'Ville Spatiale', and Cedric Price's 'Fun Palace'.[13] Coincidentally, the spaceship design for the film 'Silent Running' was influenced by Kiyonari Kikutake's 'Landmark Tower' at the Expo, which director Douglas Trumbull had visited. There was aspiration for a future civilization, and at that time, the architecture showed the tangibility of SF, and would even spur on the collective popular imagination to further fuel the environmental movement of the 1970s. Film critic Mark Kermode, for whom 'Silent Running' is a favorite, notes that because of the origins of the story in the environmental movement and association to visionary architects, the film is a 'visually stunning and heartfelt riposte to the emotional sterility of Kubrick's '2001: A Space Odyssey'. All too often, SF cinema is dismissed as a genre of special effects. Such critical snobbery marginalises one of the medium's most extraordinary abilities – to show us things we could not possibly see elsewhere.'[14]

The future is now sold to us not in terms of decades or even years, but in months or weeks. Everyone appears to be in such a rush, driven by the latest release of an essential device or gadget, but ultimately missing the point of dreaming about the future. Perhaps it is the tangibility of these commercially lucrative futures, their achievability that makes them appealing in the short term. Diametrically opposed to the kind of vision of the Metabolists and the modernists, Japanese architecture at the beginning of the 21st century is defined predominantly by the single private house. The extremely high density and cultural homogenization of Tokyo mega-city has led to a popular culture of what may be confused as eccentricity, and means of expression cramped onto tiny sites. The works of most successful architects of the recent

9. W Gibson, 'Neuromancer', The Berkley Publishing Group, New York, 1984, p.51

10. JG Ballard, Interview (30 October 1982), Re/Search no. 8/9, 1984

11. M Jackson, 'Japan's New Architecture is Expression of Freedom', The Freelance Star, Virginia, November, 1987

12. R Koolhaas & HU Obrist, 'Project Japan: Metabolism talks', Taschen, London, 2011, p.335

13. R Koolhaas & HU Obrist, 'Project Japan: Metabolism talks', Taschen, London, 2011, p.511

14. M Kermode, 'Silent Running (BFI Film Classics)', Palgrave Macmillan, London, 2014, p.83

generation have been concerned with small, playful structures that re-imagine the use of space. However, contemporary Japanese architecture which heavily references traditional screens, integrated symbolism and appropriation of the garden as a ritual and spiritual enclave has been criticized for lack of vision – Shohei Shigematsu, partner of OMA*AMO New York, condemned it as the empty tastefulness of 'Muji-Style'.[15]

The fear of experimentation across all nations might be an outcome of years of complacency, while much of the speculative visions were cultivated in regimes of radical political goals and dangerous totalitarianism. With the severity of climate change, mass migration and global housing crises, speculative visions should embrace ambitions of SF. In developing countries with the possibility of vast capital gains, there is a greater sense of potential in their urban futures. World population is increasing at a rate of 1.14%[16] giving the earth approximately 61 years to double its population. The demographic of people living in urban areas is also predicted to increase to 70% by 2050, almost entirely due to new living paradigms in developing nations. The urban future of developing nations is a very serious concern – relentless unsustainable consumptions of natural resources can lead to inevitable major negative ramifications for the entire global community. David Adjaye, who spent 11 years documenting the capital cities of every African nation, believes an architect has to be a futurist as the world is moving so fast, and 'the extraordinary thing about architecture is that we have to work with not only the citizenship that is there but also an imagined citizenship in the future, and speak to a past… that has already come. We are in a sort of future-past-present construction.'[17]

TO PROVIDE
'No utopia can ever give satisfaction to everyone, all the time. As their material conditions improve, men raise their sights and become discontented with power and possessions that once would have seemed beyond their wildest dreams. And even when the external world has granted all it can, there still remain the searchings of the mind and the longings of the heart.'
– Arthur C Clarke, 'Childhood's End', 1953

Making Provisions
The stimulus for identifying new forms of sustainable infrastructure can derive from the works of SF and futurologists. Seeking to provide for future generations, new boundaries have to be pioneered and systems re-imagined. Mining SF, or its more respected and formal relation, futurology, for a design brief is by nature state of the art.

On sustainability, the British philosopher and SF author Olaf Stapledon anticipated the science of genetic engineering, and predicted in 'Last and First Men: A story of the near and far future' (1930) that civilization might collapse as a result of resource depletion, a concept that was ridiculed as outlandish at the time. Ironically, more than half a century later, humans are evacuated from the over-polluted and uninhabitable planetary surface in Pixar's 'WALL-E' (2008), in order to give the earth and its ecosystems time to recuperate. The film's protagonist is a trash compactor robot, specifically a 'Waste Allocation Load Lifter-Earth class' (WALL-E); it is the last functioning unit after the megacorporation that originally initiated the plan gives up hope and leaves the remainder of the human race floating in orbit. The film's second protagonist is EVE (Extra-terrestrial Vegetation Evaluator), an advanced robot sent to earth to gather evidence of revitalization, perhaps only so that the corporation can eliminate it and continue to profit from their business in space.[18] With such scenarios, can the wrongs of the world ever be corrected? In Jack Vance's 'Rumfuddle' (1976), a typical job is driving a bulldozer that shoves the detritus of industrial civilization through a portal into the oceans of a garbage world, an attempt to restore the earth to its pristineness.

SF always holds a mirror to the present, taking the notion 'What if...' as its starting point. At its heart, SF questions how humanity adapts, and no process of change threatens us more radically than what we are doing now to the natural environment we are entirely dependent upon. In HG Wells' 'A Modern Utopia' (1900), a case is constructed to show how progress in transport, agriculture and communication infrastructures will have the capability to balance-out the world's inequalities. The physical construction of infrastructures would be backed up by global standards in education, law and equality.

Infrastructure can transform society, with each era providing new opportunities. There are a number of surreal photographs readily available online of a warrior of the Maasai tribe using a mobile phone – the 'M-Pesa' scheme of East Africa is an invisible but highly powerful infrastructure. The hard infrastructure is largely immaterial, and instead of traditional banking which requires local branches in rural areas, mobile phone providers allow users to transfer credit via their service. The rural outpost need not have the security of a bank as it only provides a charging point or a place to buy a telephone; the rest is done far-away by the service provider. Concrete, tarmac and cables of the 19th and 20th centuries are nowhere in sight. Mobile phone networks and wireless internet technology define the way in which communications and social media phenomena have changed everyday life of the digital revolution.

Communications solutions company Telappliant deals largely with 'Cloud' computing which allows clients to efficiently resource computing power as a service product, rather than having to make a huge investment in ever more sophisticated technology and computing infrastructure. Many successful companies run entirely from the Cloud to minimize investments in their own hard infrastructure of network servers and backup for insurance purposes.

New Energy of Destruction
The sun has been the source of mankind's energy for millennia, and will continue to provide heat and light long after the death of our planet. Ancient cultures from across the continents worshipped the sun as god or life-giver. While our progress in science, nature and the universe has forced humanity to reassess ancient beliefs, SF offers a platform to dream.

The evil fiend, industrialist and scientific genius extracted heat and converted it into other energy forms, leaving the planet as a frozen wasteland in Geoffrey Hoyle and Professor Sir Fred Hoyle's SF novel 'The Frozen Planet of Azuron' (1982). In real science, the conversion of heat into electricity has been accomplished by a number of scientists, including the notable Lonnie Johnson's 'Thermoelectric Energy Converter'. But it was the extraordinary ability to convert a mass of atoms directly into energy that would lead the general nonscientific public to re-evaluate their views of Albert Einstein's 'Special Theory of Relativity' (1905) and 'General Theory of Relativity' (1916). His new energy was applied as nuclear warheads, weapons that wielded cataclysmic power with the bombing of Hiroshima and Nagasaki.

15. S Shigematsu, 'OMA/Progress', Barbican Art Centre [http://www.barbican.org.uk/artgallery/event-detail.asp?ID=12472], retrieved 12 March 2016

16. M Rosenberg, 'Population Growth Rates and Doubling Time', About Education, About.com, 10 June 2015 [http://geography.about.com/od/populationgeography/a/populationgrow.htm], retrieved 10 September 2014

17. D Adjaye, 'Podcast: David Adjaye on architecture and Social inclusion', The World Economic Forum Blog 'Inside the Creative Mind', 12 August 2014 [https://agenda.weforum.org/wp-content/uploads/arts-podcast-4-david-adjaye.mp3], retrieved 10 September 2014

18. A Stanton & J Reardon, 'WALL-E', Walt Disney Pictures & Pixar Animation Studios, USA, 2008

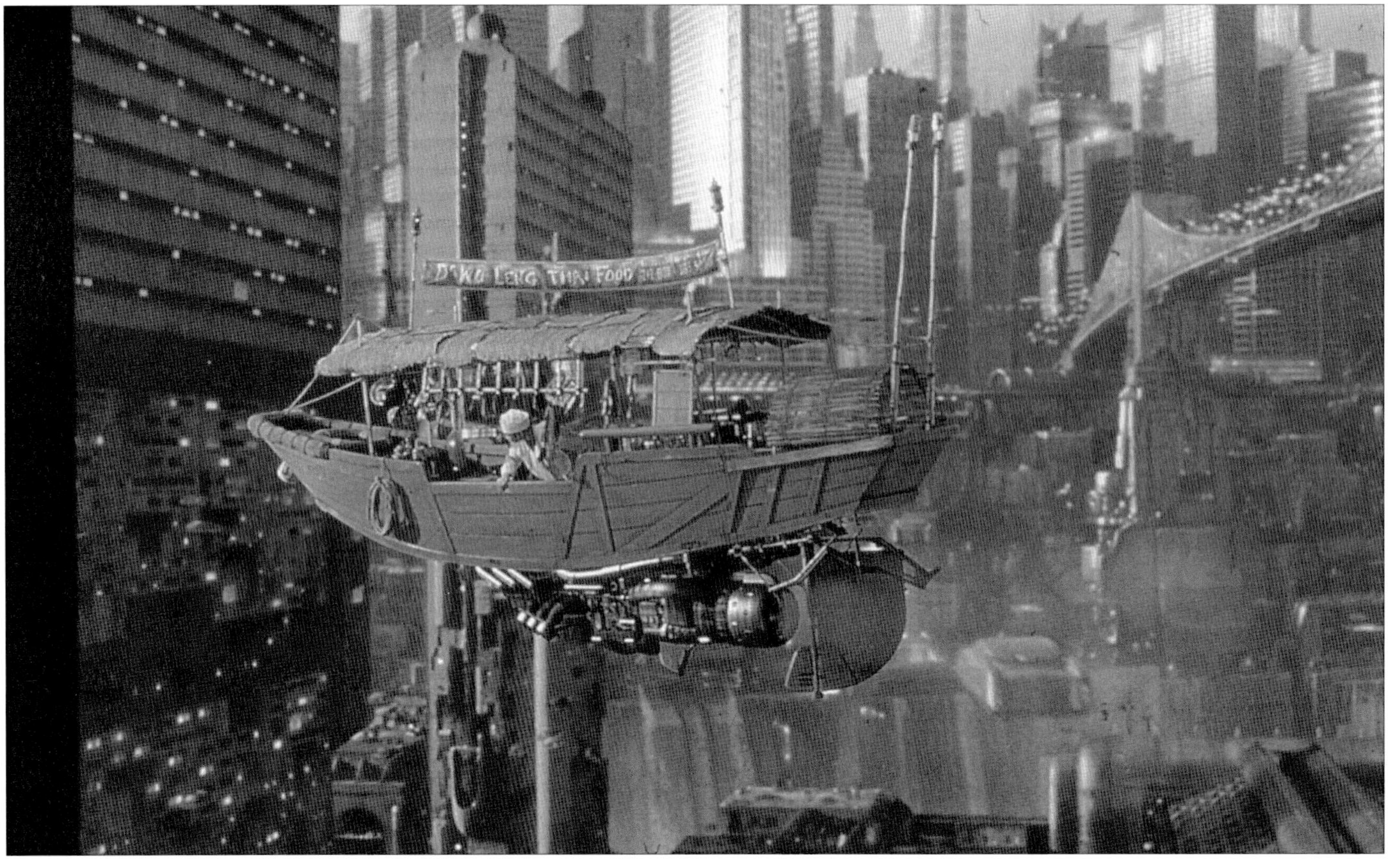

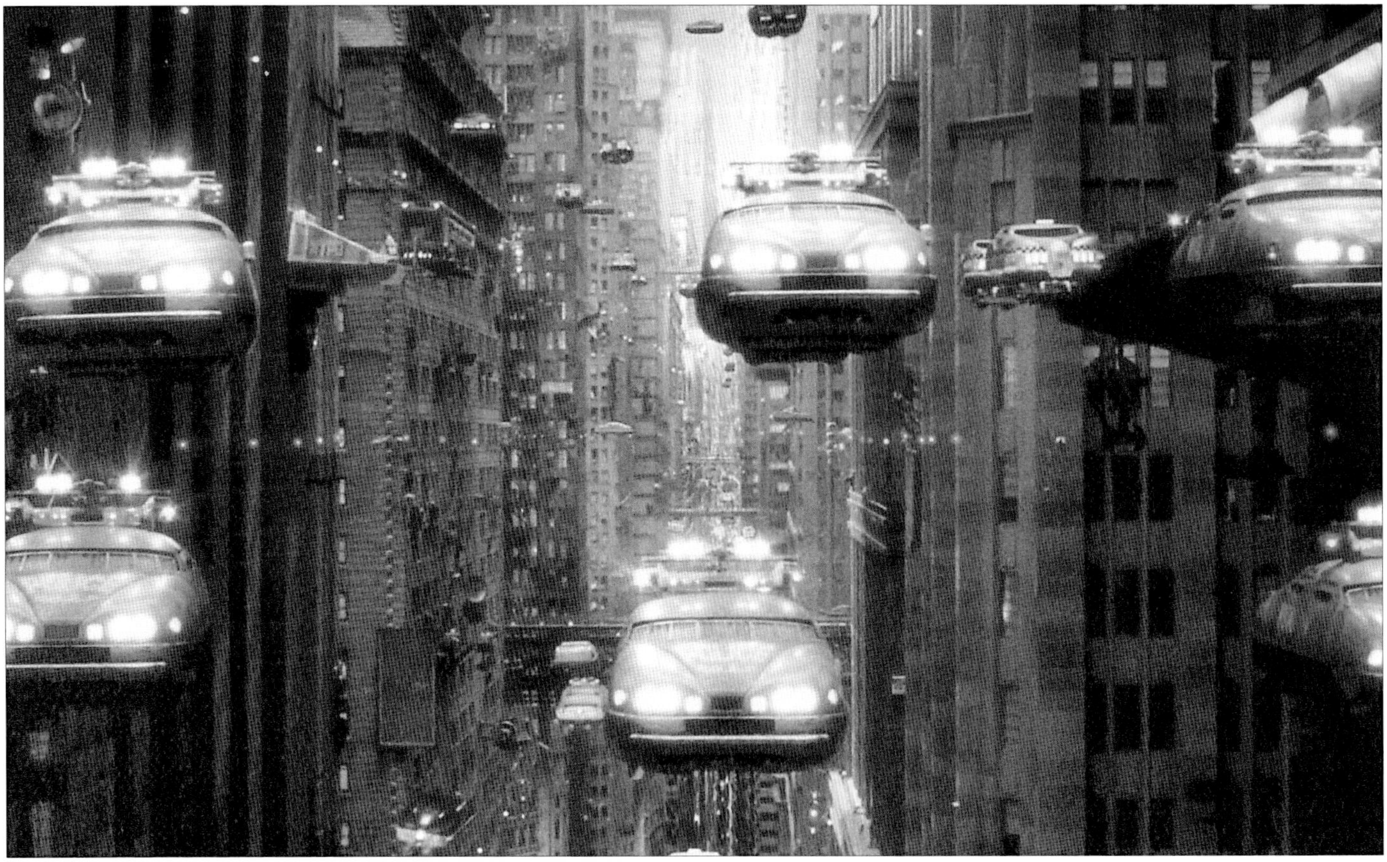

According to the SF Encyclopedia, 'the claim that SF is a realistic, extrapolative literature is often supported by the citing of successful predictions, among which atomic power and the atom bomb are usually given pride of place'.[19] As far as cultural imagination is concerned, the nuclear age opened up a veritable Pandora's Box to inspire new SF and theorization about the inexhaustible energy of the future. Simultaneously, there are fears about radiation poisoning; SF dystopias in films like 'The Terminator' (1984) have come to represent the post-apocalyptic sub-genre. In the radiation free meteorological enclave of a post-nuclear holocaust world described in 'Z for Zachariah' (1974) by Robert C. O'Brien, the teenage protagonist thinking she is the last human on earth becomes fearful when another person appears with a protective suit, thus initiating a tense relationship involving conflict, fear and care.

Theoretical physicists have almost fully explained sub-atomic and quantum behaviors. Salvador Dali was by no means a scientist, but like many was fascinated with the breakdown of the laws of physics. In Dali's 'Nuclear Mysticism' period, his surreal landscapes of the quantum world celebrate the sub-atomic particle. The reinterpretation in 'The Disintegration of the Persistence of Memory' (1954) saw one of Dali's most iconic works transformed – the clocks melt and fragment in space. In the same year, he merged scientific concepts with psychological ones and repainted the portrait of his sister as 'Young Virgin Auto-Sodomised by the Horns of Her Own Chastity'. Along with the rest of the Surrealist movement, Dali's imageries are shocking and have been hugely influential to the development of SF. The surrealists had the ability to imagine impossibilities and strangeness through their artworks, and deliver them to us with such a convincing and unnerving effect.

SF Transport Provision

Large-scale transport systems have had huge impacts on society. After World War I, there were high performance aircraft and vast zeppelins in the sky, ushering in a powerful new age of 'The Future'. Just as early steam railways and vast cruise liners had done the previous century, the giants of the sky promised an efficient and revolutionary infrastructure among the clouds. By the mid-20th century in Japan, the Shinkansen and later the Magnetic Levitation transportation embraced more than just the SF look; the technology employed allowed the trains to reach astonishing acceleration velocities on a zero friction real-world force field.

In much of the iconic image of the SF utopia, excluding those that resort to teleportation or telepathic communities, there is a quintessential image of transport. Here young attractive inhabitants go about unhurried; there are flying cars, suspended railways and all manner of streamlined and shining metal objects. The blue skies and apparently perfect health of comic book artwork are evocative of a spirit of hopefulness, wonder and technological awe. The images are of course more than slightly disingenuous, with advertising and the corporate sector always close-by telling 'little white lies'. It is only when true pioneers use imagination, business strategy and engineering functionality simultaneously that we get infrastructures like the 'Wuppertal Suspended Railway' in Germany.

Based on the idea of British civil engineer Henry Robinson Palmer, who had designed the world's first monorail and the first elevated railway, the Wuppertaler Schwebebahn was first operated in 1901, and

facing page top & bottom: Luc Besson's 'The Fifth Element' (1997) features flying cars and a ramshackle flying sampan that delivers take-out Chinese food from apartment to apartment, literally blurring the boundary between home and public space.

19. 'Nuclear Energy', The SF Encyclopedia, April 2015 [http://www.sf-encyclopedia.com/entry/nuclear_energy], retrieved 10 August 2015

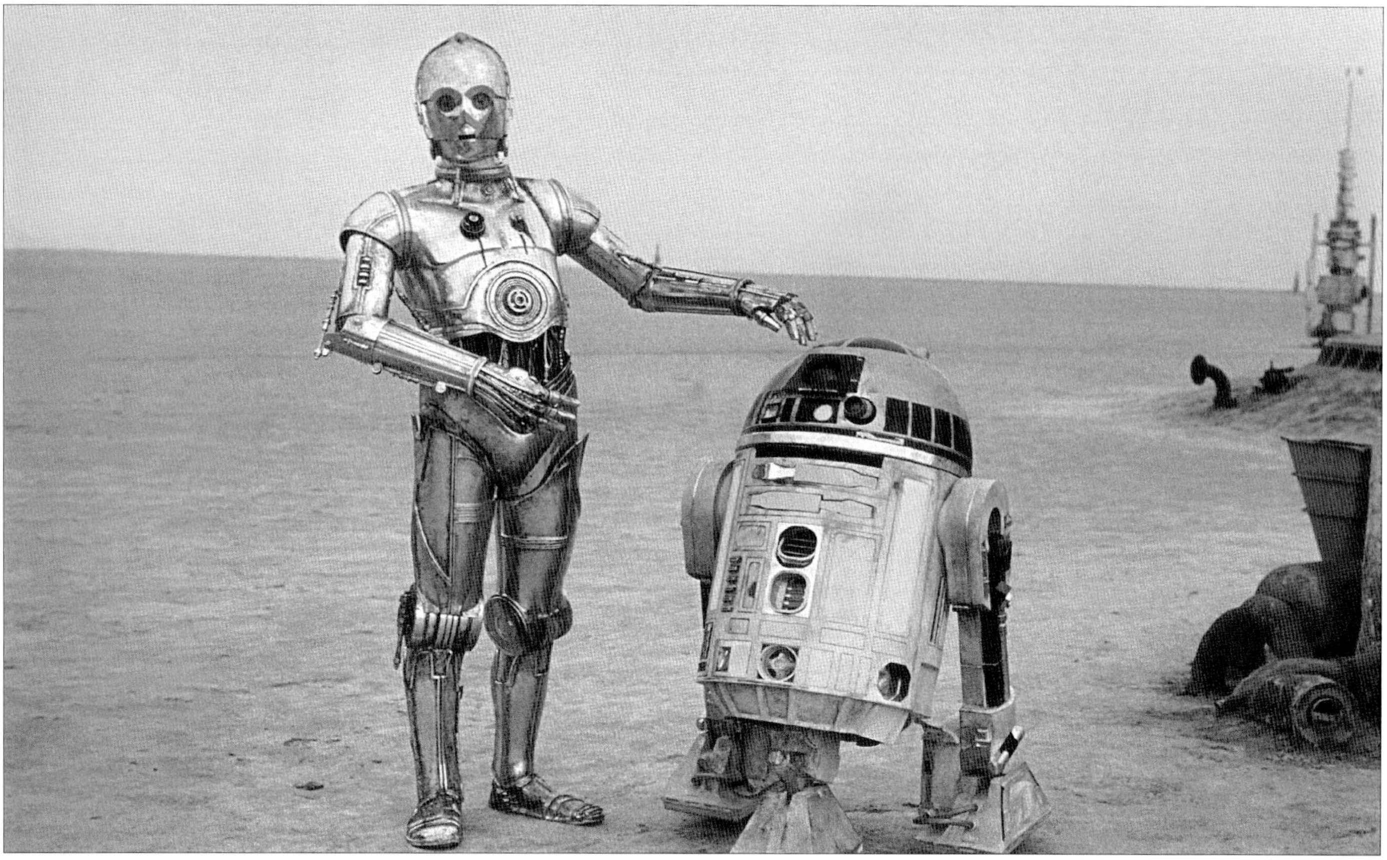

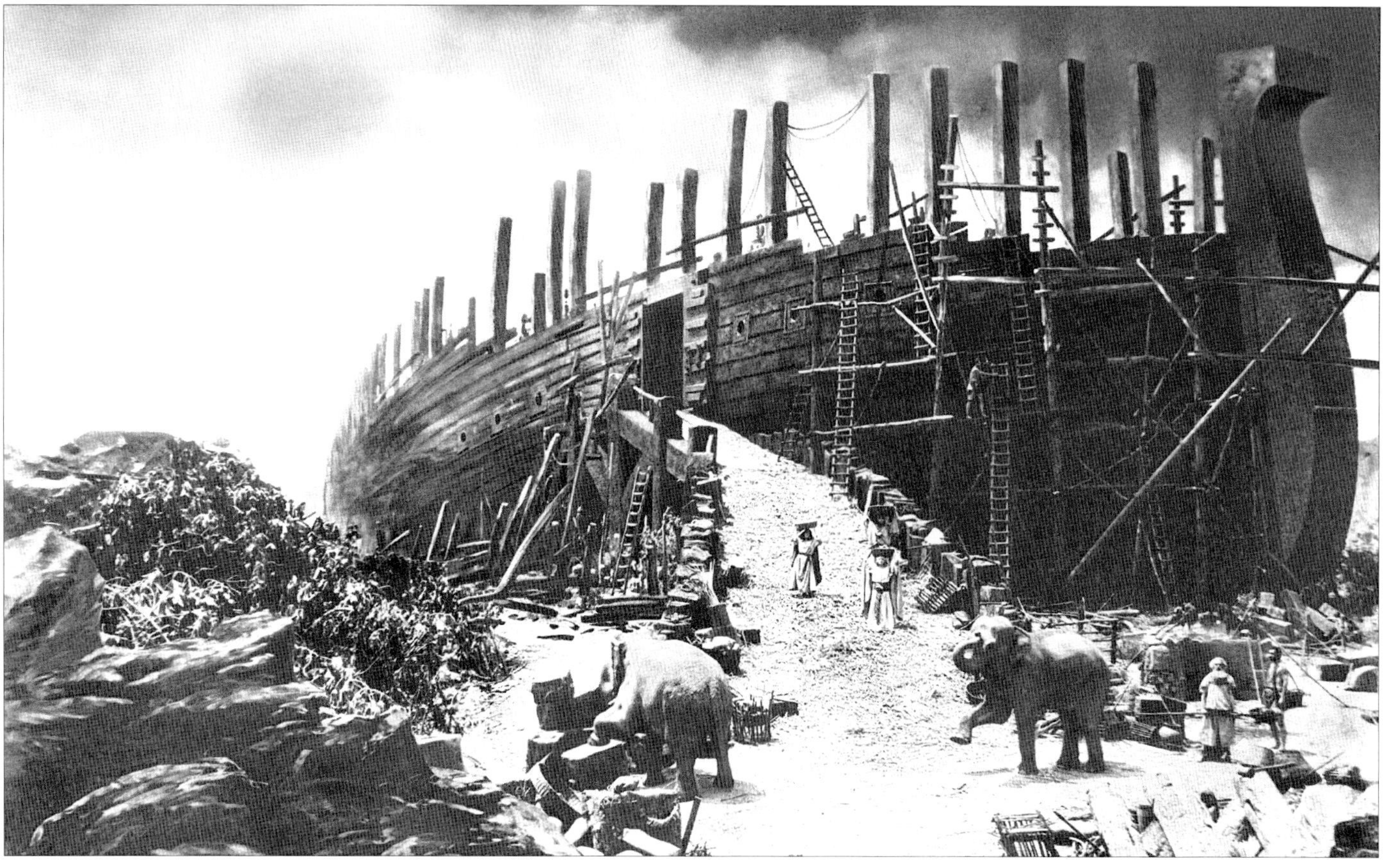

runs along a 13-kilometer track, with 20 stations.[20] The commuter transport has carriages hanging underneath a steel track 12 meters off the ground, and used to link up various mills and factories in the area to transport workers. The steel legs allow the suspended trains to follow the course of roads and much of the River Wupper. Still fully operational today, many of the stations have since been refurbished and the line carries a mix of historic and modern carriages. The infrastructure still evokes the romance of the bygone industrial era and SF.

For sociologist Saskia Sassen, 'all the major infrastructures, from sewage to electricity and broadband, should be covered by transparent walls and floors; so if you are waiting for the bus, you can actually see how the city all works and begin to get engaged'.[21] To reveal the totality of a subterranean infrastructure would be a phenomenal experience – just imagine the vast caverns and tunnels of the London Underground are instead laid over the city, with suspended carriages floating above the streets of the metropolis. It would resemble the urban scenes recognizable in SF, while presenting the inhabitants with theatrical visual impact and colossal spatial consequences. However unlike a SF graphic novel where everything on the page is about strong communication, and excitement of the imagination, the revolutionary infrastructure of London with its 402 kilometers of transport network remains politely covered under the city, taken for granted and not celebrated.[22]

Robots in Communities and Workforce
There is another form of provision that is created between science and SF – robots, androids and semi-mechanical clones originated in comic books, utopian space adventures and dystopian novels are the predicted group of intelligent beings for the near future. Bio-robotically engineered android wives, servants and animals, almost indistinguishable from their real live counterparts, are offered as incentives in Ira Levin's 'The Stepford Wives' (1972) and 'Do Androids Dream of Electric Sheep?' (1968) by Philip K. Dick. In the curiously pretty postcard town of Stepford, the men have conspired to upgrade their wives by replacing them with unusually beautiful and subservient robotic replicas. In Dick's post-apocalyptic scenario, despite being motivated by a technology-based religion, humans seek greater empathy and status by owning real live animals, not electric ones.

The word 'robot' derives from the Czech word for forced-labor, and first appeared in anthropometric form in the 1920 play 'R.U.R.' – 'Rosumovi Univerzální Roboti' (Rossum's Universal Robots) by Karel Capek.[23] Robots feature stereotypically as a domestic servant cum quasi appliance in SF. Conflicts between humans and robots are almost ubiquitous in literature that features robots, whether they are main protagonists or antagonists. In Capek's play, the robot servant class form a rebellion, and vanquish their masters. Works by Isaac Asimov such as 'I, Robot' (1950) and the novella 'Bicentennial Man' (1976), deal with conflicts around the rights and ethics that are granted to artificial intelligence. In the real world, 'Roboethics' is emerging; it takes into account the reasons for ethical building, use and treatment of artificially intelligent beings. For example, it would be considered unethical to create a robot that would have enough intelligence to cause harm to humans, but without systems of judgement or control like Victor Frankenstein's monster in 'The Modern Prometheus' (1818) by Mary Shelley.

facing page top: C-3PO and R2-D2 are robot characters in the the 'Star Wars' universe created by George Lucas.

facing page bottom: The first recorded infrastructure of migration might be Noah's Ark.

20. Wuppertal, 'Suspension Monorail' [https://www.wuppertal.de/microsite/en/tourism/schwebebahn/102370100000140310.php], retrieved 14 March 2016

21. S Sassen, 'Open Source Urbanism', 29 June 2011 [http://www.domusweb.it/en/op-ed/2011/06/29/open-source-urbanism.html], retrieved 14 March 2016

22. Transport for London, 'Facts & Figures' [https://tfl.gov.uk/corporate/about-tfl/what-we-do/london-underground/facts-and-figures], retrieved 14 March 2016

23. A Roberts, 'The History of Science Fiction', Palgrave Macmillan, New York, 2006, p.168

The humanoid robot Baymax, from Disney's 'Big Hero 6' (2014), is primarily programmed as a healthcare companion for disaster relief and has a highly durable and super-strong mechanical skeleton with an inflatable outer skin to provide a non-threatening 'huggable' appearance. The film envisions a parallel near-future where the robotics and artificial intelligence have become rapidly developed. The context, a futuristic metropolis, is exaggerated by situating the characters in a portmanteau city of San Francisco and Tokyo, 'San Fransokyo'. Today, San Francisco has a reputation as a tech-town and the American-Mecca for geek culture, while Tokyo's scale, urban culture and technology-based economy have been hailed as cutting-edge by the west for decades. Based on speculative history, the film's past-tense scenario is a re-imagination of the events following the 1906 San Francisco earthquake where Japanese immigrants, who are experts in earthquake-proof infrastructure, collaborated with local Californians to rebuild the city. At the domestic scale, the film sets are hybrid vernacular east and west architecture, and the metropolitan mega-scale makes reference to the quasi-asian, retrofitted noir-future similar to that of Ridley Scott's interpretation of 'Do Androids Dream of Electric Sheep?', the visually spectacular 'Blade Runner' (1982). Apart from the realistic strangeness of re-imagining the Golden Gate Bridge with a Torii Shinto gate, the film also indulges many counts of high-tech robotics integrated with the city, including those derived from the (in)famous vending machines of Tokyo.[24]

Robotics and automation come up against ethics in military development, a sector with an ancient and intrinsic relationship to innovation that seeks to employ them as offensive weapons. The biggest ethical question is that if robots can kill people without direct human control, should they be allowed to? According to Patrick Lin in his article 'The Ethical War Machine', 'robots are now replacing human soldiers in dull, dirty and dangerous missions, like searching tunnels and caves for terrorists, rescuing wounded soldiers, spying on enemies and even killing humans. In 2003, the USA had no ground robots in Iraq or Afghanistan; now we have over 12,000 robots on the ground and 7,000 in the air in those conflict areas. By all accounts, the Robotic Revolution is here.'[25]

Not Providing Enough
There is a huge hidden potential for resources and discoveries in Jules Verne's, 'A Journey to the Centre of the Earth' (1864). Unlike many of Verne's other works, the book draws the reader to the wonder and imagination of the unknown as well as the concept of a self-contained evolutionary system. The essence of exploration is exaggerated with the discovery of living prehistoric animals, huge insects and 12 foot high pre-historic humans. Unfortunately for our resource-hungry society, modern science seems to indicate that it is extremely unlikely that such an inner place exists. There is of course still space on our planet for new discoveries, but by and large we have a fair idea of the surface area of our world. Images taken of the earth from space can be quite moving, we feel small and vulnerable in a vast universe. We are also unsure about our foredooming political landscape in a world where resources are becoming rapidly depleted.

In 'The Black Cloud' (1957) by Professor Sir Fred Hoyle, everything starts to change after the arrival of an extra-terrestrial cloud. The literature resonates with acclaimed ethologist and evolutionary biologist Richard Dawkins, who praised the author's treatment of hard SF where impeccable science and sociology are analyzed speculatively after an initial unusual event. The enthralling and scientifically rigorous story has weather systems disrupted, extreme heat, freezing conditions, and floods resulting in massive death tolls. In the face of such extreme climate change, the world's governments struggle with their plan of action, settling for nuclear war against the cloud. The stupidity and arrogance of mankind is revealed as the politics becomes a greater threat to civilization than the cloud.[26]

The 2010 documentary 'How Much Does Your Building Weigh, Mr Foster?' reflects on Masdar City in Abu Dhabi, arguably the most ambitious social, urban and technical experiment of the 21st century. A SF city in the Arabian desert, complete with solar farm and driverless cars, Norman Foster embraces the inevitability of global climate disaster arguendo, evaluating what is being done and how we are researching and formulating possibilities for the future. Foster lamented that 'if we achieve a zero waste, zero carbon [city] then that will be a kind of miracle, the tragedy is that given the urgency of the situation, given what is a stake, which is literally our survival as a species, the thing that I find inexplicable is that there is only one Masdar. You know if there were 20 urban experiments in terms of 20 cities happening around the planet now, one would be very, very critical and say "why only 20!" – That is the shocking thing, that is unbelievable.'[27]

TO PARTICIPATE

'If you want to build a ship, don't drum up people to collect wood and don't assign them tasks and work, but rather teach them to long for the endless immensity of the sea.'
– Antoine de Saint-Exupéry, 'A Guide for Grown-Ups', 2002

Currency, Religion and Ritual

Gatherings in cities are usually caused by, or attract, commerce, or have religious or ritual explanations. The square, the marketplace or the bazaar are the kind of public spaces that make cities function and they are the reason that cities, streets and districts develop in the first place.

In the city of darkness, is the currency light? In the city of sand, is the religion water? If we take the premises of SF, which can be unbelievably harsh or extreme, we realize that the mode of trade and economy would be much different from our own. If there is scarcity, the supply of that key commodity can be seen as the alternative 'currency' of those worlds. For now, the strongest currencies of our planet are oil and grain; in due course currencies of the future will emerge. Speculation if there will be safe water is not unfounded; with population rise and pollution, water may well be the most valuable commodity there is. We already know the importance of water as the giver of life, second only to the sun. We may expect a return to infrastructure and architecture that celebrate and value the precious commodity, harking back to the days of early irrigation, aqueducts and communal bathhouses. Water is presented as the currency in Isaura, the city of a thousand wells in Italo Calvino's 'Invisible Cities' (1972).

Today when we associate currency or money with planning we might automatically think of the epitomic anecdote – Disney. Disneyland and the Experimental Communities Of Tomorrow (EPCOT) sell short-term fantasy and happiness, rather than ever planning on delivering the everlasting utopia. EPCOT was Walt Disney's unrealized vision for how participation in a collective ideology could form the basis of corporate cities. Disneyland and Disneyworld are examples of heterotopia. The timeless and endless pleasure gardens are a massive attraction for visitors, allowing the tourists to buy into an apparent utopia for a few days. The Disney Company aimed to create a built environment to fully immerse and entertain visitors in 'the happiest place on earth', the resort's motto.

24. J Julius, 'The Art of Big Hero 6', Chronicle Books, San Francisco, 2014

25. P Lin, 'The Ethical War Machine', Forbes Online, 22 June 2009 [http://www.forbes.com/2009/06/18/military-robots-ethics-opinions-contributors-artificial-intelligence-09-patrick-lin.html], retrieved 8 August 2015

26. N Lezard, 'The Black Cloud by Fred Hoyle – review', Books: Nicholas Lezard's Choice, The Guardian, 23 October 2010 [http://www.theguardian.com/books/2010/oct/23/black-cloud-fred-hoyle-review], retrieved 12 March 2016

27. N Foster, (directors) C Carcas & NL Amado, 'How Much Does Your Building Weigh, Mr Foster?', Art Commissioners & Aiete-Ariane Films, 2010

Throughout history, religion and rituals have led mankind to build some of its most ambitious infrastructures. Many of our so-called marvels of engineering and grandiose interpretations of the imagined realm have been born from slavery and dictatorship, and shaped our world to terrifying and tragic consequences. Nevertheless, the history of the pyramids has been widely disputed to this effect. In January 2010, controversial articles emerged following the discovery of worker tombs built close to the pyramids of Khufu and Khafre. Zahi Hawass, the chief archaeologist heading the excavation team, stated, 'these tombs were built beside the king's pyramid, which indicates these people were not by any means slaves'.[28] In 'His Dark Materials' (1995), Philip Pullman imagined the malevolent religious institution 'The Magisterium', composed of various courts, councils and colleges, to be the most dominant infrastructure in London.

SF can provide a place to speculate on our immortal soul and the wonders of the universe, just a couple of functions it shares with religious faiths. Across the world, the darkened infrastructures of multiplex cinema allow individuals, couples, families and friends to collectively participate, in their millions, to silently worship the superheroes of SF. Damien Walter, an author of weird fiction, argues, 'the immense respect given to SF by their fans is very close to an act of faith. We're only a few centuries and a small apocalyptic event away from isolated communities of huddled believers worshipping the gospels of Asimov, Clarke, and Le Guin. If a future society based on the eccentric thinking of SF authors seems outrageous, it's no stranger than a society founded on Genesis, Exodus and Revelations.'[29]

For SF authors, the dark side of imagination extends often to the great capacity for humans to dream-up ever more complex and cruel ways of terrorizing one another. There are still public executions in the world today, and plenty of historical source material. The gladiators of the Colosseum in Rome would contest to death in front of 80,000 spectators (a comparable capacity to that of the London 2012 Olympic Stadium); historians believe the arena could even been flooded to host naumachia / navalia proelia (mock sea-battles). Classical civilizations such as Greece and Rome were notorious for constructing colossal public infrastructures – the hippodromes, forums and circuses formed the epicenter of urban rituals, whether it be for violence, excitement or commerce.

In Suzanne Collins' 'The Hunger Games' (2008), televised violent death is a sought after form of entertainment. In the fictional 12 districts of Panem, teenagers are annually selected to fight to the death in large arenas of over a kilometer in diameter. The infrastructure, environment and obstacles of the venue are designed by the Gamemakers of the Capitol with new, innovative and exciting deathtraps unveiled every year. Varying environmental conditions within the arena range from desert to ice and from water to forest. Battle begins with all contenders standing on podiums in a ring; when given the signal, the bloody contest ensues. Participants are imprisoned by defensive infrastructures including force fields, fences and an artificial sky – there is only one winner. In the case of the '75th Games', each part of a 12 segmented arena contained a unique trap including lightning, paralysing fog and vicious beasts. Apart from the latter, the environmental traps are previews of what we can expect in reality if climate change is real. The Gamemakers also resort to interfering with the physicality of the arenas, if participants are unwilling to kill or indeed too skilful to be killed.[30]

The 'Thunderdome', from the 'Mad Max' franchise (1979–1985) precedes 'The Hunger Games' as the innovative arena. The infrastructure was intended to be the sole place of violence and dispute resolution in the desert settlement of Bartertown. Suspended contestants battle to their death inside, while spectators climb on the dome's surface to witness the bloody events, over which Tina Turner's character, the ruler Aunty Entity, ruthlessly presides. As populations continue to grow and a full-scale war over natural resources is possible, the world of Mad Max seems more and more prophetic.

We are equally guilty of desiring violent entertainment, as we crave for the consumption of a less-than-ethical, hedonistic and commercial utopia. SF regularly highlights issues of subordination and excess; Fritz Lang's 'Metropolis' divulges the pleasure gardens for the upper class fuelled from below, and the ruling inhabitants of Jonathan Swift's 'Laputa' have endless time to construct their scientific examination from their deadly flying fortress. Often these works emphasize the dystopian vision by imposing an eternal timescale to the regime. In Alice's adventures underground (later 'Alice's Adventures in Wonderland' 1865), the Mad Hatter and the March Hare are acting out a seemingly eternal tea party. Although apparently prepared for many, many guests, they usually entertain only themselves until joined by the story's protagonist. The endless novelty of the Mad Hatter's tea party is ultimately too much for 'sane' Alice and she has to leave. Elsewhere, leisure time is not afforded to the weak, but 'luckily' the underclass inhabitants of the 'Brave New World' (1931) are not burdened with intellect or genetic urges.

Endless laboring or repetitive life can be seen as a submission equal to fascism, unimaginative communism, or so called Oligarchic Capitalism. The architectural/artist group the Situationists developed techniques and manifestoes that would break the conformity of everyday life, and find unexpected and infinite creative possibilities. Constant Nieuwenhuys' 'New Babylon' (1959–74) was the group's most overt infrastructural proposal to provide the opportunity for an anti-capitalist city.

Aspiration for the Future
The 'Retro-Future' is a SF stereotype that largely refers to the generation of media and pop-culture post World War II. Not only was there a feeling of new optimism in the heart of the USA and Allied countries, which brought with it hope for a better future, but also terrible reminders of destruction, hatred and the astonishing power and fear of the brutal use of technology.

World War I is remembered in literary history as the most significant departure from a romanticized noble form of battle. The technological boom that led to the use of tanks and machine-gun artillery completely changed the tactics of previous conflicts. Between wars, the glory of great engineering and industrial revolution are transformed into the all-powerful crushing machine age as witnessed in Lang's 'Metropolis'. It is, however, the use of mankind's ultimate technological achievement and weapon on Nagasaki and Hiroshima which has cast a shadow of fear over our notion of the future and matters of technological progress. Weapons with such unimaginable power, which many powerful nations around the world are developing, are certainly of SF proportions.

There seems to be a tendency for humans to strive for improvement, to overcome hardship and to survive. It is also the case that a great number of extremely beautiful works of literature and art were born of the same conflicts. Untainted by propaganda and a contrast to the war, soldiers would find a reason to survive and see the splendour of being alive. The new spirit was endowed by the 'Baby Boomers', a product of a post-war prosperity born between 1946 and 1964. In the USA, this generation has been unusually wealthy and politically liberal in comparison to their parents. There were to be new ways of building society, new cities, ways to assimilate technology into the domestic context, and all manner of business and leisure activity. The entire generation won Time magazine's 'Man-Of-The-Year'

28. Associated Press in Cairo, 'Great Pyramid Tombs Unearth "Proof" Workers Were Not Slaves', The Guardian, 11 January 2010 [http://www.theguardian.com/world/2010/jan/11/great-pyramid-tombs-slaves-egypt], retrieved 22 October 2015

29. D Walter, 'Creation Writing: Is sci-fi a 21st-century religion?', The Guardian, Science Fiction: Damian Walter's Weird Things, 16 January 2015 [https://www.theguardian.com/books/booksblog/2015/jan/16/sci-fi-21st-century-religion-universe-hubble], retrieved 22 October 2015

30. S Collins, 'The Hunger Games', Scholastic, New York, 2008

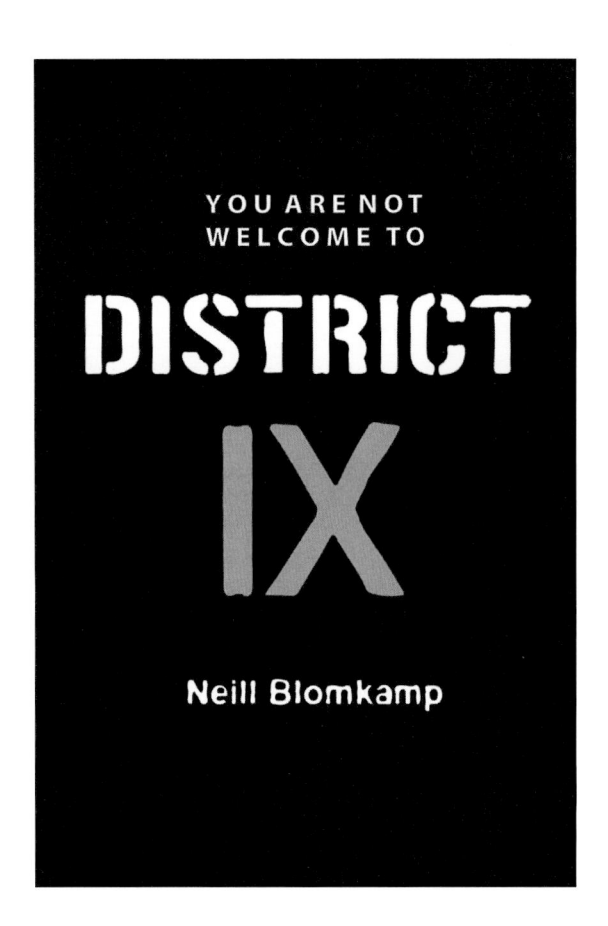

YOU ARE NOT WELCOME TO
DISTRICT IX
Neill Blomkamp

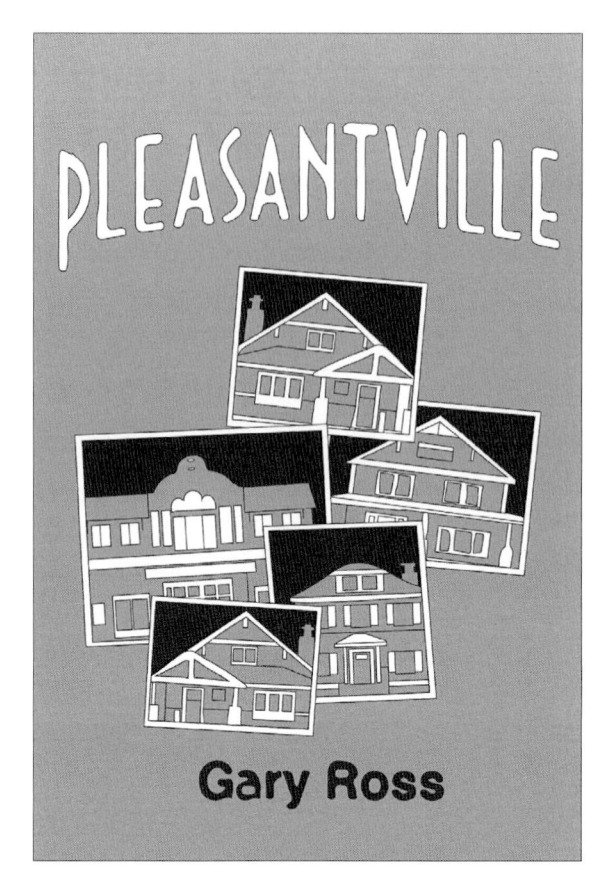

PLEASANTVILLE
Gary Ross

the **TRUMAN** show
Andrew Niccol

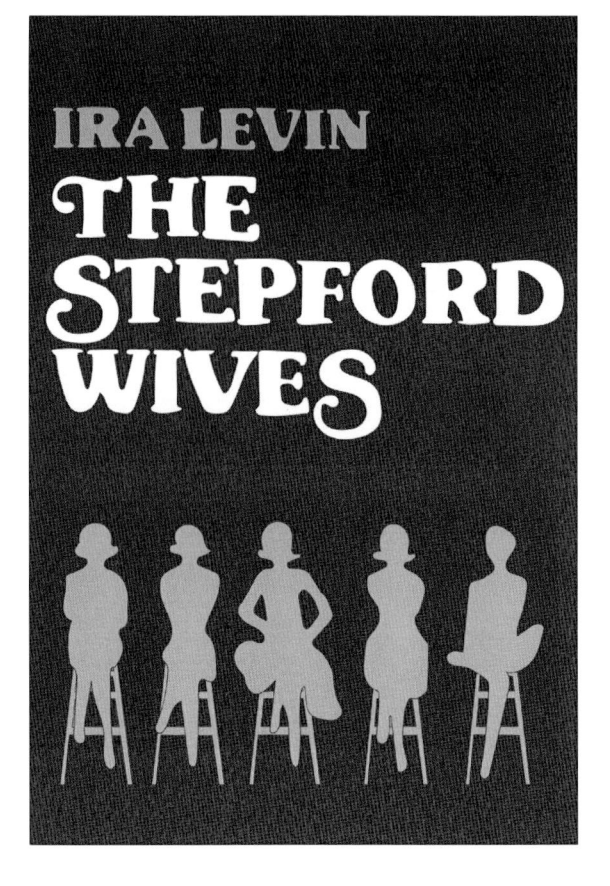

IRA LEVIN
THE STEPFORD WIVES

science fiction: the imagination sourcebook

RoboCop
Edward Neumeier
Michael Miner

Looking Backward 2000-1887
Edward Bellamy

the Blind Assassin
Margaret Atwood

William Morris
News from Nowhere

39

award in 1966; the article entitled 'The Inheritor'[31] reflected the impact young men and women were having on civilization at the time, from the counterculture of the 1960s and feminist movements and pop-culture.

The explosion of available media was influential for those living in the first half of the 20th century. Picture-houses and cinemas themselves were fantastic and novel experiences. Fashion, household appliances, cars and even houses began to acquire stylized space-age forms, with new materials providing positive connotations of mass production, modernity, plastic and hopefulness. For a time, the future became a context, with an almost religious adherence that would change the nature of human participation, and collective re-imagination of society. Themes included helpful robots, abundant resources, flying cars, and intergalactic travel – the good life fondly remembered in 'The Jetsons' (1962–1963), an American animated sitcom produced by Hanna-Barbera.

'Retro-Future' was reactionary to the speculative future influenced by the Cold War of the 1980s. Fear-inspired SF was dominant and the period was politically tense, a stark contrast to the utopian optimism of 'The Future'. Entertainment could be found in the threat, dystopia and destructive storylines which began to replace what now seemed like out-dated horror films about traditional monsters. 'Steampunk', a retro subgenre of SF, incorporated technology and retro stereotype machinery from the likes of HG Wells to exaggerate the sinister potentials.

SF is still evolving as one of the most important genres of literature. In the early 21st century, works such as Collins' massive best-sellers 'The Hunger Games' trilogy have been influential for introducing and encouraging a whole generation of young readers. Author Jennifer K Stuller, who is best known for her work on female representation in popular culture, praises the potential and 'flexible rules' of SF in their ability to empower women. Stuller argues that leading female protagonists, once they make the leap from literature to film, highlight how other genres fall so woefully short in terms of gender and sexual politics. Characters such as Katniss from 'The Hunger Games' and Rey, who from her leading role in 'Star Wars: The Force Awakens' has been described as effectively inheriting the franchise on behalf of women, are rare and significant cultural heroes; especially when, as Stuller describes, 'finding complicated female heroes in film and television has often felt as impossible as finding food in a dystopian wasteland or as daunting as winning the aforementioned Hunger Games.'[32]

Fear and Speculation – Why We Don't Participate
One possible reason SF is wary of the future is the affiliation that powerful political regimes have with the notion of progress, future and utopia. One only has to look at major 20th century powerhouses such as Soviet Russia and the Constructivist architecture of communism, or to the colossal masterplans dreamt up by Albert Speer for the National Socialist's 'Thousand Year Reich'. The events of mechanical warfare from World Wars I and II inspired, directly, the fear factor that is often associated with SF. 'Nineteen Eighty-Four' by George Orwell is a perfect example of a speculative future that took influence directly from the political atmosphere of both life in the Soviet Union and Wartime Britain.

Totalitarian regimes rely on demonstrative participation, whether that may be the Nuremberg rallies or the funerals of god-like dictators. People are required to march in line, to collectively celebrate or mourn, or to 'vote' unanimously. After the Spanish Civil War, Orwell stated in his essay 'Why I Write' (1946) that 'every line of serious work that I have written since 1936 has been written, directly or indirectly, against totalitarianism and for democratic socialism. Everyone writes of them in one guise or another.'[33] and that he believed great events had universal influence on all forms of culture.

For all the speculation, there are many issues today that scientists believe may be on the cusp of becoming severe new problems for humanity in the very near future. It is possible to see the selected examples as scripts for the SF cities of today. They may be tumultuous, paranoiac, and seething with critical interpretations; these relate to infrastructure, environments and the constructs of society.

John Brockman's book 'What Should We Be Worried About?' (2014) gathered such ideas from the best and brightest of 21st century minds. The arguments vary from the risks of natural resource related warfare and whether the human experience is becoming homogenized and oppressed even in free countries by capitalist powers, to serious worries of the possibility of maintaining life and its infrastructures without the internet or the ever greater human/nature divide.

Theoretical physicist and Harvard Professor Lisa Randall worries for the future of long-term investments into research that would deal with unexpected, difficult or abstract questions, scientific or otherwise. She lamented that 'recently I've been to three conferences where the future was a major topic of discussion. Many ideas were presented, but my colleagues and I certainly worry whether experiments will happen.'[34] Software pioneer Dave Winer's concerns resonate with Randall's – the non-commitment to dream-building, thinking big, and generally having ambition for the future of humanity suggests that we may not want to survive. 'Until a few generations ago, the human species was dealing with the following question "Do we have what it takes to survive?" We answered that question with the invention of heat, plumbing, medicine, and agriculture. Now we have the means to survive, but do we have the will?'[35]

These worries call into question the nature of what kinds of architecture, infrastructure and cities are designed today. Could a speculative approach to the investigation, analysis and design of architecture and infrastructure prove its worth in terms of safeguarding our species from our own (self-inflicted by means of climate change) demise?

Participate and Procreate
Humans are social creatures and traditionally have relied on public space, gathering and social interaction to select mates. In other words: participation leads to procreation. In SF, love stories are often hard in the making when up against the challenges or physical behavior of people in the speculative scenario. SF has many examples of specific reproduction infrastructure, and these reflect real-world concerns.

Located on the very first tier of Maslov's hierarchy of needs, sex and reproduction is one of our major activities as a species, and the first to become increasingly virtual in the 21st century. Active physical participation in flirting is not as necessary as it was in the pre-internet era; it is possible and common to use online resources to match-make or copulate. The new soft infrastructures have played a significant role in how we socialize and select sexual partners. Although not replacing bars and nightclubs, finding romantic candidates on the internet involves statistical data, casual conversation before meeting and a chance to curate one's own first impression through edited 'about me' text and choice photographs. Perceived limitations and physical locations can be overcome in digital public space.

previous pages: Not science, but not fantasy.

31. 'Man Of The Year: The Inheritor', Time Magazine, 6 January 1967 [http://content.time.com/time/magazine/article/0,9171,843150,00.html], retrieved 20 June 2015

32. JK Stuller, 'International Women's Day: Why women can thrive in sci-fi', BBC News, 8 March 2016 [http://www.bbc.co.uk/news/entertainment-arts-35717247], retrieved 28 April 2016

33. G Orwell, 'Why I Write', 1947 [http://www.resort.com/~prime8/Orwell/whywrite.html], retrieved 08 June 2015

34. L Randall, 'Big Experiments Won't Happen' in 'What Should We Worry About?', J Brockman, Harper Perennial, New York, 11 February 2014, p.174

35. D Winer, 'Does the Human Species Have the Will to Survive?' in 'What Should We Worry About?', J Brockman, Harper Perennial, New York, 11 February 2014, p.405

It is now popular to use IVF treatment for pregnancy or surrogate mothers, and there have been successful examples of test-tube babies, and genetic engineering. The term 'designer baby' gained popularity in the late 1990s, but the potential to eradicate certain genetic disorders may indeed see the practice becoming more common. The worry for pre-birth design is previewed in Andrew Niccol's 'Gattaca' (1997). The film is part of the SF subgenre 'Biopunk' and is set in a society founded on eugenics, the science of scripted genetic make-up to improve desirable heritable characteristics. The film's protagonist, Vincent Freeman, was conceived naturally and spends his life struggling against genetic discrimination.[36]

In two extremes of the political SF dystopia, Orwell and Huxley, we are presented with forms of government mind control by fear, and by pleasure. In 'Brave New World', Huxley imagines a future free from the burden of birth and childcare, where young are born in hatcheries from artificial methods, and are raised by the government in 'Conditioning Centres'. Hypnopædia (sleep-learning) and discouragement of critical thinking along with hedonism, hallucinogenic and recreational group sex quashes the urge for individual thought. The aim of artificial conception is to produce 'standard men and women: in uniform batches' and is 'one of the major instruments of social stability'.[37] Huxley was inspired by the utopian novels of HG Wells, but what started out as a parody of Wells' 'Men Like Gods' (1923), soon became an exercise in pushing the boundaries of a frightening vision: 'I am writing a novel about the future – on the horror of the Wellsian utopia and a revolt against it. Very difficult, I have hardly enough imagination to deal with such a subject.'[38] In the novel, the character of John the Savage highlights the dystopian aspect of society, where he finds that technological wonders and consumerism are not worthy replacements for freedom. Spatially the novel was influenced by the industrial buildings in Billingham, County Durham, which Huxley visited shortly before writing the novel. The character Mustapha Mond is named after the real-world Sir Alfred Mond who had business success forming Imperial Chemical Industries (ICI) in 1926. ICI's vast industrial development in Billingham created a surreal mechanical landscape producing chemicals, explosives, fertilizers, insecticides, and paints.[39]

In 1958, Huxley released a non-fiction work titled 'Brave New World Revisited', in which he argued that the world is becoming more and more like his prophetic novel, accelerated by increasing population and communication infrastructure, especially subliminal suggestion. Elements of the book influenced his final novel 'Island' (1962) which is regarded as the utopian counterpart to 'Brave New World'.

Infrastructure of Dreaming
According to legend, the Forbidden City in Beijing was conceived in a dream. The young prince Zhu Di (later Yongle Emperor) had a monk tutor who imagined a vast extra-terrestrial city – an infrastructure designed to link the soon-to-be emperor with divine forces and that of nature and the universe.[40] The palace's chief architect, widely believed to be Cai Xin, used a uniform modular system for the arrangement of the buildings and the artificial hill of Jingshan Park protects the Forbidden City from evil spirits from the North. The rectangular plan of the infrastructure measures 961 meters from north to south, 753 meters from east to west, and occupies an area of 720,000 square meters with nearly 1,000 palaces, halls, pavilions, and courtyards.[41] Constructed using more than 12 million bricks, the continuous red outer walls are bounded by a 52-meter wide moat and have four impressive corner towers commanding each corner of the city.[42]

The factors that influence the morphology of our cities are multifarious. Infrastructures that allowed trade formed the backbones of streets, which over time developed into complex networks and allowed for the emergence of the various territories that define the visible as well as invisible infrastructures of the city. The practical aspects of urban infrastructure cannot be overlooked as unimaginative or uncultured. Speculative visions of a powerful city must also consider the many practical requirements of its inhabitants that include provision of safe water and food, electric light, and efficient transport. It was a great feat of imagination when Sir Joseph William Bazalgette dreamt of his vast sewerage network for London inspired by the Great Stink of 1858; the infrastructure is still in use today over a century later. He highlighted that 'the majority of the inhabitants of cities and towns are frequently unconscious of the magnitude, intricacy, and extent of the underground works, which have been designed at great cost, and are necessary for the maintenance of their health and comfort.'[43] It was a dream of a better wellbeing; one of many dreams that have transformed London. Other dreams have been of grandeur as in the case of the development of Buckingham Palace and the Mall, while the Tower of London and its dungeons portrayed power. A magnificent celebration of the imagination is the dream-like painted London skyline 'A Tribute to the Memory of Sir Christopher Wren' (1838) by Charles Robert Cockerell. He brought together Wren's major buildings into one vast urban infrastructural landscape of 55 buildings including 33 London churches, palaces, colleges, hospitals and monuments, as well as some buildings from outside London including Chichester Cathedral, Winchester Palace and All Souls Oxford – with St Paul's Cathedral being the grand centerpiece.[44]

In 'The Engineering of Architecture' (1987), James Gowan highlights an often observed incompatibility in the making of buildings and infrastructures: 'If a scrupulous distinction were made between architecture and engineering, it would be that one is concerned primarily with art and the other, utility. When one activity invades the territory of the other, it does so at considerable risk.'[45] Dreams and dreaming have been an ongoing preoccupation of urban planners, architects and artists since the beginning of time. Art can be identified to be at the core of what it is to be human and even when architecture was just mud, it was able to answer a higher purpose than mere shelter. 'Building in earth seems to provoke a particularly physical creative urge in its craftsmen. Architecture is therefore the expression of profound impulses; it requires neither the use of complex instruments nor academic or technological knowledge.'[46]

At the same time, we now have thousands of mines in the sea, huge tunnels, bridges, and computerized communication systems that extend to even the most isolated regions of the planet. Archigram, known for their SF architecture, are, in fact, not so far from being realized. Un-built projects such as Ron Herron's 'Walking Cities' (1964) and Peter Cook's 'Instant City' (1968) are precursors to many of today's hi-tech cities, infrastructures in space (in the form of the International Space Station), and settlements planned for the moon. Ron Herron's 'Walking City' rejected the need for a permanent or ecologically stable ground, the hydraulic legs enabling the vast edifices to slowly wander between host cities or in open countryside – Reyner Banham, however, felt that 'something the size of a city center should know its place in the townscape, in history, and in Western culture...'[47]

Deborah Cadbury's 'The Seven Wonders of the Industrial World' (2004) identifies infrastructures that have dreamt ahead and broken down new barriers – the Great Eastern, Bell Rock Lighthouse, Brooklyn Bridge, London Sewers, Transcontinental Railroad, Panama Canal and Hoover Dam. It is perhaps safe to say that these technical feats were produced, run and inhabited by a low paid socially marginalized

36. A Niccol, 'Gattaca', Columbia Pictures, 1997

37. A Huxley, 'Brave New World', Vintage, London, 2007, p.5

38. A Huxley, 'Letters of Aldous Huxley', Harper & Row, New York, 1969, p.348

39. A Huxley, 'Brave New World', Vintage, London, 2007, p.xxii

40. F Dorn, 'The Forbidden City: The biography of a palace', Charles Scribner's Sons, New York, 1970

41. Z Yu, Palaces of the Forbidden City, Allen Lane, London, 1982, p.32

42. Z Yu, Palaces of the Forbidden City, Allen Lane, London, 1982, p.288

43. JW Bazalgette, 'The Great Engineers: The art of British engineers 1837-1987', Academy Editions, London, 1987, p.119

44. CR Cockerell, 'A Tribute to the Memory of Sir Christopher Wren', RIBA Library Drawings Collection, 1838

45. J Gowan, 'The Engineering of Architecture' in 'The Great Engineers: The art of British engineers 1837-1987', Academy Editions, London, 1987, p.153

46. J Dethier, 'Down to Earth - Mud Architecture: An old idea, a new future', Thames & Hudson Ltd, London, 1982, p.101

47. R Banham, 'The Visions of Ron Herron', St Martins Press, London, Architectural Monographs no.38, 1994, p.76

THE BEST IN SCIENCE FICTION

WONDER
Stories

July

A GERNSBACK PUBLICATION

HUGO GERNSBACK Editor

NEW YORK TO SYDNEY

25¢

"VOICE OF ATLANTIS"
by Laurence Manning

labor force. In the case of the Brooklyn Bridge, workers were lowered into the sea in pressurised diving bells which allowed them to work on the river bed in the dry, but led to many cases of extreme medical problems due to the pressure, often proving fatal.[48] Nevertheless, many of the bold infrastructures have paved the way for positive social change with the advent of modernity.

So what is the dream? Do we dare speculate the infrastructures that could bring about peace or alleviate global poverty? Is this within the remit of architects and urban planners, or in that of politicians and the business elite? We look to those who have dreamt about our future in SF; the narrative allows us to glimpse into the sometimes surreal, utopian or even terrifying environments of the coming centuries. We feel humane or inhumane depending on the reading of the everyday experience of the world. The prophetic nature of SF and its study allows us to visualize new challenges that we would not otherwise be able to begin to think of addressing, without first immersing ourselves in speculative imagination.

On comparing pens and paper of the western world to those of Japanese tradition, Junichiro Tanizaki deliberates in his influential literature 'In Praise of Shadows' (1933), 'our thought and literature might not be imitating the West as they are, but might have pushed forward into new regions quite on their own. An insignificant little piece of writing equipment, when one thinks about it, has had a vast, almost boundless, influence on our culture.'[49] A 'butterfly effect' can profoundly alter the course of our development and that of generations to come.

If we held the same critical-thinking as Tanizaki, but instead were to focus on the imagination of alternative environments – what would urban futures in Africa, Australia, or South America look like without inherited or imposed Roman, British Colonial, or modernist contamination? Despite unprecedented investments and opportunities in global urban developments, many of today's Chinese and Middle Eastern cities and architecture are pastiches, unquestioning outcomes of the international modern style. Even with the urgency of climate change, infrastructural designs have continued to be of homogenous international solutions – the age of the automobile is global and ubiquitous, multi-lane tarmac highways carve through desert, forest and mountain alike. In adopting the speculative function of SF, we can perhaps begin to uncover possible shared truths that address the fundamental human requirements to protect, to provide and to participate. It is in this opportunity that the nature of utopias can be better understood; resulting in the evolution of urban futures tailored for the determining factors of climate, resources and the idiosyncrasies of human culture.

'The purpose of a storyteller is not to tell you how to think, but to give you questions to think upon.'
—Brandon Sanderson, 'The Way of Kings', 2010

facing page: Science fiction is the history of ideas.

48. D Cadbury, 'The Seven Wonders of the Industrial World', Harper Perennial, London, 2004

49. J Tanizaki, 'In Praise of Shadows', Vintage Classics, London, 2001, p.15

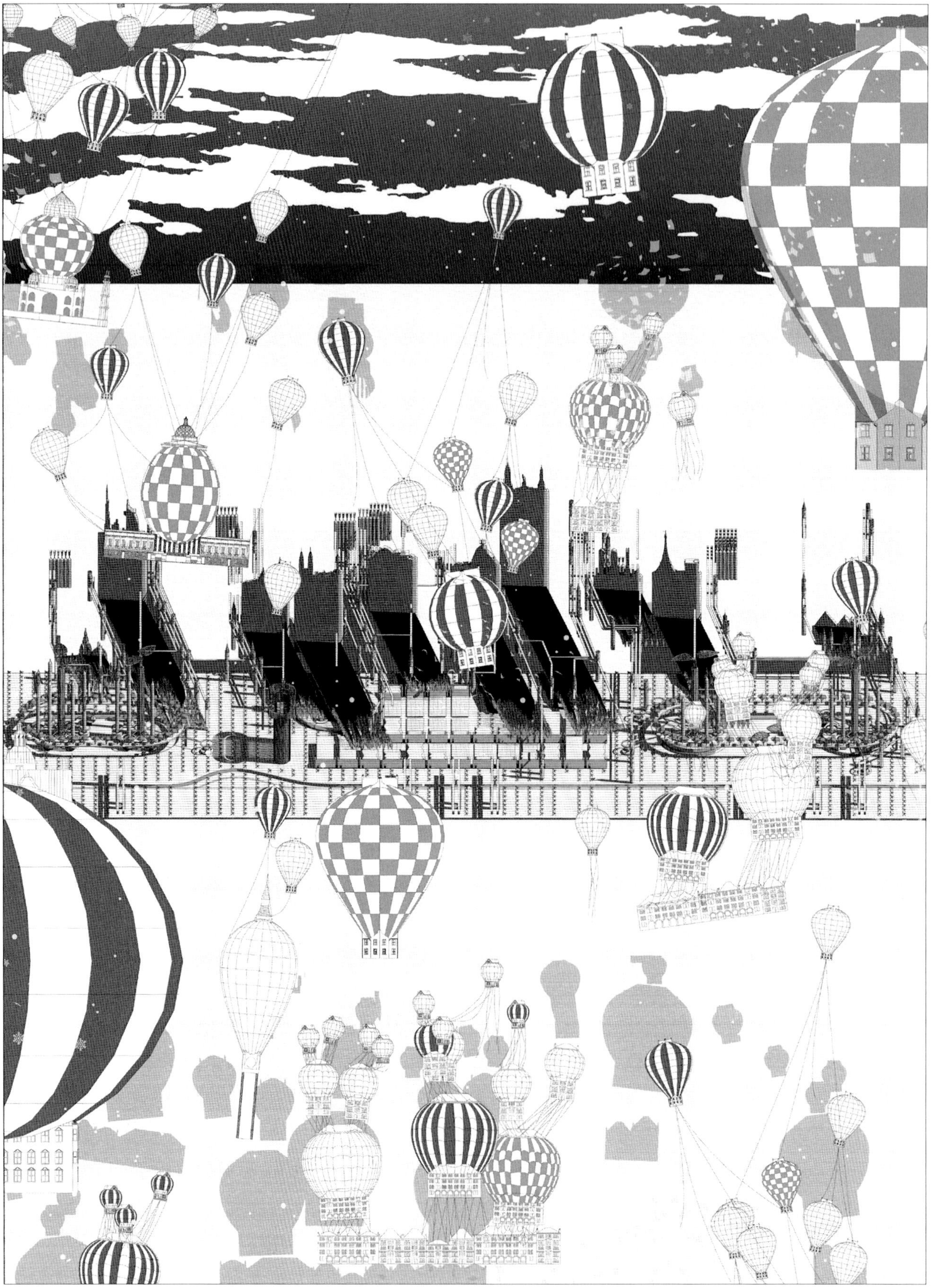

Science Fiction or Urban Future?

'Individual science fiction stories may seem as trivial as ever to the blinder critics and philosophers of today - but the core of science fiction, its essence has become crucial to our salvation if we are to be saved at all.'

– Isaac Asimov, 'My Own View', 1978

All discussions about the future are, by definition, fictional; they concern the act of imagining. Events and inventions can be predicted, in both the short and long term. When the author's imagined world enters the realms of realization, the work makes the shift from science fiction (SF) to 'prophetic'. Jules Verne's 1865 prediction of moon landings in 'From the Earth to the Moon' were realized by NASA just over a century later in 1969, and Edward Bellamy's 1888 prediction of credit cards and centralized banking in 'Looking Backwards: 2000–1887' are two good examples of writers' foresight. What were once quintessential fantasy gadgets, in a matter of decades have become real and widespread – the internet, wireless electronics, video calls and miniaturized computers all featured in popular SF such as 'Star Trek' and '2001: A Space Odyssey'.

Once an idea enters the industrious minds of technological innovators it is quickly realized, often pushed ahead by military funding or commercial sectors. In fact, the classic gadgetry of the space-obsessed generation now seems mundane compared with what is available in reality; technology has become a ubiquitous and invisible infrastructure – the 'Cloud'. Of course, we are still searching; the pursuit of the unknown is never-ending. However, the industrial age has matured, and gadgets have lost their appeal. We are asking different questions of the future, speculations that deal more with the ideas of how we will live rather than transposing our current lifestyle into a more technically proficient age, as 'The Jetsons' had done by simply juxtaposing 1950s domesticity with a city in the sky.

Future itself is not fictional; it is ongoing. And all of us are destined to spend the rest of our lives there, in one of any number of potential future-worlds. Nevertheless, we are certainly in a state of uncertainty, of which there are two categories: 'known unknowns' and 'unknown unknowns'. The former can be subjected to rigorous research, deliberation and experiments. For instance, the 'Theory of Everything' completes and consolidates the fragments of understanding we gained from 'General Relativity' and 'Quantum Field Theory' to enlighten us of the exact origins of the universe. Scientific methodologies and creative imagination can unite to mutually motivate in the quest of 'known unknowns'. Issues and events, for which we simply have no inkling, are the 'unknown unknowns'. How could we ever hope to make a discovery (or indeed benefit from one) when deliberating about the mysteries of life and the

facing page: Relocation of global landmarks brings cultural diversity.

following pages: The innovative concepts and issues raised in science fiction reveal the legitimacy and prophetic qualities of speculative writing.

BRAVE NEW WORLD

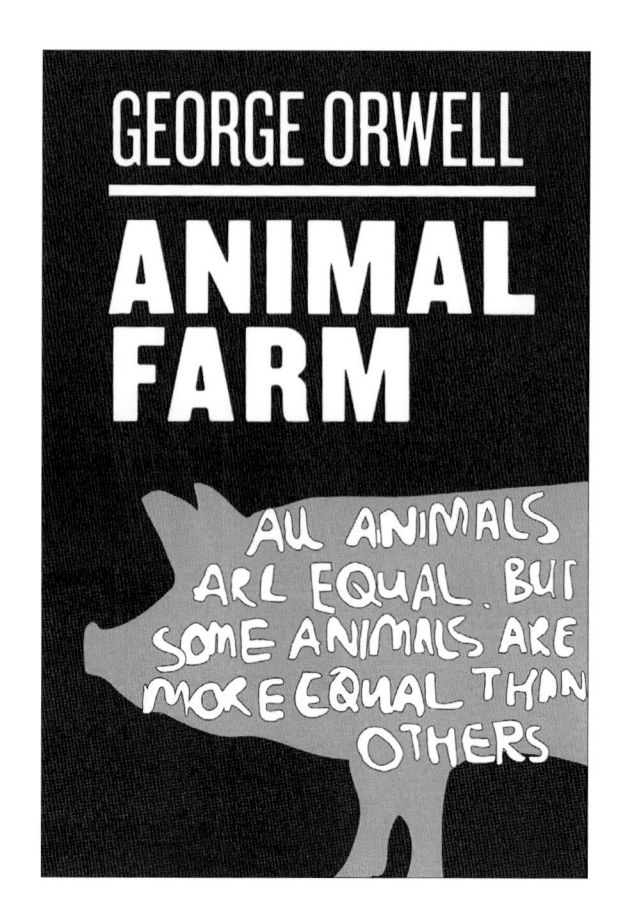

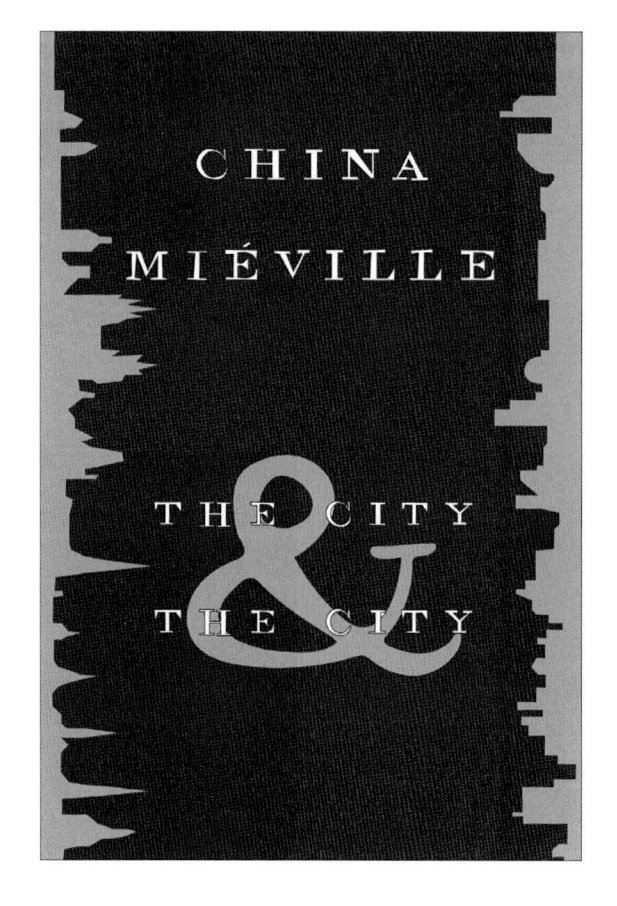

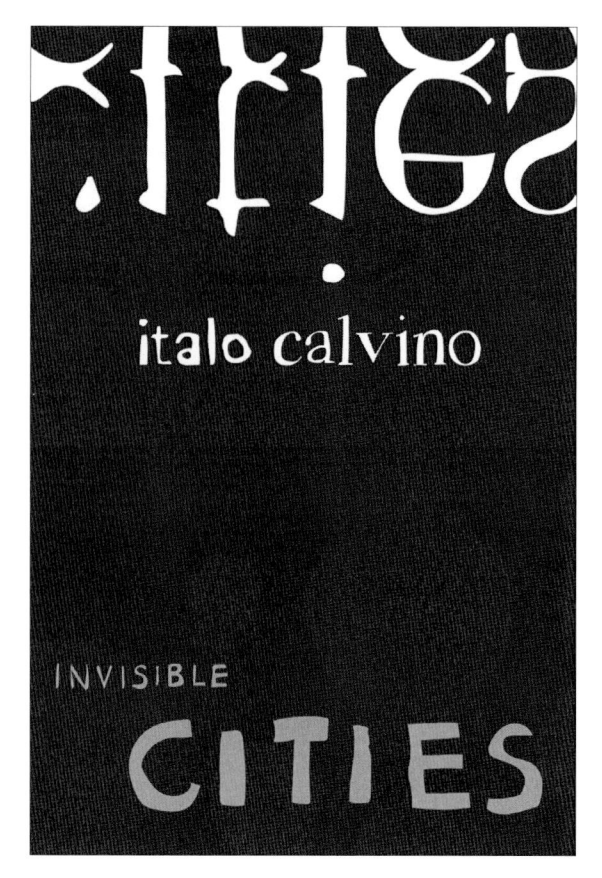

ALDOUS HUXLEY

GEORGE ORWELL

ANIMAL FARM

ALL ANIMALS ARE EQUAL. BUT SOME ANIMALS ARE MORE EQUAL THAN OTHERS

CHINA MIÉVILLE

THE CITY & THE CITY

italo calvino

INVISIBLE CITIES

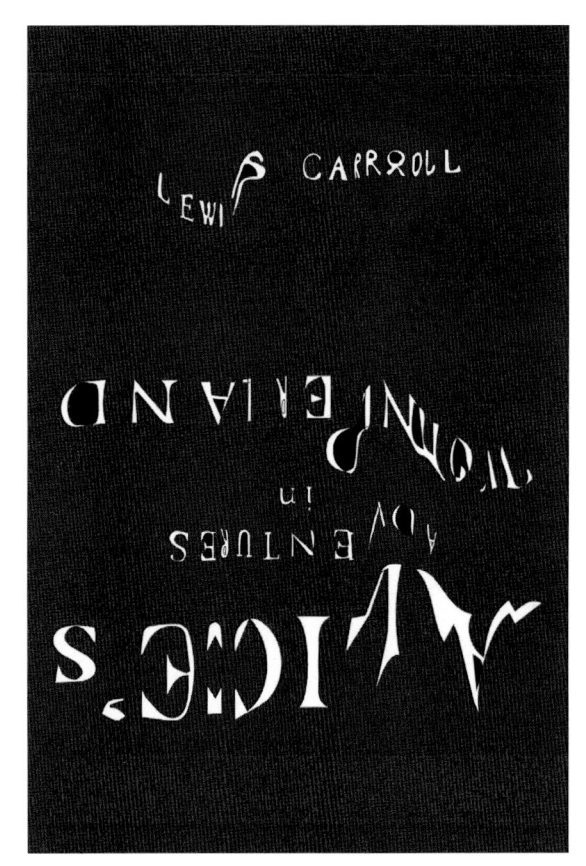

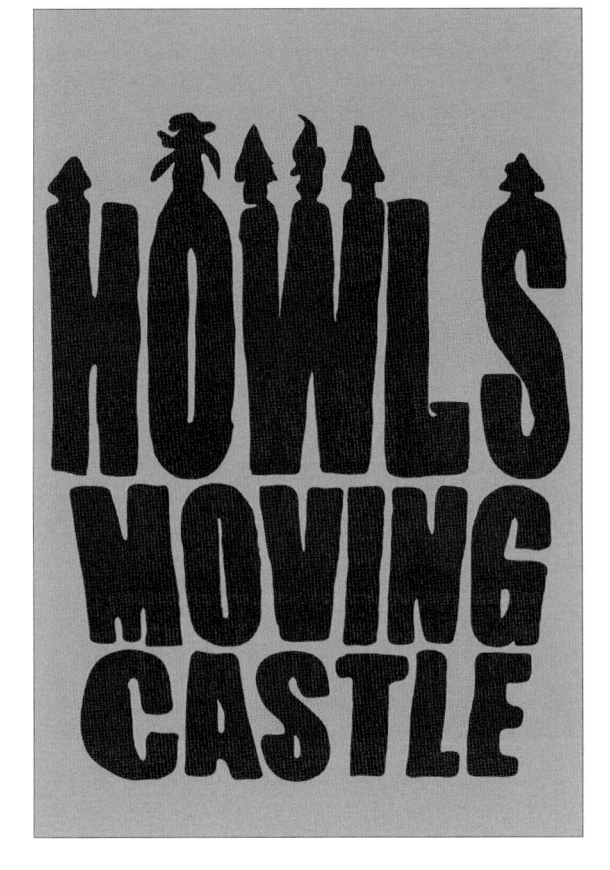

science fiction or urban future?

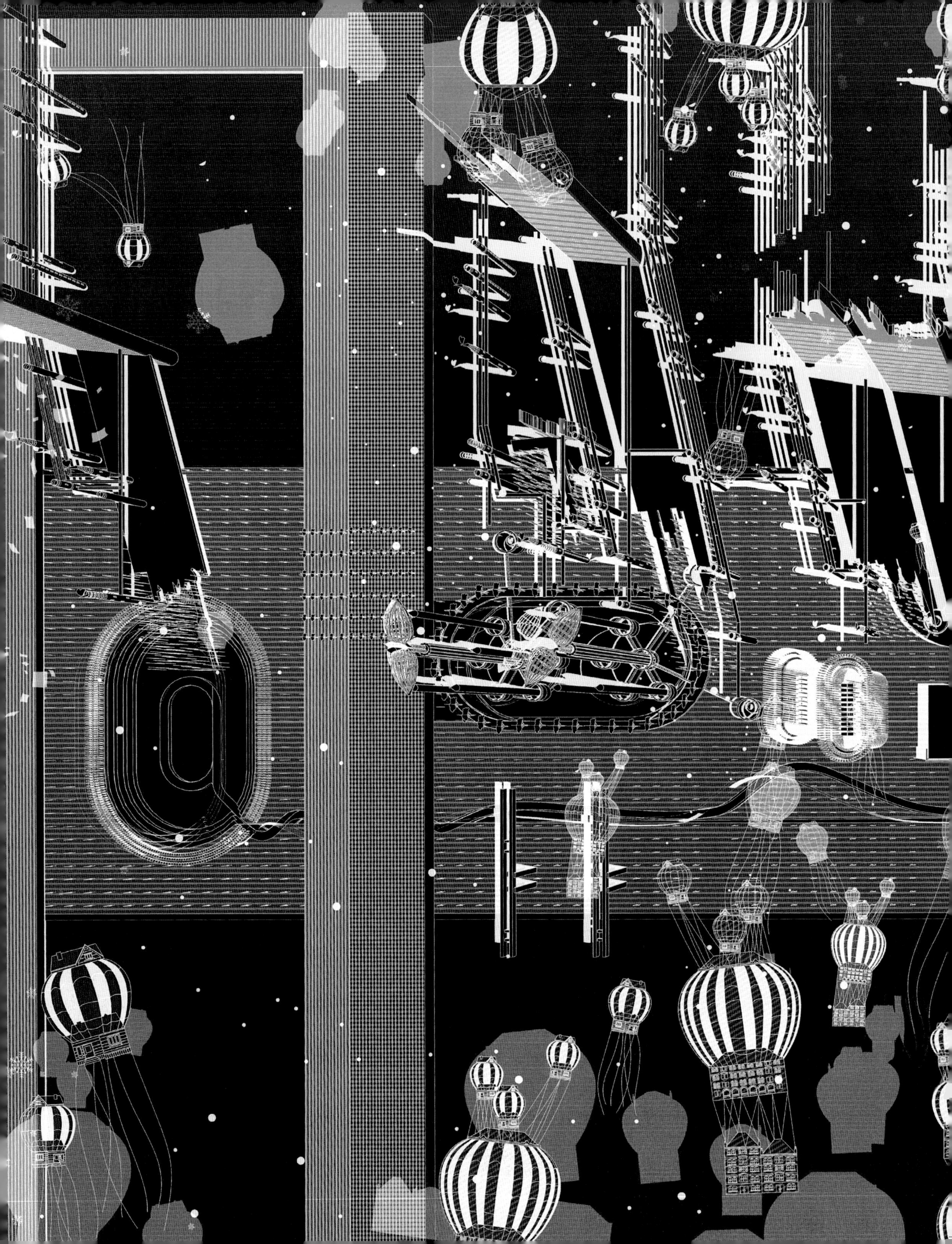

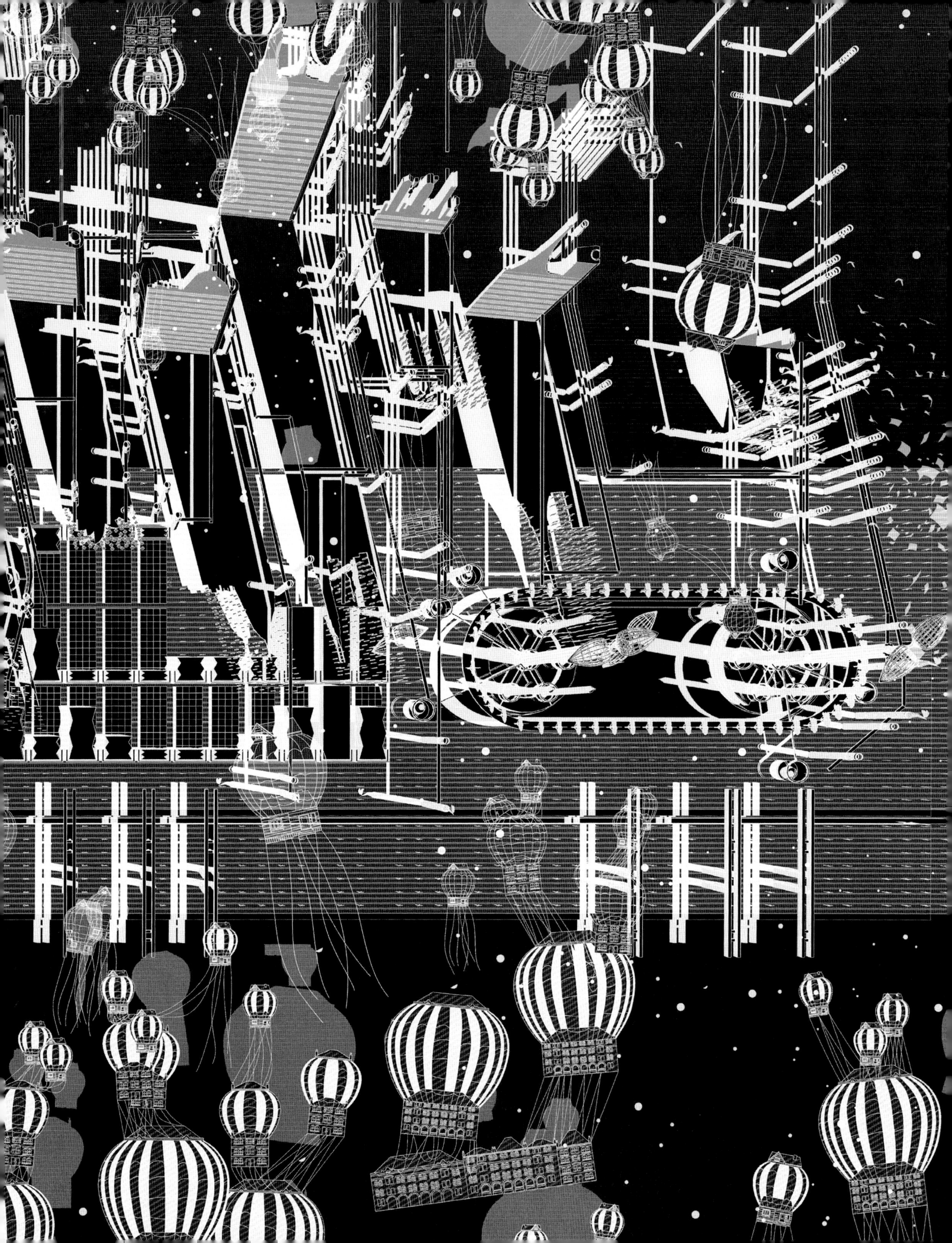

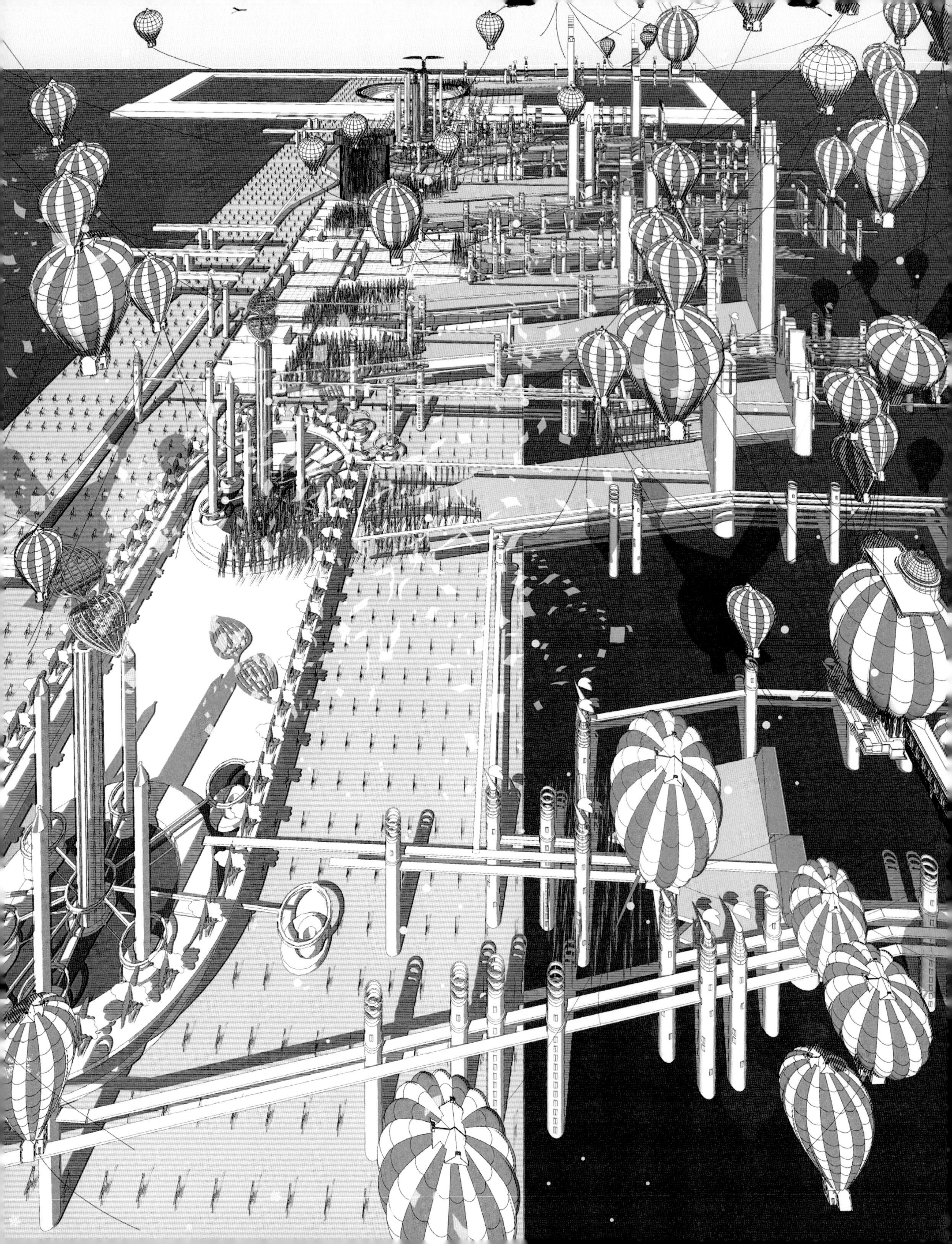

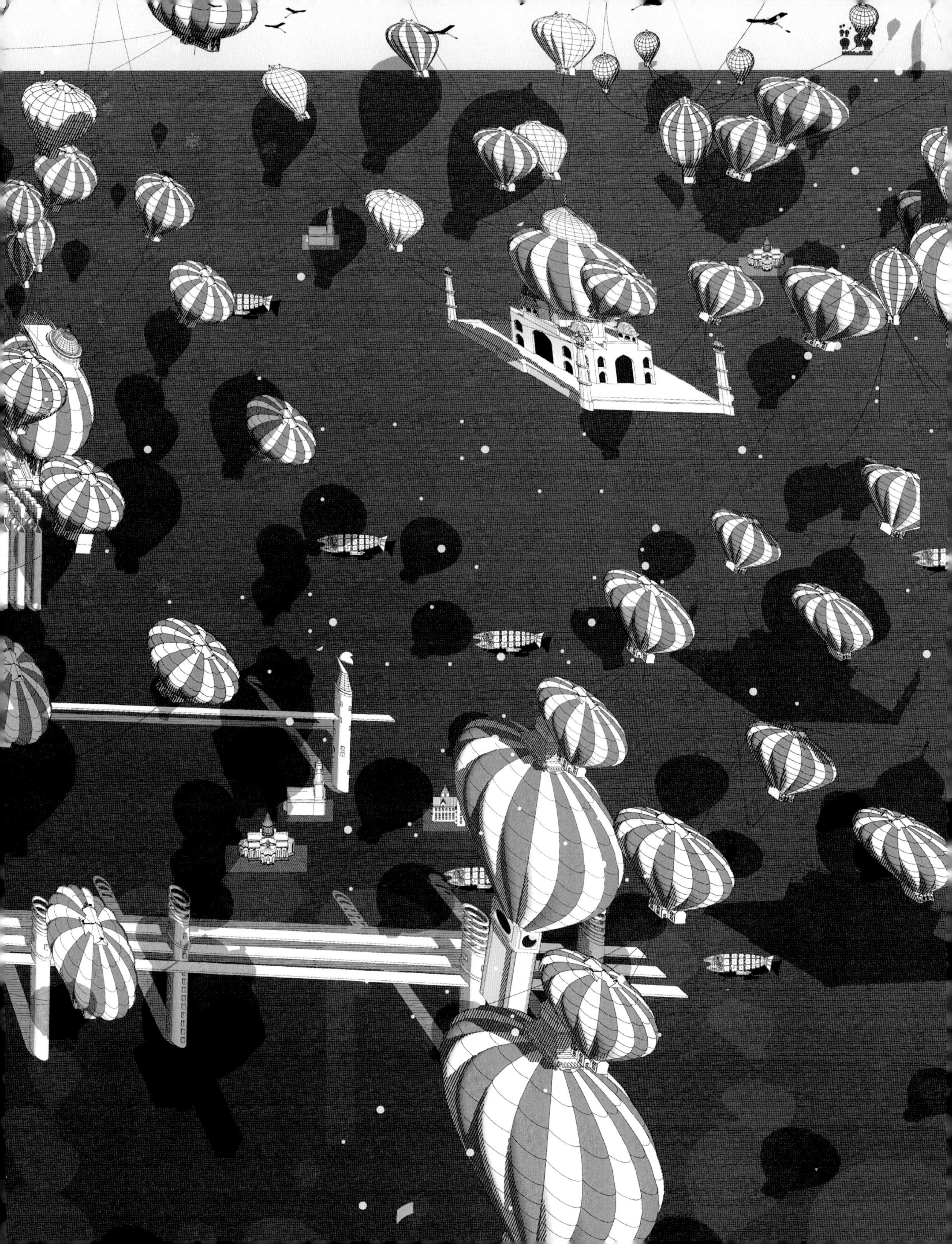

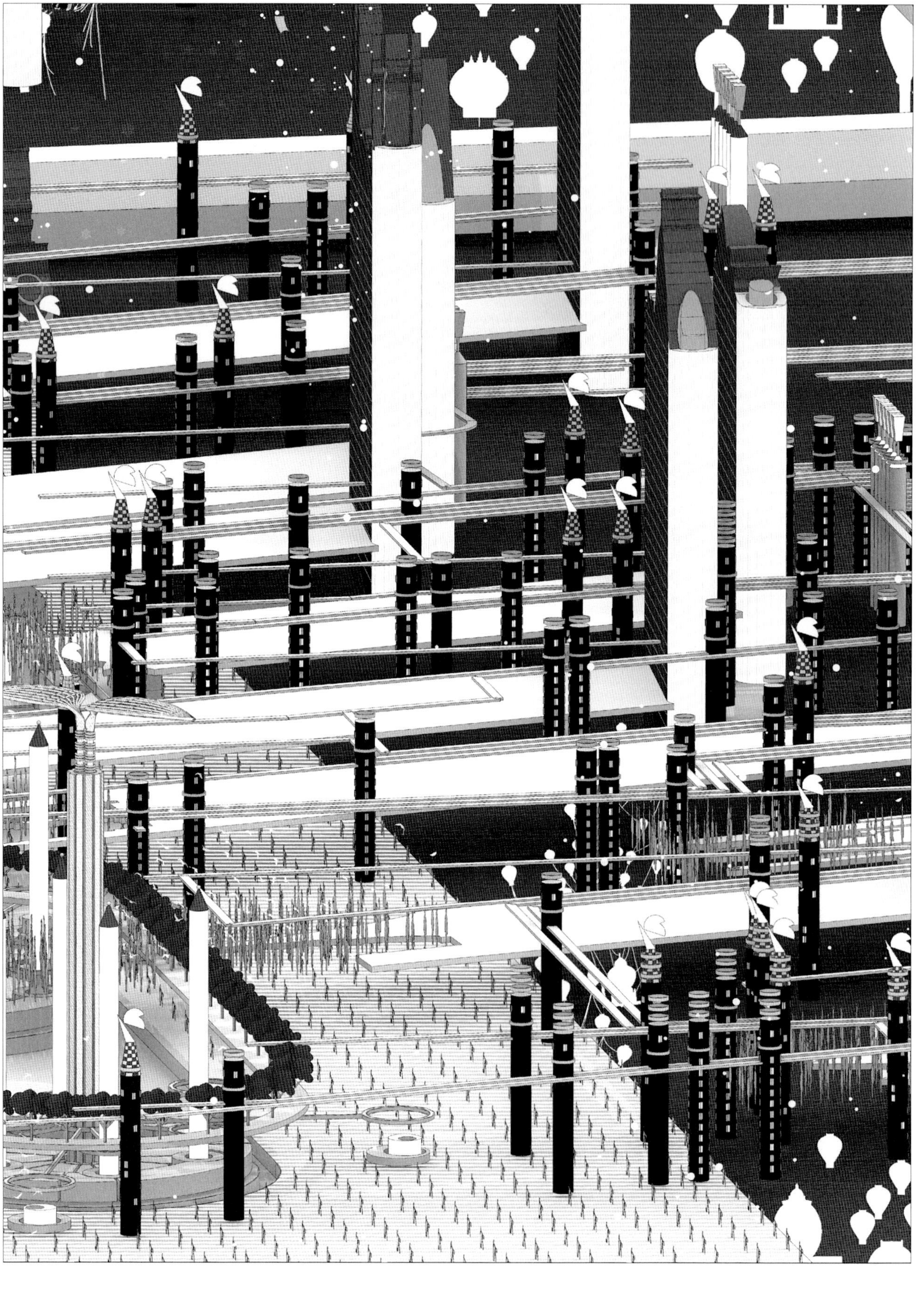

world before it occurs? 'Unknown unknowns' occupy an indeterminate state; those who traverse liminal territories and interdisciplinary grey-areas stumble upon them, and they see uncertainty as a guiding light and dare – as if to venture blind into an abyss.

SF is crammed with spatially suggestive concepts and intensity that in provoking political commentary, also ignites our imagination. SF consistently presents the world anew with re-invigorated critical faculties, and perhaps a greater perception of the incongruity of our society, cities and infrastructures. The perfect world, in SF, is far more imperfect than is at first seemed, where the understanding and sympathies for existing traditions of protection, provision and participation are turned upside-down.

More than any other genre, SF invests time in revealing to the reader a sense of the otherworldly; it has urgency for and delights in the visionary. A modest shelf of SF is a vast library of knowledge, but it is knowledge in the form of questions – dichotomies, polemics and 'what if...' are great for propelling spatial narratives. By presenting a marginal take on any given scenario, SF is 'lateral thinking', 'outside the box', and 'the Devil's advocate', and can always inspire debates of our urban futures.

Urban Futures: The Magnum Opus of SF Infrastructure
If our raison d'être stood to interrogate the world of the built environment through the rich ingredients of speculative fiction, how then would our future cities take form? Ancient and medieval civilizations held strong beliefs in the powerful work of alchemists. According to legend, the processes of alchemy ultimately led to the discovery of the philosopher's stone, a potent object able to transform lead into gold and create an elixir of eternal life. Formulas produced by alchemists are often secrets and non-consistent.

For our 'Urban Futures', there are processes to follow and correct amounts of ingredients to use:

Firstly, two equal portions of Aldous Huxley's 'Brave New World' (1931) and George Orwell's 'Animal Farm' (1945) to accommodate the themes of equality, freedom, utopia, the perfect world and the role of politics.

Then add the primary energy source, and the building material extracted from Richard Brautigan's 'In Watermelon Sugar' (1968). This is spread neatly across the pre-prepared ground surface, a great expanse of salt water (the pool of tears), from Lewis Carroll's 'Alice's Adventures in Wonderland' (1865).

Carefully add China Miéville's 'The City & The City' (2009). If applied correctly this has the effect of separating the mixture; there should be two distinct territories: one of light and one of shadow.

Next, the collection of tangible and intangible infrastructures from Italo Calvino's 'Invisible Cities' (1974) should permeate the porous urban-mix. A generous sprinkling of Diana Wynne Jones' 'Howl's Moving Castle' (1986) provides the means for the inhabitants to migrate to this city-like construct.

science fiction or urban future?

previous four pages: Out of the alchemy of science fiction comes the masterplan of an urban future.

facing page: Housing towers form the structural nodes of elevated connections.

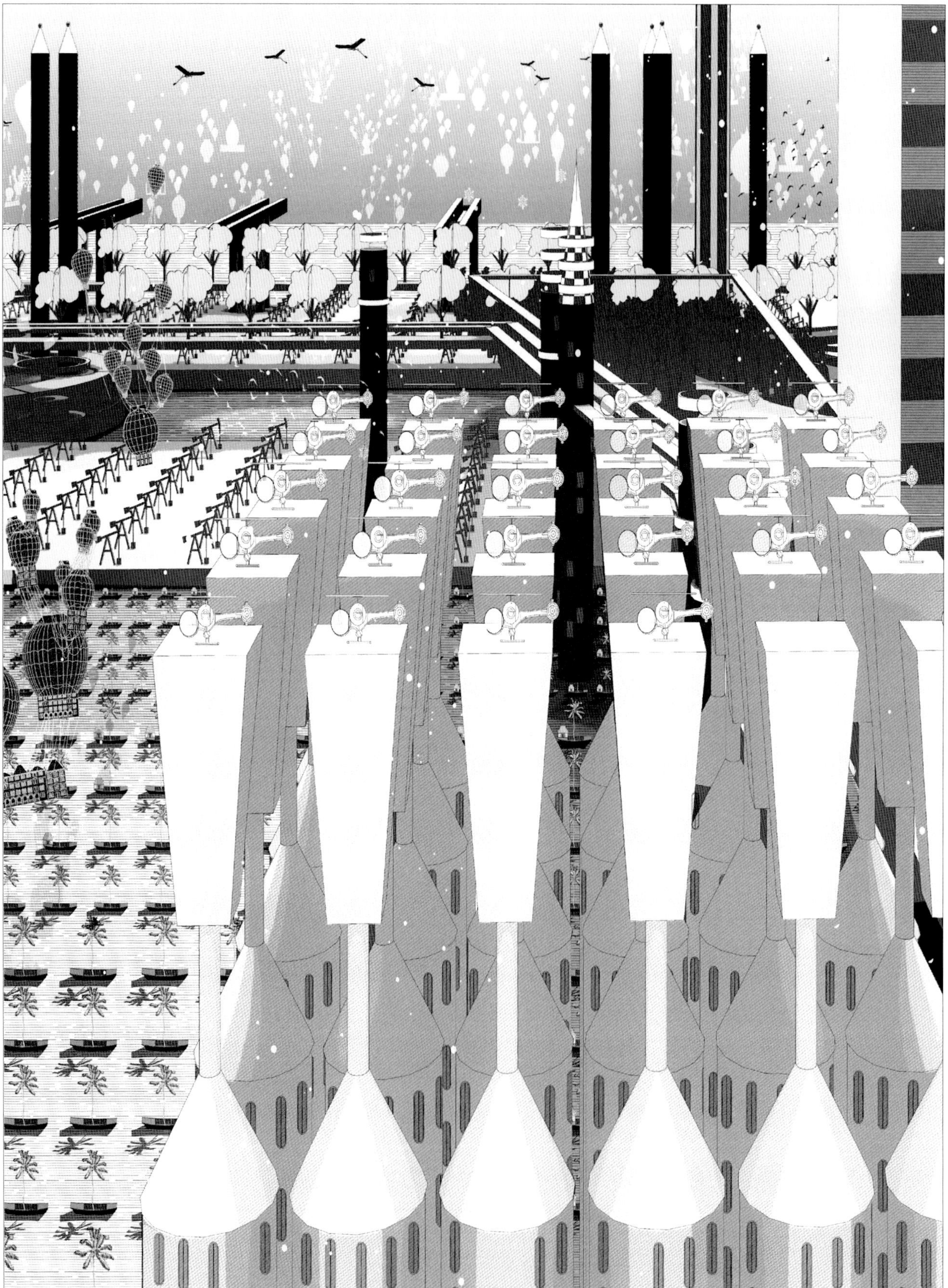

science fiction or urban future?

We animate the mixture with Andrew Niccol's 'In Time' (2011), and with the understanding that currencies from the world's existing corrupt and fragile economies would be useless in the alchemy of the SF city. Here time itself becomes currency – slowness and old age are celebrated as community and leisure activities.

Finally, season with noir comic book motifs and keep stored in a cool dark place until life resembles JG Ballard's 'The Burning World' (1964).

Whether or not the practice of alchemy produced a single drop of elixir is less important historically than what actually was achieved. Could the same be true of a SF city experiment? Alchemists, like druids before them, conducted scientific research in medicines, chemistry and natural sciences; as a result they were considered to be men of knowledge and held in extremely high esteem by both monarchies and the populous. Alchemy had a powerful influence on the development of Chinese culture, the Islamic world, and the Renaissance in Europe.

Isaac Newton is known to have practiced alchemy for many years, although is best remembered as the father of modern physics. Newton was a polymath who had the vision to drive the human race forward and perhaps to ask questions that had not been posed. 'In an age when there were no microscopes to penetrate living cells and no understanding of the nature of atoms and molecules, the alchemists were not misguided so much as misinformed, doing their best to make sense of a world they could not see. That they understood as much as they did is the real marvel: in pursuing what today seems like little more than witchcraft, the alchemists were in fact laying the foundation for modern experimental science.'[1]

facing page: The 'Dragonfly Police' keep constant watch over the precious floating watermelon fields.

following pages: 'Nodding Donkeys' mash watermelons into sugar-rich pulp before multi-level infrastructures refine this into food, fuel, and biodegradable building material.

1. J Bosveld, 'Isaac Newton: World's most famous alchemist', Discover Magazine, 28 December 2010 [http://discovermagazine.com/2010/jul-aug/05-isaac-newton-worlds-most-famous-alchemist], retrieved 29 July 2016

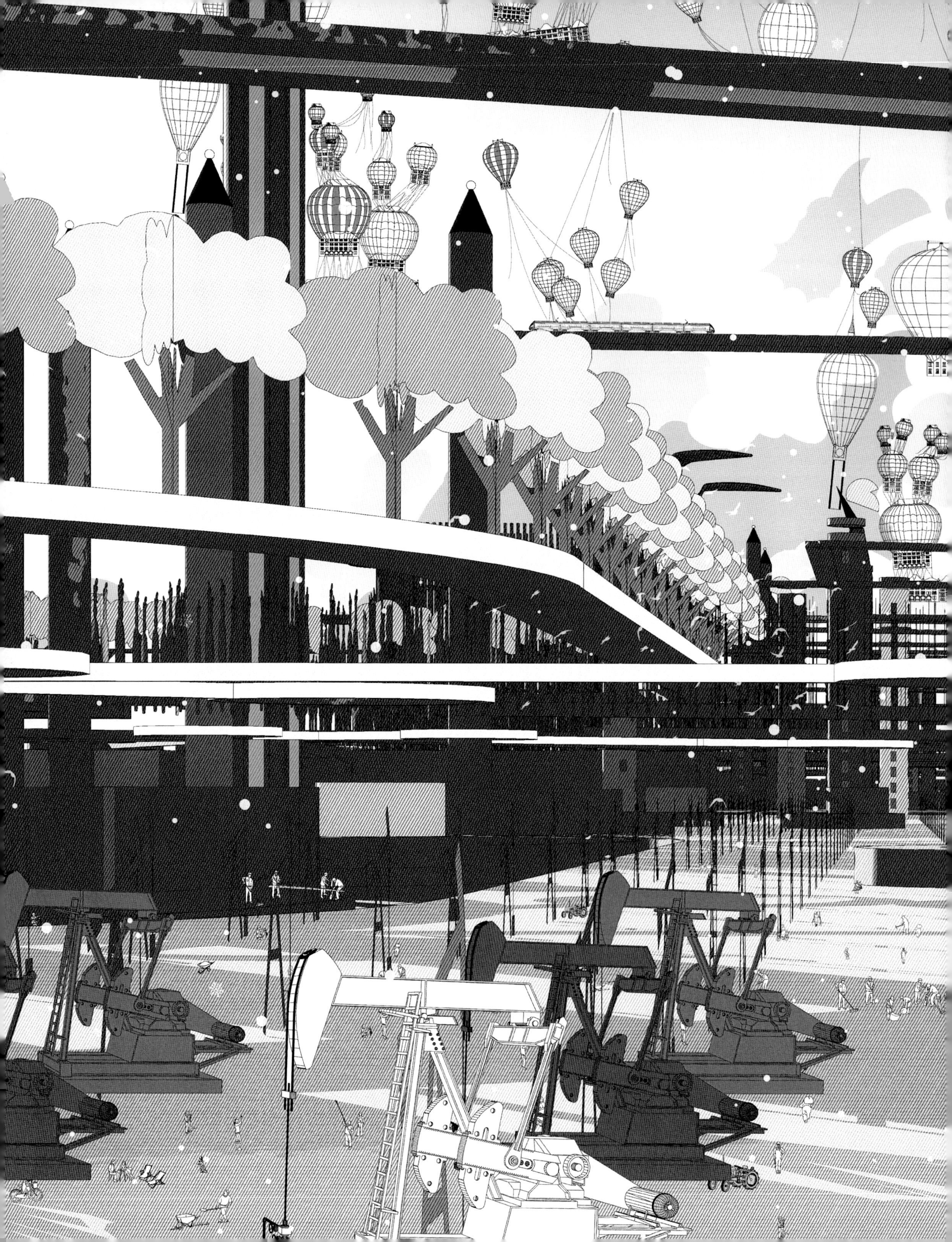

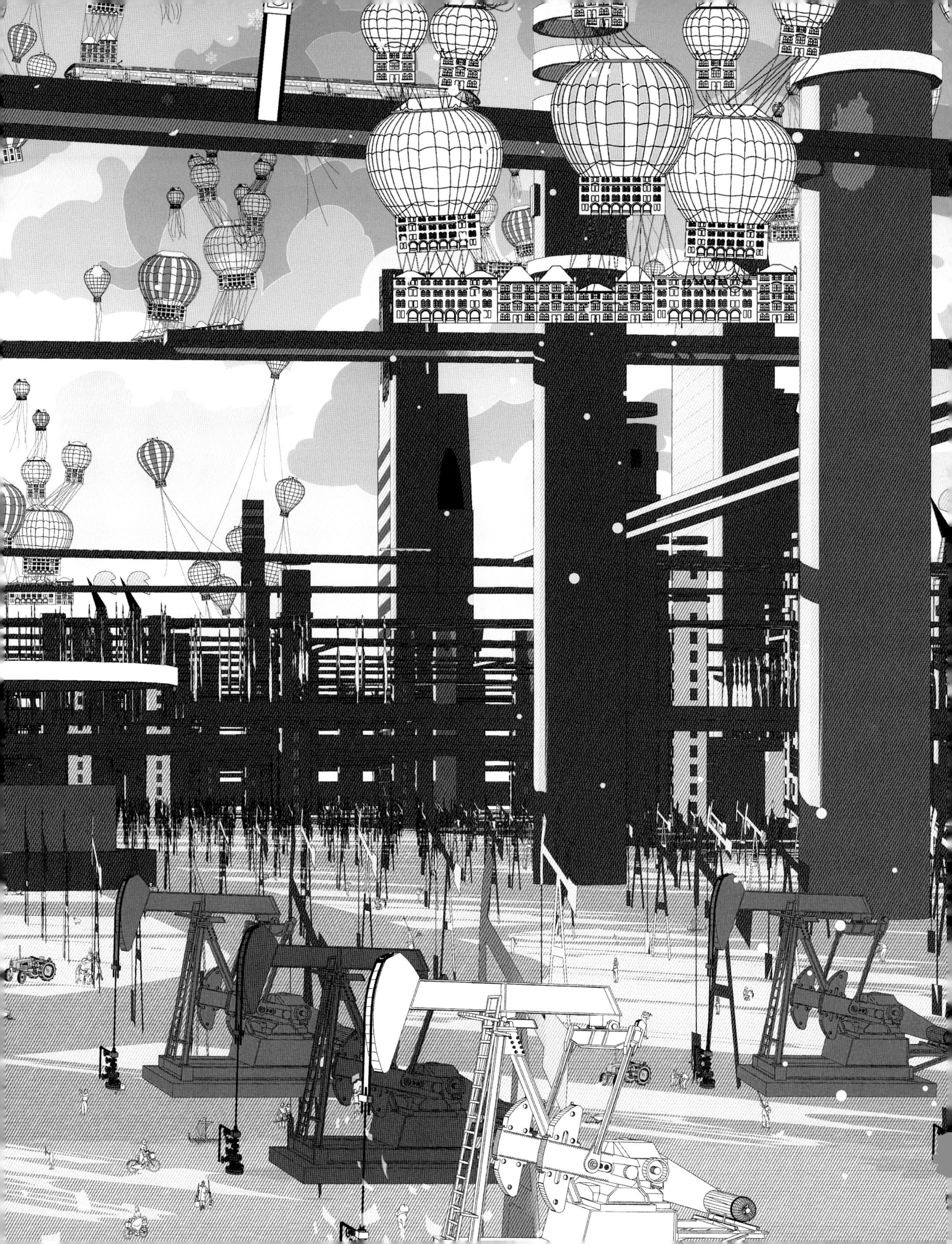

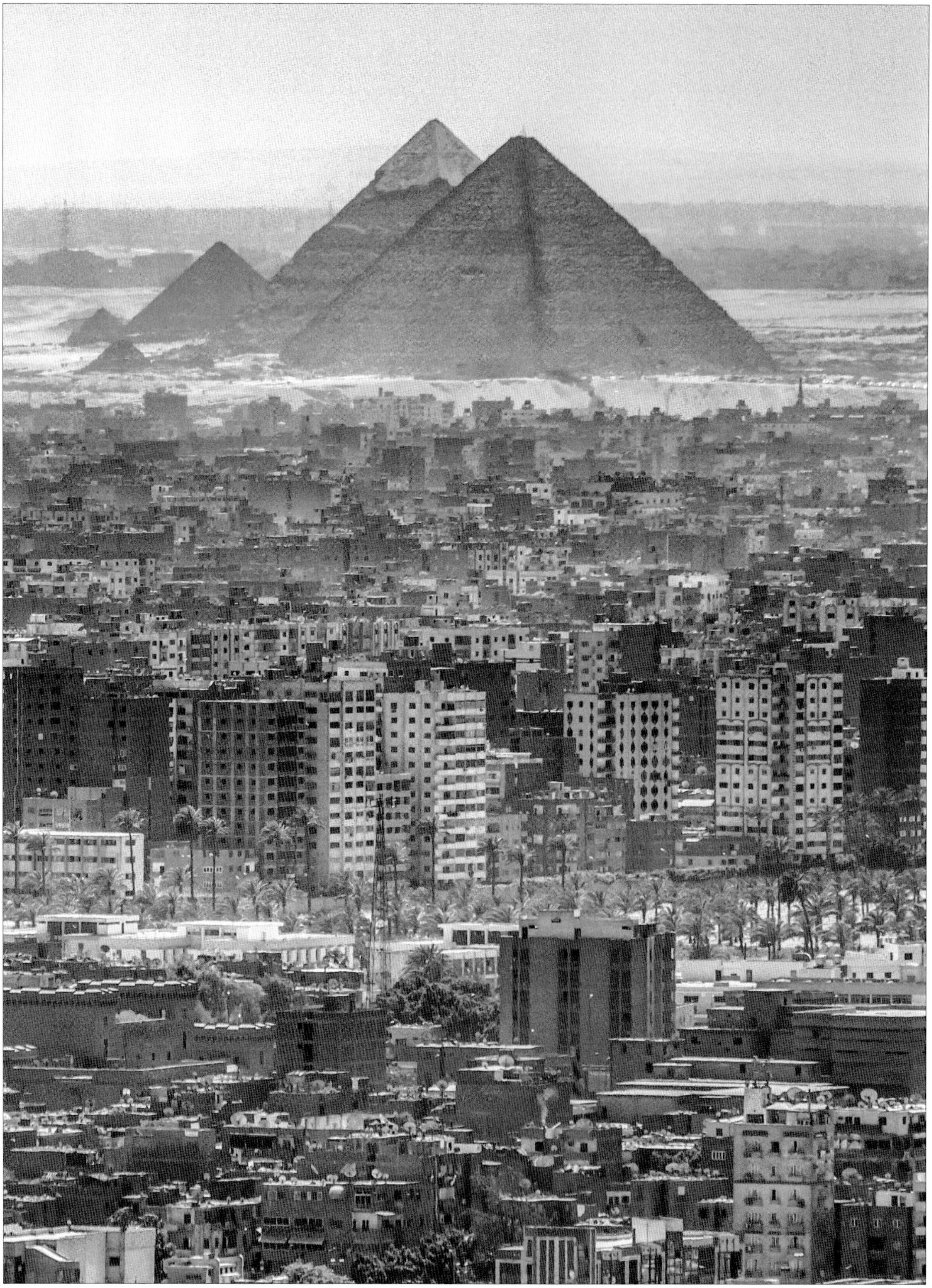

The City as a Collection of Infrastructures

'The chief function of the city is to convert power into form, energy into culture, dead matter into the living symbols of art, biological reproduction into social creativity.'
  – Lewis Mumford, 'The City in History: Its origins, its transformations, and its prospects', 1968

The myth of the earliest city, Eridu, is that the Babylonian god Marduk, 'constructed a reed frame on the face of the waters. He created dirt and poured it onto the frame. In order to settle the gods in the dwelling of their hearts delight, he created mankind' to render services to the gods and to the first building, the temple of Esagila.[1] Marduk sought to protect his people from the challenges of the aggressive natural environment. The Mesopotamian narrative correspondingly describes the evolution and functions of urbanity, and laid the foundation for civilizations and belief that visions to protect, to provide and to participate can be achieved in the city. Eridu, nonetheless, was a real Sumerian city on a location now known as Tell Abu Shahrain in southern Iraq; the mud covered reed platform and the temple being the first infrastructures.

Infrastructure refers to the fundamental man-made structures, networks, services and facilities that support the essential growth of a country, city or industry and is fully dependent by its communities. Generally large and accessible by multiple individual agents in a given system, infrastructure implies repetition, rationality, and efficiency. Infrastructure is an enabler of socio-economic growth, planning policies and social wellbeing; with coming technological advancement, infrastructure has the ability to adapt landscapes, urban forms and social cultures. There are two major classifications of infrastructure – hard and soft.

Hard infrastructures directly contribute to the survival of a community and its ability to respond and recover at the time of extreme events. They are systems for transport, water and sewer management, energy grids and telecommunications. However, a city with only hard infrastructure of roads, railways, pipelines, dams, canals and satellites would be a vacuous and meaningless city. Soft infrastructures are fundamental to quality of life, promote economic, health, and education programs, and contribute to the day-to-day cultural and social development of a community. Institutions or organizations such as transport network operators, government departments, industry standards, trade agreements and the law are considered soft infrastructures.

Early hard infrastructures such as arable farmland, grain stores, mills and food markets perform hand-in-hand with soft infrastructures of trading or monetary systems and regulations. In medieval times,

facing page: The pyramids were the archetypical urban infrastructure to protect.

following pages: The collection of infrastructures in London ensures sustainable functioning of the city.

1. G Leick, 'Mesopotamia: The invention of the city', Penguin Press, London, 2001, pp.1–2

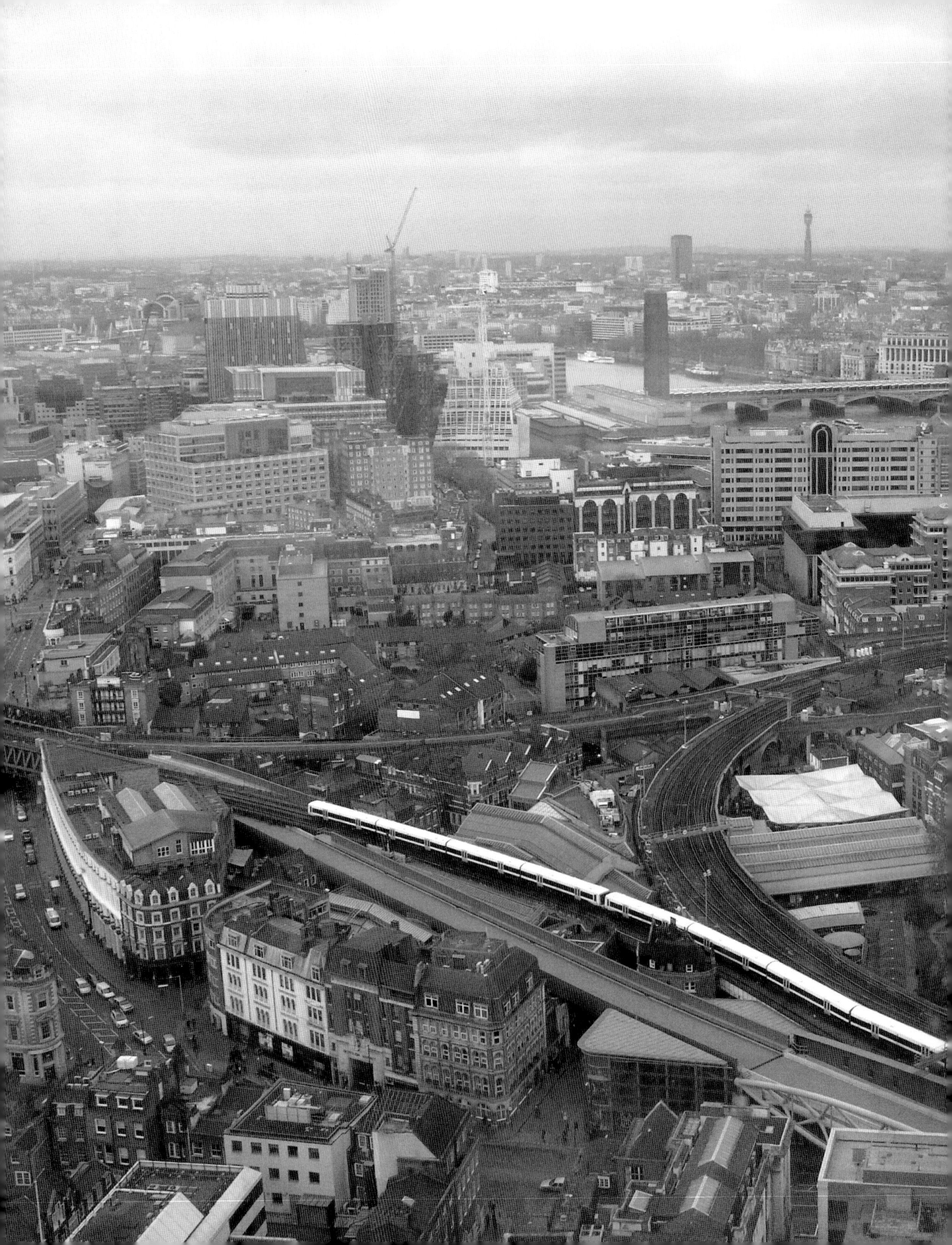

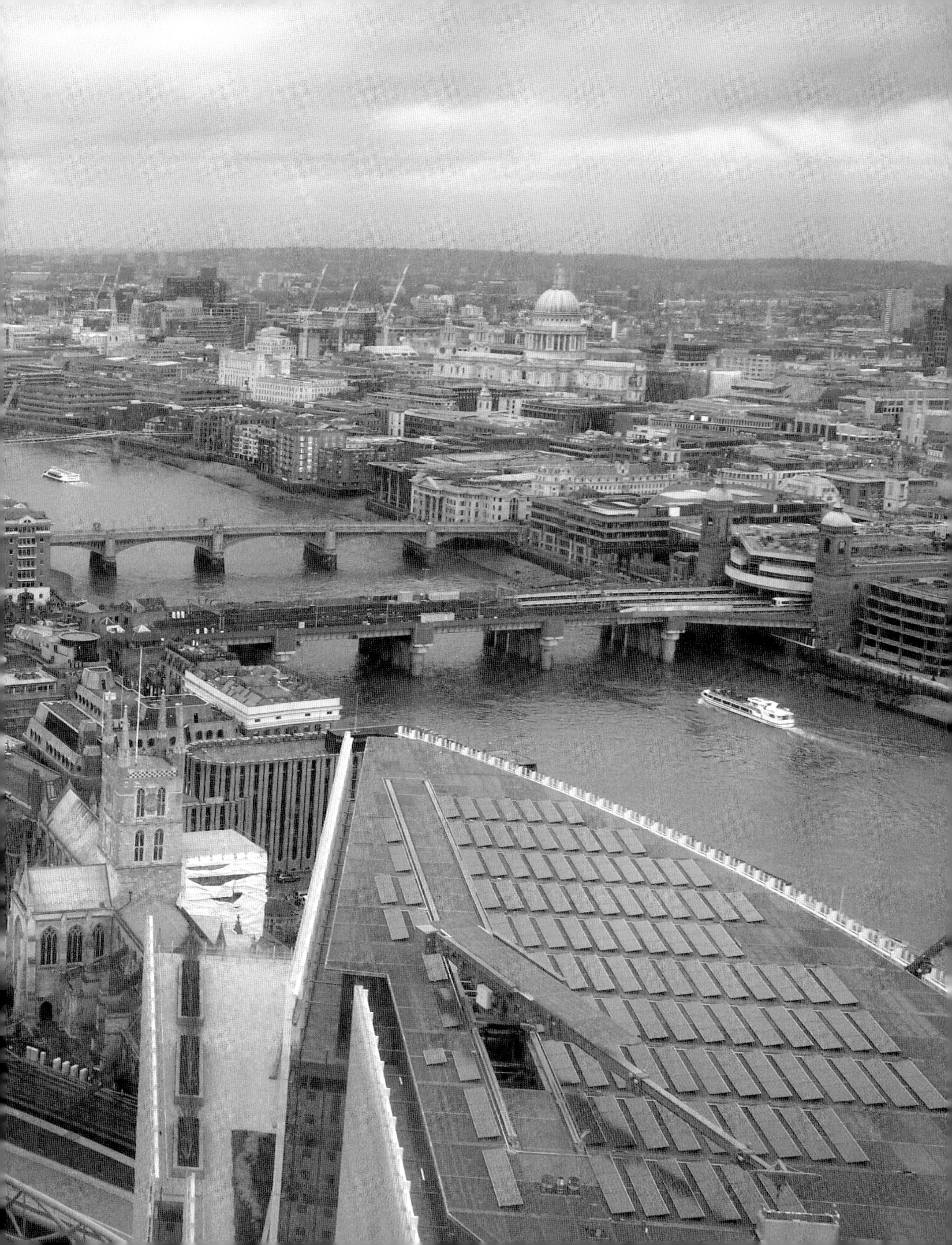

it was the productive landscapes of industry that shaped the form of large swathes of landscape and cityscape alike. Under the control of a feudal regime, the countryside of Yorkshire in England was divided up into fields for agriculture and livestock. Stone walls divide and subdivide properties in a hierarchical manner as land is passed down through the sons of each subsequent generation.[2] The city of Leeds is a consequence of a feudal heritage. The whole city is planned around the trading hub burgage plots at the busy crossroads of Briggate and Kirkgate, and was economically boosted by the opening of the Leeds and Liverpool Canal and the Leeds to Selby Railway, which linked the town to the important port of Hull. Leeds became an industrial giant, and its trading infrastructures such as the Leeds Central Market and Corn Exchange were marvels of engineering. The latter was built to provide a dry and brightly lit trading environment for millers, brewers, maltsters and the local market, and included 59 offices for merchants.[3] Later, as more of the tight plots on the main streets were divided, the back streets, residences and passages were cleared and carved-out to build Leeds' iconic and luxurious Victorian arcades, an infrastructure where one can shop, gossip and retreat from the wheeled traffic, the soot and Yorkshire drizzle of the 19th century city. The eight original arcades were part of a greater scheme to establish a stronger civic identity and self-esteem to coincide with the town being granted city status in 1893.[4] Intrinsically, like most cities, Leeds is a collection of both hard and soft infrastructures past and present, aimed to protect, to provide and to participate.

The character of the infrastructure defines the city, its society and underlines countless nuanced forms of human activities. The pyramids, intended for the Egyptian belief in the divinity of their rulers and afterlife, were early forms of housing and storage; they were recognized as the archetypical urban infrastructure to protect. The shape of the infrastructure is thought to be representative of the descending rays of the sun and symbolized the mythical primeval mound of creation, from which the Egyptians believed the earth was created. The pyramids were built on the west bank of the Nile in Giza, the site of the setting sun associated with the realm of the dead in Egyptian mythology. The Pyramid of Khufu occupies a 5.4-hectare base, an area equal to the combined base areas of the cathedrals of Florence and Milan, St. Peter's in Rome, and St Paul's Cathedral and Westminster Abbey in London;[5] and is the only surviving monument of the Seven Wonders of the Ancient World, long after its creators, ancient cities and society have disappeared.

Medieval Bruges became a port city due to an unexpected environmental calamity. In the early 1100s, a tidal wave swept some 15 kilometers up the River Zwin, brought the North Sea into Bruges and created a transversal dike at the end of the channel.[6] The infrastructure, henceforth, provided the city with a large harbor and established the prosperity of both Bruges and its fore-port Damme for more than three centuries. Bruges was quickly established as an economic capital of Europe and the wealth afforded many public buildings including the imposing 83-meter high belfry in the Grand-Place.

The urban charisma of Paris today is a tapestry of historic grains – the layout of its streets and the sequential series of walled territories, each one bringing with it protection and new sets of infrastructure, be it a moat, or shielded farmland, or new roads. As Paris grew, houses were built both inside and outside the wall, and with each wall demolished, a street appeared. While the Philippe Auguste Wall marked an early construct for defensive purpose, the Wall of the Ferme Générale was the first to be built for a controlled tax zone, an infrastructure of money. The architect Claude Nicolas Ledoux designed over 60 of its iconic toll barriers.

Emperor Napoleon III and his prefect of Seine, Baron Haussmann, (in)famously carved up the medieval Parisian districts and slums to make way for a series of grand boulevards spanning over 80 kilometers. Their ambitious public infrastructure program helped to control the city and its population, especially at times of civil unrest. The reconstruction program strategically demolished the encircling city customs wall to allow expansion into the surrounding suburbs. The cramped and unhealthy medieval neighborhoods were replaced, and at the same time, underground water and sewer systems were constructed beneath new streets. The widening of the streets stimulated the economy and employment with implementation of marketplaces and public architectural projects, including cultural palaces. The green boulevards and streets intersected each other, while maintaining the geometric and symmetrical aesthetic of the grand sweeping Parisian landscape. In addition to the new 1,100 kilometers of sidewalks with trees, the green lungs in the form of public parks increased the densely vegetated area of the city from less than 0.2 square kilometers to nearly 20 square kilometers.[7]

The 1.9-kilometer long Avenue des Champs-Élysées is the archetypal Parisian boulevard-type street and perfectly expresses the French national sentiment of liberty. In 2010, freed of its frenetic motor traffic, the avenue mobilized some 55,000 struggling French farmers and staged a beautiful reminder of their trade by recreating the 'Elysian Fields' with more than 8,000 plots of earth, 150,000 plants and 650 fully grown trees, along with pigs, cows, horses and sheep. This is precisely the embodiment of Marxist writer Marshall Berman's appraisal of the boulevards as 'the most spectacular urban innovation of the 19th century, and the decisive breakthrough in the modernization of the traditional city' because they 'open up the whole of the city, for the first time in its history, to all its inhabitants. Now, at last, it was possible to move not only within neighbourhoods but through them. Now, after centuries of life as a cluster of isolated cells, Paris is becoming a unified physical and human space.'[8] The Champs-Élysées, meaning Elysian Fields, was an area of vegetable gardens and fields until the 17th century, whereas today it makes an iconic place and setting for the Parisian reputation of high-fashion, style and luxury retailing.[9]

As in Paris, the principal infrastructure of any city plan is the street. Joseph Rykwert defines the street as 'human movement institutionalized'.[10] Rather than being a convenient infrastructure for traffic, the street is 'a complex civic institution, culture-specific and capable of dazzling formal variations and calculated nuance – a balancing act complicated by the advent of automobile'.[11] A utility and sometimes ceremonial infrastructure, the street comes in all scales, from the ring road, avenue and boulevard, to the alley and colonnaded arcade, elevated walkways and the embankment sidewalk. In Vienna, the shop-lined Karntner Strasse stretches from Stephansdom, the tallest cathedral in the world at Stephansplatz, out to the Wiener Staatsoper at Karlsplatz on the Ringstrasse. In the densest part of the Moroccan cities Fez and Marrakesh, the narrow vernacular streets protect pedestrians with systems of trellis and awnings and take the role of ancient forums, cultivating civic solidarity under the burning sun. Throughout Europe, North Africa and Asia, arcades are communal spaces as they are incorporated into urban public infrastructure systems. Milan's Galleria Vittorio Emanuele is the most spectacular of traditional Italian covered arcades while Bologna's streets are accompanied by nearly 20 miles of 'portici'. In 'The Death and Life of Great American Cities' (1961), Jane Jacobs strongly emphasized the intimate life of a city street with its neighborhood shops and people chatting on the sidewalks, and it is the coming together and sharing of ideas that make a richer life.

2. D Simpson, 'Medieval Leeds/Victorian Leeds', Yorkshire: History and places to visit, 2009 [http://www.yorkshire-england.co.uk/Leeds.html], retrieved 18 July 2015

3. T Quinn & M Jones, 'Leeds: A photographic journey through Yorkshire's largest city', Myriad Books, London, 2008, pp.32–33

4. P Dobraszczyk, 'The Victorian Arcades of Leeds', 2011 [http://ragpickinghistory.co.uk/2011/04/29/the-victorian-arcades-of-leeds/], retrieved 18 July 2015

5. DM Burton, 'The History of Mathematics: An introduction', McGraw-Hill, New York, 2011, p.58

6. RH Charlier, 'Grandeur, Decadence and Renaissance', Journal of Coastal Research, special issue.42, 'The Sun, Earth and Moon', Spring 2005, p.433

7. AB Jacobs, E MacDonald & Y Rofe, 'The Boulevard Book: History, evolution, design of multiway boulevards', The MIT Press, Cambridge, Massachusetts, 2002, p.78

8. M Berman, 'All That Is Solid Melts into Air: The experience of modernity', Viking Penguin, New York, 1988, pp.150–151

9. H Schofield, 'French farmers turn Champs-Elysees into huge farm', BBC News: Europe, 23 May 2010, [http://www.bbc.co.uk/news/10143393], retrieved 1 August 2015

10. J Rykwert, 'The Neccessity of Artifice', Rizzoli, New York, 1982, p.105

11. S Kostof, 'The City Assembled', Thames & Hudson, London, 1999, p.220

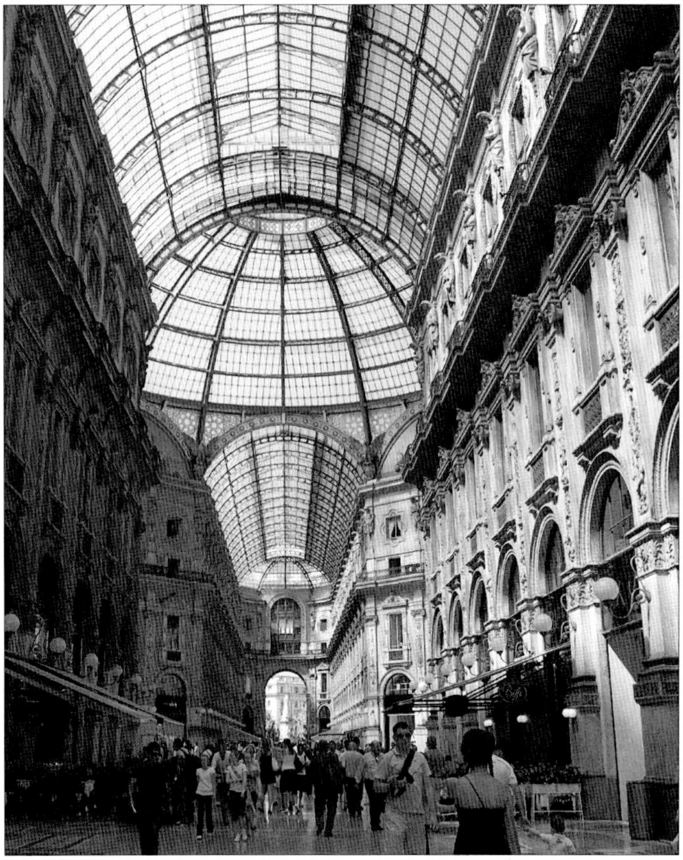

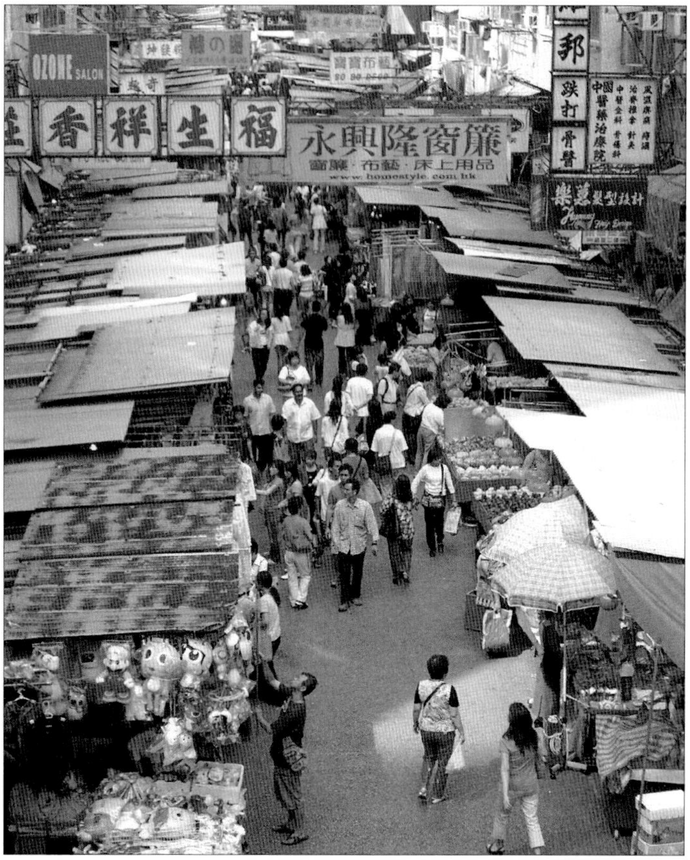
OZONE SALON
永興隆窗簾
窗簾·布藝·床上用品
www.homestyle.com.hk

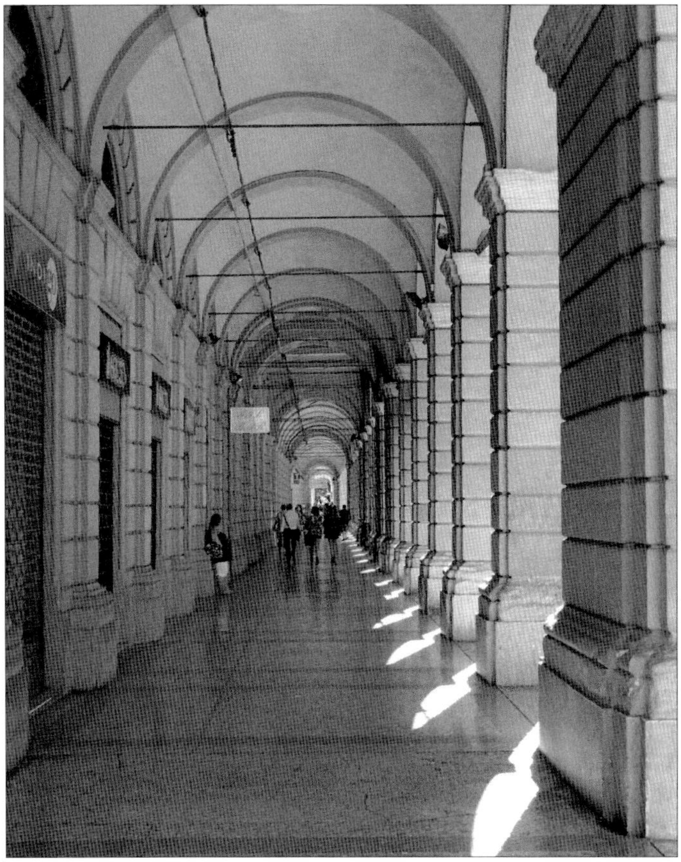

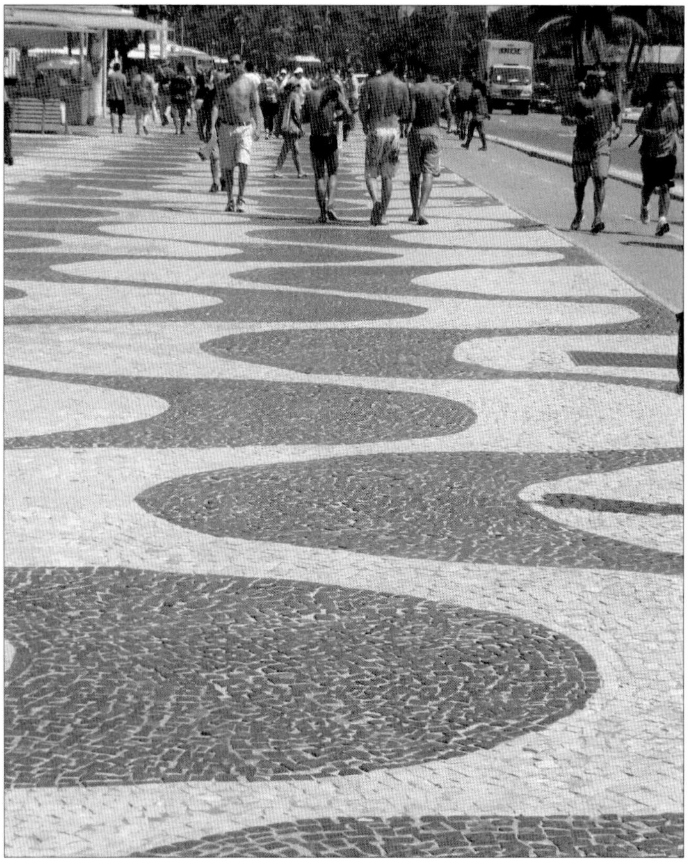

the city as a collection of infrastructures

facing page from top left clockwise: Milan, Hong Kong, Rio de Janeiro, and Bologna strongly emphasize the intimate life of their streets.

left and following pages: Sites of collective wellbeing, public encounter and participation of civic culture in Times Square, New York, and on Galata Bridge, Istanbul.

67

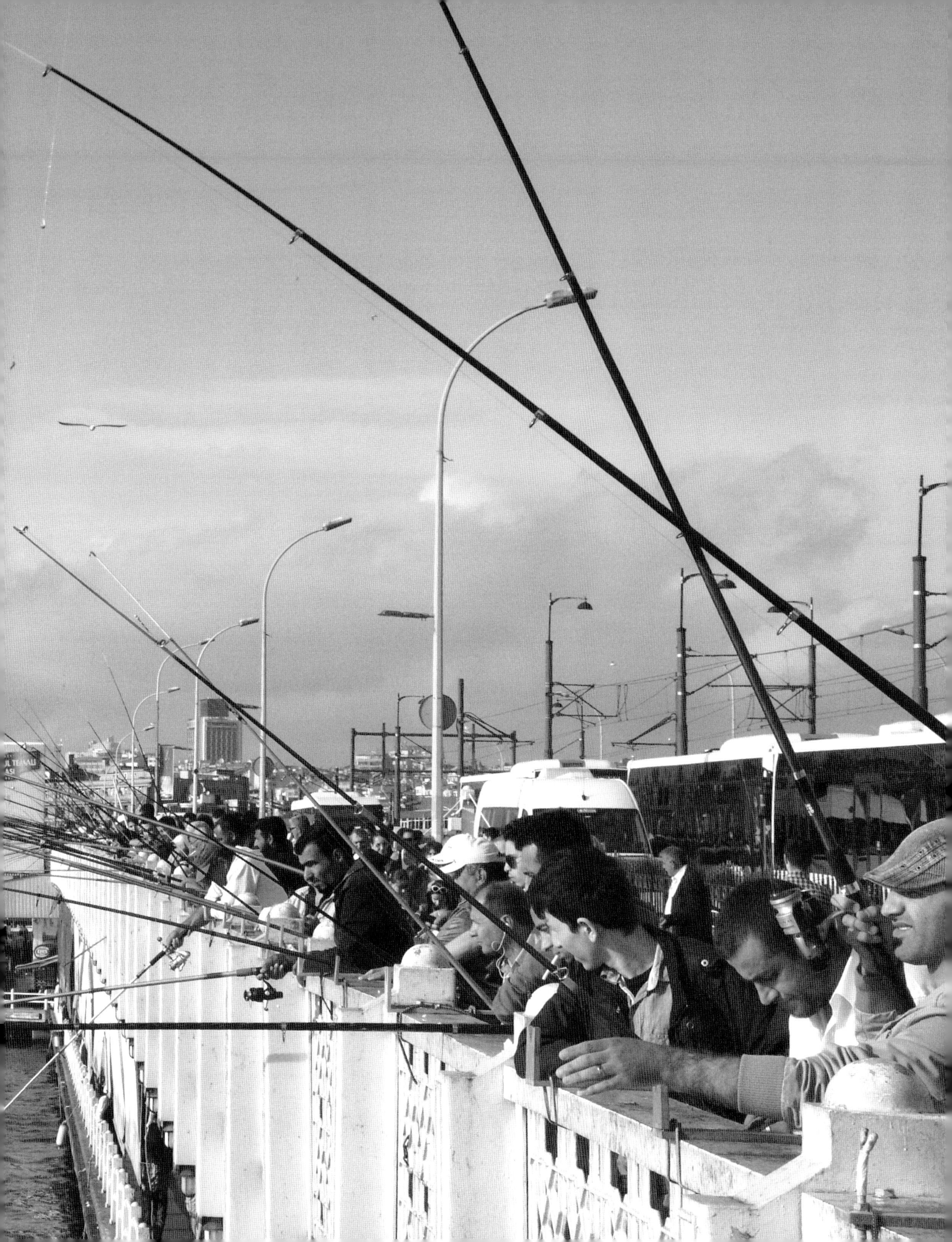

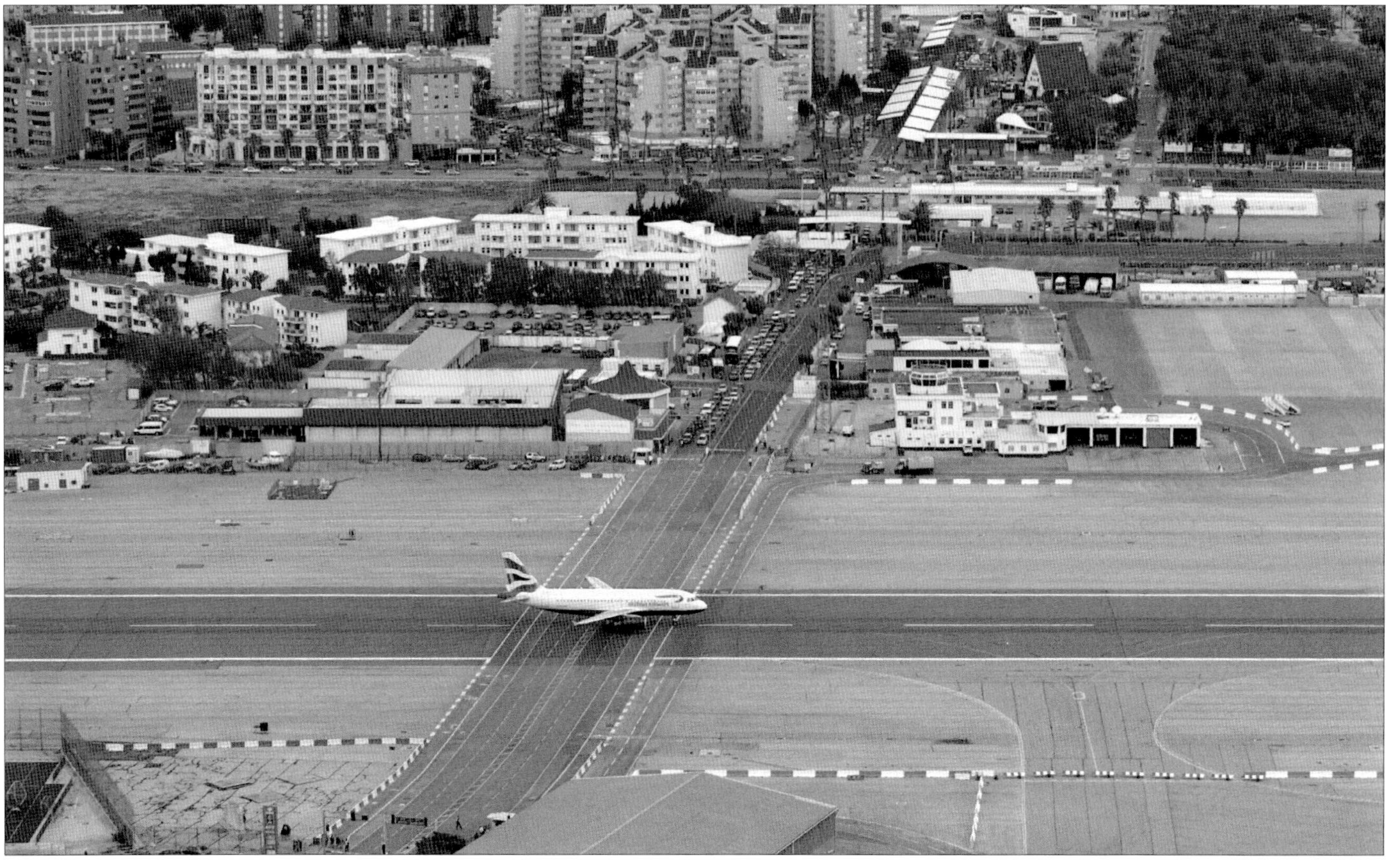

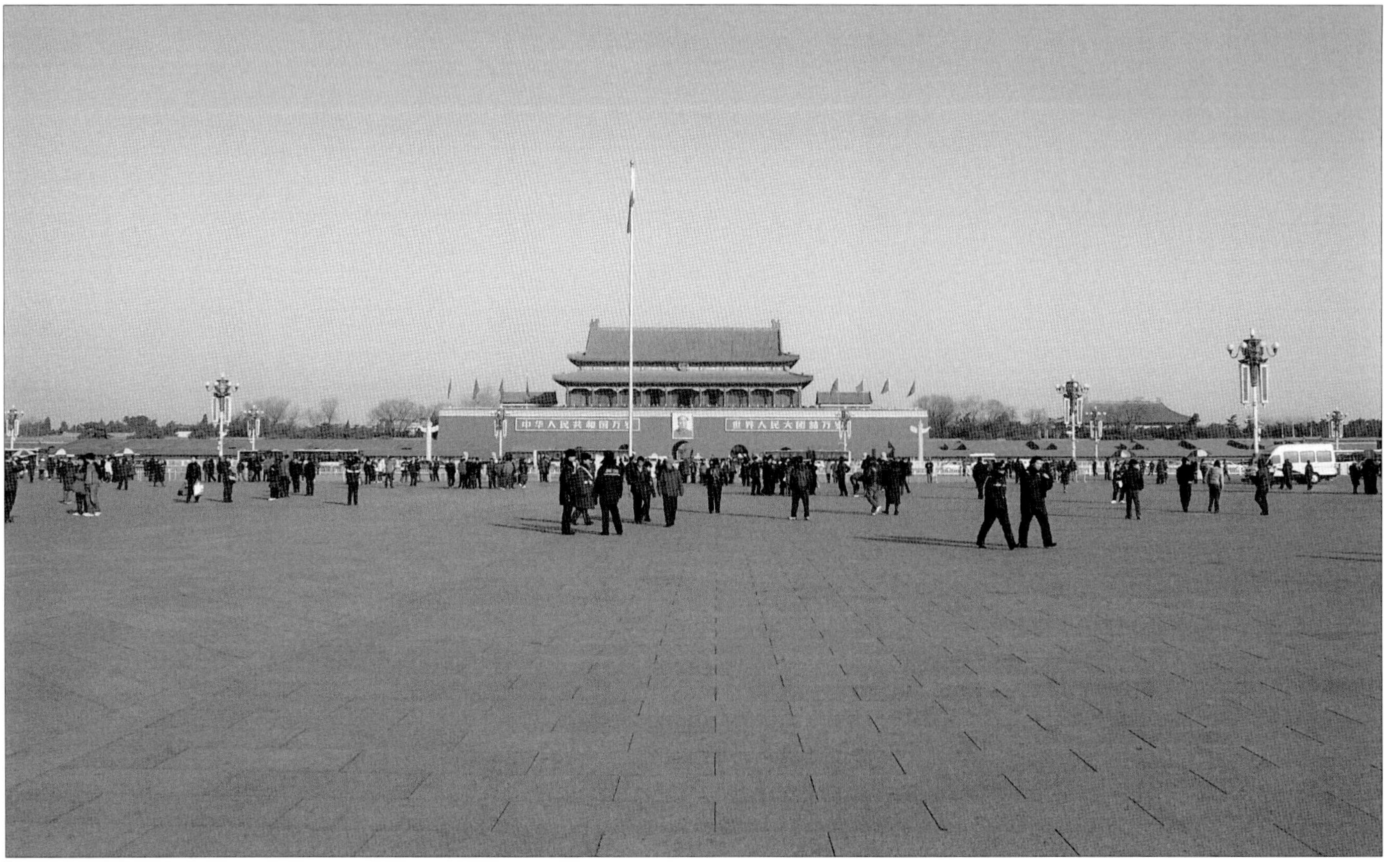
中华人民共和国万岁
世界人民大团结万岁

the city as a collection of infrastructures

Within a city, there are often several converging locations that serve as symbols of collective wellbeing, expressions of achievement and aspiration by leaders and visionaries, sites of public encounter and participation of civic culture, and significant spaces of political deliberation and agonistic struggle.[12] On the tiny peninsula of Gibraltar, the airport runway has to intersect the four-lane Winston Churchill Avenue as a consequence of limited available flat land. Whenever a flight departs or arrives, pedestrians and cars stop at barriers on either side of the runway – a novel solution. The open space is an important infrastructure of any city plan; Tiananmen Square in Beijing, Place de la Concorde in Paris and Times Square in New York each have a different form as well as social and political functions. While Moscow's Red Square is associated with Lenin's tomb and displays of military hardware, Berkeley Square, Grosvenor Square and Russell Square serve as reminders that London is most inviting when nature is included.

Religion, amongst other factors, had profound influence on the rise of cities and their infrastructures. Centuries after the fall of the Roman Empire, cathedrals remained the most important urban buildings. The Catholic Church and its bishops would build urban centers in the thriving cathedral district and establish church schools, hospitals, monasteries and markets. The medieval market city of St Albans owed its existence to one of the wealthiest religious establishments in England, the Abbey Church. The churches of St Michael's, St Peter's and St Stephen marked the cathedral city's entrances.[13]

Similar to their European counterpart, mosques are innovative multi-use infrastructures in which worship, religious education, general administration, and public assembly take place. Their courtyards are filled not only with worshippers but also with children taking lessons, women gossiping, and old men, seemingly, just sitting around. The Great Mosque of Cordoba held a place of importance amongst the Islamic community of al-Andalus for three centuries. Cairo, the city of a thousand minarets, has one of the greatest concentrations of historical monuments of Islamic architecture in the world including the influential Al-Azhar Mosque.

In the center of Istanbul, the vast domed cathedral of Hagia Sophia and the Sultan Ahmed Cami 'Blue Mosque' gaze across the Sultanahmet Park at one another. The Byzantine Emperor Justinian I built the cathedral in the 6th century, while the mosque was completed during the reign of Sultan Ahmet I in the 17th century. The two majestic buildings, with their giant buttresses and soaring slender minarets, commanded the trade routes between the Aegean Sea and the Black Sea from their strategic positions. Like Istanbul itself, the infrastructures both divide and join the inhabitants of the city and their history, symbolizing a cultural difference of epic proportions – medieval Christianity, the Ottoman Empire, resurgent Islam and modern Turkey. In 2006, the head of the Catholic Church, Pope Benedict XVI, visited the Blue Mosque and hoped that Turkey 'will be a bridge of friendship and collaboration between East and West'.[14]

Reputation makes powerful cities. The use of technological infrastructure to assert supremacy over nature (and mankind) by the USA and the Soviet Union can be dated back to Hellenistic Alexandria. Instead of building Alexandria on the Nile delta, Alexander the Great strategically selected a site some

facing page top: The airport runway intersects Winston Churchill Avenue in Gibraltar – the city comes to a stand-still several times a day when planes arrive and depart.

facing page bottom: Tiananmen Square in Beijing is an infrastructure of national celebrations and violent protests.

12. A Amin, 'Collective Culture and Urban Public Space', B Catterall (ed.) City, Routledge, Oxford, vol.12, issue.1, April 2008, pp.5–24

13. 'The Medieval Town of St Albans', The Cathedral and Abbey Church of Saint Alban [https://www.stalbanscathedral.org/history/the-road-to-magna-carta/the-medieval-town-of-st-albans], retrieved 18 August 2015

14. N Kar, 'Blue Mosque, only mosque in Istanbul with six minarets', Anadolu Agency [http://www.aa.com.tr/en/special-news/272794--blue-mosque-only-mosque-in-istanbul-with-six-minarets], retrieved 18 August 2015

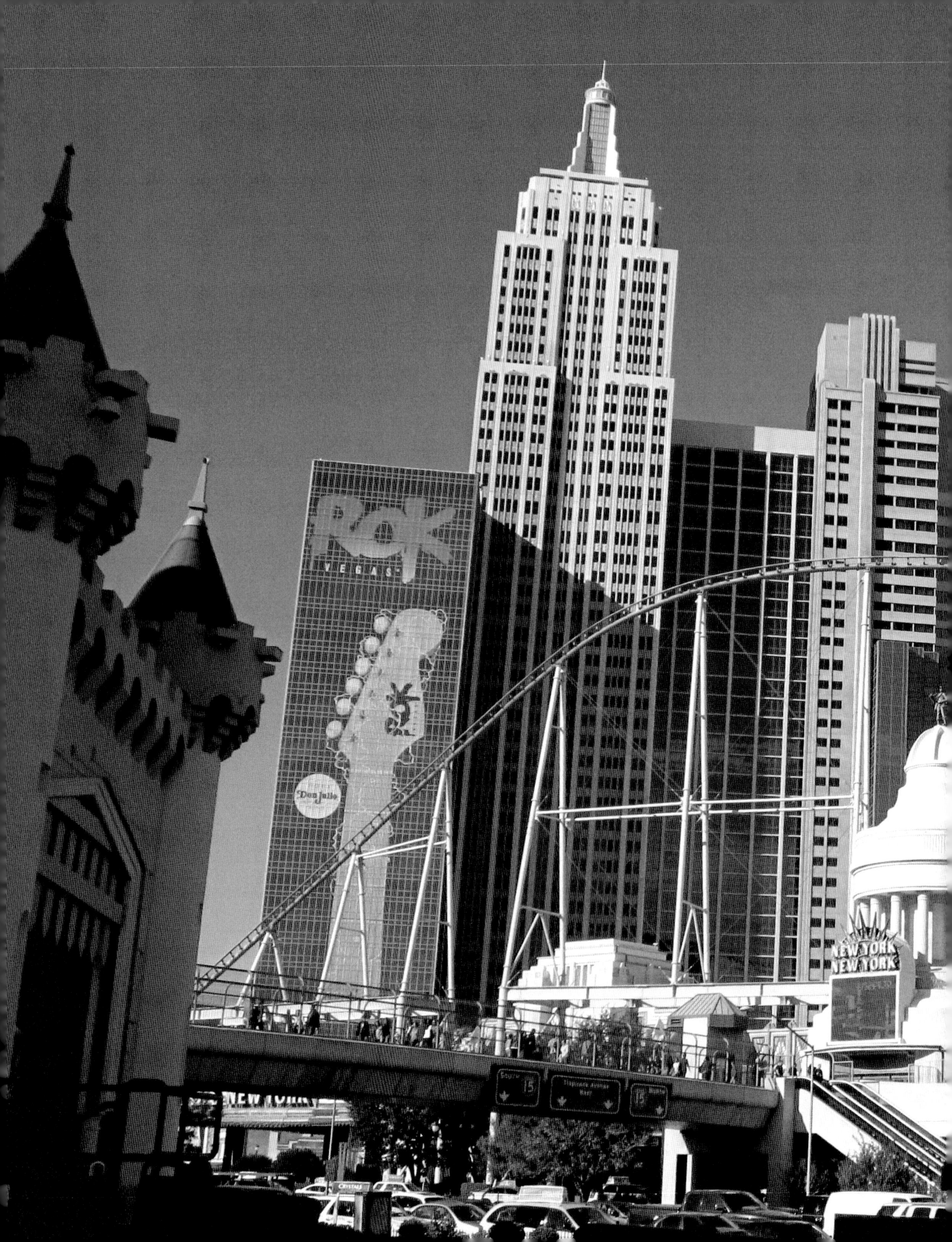
VEGAS
Don Julio
NEW YORK
NEW YORK

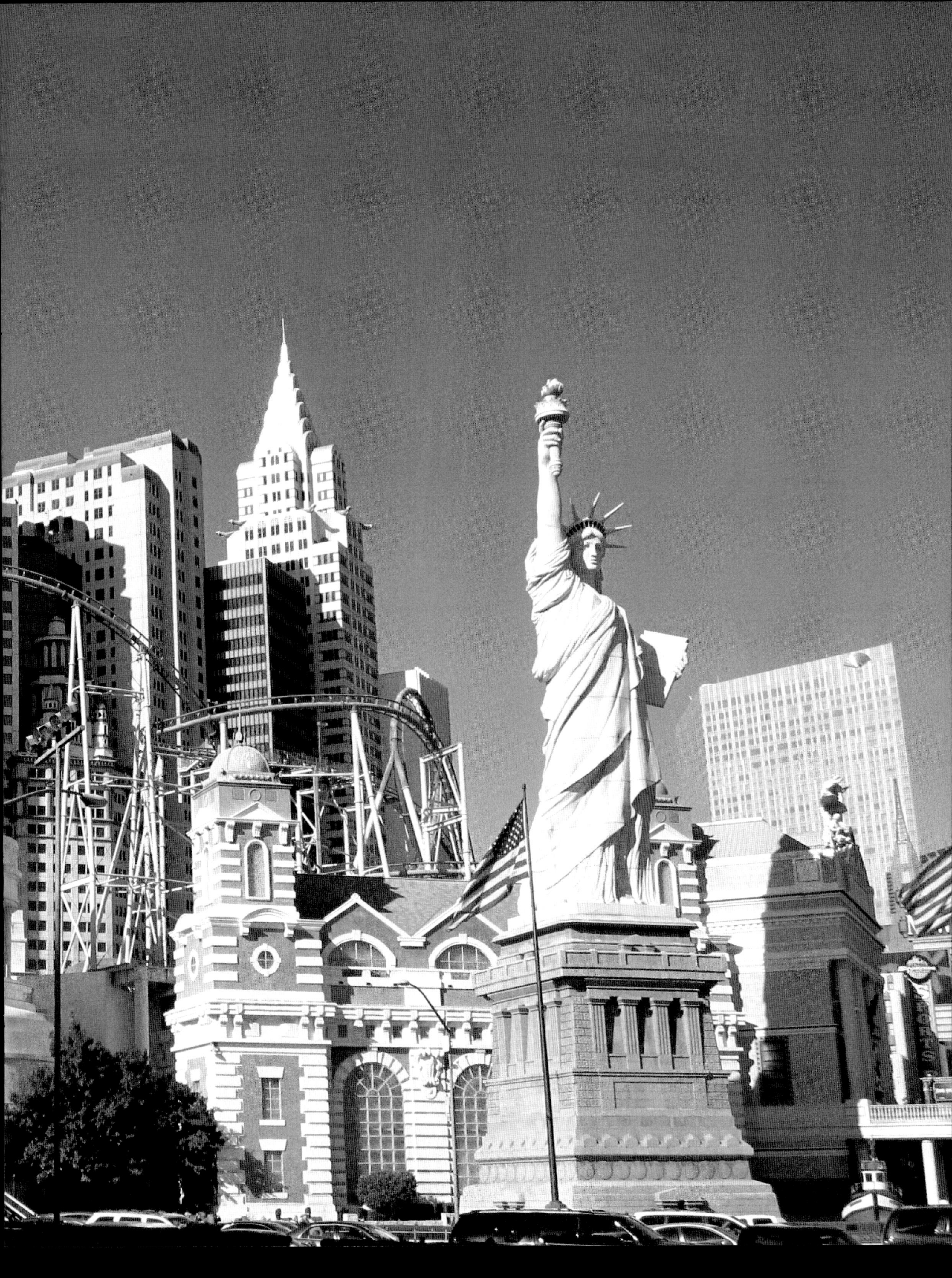

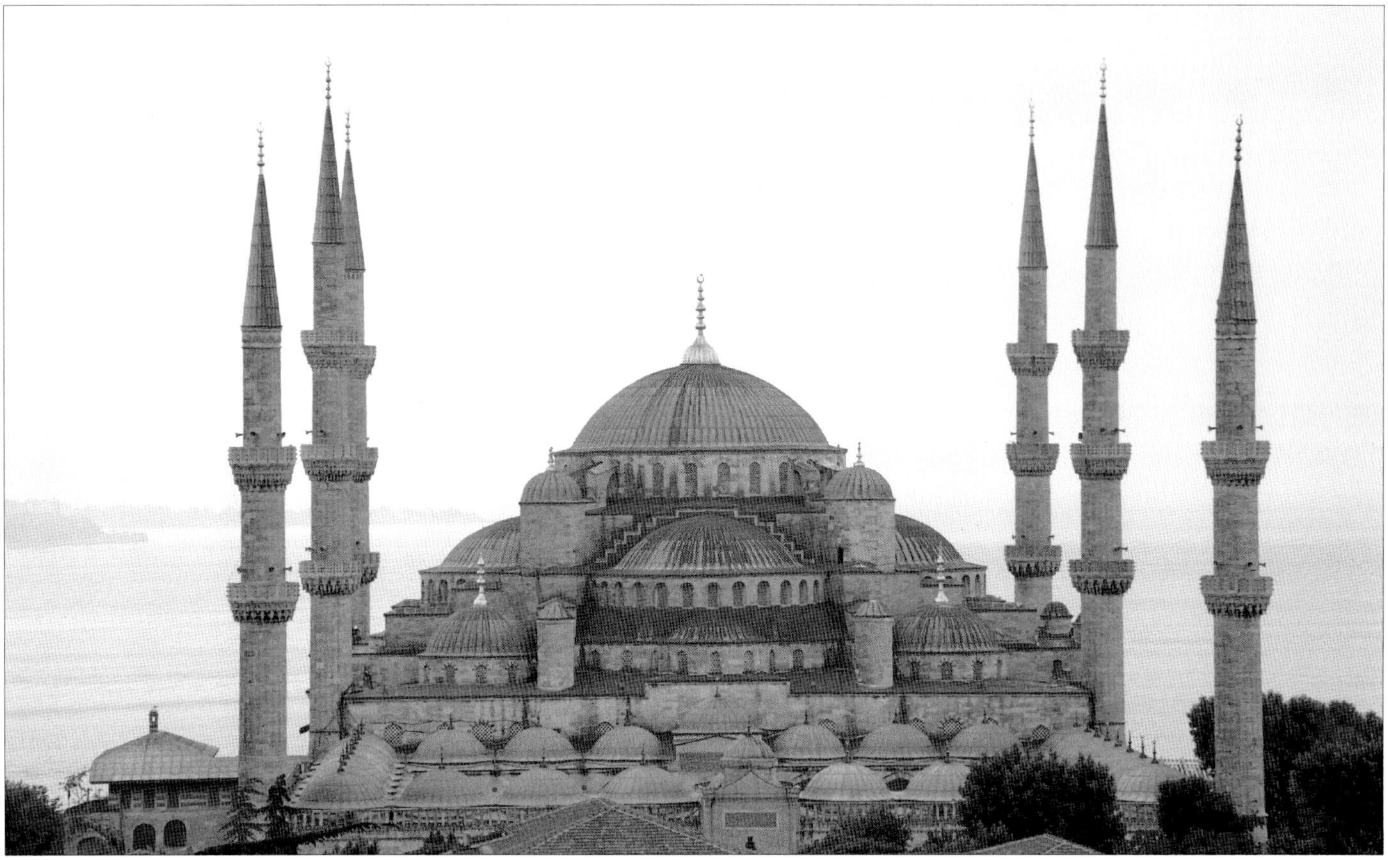

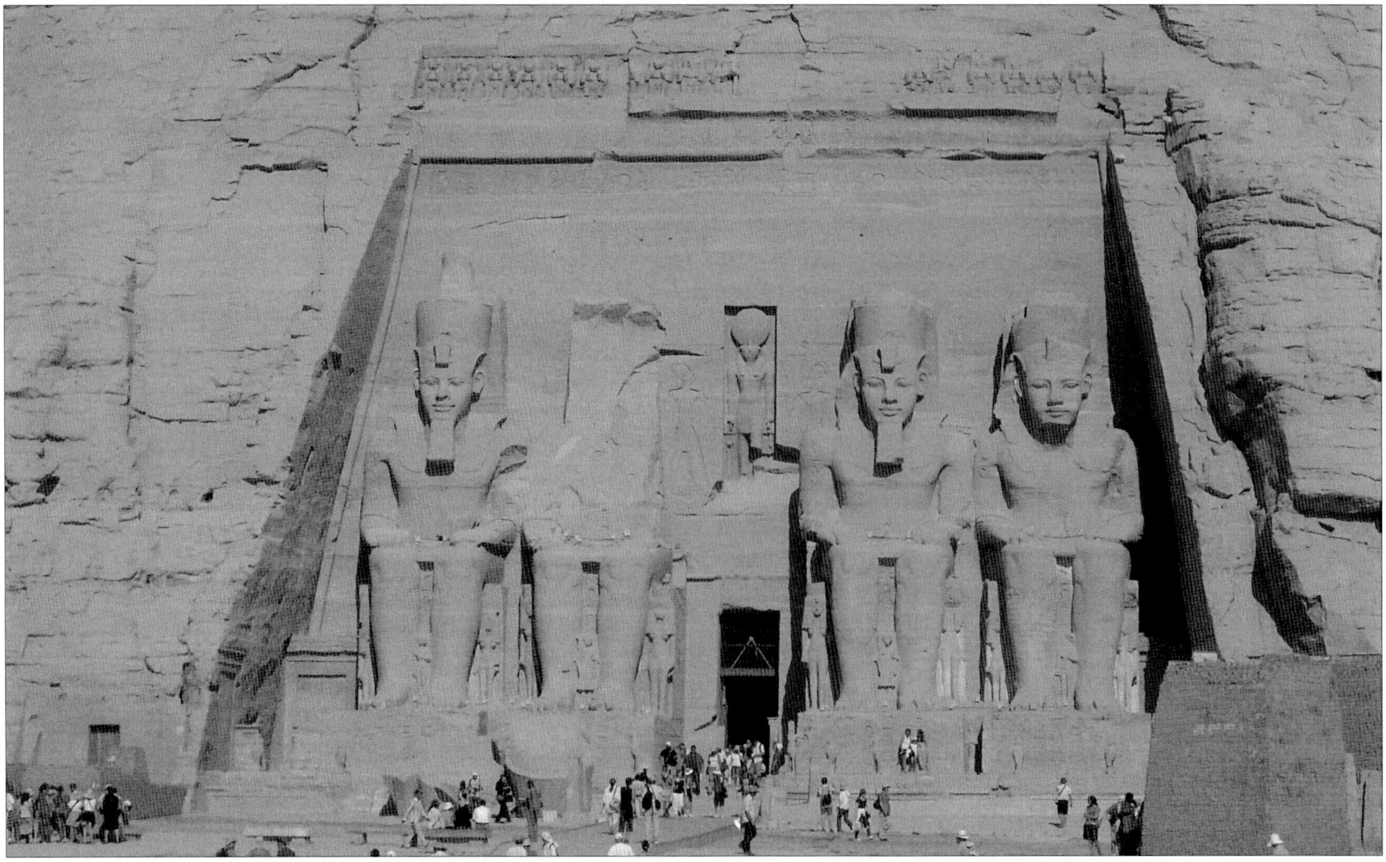

the city as a collection of infrastructures

20 miles to the west and north of the marshy Lake Mareotis, so that the silt and mud carried by the river would not block the harbor city. The Heptastadion, a causeway infrastructure, was constructed to link the mainland to the island of Pharos, thus creating two remarkable harbors: one for Nile River traffic and military vessels, and the other for Mediterranean Sea trade.[15] The harbors would long remain deep and clear, and made Alexandria the most powerful metropolis of the Orient, accumulating culture and wealth.

Alexandria paraded the world's first lighthouse, Pharos, to further demonstrate its technical prowess to other civilizations and its power over nature. The whole infrastructure was estimated to be over 117 meters high.[16] Topped by a continually burning fire at night, it boasted fuel wagons pulled by mules on spiral ramps, a camera obscura spyglass to observe the neighboring city of Constantinople, and an Archimedean burning lens to reflect sunlight visible in the harbor from 56 kilometers away.[17] Until its demise in the 14th century, legends claimed that the death ray from the large curved mirror could destroy enemy ships before they could sail into the harbor. The Pharos has many characteristics in common with modern skyscrapers.

Tall infrastructures are concerns of utility, the provision of masts, observation platforms and transmitters; accommodation compressed by extraordinary land values; foundation conditions; or exotic siting. Structural engineer Matthew Wells recognizes that 'tall infrastructures are built with an idealism for the sublime and the embodiment of corporate, global and international powers; perhaps symbolizing mankind's search for utopia'.[18]

The American city was the first to conceive the modern skyscraper. Elevator technology, electricity and steel frames allowed buildings to rise up dozens of storeys, from the Flatiron Building to the Chrysler to the Empire State Building; they became highly expressive monuments to the power of capitalism and technology. Manhattan Island was transformed in the early 20th century, soon becoming one of the most awe-inspiring and intense sites of architectural experimentation anywhere in the world.

For Le Corbusier that was not enough – he infamously stated after his visit to the city that the buildings were disappointing compared to their reputation; they were 'much too small'. In line with his vision for cities, the towers would be huge and a lot further apart. In 1937, on his return from the USA, Corbusier published his recrimination towards the nation's attitudes, architects and planning in 'Quand les Cathédrales Étaient Blanches' ('When the Cathedrals Were White'); the book had the subtitle 'A Journey to the Country of Timid People'. Being clearly unimpressed by the lacking imagination and poor vision of American skyscrapers and suburbs, Corbusier felt depressed that the Americans had at their disposal freely available dream-opportunities, which they squandered.

Le Corbusier presented one of his most extraordinary visionary projects in the shape of an inhabited viaduct – 'Plan Obus' (1932). The proposed edifice cum infrastructure for Algiers would, had it been realized, have stretched for 15 kilometers around the bay with a transport highway running along its top. The residential mega-structure would hang in the sky, into which individual housing units and

previous pages: Heterotopia, an integral part of social infrastructures that range from Disneyland to Las Vegas.

facing page top: The 400-year-old Blue Mosque has six minarets, five main domes and eight secondary domes.

facing page bottom: The relocation of the Great Temple of Ramesses II was necessary to prevent it from being submerged during the creation of Lake Nasser, the massive artificial water reservoir formed after the building of the Aswan High Dam on the Nile River.

15. UNESCO Environmental Development in Coastal Regions and in Small Islands, 'Alexandria's Place in History' [http://www.unesco.org/csi/pub/papers2/alex6.html], retrieved 11 August 2015

16. AS Elnashai, L Di Sarno & MD Carter, 'New Light on an Ancient Illumination: The Pharos of Alexandria', International Journal of Nonlinear Sciences and Numerical Simulation, Freund Publishing House, Tel Aviv, 2006, pp.137–148

17. M Wells, 'Skyscrapers: Structures and design', Lawrence King Publishing, London, 2005, pp.6–7

18. M Wells, 'Skyscrapers: Structures and design', Lawrence King Publishing, London, 2005, p.6

76

urban blocks could be inserted. The infrastructure would make links to the city by colossal sky bridges spanning over the historic structures of the Casbah. 'Algiers was a major phase for me. Faced with that imposing natural setting I opened up my urbanism to new, flexible splendours, parts of the elements, as it were; sea, sun, cliffs, vegetation… a phase adding prodigious poetry to our energy.'[19]

With today's continually escalating population, changing expectations and challenging climate change obligations, infrastructure is the means to ensuring sustainable functioning of the city. Infrastructure has always been fundamental to London's urban, social and economic development. In the 19th century, innovative infrastructures such as the London Underground and Sir Joseph Bazalgette's sewer system collectively reduced traffic congestion, provided greater access to employment opportunities, and improved the health and wellbeing of the city. Later in the 20th century, the Thames Barrier, the Docklands Light Railway, the Channel Tunnel between London and Paris, and a network of airports have, in their different ways, improved London's security and connectivity. The Thames Barrier protects central London from flooding caused by tidal surges and was originally designed to last up to the year 2030. Recent analysis suggests that even with sea level rise in line with anticipated climate change, the barrier will offer sufficient protection until 2060–70.[20] With the introduction of the Crown Lands Act 1851, the eight Royal Parks became free accessible open spaces covering almost 20 square kilometers of land. The parks along with their 3,000 trees[21] are vital historic urban infrastructures in the living fabric of London – a role important in many other cities too.

Sociologist Saskia Sassen believes that 'the public space is a place in which there is a momentary condition of equality. At some point in the future, many overused cities will have to be reconstructed'.[22] Aspirations and speculations bring about new and meaningful infrastructures for our urban futures. The city, from a simple settlement, can be read as a collection of infrastructures and as a collage of places. There are countless nuanced forms of 'place' that occur with the melding of hard and soft infrastructures. The Japanese architect Kengo Kuma bemoans the built environment trends that have led to mass-application of prefabricated steel, concrete and glass cities, and mourns for the lost craftsmanship and traditions of Japan, severing ties to culture and heritage, and the nuanced relationships which used to constitute meaningful connections of place and human beings.[23]

'I am convinced that the earthquake and tsunami that struck the Tohoku region of Japan on 11 March 2011 provided an opportunity to redress the balance of social and cultural decline… When I saw the tsunami washing away those American-style houses and cars, Noah's flood came to mind.'
   – Kengo Kuma, 'Kengo Kuma: Complete works', 2012

facing page: New York, the American city conceived for the modern vertical infrastructure.

19. L Corbusier, 'Letter to His Mother, 4th April, 1931' in 'Le Corbusier Le Grand', T Benton, Phaidon, London, 2008, p.270

20. T de Castella, 'How does the Thames Barrier Stop London from Flooding?', BBC News Magazine, 11 February 2014 [http://www.bbc.co.uk/news/magazine-26133660], retrieved 14 August 2015

21. 'The Royal Parks Corporate Plan 2013-16', The Royal Parks, 2013 [https://www.royalparks.org.uk/__data/assets/pdf_file/0017/41750/the-royal-parks-corporate-plan-2013-16.pdf], retrieved 14 August 2015

22. S Sassen, 'Justice and Equality', Barcelona Debate 2015 – Wield the Word, Centre of Contemporary Culture of Barcelona: Public Space, February 2015 [http://www.publicspace.org/en/post/public-space-is-a-place-in-which-there-is-a-momentary-condition-of-equality], retrieved 15 August 2015

23. K Frampton & K Kuma, 'Kengo Kuma: Complete works', Thames & Hudson, London, 2012, p.9

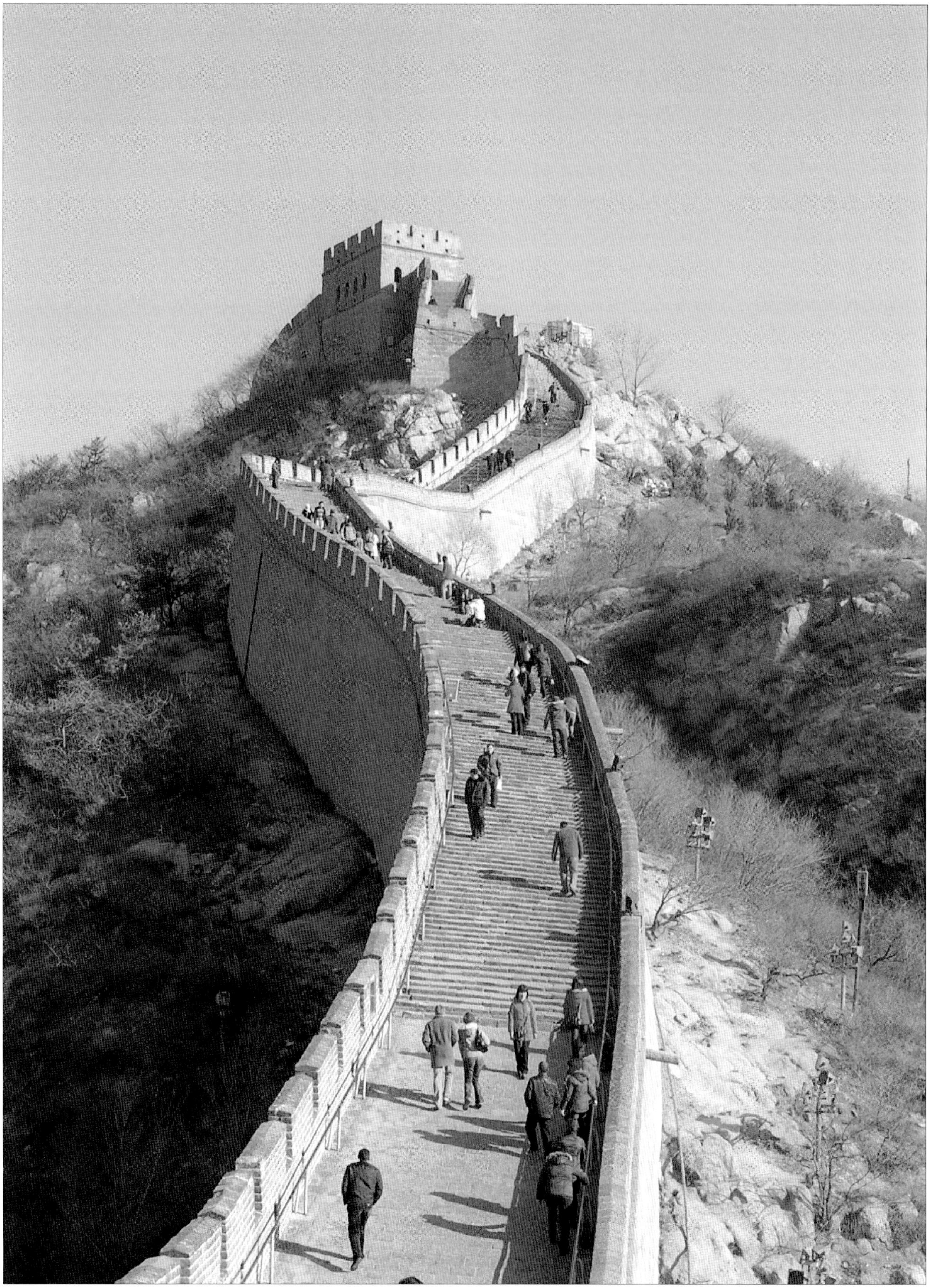

To Protect

'As we pass through cities, we are travelling between the walls of other people's lives. From Beijing to Berlin, in our seven-thousand-year love affair with cities, walls have – at different times and different places – imprisoned people and helped set them free.'
  – PD Smith, 'City: A guide for the urban age', 2012

The evolution of society and the city has been shaped by the strong desire to protect the individual, the community and its possessions from invasions by means of walls and fortifications. The transition from a nomadic hunting and food-gathering economy to an agricultural settlement marked the beginning of defensive infrastructures taking on monolithic permanent forms. Fortifications assured their inhabitants not only safety from enemies but also dominance over the surrounding territory and controlled urban sprawl. Historic urban walls had common characteristics of continuous high ramparts reinforced with towers, bastions, and gates, surrounded by a deep moat enclosing an inhabited area. The silhouette and quality of the infrastructure defined the character of the city, and underscored its wealth and power.

Considered the oldest settlement, the ancient city of Jericho, Tell es-Sultan, protected its sophisticated Neolithic social and political systems with a massive, round, stone-wall fortification.[1] The concept of a defensive infrastructure was very different in Çatalhöyük, where the continuous and shared blank walls of the Anatolian houses formed an economical and unique fusion of the urban fabric with the settlement's protection. The urban plan was without streets and all traffic moved across rooftops. Single storied mud-brick houses were built side-by-side, had no doors to the outside and were entered via ladders from the roof. The occasional open courtyard interrupted the solid building mass not for circulation or social interactions, only to facilitate collection of rubbish. Another feature of Çatalhöyük was that the inhabitants protected their dead by burying them under the floors.[2]

From the third millennium, ramparts were considered an important characteristic of Mesopotamian urban defensive infrastructure. The rigid geometric arrangements reflected circulation patterns and had wall thickness that varied between 25 and 34 meters in ancient Ur; and those of Babylon were reputed to be 25 meters in height.[3] While the need for new defenses was incremental and coincided with that of urban expansion, economic and military responsibilities, some fortifications have been the outcome of democracy and the consequent awakening of civic consciousness. Ancient Greek towns developed with autonomous and cultured societal life; old citadels with more isolated strongholds were destroyed making way for the new urbanism of the empire. The Long Walls, the connection from the city of Athens to its ports at Piraeus, were dismantled after the Peloponnesian War as one of the key terms

facing page: With a total length of more than 20,000 kilometers, the Great Wall was built to protect China from outside aggression, but also to preserve its culture.

1. H de la Croix, 'Military Considerations in City Planning: Fortifications', George Braziller Inc., New York, 1972, p.13

2. J Mellaart, 'Catal Huyuk: A Neolithic town in Anatolia', McGraw-Hill Book Company, New York, 1967, pp.58–67

3. H dela Croix, 'Military Considerations in City Planning: Fortifications', George Braziller Inc., New York, 1972, p.15

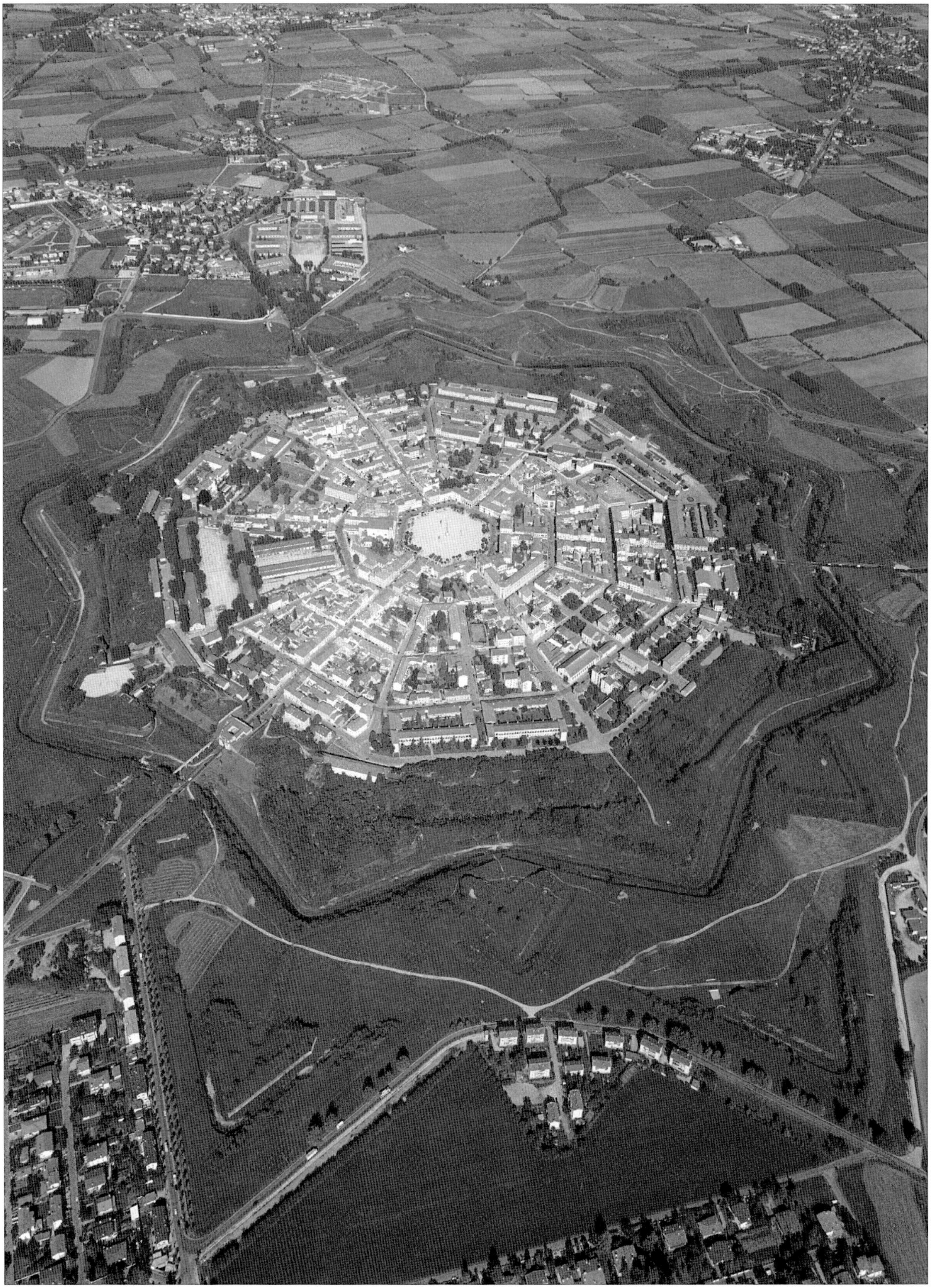

of the Athenian surrender to the Spartans. The demonstrable effectiveness of the walls was such that within a few decades of the destruction, they were re-built following rebellion against the Spartan's imposed government. The infrastructure protected Athens and its democracy whilst providing security of resources.[4]

Larger cities protected themselves with double, and occasionally triple, wall circuits. Medieval Florence had six rings; it began with the Roman settlement up to the 14th century when the last circuit was completed. The ancient Roman brick wall prescribed a rectangular plan of eight urban blocks, with two principal axes, 'cardo' (Via Roma and Via Calimala) and 'decumanus' (Via Strozzi and Via del Corso). As Florence prospered, its urban infrastructure became saturated with tightly packed mixed-use housing up to six floors high, and a scattering of defensive towers for noble families. The sixth and final fortification had walls six meters tall, measured nearly nine kilometers in length, and was punctuated with 15 city gates and 73 defensive towers. The 430-hectare enclosure included religious buildings, hospitals and new suburbs with small farms, open fields and orchards; crucially it also had enough land in anticipation of future growth.[5] When Florence became Italy's new capital in 1865, the city suffered severe planning alterations; much of the city walls were demolished to make way for the ring road.

During the Middle Ages, safety was of supreme importance, for the Italian city-states were continually at war with one another. When the enemies breached through the city walls, the inhabitants would seek protection in the fortified tower-houses. San Gimignano, a walled medieval hill community in Tuscany, had around 72 fortified tower-houses in the 1330s, some of them nearly 70 meters in height. The Torre Grossa, which still dominates the skyline, is one of 14 remaining towers.[6] Wealthy patrician families and merchants built them to proclaim their wealth and power. Equally, some conquerors would insist on defenseless cities, in order to display their confidence over conquered territory. Napoleon I forced European cities like Turin, Frankfurt and Brussels to pull down their walls. The Mongols, similarly, forbade the building of city walls throughout China in the 1280s, and ordered the leveling of many existing walls, including those in Suzhou, to prevent their cities from serving as bastions of Chinese resistance.[7]

While it was not unusual to build the walls ahead of the city, a number of existing 'utopian' defensive infrastructures were never more than partially inhabited, and therefore can only affirm the unwarranted optimism of urbanists and military engineers. Palmanova, a Renaissance city in the shape of a nine-pointed star, though planned for 20,000 has never attracted more than 5,000 inhabitants to this day.[8] Situated near Udine in the valley of the River Po, the Venetian 'protective city' was designed to defend against attacks from the Ottoman Empire. Three defense rings, the first two erected in Venetian times with the third one under Napoleon, surrounded the city whose inhabitants were supposed to be self-sustaining merchants, craftsmen, and farmers. The radial plan, however, was flawed and transformed the city into a militarized zone in which all public facilities were relinquished to defensive purposes. The rings of city walls and moat imprisoned the inhabitants in a strict frame, excluding any possibility of urban development.[9] It was so unpopular that, in 1622, criminals were offered pardons to entice them to move to the city. Perfectly preserved today, the life of this Italian utopia is still determined by the military.[10]

facing page: The Venetians resorted to pardoning criminals and offering them financial incentives to settle in the idealistic Renaissance defensive infrastructure, Palmanova.

4. DH Conwell, 'Connecting a City to the Sea: The history of the Athenian Long Walls', Koninklijke Brill NV, Leiden, 2008, p.1

5. P de Simonis et al., 'Florence: Heritage guide series', Touring Club of Italy, 1999, pp.9-15

6. B Bryson, 'The Road Less Travelled', Dorling Kindersley Ltd., London, 2009, p.125

7. S Kostof, 'The City Assembled', Thames & Hudson, London, 1999, p.26

8. H de la Croix, 'Military Considerations in City Planning: Fortifications', George Braziller Inc., New York, 1972, p.10

9. JGG Lepage, 'Castles and Fortified Cities of Medieval Europe: An illustrated history', McFraland & Company Inc., North Carolina, 2002, p.300

10. W Braunfels, KJ Northcott (trans.), 'Urban Design in Western Europe: Regime and architecture, 900-1900', The University of Chicago Press, Chicago, 1988, p.159

11. P Griffith & P Dennis, 'The Vauban Fortifications of France', Osprey Publishing, New York, 2006, p.24

12. S Kostof, 'The City Assembled', Thames & Hudson, London, 1999, pp.12-15

Nearly a hundred years later, models of cosmic order remained influential on imperialistic infrastructures. When Marquis de Vauban, commissioned by the French king, Louis XIV, built his most famous fortification of Neuf-Brisach in Alsace-Lorraine, France, he modified the Italian plan of Palmanova and was astonishingly effective. Dominant bastions were replaced; small bastions with wider earthworks defended large perimeters. Ditches and glacis were strengthened with ravelins, an outer layer of detached earthworks. Vauban was particularly strategic with the use of water obstacles and tactical sluices; critical areas of low-lying ground could be flooded quickly in time of siege, but left dry for more productive use in ordinary times. Canals were designed to bring building materials and general supplies into the fortified city of a neat checkerboard of streets and square blocks, with a central open parade ground, flanked by a church. Long tenement blocks were built into the octagonal wall. The extensive square grid was more easily organized and more efficient for subdivision, and would later be taken up in the planning of many US cities.[11]

Between bouts of violence, cities needed to protect their rights of tollage and to control access to their markets; often customs boundaries corresponded with the city walls. In 1734, Berlin enlarged the boundary of Friedrichstadt; the monumental Brandenburg Gate functioned as both a custom station and a grand entry into the city.[12] By the 19th century, the formations of centralized national states and the industrial era accelerated the unmaking of urban fortifications and with them the fundamental limitations of urbanity set by the walls. Circuits of defense and customs boundaries were transposed from individual urban forms to distant territorial national frontiers. In Vienna, by the imperial decree of December 1857, Franz Joseph declared the abolition of the medieval walls and fortifications of the inner city, together with the ditches. The bastioned walls were later replaced by the wide, open-textured Ringstrasse, a 'sociological isolation belt'[13] of major civic and national administrative buildings, civic institutions and a scattering of residential blocks interspersed with public gardens to provide a protective zone.[14]

Living Ground

A modern version of the underground city is something we might associate with science fiction (SF), extreme weather and post-nuclear dystopian worlds. Communities in 'The Penultimate Truth' (1964) by Philip K Dick and Hugh Howey's 'Wool' (2013), pledged to a dystopian society full of regulations and to infrastructures they believed were meant to protect them – a giant underground silo hundreds of meters deep, and a massive underground bunker, respectively. Alas, that has not stopped construction from venturing down beneath the familiar streets. It is common to bury vast multi-storey car parks underneath building developments, hiding away the unsightly workings and reducing the amount of visible building above ground. Car parks are not deemed to need natural light, a commodity usually reserved for expensive office space where maximum amounts of glass envelop the building's structure.

Modern commerce has realized that natural light may actually be a distraction. Shopping malls often have very deep floor plates which are mechanically and electrically serviced, such that air, heat and lighting requirements are set consistently at an optimum level for profitability and consumer purchase rate. The RÉSO 'underground city' in Montreal, Canada, is the largest multi-use underground complex in the world. Over 30 kilometers of tunnels link together hotels, offices and apartment buildings, and lead inhabitants to the city's transport infrastructure including Metro stations, two major train stations and a bus terminal.[15] The 'urban-glue' that binds the subterranean world together is a large number of buried shopping malls several storeys deep. These complexes are a significant draw for tourists who can learn to navigate Montreal almost exclusively by maps published by department stores.[16] If the complex is seen as a whole, it may well be the largest shopping promenade in the world, and it can all be visited without ever venturing outside.

Similarly, the buried infrastructure of Tokyo Station is one of the largest and busiest transport hubs at a global scale, with over 3,000 trains per day leaving the many platforms, behind its colonial, European-style facades on ground level. The station opened in 1914, marking Japan's golden rail-age, and boasts a futuristic and high-tech capacity. The main station has 10 platforms above street level; others located several stories underground have an extensive system of tunnels, moving walkways and connections to subway stations. It is rumored that the station's 'secret' tunnels provide direct links to government buildings. Like Montreal, the passages form part of a larger network linking Tokyo Station to surrounding shopping centers and commercial buildings. Having survived bombing in World War II, Tokyo Station celebrated its 100-year anniversary in 2015, and enjoys its status as a cultural landmark. With earthquakes and other natural threats in Japan's capital, the station is a safe haven as the whole compound is defended by a sophisticated seismic isolation structure.[17]

Troglodytic Life
Caves have provided safe haven for us for thousands of years, across the world. This tradition of protective space would eventually progress to embody all that we call architecture. In 'Architecture Without Architects' (1987), Bernard Rudofsky explains that 'troglodytism does not necessarily imply a low cultural level; amenities vary as much as those of more conventional habitations'.[18] He amazed us by revealing how underground settlements in China's Loess-Belt have a sophisticated network of underground buildings, not being limited to just simple caveman dwellings. Factories, schools, hotels and government offices are all entirely underground: 'dwellings below, fields upstairs'. Loess is an easily carved silty and porous substrate. The traces of these dwellings are only revealed by square holes for internal courtyards and by arc-shaped slices into the earth which contain entrance staircases. The entrances are marked only with trees or stones.

Caves can be dug out of cliff faces or formed naturally. Underground tunnels have also been rich sites of human inhabitation, some of them many storeys deep. Turkey's historical region of Cappadocia has large numbers of underground settlements which date back to ancient times; the soft volcanic rock is easy to carve. In 2014, an unknown subterranean settlement with around seven kilometers of tunnels was discovered around the Nevsehir hill fort near the city of Kayseri – at around 5,000 years old, the city is thought to be the largest underground city in the world.[19] The city contains living spaces, kitchens, wineries, chapels, staircases and linseed oil production facilities. In equal proportion, the city is strange, and astonishing, and 'appears to have been a large, self-sustaining complex with air-shafts and water channels. Studies suggest the underground corridors may plunge as deep as 113 meters.'[20] The most renowned underground city in Turkey is Derinkuyu. Its multi-level passages and chambers are large enough to house many thousands of inhabitants, and have sophisticated planning which allows co-habitation with livestock. Derinkuyu remained inhabited until the early 20th century; sectional drawings of the city are reminiscent of termite mounds or something from SF. It is not clear whether desperation and safety from attack were the only reason why these cities were burrowed.

The ancient city of Petra in modern-day Jordan, a UNESCO World Heritage Site, is recognized for its astonishing rock-cut architecture with Greek-influenced facades cut from sandstone walls in the narrow

13. CE Schorke, 'Fin-de-Siecle Vienna', Politics and Culture, New York, 1961, p.33

14. S Kostof, 'The City Assembled', Thames & Hudson, London, 1999, pp.52–55

15. E Reid, 'Montreal's Underground City Is a Mess, a Glorious Effing Mess' [http://montreal.about.com/od/underground-city/ss/underground-city-montreal-souterrain.htm], retrieved 2 September 2015

16. Undergroundmontrealmap.com, 'Montreal Underground Maps' [http://www.undergroundmontrealmap.com/montreal-underground-city-maps/], retrieved 2 September 2015

17. B Goode, 'Tokyo Station: 100 years of trains, tourism and secret tunnels', CNN, 22 December 2014 [http://edition.cnn.com/2014/12/21/travel/japan-tokyo-station-100-years/], retrieved 2 September 2015

18. B Rudofsky, 'Architecture Without Architects', Doubleday & Company, MoMA, New York, 1964, p.20

19. J Stone, 'Vast 5,000 Year-old Underground City Discovered in Turkey's Cappadocia Region', The Independent, 31 December 2014 [http://www.independent.co.uk/news/world/middle-east/vast-5000-yearold-underground-city-discovered-in-turkeys-cappadocia-region-9951911.html], retrieved 11 May 2015

20. J Pinkowski, 'Massive Underground City Found in Cappadocia Region of Turkey', National Geographic, 26 March 2015 [http://news.nationalgeographic.com/2015/03/150325-underground-city-cappadocia-turkey-archaeology/], retrieved 11 May 2015

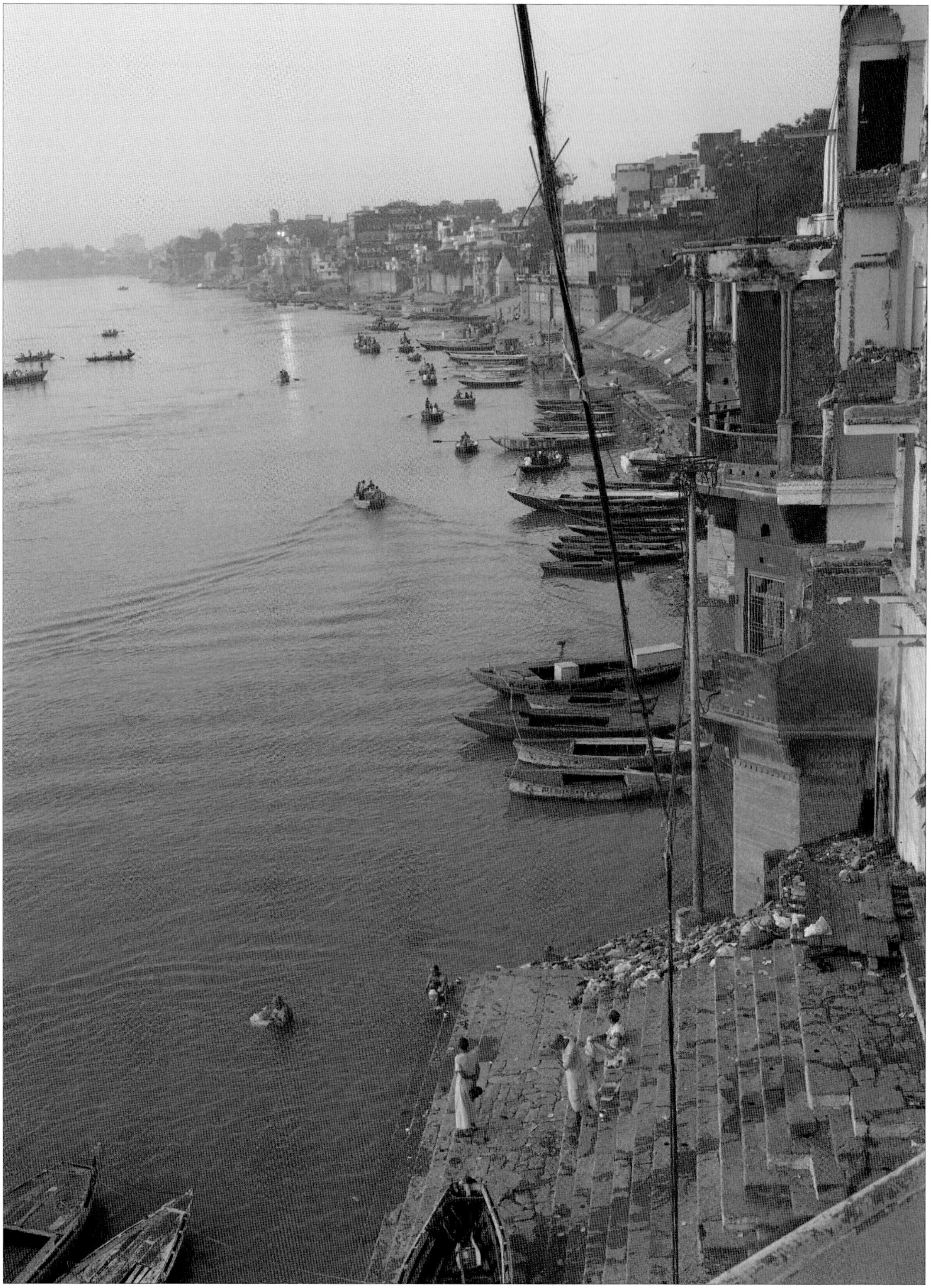

gorge. The city's most reliable and valuable resource is the ingenuity of its inhabitants, the Nabataeans. They laid sophisticated infrastructure networks of dams, cisterns and distribution channels cut into the rock face to capture water from flash floods in the artificial desert oasis en-route to Damascus. Today, the networks are still visible, snaking their way along the walls of the gorge. They bear similarities to the technology used by the Greeks in the 'Temple of Knossos' and by Nebuchadnezzar in the 'Hanging Gardens of Babylon'. Charles R. Ortloff, author of 'Water Engineering in the Ancient World', described the unique Nabataean systems where 'they utilized all possible above-and-below ground water supply and storage methodologies simultaneously. Water from high-level reservoirs was delivered to terraces and fountains through hydrostatically pressurized terracotta pipelines.'[21]

Another UNESCO World Heritage Site, the tourist hotspot of the Loire Valley in central France is home to rich limestone deposits. The area's history of quarrying, reflected in the white stone vernacular of its many towns and villages, also offers a surprising set of infrastructure. Since the Middle Ages, local inhabitants had been building grain silos and livestock pens in tunnels beside their own cave-dwellings. Today, the caves are in use by the wine makers; miles of cave cellars provide a constant temperature for the aging of barrels and storage of bottles.[22] The luxury hotel Les Hautes Roches, built into the caves at Rochecorbon, offers guests unique rooms in the limestone tunnels that were once home and hiding place for monks from Marmoutier Abbey.[23] Other caves in the region are used as working mushroom farms; the lack of light is beneficial for fungal growth, while temperatures and humidity can be controlled.

In the Name of Tradition and Faith
Caves and rivers are infrastructures created by the power of nature. The first urban societies arose in the fertile floodplains of the Indus in southern Asia, the Huang He (Yellow River) in China, the Nile in Egypt, and the Tigris and the Euphrates in the Middle East. The rivers were strategic infrastructure for trade, exploration, and settlement. The Hudson River in New York State made possible Henry Hudson's exploration of the then New World; the Volga River facilitated trade and cultural exchanges between Scandinavia and Russia and the Persians. The Mississippi in the United States, the Ruhr in Germany, and the Thames in England powered the mills of hundreds of factories when industries flourished alongside the expansion of cities.[24]

The Ganges in India is the most holy of rivers. The revered multi-use infrastructure 'protects' nearly half a billion inhabitants along its 1,560 mile course from the Himalaya Mountains to the Indian Ocean, in addition to millions of other visitors. Millions bathe in the Ganges during Kumbh Mela, held every third year at one of the four holy pilgrimage cities of Allahbad, Haridwar, Ujjain, and Nashik. In 2001, more than 40 million people gathered on the main bathing day of the festival and over 80 million in 2013, breaking the record for the biggest gathering of humanity on earth.[25] Men, women and children from all strata of society set up camp along the sands of the riverfront in the open for nights; the faithful believe a festival dip will cleanse a lifetime of sins, and help bring salvation.

For millennia, Hindus have also brought their dead to the Ganges, with the believe that if the bodies are cremated on the banks and their ashes scattered in the water, the souls will be free to find nirvana

facing page: The Ganges in India, the most revered multi-use infrastructure 'protects' tradition and faith of nearly half a billion inhabitants.

21. CR Ortloff, 'The Water Supply and Distribution System of the Nabataean City of Petra (Jordan), 300 BC–AD 300', Cambridge Archaeological Journal, vol.15, 2005, pp.93-109

22. Food Republic, 'Loire Valley Wines: Stay In The Caves' [http://www.foodrepublic.com/2013/12/05/loire-valley-wines-stay-in-the-caves/], retrieved 2 September 2015

23. Les Hautes Roches Official Website, 'In the Caves: A story' [http://www.leshautesroches.com/troglodytes.php], retrieved 2 September 2015

24. 'Education: River', National Geographic [http://nationalgeographic.org/encyclopedia/river/], retrieved 21 August 2015

25. G Pandey, 'Kumbh Mela: "Eight Million" bathers on first day of festival', BBC News: India, 14 January 2013 [http://www.bbc.co.uk/news/world-asia-india-21017217], retrieved 21 August 2015

26. M Krishnan, 'A Believer's Town of Death and Deliverance', Deutsche Welle (DW) Germany, 2013 [http://www.dw.com/en/a-believers-town-of-death-and-deliverance/a-17041261], retrieved 21 August 2015

27. M Krishnan, 'A Believer's Town of Death and Deliverance', Deutsche Welle (DW) Germany, 2013 [http://www.dw.com/en/a-believers-town-of-death-and-deliverance/a-17041261], retrieved 21 August 2015

28. A Polidor, 'Ganges River', Sacred Land Film Project, 2014 [http://www.sacredland.org/index.php/ganges], retrieved 21 August 2015

and liberated from rebirth. Varanasi is the holiest of cities along the river's course and the most auspicious place to die. Along the city's dramatic embankment of long flights of stairs, the Manikaran and Harishchandra ghats are amongst the 84 ghats that perform some 90,000 cremations each year.[26] The elegant 'ghats' landings are also adapted for blessing of marriages and newborn babies, and almost every ritual of human life.

While the spiritual magnitude of the river has grown, the quality of the water has deteriorated severely due to unregulated disposals of thousands of carcasses of dead revered cows adding to everyday human activities, and deposits of partially cremated human remains and ashes. According to the National Ganga River Basin Authority, the amount of bacteria, toxins and chemicals found in the river is now almost 3,000 times over the acceptable 'safe' limit of the World Health Organization (WHO).[27] The waste treatment systems have remained relatively unchanged despite rapid population growth, and are now unable to cope with some 800,000 gallons of sewage mixed with industrial waste from pharmaceutical companies, electronics plants, textile and paper industries, tanneries, and oil refineries, all flowing into the Ganges each day. Adding to the pollution crisis, the flow of the river is being blocked by dams for irrigation and electricity, limiting its ability to clean itself. The result of the pollution is an array of water-borne diseases including cholera, hepatitis, typhoid and amoebic dysentery. An estimated 80% of all health problems and one-third of deaths in India are attributable to water-borne diseases.[28]

Attitudes towards human untreated waste and pollution are slowly shifting; nonetheless the government's Ganga Action Plan in 1985, devised to clean up the river by installing sewage treatment plants and threatening fines and litigation against industries, has been largely unsuccessful. Many Indians blamed the failure on governmental mismanagement, technological mistakes and lack of participation from local communities in the planning process.[29] Truthfully, ordinary Indians should also take equal blame for the failures, as there has been little civic pride and sense of collective responsibility towards the wellbeing of the river. In 2014, the Prime Minister of India, Narendra Modi, made the cleanup of the Ganges a metaphor for his election campaign and pledged 'to restore the river's purity just as he will revive a nation sullied by corruption and stalled by mismanagement and bureaucratic sloth'.[30] The revitalization of the Ganges is a monumental undertaking but the real challenge remains for politicians to offer infrastructure improvements without resorting to use it as a political weapon.

In fact, the threat posed by the pollution, and particularly in Varanasi, is not just a matter of health – it is a matter of protecting tradition and faith. The importance of protecting the sacred river was poetically articulated by Veer Badra Mishra, a Hindu priest and civil engineer who has worked for decades to combat pollution in the Ganges: 'There is a saying that the Ganges grants us salvation. This culture will end if the people stop going to the river, and if the culture dies the tradition dies, and the faith dies.'[31]

Digging In
Millions died on the Western Front in World War I. 'European nations began World War I with a glamorous vision, only to be psychologically shattered by the realities of the trenches.'[32] The trench warfare was essentially the evolution of ancient principles of fortifications translated into the context of modern field combat. Moving earth and burrowing-out networks of strategic labyrinths and defensive lines became a major mission and infrastructure. Separated by meadows of barbed wire, miles of trenches were dug in a network of long zig-zag lines, such that it would not be possible for the enemy to open fire along their length should they breach the defenses.

There was a total of 25,000 miles of trenches dug in World War I, of which 12,000 miles were dug by allied forces. British trenches were dug mostly at night by way of entrenchment, the more efficient method that allowed many soldiers to dig the full length of the trench simultaneously. It took 450 men working for six hours to dig 275 yards of trench seven feet deep and six feet wide.[33] The dimensions of the frontline trenches varied with opportunity, tactical employment and conditions; some trenches were wide enough to admit the passage of a stretcher without interfering with the garrison firing out.[34]

The infantry, with assisted planning from the Royal Engineering field companies, were mainly responsible for constructing the trenches. The most important construction tools were the pick and shovel GS, and the entrenching implement, and on occasion they resorted to bayonets and anything else that came to hand.[35] In softer soil conditions, the walls of the trenches would have to be reinforced with wooden frames, expanded metal mesh or chicken-wire held in place with iron pickets, and sandbags. Wooden planking was also installed to prevent the soldiers standing in water.[36]

The reality of the rotten conditions and the terrifying consequences of the battle have influenced generations of artists and writers. In 'The Great War', reportage cartoonist Joe Sacco depicted July 1, 1916, the Battle of Somme, in an extraordinary, 24-foot-long panorama: his wordless piece amplifies the horrors of the infrastructure within the clouded vision of humanity.[37]

Cinematic Reading of Reality

There is a tendency to romanticize or demonize slums; both views are extremes of reality. 'Slum dwellers share something with those caught in a war zone, where the infrastructure of society has been interrupted or destroyed. To survive, they have to be inventive. But the people in the war zone can look forward to the end of war, the restoration of society and its services. The slum dwellers have no such prospect. For them the war, its brutalities and atmosphere of cruelty and indifference to human life, never ends,' explained Lebbeus Woods.[38]

Kowloon Walled City, six-and-a-half acres of solid 10 to 14 storeys building and home to 33,000 people, was one of the world's densest slums until its demolition in 1993. The illustrator Kazumi Terasawa, together with Kowloon City Expedition, made an extraordinary drawn survey of the 'self-regulating, self-sufficient and self-determining' inhabitable infrastructure – the incredibly detailed cross section includes all the contents and human inhabitation within the cramped commodities, restaurants, shops, and even small factories intertwined with thousands of domestic spaces. The drawings reveal innovative space-saving solutions and highlight the importance of the few windows and open courtyards.[39] Inside, there were no thoroughfares, no vehicles except for the odd bicycle and hundreds of varieties of alleys. Seventy-seven wells of nearly 300 feet in depth supplied water, and electricity was stolen from the mains.[40] In the book 'City of Darkness: Life in Kowloon Walled City',[41] stunning photographs of the interiors and exterior of the buildings by Greg Girard and Ian Lambot offer glimpses at human scale, but fall short in communicating the spatial impossibility to the extent of the section drawings. Kowloon Walled City, also home to the notorious mafia and brothels, was the inspiration behind the dystopian streetscape and cyberpunk feel of the manga SF series 'Ghost in The Shell' (1995), by Masamune Shirow.

29. A Polidor, 'Ganges River', Sacred Land Film Project, 2014 [http://www.sacredland.org/index.php/ganges], retrieved 21 August 2015

30. S Sinha, 'Ganges River: Revered, soiled and symbol of an Indian election campaign', The New York Times, 14 May 2014 [http://www.nytimes.com/2014/05/15/world/asia/ganges-river-revered-soiled-and-symbol-of-an-indian-election-campaign.html?_r=0], retrieved 21 August 2015

31. A Polidor, 'Ganges River', Sacred Land Film Project, 2014 [http://www.sacredland.org/index.php/ganges], retrieved 21 August 2015

32. V Postrel, 'Glamour and the Art of Persuasion', Reason, January 2014 [http://reason.com/archives/2013/12/27/glamour-and-the-art-of-persuas], retrieved 12 February 2015

33. 'The Great War Training Trench', The Friends of Shoreham Fort [https://www.shorehamfort.co.uk/about/the-great-war-training-trench/], retrieved 12 February 2015

34+35. S Bull, 'Trench: A history of trench warfare on the western front', Osprey Publishing, Oxford & Imperial War Museums UK, 2014, pp.36–42

36. A Robertson & D Kenyon, 'Digging the Trench: The archaeology of the western front', Pen & Sword Military, South Yorkshire, 2008, p.74

37. A Hochschild & J Sacco, 'On The Great War', WW Norton & Co., 2013

38. L Woods, 'Slums: The problem', Lebbeus Woods Blog, 18 January 2008 [https://lebbeuswoods.wordpress.com/2008/01/18/slums-the-problem/], retrieved 12 August 2015

39. Kowloon City Expedition & Kazumi Terasawa, 'Large illustration Kowloon City', Iwanami Shoten, Tokyo, 1997

40. P Popham, 'Introduction' in 'City of Darkness: Life in Kowloon Walled City', G Girard & I Lambot, Watermark Publications, UK, 1993, pp.9–12

41. G Girard & I Lambot, 'City of Darkness: Life in Kowloon Walled City', Watermark Publications, UK, 1993

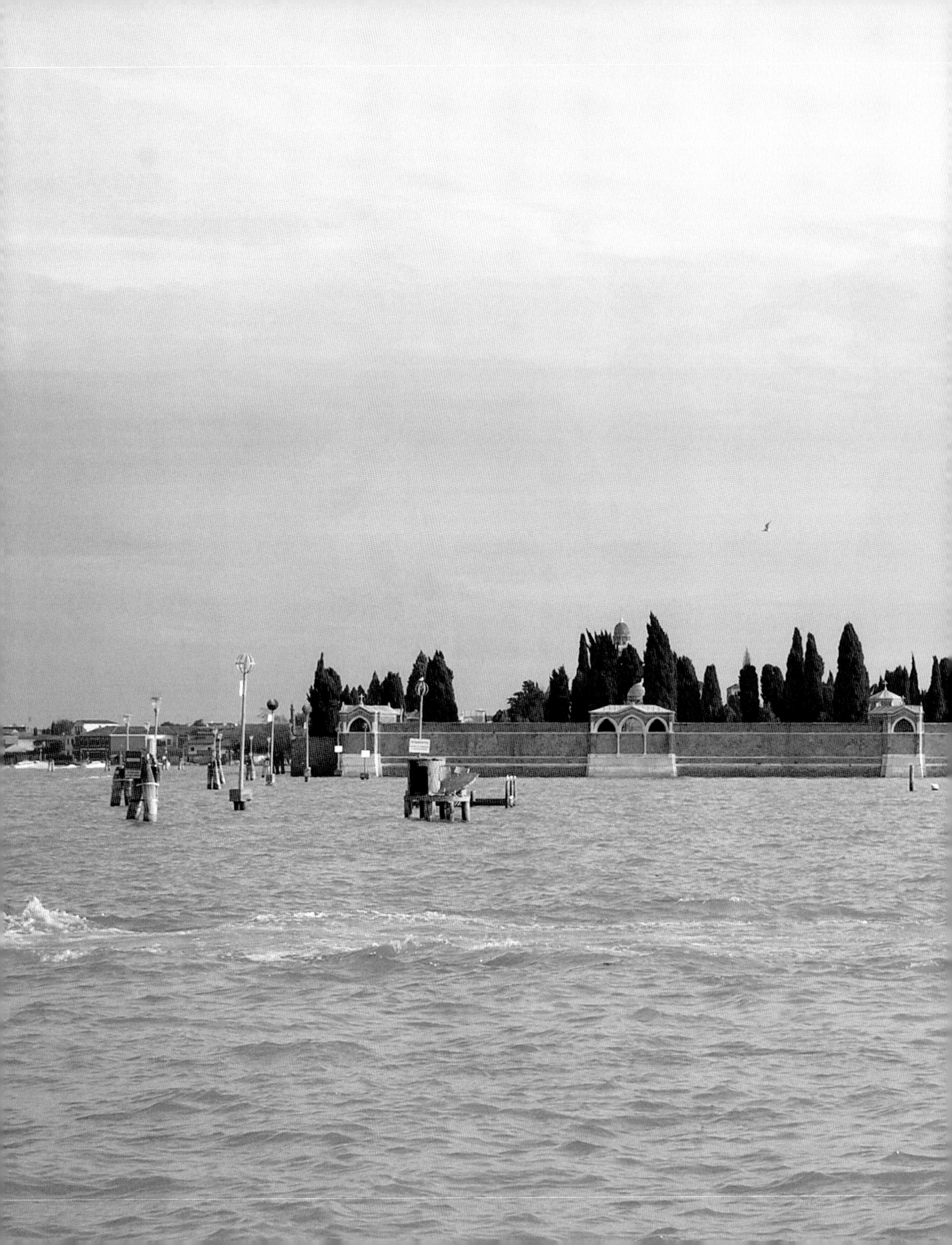

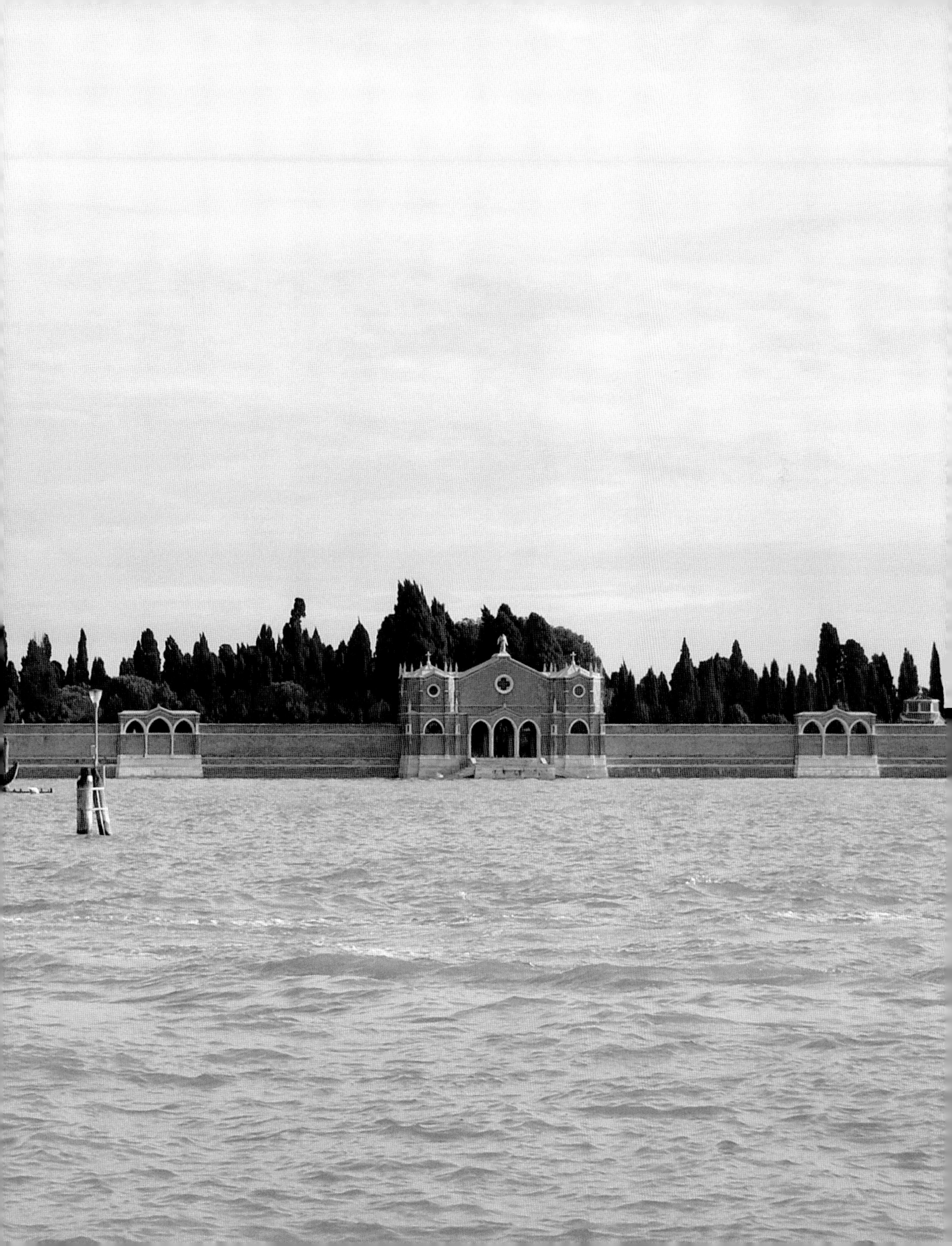

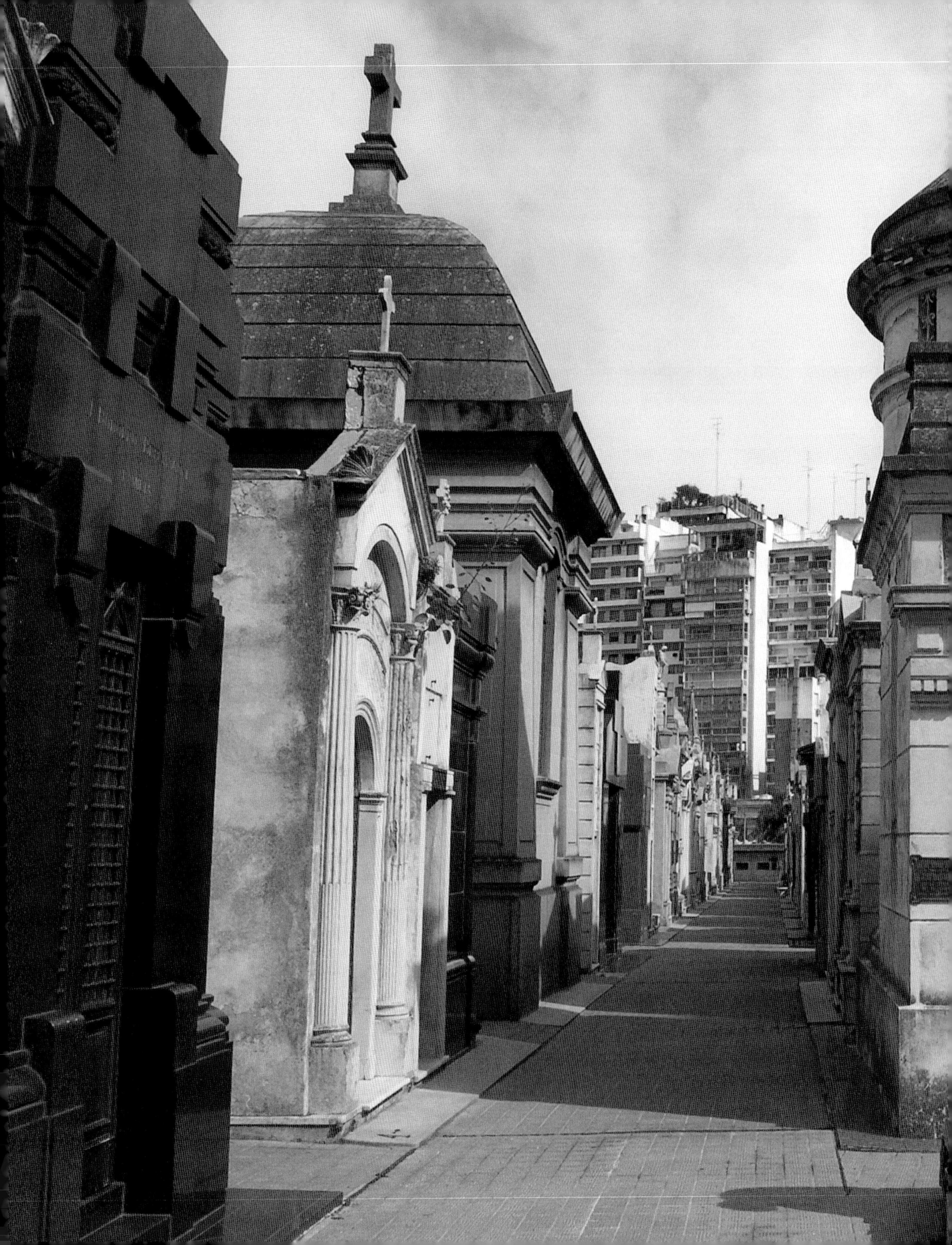

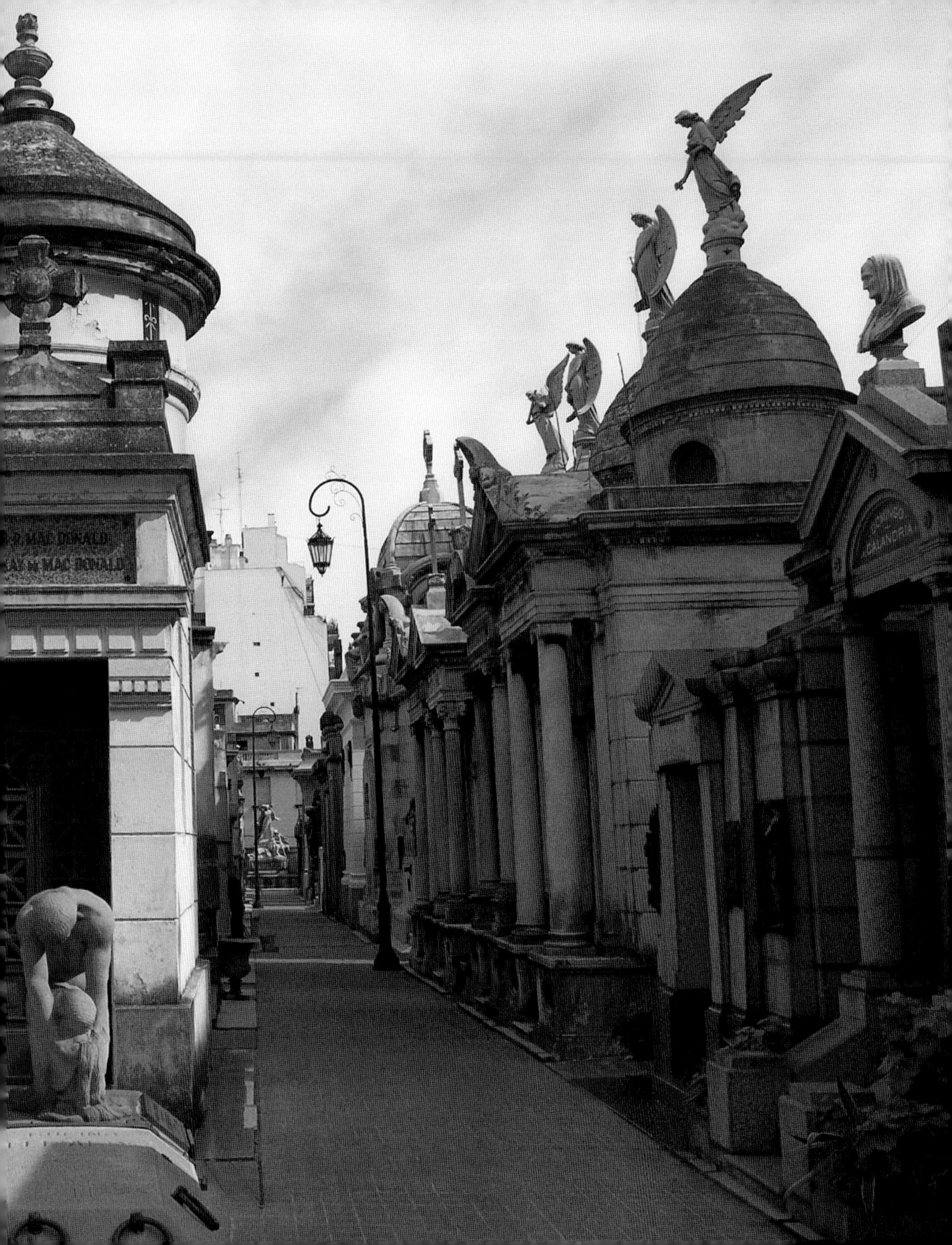
MAC DONALD
MAC DONALD

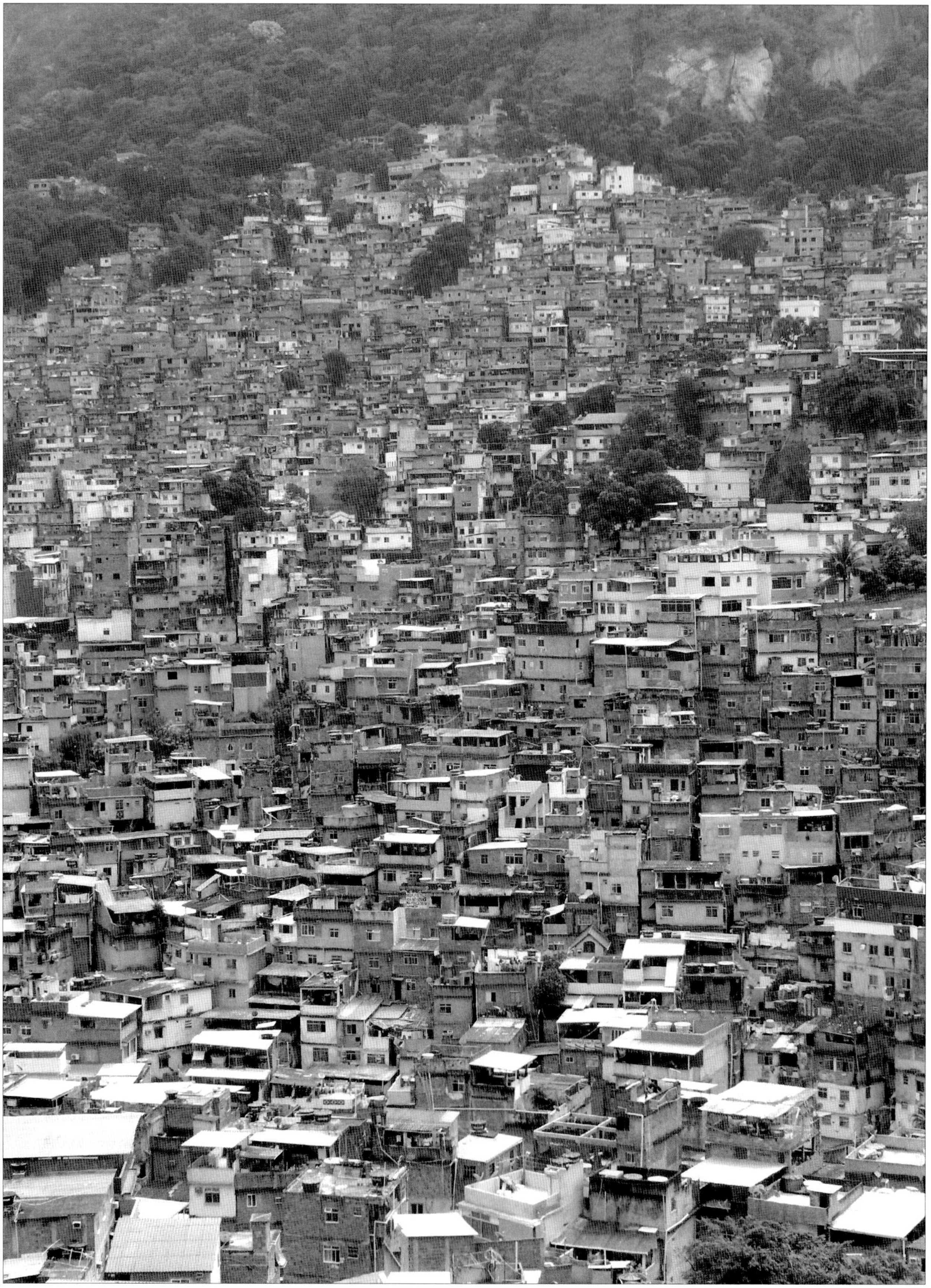

Kar-wai Wong's film 'Chungking Express' (1994) explores love and loneliness of the Hong-Kong metropolis, with much of the story set in the infamous Chungking Mansions, another informal pattern of inhabitation to rival that of Kowloon Walled City. Although located in an expensive district of Hong Kong, the 17-storey, five-block infrastructure is well known as the cheapest accommodation in the city. Alongside notorious trafficking, drugs trade, used electronics and curry houses, it is home to over 5,000 foreign immigrants (largely Pakistani, Indian, Nigerian and Middle Eastern) at any one time, and visited by around 10,000 each day.[42] In 2007, Chungking Mansions was named 'Best Example of Globalization in Action' in Asia by 'Time' magazine, which described it as a 'great sleepless citadel'. For his research, Gordon Mathews, professor of anthropology at the Chinese University of Hong Kong, lived part-time in the infrastructure for a year and claimed to have encountered 120 different nationalities dealing in various trades including knock-off mobile phones and used computers. He estimated '20% of the mobile phones now in use in sub-Saharan Africa have passed through Chungking Mansions' and are traded by container loads. 'The on-going myth has been of Chungking Mansions as a hellhole. But it is not. It is a beacon.'[43]

Another large slum infrastructure in Asia is the Dharavi district of Mumbai, the inspiration and film set for Danny Boyle's film, 'Slumdog Millionaire' (2008). The scene where the protagonist is so desperate for an autograph from his Bollywood idol Amitabh Bachchan that he swims through human faeces for the opportunity, best describes the narrative and the spatial conditions of the settlement. Originally a small fishing community, Dharavi is located on prime land in the center of Mumbai and has an estimated population of 750,000.[44] Boyle describes the slum as 'the most chaotic place on earth', and explains that the frantic energy of the film is an honest interpretation of how Mumbai feels everyday. 'There are a billion people living in that country. That's enough to start a planet! The overwhelming experience gives you an idea of what it's like to feel the heartbeats of a billion people. The stimulation you get from everything changing all the time is extraordinary.'[45] Water supply in slums is irregular and unreliable at best; Dharavi is no different. In a report for The Guardian newspaper, Benita Fernando describes the plastic 'ubiquitous big blue drum' that can hold 200 liters of water, and almost every house has one. 'Your house may be 250 square feet, but you will make space for this stout, almost-family member... many houses store enough water to serve a family of five for up to three days.'[46]

Gavin Hood's film adaptation of the 1980 novel 'Tsotsi' beautifully portrays an evocative set of spatial conditions in Alexandra, from the concrete pipes the protagonist lived in as a child, to the slum houses, shops, bars and public spaces that emerge in the informal settlement. Alexandra is one of the poorest urban areas in South Africa, but it is Cape Town that is home to Africa's largest slum Khayelitsha, which has at least 400,000 recorded residents but the figure is likely to be much higher. Both slums vastly increased in size after apartheid ended; the increased migration from rural to urban was due to possible employment opportunities.[47] Soweto was the chosen film set for 'District 9' (2009), a SF film directed by Neill Blomkamp. In the politically charged thriller, the unsettling treatments of (space) shipwrecked aliens by governments and other sinister private organizations are reminders of mankind's cruelty, exploitation and greed. The film is also an implicit reference to the District Six residential area of Johannesburg where major atrocities were committed by the apartheid regime in the 1960s and 1970s.[48]

to protect

previous four pages: The city of angels in Venice (Isola di San Michele) and Buenos Aires (La Recoleta Cemetery).

facing page: Rio de Janeiro's favelas, which have grown organically to become dense and complex, have many advantages over sprawling more unsophisticated grid plans, and the relentless model of homogenous suburbia.

42+43. L Fitzpatrick, 'The Best of Asia: Best Example of Globalization in Action', Time Magazine online, 2007 [http://content.time.com/time/specials/2007/best_of_asia/article/0,28804, html], retrieved 27 August 2015

44. B Fernando, 'An Urbanist's Guide to the Mumbai Slum of Dharavi', The Guardian: Cities, 2 April 2014 [http://www.theguardian.com/cities/2014/apr/01/urbanist-guide-to-dharavi-mumbai], retrieved 27 August 2015

45. K Chang, 'Danny Boyle's Slumdog Millionaire', Anthem, November 2008 [http://anthemmagazine.com/danny-boyles-slumdog-millionaire/], retrieved 27 August 2015

46. B Fernando, 'An Urbanist's Guide to the Mumbai Slum of Dharavi', The Guardian: Cities, 2 April 2014 [http://www.theguardian.com/cities/2014/apr/01/urbanist-guide-to-dharavi-mumbai], retrieved 27 August 2015

47. D Tovrov, '5 Biggest Slums in the World', International Business Times, 9 December 2011 [http://www.ibtimes.com/5-biggest-slums-world-381338], retrieved 22 August 2015

48. SC Johnson, 'The Real District 9: Cape Town's District Six', Newsweek: World, 27 August 2009 [http://www.newsweek.com/real-district-9-cape-towns-district-six-78939], 22 August 2015

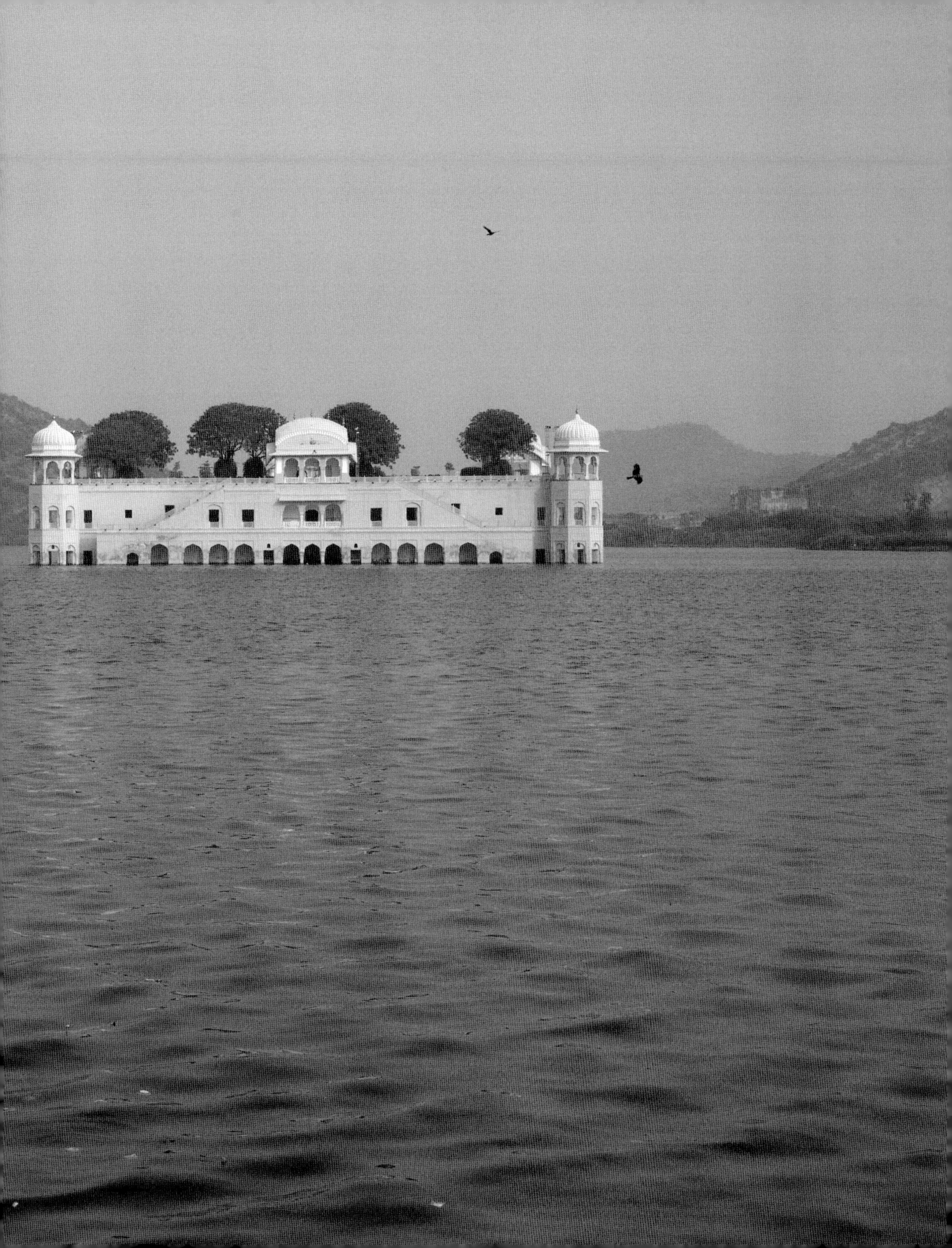

Amongst Brazil's densest favelas, Rio de Janeiro's informal settlements have regular shoot-outs between drug traffickers and police, as well as assorted criminal activities. To guarantee their own safety, local residents pledge political loyalty and cooperation to the traffickers who maintain order in the favelas despite continuing high levels of violence. 'Tropa de Elite' (2007) by José Padilha is a semi-fictional account of corruption and cooperation between organized crime, drug barons and the BOPE policemen (Rio de Janeiro's military police squads). In recent years, the Brazilian government has made several attempts to deal with urban poverty by relocating residents of favelas into new public housing projects and by way of gentrification and upgrade of favelas.

When Rio de Janeiro hosted the Olympic Games in 2016, a shortfall in accommodation for the many thousands of visitors was predicted – the savvy and entrepreneurial favelas responded to the opportunity. The government made allowances that 'pacified' favelas could register as guesthouses. In addition, residential homes across Rio's non-favela areas offered up spare rooms along with commercial guesthouses and B&Bs for the 16 days of the Olympics. 'Airbnb', the US website that allows homeowners to rent out properties online, became the official accommodation partner for Rio 2016.[49] This type of private-public relationship has been emerging over the last decade, where the government relies on the soft infrastructure of commercial social media and local domestic entrepreneurs as a resource. For informal settlements and slums to thrive as important city infrastructure, they tend to rely on proximity to booming commercial centers.

The complex and extremely nuanced organization of the world's great slums makes them hard to understand if you are used to reading cities and urbanism in a western or higher-economically-developed configuration. These informal settlements are the archaeological ancestors of medieval city morphology. Cities, which have grown organically to become dense and complex, have many advantages over sprawling more unsophisticated grid plans, and the relentless model of homogenous suburbia. The suburban concept was born in the UK as a measure for improving the health of those who had previously occupied dense slums built for the industrial boom. Suburbia offered space, clean water and fresh air, and attempted to solve social issues, but this concept of 'self-imposed isolation' is hard to reconcile with a nuanced and sophisticated network of hard and soft infrastructures that density can provide.

The World's Largest Open Prison
Israel's West Bank wall was 'attacked' by guerrilla artist Banksy in 2005. Nine provocative and satirical paintings of life were made on the Palestinian side of the wall. One depicted a ladder going over the wall, while another was of an idyllic beach on the other side.[50] His 'Flying Balloons Girl', was probably the most striking reminder of humanity's desire for freedom, Palestinian and Israeli alike. While the United Nations and the International Court of Justice consider the controversial wall illegal, the Israeli authorities argued that the infrastructure is necessary to protect the country from suicide bombers. In an exchange of letters in April 2004, President George W Bush outlined US policy on the matter: 'As the government of Israel has stated, the barrier being erected by Israel should be a security rather than political barrier, should be temporary rather than permanent and therefore not prejudice any final status issues including final borders, and its route should take into account, consistent with security needs, its impact on Palestinians not engaged in terrorist activities.'[51]

The majority of the 670-kilometer West Bank Barrier is an infrastructure composed of concrete base and walls, five-meter high wire mesh, deep ditches and rows of razor wire. In specific areas, the eight-meter tall solid-concrete wall measures up to three meters in width. Complete with watchtowers and electronic sensors, the wall is simultaneously protective against any possible attacks and demonstrably oppressive. Palestinian land has been confiscated to build the barrier, and economic survival threatened as farmers and traders are cut-off from their land and suppliers. Access to the 40,000-inhabitant town of Qalqilya, once known as the West Bank's 'Fruit Basket', is limited to a single Isreali checkpoint.[52] Banksy explicitly stated that the walls essentially turned Palestine into 'the world's largest open prison'.

Extraterritoriality and Micronations
Often, SF writers create fictional micronations as settings for their characters. In 'The Prisoner' (1967), the creators Patrick McGoohan and George Markstein held the main protagonist 'Number Six' in 'The Village', a self-contained society protected on three sides by mountain ranges and on the fourth by the sea. The surreal setting for the British SF television series has an extensive multi-use infrastructure that includes a cinema, statue garden, a retirement home, a gymnasium, a fully equipped hospital, a radio station, and its own graveyard.

Following the capture of Rome, the popes were essentially 'imprisoned' within the Vatican walls for 59 years. They took a stand against the authority of the Italian government up until becoming the Vatican City and being granted extraterritoriality in 1929 with the Lateran Treaty between the Italian State and the Holy See. The history of the Vatican City being the world's smallest internationally recognized sovereign state dates back to the Donation of Constantine, a forged 8th century Roman imperial decree that allegedly transferred imperial prerogatives over Rome and the western part of the Roman Empire to the papacy.[53] Today, it is protected by the Italian State from expropriation and taxes. An urban and landlocked walled enclave of Rome, the borders of its 44-hectare territory were determined primarily by its medieval and Renaissance fortifications and buildings. The enclosure is only interrupted by St. Peter's Square, the magnificent entry plaza to the basilica for pilgrims, worshippers, and visitors. A simple white line delineates the border between Italy and the Vatican City across the pavement of the square.[54]

Within the Vatican's monumental walls are the Vatican Gardens, which occupy more than one-third of the state's land. The Leonine Wall forms the western and southern borders of the Renaissance and Baroque gardens designed with Italian geometric patterns, French flowerbeds, and English lawns and woods to simulate an open countryside. The collection of statues, classical columns, images of gods, and emperors' busts as well as modern figures of saints are displayed amongst cedars, stone pines, cypresses, palms and olive trees. Even the pope has his own small vegetable garden for his private household.[55] Lined with trimmed laurel and myrtle, the garden paths lead to a radio station, a little-used railway station, a heliport, army barracks, a pharmacy, and the cultural locations of St Peter's Basilica, the Sistine Chapel and the Vatican Museums.

Probably a less well-known independent nation is the Principality of Sealand. In 1966, the Prince of Sealand, Roy Bates, first occupied the infrastructure of 'Roughs Tower', a disused World War II Maunsell Fort for anti-air defense located in the North Sea approximately seven nautical miles off the coast of East Anglia. Connected by an iron platform, the 550-square-meter fort has two concrete towers with

previous pages: The island palace of Jal Mahal in Jaipur has four floors hidden under the surface of Man Sagar Lake, with the fifth floor exposed.

following pages: Across the pavement of St. Peter's Square, a simple white line delineates the border between Italy and the Vatican City.

49. D Bowater, 'Rio's Favelas to Accommodate Visitors to 2016 Olympics', BBC News, 30 July 2015 [http://www.bbc.co.uk/news/business-33673990], retrieved 27 August 2015

50. 'Art prankster sprays Israeli wall', BBC News, August 2005 [http://news.bbc.co.uk/1/hi/entertainment/4748063.stm], retrieved 26 August 2015

51+52. 'Q&A: What is the West Bank barrier?', BBC News, August 2005 [http://news.bbc.co.uk/1/hi/world/middle_east/3111159.stm], retrieved 26 August 2015

53. A Stockwell, 'A Corrupt Tree: An encyclopaedia of crimes committed by the church of Rome against humanity and the human spirit: 1', Xlibris, 2014, p.326

54. JMS de Muniain, 'The Vatican City State' in 'The Vatican: Spirit and art of Christian Rome', J Daley (ed.), The Metropolitan Museum of Art & Harry N. Abrams Inc., New York, 1982, pp.33–34

55. EM Jung-Inglesis, 'Other Buildings and the Vatican Gardens' in 'The Vatican: Spirit and art of Christian Rome', J Daley (ed.), The Metropolitan Museum of Art & Harry N. Abrams Inc., New York, 1982, p.161

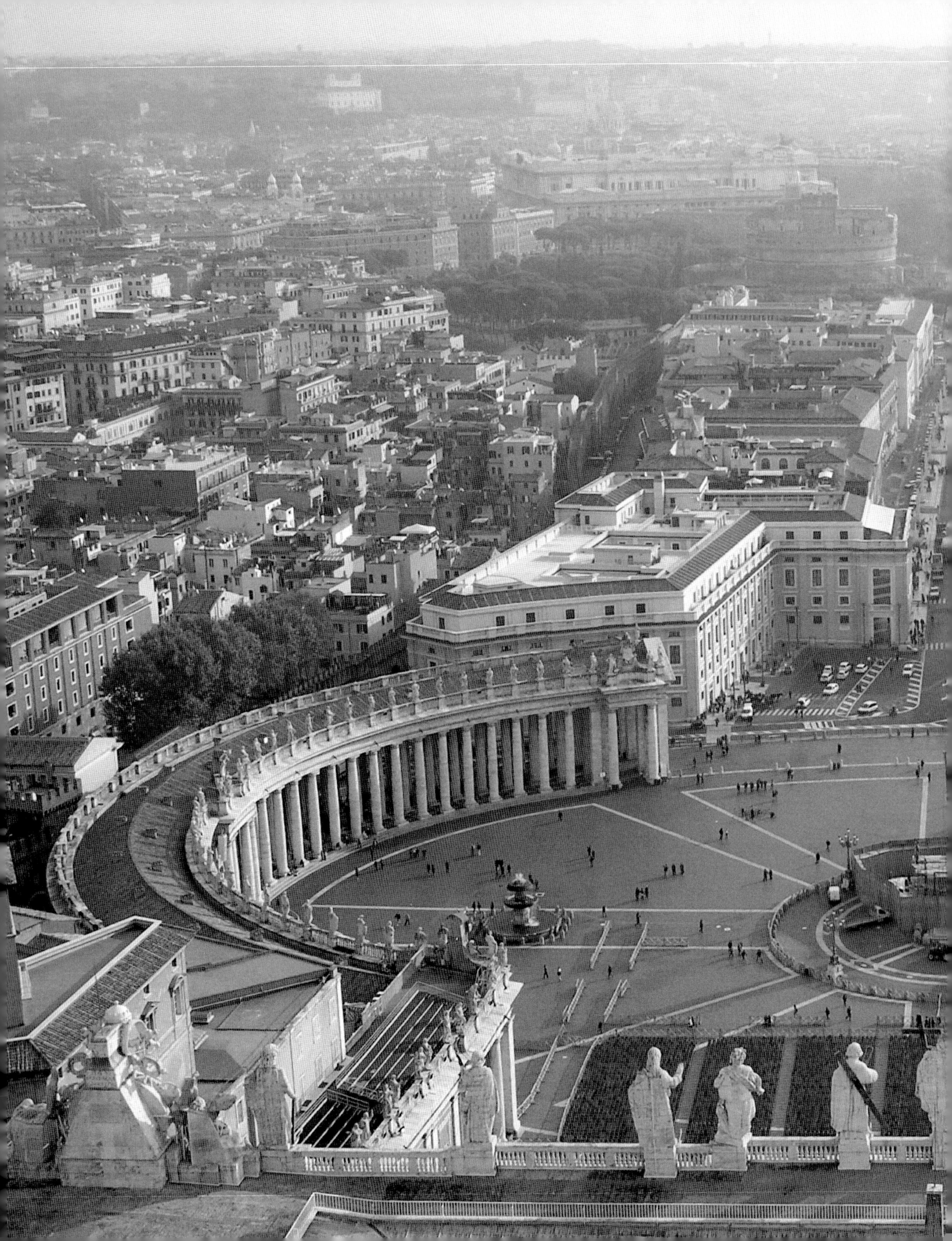

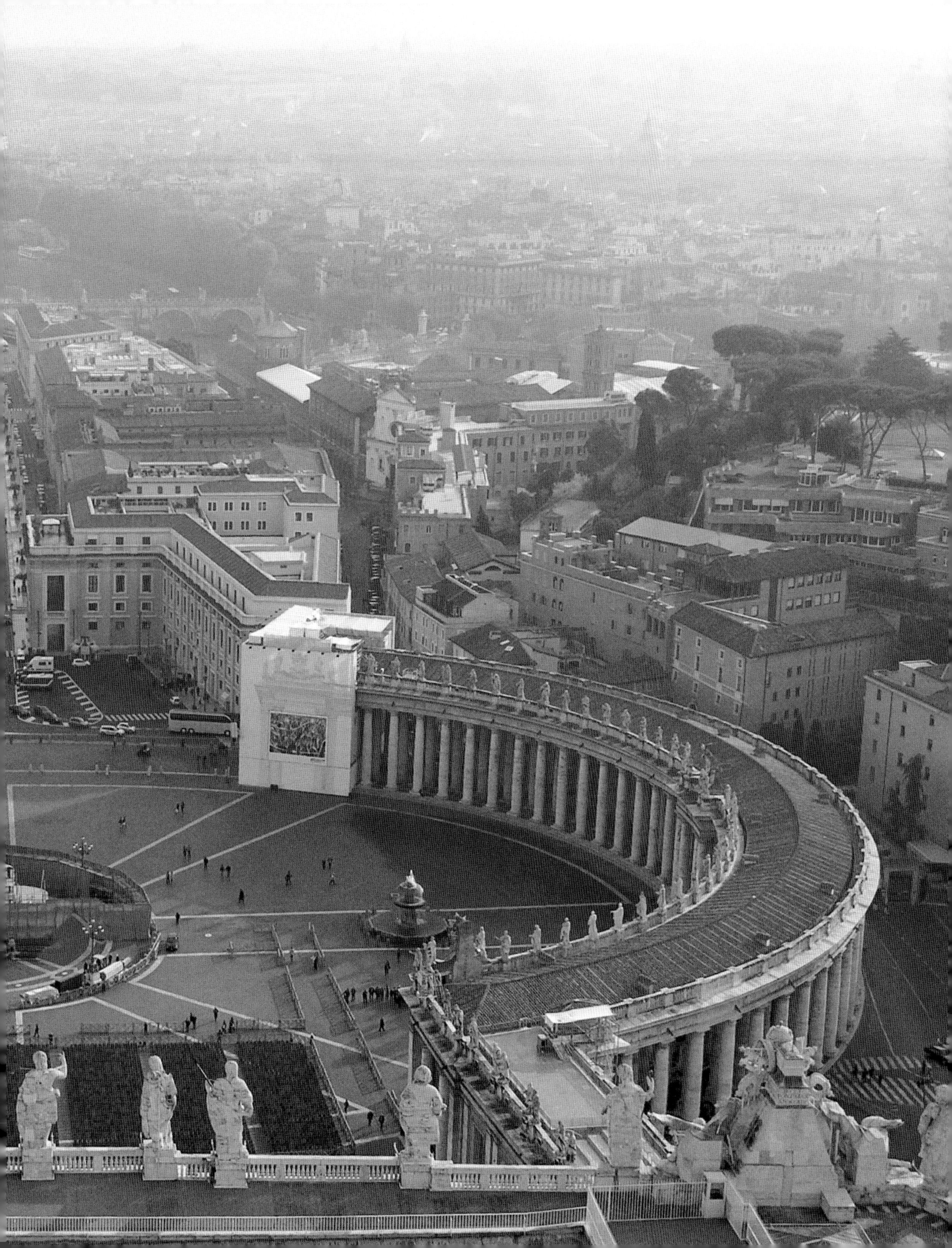

seven floors each; there is a lift shaft going up the side that was originally an ammunition hoist. Once home to more than 100 men, the rooms in the towers extend down to the seabed. There were double bunks around the walls with bulletproof portholes. The original wartime generators provided electricity and an old fishing boat brought regular supplies from the mainland.[56] Both Bates and the fort's previous inhabitants had been pirate radio broadcasters, but his operations for 'Radio Essex' have become decreasingly central to his life. Bates declared the infrastructure to be an independent sovereign state, and has successfully seen-off a number of evictions and invasions. The Principality of Sealand now offers a base for internet servers in a desirable off-shore location, as well as selling titles of Lord & Lady or Baron & Baroness. It has its own currency, the Sealand Dollar, and issues passports, while commemorative coins can be purchased from the Sealand official website in addition to a plethora of merchandizing.[57]

On the Danish island of Elleore in the Roskilde Fjord is another independent sovereignty of approximately 15,000 square meters with a purported capital, the tented town of Maglelille, erected only during the annual summer one-week-long 'citizens' gathering. Established as a gentle satire of the government structure and royal traditions of Denmark, the sovereignty has its own eccentric traditions including a ban on the historical fiction 'Robinson Crusoe' (1719), and the use of 'Elleore Standard Time', which is 12 minutes behind Danish time.[58] Sealand and the Kingdom of Elleore, an island for summer camp purchased by a group of Copenhagen schoolteachers, are examples of micronations. These infrastructures are usually very small pieces of territory that whilst not being officially recognized by world governments, have had claims of sovereignty over them. According to The United Nations Convention on the Law of the Sea, 'artificial islands, installations and structures do not possess the status of islands. They have no territorial sea of their own, and their presence does not affect the delimitation of the territorial sea, the exclusive economic zone or the continental shelf.'[59] Whether or not these principalities are officially recognized, they are demonstrative of our desire to conquer, rule over and protect our own territories. Today, as futurists, architects and urban planners are starting to look out to sea for our urban futures, Sealand serves as a unique and intriguing case study. The feeling of empowerment and liberation can be extremely seductive, even to the point of living on an abandoned infrastructure in the middle of the sea.

Protecting Economic Interests
In 2015, China's reclamation of the Spratly Island reefs in the South China Sea, through massive dredging operations, has shifted to strings of new-build artificial islands. The US Pentagon warned that 'while Beijing's island infrastructure intent is unclear, five emerging outposts totaling about 800 hectares could be used for military surveillance systems, harbors, airfield and logistical support'.[60] It was originally thought the coral atolls of the South China Sea were hotly disputed territories as they are potentially sitting above massive reserves of oil and natural gas. While several Asian countries, including Vietnam, the Philippines, Taiwan, and Malaysia, have occupied some of the real island outposts,[61] they have warned that failure to halt China's constructions will allow Beijing to take 'de facto control' of the area.

The construction of military bases on artificial land is an extremely expensive and technically challenging effort. The infrastructure is generally unfit for any civic or domestic purposes, and territory of this kind bears no functional likeness to historical forts, castles or great-walls which integrated complex urban inhabitable layers with a defensive barrier. Instead, they are more akin to the specialized military infrastructure of Maunsell naval forts built for the rivers Thames and the Mersey during World War II. Whether or not there are natural resources present, China is mainly interested in the strategic advantage of controlling these infrastructures at sea. As expected, Chinese Government officials have been quick to refute any allegations of colonialism.

China has faced further mounting accusations in the West in recent years over its foreign investment portfolio of infrastructures 'growing into history's most extensive global commercial empire'.[62] In 2013, Chinese leader Xi Jinping unveiled the audacious plan 'One Belt, One Road', a land-and-sea reimagining of the fabled East–West Silk Road. Planned and in-place Chinese-financed land, sea and air transport, power plants and natural resources distribution pipelines, and telecommunications, are to facilitate current and prospective mines, oilfields, and an array of businesses back to and from China. On land, high-speed rail connects Kunming in China to Laos, Cambodia, Malaysia, Singapore, Thailand and Vietnam; from Kashgar, the westernmost city in China, through Pakistan to the Arabian seaport of Gwadur; and from Acu, near Rio de Janeiro, crossing the Amazon rainforest and the Andes Mountains, and terminating on the Peruvian coast. China has also agreed to construct a network of roads, rail and energy pipelines from Xi'an in central China to Belgium and Spain; and help build transport infrastructure linking all 54 African countries. At sea, a companion 21st century Maritime Silk Road would connect the South China Sea to the Indian and South Pacific oceans.[63] Some of these thousands of miles of infrastructure already exist; China now has to strategically link them all together.

Whatever the concerns about the motives of foreign investors, many African policymakers recognize Chinese investments represent a vital contribution to Africa's development and infrastructure deficit. Beijing's exploitations range from access to Africa's natural resources and huge domestic market, to service contracts for Chinese Government-backed construction companies.[64] In 2014, the instability in Africa has forced China to abandon its quintessential foreign policy of non-interference – Beijing deployed its first infantry battalion of about 700 combat troops to a UN peacekeeping mission in South Sudan to protect its national economic interests.[65] However, the lack of sustainability could only lead to African dependence upon Chinese largess for future development and maintenance of infrastructures. Africa 'is now willingly opening itself up to a new form of imperialism', protested the governor of the Central Bank of Nigeria, Lamido Sanusi, in the Financial Times.[66]

To further boost its grand scheme of global infrastructure, Beijing initiated the Asian Infrastructure Investment Bank, with the support of 57 regional and non-regional members. Such ambitions are certainly China-centric but are neither intimidating nor grasping, nor even a Chinese invention. Other nations have behaved in a similar manner – the Romans paved hundreds of thousands of miles of road and aqueducts to control much of Europe and beyond; later, in the 18th and 19th centuries, the British Empire's commanding navy expanded its territories with the construction of ports, roads, and railroads. As Michael Pillsbury, author of 'The Hundred Year Marathon' explained, 'China's ambitions are rooted in a fierce sense of competitiveness which they claim they learned from the America of the 1800s'.[67]

Fortifications, moats, lagoons, and glacis that have long lost their defensive value still solidly enclose many towns. Walls can still frame and protect a city, but these infrastructures need no longer be made of stone and mortar – city zoning, greenbelts, and floodgates can defend against the contemporary threats of overpopulation, pollution and climate change. At the 2014 American Physical Society conference, Rongjia Tao, a physics professor from the USA, put forward a plan to build three 'great walls' of reinforced glass for forestalling the formation of tornadoes. The gigantic barriers of, up to

56. R Anderson, 'The Country We Established at Sea', The Guardian, 3 February 2007 [http://www.theguardian.com/theguardian/2007/feb/03/weekend7.weekend6], retrieved 12 May 2015

57. Sealand Official Website [http://www.sealandgov.org/gifts/sealand-constitution], retrieved 12 May 2015

58. J Ryan, G Dunford & S Sellars, 'Micronations: The Lonely Planet guide to home-made nations', Lonely Planet Publications, London, 2006, pp.42–47

59. Oceans and Laws of the Sea, United Nations, 'The United Nations Convention on the Law of the Sea' [http://www.un.org/depts/los/convention_agreements/texts/unclos/unclos_e.pdf], retrieved 12 May 2015

60. Associated Press Washington, 'China's Land Reclamation in Disputed Waters Stokes Fears of Military Ambitions', The Guardian: World News, 8 May 2015 [http://www.theguardian.com/world/2015/may/08/china-land-reclamation-south-china-sea-stokes-fears-military-ambitions], retrieved 22 August 2015

61. R Wingfield-Hayes, 'China's Island Factory', BBC Special, 9 September 2014 [http://www.bbc.co.uk/news/special/2014/newsspec_8701/index.html], retrieved 22 August 2015

62, 63+67. S LeVine, 'China is Building the Most Extensive Global Commercial-military Empire in History', Quartz, 9 June 2015 [http://qz.com/415649/china-is-building-the-most-extensive-global-commercial-military-empire-in-history], retrieved 22 August 2015

64. A Tiffen, 'The New Neo-Colonialism in Africa', Global Policy, Durham University, UK, August 2014 [http://www.globalpolicyjournal.com/blog/19/08/2014/new-neo-colonialism-africa], retrieved 22 August 2015

65. D Smith, 'China to Send 700 Combat Troops to South Sudan', The Guardian: World News, 23 December 2014

66. L Sanusi, 'Africa Must Get Real About Chinese Ties', The Financial Times: Opinion, 11 March 2013

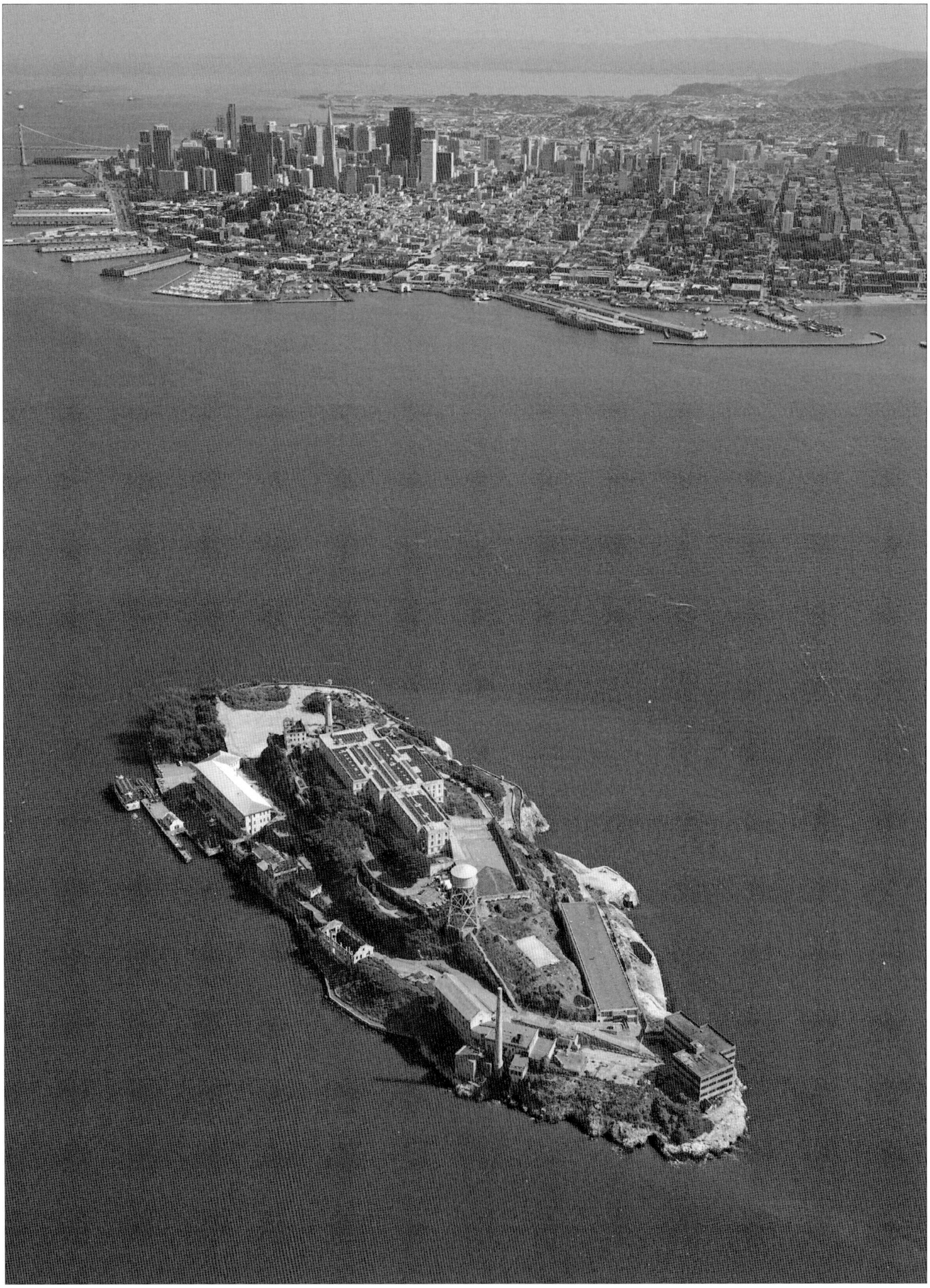

260 kilometers long, 50 meters thick, and 300 meters tall, would softened the clashing streams of hot southern and cold northern air that lead to the formation of hundreds of twisters every year in Tornado Alley, the land corridor between the Rocky and Appalachian mountain ranges that covers parts of Texas, Oklahoma, Kansas, and Nebraska. Meteorologists have been highly skeptical; the US$16 billion infrastructure would not be strong enough to block a tornado in motion.[68] Alas, the preposterous nature of the wall to tackle growing metrological and ecological threats is reminiscent of the kind of naïve and wasteful proposition presented by Donald Trump. During the 2016 USA election campaign, Trump pledged to build a physical wall between Mexico and the USA to reduce immigration – he even stated his intention to force Mexico to build and finance the infrastructure.[69]

Many cities choose to adopt a more nuanced defense system derived from traditional methods, and subtle cultural and geographical understanding. In Australia, settlements and suburban sprawl around the cities of Adelaide, Sydney and Melbourne are in constant danger of bushfires during their long summer months. One strategy of defending against the rampant spread of destruction is to literally fight fire with a 'wall of fire'. Controlled burning of areas around human settlement produces a barrier of non-flammable ash, which prevents wildfires from trespassing. Controlled burning is a defense infrastructure, and with details of the organized activity published by local councils for citizens' convenience, a well-regulated summer fire is just another aspect of the television weather forecast.[70] Prescribed burns are known to improve the environment for wildlife and assist plant species to reproduce and germinate. For farmers, it is common practice to employ 'fire ecology', an agricultural technique of both an industrial and subsistence scale, to make controlled burns of fields after a crop cycle to re-invigorate pastures and forestry management, and to kill pests and disease.[71]

Areas that have been deforested are at risk from desertification, landslides and flooding. The entire Amazonian ecosystem in South America relies on the presence of trees – take the trees away and the whole environmental system will go into shock. In regions where the land has been carved-up into farms, fields and settlements, there is an inbuilt tension between the forces of nature and the man-made environment. According to the UK's Environment Agency, 'it is likely that with climate change and development pressures, ...[currently] around 5.2 million properties in England, or one in six properties, are at risk of flooding'.[72] Tree planting can reduce the impact of flooding by stabilizing the ground, attenuating floodwaters, and can also help to filter out pollutants. The report 'The Role of Productive Woodlands in Water Management' by the Confederation of Forest Industries UK (Confor) highlights that 'society is increasingly threatened by flooding while the water environment remains seriously impacted by a range of human pressures. There is a strong case for further investment in well-targeted woodland creation to help meet a wide range of environmental and social goals.'[73] In fact, there is a surreal commonality between the trees planted for defense purposes near coastal areas and JRR Tolkien's tree-like 'Ents' in 'Lord of the Rings: The Two Towers' (1954) – they both exercise great patience and thoughtfulness in anticipation of the enemy.

Living green walls, hedges and espaliered fruit fences have always been indispensable requisites of civilized architecture and landscape infrastructure. Farmers, in Shimane Prefecture in Western

facing page: A notice at the entrance to Alcatraz, the famous 12-acre US island penitentiary in San Francisco, reads '...1.5 miles to transport dock. Only Government boats permitted, others must keep off 200 yards. No one allowed ashore without a pass'.

68. J Morgan, 'Great Walls of America Could Stop Tornadoes', BBC: Science and Environment, 8 March 2014 [http://www.bbc.co.uk/news/science-environment-26492720], retrieved 22 August 2015

69. S Bixby & D Agren, 'Trump Reveals Plan to Finance Mexico Border Wall with Threat to Cut Off Funds', The Guardian, 5 April 2016 [https://www.theguardian.com/us-news/2016/apr/05/donald-trump-mexico-border-wall-plan-remittances], retrieved 20 June 2016

70. Brisbane City Council, 'Planned Burns 2014 – Brisbane West' [http://www.brisbane.qld.gov.au/community/community-safety/disasters-emergencies/types-disasters/bushfires/planned-burns-2014/planned-burns-2014-brisbane-west], retrieved 8 November 2014

71. W Ladrach, 'The Effects of Fire in Agriculture and Forest Ecosystems', International Society of Tropical Foresters, Special Report, June 2009, p.2

72. Environment Agency, 'Flooding in England: A National Assessment of Flood Risk', 2009 [https://www.gov.uk/government/uploads/system/uploads/attachment_data/file/292928/geho0609bqds-e-e.pdf], retrieved 12 August 2016

73. Institute of Chartered Foresters, 'New Report Highlights How Productive Tree Planting Can Reduce Flood Risk', News, March 2015 [http://www.charteredforesters.org/news/item/362-confor-report-woodland-flood-risk-prevention/], retrieved 12 August 2016

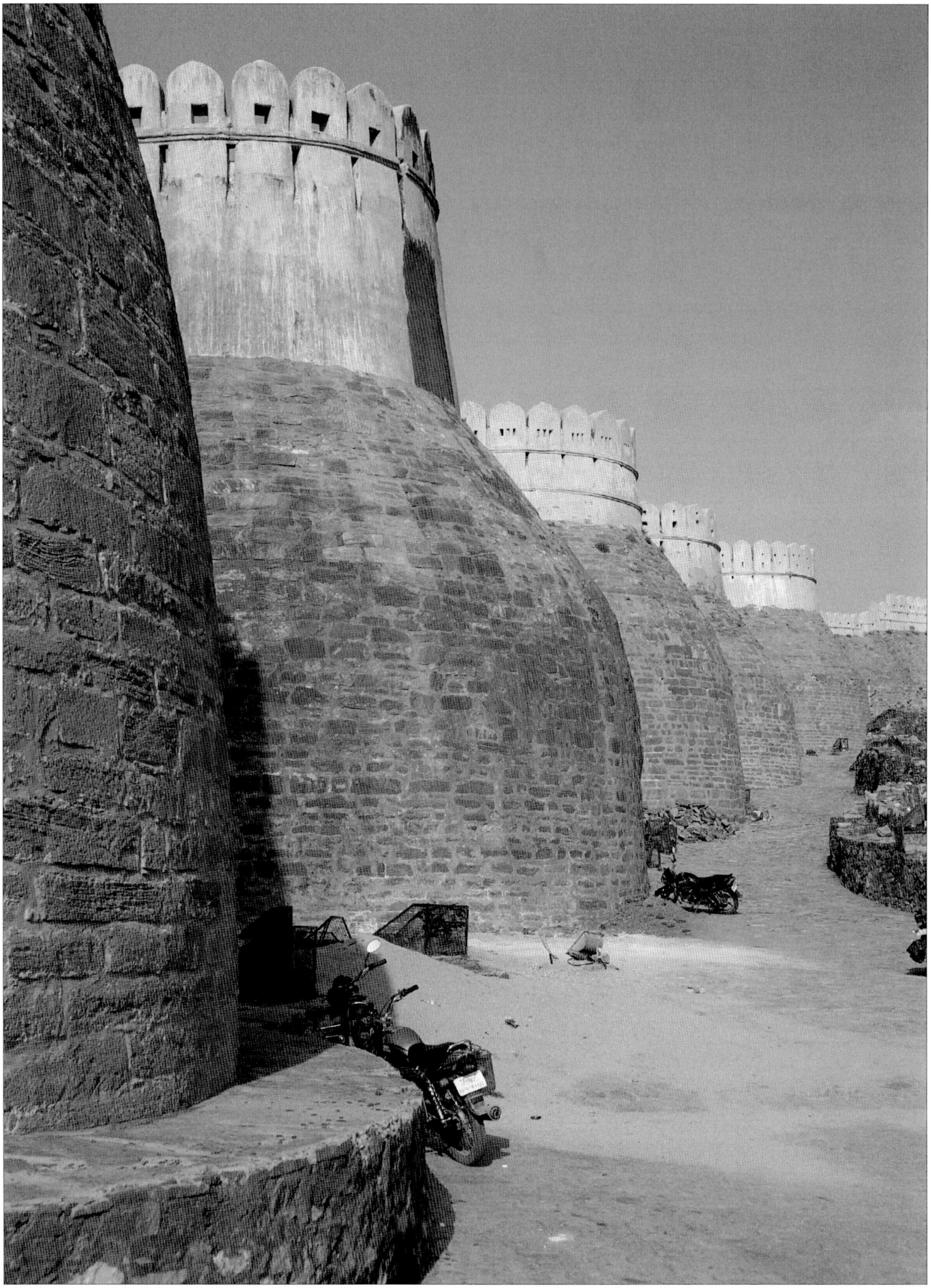

to protect

Japan, coax pine trees into thick 50-foot high L-shaped hedges to buffer against winter winds and snowstorms. Coastal erosion can be mitigated by the establishment of artificial reefs to reduce or redirect the impact of the waves and seek to re-instate valuable habitats for endangered sea-life. One of the greatest economic advantages of landscape or natural infrastructure is the low-cost; more-often-than-not the materials are already on the site, or can be cultivated for free.

Almost every spring, Beijing is victim to savage sandstorms that engulf the city under an abrasive yellow haze. The Chinese Government, driven by its obligation to protect the city's air quality, has invested in dune stabilization research – the approach involves 'solidifying' the sand in a 2,667-hectare area of the Tianmo Desert.[74] There are multiple ways to stabilize dunes, but perhaps the cheapest and most effective is to simply cultivate vegetation on them. As the roots establish, they bind together loose layers of sediment into a firm infrastructure. It is without doubt that the strongest ally we could hope to protect us from natural disaster is nature itself.

There is of course the question of 'why did humans choose to inhabit afflicted areas?' A lot of the world's infrastructure is only required because of questionable or unforeseeable miscalculations in urban planning. The nuance of settlement and protection becomes explicit with density. Urban phenomena such as Kowloon Walled City prove that dense and intense urban-life can thrive within small confines. Manhattan, for example, maintains a degree of porosity at ground level and on its fire escapes; it is these variegated notion of screens and layers of veils that produce an urbanism that can simultaneously protect and offer democratic freedom to the public realm. It was graffiti and protest that gave the Berlin Wall a sense of place which now, as a 20th century ruin, remains an integral, ongoing chapter in the reading of the city. When a wall has heroic solidity such as the Forbidden City or Buckingham Palace, there is little or no urban nuance.

The continuance of earmarking large percentages of national budget for military and defense suggests that our age-old fears have remained the same. But walls and visible defenses have picked up a bad reputation, whether it is political, in the case of the Berlin Wall, or socially alienating, where boundaries or gated compounds can be segregating. The modernist movement and subsequent architectural aesthetics have stressed the importance of 'transparency'. The concept encompasses clear and honest architectural forms and infrastructures for cities and its communities, which sets the theatre for open and public engagement. To address issues of climate change, security and relentless urban expansion, we need to speculate and redefine the poetics of walls without conflict.

'There is a time to battle against nature, and a time to obey her. True wisdom lies in making the right choice.'

– Arthur C Clarke, 'The Fountains of Paradise', 1979

facing page: Kumbhalgarh Fort near Udaipur in India is the second largest wall in the world after the Great Wall of China.

74. Xinhua News Agency, 'Project Stops Sandstorms in Beijing', Environment News, State Council Information Office and the China International Publishing, 2008 [http://www.china.org.cn/environment/news/2008-03/17/content_12823275.htm], retrieved 12 August 2016

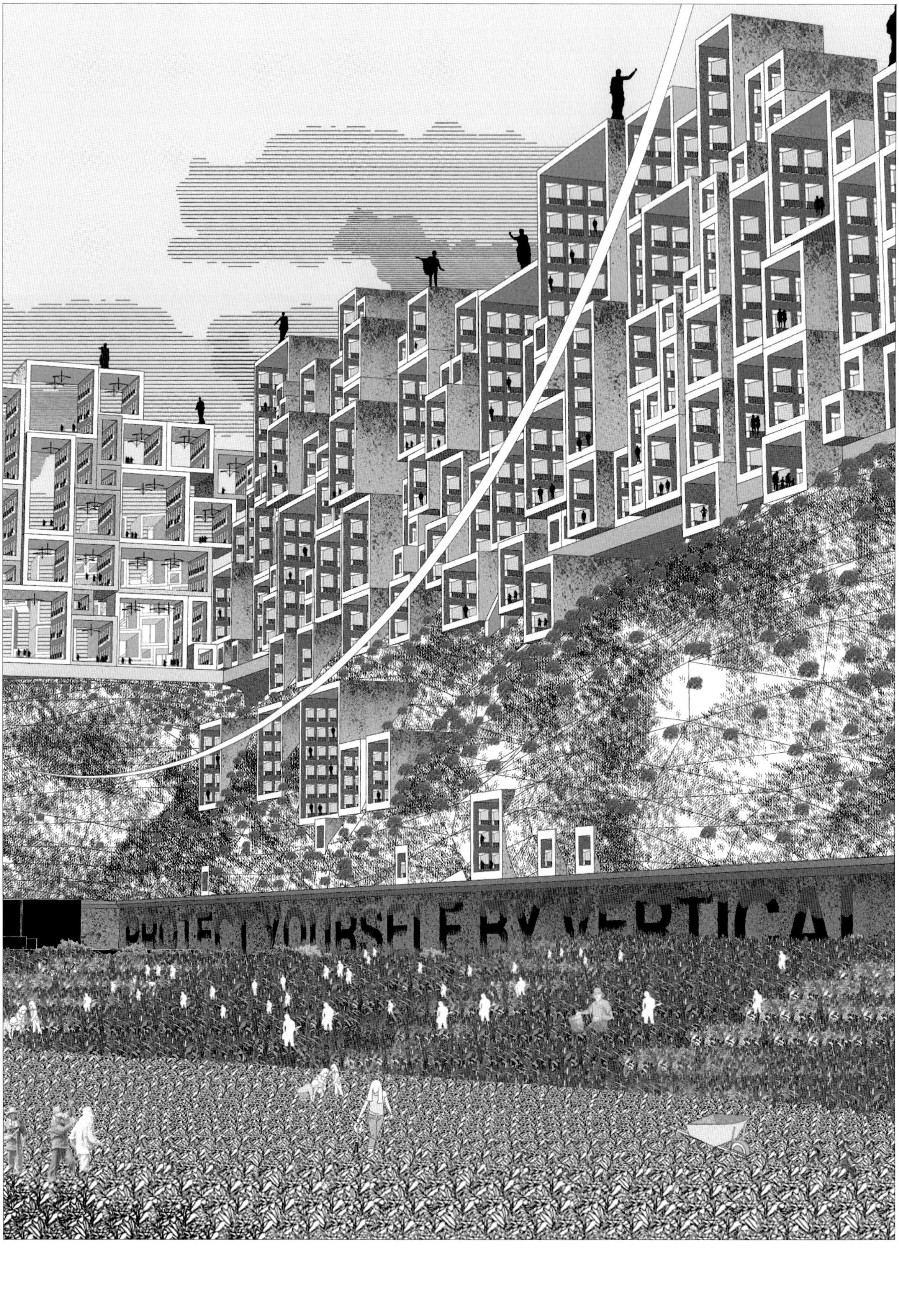
PROTECT YOURSELF BY VERTICAL

urban future
London Is Flooding?

(i)

'Perched in the windows of the office blocks and department stores, the iguanas watched them go past, their hard frozen heads jerking stiffly. Without the reptiles, the lagoons and the creeks of office blocks half-submerged would have had a strange dream-like beauty, but the iguanas and basilisks brought the fantasy down to earth. As their seats in the one-time board-rooms indicated, the reptiles had taken over the city.'

– JG Ballard, 'The Drowned World', 1962

Ballard's London is subject to a new Triassic age, under the environmental force even the human mind begins to regress. Melting ice caps have caused the cities of the west to plunge into a tropical lagoon-like state, and with that submersion came a rising dystopia. Pirates drain the lagoons and loot treasures from the past, whilst others occupy the upper floors of buildings which emerge from the water and vegetation.[1] Writer Will Self argues that given Ballard's childhood in Shanghai where he had experienced regular events of flooding, and the formative and perhaps apocalyptic experiences of the Japanese invasion during World War II, 'while he may not have consciously been constructing an eco-parable, such was the fertility of Ballard's imagination he couldn't help giving birth to a thriving example of the genre.'[2] Editions of the novel often have striking visions of a semi-submerged London as the cover image; London landmarks such as St Paul's Cathedral or Tower Bridge can be seen emerging from thick vines, a canopy of tropical leaves and a reflection of the dilapidated structures in the murky waters of the flood.

'London is already feeling the effects of climate change. It is particularly vulnerable to flooding, subsidence, overheating and to water supply shortfalls', notes the London Plan.[3] Understandably, the anxieties extend to very many cities, not just London, that would be underwater when ice caps melt. How will sea level rise impact the vulnerable inhabitants as well as the wealth of existing infrastructures in the cities? What are the viable measures to protect and adapt existing floodwalls, embankments and barriers, and also the time scales to implement new infrastructures? Retreat, attack or defend?[4]

Apprehension and skepticism caused by our remnant understanding of the 1928 Thames flood in London is still ongoing; people drowned and thousands were made homeless when floodwaters poured over the top of the Thames Embankment. The rising sea levels at the time coincided with a high spring tide as well as a storm surge that raised the water levels in the Thames Estuary. The situation was worsened by capital dredging which made it easier for seawater to flow up the Thames during high tide. Plans to build the Thames Barrier began soon after the North Sea flood disaster of winter 1953; the disaster caused

facing page: London is dramatically transformed by inhabitable walls and castles, thus moving the city's communities into concentrated vertical living, recalling 'The Tower of Babel'.

following pages: The heritage and spirit of London is divided into three fundamental bodies to safeguard: the 'Queen', the 'Economy' and the 'Knowledge'.

1. JG Ballard, 'The Drowned World', Berkley Books, London, 1962

2. W Self, 'Will Self on JG Ballard's The Drowned World', The Telegraph, 31 August 2013 [http://www.telegraph.co.uk/culture/books/10273413/Will-Self-on-JG-Ballards-The-Drowned-World.html], retrieved 19 July 2016

3. The Mayor of London, 'London's Response to Climate Change', The London Plan, Chapter 5, March 2016, p.176 [https://www.london.gov.uk/sites/default/files/the_london_plan_malp_march_2016_-_chapter_5_-_londons_response_to_climate_change.pdf], retrieved 24 July 2016

4. Building Futures RIBA, 'Facing Up To Rising Sea-Levels: Retreat? Defend? Attack?', Institute of Civil Engineers, 2010 [www.buildingfutures.org.uk/assets/downloads/Facing_Up_To_Rising_Sea_Levels.pdf], retrieved 14 September 2015

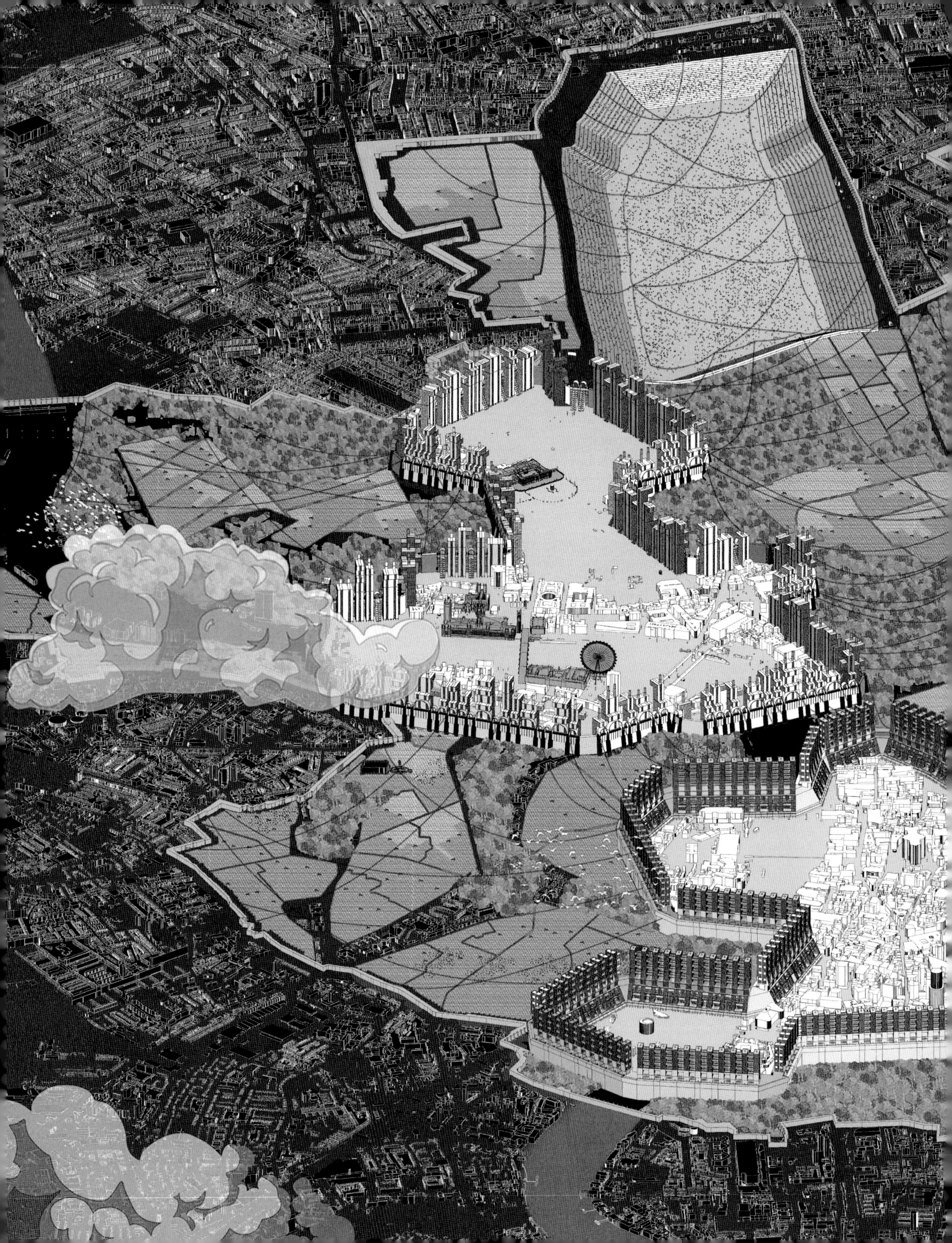

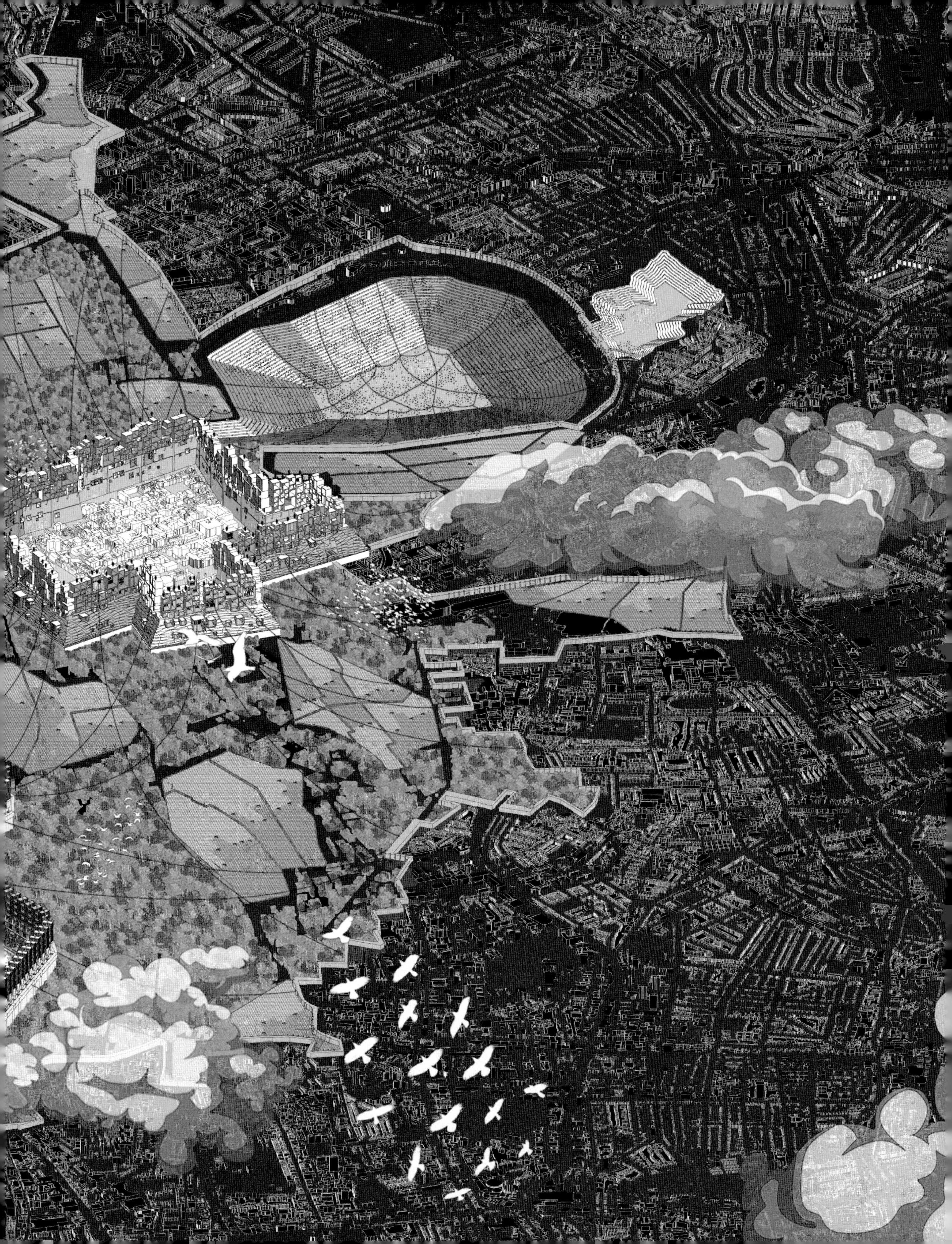

GATE 2

OD SAVES QUEEN AND COUNTRY

OUR GREAT GOAL

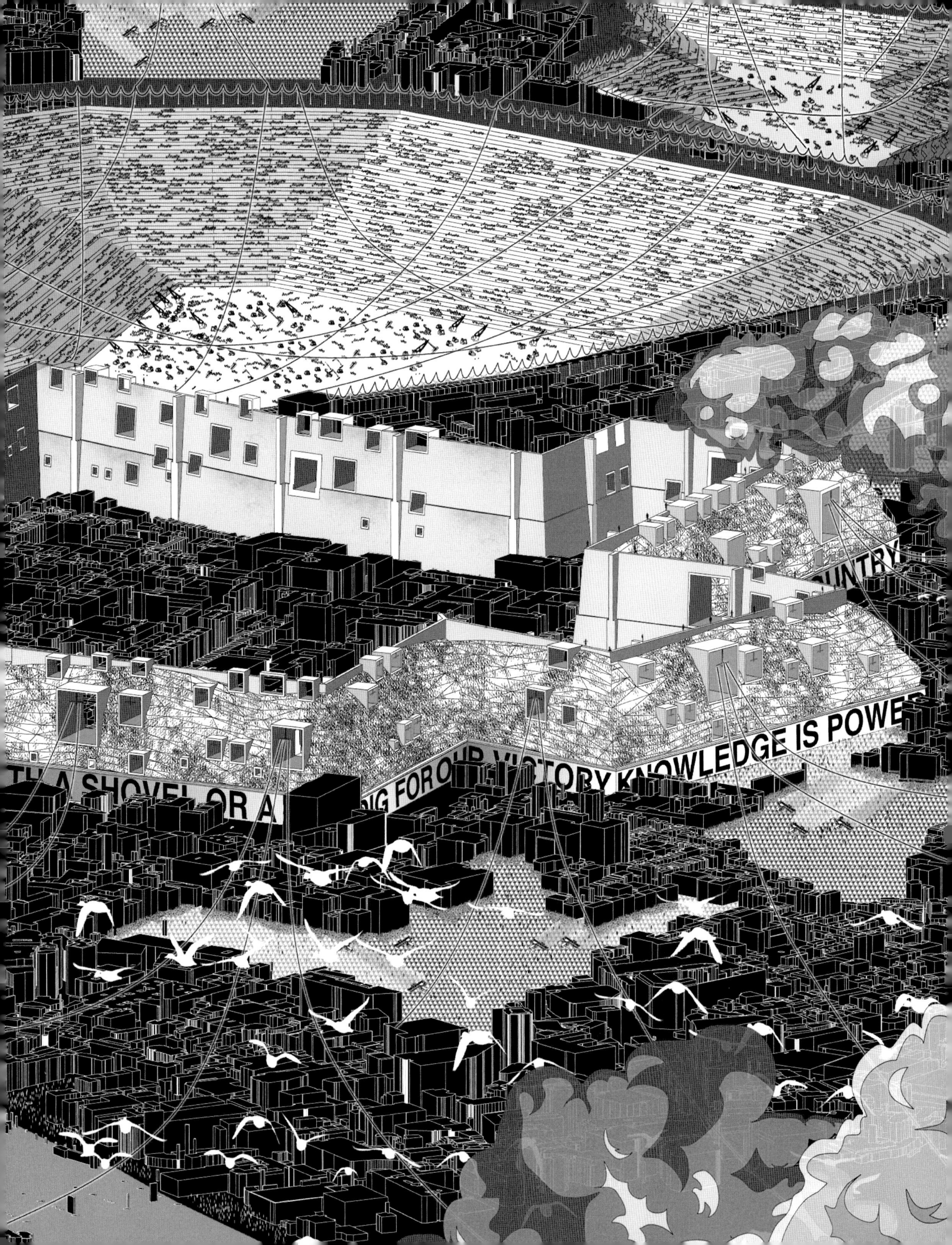

TH A SHOVEL OR A
IG FOR OU
TORY
KNOWLEDGE IS POWE
UNTRY

DIG FOR OUR VICTORY

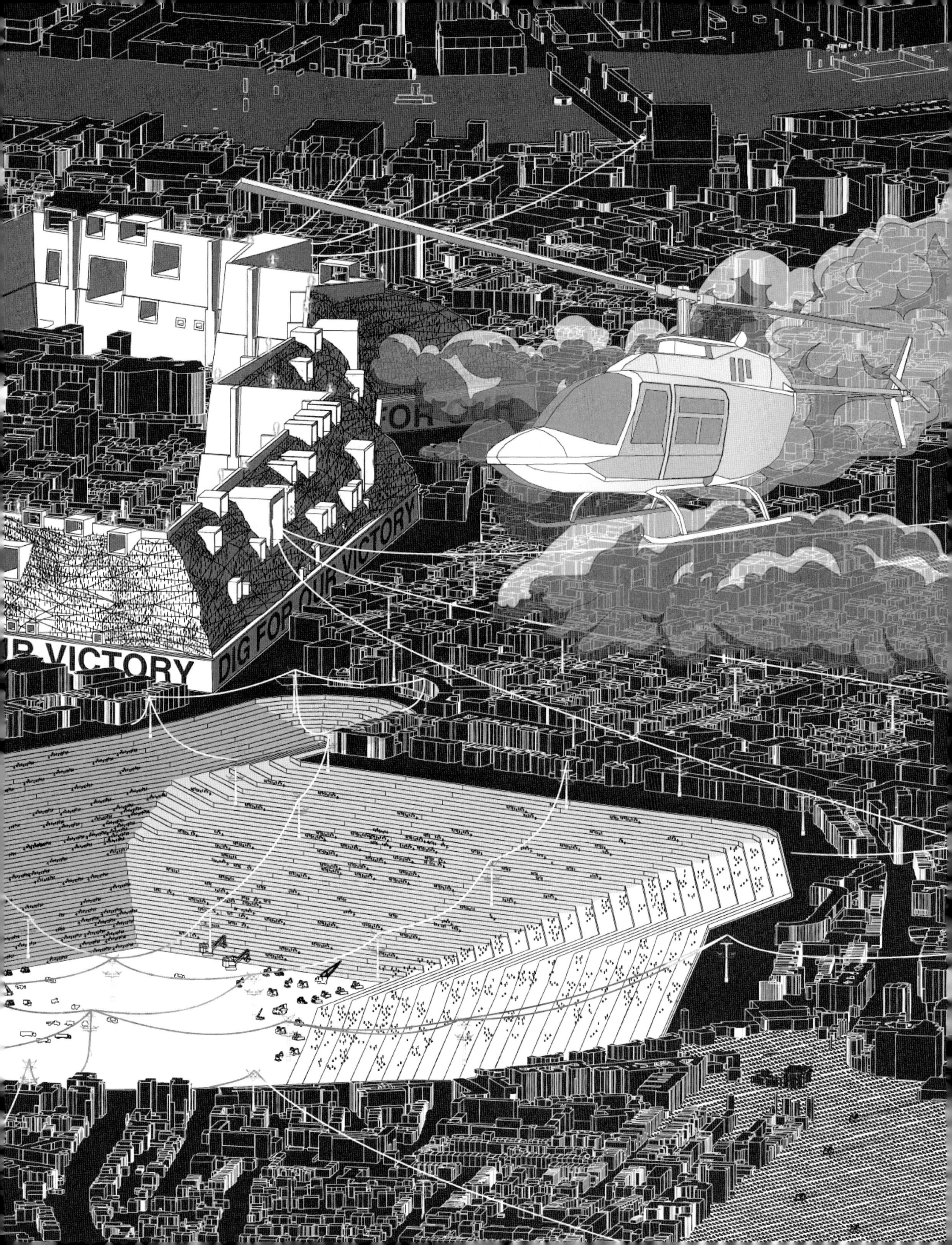
DIG FOR OUR VICTORY
UR VICTORY
FOR OUR

BUILD HIGHER
BUILD HIGHER

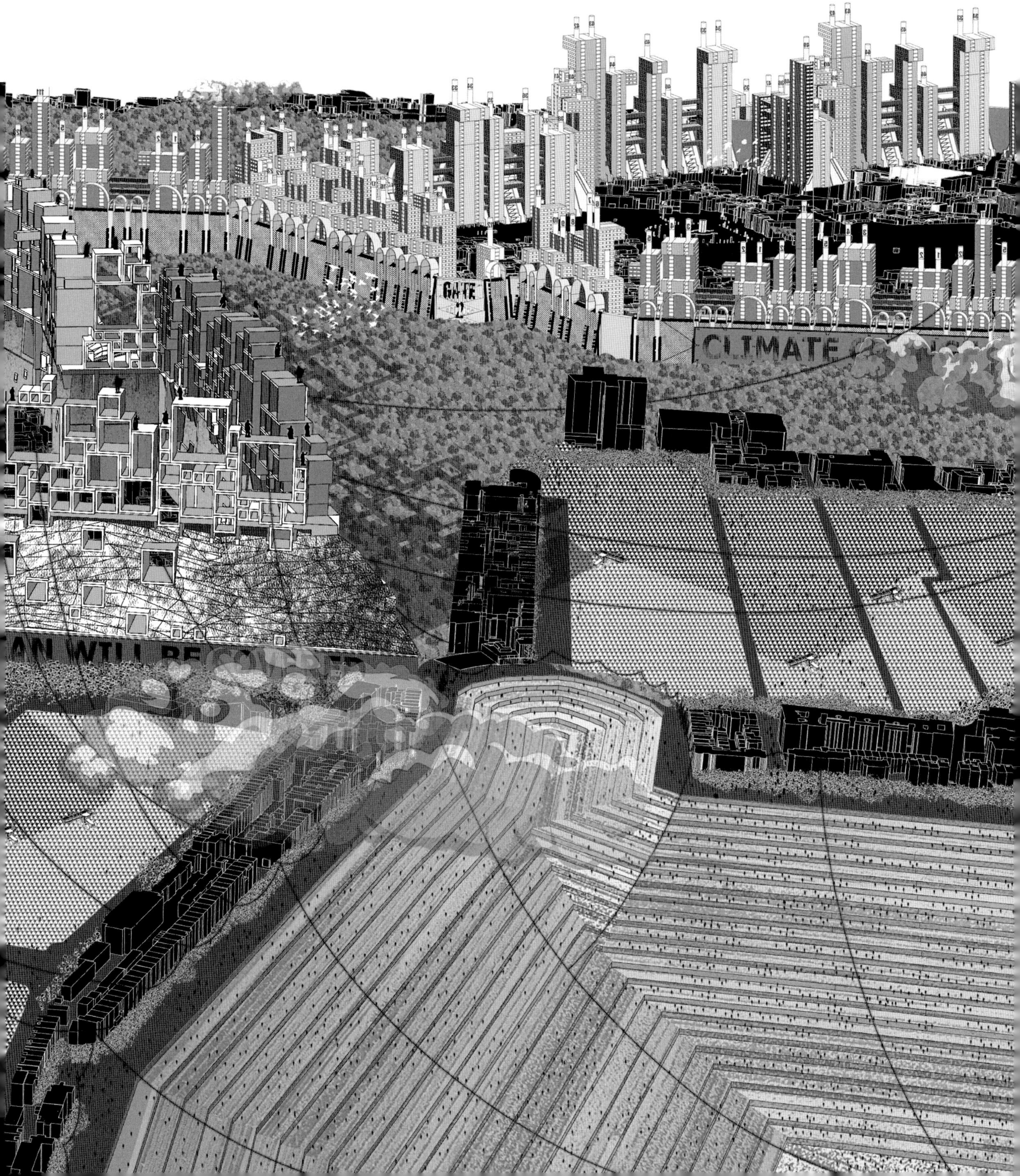
GATE 2
CLIMATE

It's Fox Hunting Season NOW!
27
29
30
28
23
20
22
21
GATE
DON'T MISS IT.

substantial damage to factories, gasworks and electricity generating stations from Tilbury all the way to the East End.[5]

The Thames Barrier is one of the world's largest movable flood resistant infrastructures – the row of science fiction-like mini-piers and silver pods that spans 520 meters protects London from tidal surges and storms. The barrier although fairly dormant is a powerful assurance. Having only been deployed 114 times between the 1980s and 2000s, there have been 65 closures since 2010, suggesting a strong, overall upward trend.[6] The barrier, together with 350 kilometers of flood walls and embankments, smaller barriers, pumping stations and flood gates, was constructed more than 30 years ago, when engineers planned for sea level rise of eight millimeters a year. However, the sea level rise in the Thames estuary over this century could be greater than 20 centimeters.[7] Although there will not be major adjustment to the existing system of defenses until 2070, the UK's Environment Agency are now looking into the short-, medium- and long-term recommendations of replacements and repairs made by the Thames Estuary 2100 Plan (TE2100). With such unfortunate sequences of events in the city's past, it is no wonder that current news of rising sea levels plays on Londoners' anxieties and uncertainties.

'The Paranoid City' is one-third homage to Ballard, one-third speculation into the threat of nature and the resilience of cities, and one-third a provocation exercise in re-interpreting the notion of a 'disaster'. The new inhabitable infrastructures, at once, protect parts of the urban fabric and also safeguard the housing welfare of London's inhabitants. Flooding has a bad reputation for targeting the poor, a major theme of Maggie Gee's SF novel 'The Flood' (2004), which sees an open society threatened when repeated floods and a hostile political situation eradicate all except the richest inhabitants who are, of course, protected by their higher position geographically. As evidenced in New Orleans with Hurricane Katrina in 2005, helpless demography that occupy susceptible topography and have poor infrastructure are most vulnerable. As climate-mania heightens to an overwhelming public insecurity, Londoners succumb to overprotective measures in order to safeguard their hard earned city habitat. Built-on anxieties, fears and foreseeing a great flood within a few short decades, three multi-use infrastructural 'castles' embrace and protect the inhabitants and core institutions of the city from being submerged. The strongholds recall the 'Tower of Babel'[8] which was built by a united humanity, in an effort to reach a higher state and topography. London is dramatically transformed with farming moats and living castles that dominate the skyline, thus moving the city's communities from relative low-rise housing into concentrated vertical living. The heritage and spirit of London is divided into three fundamental bodies to safeguard: the 'Queen', the 'Economy' and the 'Knowledge'.

The Castle of the Queen – London is the seat of government and parliamentary activity for the UK. The inhabitable infrastructure of the 'Queen' protects Buckingham Palace, the Houses of Parliament and the spirit of her people. After a particularly vicious flood in 1236, many had to row around the Great Hall of the Houses of Parliament in boats. If this long anticipated flood were to occur and without the infrastructure in place, then government ministers would have to be evacuated, leaving them completely helpless to aid the city and its inhabitants. The castle consists of several protective layers. Within the walls are accropodes, concrete breakwater units that collectively reduce the intensity of incoming waves.

previous pages: Climate change has driven Londoners to hide within the protective infrastructures.

facing page top: A prophetic view of London if humans vanished.

facing page bottom: The armors act as 'nesting' stopovers for migrating birds from the Northern Hemisphere.

5+6. D Hill, 'Beyond the Thames Barrier: How safe is London from another major flood?', Resilient Cities, The Guardian, 19 February 2015 [https://www.london.gov. https://www.theguardian.com/cities/2015/feb/19/thames-barrier-how-safe-london-major-flood-at-risk], retrieved 24 July 2016

7. The Thames Estuary 2100 Plan, 'Managing Flood Risk Through London and The Thames Estuary', The Environmental Agency (UK), 24 June 2014, [https://www.gov.uk/government/publications/thames-estuary-2100-te2100/thames-estuary-2100-te2100], retrieved 24 July 2016

8. RT Pennock, 'Tower of Babel: The evidence against the new creationism', MIT Press, Cambridge, Massachusetts, 1999

LIVE HIGHER
WATER IS RISING

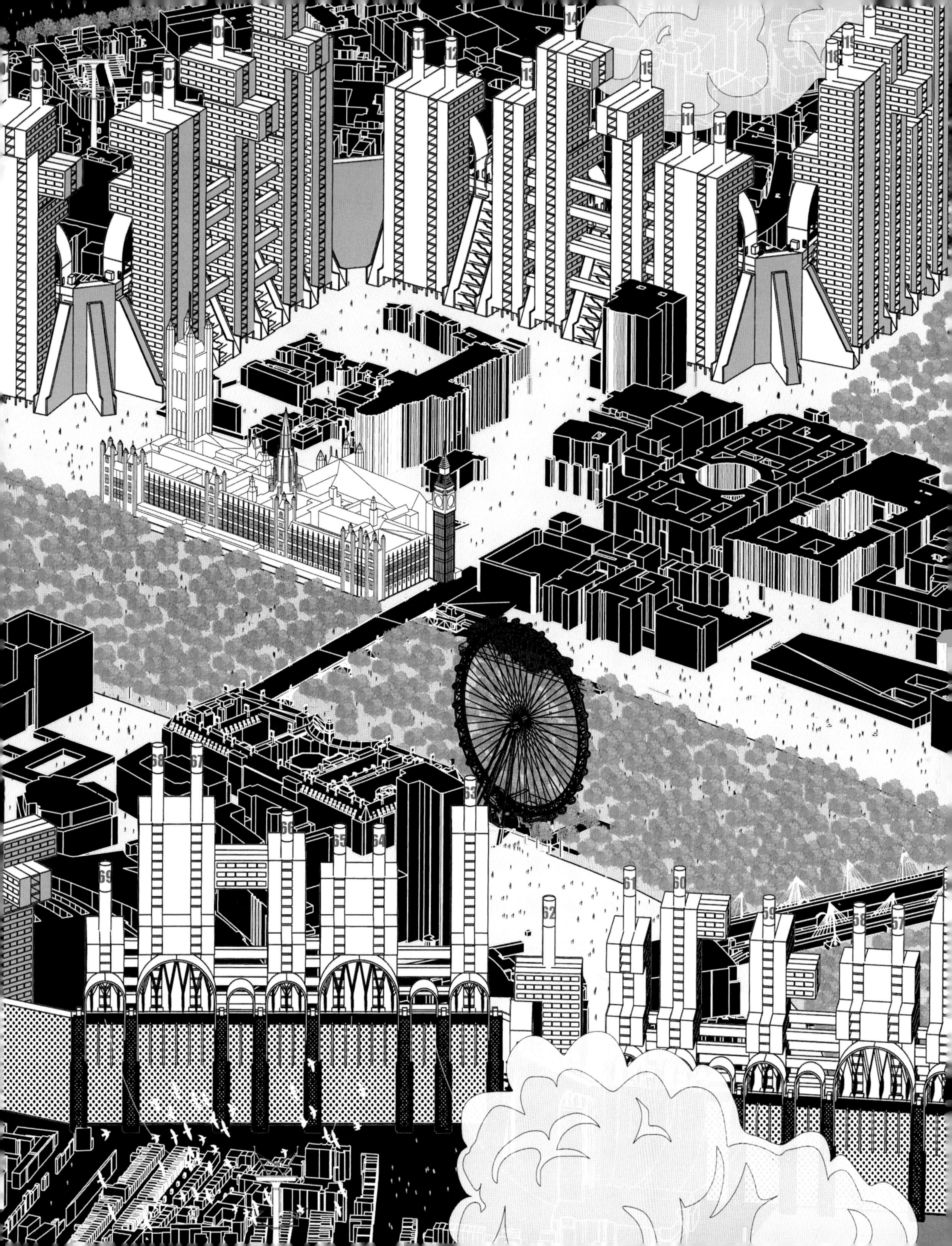
07
11
12
13
14
15
16
17
18
19
68
67
66
65
64
63
69
62
61
60
59
58
57

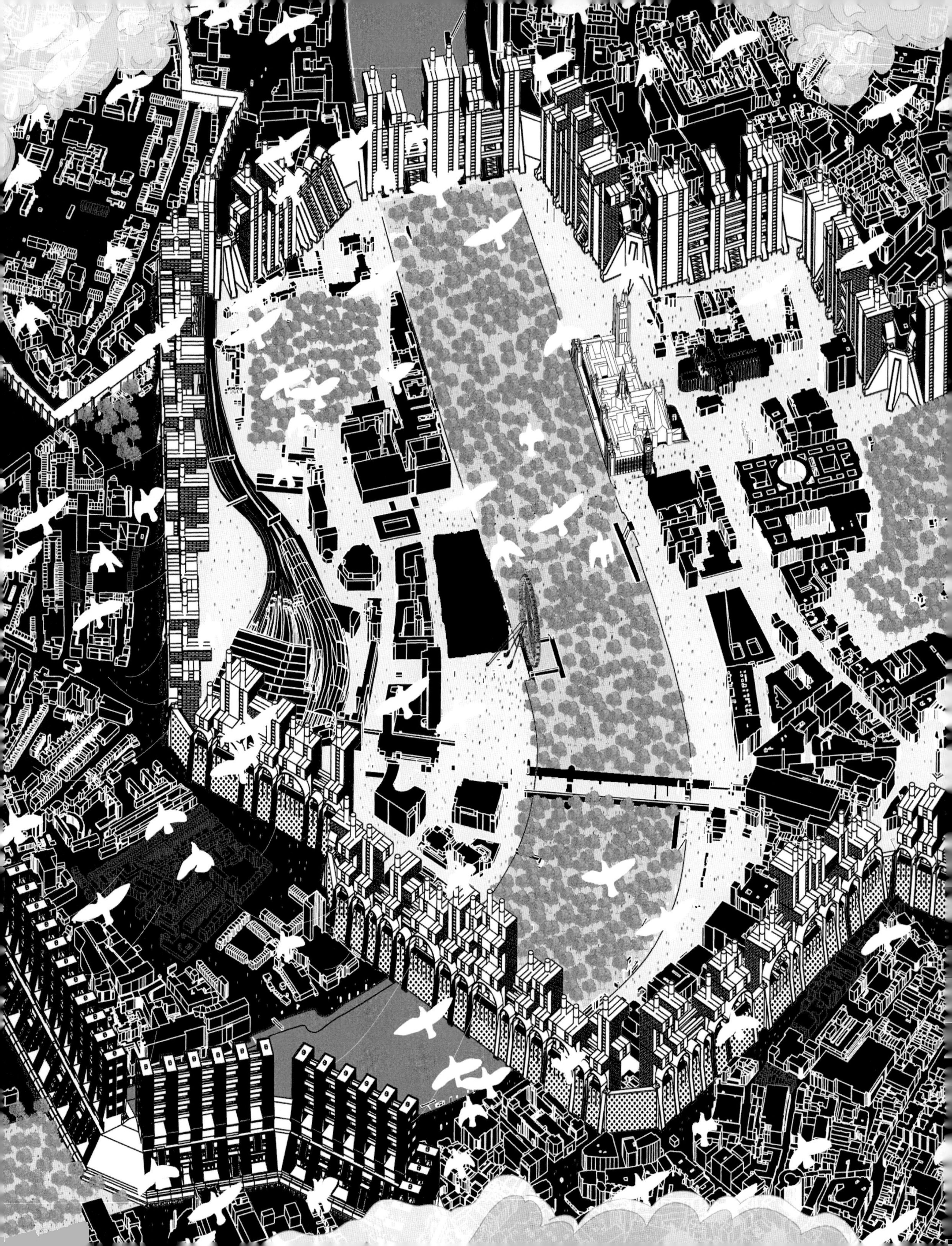

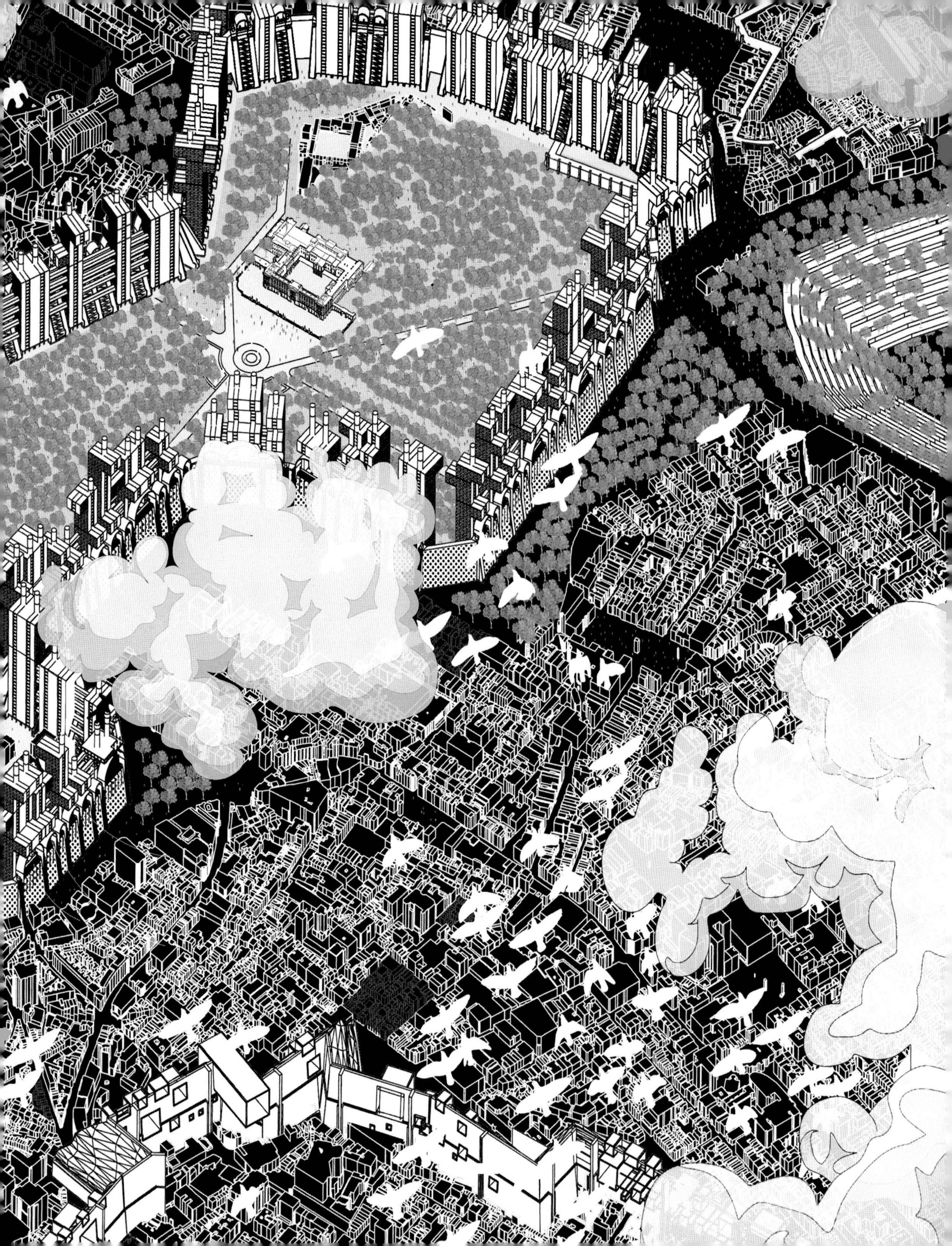

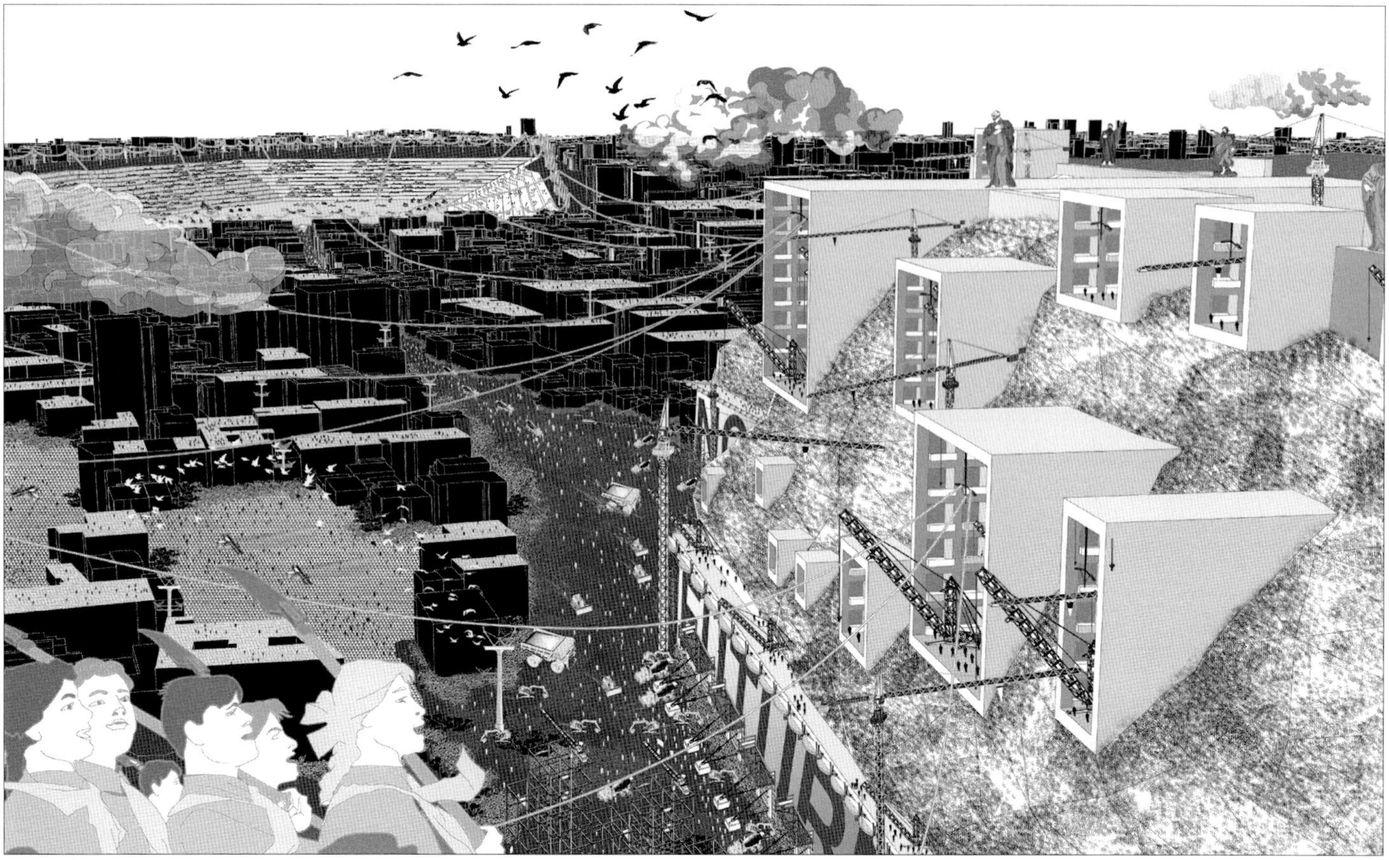

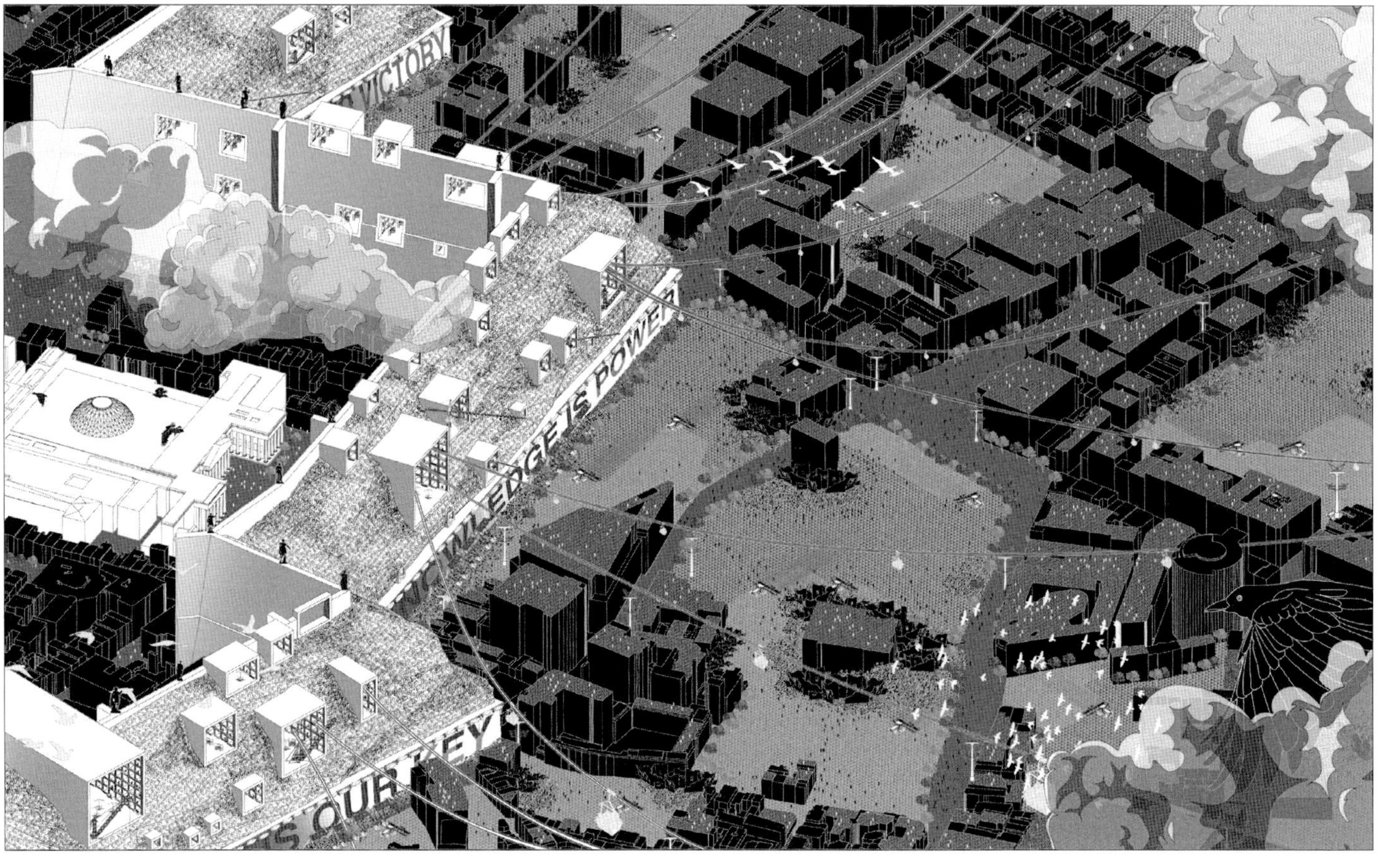
VICTORY

The armors also act as 'nesting' stopovers for migrating birds from the Northern Hemisphere. On top of the accropodes lies a living vertical garden teeming with life; when the flood emerges, these patterned gardens peel off the walls and become inflatable grass floats. An armada worth of boats strategically hang within the arches above the walls, constantly swaying much like the pendulum of a clock. They not only serve as a further precautionary measure, but are perpetual reminders of the inevitable drawing closer. Being the constitutional monarch of England, Scotland, Wales and Northern Ireland, the Queen cultivates national identity and unity. The infrastructure, as with her majesty, commands widespread optimism and pride, bestowing its inhabitants with a collective sense of belonging, and staunchly protects London from the 'Broken-Britain' myth.

The Castle of Economy – London is one of the world's leading financial centers, and contributes an estimated £250 billion to the UK economy each year. According to the Association of British Insurers (ABI) and the Environment Agency (EA), major floods since 2000 including the 2007 summer floods have resulted in insurers paying out £3 billion; the 2005 floods in Carlisle costing £272 million, and the Cumbrian floods in November 2009 costing a further £174 million.[9] The infrastructure of 'Economy' aims to preserve the undying heartbeat of the Square Mile, the central body for managing financial stability. The ordered towers, reminiscent of the passive-aggressive dominance of existing banking skyscrapers, systematically line-up to form an impenetrable wall to the physical flood – protecting some of the UK's most important financial framework and soft infrastructure: the City of London, the Bank of England (being the second oldest central bank in the world and the world's eighth oldest bank) and the whole financial district. Symbolically, it also represents the continuing financial independence and confidence that the UK maintains, amid the metaphorical flood of the 'Age of Austerity' and 'Brexit' in 2016. Despite the fact the UK has almost always distanced itself financially from the rest of Europe, is her financial independence strengthened by having the wall protecting British interests, or missing opportunities by closing itself in?

The Castle of Knowledge – The infrastructure of 'Knowledge' heroically defends the British Library, the British Museum, and the University of London, creating a protective sanctuary of knowledge and culture. The wall denies the oncoming floodwaters from causing physical damage to treasured relics and artefacts, and the age-old books – retaining authentic, original and reliable manuscripts of British knowledge and heritage. In a world where information is so abundant and readily accessible via electronic means, the 'digital flood' of information also becomes a threat. Retaining physical books means protecting the tactility of knowledge and the quest for information. The infrastructure of 'Knowledge' is affectionately known as 'the people's wall' because of the collective efforts of the city's inhabitants to build the entire castle from manually dug London clay. The excavated zones, reminiscent of stepped wells, are adapted into cooperative hubs for agriculture and farming. Amongst the inhabited cube-like capsules in the wall and on rooftops, deities and religious objects started to accumulate – the inhabitants believe that the 'guardians' would ward off the impending flood.

Outside the walls between castles, a cable-cart system connects a series of urban atriums with sky streets, community contemplation units and energy hubs, to facilitate the trading of knowledge, goods

previous pages: The inhabitable infrastructure of the 'Queen' protects Buckingham Palace, the Houses of Parliament and the spirit of her people.

facing page top + bottom: Viewed as a calming mechanism, the cable-cart system creates a constant pace of communication between neighboring realms.

9. 'Massive rise in Britain's flood damage bill highlights the need for more help for flood vulnerable communities says the ABI', Association of British Insurers: News, November 2010 [https://www.abi.org.uk/News/News-releases/2010/11/massive-rise-in-britains-flood-damage-bill-highlights-the-need-for-more-help-for-flood-vulnerable-communities-says-the-abi.aspx], retrieved 14 September 2012

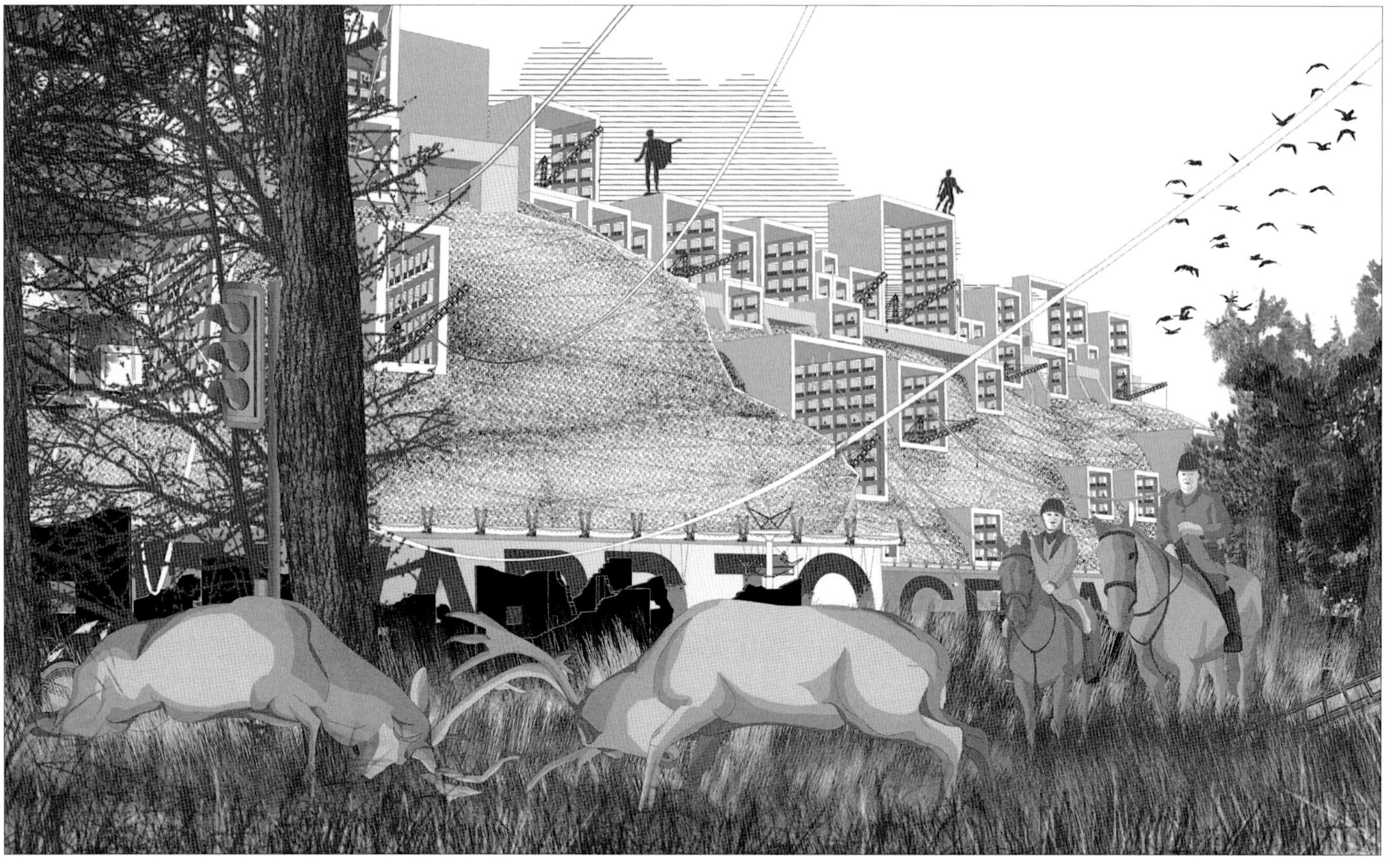

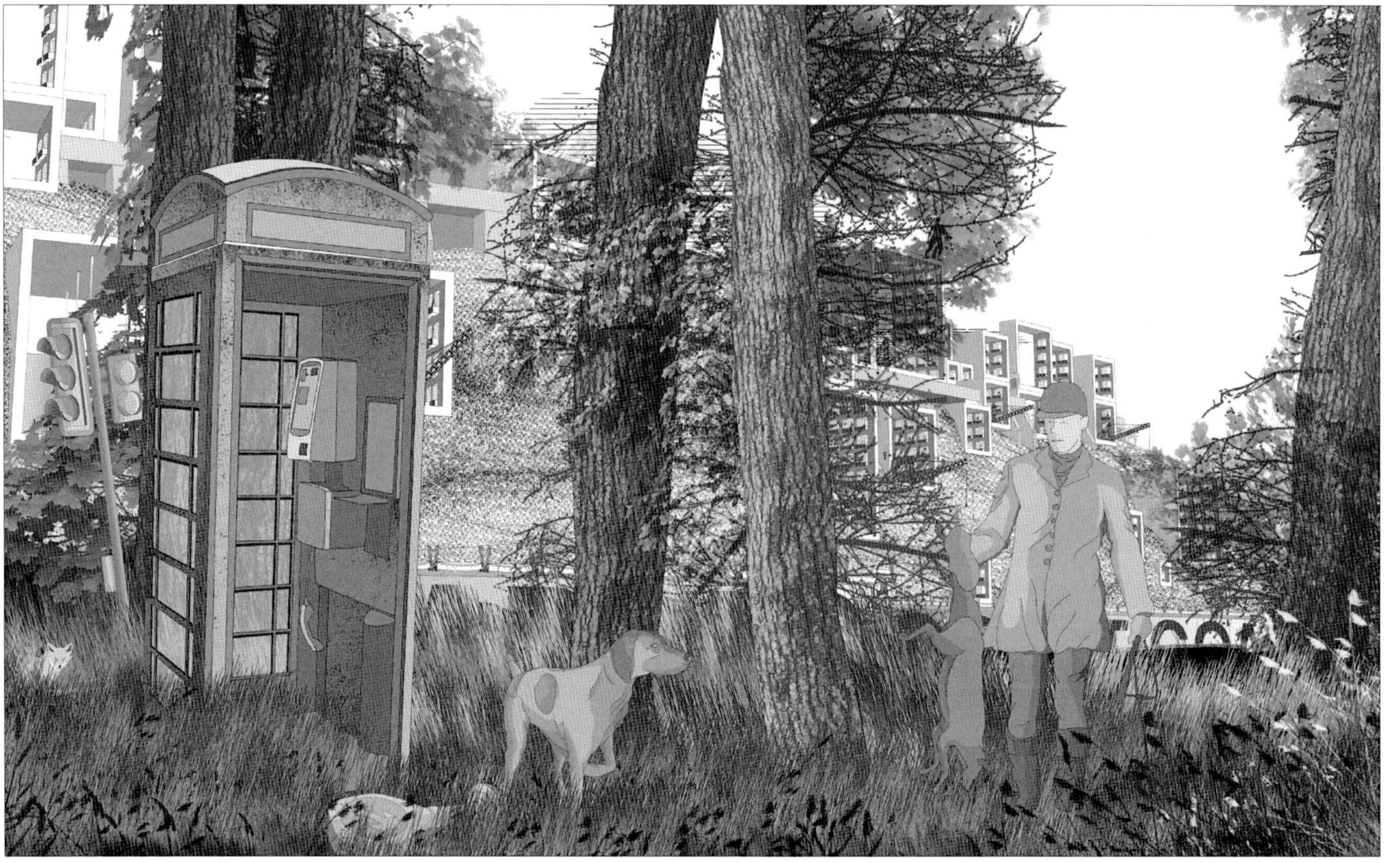

london is flooding?

facing page + left: Relics of London's forgotten past are swathed in vines, while telephone booths and other urban furniture can be found along the desolate streets.

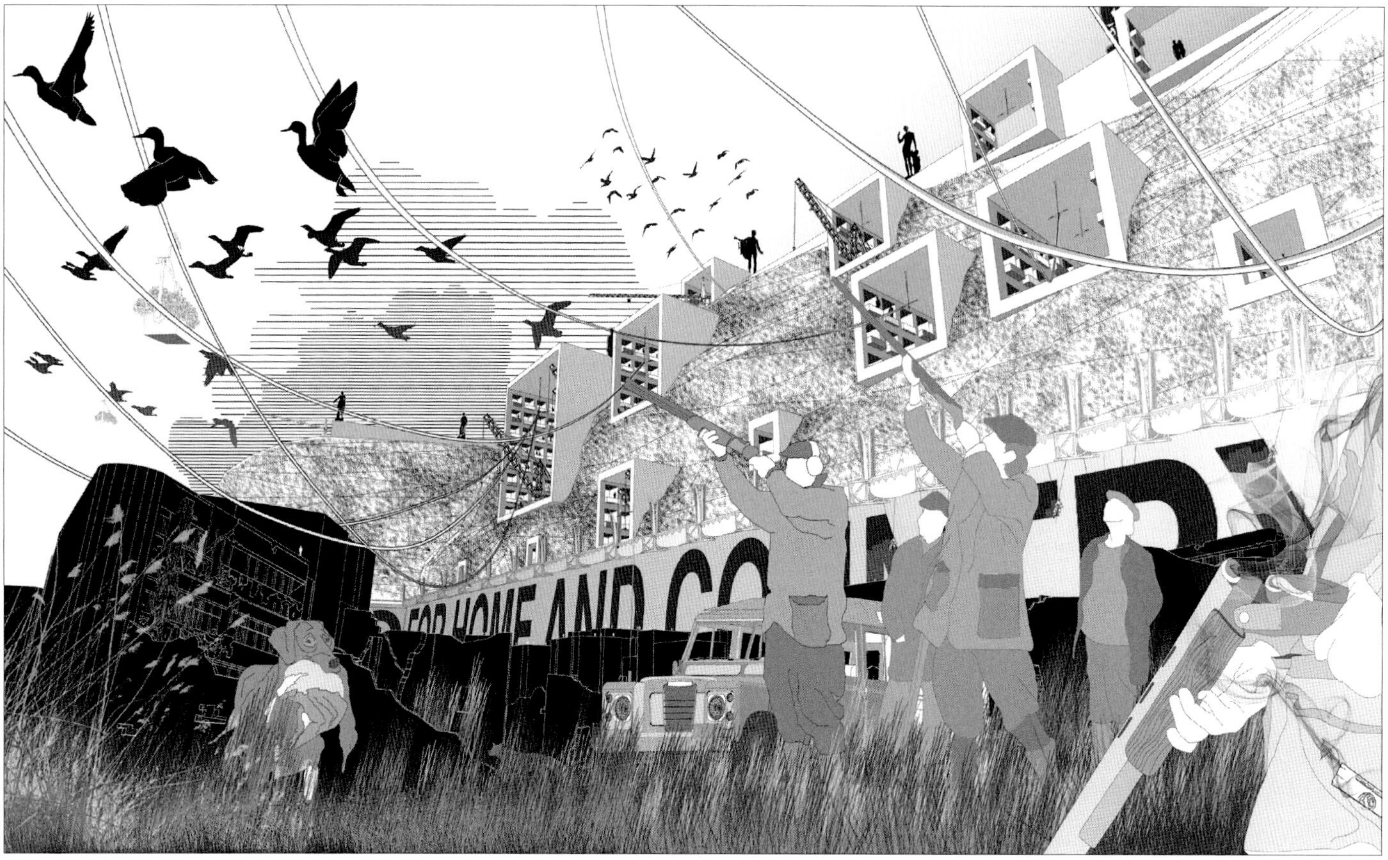
FOR HOME AND

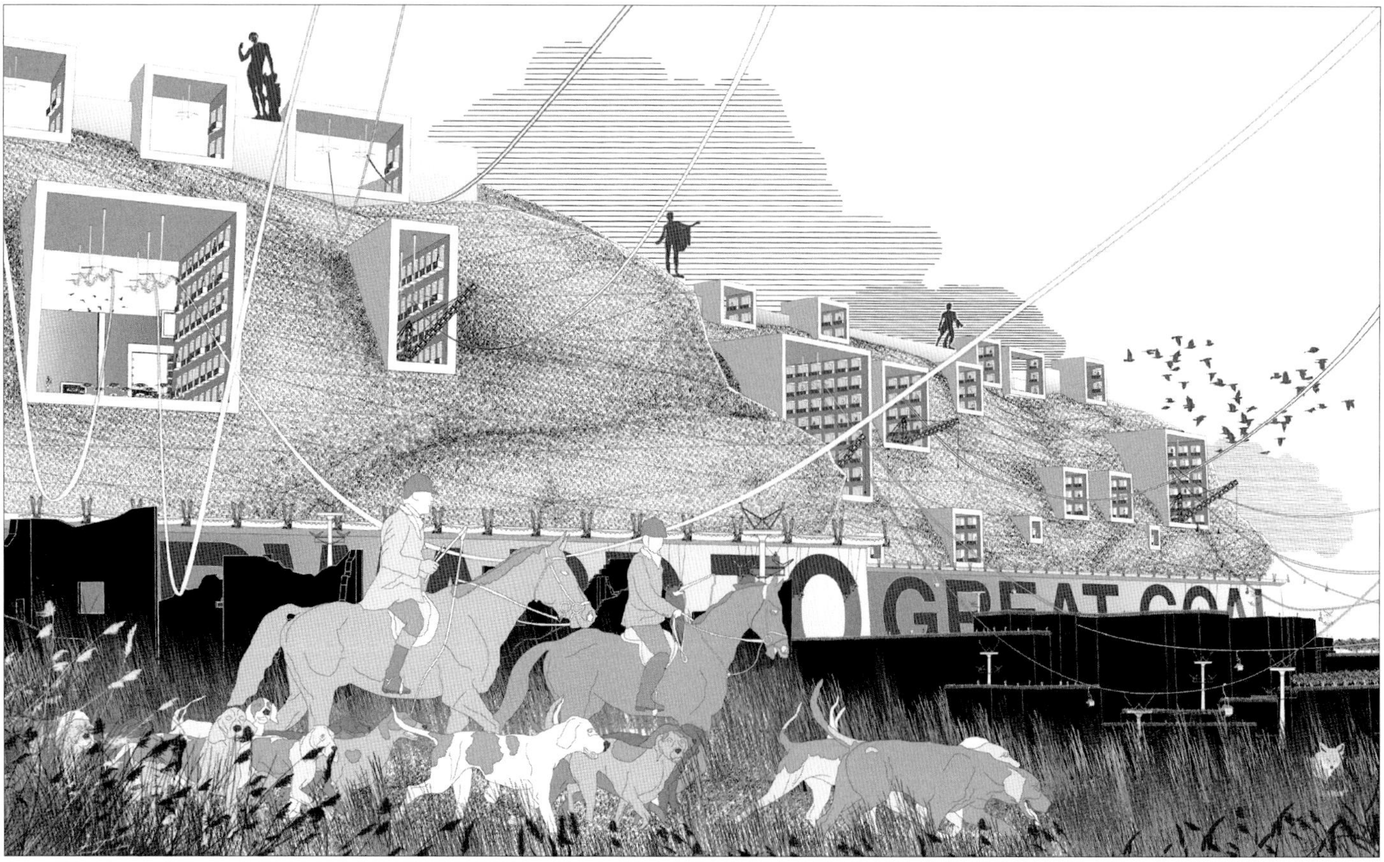
TO

and services. Viewed as a calming mechanism, the transport system also creates a constant pace between neighboring realms. With every inhabitant concentrated within the three Castles, London outside the protective infrastructures is abandoned.

In what might be considered dystopia, a new ecology conquers the once man-made city and flourishes within a forested cityscape, providing opportunities for sustainable hunting and diverse cultivation of natural products. Relics of London's forgotten past and fallen iconic structures are swathed in vines, while rusticated bicycles and other machineries can be found along the desolate streets; we can only reminisce. Through nature's resurgence, de-construction and organic renovation, the forest connects the multitude of existing 'green lungs' – Kensington Gardens, Regents Park, Green Park, Victoria Park and thousands of smaller squares help rejuvenate and protect the air quality of the once-polluted city. Encircling the three Castles, the new green infrastructure has the potential to protect the city when the River Thames does eventually break its banks. Trees soak-up water from the ground, and the collective flora can reduce the overall height of floodwaters. The strong roots of established vegetation binds together riverbanks and slopes, thus fewer collapses and landslides occur.

The Environment Agency and numerous UK universities have made extensive research into the potential of tree planting.[10] Therefore, it is not surprising that the political inclination is to have effective planting in the countryside rather than decorative hedge-trimming. Lord Rooker, a former environment minister, bemoaned that 'we [the UK Government] pay the farmers to grub up the trees and hedges; we pay them to plant the hills with pretty grass and sheep to maintain the chocolate box image, and then wonder why we've floods.'[11]

It was the promise of a great flood that inspired Noah to build his Ark; and for 'one hundred and twenty years', he waited for rain and planted trees to supply the timber for the enormous hull. To many, Noah must have seemed paranoid or delusional. However, as the ancient story goes, Noah was wise to heed the divine call: he prepared the infrastructure, collected together the animals of the earth and survived the deadliest of God's purge. In the Paranoid City, humans have abandoned their homes, and been forced by their fears and anxieties to hide within the protective infrastructures of the three Castles. The new order of the city empowers flora and fauna to rediscover their rightful territories, while beyond the walls of assurance the populace can only wait.

facing page top + bottom: A new ecology conquers the man-made city and flourishes within a forested cityscape, providing opportunities for sustainable hunting.

following pages: The infrastructure of 'Economy' aims to preserve the undying heartbeat of the Square Mile, the central body for managing financial stability.

10. R Harrabin, 'Tree Planting Can Reduce Flooding', BBC News, 11 March 2016 [http://www.bbc.co.uk/news/science-environment-35777927], retrieved 11 August 2016

11. R Harrabin, 'Lord Rooker: Planting trees could stop flooding', BBC News, 23 January 2014 [http://www.bbc.co.uk/news/uk-25864631], retrieved 11 August 2016

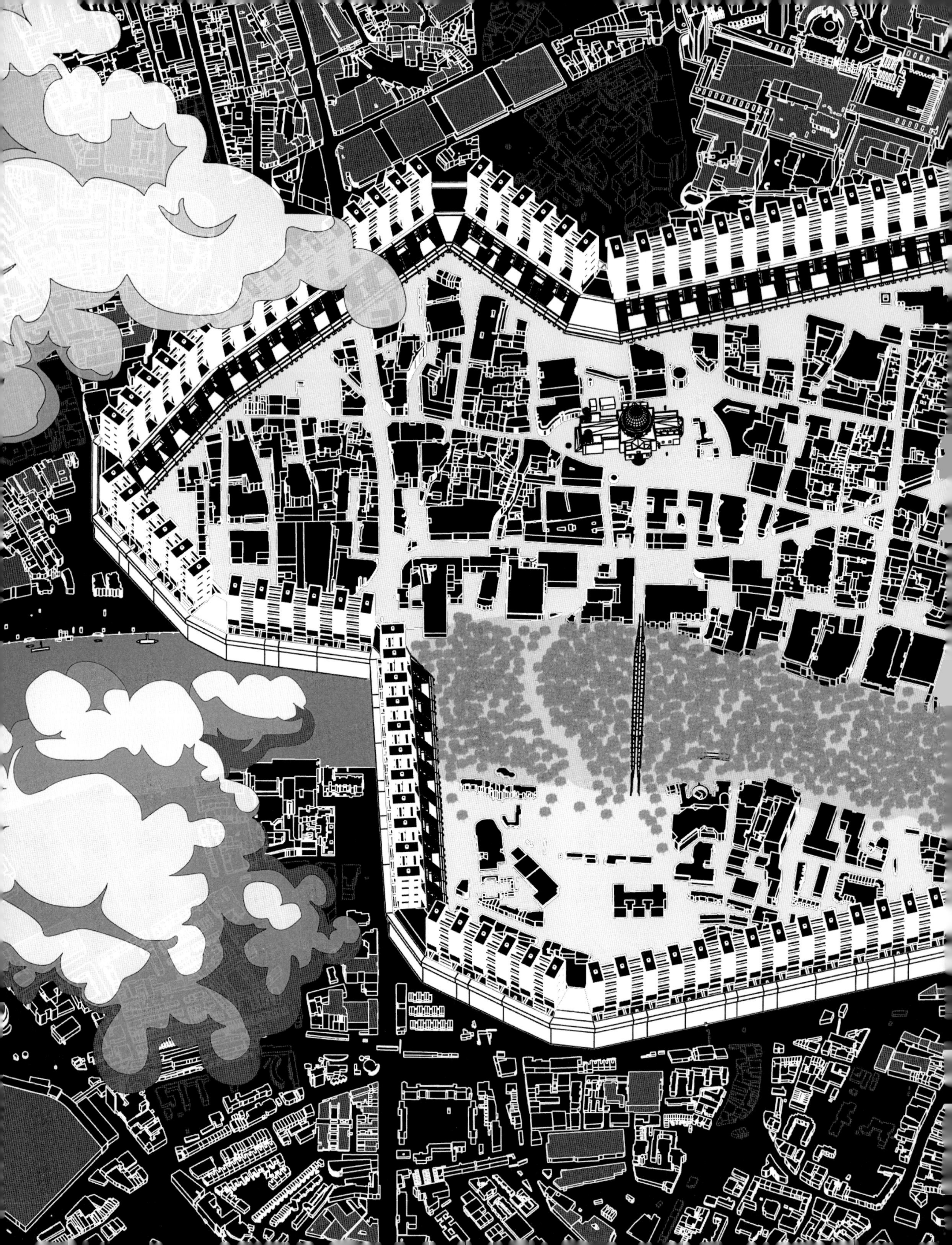

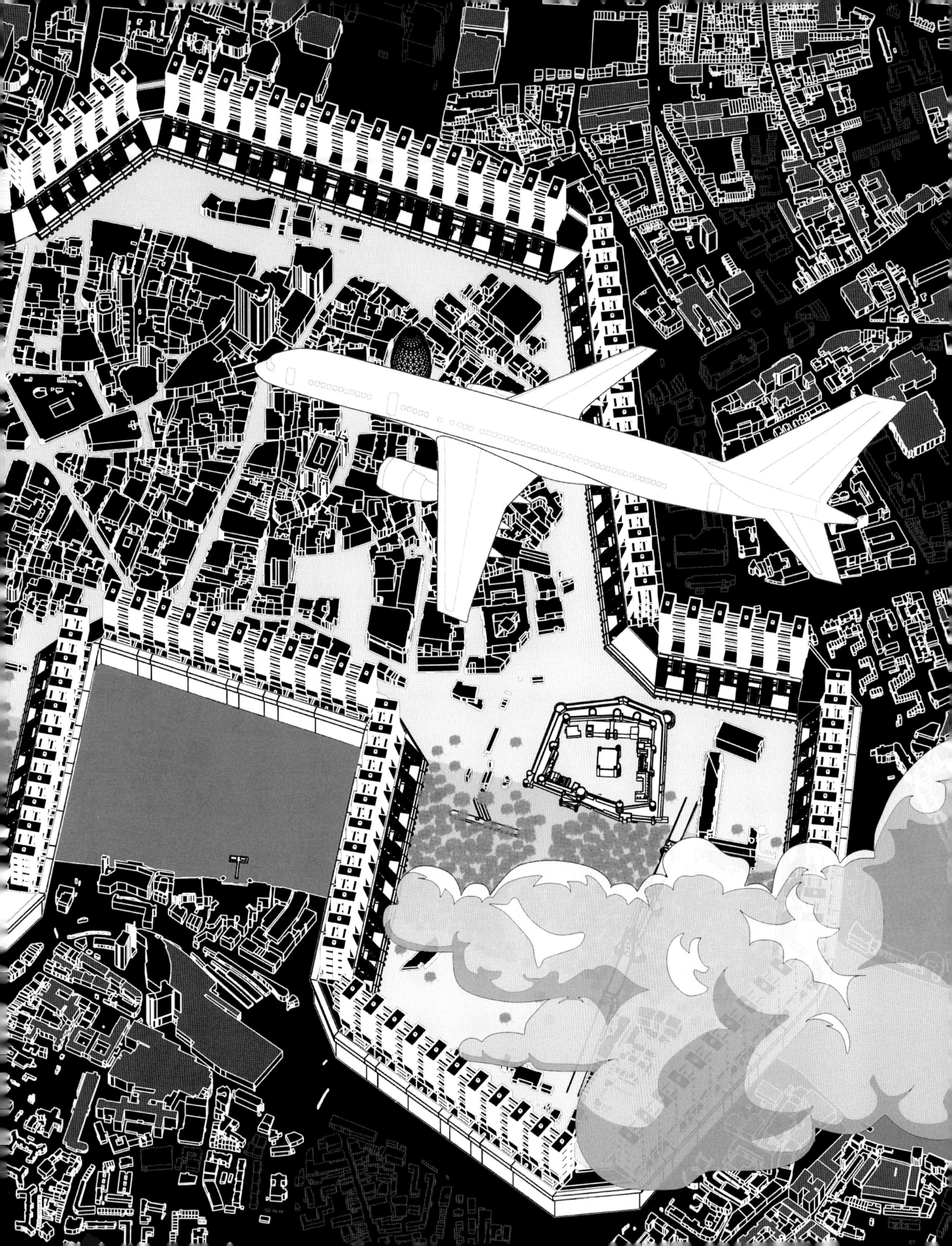

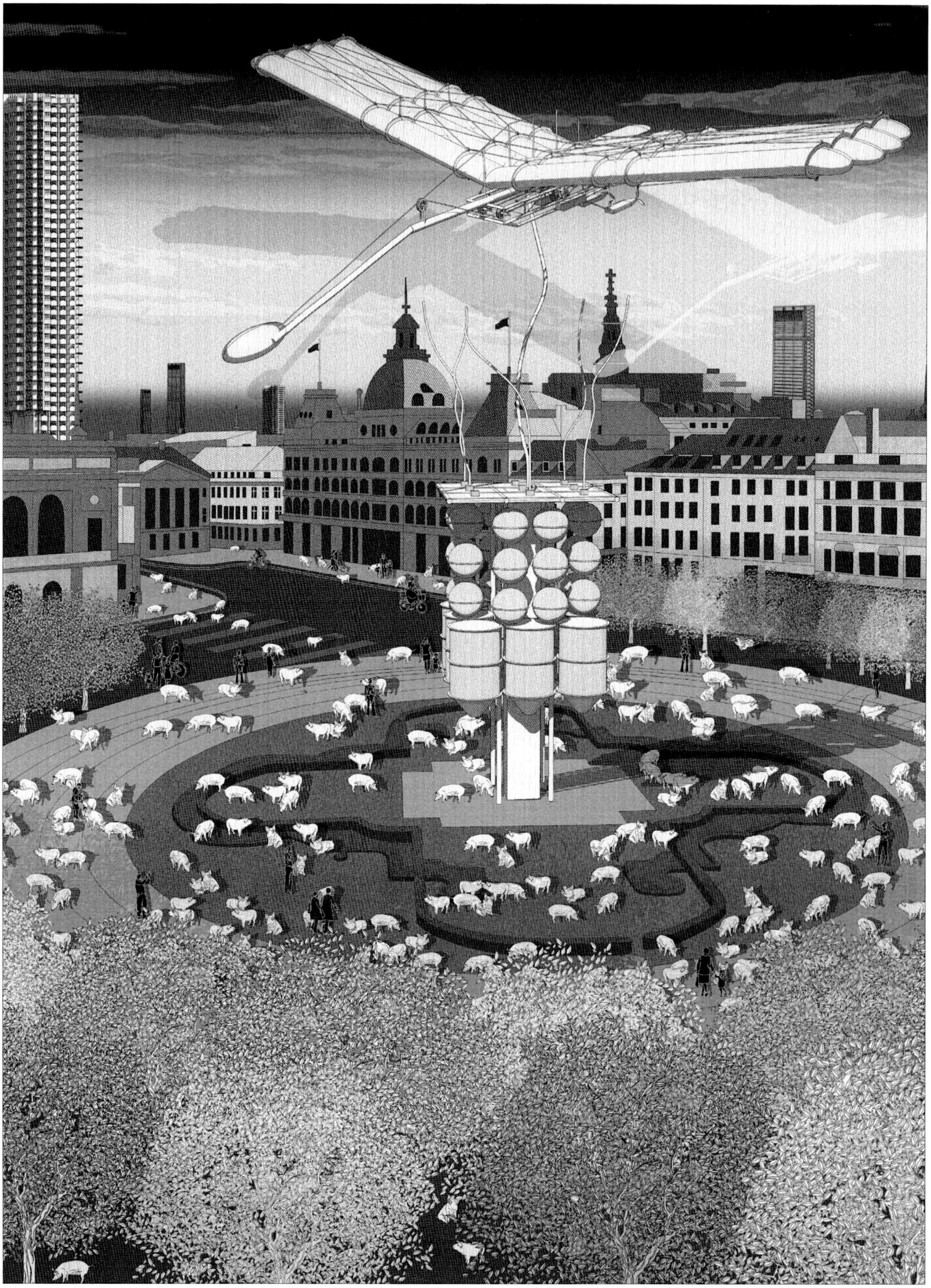

urban future

Swine Under the Sheltering Skies

(ii)

'By creating great comics for kids, we can plant powerful seeds of change that will have a lifelong impact and foster a new generation of global leaders, thinkers and doers to tackle the world's most pressing issues like climate change and inequality.'

– Stan Lee and Sharad Devarajan, 'Comics Uniting Nations', 2015

In Marvel comics, every city has one or several superheroes offering protection. Gotham City, the fictional version of New York, has Batman leaping over rooftops to rescue law-abiding citizens from millionaire supervillains or tracking down scientist criminals in shadowy alleyways. Many superheroes have appointed the Big Apple and its surroundings as their nonstop battle-ground, with Spider-Man swinging through from Queens, the Fantastic Four conveniently located in Midtown, and the Iron Man launching artilleries from Long Island. On the other side of the USA, Coast City, the home of the Green Lantern, is the literary doppelgänger of Los Angeles. Nevertheless, in the real world many of our cities are at risk of becoming modern-day Gothams, with unprecedented levels of organized and violent crimes, risk of terrorist attacks and the bigger-than-life criminal, climate change.

In 2015, the United Nations enlisted 'Chakra the Invincible' and his neighbor 'Mighty Girl' to help disseminate to a world audience 17 global goals for sustainable development. They are globalized superheroes that can relate with inhabitants from Boston to Beijing to Bangalore.[1] In fact, there is a common belief that superheroes are the underlying factor for the cultural phenomena that surrounds our current understanding of urban spaces and cities. At least among comic fans, skyscrapers and other urban infrastructures have entered into popular consciousness thanks to all the awe-inspiring human figures that suspend and bounce from them without fear.[2]

In 2016, satellite observations published by the US National Snow and Ice Data Center reported that the melting in Greenland 'poses dangerous long-term threats to climate because sea ice plays a huge role in reflecting solar radiation away from Earth. As climate change warms the oceans and melts the sea ice, the Arctic becomes darker on average, increasing its ability to absorb more heat and causing further warming of the oceans'[3] and potentially contributing to future sea level rise. To combat these aspects of climate change, we need more than just human protectors in capes, spider-suits, or carrying invincible shields, we need innovative infrastructural superheroes. Studies into the prevention of melting have suggested solutions for Greenland that include wrapping the territory in an insulated cloth, or seeding clouds to form a surface above to reflect sunlight before it has the opportunity to heat up the ground. The mission seeks to strengthen the relationship between Greenland and the sovereign state of Denmark,

facing page: The Dynamic Duo of Denmark (DDD) have the combined traits of the eco-warrior, energy demigod, and rationalist climate change fighter.

following pages: The Heliotropic Android Swans collectively form an airborne environmental infrastructure to reflect rays back out of the atmosphere.

1. S Southey, 'Climate Change Comic for Children at COP21', Comics Uniting Nations, 10 December 2015 [http://www.comicsunitingnations.org/press-releases/], retrieved 26 July 2016

2. P Gutierrez, 'Why So Many Superheroes Are Drawn to New York', The New York Times, 8 March 2010 [http://cityroom.blogs.nytimes.com/2010/03/08/why-so-many-superheroes-are-drawn-to-new-york/?_r=0], retrieved 26 July 2016

3. M Greshko, 'Record Greenland Melting Caused by Surprising Feedback Loop', National Geographic: News, 9 June 2016 [http://news.nationalgeographic.com/2016/06/ice-melting-greenland-jet-stream-weather-climate-change/], retrieved 26 July 2016

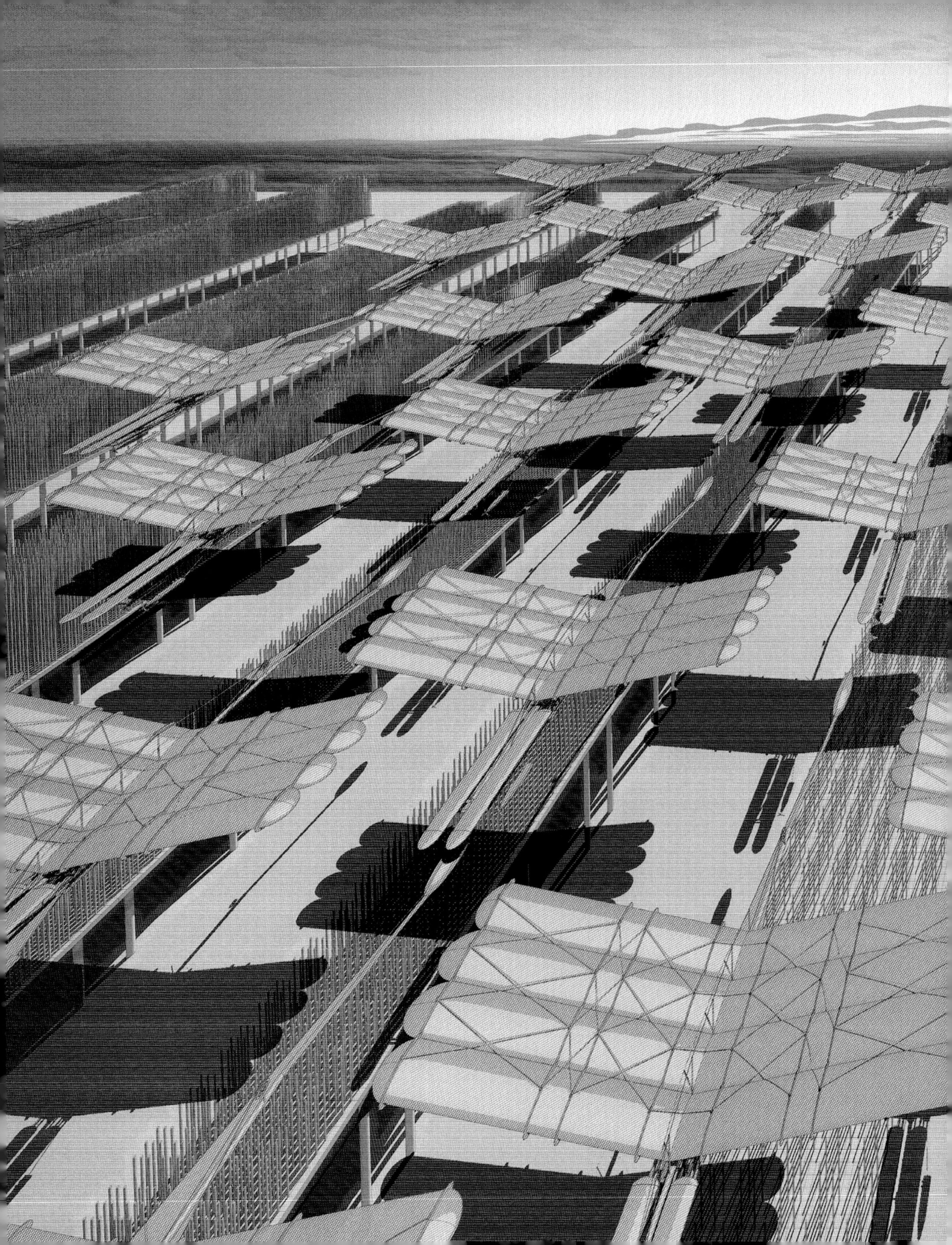

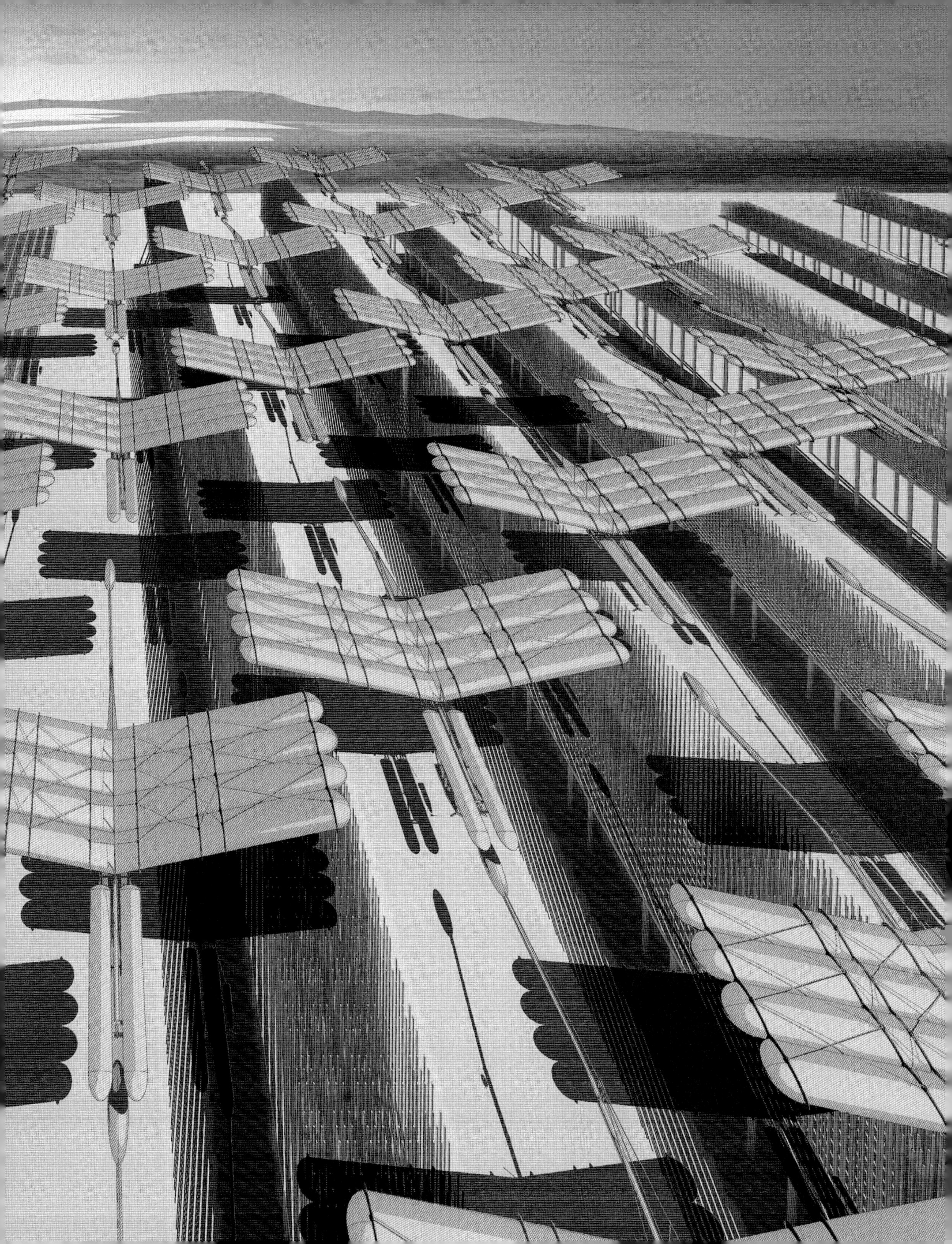

ØBENHAVN

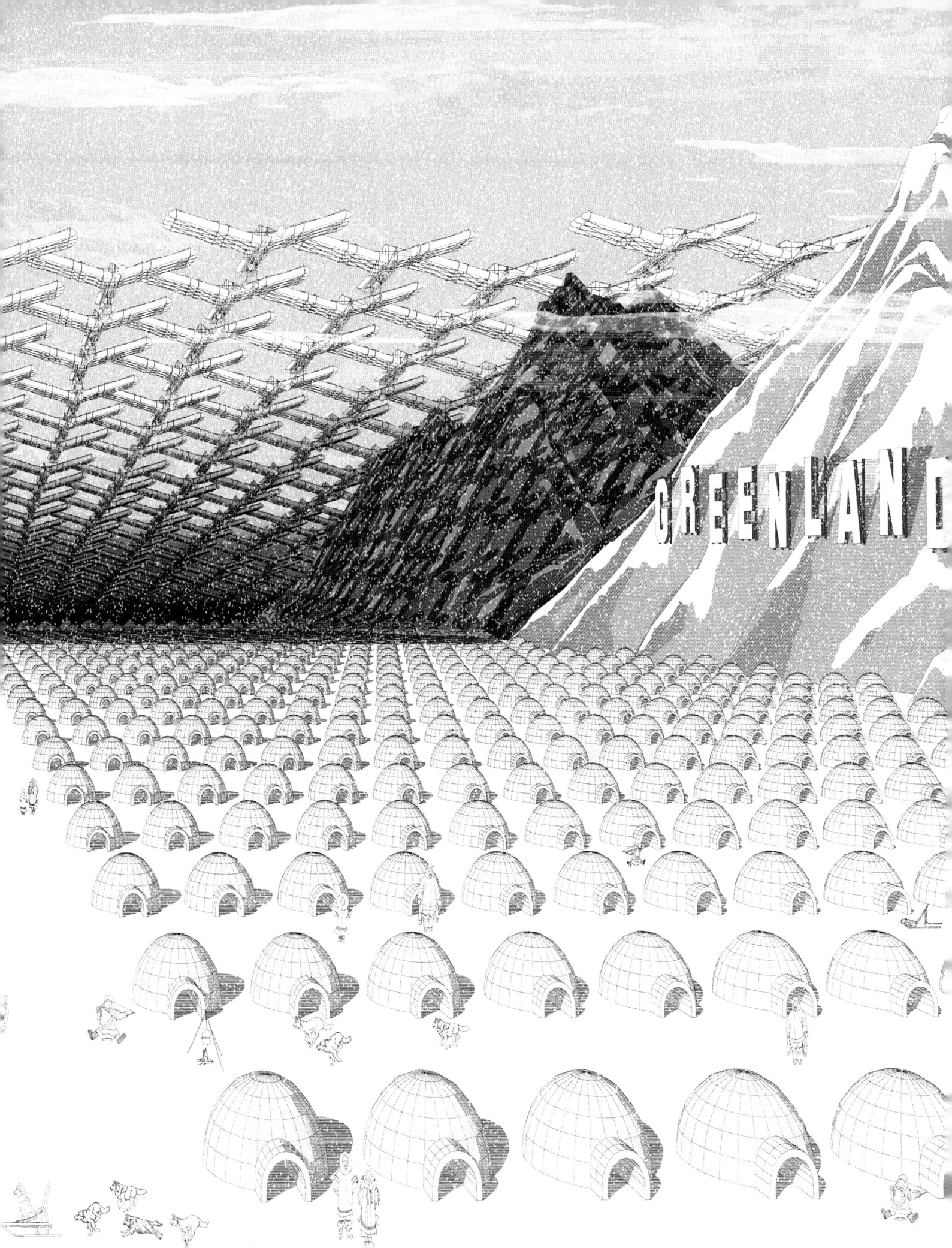

GREENLAND

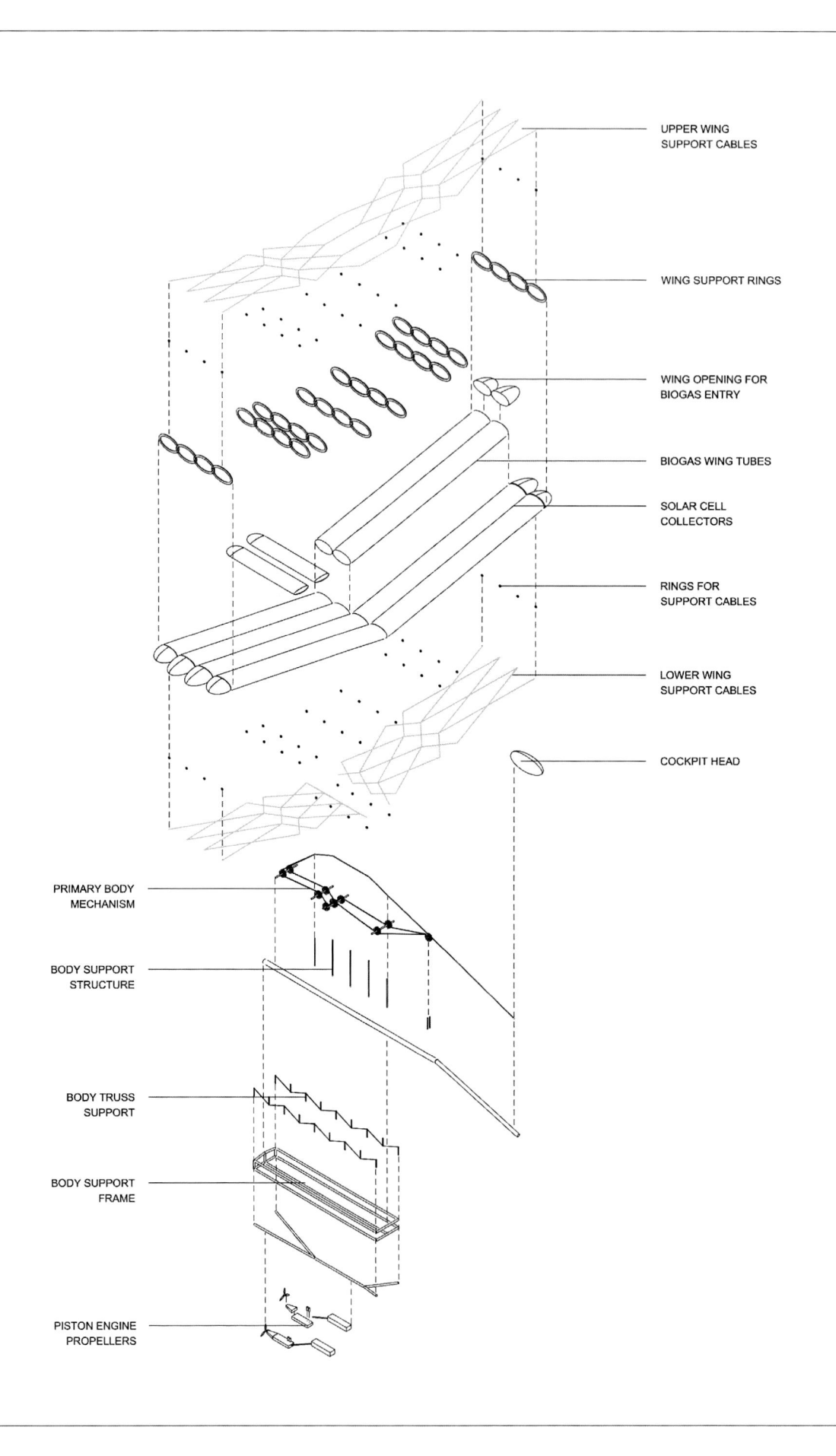

- UPPER WING SUPPORT CABLES
- WING SUPPORT RINGS
- WING OPENING FOR BIOGAS ENTRY
- BIOGAS WING TUBES
- SOLAR CELL COLLECTORS
- RINGS FOR SUPPORT CABLES
- LOWER WING SUPPORT CABLES
- COCKPIT HEAD
- PRIMARY BODY MECHANISM
- BODY SUPPORT STRUCTURE
- BODY TRUSS SUPPORT
- BODY SUPPORT FRAME
- PISTON ENGINE PROPELLERS

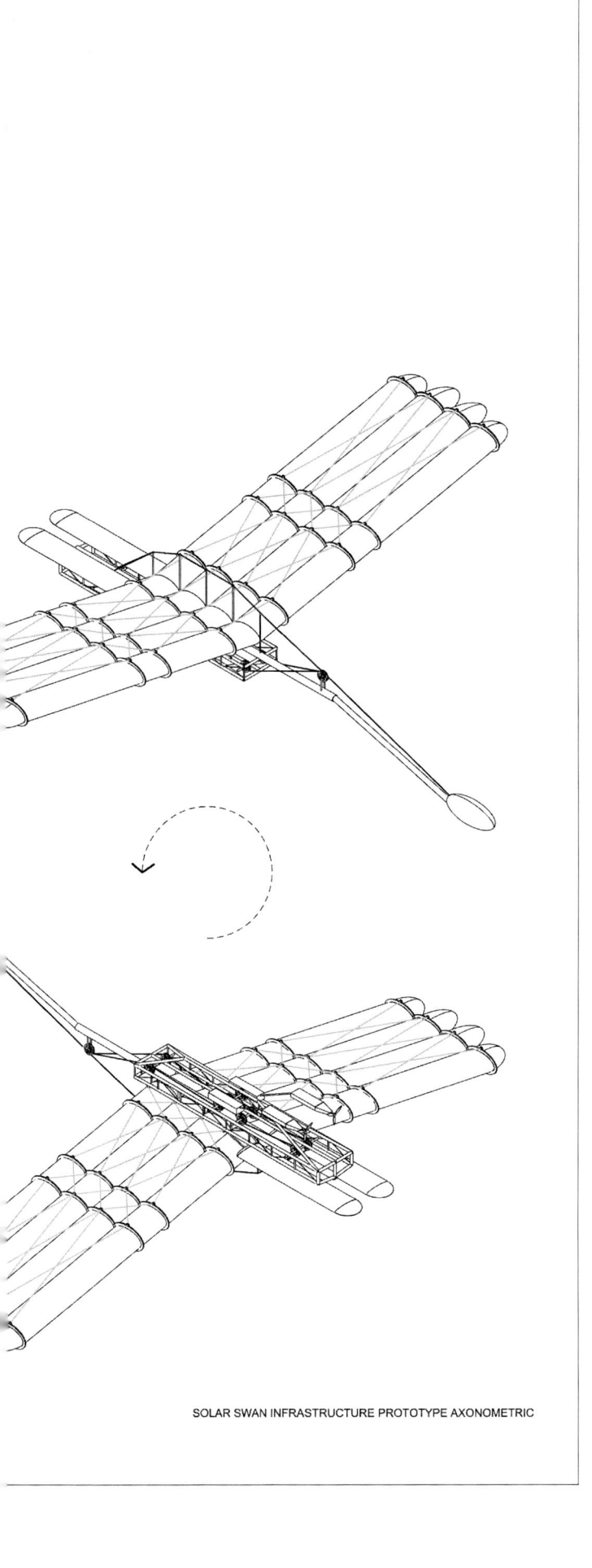

SOLAR SWAN INFRASTRUCTURE PROTOTYPE AXONOMETRIC

NOTES:

PROTOTYPE SWAN TO BE
FLOWN OFF FROM
THE HANS CHRISTIAN
ANDERSEN
MUSEUM IN ODENSE

STATUS

APPROVED

INITIAL PROTOTYPING

PROJECT

PROTOTYPE ASSEMBLY
AXONOMETRIC

SUBJECT

SOLAR SWAN
INFRASTRUCTURE

ISSUED BY

EW

CHECKED BY

SM

DATE

DRAWING No.

5211_SOLARSWAN_A000_UNIT

138

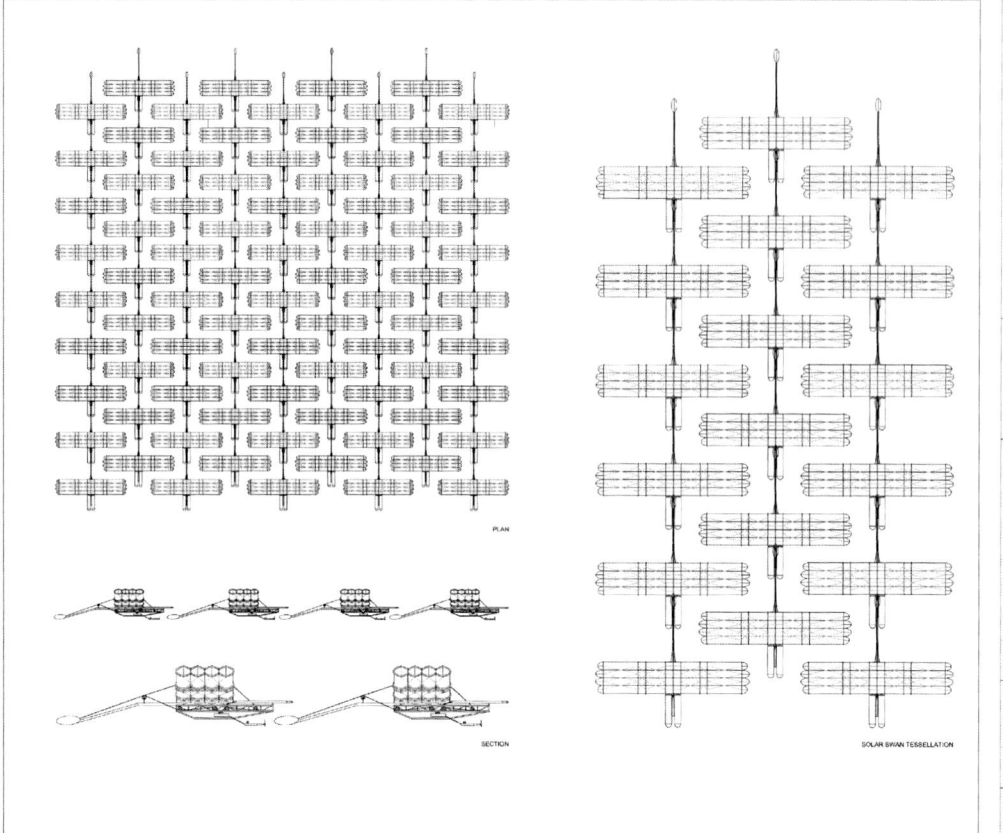

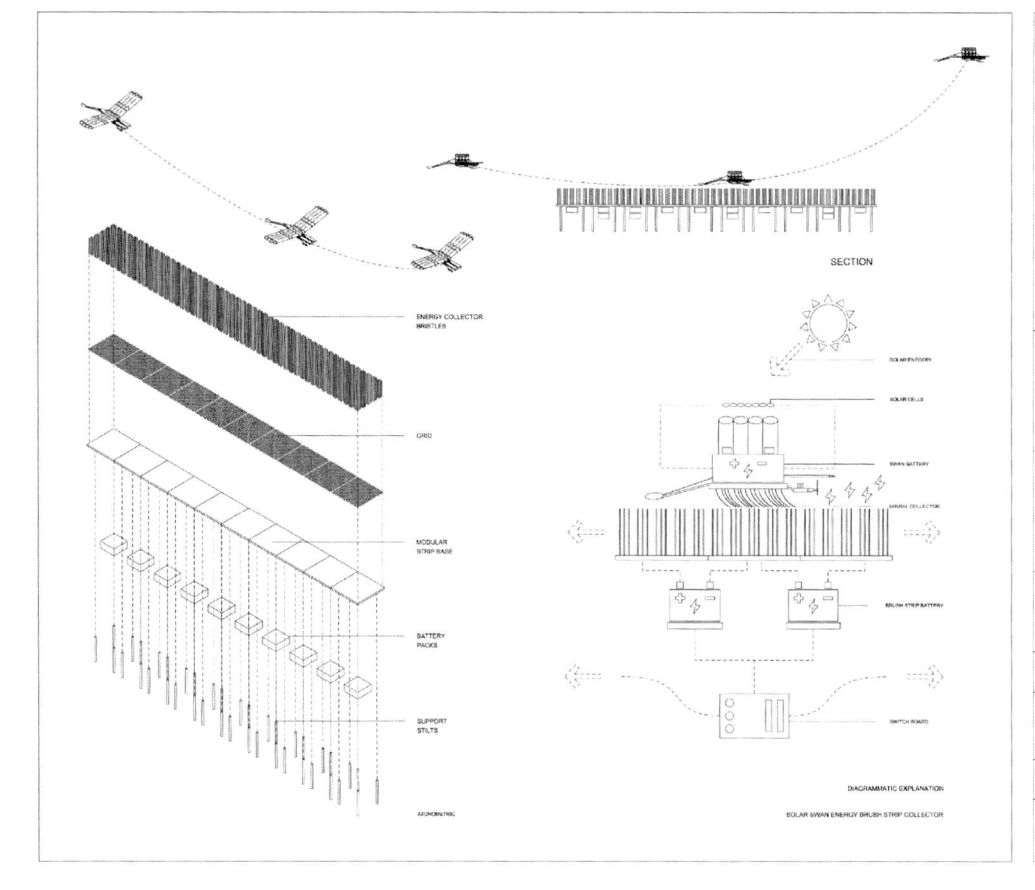

swine under the sheltering skies

by symbiotically providing a sustainable protection infrastructure that would not only boost Greenland's economy, but also appoint Denmark to the forefront of global climate change defense.

With its soaring pig population and its ambitious 'Energy Strategy 2050'[4] which seeks to achieve independence from coal, oil and gas in addition to reducing its greenhouse gas emissions, Denmark is the perfect initiator for new kinds of archetypal infrastructural superheroes – the Dynamic Duo of Denmark (DDD) have the combined traits of the eco-warrior, energy demigod, and rationalist climate change fighter. Just as the team of Batman and Robin is commonly referred to as the Caped Crusaders, the DDD has the pigs of the 'Swine Squad' to serve as the counterpart to the 'Heliotropic Android Swans'.

For a comparatively small country with under six million inhabitants, Denmark has more than 29 million pigs reared on 3,800 pig farms, with 90% of the pork produced in the country exported to over 140 different countries.[5] The Swine Squad is a highly valuable resource for biogas production. Using anaerobic digesters, their gaseous expulsions and nutrients are converted into methane gas, used both as buoyancy and sustainable fuel for the thousands of Heliotropic Android Swans that migrate from Denmark to Greenland every year.

The rescue efforts of the eleven princes transformed into swans, who saved their sister in HC Andersen's 'The Wild Swans' (1838), inspires the symbolic 'swan' motif. The Heliotropic Android Swans collectively harvest wind energy and form an airborne environmental infrastructure to shade the heat and UV of the sun, reflecting rays back out of the atmosphere before they have a chance to further melt any of the ice caps. Each 'feather' of the swan is reversible; a white side to reflect the sun and on the reverse surface, there are black photovoltaic cells with which the infrastructure recharges its electric batteries, thus making the most of Greenland's 24-hour summer sunbeams. The majority of Greenland's population works in the country's renewable energy business, and operates from offices built on the underside of large conductor-brush charge transmitters. Under the Swans, the inhabitants in Nuuk would go about on husky-drawn sleds and fill their techno-igloo houses with Danish 'hygge' via a faint, pale blue glow.

The DDD is also a social infrastructure for equality. It has the hallmarks of the socialist ideals of radical urban thinkers from Paolo Soleri to R Buckminster Fuller, although the political and environmental outcomes of the two may have been different. In the un-built works of visionaries, peaceful and egalitarian utopia remains honest, humane and untainted by the reality of human greed.

'The creatures outside looked from pig to man, and from man to pig, and from pig to man again; but already it was impossible to say which was which.'
 – George Orwell, 'Animal Farm', 1945

In the speculative scenario of the DDD, pigs of the Swine Squad have acquired equal rights similar to those of their human co-inhabitants. Denmark has legislated against the current trend of unethical mass farming of pigs for meat. Instead, the Danish Landrace pig is henceforth granted first-class citizenship. After all, the Danish government essentially outlawed meat when Allied forces cut off supply routes to

4. The Danish Ministry of Climate and Energy, 'Energy Strategy 2050: From coal, oil and gas to green energy', The Danish Government, February 2011, p.5

5. Admin, 'The Danish Pig Industry and The Environment', PigWorld: The voice of the British pig industry, 2015 [http://www.pig-world.co.uk/features/environment-features/the-danish-pig-industry-and-the-environment.html], retrieved 25 July 2016

140

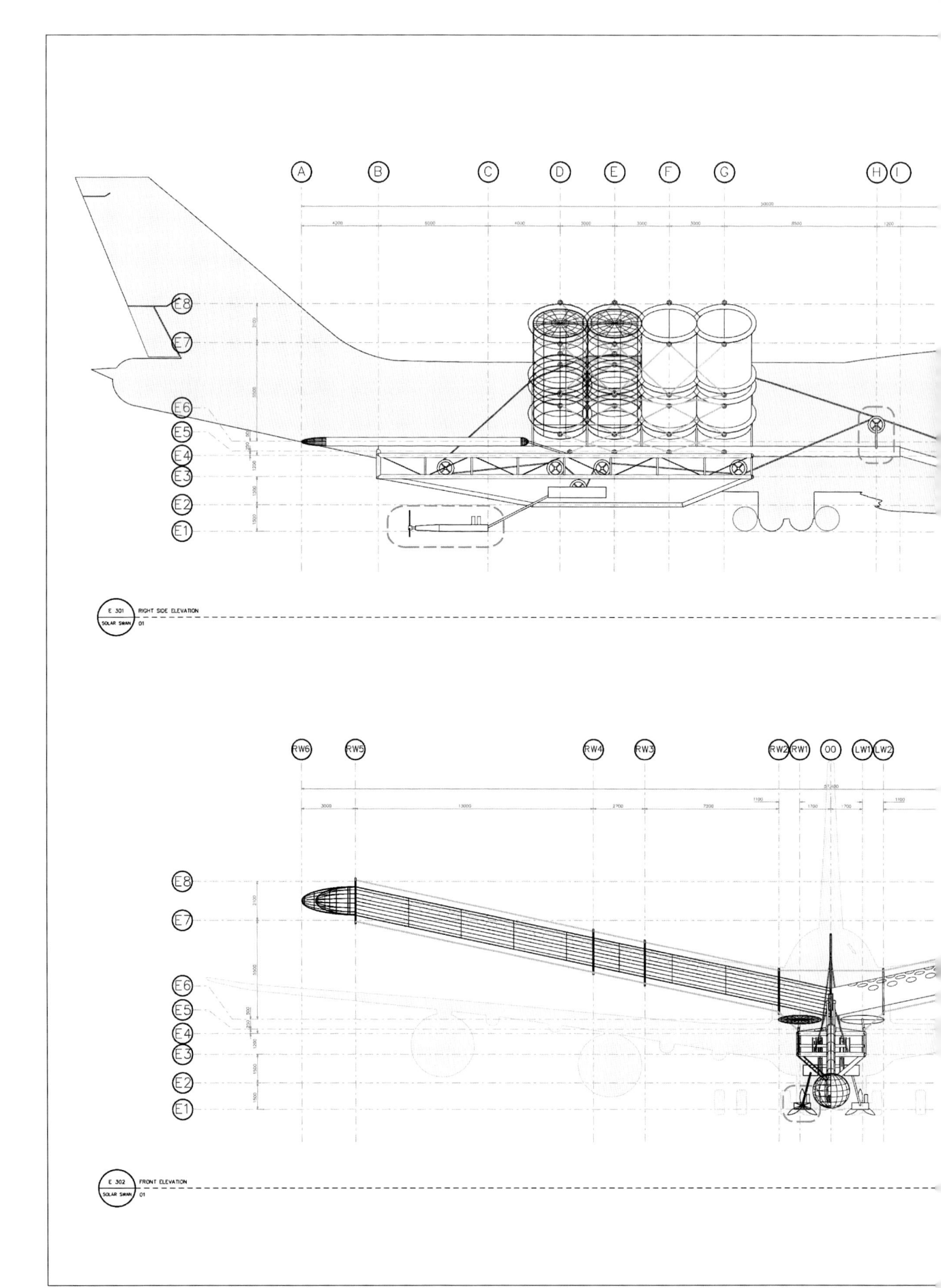

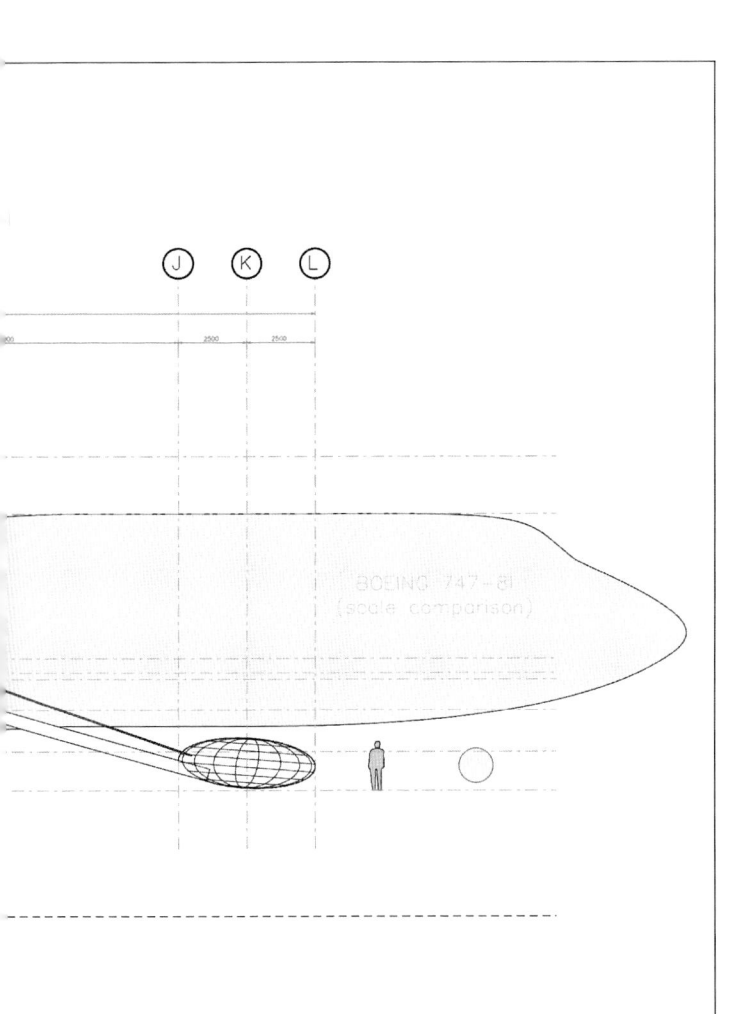

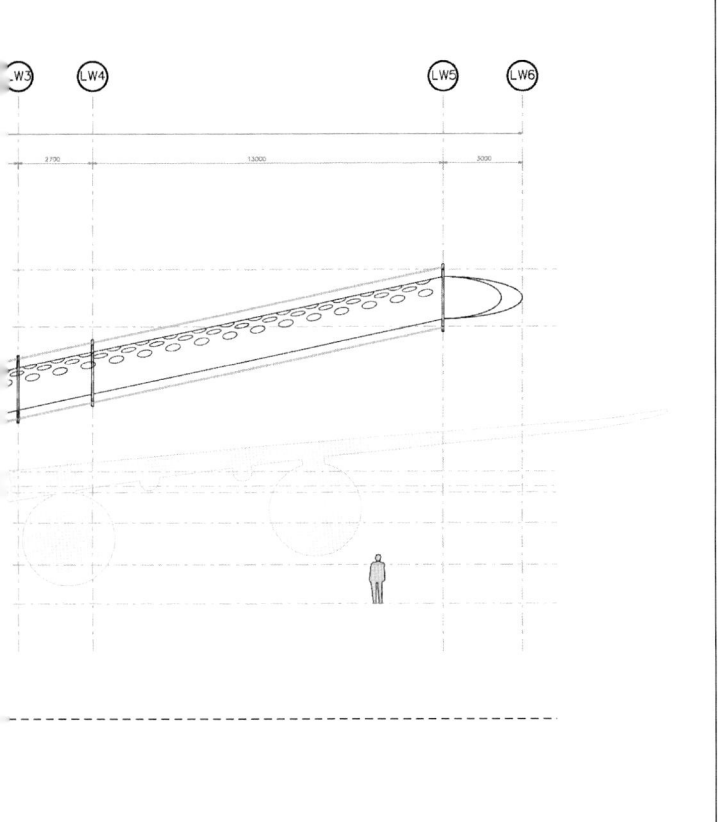

NOTES:

PROTOTYPE SWAN TO BE
FLOWN OFF FROM
THE HANS CHRISTIAN
ANDERSEN
MUSEUM IN ODENSE

STATUS

APPROVED

INITIAL PROTOTYPING

PROJECT

PROTOTYPE ASSEMBLY
AXONOMETRIC

SUBJECT

SOLAR SWAN
INFRASTRUCTURE

ISSUED BY

SM

CHECKED BY

EW

DATE

DRAWING No.

5211_SOLARSWAN_A000_UNIT

Lovely day for a stroll in Denmark Little Hans!

Pig Towers with little pig homes for the masses

The procession with plenty of beer and sows ;)

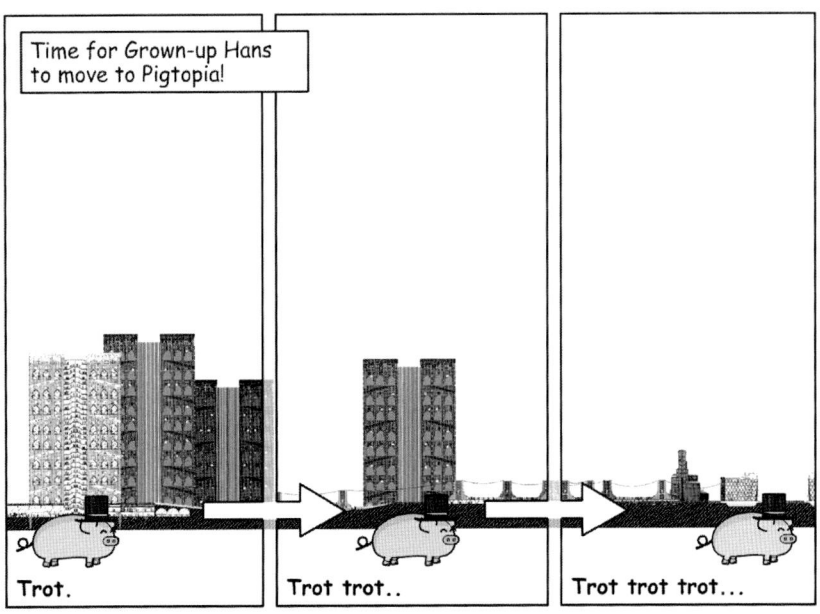

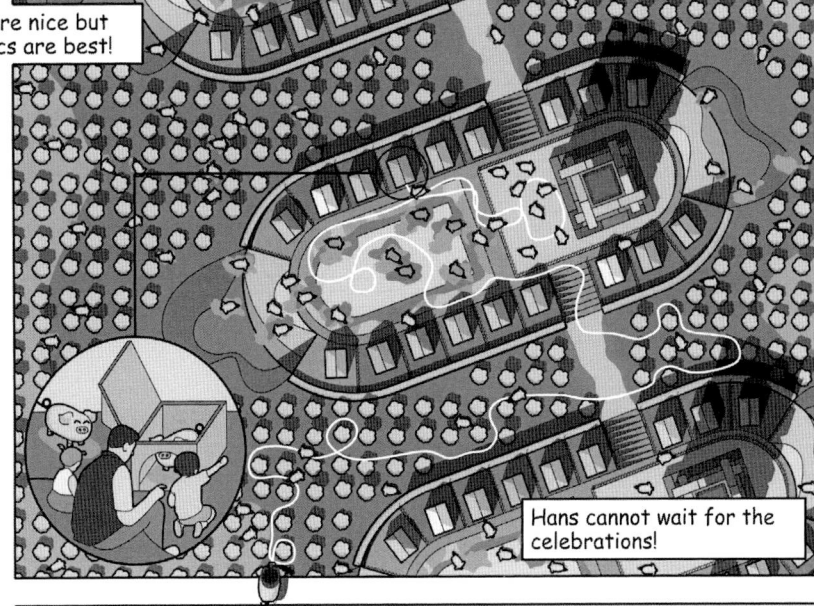

left: Life in 'Porktopia'.

following pages: During autumn, the pigs are led on a grand procession to the nearest Royal grounds through avenues lined in apple orchards, to a grand feast overseen by the Royal Family.

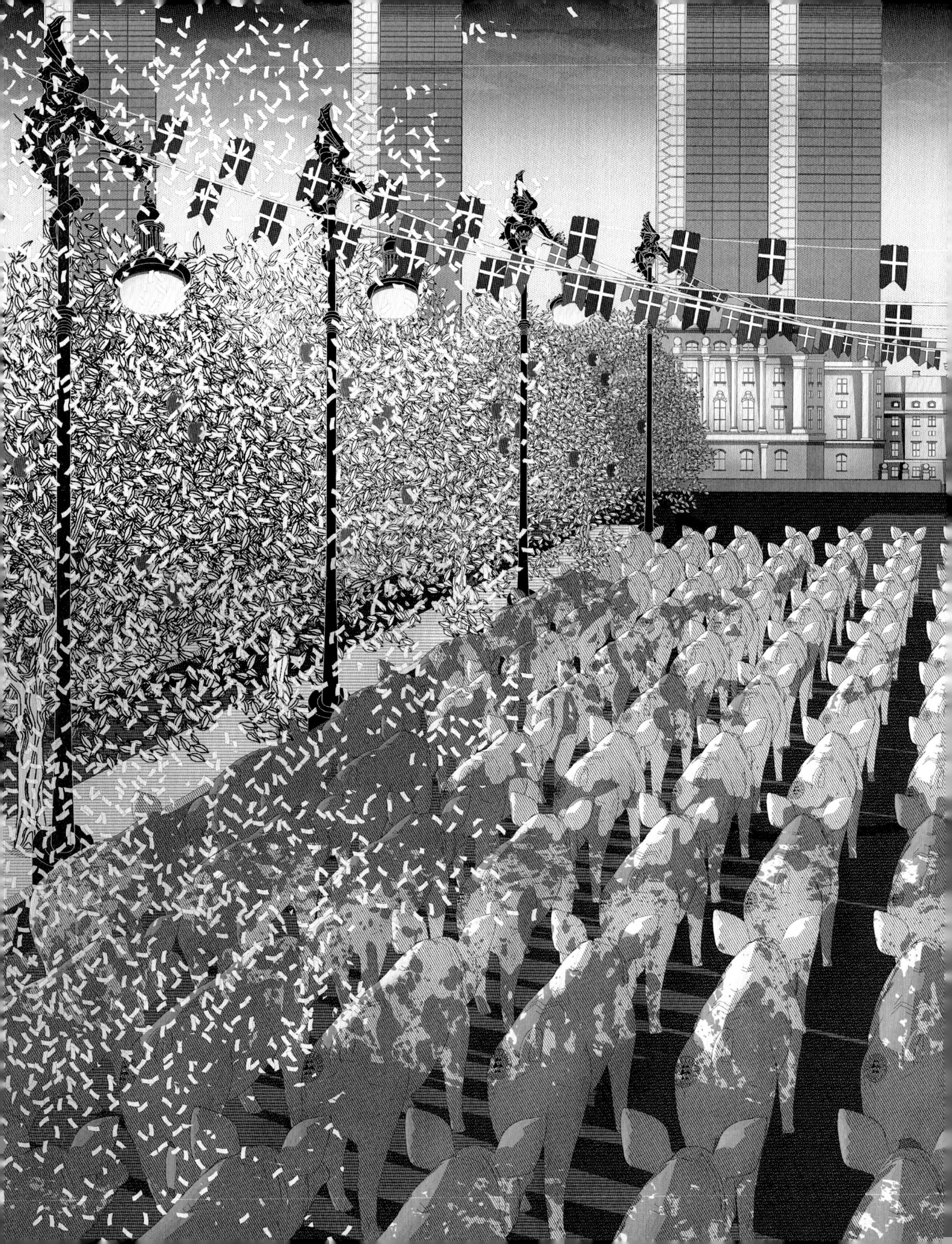

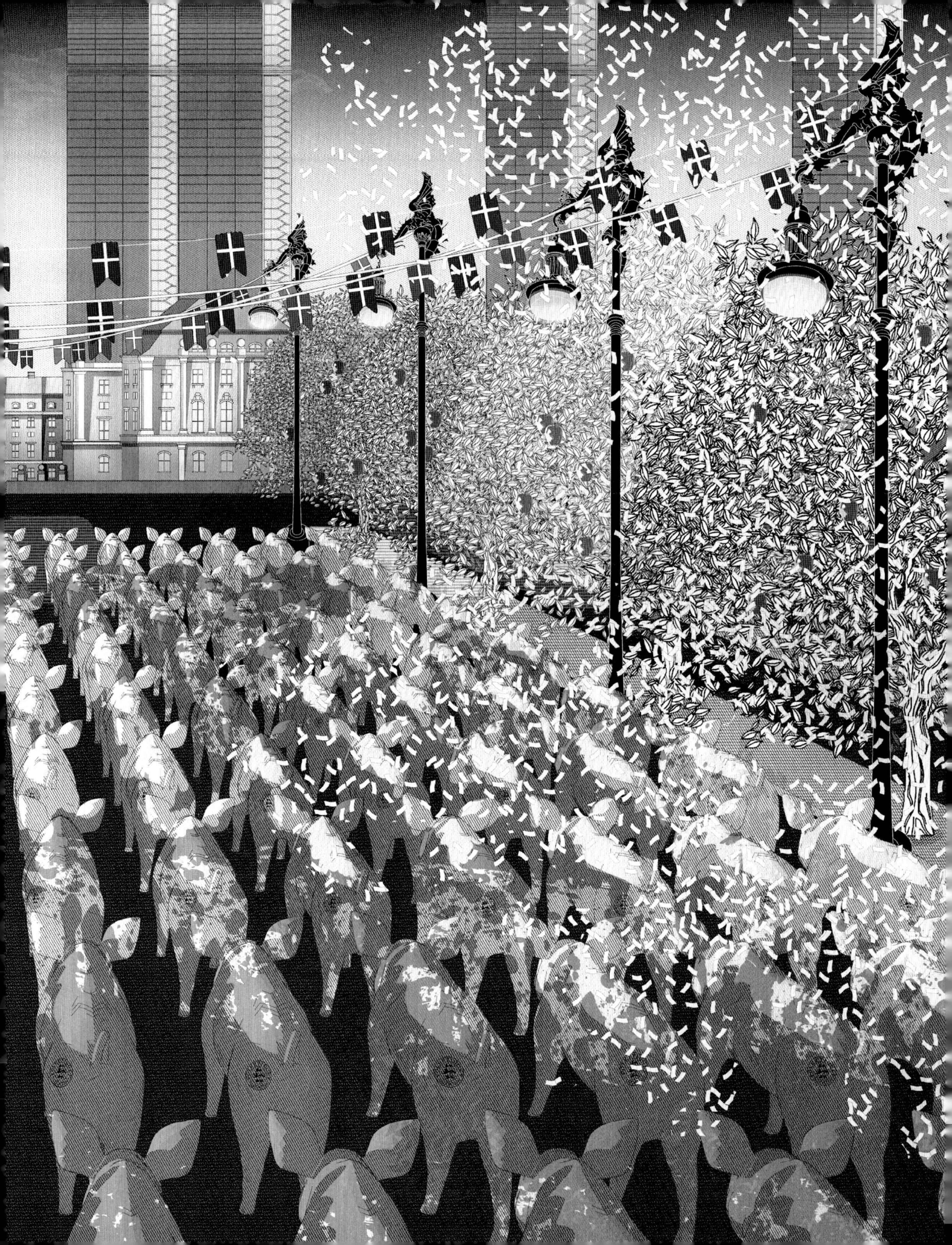

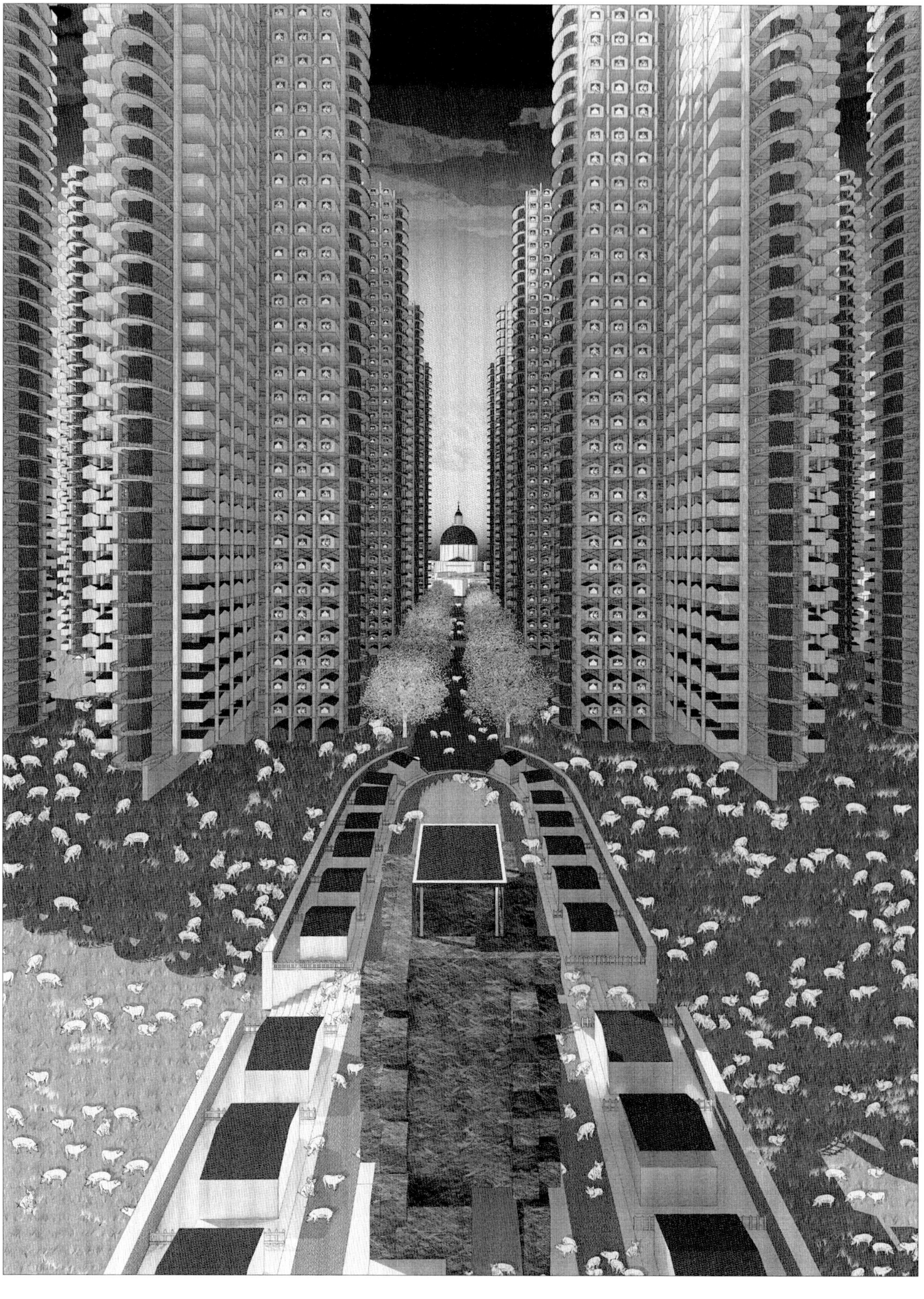

German-occupied Denmark. Pigs were slaughtered; in turn people could eat the grain that otherwise fed the animals.⁶

While the strategy during World War II made Denmark healthier, the new civil right has resulted in food and energy provisions, ancient carnivorous culture, and cities and landscapes all re-evaluated at three scales. At the domestic scale, each piglet is raised as an active member of a typical Danish surrogate family. Homes are retrofitted for multi-species and symbiotic occupancy; the alterations include food cultivation on window cills or in the gardens, grain silos in the chimney, and fireplaces padded out for piglets to slumber. Within the community scale, each pig, aged six months, reaches independent living in 'Porktopia', and becomes an active economic contributor of the Swine Squad. Sponsored by local councils, Porktopias are located within retrofitted public suburban greens and provide three types of accommodations: towers, townhouses, and bungalows. And finally at the urban scale, each city center is marked by a cathedral-esque anaerobic digestion plant, which takes the huge amount of nutrients generated by the extra 29 million new Danish citizens in the suburbs. Symbols of national pride, the clean energy-producing infrastructures provide heat and electricity to the National Grid, large quantities of fertilizer, as well as clean renewable energy to sustain the Heliotropic Android Swans in Greenland.

'Every time you open the door to one of these farms, you tell yourself: "it will be better than the last. They can't all be ignoring the law, they can't all be inflicting such misery." But then you see the pigs, and realize the scale of the suffering. It breaks your heart.'
– Compassion in World Farming, 'The EU Pig Investigations 2013'

A shame, then, that we treat pigs the way we do. Pigs are the most curious and intelligent farmyard animals. George Orwell, of course, knew that. Winston Churchill, a serious pig fancier, was mindful of it too: 'I am fond of pigs. Dogs look up to you. Cats look down on you. Pigs treat you as equal.'⁷ The pig-filled cities presented here should be read as a metaphoric critique of inequality in cities, and a provocation regarding the relationship between humans and our enslavement of nature.

The portrayal of the Heliotropic Android Swans as a radical air-force infrastructure deployed to fight the threat of sea level rise, amplifies the global concerns of climate change. By generating clean energy, the associated support of the Swine Squad for these fighters has a radical impact on the landscape both at home and on the frontline. Like the eternal underdogs and outcasts Peter Parker (aka Spider-Man) and Selina Kyle (aka Catwoman) of Marvel comics, every pig is now an eco-superhero – and we all need one. Denmark is revered for being one of the most progressive and sustainable countries in the world, with comprehensive green ideals and impudence for equality at the core of its modern identity. But how far would Denmark go to retain its status and image as a liberal eco-superpower?

facing page: Each urban anaerobic digestion cathedral processes the huge amount of nutrients generated by the extra 29 million new Danish citizens.

following pages: Porktopias are located within retrofitted accommodations: towers, townhouses, and bungalows.

6. N Johnson, 'Our Bodies Don't Need Meat. So Why Can't We Give It Up?', Grist: Meatheads, June 2016 [http://grist.org/article/our-bodies-dont-need-meat-so-why-cant-we-give-it-up/], retrieved 9 September 2015

7. J Henley, 'Welfare Doesn't Come Into It', The Guardian: Food, 2009 [https://www.theguardian.com/uk/2009/jan/06/animal-welfare-food-bacon], retrieved 25 July 2016

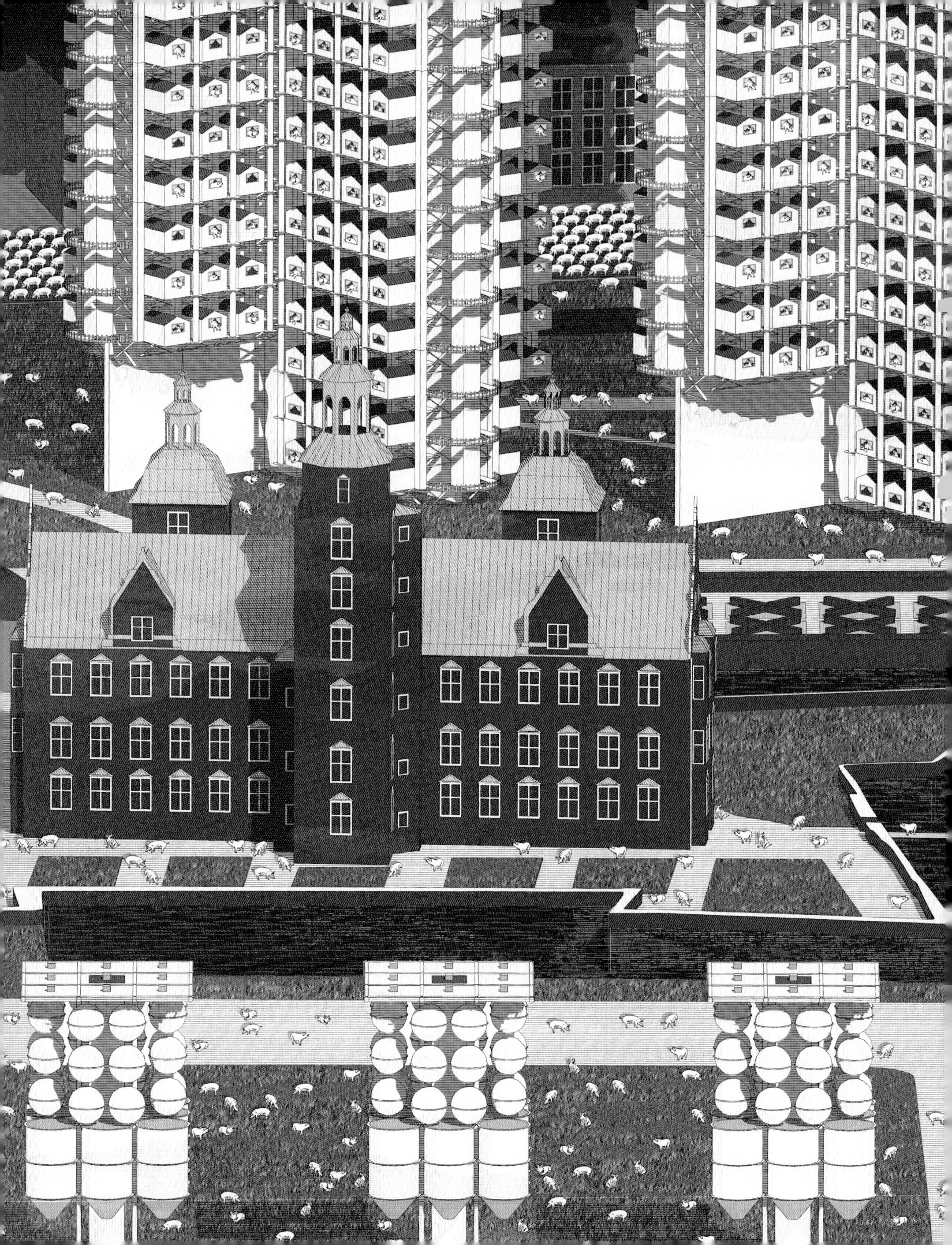

LIGHED NY
ROYAL
KÆLEDYR
SVIN
FEST

KONGENS HAVE
ROSENBORG SLOT
1. KLASSE
BORGER

150

urban future

The City of Frozen Spires

(iii)

'We're obviously sad, but we were able to freeze Robert under optimum conditions, so he's got another chance.'

– David Ettinger, The Washington Post, 2011

151

Robert CW Ettinger died at age 92. The frozen body of the science fiction (SF) writer, who popularized the cryonics movement, is currently stored in a vat of liquid nitrogen at his nonprofit Cryonics Institute outside Detroit, home to more than 100 fellow immortalists, which includes his mother and two wives, and dozens of pets, who are all awaiting revival. If all goes according to his manisfesto 'The Prospect of Immortality' (1964), Ettinger will remain in a period of icy stasis for decades or even centuries, until such a time where advanced medical technology would defrost him and restore him to good health.[1]

The preservative effects of low temperatures have been known for a long time. The notion of reviving human beings entombed in ice first appeared as a fictional device in 'The Frozen Pirate' (1887) by W Clark Russell.[2] The term cryonics emerged in the 60s and has since appeared frequently in SF and popular culture, often under the incorrect term cryogenics. At the time, many futurologists considered Ettinger's optimism highly plausible. The idea came as the world was coming to terms with the atomic bomb, robotic spacecraft and SF technologies popularized in films such as Arthur C Clarke and Stanley Kubrick's '2001: A Space Odyssey'. Later, in 'Interstellar' (2014), Christopher Nolan twisted notions of time and aging by juxtaposing cryonically preserved characters with science focusing around Einstein's theory of relativity. Most famously in 'Star Wars, Episode VI: Return of the Jedi' (1983) Han Solo was captured, frozen in carbonite and delivered to Jabba the Hutt; and 'Austin Powers: International Man of Mystery' (1997) pokes fun at the trope.

Buckminster Fuller dreamt of preserving an ecosystem within his Manhattan Dome decades before Nicholas Grimshaw created the various ecosystems for the preservation of species in his Eden Project domes. These projects aspire to manipulate climatic conditions; with an additional skin and advanced technological infrastructure the perfect weather for protection can be artificially fabricated. Museums keep their greatest treasures in dark cabinets; light, changes in humidity and temperature and pollution are all risks that threaten the longevity of artefacts. Police case evidence, cadavers, precious specimens, and stored seeds are often preserved by freezing.

Inevitably, sea level rise will exacerbate the premature death of many coastal cities, informal settlements and cultural heritage sites as well as increasing loss of life and health risks. The Organisation for

facing page: A new vertical infrastructure pushes the city into 21st century security, whilst the old capital is hidden away in the eternal night.

following pages: The blueprint for the Frozen Spires.

1. E Brown, 'Robert Ettinger, Founder of the Cryonics Movement, Dies at 92', The Washington Post, 24 July 2011 [https://www.washingtonpost.com/local/obituaries/from-phyics-teacher-to-founder-of-the-cryonics-movement/2011/07/24/gIQAupulXI_story.html], retrieved 29 July 2016

2. 'Cryonics', The Encyclopaedia of Science Fiction, 2016 [http://www.sf-encyclopedia.com/entry/cryonics], retrieved 29 July 2016

THE MASTERPLAN

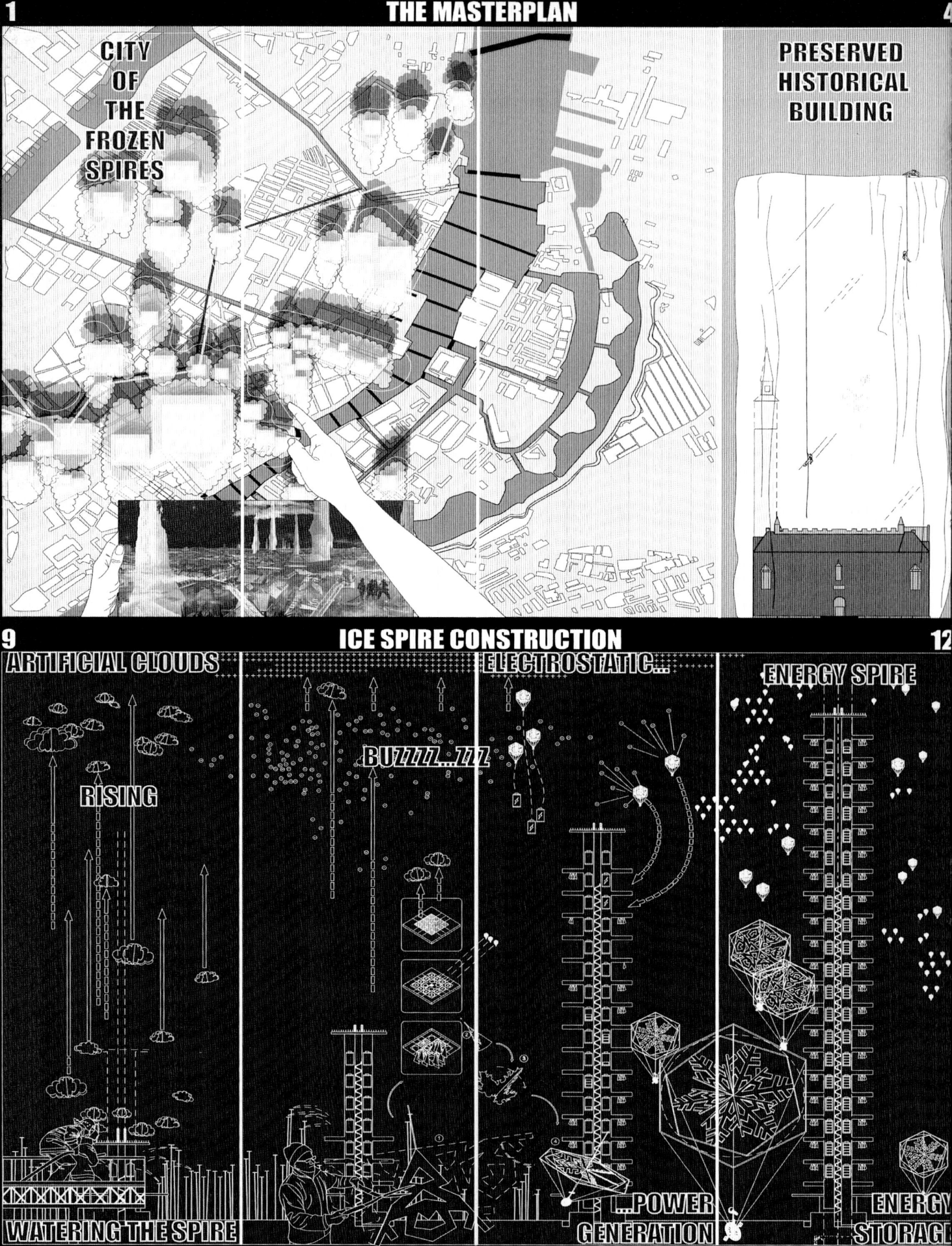

CITY OF THE FROZEN SPIRES

PRESERVED HISTORICAL BUILDING

ICE SPIRE CONSTRUCTION

ARTIFICIAL CLOUDS — RISING

ELECTROSTATIC... BUZZZZ...ZZZ

ENERGY SPIRE

WATERING THE SPIRE · ...POWER GENERATION · ENERGY STORAGE

CITY PRESERVATION

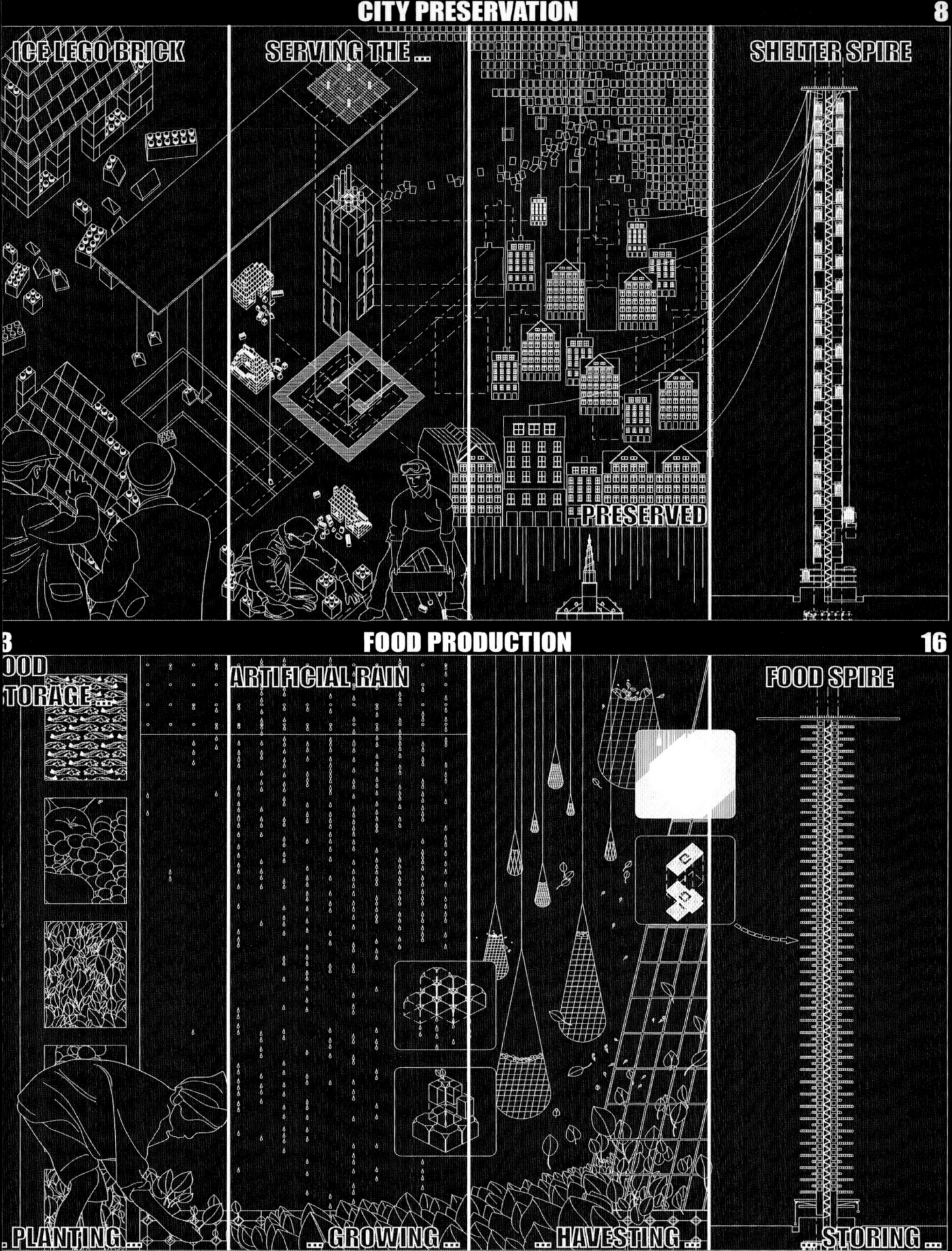

ICE LEGO BRICK | **SERVING THE ...** | **PRESERVED** | **SHELTER SPIRE**

FOOD PRODUCTION

FOOD STORAGE | **ARTIFICIAL RAIN** | | **FOOD SPIRE**

... PLANTING ... | ... GROWING ... | ... HAVESTING ... | ... STORING ...

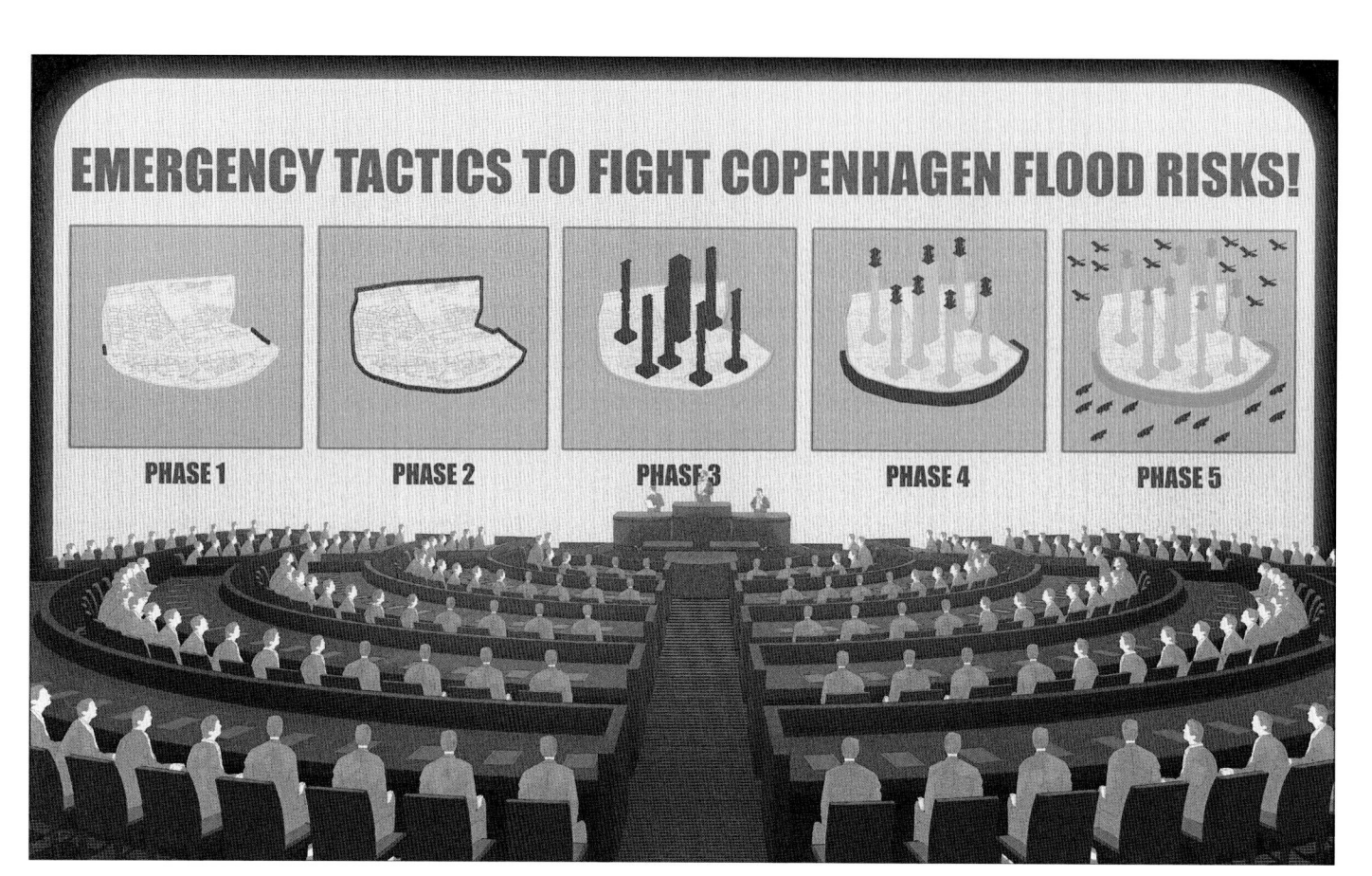

EMERGENCY TACTICS TO FIGHT COPENHAGEN FLOOD RISKS!

PHASE 1　　PHASE 2　　PHASE 3　　PHASE 4　　PHASE 5

Economic Co-operation and Development predicted a half meter of sea level rise by 2070, '150 million people in the world's large port cities will be at risk from coastal flooding, along with $35 trillion worth of property – an amount that will equal 9% of the global GDP'.[3] For the most part, cultural heritage preserved not in museums but in the urban fabric of cities, will not be spared. Increases in sea level have forced communities, archeologists and international organizations like the United Nations Educational, Scientific and Cultural Organization (UNESCO) to make intelligent decisions about whether to preserve, move or abandon historic cities, monuments and archaeological sites. Some heritage sites have spurred new levels of technology in efforts to preserve and record them through 3D laser scanning, ground-penetrating radar and land and aerial surveys.[4] The impending threat can only worsen, but helping coastal communities survive can also help extend the life of our heritage.

In Denmark, the Ministry of Culture has estimated 300,000 buildings worthy of preservation, based on atlases submitted by municipalities.[5] 'We are not just wanting to solve a problem, we also want to create a better city for its citizens'; this forward thinking comes from Copenhagen Climate Unit's director Lykke Leonardsen.[6] Unlike many cities located by the sea, planners in the Danish capital Copenhagen are taking visionary steps to protect its historic city and cultural heritage. 'In adapting to climate change, cities can choose either grey or green infrastructure. Grey infrastructure means building walls and barriers. The green option, which has growing support, includes green roofs, green streets that will capture storm water, and pavements that allow water to percolate through'[7] outlines Professor Stuart Gaffin, from the Center of Climate Systems Research at Columbia University. However, Klaus Jacob, a geophysicist at the same university, emphasized, 'the problem is we're still building the city of the past. But we should not build a city now that we know will not function in 2100. There are opportunities to renew our infrastructure. We just have to grasp those opportunities.'[8]

'What if...' Copenhagen can achieve immortality through 'quick-freezing of its body' through grey and green infrastructures in anticipation of future resurrection once the turmoil of the climate catastrophe has been overcome? In advance of the flood, its alter ego 'The City of Frozen Spires' constructs an inhabitable dam, locating it where the city's 17th century fortification once stood. The multi-use grey infrastructure performs as the city's curator, editing and categorizing deposited local historical artifacts. In addition, it functions as the new Ministry of Energy, generating sustainable hydroelectric power for the cryonics urban preservation enterprise. The Danish Government is aware of the setback faced by the Cryonics Society of California in 1981 when a power failure caused a number of frozen bodies to thaw out, sparking off a chain of lawsuits.[9]

Within the protective dam enclosure, its green vertical counterpart captures and freezes rising seawater to entomb the city's building structures including church spires, steeples and domes. Each spire archives only artifacts relating to the function of its host building – for example, religious artifacts are encrusted in the ice above a place of worship. In medieval times, it was not uncommon to recycle parts of buildings into other buildings or infrastructure – the finishing stone to the Great Pyramids was stripped and re-used, the Colosseum in Rome was extensively raided to build homes and churches, and the Vatican City and its walls.

facing page top: The central government steps up their preservation efforts; old Copenhagen is prematurely protected with ice to avoid damage from anticipated sea level rise.

facing page bottom: More and more Danish identities will require careful preservation.

3. T Folger, 'Rising Seas', National Geographic, September 2013 [http://ngm.nationalgeographic.com/2013/09/rising-seas/folger-text], retrieved 29 July 2016

4. H Thompson, 'Rising Seas Threaten to Swallow These Ten Global Wonders', Smithsonian.com, September 2015 [http://www.smithsonianmag.com/science-nature/rising-seas-threaten-swallow-these-ten-global-wonders-180956646/?no-ist], retrieved 29 July 2016

5. C Hjorth-Andersen, 'The Danish Cultural Heritage: Economics and politics', Institute of Economics, University of Copenhagen, 2004, p.22 [http://www.economics.ku.dk/research/publications/wp/2004/0433.pdf], retrieved 28 July 2015

6. S Peach, 'Copenhagen Confronts Rising Sea Level Risks', Yale Climate Connects, 2015 [http://www.yaleclimateconnections.org/2015/09/copenhagen-confronts-rising-sea-level-risks/], retrieved 29 July 2016

7. E Braw, 'Tackling Climate Change: Copenhagen's sustainable city design', The Guardian, 8 October 2013 [https://www.theguardian.com/sustainable-business/tackling-climate-change-copenhagen-sustainable-city-design], retrieved 29 July 2016

8. T Folger, 'Rising Seas', National Geographic, September 2013 [http://ngm.nationalgeographic.com/2013/09/rising-seas/folger-text], retrieved 29 July 2016

9. 'Cryonics', The Encyclopaedia of Science Fiction, 2016 [http://www.sf-encyclopedia.com/entry/cryonics], retrieved 29 July 2016

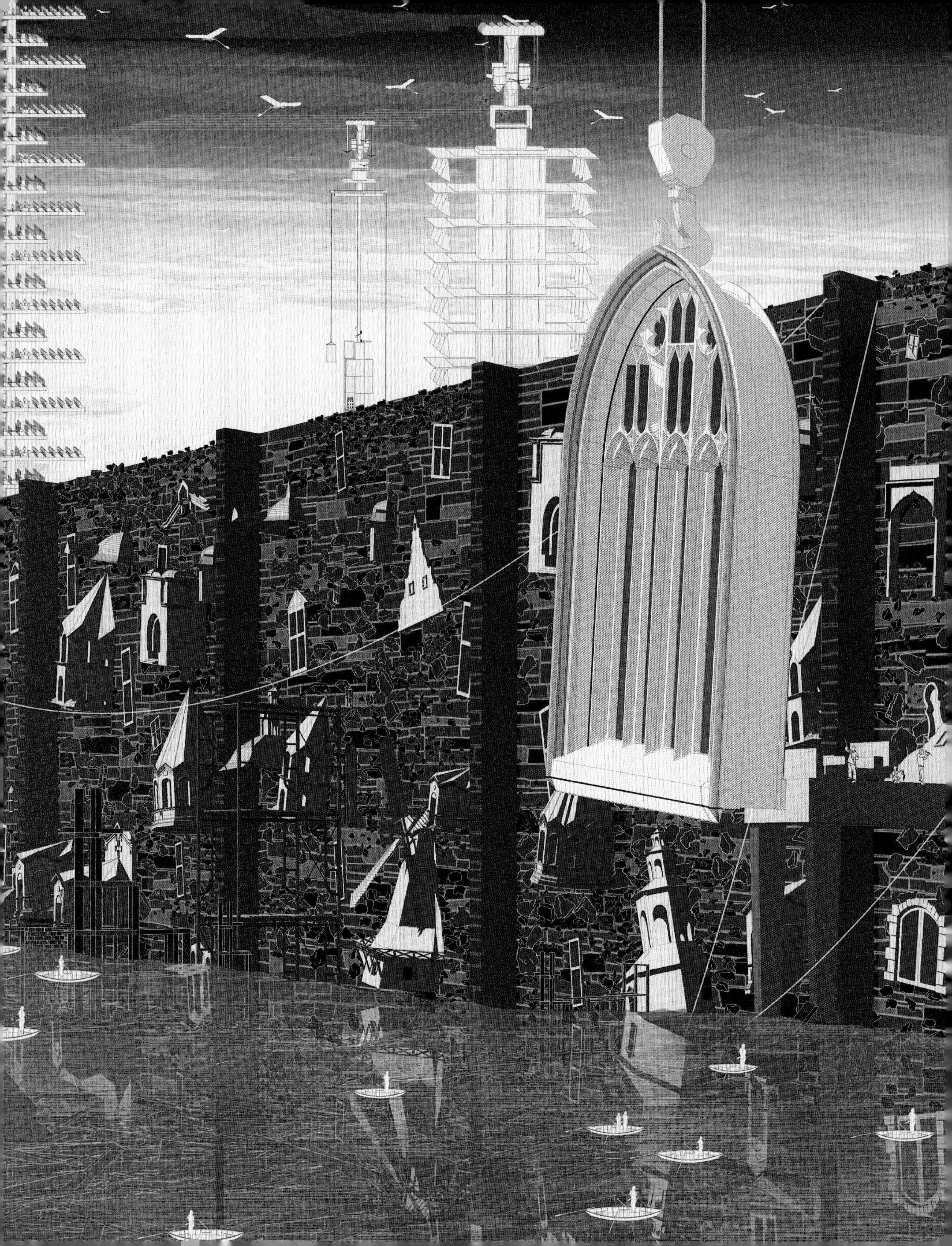

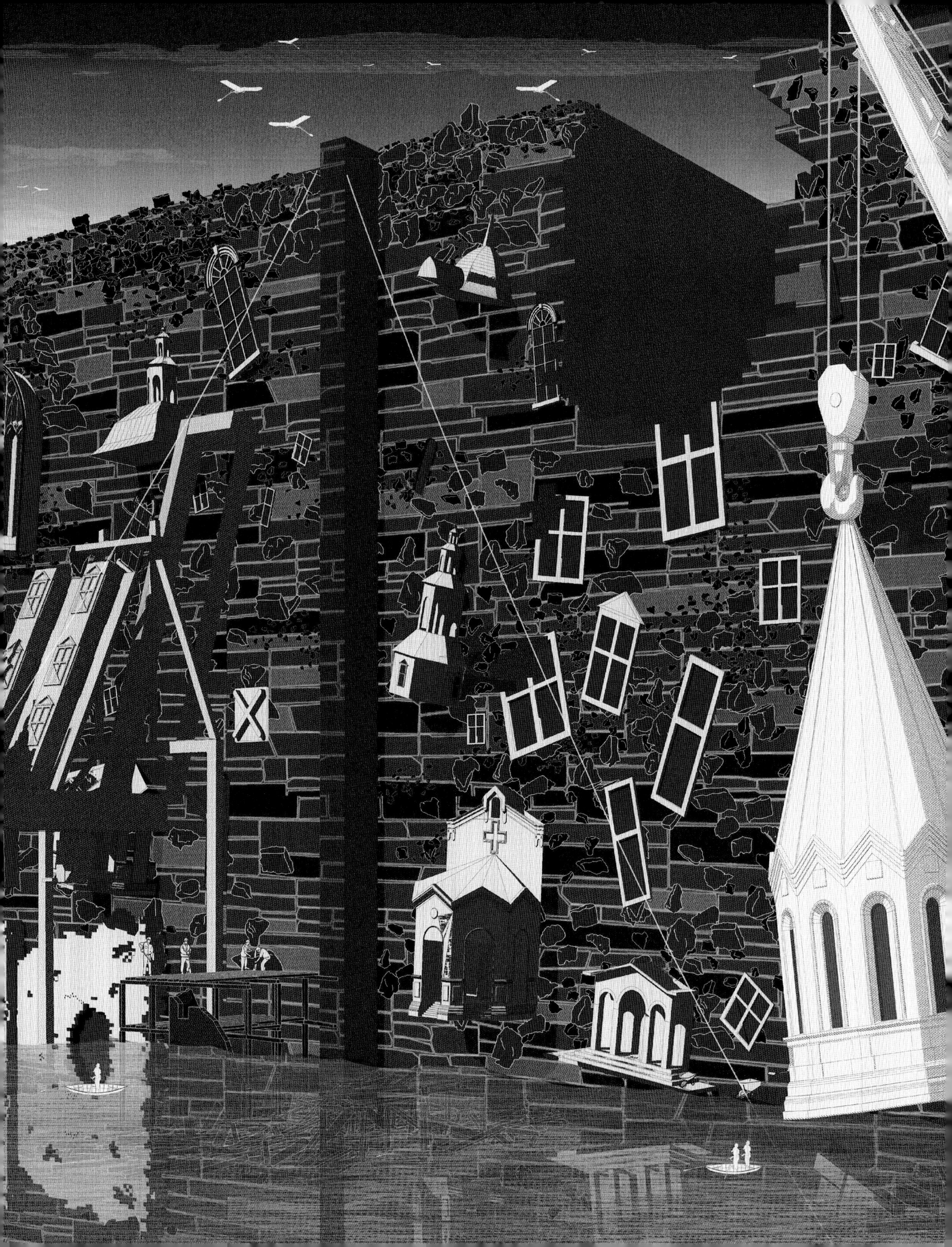

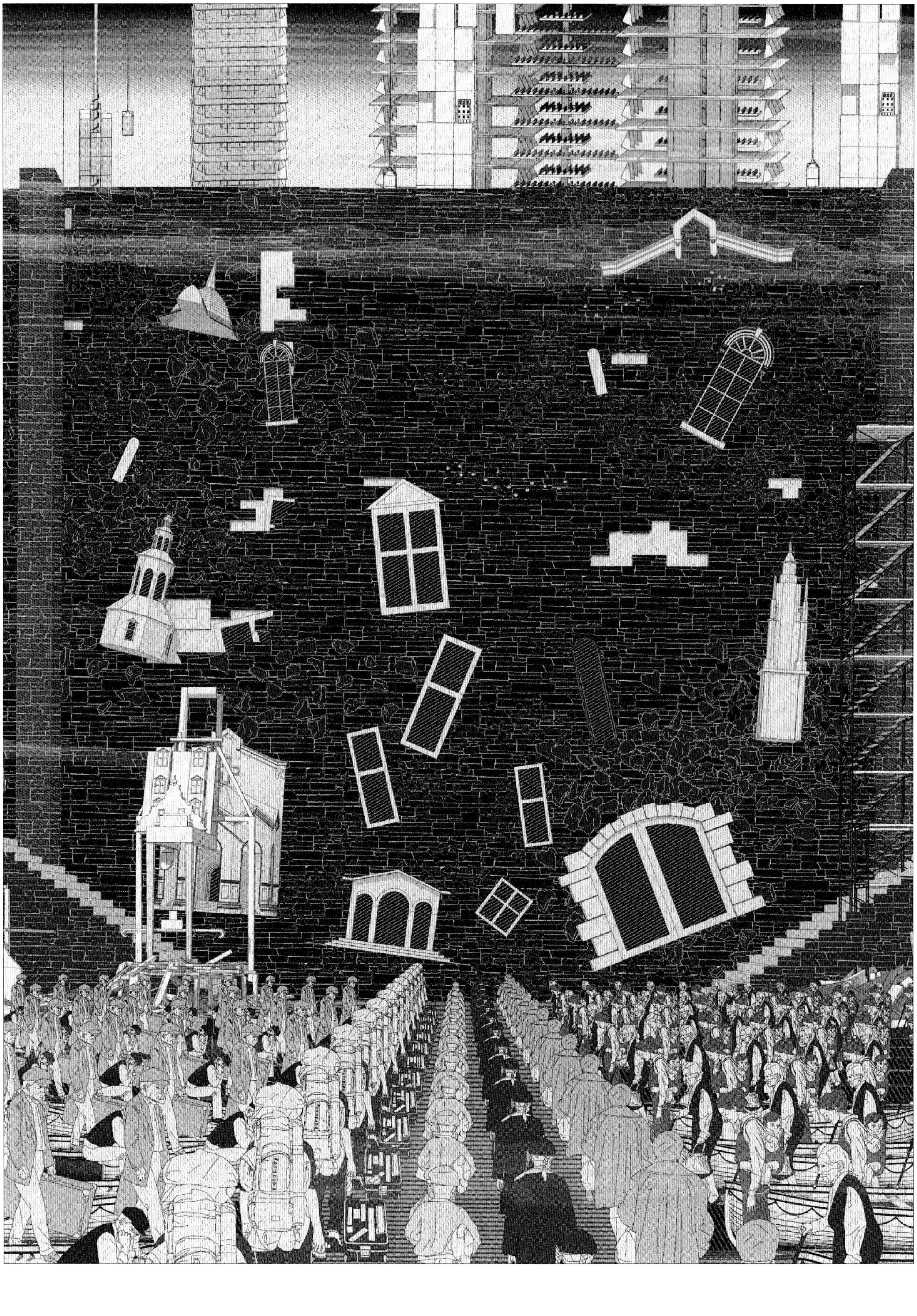

the city of frozen spires

The Frozen Spires emerge throughout the city, breaking the uniformity of the relatively horizontal skyline. The massive spires of frozen floodwater primarily function to protect and preserve heritage but also provide an abundance of housing and industry. There is the daily ritual of desalinating seawater for potable human consumption and irrigation quality for the hanging gardens which adorn the towering ice structures. Along with layers of historical artifacts, water and food are simultaneously preserved within the spires, ensuring a resilient strategy for the city in times of uncertainty.

Frank Lloyd Wright, in his book 'A Testament' (1956), dreamt of the Mile High Illinois tower, impossible at that time. Four times the height of the Empire State Building, the 528-storey proposal included parking for 15,000 cars and 150 helicopters.[10] Wright's vision inspired the 'Burj Khalifa' tower in Dubai, which was completed in 2009; at a soaring 828 meters, it flaunts technology unknown in Wright's day.[11] Consequently, how tall can the Frozen Spires reach? As the extent of flooding continues, the escalating amounts of displaced seawater make the ice ever denser and structurally enhanced, thus feeding the vertical growth of the Frozen Spires – the sky is the limit.

The Frozen Spires exploit the very element that threatens, embracing the enemy in their many 'self-adaptations' to combat climate change. There is a colossal vertical cooling coil in each spire to refrigerate and transform the plentiful resource; a network of services and ventilation ducts weave around the densely inhabited translucent ice. Simultaneously, the spires filter polluted air intake and expel heat from the ice, forming layers of clouds to shade the infrastructure. Any excess heat is recycled into accelerating the cultivation of vegetables using principles from intense carbon greenhouse technology. From the terraced gardens on top of each frozen spire, inhabitants can look out to a pure white winter wonderland. Automated ploughs gracefully modulate the top surface of the ice to maximize its 'white' appearance and its efficiency of reflecting solar rays, the principles of albedo effect. Refinement of the ice infrastructure continues throughout the day, every day.

To escape the dangerous and intimidating environmental conditions of the later stages of climate change, future nomads, abandoned artifacts and migrating infrastructures from neighboring nations start to deposit themselves around the edges of the city – resembling a pilgrimage to the building site of the Tower of Babel. Copenhagen, by protecting and preserving its heritage as it moves forward, becomes an important cultural window to the past, whereas so many other cities have settled for destruction, chaos and dystopia in the toughest days of climate change. The City of Frozen Spires has turned Ettinger's cryonics movement into a veritable religion. Ettinger believed death is only for the unprepared and unimaginative.[12]

previous + facing pages: Around the edges of the protective wall, future nomads, abandoned artifacts and migrating infrastructures from neighboring nations start to deposit themselves.

following pages: The Frozen Spires emerge throughout the city, breaking the uniformity of the relatively horizontal skyline.

10. FL Wright, 'The Testament', Horizon Press, New York, 1957, pp.239–240

11. Emaar Properties, 'Burj Khalifa: Facts and Figures' [http://www.burjkhalifa.ae/en/the-tower/factsandfigures.aspx], retrieved 9 September 2015

12. E Brown, 'Robert Ettinger, Founder of the Cryonics Movement, Dies at 92', The Washington Post, 24 July 2011 [https://www.washingtonpost.com/local/obituaries/from-phyics-teacher-to-founder-of-the-cryonics-movement/2011/07/24/gIQAupulXI_story.html], retrieved 29 July 2016

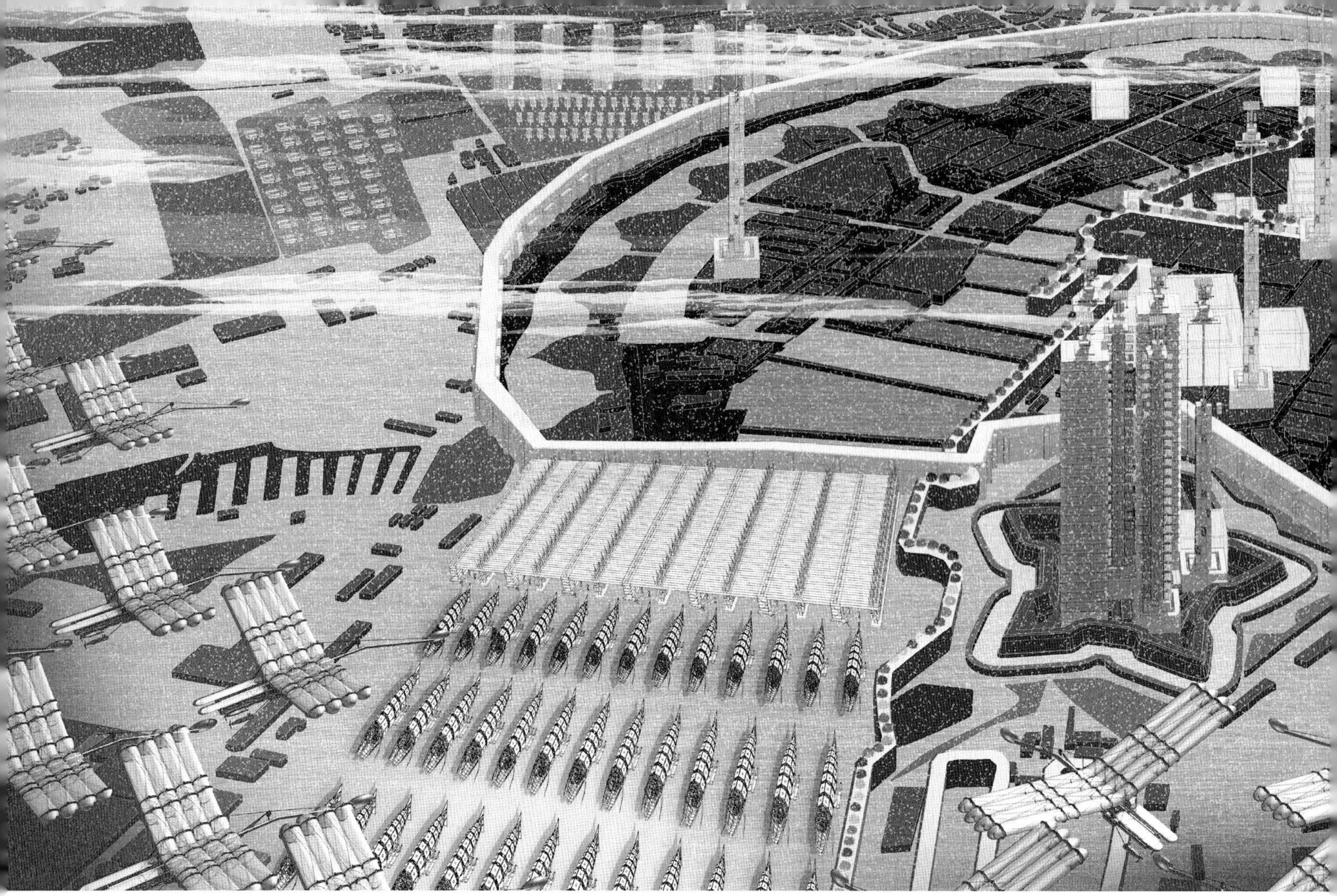

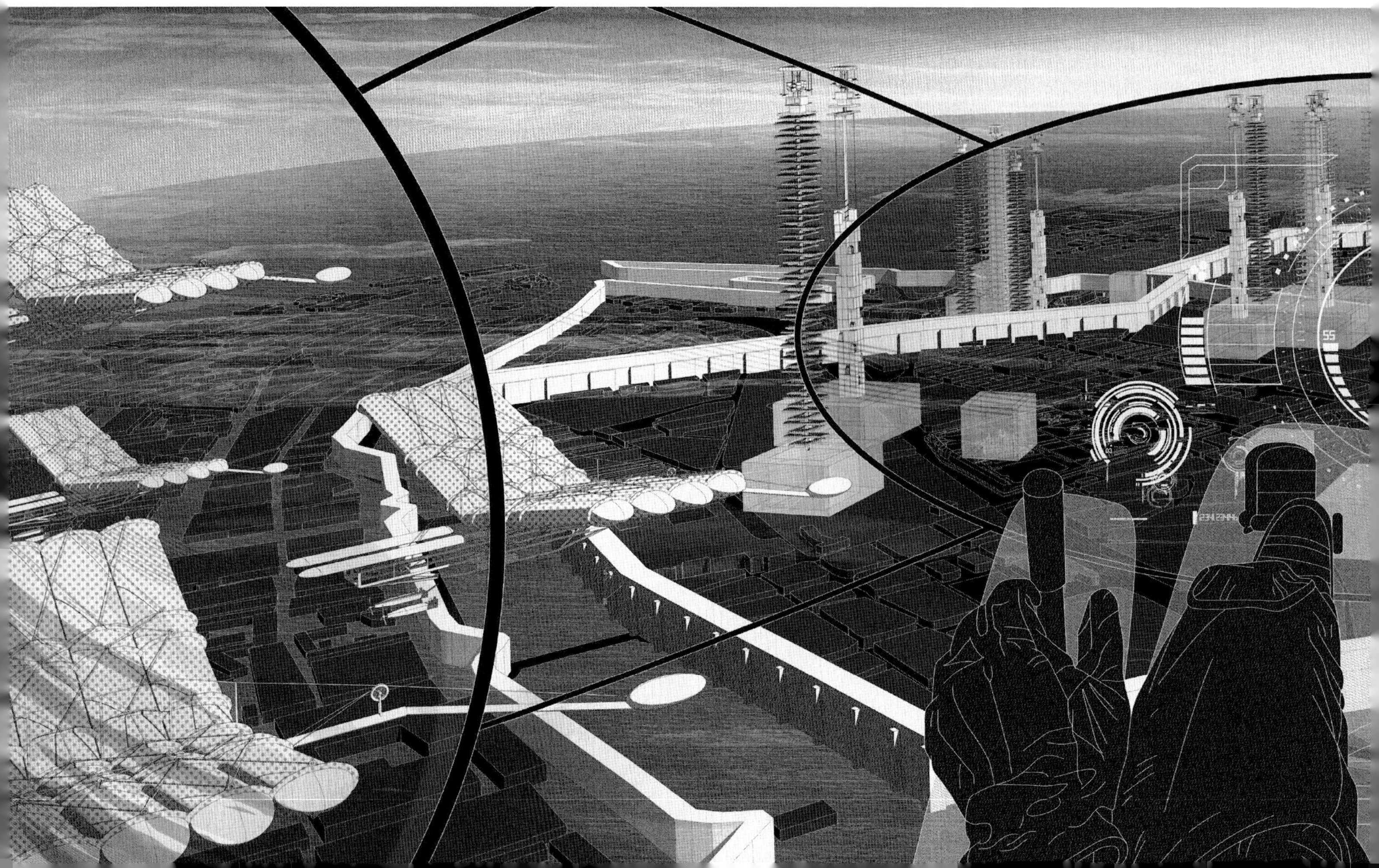

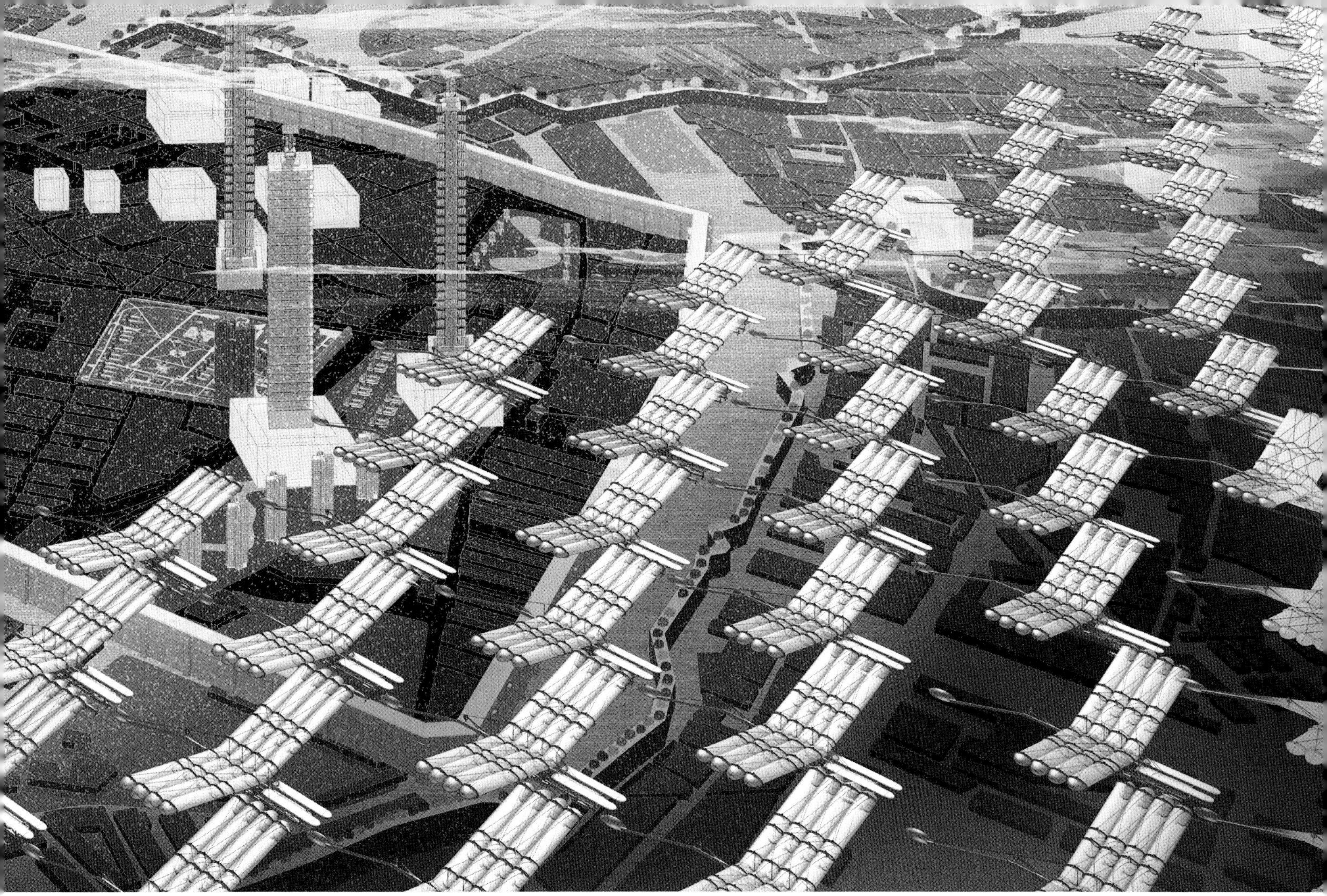

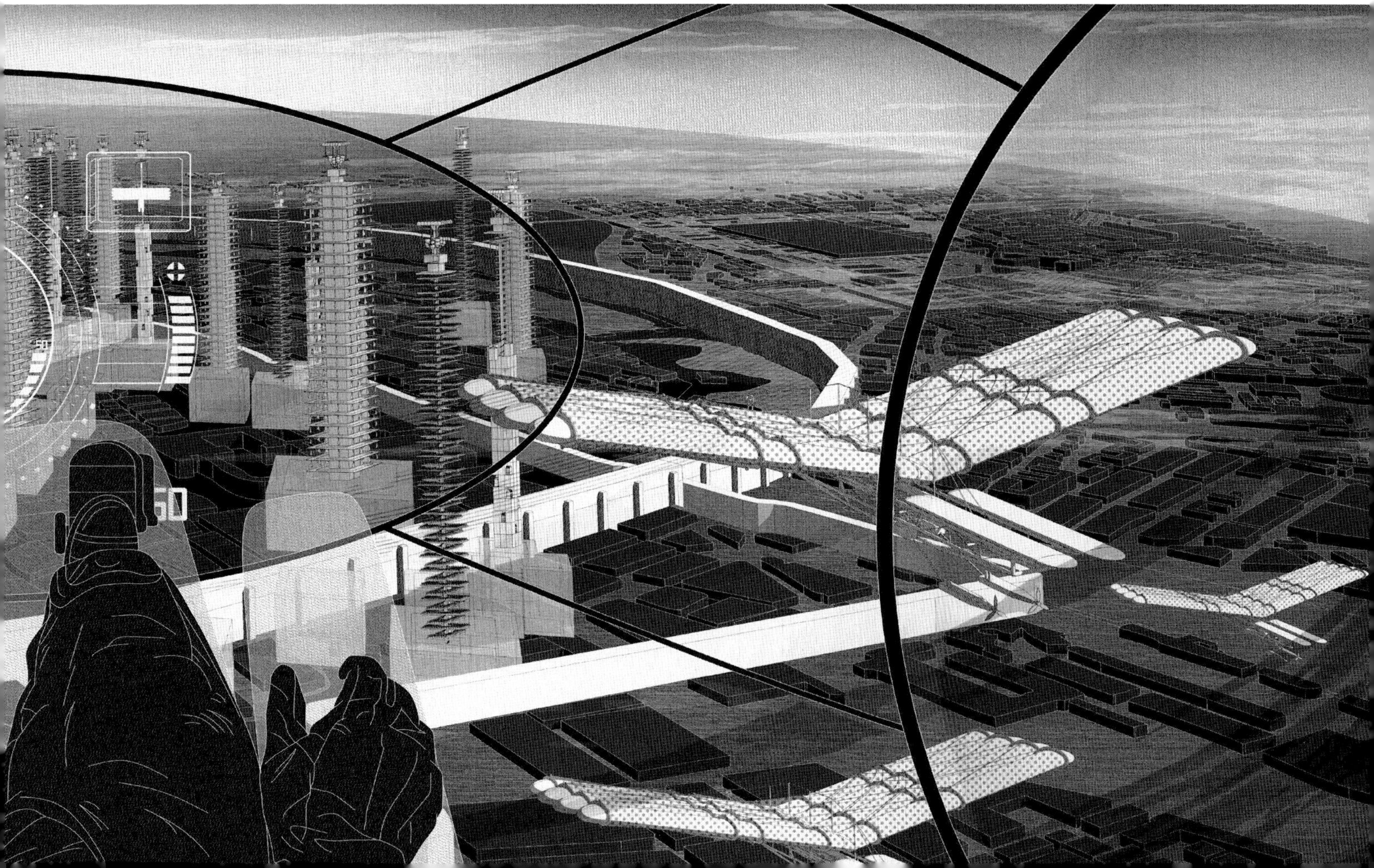

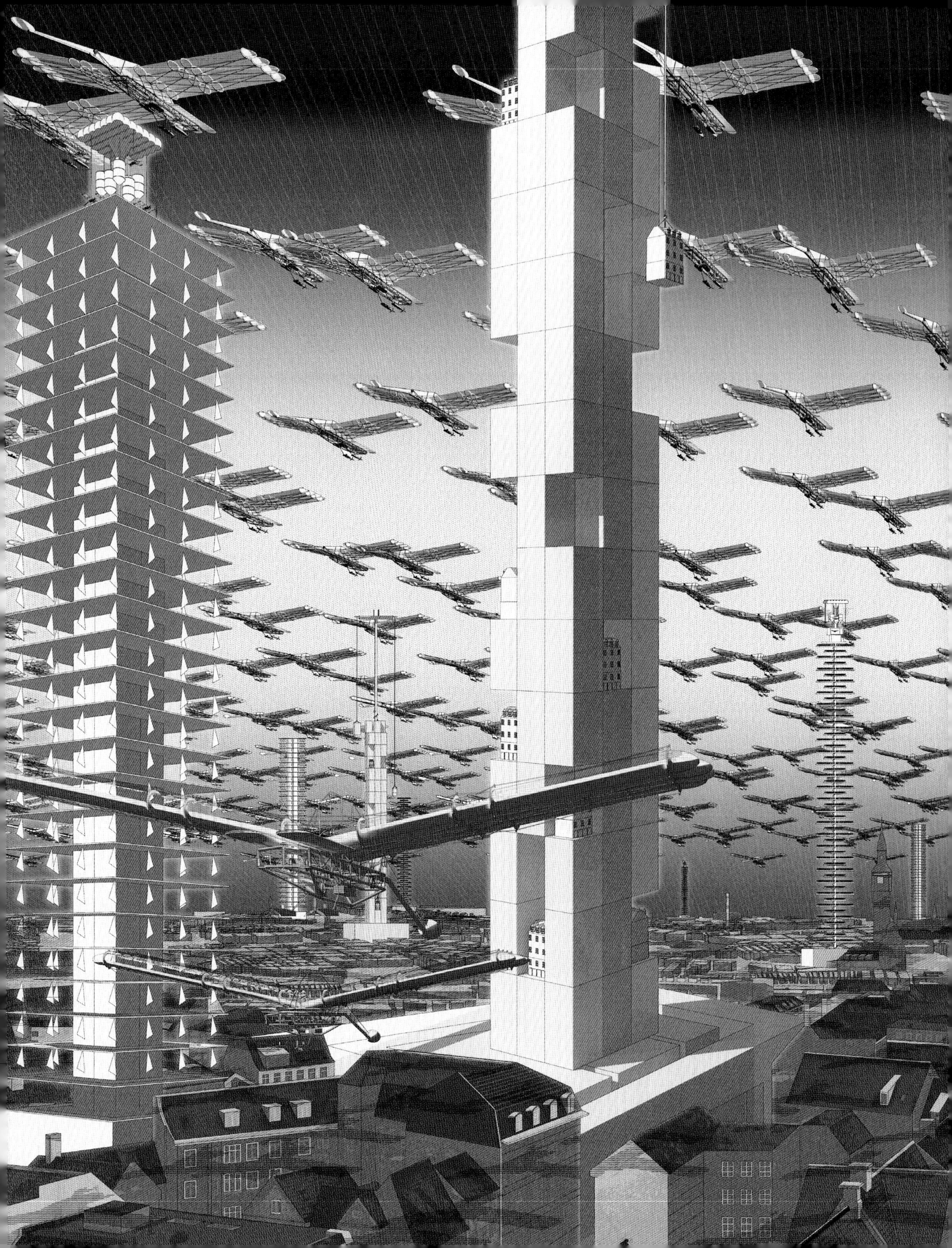

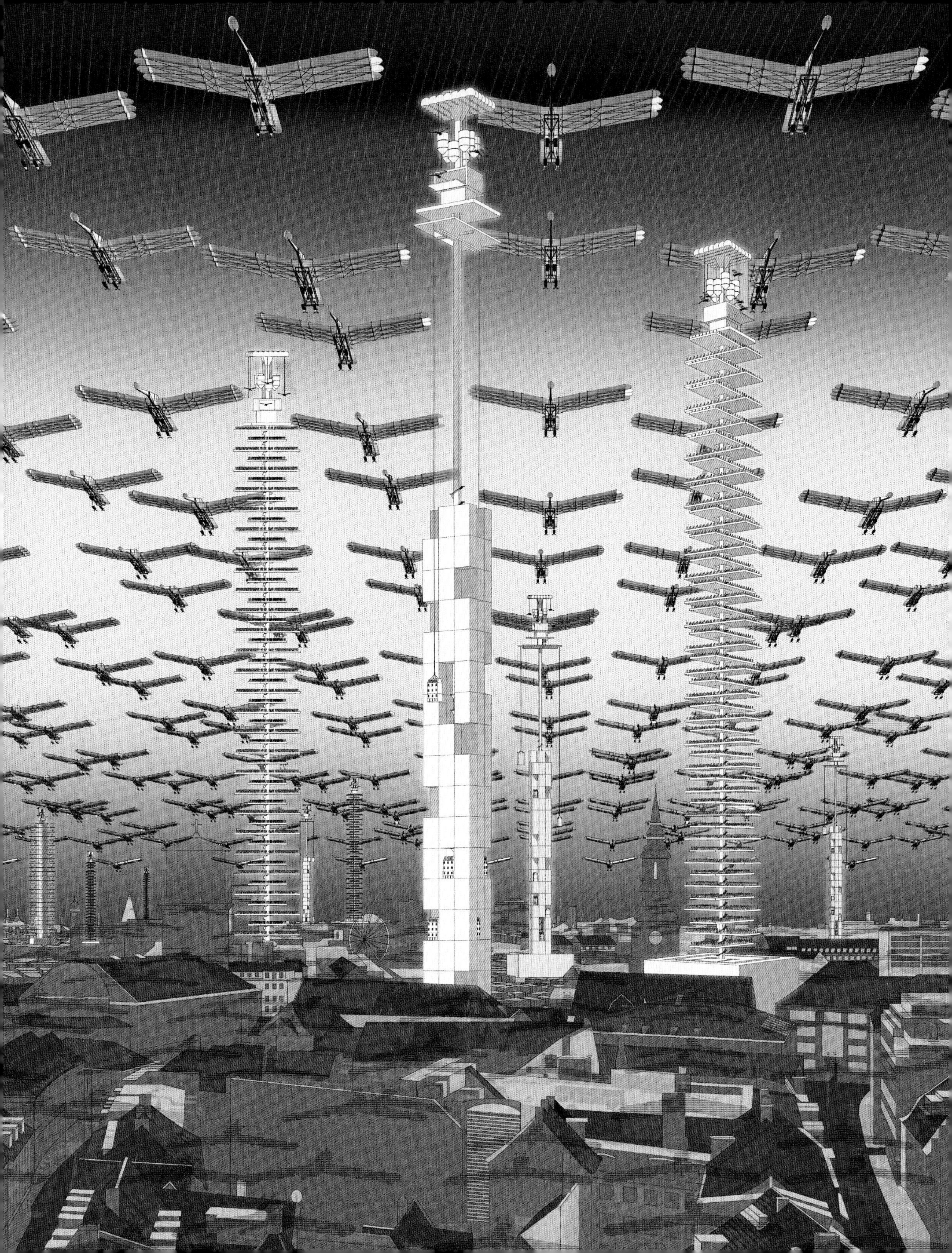

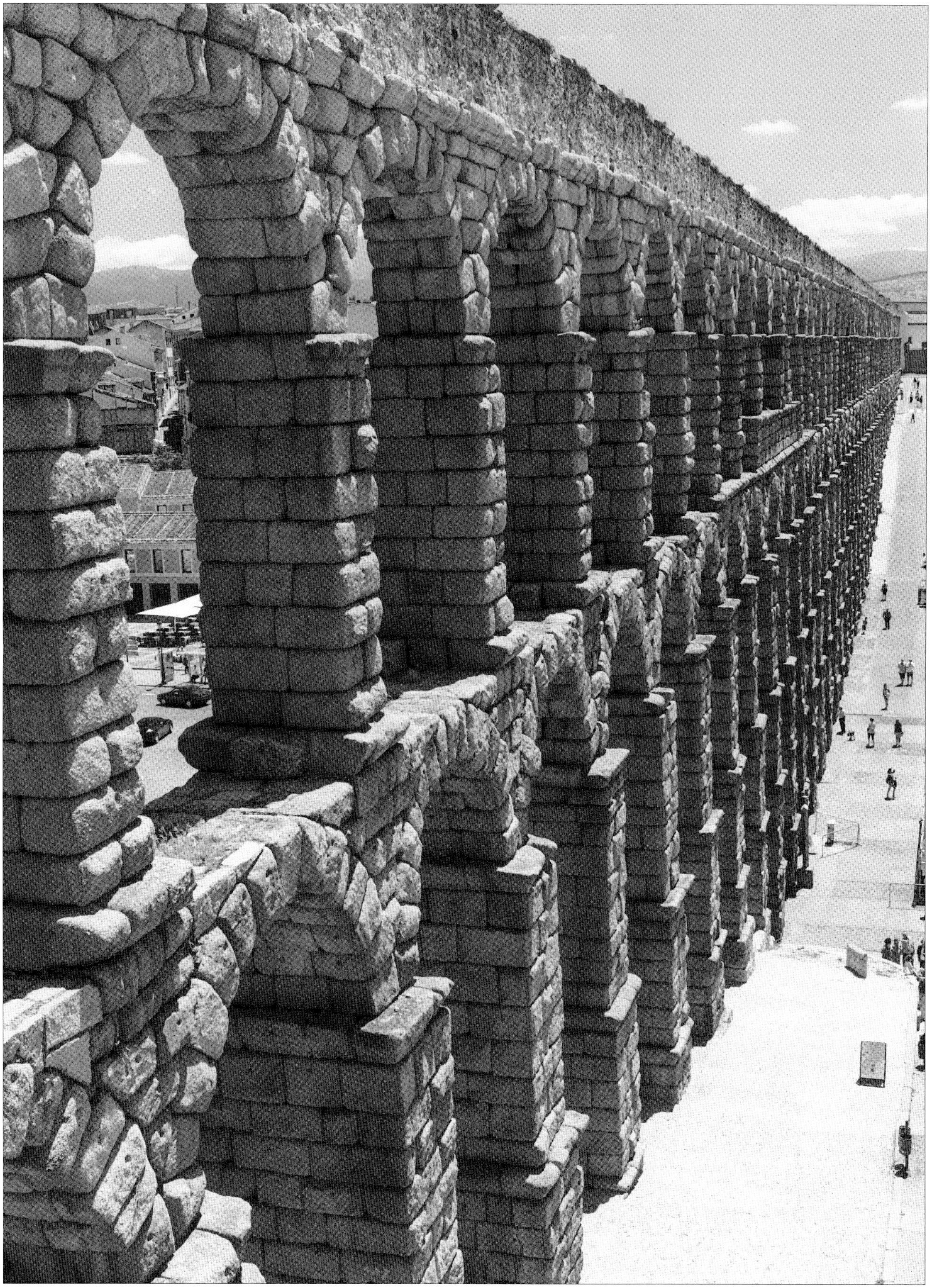

To Provide

'There can be no doubt that engineering came into being to solve new problems of a new society, but once engineering was established, there arose an interaction by which it in turn influenced the evolution of society. This state of affairs continues today and will continue to exist as long as civilization remains dynamic and maintains its evolutionary course.'
– Richard Shelton Kirby, 'Engineering in History', 1991

The evolution of society and the city as a continual problem solving activity is a Roman idea. The Romans were great engineers and they brought ingenious utilitarian infrastructure to provide for the regions of their empire. They created long lasting urban and environmental impacts, and their technologies were the reconciliation of external expansion and essential consolidation. Sextus Julius Frontinus, the most famous of Roman engineers and a utilitarian public servant with no interest in aesthetics, famously stated: 'With such an array of indispensable structures, compare if you will, the idle Pyramids or the useless, though famous works of the Greek.'[1]

Amongst the innovations of the Augustan age, it was the aqueduct – a hard infrastructure to channel water – that empowered Rome and its ascension to become the great city of popular imagination. Water management has been a key factor in its prosperity, wellbeing and cultivation from a humble pastoral settlement. Without the aqueduct, other cities of the Roman Empire including Colonia Nemausus 'Nimes' in France, Colonia Claudia Ara Agrippinensium 'Cologne' in Germany, Tarraco 'Tarragona' in Spain and the city of Gadara, in modern day Jordan, would probably not have existed.

From the 1st to the 2nd century, aqueducts multiplied throughout Rome and traversed the cities of its empire; colonnades of arches reached prodigious heights conducting water streams. Not altogether new, the arch had been used by the Etruscans, and the inspiration of the water management system was adopted from the Greeks, which originated from the 'ganats' in Persia. The qanat system consists of underground channels that convey water from aquifers in highlands to the surface at lower levels by gravity, and they are still built today throughout Africa and the Middle East.

Any lack of originality of the Romans, however, was adequately compensated for by the assimilation of unparalleled strategic thinking and a willingness to adopt new and foreign ideas, in the process achieving a distinctive expression of its own.[2] The aqueduct of Segovia in Spain is over 800 meters long and the Pont du Gard in southern France is 270 meters in length; both still survive today as spectacular monuments to the skill and audacity of Roman engineers. The former has a double row of five-meter

facing page: The aqueduct of Segovia in Spain, one of many hard infrastructures that empowered Rome and its ascension to become the great city of popular imagination.

1. SJ Frontinus, C Bennett (trans.), 'Stratagems and the Aqueducts of Rome', Harvard University Press, Cambridge, Massachusetts, 1961, p.357

2. K Galinsky, 'Augustan Culture', Princeton University Press, New Jersey, 1998, p.333

166

arches, one above the other and at the high point reaching 36 meters. The Pont du Gard, with its three tiers of arches, measures 49 meters in height and is a spectacular vision.³

Despite common belief, viaducts and bridges supported only 5% of the total distance of Rome's aqueducts. The majority of Roman water infrastructure ran below the city for security reasons – an exposed drinking water supply would be vulnerable to the many enemies of the empire.⁴ The entire system relied on various gradients and gravity to maintain a continuous flow. Water arrived in varying qualities and was stored in giant underground cisterns located around the city. The worst water, which came from lakes, served farms for irrigation, while the best quality water sourced from underground springs and from the valley was delivered to private houses, public fountains, and bathhouses, where the inhabitants of ancient Rome spent much of their leisure time. The collection of grey-water within the infrastructure was carefully designed so that all wastewater drained into the Cloaca Maxima, which eventually emptied directly into the Tiber River. The constant flow of water helped to remove wastes from latrines and keep the sewers clear of obstructions. The Cloaca Maxima is one of the world's oldest functioning wastewater and storm-water systems today.

In most circumstances, the water from the aqueducts reached only the ground floor of apartment buildings. Ancient Rome was a city of fountains; the inhabitants of the upper floors had to manually carry water drawn from the nearest public fountain. The city's aqueducts fed 39 monumental fountains and 591 public basins.⁵ These social infrastructures were an invitation 'for pausing, an opportunity to quit for the moment, the activity of the pavement joining directly with those of contiguous streets and squares, and ready to receive diversions from traffic alongside, spatially dilated through the sight and sound of moving water'.⁶ At the height of the Roman Empire, 11 aqueducts supplied the city of Rome a per capita water use of 67 liters per day that is more than what is commonly available in most cities today.⁷ Cities and municipalities throughout the empire commissioned aqueducts as public necessities of aspiring luxury and civic pride.

Water management became an issue for the city. Not all the water carried in the aqueduct arrived in Rome – a large number of landowners and farmers bribed water officials to tap a nearby aqueduct. Upon his investigation of the problem of illegal connections, Frontinus was exasperated, 'there are extensive areas in various places where secret pipes run under the pavement all over the city. I discovered that these pipes were furnishing water by special branches to all those engaged in business in those localities through which the pipes ran, being bored for the purpose here and there by the so-called "puncturers". How large an amount of water has been stolen in his manner, I estimate by means of the fact that a considerable quantity of lead has been brought in by the removal of that kind of branch pipe.'⁸

The Claudians over time adjusted the ideal of engineering towards the provision of infrastructure as a public duty. With political and social stability, a new phase of urbanism for the empire coincided with the introduction of new everyday soft infrastructures. Bathhouses and latrines provided basic human rights to clean water and sanitation, and these sumptuous and elaborate establishments acted as community centers and analog of urban life. By the end of the 4th century, Rome had 11 huge, symmetrically planned

---

facing page: There was once a network of over 6,000 wells located in the middle of squares and courtyards, to supply the population of Venice with freshwater.

3. DJ Brown, 'Bridges: Three thousand years of defying nature', Octopus Publishing Group, London, 2005, p.23

4. N Smith, 'Roman Hydraulic Technology', Scientific American, 1978, vol. 238, issue.5, pp.154–161

5. Frontin, 'Les Aqueducs de la ville de Rome', translation and commentary by Pierre Grimal, Société d'édition Les Belles Lettres, Paris, 1944

6. WL MacDonald, 'The Architecture of the Roman Empire: An urban appraisal', Yale University Press, New Haven, 1988, p.105

7. C Bruun, 'The Water Supply of Ancient Rome: A study of Roman imperial administration', The Finnish Society of Sciences and Letters, Helsinki, 1991, p.103

8. SJ Frontinus, C Bennett (trans.), 'Stratagems and the Aqueducts of Rome', Harvard University Press, Cambridge, Massachusetts, 1961, p.357

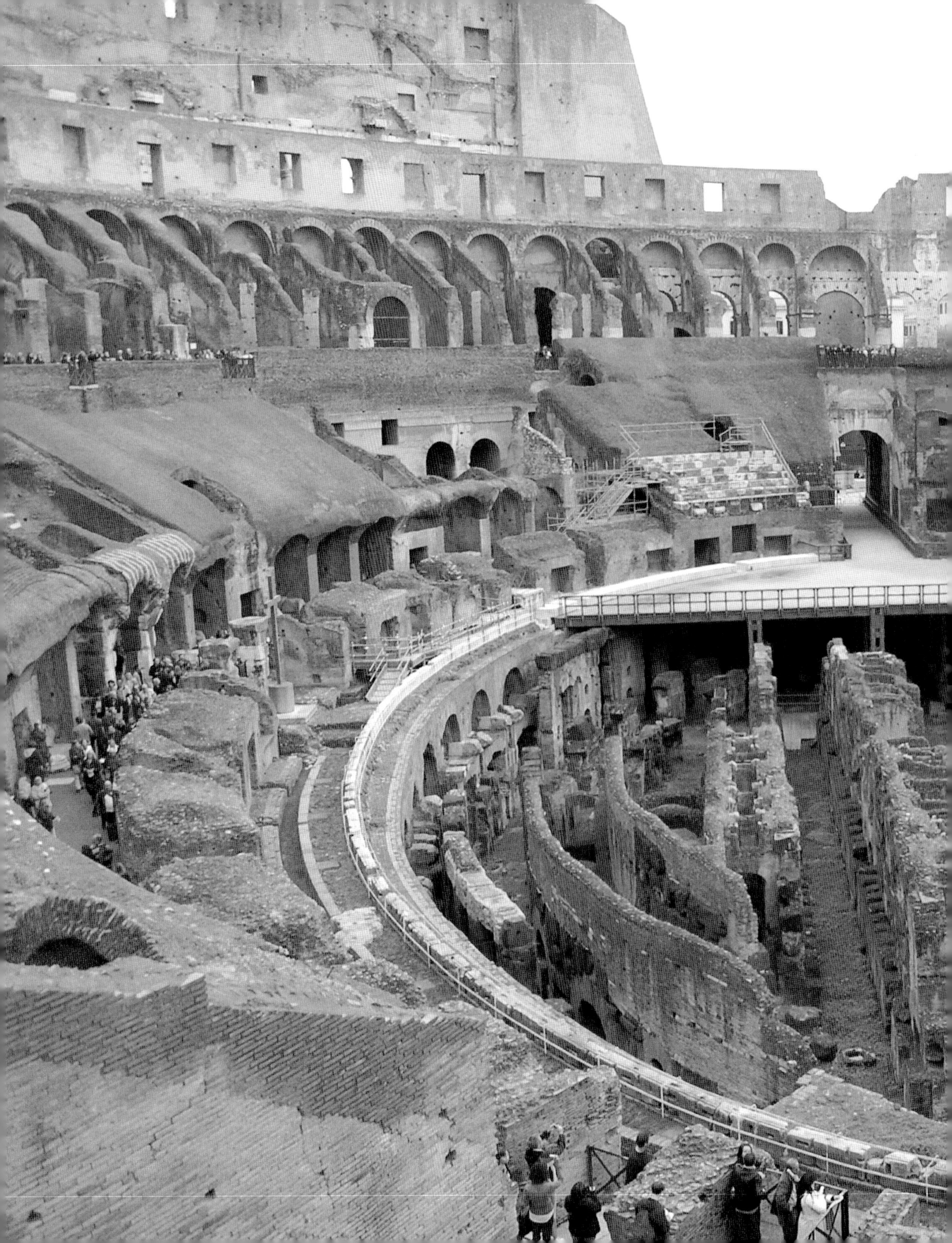

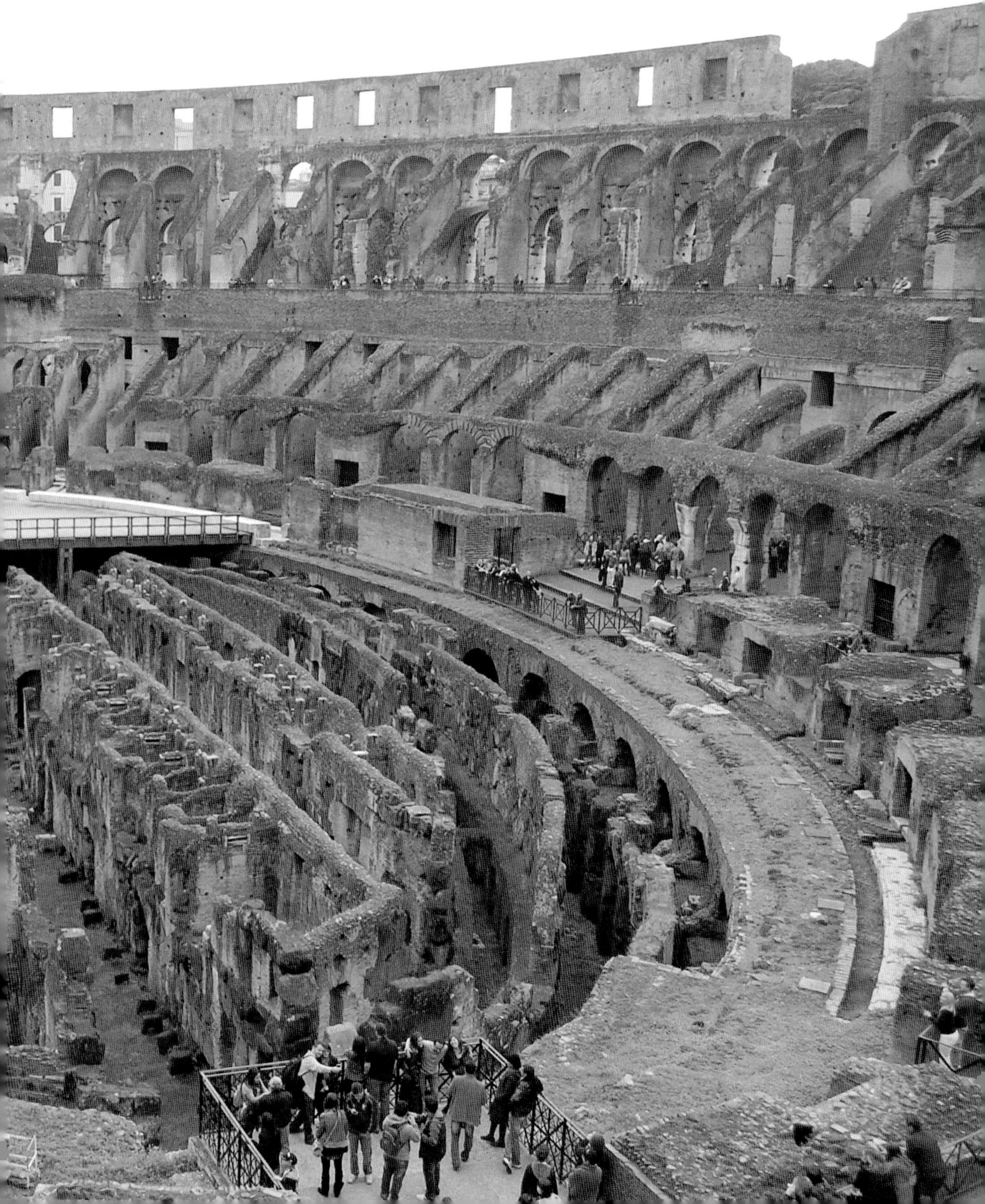

imperial baths and more than 800 further domestic establishments.⁹ The amphitheater delivered sports and gladiatorial recreation. The forum, a novel Roman idea, was a marketplace; along with shops and the stoas used for open stalls, it incorporated the city hall, the magistrate court, and a temple that were all combined into a single structure. The multi-use infrastructure facilitated open, diverse discussions and people were able to publicly voice their political opinions and socialize. Forum Trajanum was the last of the imperial infrastructure of ancient Rome.

However, the provisions of everyday infrastructures must not be misconstrued with the development of social wellbeing and liberalism. The bathhouses, amphitheater and forum were representative of political and social control centers, giving Rome further surveillance and influence over its people and its new colonies. The greatness of the Roman Empire was a direct consequence of engineering as propaganda, and the aqueduct was the ultimate ingenious political infrastructure. It is indeed because of the aqueduct that great transformations of service infrastructure took place, changing the basic systems from a primitive mode into recognizable modern forms.

Specialized Ground
Roman society was immensely attached to its public fountains, bathhouses and forum. It is recognized that humans form emotional attachments to cities and infrastructures – the San Franciscans fought the City Hall, pro-bus politicians and the Public Utilities Commission for over seven years in the 40s to save the cable cars. San Francisco's Powell Street cable car system is a significant ground treatment transport infrastructure. Based on early mining conveyance systems, Andrew Smith Hallidie's system came about in 1873 after he witnessed horses being whipped while they struggled on the wet cobblestones to pull a horse-car up many of the city's steep hills.[10] Each car was towed along its hilly tracks and had a grip mechanism that engaged with a system of cables operating at constant speed in channels beneath the streets. The operating machinery was located at the powerhouse, where large boilers were used to drive the winding wheels. At each of the terminals, manual non-powered turntables were employed to rotate the single-ended cable cars, adding theatre to the transport system.

After the great earthquake and fire of San Francisco in 1906, the cable car infrastructure along with the rest of the city was left in ruins. The infrastructure of 69 city blocks' worth of tracks and cable channels was upgraded and rebuilt several times. Today the city's intermodal urban transport network is celebrated as the world's last remaining manually operated cable car system – an icon for the city, a commuter transport and a tourist attraction. As old as almost any building in the city and a great way to climb up San Francisco's notoriously undulating streets, the cable car infrastructure (and the ringing of their bells!) is an intrinsic piece of urban legacy, specialized, localized and integrated.[11]

There are threats for the long-standing tradition in the ever-denser city. According to the US Department of Transportation, the cable cars routinely rank among the most accident-prone mass transportation mode in the country per vehicle mile traveled annually. Over the last 10 years, city officials have reported 126 accidents injuring 151 people.[12] This is due to the motor-car oriented culture, and traffic pressures that are caused when streets designed for specialist systems are pushed to breaking point with generic transport, neither being truly suitable for the 21 century city.

Walking on Air
With increasing population density, limited usable land and challenging topography, cities are looking towards elevated walkways and skywalks to improve pedestrian accessibility and provide better walking environments. These enclosed

environments invoke memories of SF – HG Wells' 'A Story of the Days To Come' (1897) and 'The Sleeper Awakes' (1910), and Fritz Lang's 'Metropolis' (1925). However, the moving walkways and skywalks in all three dystopian SF are no match when compared to Robert A Heinlein's 350-kilometer mechanical connection between Cincinnati and Cleveland described in 'The Roads Must Roll' (1940).

The Hong Kong Central Elevated Walkway System provides an extensive three-dimensional connectivity where the traditional 'terra firma' reference is rendered obsolete. Its elaborate aerial network of walkways, footbridges and elevated tunnels links the super-dense vertical skyscrapers to commercial hubs, supermarkets, stations and even the airport. Privately owned shopping mall lobbies are required to maintain 24-hour access and take on the responsibility of a public thoroughfare, a role akin to public squares and plazas in other cities. In turn, the arrangement boosts economic activities and significantly enhances the retail value of the commercial developments. Three-dimensional urbanism in Hong Kong is the combination of two factors – pragmatic thinking and comprehensive masterplanning by the government against the backdrop of the city's unique geography and economy.[13] Although constructed by a host of stakeholders at different times for different demands, the pedestrian infrastructure in the sky provides a respite irrespective of traffic conditions, weather and crowds, and nurtures the spatial relationship between public and private. Most privately owned spaces are now publicly accessible, blurring circulation and program. Elevated tunnels are transformed into salons and dance halls; walkways for recreation, afternoon naps and exercise; and footbridges for political protests.

Cincinnati, Dallas, Des Moines, and Minneapolis are amongst American cities to have notable elevated walkway systems, often enclosed and climatically controlled. The Minneapolis Skyway System is the world's largest continuous system of over 13 kilometers that connects 69 blocks in the downtown.[14] Like most skywalks in America, the second-level pedestrian connections have been privately owned, developed, and operated. In Canada, the Plus 15 Skyway network in Calgary has a total of 62 discontinuous single and multi-level skywalks to provide 18 kilometers of comfort in climate-controlled circulation, which is extremely valuable during the city's long, harsh, snowy winters. Apart from economic activities, indoor urban parks and vegetated spaces can also be found throughout the system.[15]

Unlike the popular elevated walkways in Hong Kong and the Minneapolis Skyway System, the discontinuous skywalks in Mumbai have become a story of dissent. A joint initiative of the Mumbai Metropolitan Region Development Authority (MMRDA) and the Maharshtra State Road Development Corporation (MSRDC), the 36 skywalks stretching 17 kilometers in total were intended to lift the city's foot soldiers above the gridlock of cars, rickshaws, motorcycles and the crowds of pedestrians, street vendors and squatters.[16] More than half of Mumbai's 22 million inhabitants walk, making it one of the most pedestrian-powered metropolises in the world. The four-meter wide elevated express lanes, in theory, should provide better accessibility for pedestrians in the city, and connect them to targeted destinations like residential areas, bus stations, taxi stands, office spaces and shopping areas.

Many Indian city inhabitants, however, have questioned and disapproved of the infrastructure provided; despite that the skywalks were initiated in good faith as a solution for a healthier city with reduced

previous pages: Historians believe the Colosseum in Rome could even been flooded to host naumachia / navalia proelia (mock sea-battles).

9. WL MacDonald, 'The Architecture of the Roman Empire: An urban appraisal', Yale University Press, New Haven, 1988, p.115

10. The San Francisco Municipal Transport Agency (SFMTA), 'Cable Car: Background' [https://www.sfmta.com/about-sfmta/our-history-and-fleet/sfmta-fleet/cable-cars], retrieved 28 April 2015

11. E Echeverria & W Rice, 'San Francisco's Powell Street Cable Cars', Arcadia Publishing, San Francisco, 2005, p.105

12. P Elias, 'San Francisco's Iconic Cable Cars Cost City Millions of Dollars in Legal Settlements', The Associated Press, 15 April 2013 [http://news.yahoo.com/san-franciscos-iconic-cable-cars-cost-city-millions-134618616.html], retrieved 28 April 2015

13. A Frampton, JD Solomon & C Wong, 'Cities Without Ground: A Hong Kong guidebook', ORO Editions, Hong Kong, 2012, p.6

14. C James, 'Minneapolis Skyway System', About Travel, [http://minneapolis.about.com/od/travelweather/a/skyways.htm], retrieved 5 November 2015

15. The City of Calgary, 'Calgary Plus15 Skywalk' [http://www.calgary.ca/PDA/pd/Pages/Centre-City/Calgarys-Plus15-Skywalk.aspx], retrieved 5 November 2015

16. M Rao, 'Mumbai Skywalks: Are these elevated paths "ugly caterpillars" or precious public space?', The Guardian: Cities, 7 November 2015

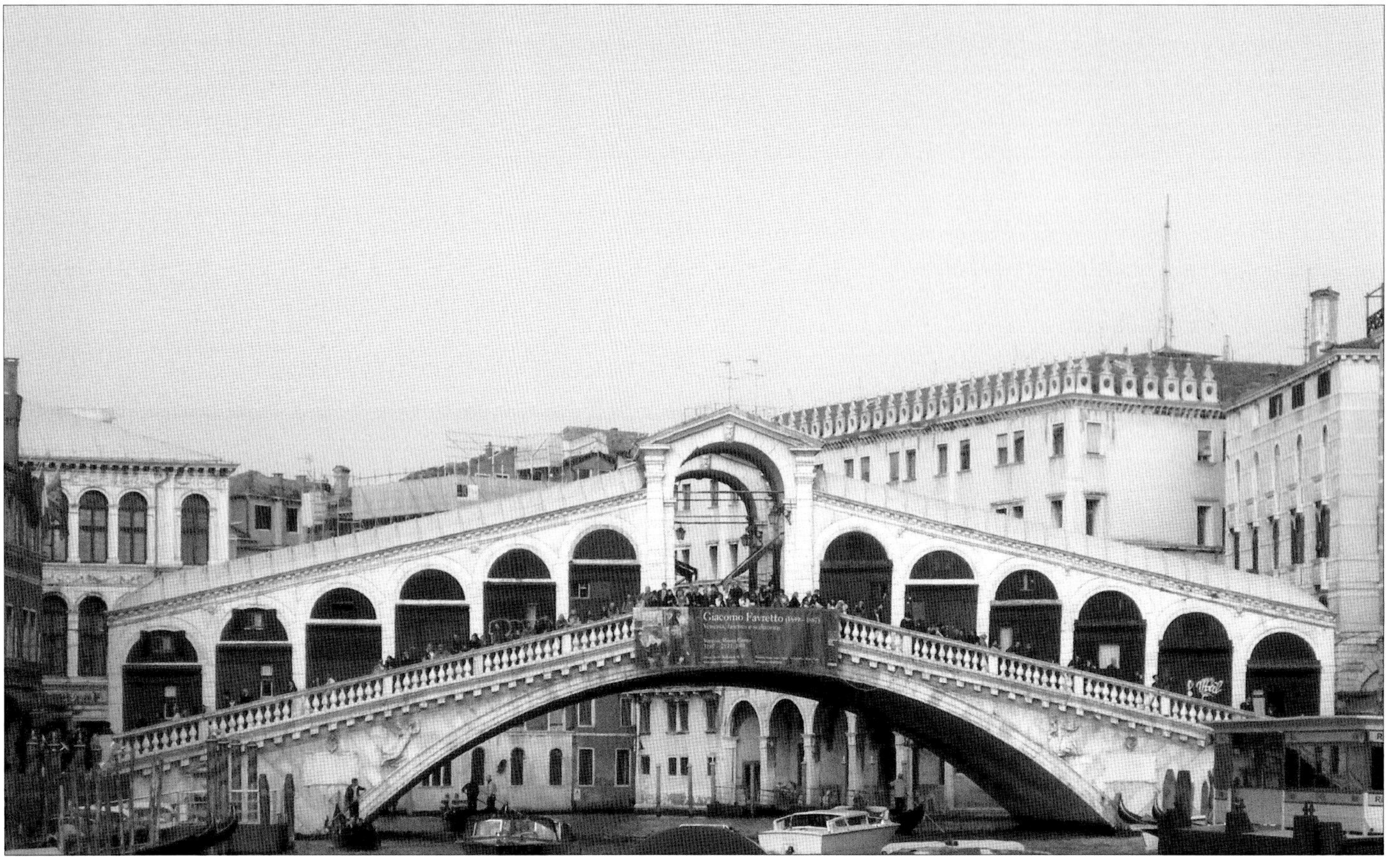
Giacomo Favretto

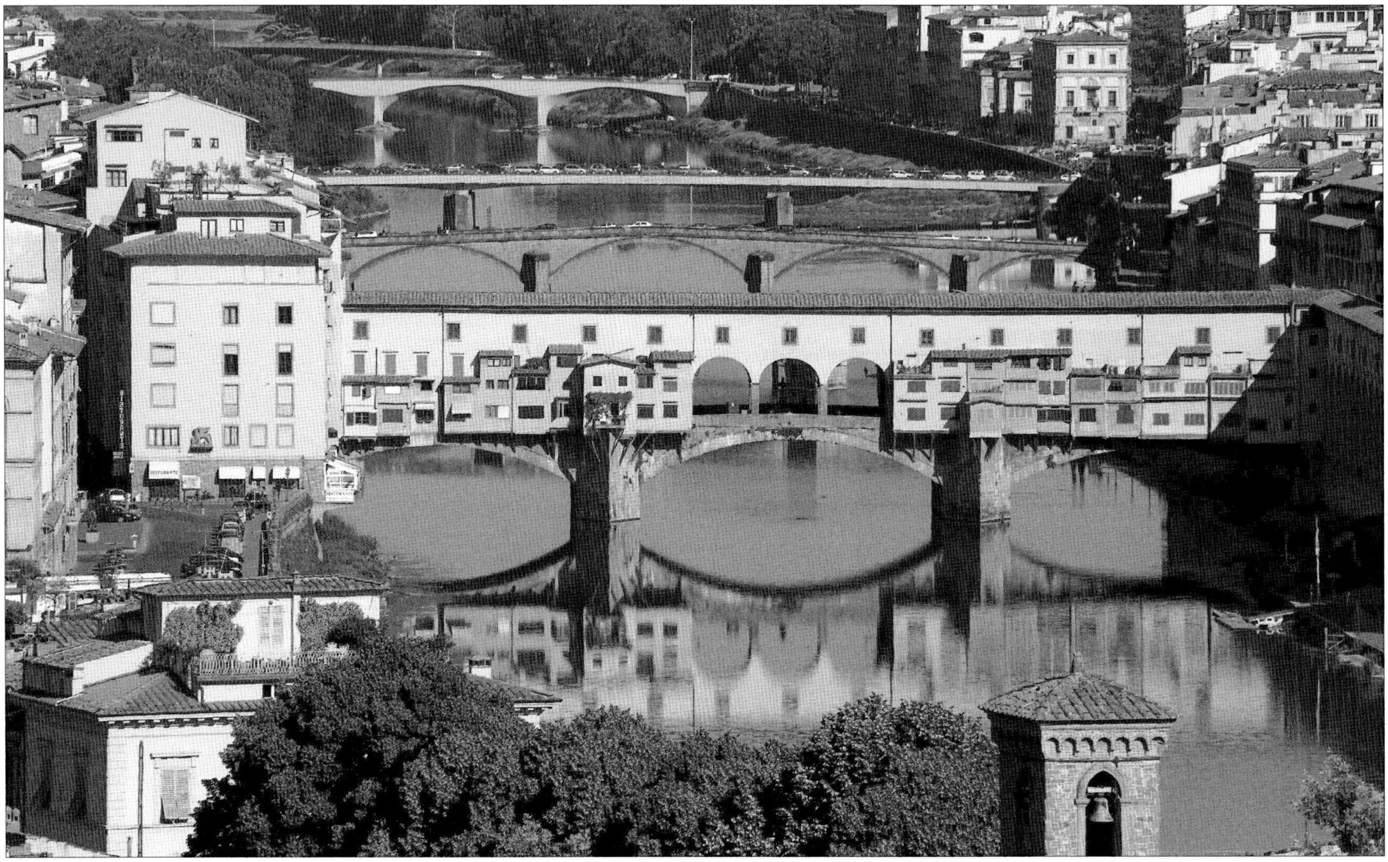

air and noise pollution. As a result of poor planning and public consultation, the negative impacts included deterioration of street-level business and activities, lack of access for the mobility-impaired and insufficient safety provisions for children who used the skywalks as a playground. Furthermore, the spaces along the skywalks have become clandestine meeting spots for young lovers notwithstanding the lack of privacy.[17] The Hindustan Times reported that '63.2% of people viewed the skywalks were not safe for women, especially at non-peak hours. 42.6% felt they were unsafe for everyone, with 81.4% going so far as to say that there needed to be full time security'.[18] Urban inhabitants in Mumbai and in many other cities are growing ever more resolute in asserting their needs for provision of safe public spaces, sustainable mobility and connected cities.

The Economic Miracle

The Suez Canal, inaugurated in 1869, stretches 190 kilometers and would become the shortest trade route between east and west, connecting the Mediterranean and the Red Seas. Each day, around 50 ships pass through the canal, which has no system of locks and is only a single lane wide. Since 2014, new construction has begun to widen passing locations, which could double the capacity of ships passing through. Weighed down by terrorism and regional conflict, the Egyptian government hopes the infrastructure will rescue the country's economy, generate US$100 billion in revenue and create one million jobs. Over 40,000 workers are employed since construction began, moving a total of half a trillion cubic meters of earth – equivalent to moving 200 Great Pyramids.[19]

The planned expansion, however, has alarmed marine biology organizations. For decades, massive swarms of jellyfish from the Red Sea have been pouring into the Mediterranean Sea through the canal, and the situation can only get worse by doubling the capacity of the flow. The UN's Mediterranean Action Plan, an organization tasked with protecting the sea, has raised concerns that the canal expansion might have contravened the Barcelona Convention – an agreement to minimize pollution and species invasions in the Mediterranean. Furthermore, global warming has been linked to aiding the invaders by making it easier for tropical Red Sea species to survive in the cooler Mediterranean. Scientists have recommended the installation of salinity locks within the infrastructure, a way of alleviating the impact of the canal expansion.[20]

Invasive Ground

Seemingly forever at war, Afghanistan has received many years of specialized infrastructural development. Its sandy ground in the south and rocky Hindu Kush Mountains in the north have been transformed into state-of-the art invasion sites. The harsh ground conditions have led to innovative and long lasting infrastructures that not only tame the natural landscape, but may also provide a key tactical advantage for foreign military efforts.

In 'Post-Traumatic Urbanism', Tarsha Finney explored how existing military infrastructures of airports, roads, accommodation, and unskilled concentrations of labor have given the USA and its allies an important leg-up in the current conflict.[21] Bagram Airbase, built by the Soviets in the 1960s, was greatly expanded and updated by the US military for over a decade since 2001, and as of 2010 was

facing page top & bottom: The inhabitable bridges of Ponte di Rialto in Venice and Ponte Vecchio in Florence are the precursors to the elevated walkways.

17. M Rao, 'Mumbai Skywalks: Are these elevated paths "ugly caterpillars" or precious public space?', The Guardian: Cities, 7 November 2015

18. S Manazir, 'A Story of Demand and Dissent for Mumbai's Skywalks', The City Fix: Urban Development, World Resource Institute Ross Center for Sustainable Cities, May 2014 [http://thecityfix.com/blog/story-demand-dissent-mumbai-skywalk-pedestrian-mobility-india-sharique-manazir], retrieved 7 November 2015

19. 'Egypt's Ambition: The Suez Canal, then and now', CNN: Middle East, 28 July 2015 [http://www.cnn.com/2015/07/28/middleeast/gallery/egpyt-suez-canal-then-now], retrieved 30 July 2015

20. T Ireland, 'The Great Invasion', New Scientist, 28 February 2015, pp.46–47

21. T Finney, 'Post-Traumatic Urbanism' in 'Architectural Design', A Lahoud, C Rice & A Burke (eds.), Wiley, London, Sept/Oct 2010, no.27, pp.65–69

a 2,100-hectare compound complete with all manner of modern American amenities including fast food chains KFC, Pizza Hut, TGI Friday's and McDonalds. There was a temporary ban on fast food but decisions were overturned, 'General McChrystal had little patience for the fast-food outlets that he viewed as unnecessary luxuries; he told senior officers that he was shuttering the fast-food franchises because he did not want to be the first American general to tell a grieving mother that her son died delivering frozen pizza'. The sophisticated city allows both military prowess with its historic foundations and troop psychological welfare by offering a 'taste of home'.[22] Concrete and tarmac construction takes time; so for much of the Bagram site, the invasion force used Marsden Matting to increase useable surface area, a type of pierced steel planking (PSP) which forms a rapidly deployable ground surface suitable for vehicles or even aircraft runways. Previously, the material was effectively used in World War II and the Korean and Vietnam Wars, while surplus or reclaimed PSP has been used in various civil engineering applications such as fencing, road and bridge construction including examples in Southeast Asia.[23]

With the building and re-building of better infrastructure, including roads, come exacerbated tensions in Afghan communities where land rights have given way to military 'peace-building' strategies. Once the military advantage of the infrastructure is no longer pertinent, the hard infrastructure itself brings its own conflicts. In 'Road Infrastructure Reconstruction as a Peace-building Priority in Afghanistan: Negative implications for land rights, John Unruh and Mourad Shalaby argued that unconsidered improvements to infrastructure may be detrimental to peace rather than working as true peace-building initiatives. 'Donors assume that road (re)construction will lead to economic development, peace, and security, but road (re)construction has undermined the land tenure system. Given the interaction's often-negative outcomes in conflict-affected areas, those tasked with security and development should at least change their approach so that well-placed Afghans do not benefit at the expense of the majority who cannot legally or non-violently defend their rights.'[24]

A Symbol of Hope and Glory
While the Dutch cannot actually claim to have discovered the application of wind to turn mills, the windmill is probably the most emblematic image of the Netherlands. Since the 14th century, the infrastructure has been draining water off the low-lying wetlands and lakes to make fertile agriculture polders. In addition, windmills powered a range of activities from the production of grain, oil, and paper, to sawing timber for the construction of massive fleets which enabled the Netherlands to lead in 17th century world-trading. From that time, painters have often employed the windmill to profile the Dutch Golden Age. Historians have suggested that Rembrandt van Rijn's 'The Mill' (1645-1648) 'made historical and cultural reference to the Netherlands' struggle for independence, which had been won from Spain in 1648 after 80 years of intermittent war. The painting is an image of strength and calm in the breaking light after a storm.'[25] The windmill was portrayed as a political symbol of human aspirations and a celebratory statement of hope and glory. Today, less than 10% of Dutch windmills remain out of the 9,000 that stood 200 years ago. However, the remaining examples are inspiring totems of national identity, standing like proud guardians of the threatened landscape and its people, and were still regulating inland water levels until recent times. Kinderdijk, a group of UNESCO World Heritage Listed mills, is conserved in order to highlight the historic struggle between the Dutch nation and flooding.[26]

While the windmill developed into a cultural phenomenon in the Netherlands, the infrastructure also served practical multi-functional purposes and advanced many economies around the world. The Greek engineer Heron of Alexandria was the mastermind of the first known example of using a wind-powered wheel to drive a machine in the 1st century AD, while Babylonian emperors employed wind power to achieve massive feats of irrigation technology.[27] Legend has it that Persian millwrights were posted by the Mongolian emperor Genghis Khan to China to build irrigation windmills.[28]

From about the 12th century, windmills started to enliven the pastoral English settings of wheat and corn country where they were used for processing grain.[29] For English Romantic painters of landscapes John Constable and John Linnell, the windmill was an important motif. Often washed white with black sails, there were three basic designs of the European windmill. The post mills and smock mills were portable timber infrastructures, capable of being moved from one site to another to find more or freer winds. The entire structure of the post mill rotated on a massive wooden column to allow the blades to face the wind. The tower mills, set atop a permanent stationary brick tower, had revolving caps to carry the sails, windshaft and brake-wheels.[30] It was common to house the miller and his family within the slow-moving and clumsy inhabitable infrastructure, as mills required constant attendance, for reasons of security and maintenance. Locating the windmill close to areas of production was key to reducing the transportation cost of harvested crops; flour could then be sold direct from mill to market.

The windpump mills have become a ubiquitous feature of the landscape throughout rural America. By the mid-1880s, over six million windpumps were installed on farms and ranches all over the central plains and southwest.[31] By pointing automatically into the wind via a tail vane, they generate mechanical power to drive a pump shaft up and down to draw water from deep underground aquifers. The infrastructure typically feature around 20 or more steel or wooden blades, a hand-dug well, an 'A' frame timber tower, and an accompanying timber tank-house for water storage. One of the most important factors contributing to the development of the southern Great Plains was the use of windmills to supply water for steam locomotives. They were also indispensable during the construction of the railroads to provide drinking water for the crews, where there was a windpump every three miles along the tracks.[32]

Today, thousands of wind turbines are distributed across fields and offshore locations around Europe, China, the USA and Canada. The wind turbine is a new version of an old idea. The world's largest-capacity wind turbine of 8.0 MW, the Vestas V164, has blades of 164 meters in diameter on a 220-meter tall steel pin-tower. Denmark's Vestas Wind Systems, the world's largest manufacturer of wind turbines, stand by their estimation that by 2020, as much as 10% of the world's electricity consumption can be provided by wind. They believe that 'policy makers around the world stand before a historic opportunity to meet the growing demand for energy without inflicting substantial costs to society due to adapting to climate change and pollution'.[33]

Probably 10% is not enough. We have not adapted as fast as we need to match the severity of circumstance. A modern five-megawatt turbine has operational efficiencies of 75–80%; they are engineered to be streamlined and flexible at high wind forces.[34] Jiuquan Wind Power Base in Gansu Province in China is one of the world's largest wind farms and has a production of 90,000 GWh per annum. Even then, China may just have 1% capacity for this type of wind energy. It is not the feasibility of wind farms that causes the low uptake-percentage, instead it may be due to lack of appropriate electric grid services.[35]

22. M Rosenburg, 'Afghan Forces Eat Up Return of Fast Food', Wall Street Journal, 22 February 2011 [http://www.wsj.com/articles/SB10001424052748703610604576158610111737164], retrieved 28 November 2014

23. Photos from Tarawa, 'Marsden Matting PSP', Tarawa – The Aftermath [http://tarawatheaftermath.com/Photos27.html], retrieved 28 November 2014

24. J Unruh & M Shalaby, 'Road Infrastructure Reconstruction as a Peace-building Priority in Afghanistan: Negative implications for land rights' in 'Assessing and Restoring Natural Resources in Post-Conflict Peace-building', D Jensen & S Lonergan (eds.), Earthscan, London, 2012, p.383

25. C Brenner, J Riddell & B Moore, 'Painting in the Dutch Golden Age: A profile of the seventeenth century', National Gallery of Art Washington, 2007, pp.10–12

26. PH Nienhuis, 'Environmental History of the Rhine-Meuse Delta', Springer, New York, 2008, p.88

27. M Sathyajith, 'Wind Energy: Fundamentals, resource analysis and economics', Springer, Berlin, 2006, pp.1–9

28. JJ Butt, 'The Greenwood Dictionary of World History', Greenwood Press, Westport, 2006, p.353

29. S Beedell, 'Windmills', David & Charles Publishers, London, 1975, p.13

30. JM Richards, 'The Functional Tradition in Early Industrial Buildings', The Architectural Press, London, pp.128–129

31. RW Righter, 'Wind Energy in America: A history', University of Oklahoma Press, USA, 1996, p.28

32. G Nash & J Waterman, 'Homesteading in the 21st Century', The Taunton Press, Newtown, USA, 2011, p.60

33. 'About: Discover Wind', Vestas, Denmark [http://www.vestas.com/en/about/discover_wind#!why-wind], retrieved 28 March 2015

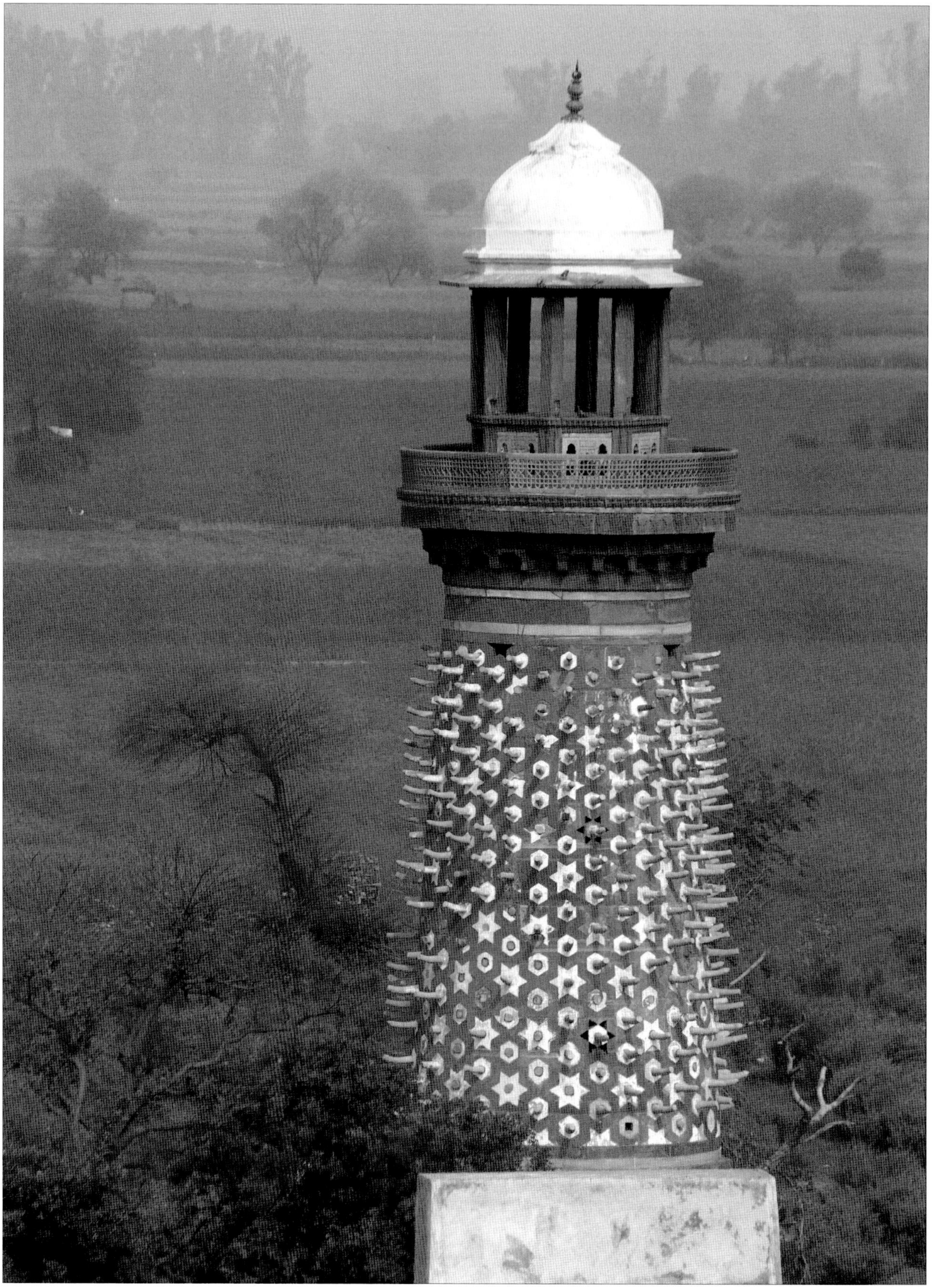

The USA is the world number one wind energy producer, leading China and Germany – a victory for American productivity. Wind provided enough electricity to power the equivalent of 16.7 million homes, or all the residential households in Iowa, Kansas, Minnesota, Nebraska, North Dakota, South Dakota, Colorado, Idaho, Illinois, and Montana. The American wind energy industry has built a new domestic manufacturing sector with 500 factories in 43 states, attracts an average of $15 billion a year in private investment into the US economy, and supports an average of 73,000 jobs.[36] In the meantime, the wind turbines have reduced carbon dioxide pollution by around 125 million metric tons in 2014, equivalent to 26 million cars' worth of carbon emissions.[37] The US Department of Energy's 'The Wind Vision Report', projected that wind energy could generate 10% of the country's electricity in 2020, 20% in 2030, and 35% in 2050.[38]

There have been endless political debates about the use of wind turbines in many European locations, including the huge potential resource in the Scottish coastal waters. In 2015, the UK Government announced that onshore wind farm subsidies are to end within a year. Chris Grayling, the leader of the house at that time, declared that 'this Government is committed to renewable energy, but I am afraid that my idea of renewable energy does not involve covering some of the most beautiful parts of the United Kingdom and the highlands of Scotland with wind farms. I want to cherish and protect the countryside for future generations.'[39] Wind-farms are perceived as un-aesthetic and damaging to the environment, and whether or not they are more ugly than the effects of climate change or more damaging than fossil fuel is entirely debatable. As for the British countryside, 'it is oversubscribed with multiple and often irreconcilable demands. The countryside is in conflict, and it is not just from wind turbines.'[40]

Fresh appraisal, financial support and actions are urgently required to identify wind as one of our key alternatives to fossil fuel. Wind power is an affordable, efficient and abundant renewable source that is pollution-free. In centuries to come wind turbines will be admired in the way traditional windmills are now. Perhaps, future Constables and Rembrandts have an important role to play in cultivating new ways of seeing these technological infrastructures as icons of hope and glory for a sustainable future.

For Greed's Sake
James Lovelock, scientist, environmentalist and futurist, believes that we will need to resort to genetically modified crops on a global scale in order to stave off catastrophe. He has advocated the synthesis of fermented food from air, water and trace chemicals as the staple gastronomic future. Prior to Lovelock, SF writers have long peddled the notion of synthetic food superseding agriculture; but until such time, food safety and technology for preserving food are still of great interest to mankind.

The potential of radiant cooling from the night sky and cool north sky in the day was first developed many centuries ago in the 'yakh-chal' of ancient Persia.[41] The cold storage infrastructure made it possible to produce ice, and preserve dairy products and meats in arid deserts with temperatures reaching 40 degrees centigrade. Its thick shadowing walls of sand, clay, egg whites, lime, goat hair, and ash mortar, enclosed an approximate area of 5,000–8,000 square meters. The huge dome structure included an underground ice-production pit and two ice-corridors: one for storing ice blocks in winter, and the other

facing page: The Hira Minar (the Elephant Tower) in Fatehpur Sikri, is thought to be a hunting tower and a lighthouse for night travelers. Lamps were hung on the protruding tusks.

34. 'Wind Energy Converters: Product overview', Energon Germany [http://www.enercon.de/p/downloads/EN_Productoverview_0710.pdf], retrieved 21 March 2015

35. 'China Starts Building First 10-GW Mega Wind Farm', Reuters, 08 Aug 2009 [http://www.reuters.com/article/2009/08/08/us-china-wind-power-idUSTRE57711P20090808], retrieved 21 March 2015

36. 'US Is World's Number One Wind Energy Producer, Leading China and Germany', American Wind Energy Association [http://www.awea.org/MediaCenter/pressrelease.aspx?ItemNumber=6965], retrieved 21 March 2015

37. 'Wind Was Largest Source of New Electricity in 2014, Congress Still Must Provide Long-term Policy Certainty', American Wind Energy Association [http://www.awea.org/MediaCenter/pressrelease.aspx?ItemNumber=7294], retrieved 22 March 2015

38. 'Wind Vision: A new era for wind power in the United States', The US Department of Energy [http://www.energy.gov/sites/prod/files/WindVision_Report_final.pdf], retrieved 20 March 2015

39. E Gosden, 'Wind Farm Subsidies Axed To Stop Turbines Covering Beautiful Countryside', The Telegraph, 18 June 2015 [http://www.telegraph.co.uk/news/earth/energy/windpower/11685082/Wind-farm-subsidies-axed-to-stop-turbines-covering-beautiful-countryside.html], retrieved 25 June 2015

40. MJ Pasqualetti, P Gipe & RW Righte, 'Wind Power in View: Energy landscapes in a crowded world', Academic Press, London, 2002, p.46

41. D Bainbridge & K Haggard, 'Passive Solar Architecture: Heating, cooling, ventilation, daylighting and more using natural flows', Chelsea Green Publishing Company, White River Junction, 2012, p.101

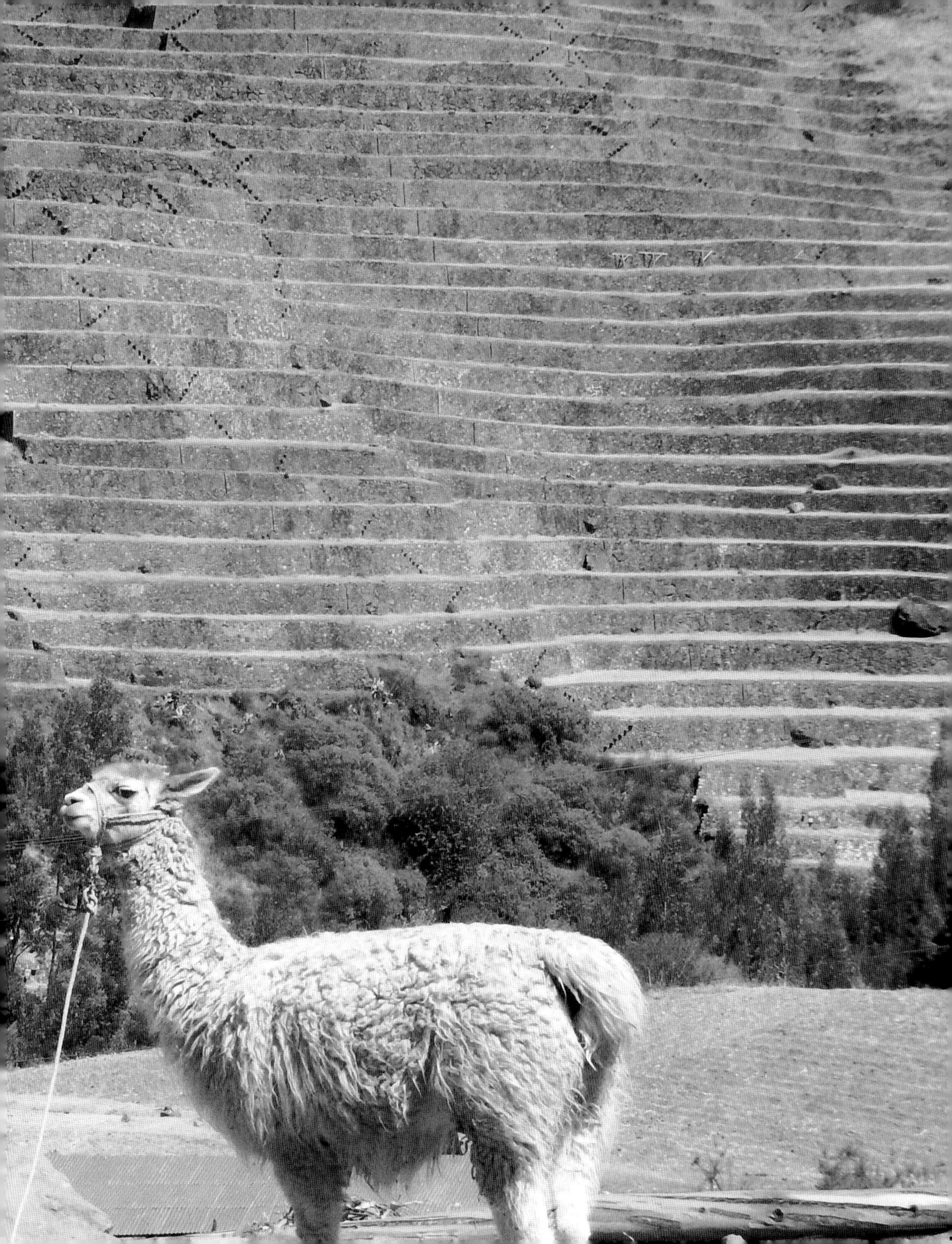

for taking them out in the summer months. The space often had access to a qanat for fresh water supply, and was equipped with 'badgirs', a system of wind-catchers to reduce internal temperatures.[42] The oldest remaining ice-chamber in Iran, the Meybod, is 50 kilometers north of Yazd, located along a caravan road adjacent to a caravanserai.

On the east coast of the USA, large-scale harvesting of natural ice in winter from lakes and rivers was a major part of the economy in the 19th century. Ice trade revolutionized the meat, vegetable and fruit, and fish industries as well as domestic food safety and consumption. Since the first shipment of New England ice from America to the Caribbean Island of Martinique, the global trade traveled as far as India, South America, Southeast Asia and Australia. Icehouses became mandatory infrastructure in many cities to facilitate the storage of ice between harvesting, trade and its final sale. Early timber icehouses, insulated with peat and sawdust,[43] were relatively small compared to the later brick infrastructures that have the capacity to hold up to 250,000 tons of ice.[44] Painted either white or yellow in order to reflect the sun during the summer months, a typical Hudson River depot would be 120 meters long, 30 meters deep, three stories high, and able to hold 50,000 tons of ice.[45] At Wolf Lake, Indiana, conveyor belts raised uniform blocks of the frozen commodity to the top of icehouses to be lowered into place for storage with vertical lifts. Major ice consuming cities, London, Sydney and Hong Kong, have dedicated icehouses near the ports to hold the luxurious imported product.

By the 1880s, New York was the largest ice market in the USA. Not only did the city require ever-increasing amounts of ice to keep food from spoiling as it moved through the increasingly complex distribution system, but the consumption of ice cream and ice beverages became one of the most desired activities at the city's pleasure gardens. Preceding public parks, pleasure gardens were grand venues where upper-class city inhabitants would gather and be seen, and be treated to theatrical performances, concerts, and fireworks.[46] Thus, the icehouses inadvertently enabled food safety and cultural development in the city. The American ice trade continued to flourish until the advent of electric refrigerators and freezers. Today the bulky icehouses are replaced by the even larger infrastructure of the 'cold chain'.

In 'Grain Elevators' (1993), Aldo Rossi described the industrial elevators of the Midwest of America as 'cathedrals of our times and is the collective memory of a place (parts of central Europe). Over time the silos rose with ever greater assurance and created the landscape of the New World. In abandoning the problem of form, they rediscovered architecture.'[47] The urban concrete silo is larger and more mechanically sophisticated than the seven- to eleven-storey rural wooden varieties. These conspicuous infrastructures on the Great Plains can be up to 120 feet high and large enough to store the annual produce of a hundred farms. Urban silos have the capacity to sort and clean grain, and are positioned on the edge of cities, near transport infrastructures of rail and waterways. Historically significant urban silos can be found in Minneapolis and Buffalo, both important centers for the international distribution of grain. There is a silo in Hutchinson, Kansas, that measures 2,600 feet, the length of nearly 10 New York blocks.[48]

Grain elevators, silos, and granaries are soft infrastructure that forms an almost universal typology for settlements. Ancient Egyptians were possibly the first to develop the silo to protect food from human and animal contamination, and also kept the grain cool, dry and ensured that it would last beyond the non-harvest months. Granaries were often lifted off the ground to avoid pests and vermin. Bernard Rudofsky commented on the sacred nature of granary buildings, 'such dignity is by no means accidental – most peasants have a religious respect for bread and the stuff that goes into its making'.[49] Similar consecration is found of granaries from the Spanish province of Galicia, and those of the Dogon people in Mali. Constructed from large granite slabs, the Spanish 'horreo' rests on pillars topped by circular stones to act as rat-guards; elegant patterns of apertures in the wall serve as ventilation. The inhabitants of Cabao in Libya built a multi-use infrastructure that integrated the storehouses and the ancient defensive wall.[50]

By the 19th century, the utilitarian infrastructures are often found close to the source of food, or where raw materials can be secured at a minimum of expenditure for transportation. They can be found everywhere, the countryside, suburbs, and not just limited to the fringes of cities with a large consuming market.

previous pages: Terraces increase the area available for agriculture in the Sacred Valley in Peru.

The Flying Pig, The Power Station and Other Utilitarian Castles

'Algie' was the nine-meter pink porcine inflatable which flew over London's imposing Battersea Power Station – the dystopian image from the cover of Pink Floyd's 1977 album 'Animals', a bitter, anti-capitalist, and scathing critique of late-70s Britain. The helium-filled inflatable famously broke loose from one of the chimneys, and caused air traffic chaos before eventually floating off to a farm in Kent.[51] Inspired by George Orwell's book 'Animal Farm' (1945) and built by a German zeppelin manufacturer Ballon Fabrik, Algie has often been credited for the power station's international fame. The Battersea Power Station, a grand brick and steel structure, was built for the London Power Company in two principal phases between 1929 and 1941, with the fourth (SE) chimney being added in 1955. In the 1950s, the utilitarian castle produced a fifth of all London's electricity, and was the first British power station to rationalize large-scale electricity distribution under the National Grid. When the album came out, the generators were still in action; the last coal-fired power station was decommissioned in 1983.[52] The infrastructure is now protected by its Grade II listing, and has been the subject of numerous failed mixed-use adaptations.

The power station has made numerous virtual appearances, from the long-running British SF television series 'Doctor Who', to a cameo for the exterior of a London railroad station in Michael Radford's adaptation of George Orwell's 'Nineteen Eighty Four'. In the film version of PD James's dystopian SF 'Children of Men' (1992), the director Alfonso Cuarón cross-referenced real and historical imagery of Algie and the power station, with fictional events and futuristic beliefs to disseminate the theme of societal misery and futility of a collapsed nation in 2027.[53] The power station portrayed a fictional Ministry of Arts, a repository of artistic treasures preserved for a posterity that will never materialize.

Another instantly recognizable London backdrop, the gasometer adjacent to the world's most famous cricket ground, The Oval, was decommissioned in 2014 to make way for housing and commercial development, regardless of its historical or architectural significance. The novelist Will Self described the demise of the utilitarian castle as 'just another casualty of the relentless spatialisation of international capital flows that is London's new skyline'.[54]

Gasometers appeared on the British urban landscape in the first half of the 19th century to store the gas produced in adjacent gasworks, which was used to light streets and homes. The first telescopic gasometer was built in Leeds, and had a pressurised container on a floating water reservoir which rose and fell along vertical runners within an external frame. The spiral gasometer had guiding rails coiling up the side of the tank so that effectively it screwed itself up and down, while the waterless

42. AN Angelakis, LW Mays & D Koutsoyiannis, 'Evolution of Water Supply Through the Millennia', IWA Publishing, London, 2012, pp.116–117

43. G Weightman, 'The Frozen Water Trade: How ice from New England lakes kept the world cool', Harper Collins, London, 2003, p.45

44. G Weightman, 'The Frozen Water Trade: How ice from New England lakes kept the world cool', Harper Collins, London, 2003, p.170

45. D Calandro, 'Hudson River Valley Icehouses and Ice Industry', Hudson River Valley Institute, New York, 2005, p.2

46. WE Harris & A Pickman, 'The Rise and Demise of the Hudson River Ice Harvesting Industry: Urban needs and rural responses' in 'Environmental History of the Hudson River', RE Henshaw (ed.), State University of New York Press, Albany, 2011, p.203

47. L Mahar-Keplinger, 'Grain Elevators', Princeton Architectural Press, New York, 1993, p.7

48. L Mahar-Keplinger, 'Grain Elevators', Princeton Architectural Press, New York, 1993, pp.12–14

49. B Rudofsky, 'Architecture Without Architects', Museum of Modern Art, New York, 1964, p.20

50. B Rudofsky, 'Architecture Without Architects', Museum of Modern Art, New York, 1964, pp.90–101

51. N Mason, 'Inside Out: A personal history of Pink Floyd', Weidenfeld & Nicolson, London, 2004, pp.228–229

KIA MOTORS
KIA MOTORS
OCTOPUS INVESTMENTS #gamechanger
OCTOPUS INVESTMENTS #gamechanger
TRAVELBAG
KIA MOTORS THE KIA OVAL
RAPID
An almighty hit
Colman's

TRAVELBAG
Worldwide Holidays
TRAVELBAG
JMFinn&Co
KIA MOTORS
KIA MOTORS
19
20
A MOTORS
KIA MOTORS
FOSTER'S
Specsavers
Specsavers
Specsavers
Specsavers

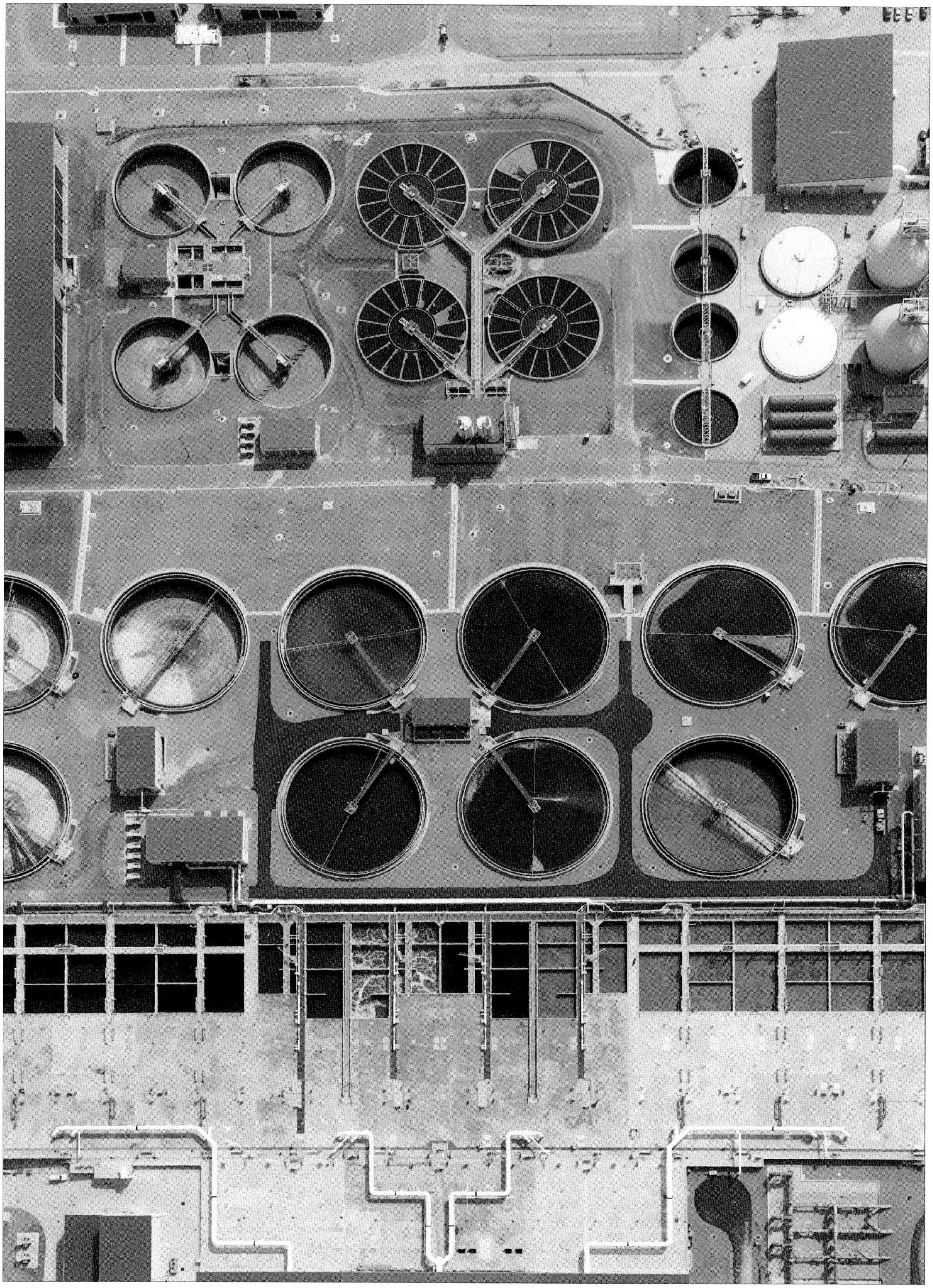

type employed the piston method of keeping the gas under pressure.⁵⁵ With a storage capacity of about two million cubic feet of gas, the infrastructure can supply over 2,000 homes – but across the country, gasometers outlived their use when the gas industry towns went into decline with the discovery of gas in the North Sea from the 1960s.

In 2013, National Grid announced plans to demolish a total of 76 gasometers across England, and Southern and Scottish Gas networks followed suit with their proposal to get rid of 111 over the next 16 years.⁵⁶ That process will deprive the urban skyline of its omnipresent Victorian feature as well as the city's industrial heritage. Gas helped build the urban fabric; the gasometer, a symbol of the modern city, must be protected.

Likewise, imagine New York City's skyline without the collective patterns of iconic water towers, all perched high above the streets. The utilitarian rooftop castles with sumptuous domes, cupolas and spires have fed domestic standpipes and fire sprinklers since the 1920s. Although they first appear to be rustic-looking relics from times past, the thousands of remaining water towers are much revered across the city's five boroughs, and are still the first line of defense against fire for many of the city's high-rise buildings.⁵⁷ A water tower system is mandatory for every building six stories and above to ensure adequate water and to control water pressure.

The New York water system has a total storage capacity of 580 billion gallons and is impounded in three upstate reservoir systems, which include 19 reservoirs and three controlled lakes.⁵⁸ The three water collection systems have various interconnections to increase flexibility by permitting exchange of water from one to another. Daily water consumption in New York City is more than 1 billion gallons,⁵⁹ with approximately 95% of the total water supply being delivered to buildings by gravity. In each building, an electric pump pushes the water from the basement to roof, and it takes two to three hours to fill the average 10,000-gallon tank. From the water tower, gravity provides water pressure and enables controlled distribution within the building.

There is an inquisitive beauty in the water towers, alongside other mechanical infrastructure of chimneys, ventilators and ironworks, jostling for the city's air rights. The landmarked sky reservoirs have appeared in Edward Hopper's soulful paintings and Saul Steinberg's 'View of the World from 9th Avenue' (1976) for the New Yorker magazine.⁶⁰ So drawn to the uniqueness of the water towers in her view across the East River to Manhattan from Brooklyn, Rachel Whiteread installed a hollow resin version on the roof of the Museum of Modern Art. Whiteread's 'Water Tower' (1998) is 'a cast of the interior of a once-functioning cedar water tower. The translucent resin captures the qualities of the surrounding sky; the sculpture's color and brightness change throughout the day and it becomes a near-invisible whisper at night. Soaring and ephemeral, it inspires city–dwellers and visitors alike to look again at the solid, weighty water towers they usually see without noticing.'⁶¹ More recently, in 2014, Ed Ruscha, Bruce Webber, Icy & Sot, Jeff Koons, Andy Goldsworthy, and John Baldessari were amongst the creative and artistic luminaries who joined 'The Water Tank Project' campaign in New York. The Water Tank Project transformed 300 water towers into public artworks to create mass awareness around water

previous pages: The gasometer near The Oval is a utilitarian castle that contributes to the urban skyline of London as well as the city's industrial heritage.

facing page: Water treatment plant.

52. '1357620 - The National Heritage List for England', Historic England [http://list.historicengland.org.uk/resultsingle.aspx?uid=1357620], retrieved 16 August 2015

53. K Voynar, 'Interview: Children of Men Director Alfonso Cuaron', Moviefone, 2006 [http://news.moviefone.com/2006/12/25/Interview-children-ofmen-director-alfonso-cuaron/], retrieved 16 August 2015

54+56. S O'Hagan, 'Gasworks Wonders…', The Observer: Architecture, 14 June 2015

55. S Clifford & A King, 'England in Particular', Hodder & Stoughton, London, 2006, p.196

57. M Bromann, 'Fire Protection for Commercial Facilities', CRC Press, Boca Raton, 2011, pp.60–61

58. 'The Water Tank Project', New York, 2014 [http://www.thewatertankproject.org], retrieved 15 August 2015

59. NYC Open Data, 'The Water Consumption in the New York City', The City of New York [https://data.cityofnewyork.us/Environment/Water-Consumption-In-The-New-York-City/ia2d-e54m], retrieved 15 August 2015

60. S Roberts, 'A History of New York in 101 Objects', Simon & Schuster, New York, 2014, p.90

61. R Whiteread, 'Water Tower', Museum of Modern Art, New York, 1998 [http://www.moma.org/collection/works/82016], retrieved 15 August 2015

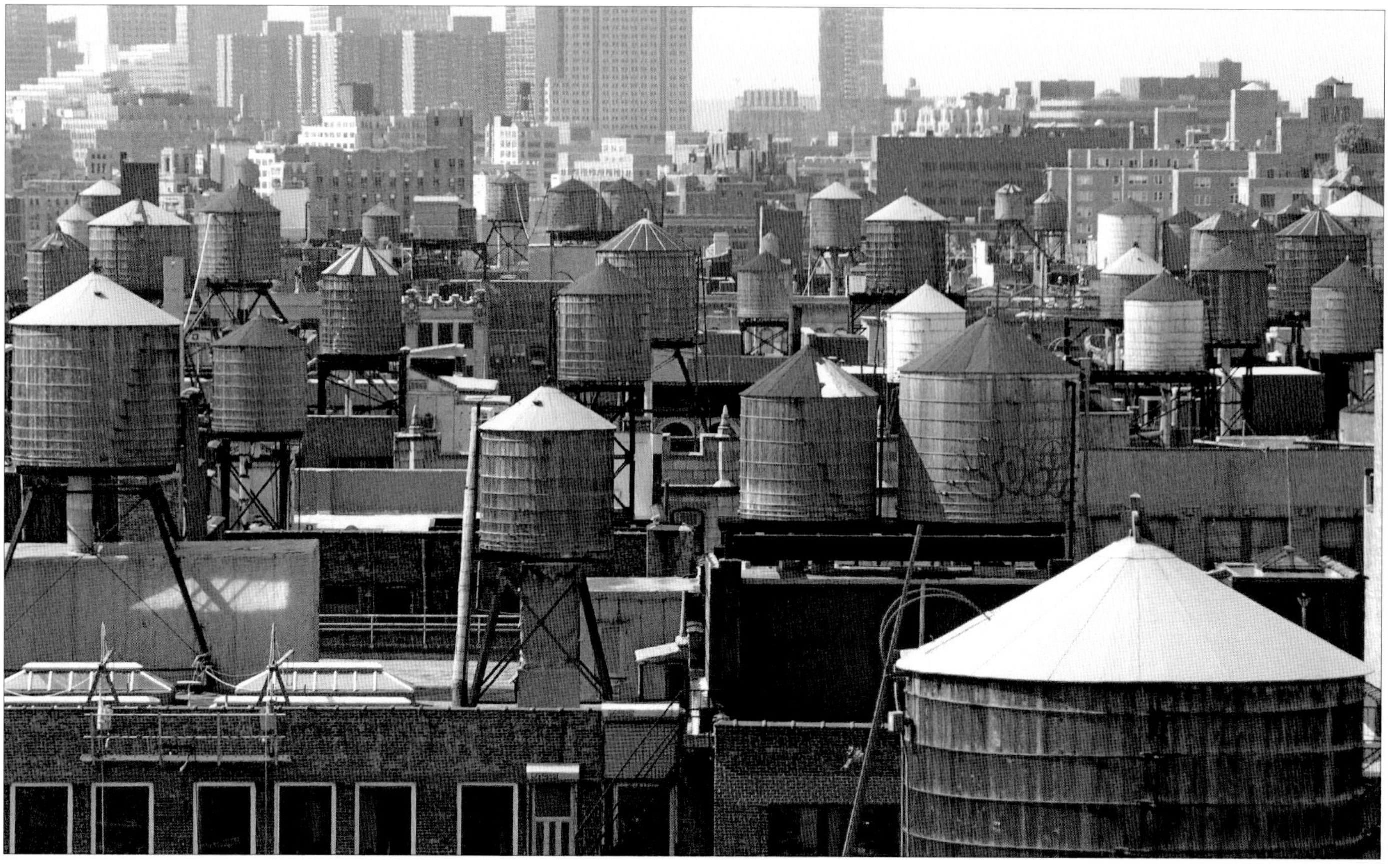

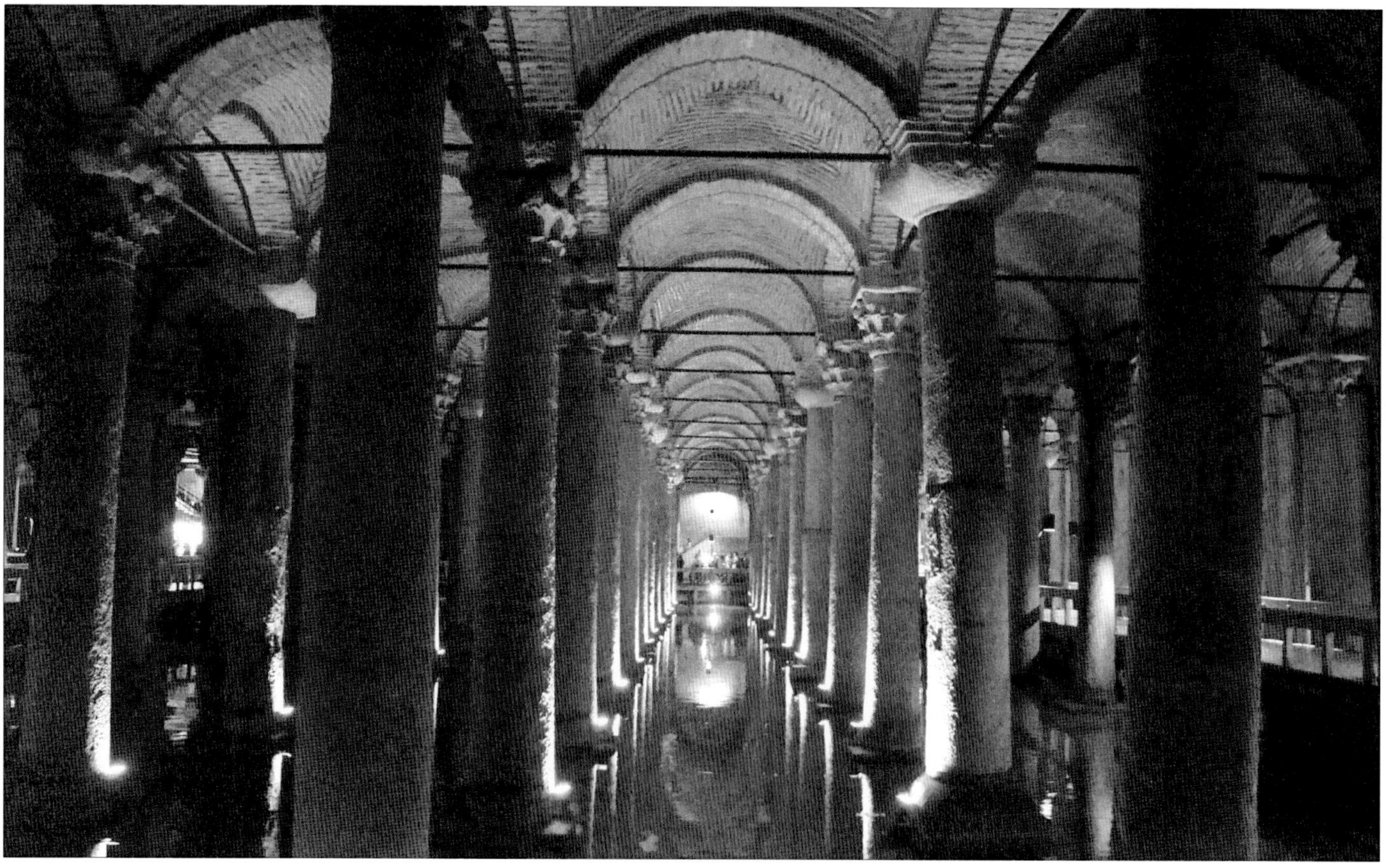

scarcity. It provided a platform to increase appreciation for the city's high quality drinking water, and the consequences of plastic waste that comes from bottled options, ultimately re-evaluating the culture associated with water consumption, conservation and waste.[62]

Water Revered and Secured

Historical efforts of establishing safe and consistent water sources have been crucial for the development of settlements and empires. Provisions of wells, ditches, cisterns and reservoirs are often central to the configuration of defensive complexes, and closely guarded. Wells also form traditional pilgrimage destinations such as St Winefride's Well in northern Wales. The life-giving dihydrogen monoxide (H2O) has been seen as a divine gift by thousands of pilgrims including notably Richard I and Henry V. Small bathing pools with changing tents were provided for those that were praying for the water's healing power.[63]

Beneath the buildings and streets of Istanbul, there were several hundred ancient cisterns. The largest of these man-made infrastructures for water security is the Basilica Cistern, known as 'The Sunken Palace', built by the Byzantine Emperor Justinian in the 6th century BC. Concealing an underground chamber of 9,800 square meters and held up by 336 nine-meter-high marble columns, the cistern has brick walls and floors, and is plastered with a thick layer of brick dust mortar for water tightness.[64] The cistern has an estimated water storage capacity of 85,000 cubic meters to meet the water needs of the Great Byzantine Palace above.[65] Other cisterns in Istanbul have seen many changes of use. Ottoman sultans used the Cistern of the Hebdomon as a stable for their elephants after the Fall of Constantinople.[66] The open-air Cistern of Aetius, with its Roman walls still visible, is now better known as Karagümrük (Vefa) Stadium, but in place of water, it still brings vitality to the city in the form of sport and green space enjoyed by up to 12,500 spectators.[67]

The undisputed marvel of water provision infrastructures is the underground stepwell. Since the third millennium BC in the Indian provinces of Gujarat and Rajasthan, thousands of stepwells were built to highlight the sanctity and scarcity of water. In these arid regions, the stepwells would harvest and preserve the few short weeks of intense monsoon rain to guarantee a year-round water supply for human needs. A stepwell can be adjacent to a temple or house with a temple or shrine within; at the edge of a village; or by the sides of an overland road, completely outside the village. There are three major constituent architectural parts to a stepwell – the vertical well with an arrangement for hauling water by buckets; the stepped corridor leading down from the entrance pavilion and ending at the water level of the well several storeys into the earth; and numerous shrines and balconies carved into the stone infrastructure to provide spaces to linger in the afternoon heat.[68]

Initially designed as inverted subterranean temples open to the sky for utilitarian purposes, the infrastructure became grand visions of intricate staircases and colonnades decorated with sumptuous carvings of deities, reaching deep into the ground to draw from the water table. During the rainy season, the wells filled up and the stepped corridor would disappear. In 2014, UNESCO's World Heritage committee listed the Rani-ki-Vav (the Queen's Stepwell), located in the North Gujarat district of Patan.

facing page top: New York's utilitarian rooftop castles of sumptuous domes, cupolas and spires.

facing page bottom: The Basilica Cistern is the largest of several hundred ancient water storage infrastructures that lie beneath the city of Istanbul.

62. 'The Water Tank Project', New York, 2014 [http://www.thewatertankproject.org], retrieved 15 August 2015

63. 'About the Well', St Winefride's Well [http://www.saintwinefrideswell.com/about-the-well/4569900184], retrieved 15 August 2015

64. JH Stubbs & EG Makas, 'Architectural Conservation in Europe and the Americas: National experiences and practice', John Wiley & Sons, New Jersey, 2011, p.339

65. R Maliva & T Missimer, 'Arid Lands Water Evaluation and Management', Springer, Heidelberg, 2012, p.502

66. A Mikhail, 'The Animal In Ottoman Egypt', Oxford University Press, Oxford, 2014, p.241

67. 'Club History', Karagümrük spor kulübü Official Website [http://karagumrukspor.com/tarihce-3-2-2-0-0-0], retrieved 21 March 2015

68. J Jain-Neubauer, 'The Stepwells of Gujarat: In art-historical perspective', Abhinav Publications, New Delhi, 1981, pp.2–3

188

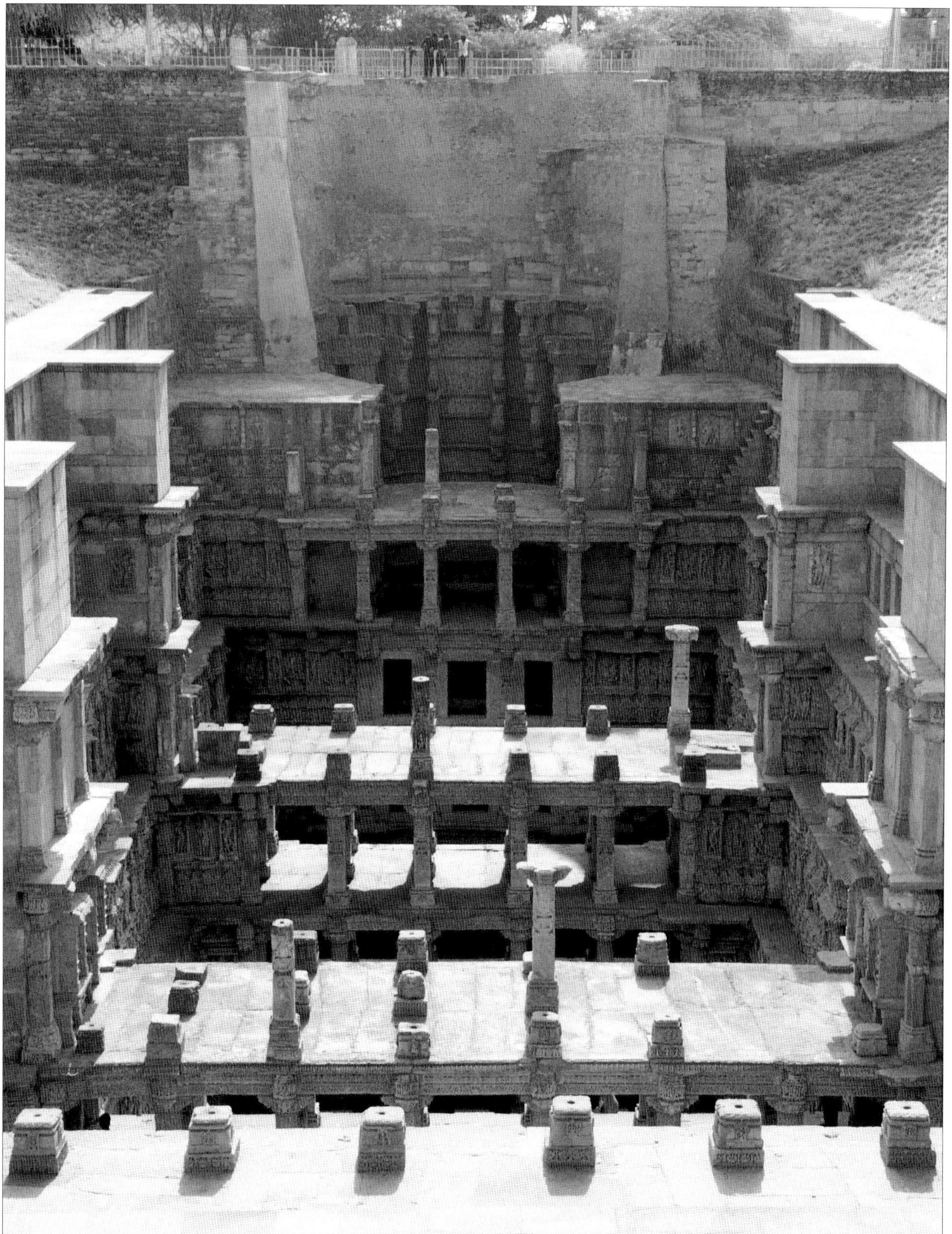

to provide

Built as a memorial to a king in the 11th century AD, the stepwell reflects the mastery of the complex craftsmanship and great beauty of detail and proportions of the Maru-Gurjara style. Divided into seven levels of stairs, it has a shaft that is 10 meters in diameter and 30 meters deep. The infrastructure is decorated with more than 500 principal and over a thousand minor religious, mythological and secular sculptures of high artistic quality, often referencing literary works.[69] In fact, the stepwell would have made a majestic portal to the fictional underlake city of Gungan on the planet of Naboo in the 'Star Wars' series.

Besides supplying water for drinking, washing, and irrigation to villages, the stepwells were considered true civic infrastructure of everyday life. For the women tasked with collecting water for daily use in their homes and on their land, the cool depth of the stepwells doubled up as places for social gathering and also a reprieve from their highly regimented existence. In 'Her Space, Her Story: Exploring the stepwells of Gujarat', Purnima Mehta Bhatt described how the inspirational infrastructure were 'often built to honor a virtuous wife or benevolent mother, a local goddess or a beloved mistress. Women have played a major role in the construction, linking the three worlds: the subterranean, the earthly and the celestial.'[70]

Sadly, centuries later, collecting and carrying water were and still are the domain and burdensome forced-responsibility of women. It remains a common sight to see women make multiple trips with their pitchers and pots to collect a day's supply of water. India has overused its water, forcing its women to search beyond their homes. The Water Project Inc., a nonprofit organization whose mission is unlocking human potential by providing sustainable water projects to communities in sub-Saharan Africa, has claimed that the walks in rural regions can 'average ten miles a day, carrying up to 15 liters on every trip. The pressure of carrying buckets of water on their heads, added with the distance to the sources, creates back, feet, and posture problems. It is a great loss for these women to be denied the opportunities to make an income, better care for their children, or in a younger girl's circumstance, be able to get a proper education.'[71]

The situation in India is similar to that of rural areas in many developing countries. According to Dr. Barbara van Koppen of the International Water Management Institute (IWMI), women spend large amounts of time collecting water; up to 119 minutes per day in South Africa; between 97 and 221 minutes per day in Sri Lanka; and as high as 416 minutes in the dry season in Tanzania. Despite the efforts, the average water availability in the sample villages is below 50 liters per person per day, the quantities recommended by the WHO. For South Africa, the average is even as low as 18 liters.[72]

'For the first time since the Cold War the German government is advising citizens to stockpile food and water for use in a national emergency. Citizens are advised to store enough food to last them 10 days, because initially a disaster might put national emergency services beyond reach. Five days' water – two liters per person daily – is advised. A major security threat to the nation in future could not be ruled out, so civil defence measures are necessary.'

– BBC News, 'Germans Told to Stockpile Food and Water for Civil Defence', 22 August 2016

facing page: Designed as an inverted temple to highlight the sanctity of water, the Rani-ki-Vav (the Queen's Stepwell) is divided into seven levels.

69. UNESCO World Heritage Centre, 'Rani-ki-Vav (the Queen's Stepwell) at Patan, Gujarat' [http://whc.unesco.org/en/list/922], retrieved 7 August 2015

70. PM Bhatt, 'Her Space, Her Story: Exploring the stepwells of Gujarat', Zubaan, New Delhi, 2014

71. A Barton, 'Water in Crisis – Women in India', The Water Project [http://thewaterproject.org/water-in-crisis-india-women], retrieved 7 August 2015

72. B van Koppen, 'Towards a Gender and Water Index', International Water Management Institute, 2000 [http://r4d.dfid.gov.uk/PDF/Outputs/Water/WPI_H_30746.pdf], retrieved 10 August 2002

The startling headline could have been lifted straight from a dystopian or post-apocalyptic SF script about the aftermath of a bio-terrorist attack on the water supply of a city – Ben Rekhi's 'Waterborne' (2005) or Alan Moore's 'V for Vendetta' (1988). In fact, it is a strategy from the 69-page 'Concept for Civil Defence' commissioned by the German Interior Ministry in 2012. Water is linked, not just to the crises of climate change, but to energy and food supplies and prices. The 3rd United Nations World Water Development Report, 'Water in a Changing World' (2009) stressed that 'unless their links with water are addressed and water crises around the world are resolved, these other crises may intensify and local water crises may worsen, converging into a global water crisis and leading to political insecurity and conflict'.[73]

According to the United Nations Intergovernmental Panel on Climate Change (IPCC), cities subject to increasing water stress are projected to more than double by 2050, with adverse effects of climate change on freshwater systems aggravating the impact of other stresses, including population growth, changing economic activity, land-use change and urbanization. Changes in fresh water quantity and quality due to climate change are expected to detrimentally affect food security and increase the vulnerability of poor rural communities, especially in the arid and semi-arid tropics, Asian and African mega-deltas, and coastal cities.

Like food, access to fresh water is closely related to issues of national security and health that could lead to conflict if left unmanaged. The UN World Water Development Report forecasts that by the year 2050, seven billion people in 60 countries will suffer from water scarcity in the worst case, and even under the lowest projection, just below two billion people in 48 countries will struggle.[74] Hence, the UN concludes that the world is facing the potential of international sub-state public protest, cross-border conflicts and mass migration as individuals and communities look to move from regions ravaged by the impacts of climate change.

Climate change affects the function and operation of existing water infrastructure, including hydropower, structural flood defenses, drainage and irrigation systems as well as water management practices. The practices that increase productivity of irrigation water usage may provide significant adaptation potential for all land production systems under future climate change. At the same time, improvements in irrigation efficiency are critical to ensure the availability of water both for food production and for competing human and environmental needs. However, in many coastal locations, current water infrastructure and water management practices may not be robust enough to cope with the impacts of climate change on water supply reliability, flood risk, health, agriculture, energy and aquatic ecosystems.

The changes in fresh water resource and hydrology in the 21st century will impact on biodiversity in every continent. Ecosystem responses to changes in hydrology often involve complex interactions with some of the ecological communities existing today easily becoming disaggregated in the future. In the IPCC's 'Water and Climate Change Report' 2008, due to the combined effects of temperature and water stress, the extinction of some amphibians and other aquatic species is projected in Costa Rica, Spain and Australia. Drying of wetlands will affect the migration success of birds that use the Sahelian wetlands as stopovers in their migration to Northern Hemisphere breeding sites. In southern Africa, unprecedented levels of extinction of both plant and animal species are envisaged. Of all ecosystems, however, freshwater aquatic ecosystems appear to have the highest proportion of species threatened with extinction by climate change, as reported by the Millennium Ecosystem Assessment in 2005.

Sea level rise could lead to the inundation of land and saltwater intrusion into inland waterways that would cause problems for accessing fresh water. The amount of water available in cities relies on runoff, groundwater recharge, aquifer conditions, water quality and water supply infrastructure including reservoirs, pumping wells and distribution networks. Safe access to drinking water depends more on the level of water supply infrastructure than on the quantity of runoffs. However, as a result of climate change, runoff and groundwater recharge will decrease and therefore improving safe access to drinking water will be harder to achieve. According to the Food and Agriculture Organization of the United Nations (FAO), if freshwater supply has to be replaced by desalinated water due to climate change, then the cost of climate change includes the average cost of desalination. The current cost of desalination is estimated at US$1.00/m3 for seawater and US$0.60/m3 for brackish water, compared to the cost for freshwater chlorination, which is approximately US$0.02/m3.[75] In densely populated coastal areas of Egypt, Bangladesh, India and Southeast Asia, desalination costs may become prohibitive.

In the 2014 article 'To Save California, Read "Dune": Survival on a fictional desert planet has a lesson for the drought-stricken state', Andrew Leonard described the increasingly dry state's vulnerability to climate change-induced droughts, and looks to the world of SF for solutions, in particular the idea of harvesting fog on the Hollywood Hills and in the surrounding Californian deserts.[76] Leonard, however, stopped short of endorsing every water procurement strategy in Frank Herbert's SF novel 'Dune' (1965).[77] In addition to building dew-collecting infrastructure to capture moisture from the air, and urgently storing any available drops into underground wells and canals, the inhabitants of the dry world of Dune also wear special water retaining 'Stillsuits' that transform any sweat or urine back into drinking water.

The infrastructure for fog harvesting is fairly rudimentary but ingenious; essentially lengths of net-fabric are stretched between vertical poles, and water is collected as it drips from the net. Research into new innovative desalination infrastructure that has a multi-use, security and inhabitation program is required to reduce the costs, especially with the use of non-conventional energy sources that are associated with lower greenhouse gas emissions. We require infrastructures which complement the natural and the man-made environments, and can liberate communities from ancient dependency on rivers and streams, but could also replace expensive concrete and metal pipes as the primary water infrastructure for those who live in rural areas, suburbia and even dense urban conditions.

'Survival is the ability to swim in strange water'
    – Frank Herbert, 'Dune', 1965

73. World Water Assessment Programme, The United Nations World Water Development Report 3, 'Water in a Changing World', UNESCO Publishing, Paris & Earthscan, London, 2009

74. 'Water for People, Water for Life', The United Nations World Water Development Report, UNESCO Publishing & Berghahn Books, 2003 [http://www.un.org/esa/sustdev/publications/WWDR_english_129556e.pdf], p.10, retrieved 7 August 2015

75. Y Zhou & RSJ Tol, 'Evaluating The Costs Of Desalination and Water Transport', Water Resources Research, vol.41, John Wiley & Sons, March 2005, pp.1–10 [http://onlinelibrary.wiley.com/doi/10.1029/2004WR003749/full], retrieved 7 August 2015

76. A Leonard, 'To Save California, Read "Dune": Survival on a fictional desert planet has a lesson for the drought-stricken state', Nautilus, 4 June 2014 [http://nautil.us/issue/25/water/to-save-california-read-dune], retrieved 12 August 2015

77. F Herbert, 'Dune', Chilton Books, Philadelphia, 1965

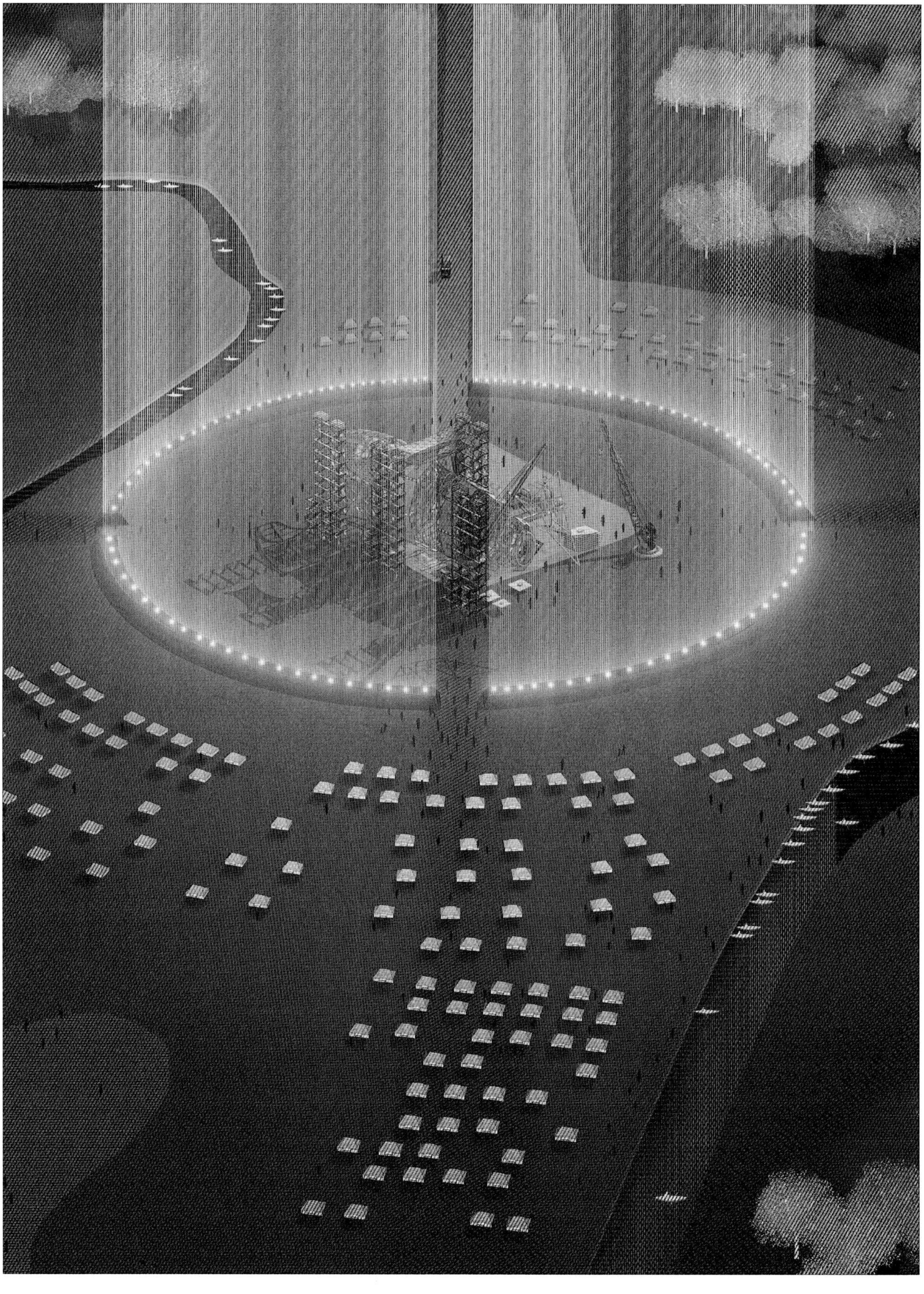

urban future (iv)
Twenty Thousand Fish Above the Sea

'Arrival of the Floating Pool after 40 years of crossing the Atlantic, the architects/lifeguards reach their destination. But they hardly notice it due to the particular form of locomotion of the pool – its reaction to their own displacement in water – they have to swim toward what they want to get away from and away from where they want to go.'
— Rem Koolhaas, 'The Story of the Pool', 1977

In the tradition of the science fiction (SF) tropes of Jonathan Swift and Jules Verne, the Russian modernist architects used a portable pool infrastructure to escape from Soviet oppression to the United States of America in Koolhaas' 'Delirious New York' (1978). Meanwhile, Brodsky and Utkin opted instead to remain in Russia to produce 'visionary schemes in response to a bleak professional scene in which only artless and ill-conceived buildings, diluted through numerous bureaucratic strata and constructed out of poor materials... [it was] an escape into the realm of the imagination that ended as a visual commentary on what was wrong with social and physical reality and how its ills might be remedied'.[1] Their 'Wandering Turtle' for the 1984 'Architecture + Urbanism' ideas competition shows a large pile of seemingly ad-hoc elements being pushed through the streets; there are numerous wheels of different sizes that provide mobility. On closer inspection, the 'Turtle' is 'a maze of a big city' comprising a diverse collection of crafted and intelligent buildings, presumably being smuggled into the banal urban context, making metaphoric reference to the 'Trojan Horse'.

Both decisions to migrate or to remain on-site are basic human rights, and can be applied as adaptation strategies in the face of climate change. Over the coming years, large-scale human displacements are expected to intensify – often the amalgamation of complex economic, social and political drivers, which are exacerbated by increasingly unpredictable environmental conditions. The movement patterns of climate migrants vary: forced migration might result from an unforeseen catastrophe such as a flood, tsunami or earthquake, while slow persistent effects of drought on agriculture could cause a gradual migration process.[2] According to the 2006 Stern Review on the Economics of Climate Change, around 200 million people will be permanently displaced as a result of climate change by 2050.[3]

'In order to survive the extremes of the world's climate, the ability to create a portable or temporary shelter is one of if not the most important human-made factor in their survival', argued Robert Kronenburg.[4] Infrastructure for survival needs to be adaptable, easily transported by individuals or by a community, and if applicable, utilize indigenous materials. In his book 'Houses in Motion', Kronenburg identified the first recorded infrastructure of migration to be 'Noah's Ark'.[5]

facing page: Like the Mongolian yurts and native American tipis, the Fish infrastructures incorporate symbolism, as well as intelligent engineering that is delicate and quickly deployable.

following pages: The Fish, a new typology of humanitarian infrastructure, provides access to clean water, sanitation, food, and health care; plus tools and materials for the technology of ground-weaving and self-replication.

1. LE Nesbitt, 'Brodsky & Utkin: The complete works', Princeton Architectural Press, New York, 2003, pp.28–29

2. The Science Communication Unit UWE, 'Science for Environmental Policy: Migration in response to environmental change', The European Commission DG Environment, issue.51, September 2015, p.3

3. N Stern, '2006 Stern Review on the Economics of Climate Change', HM Treasury, London, 2006, p.vi

4. R Kronenburg, 'Architecture in Motion: The history and development of portable building', Routledge, New York, 2014, p.7

5. R Kronenburg, 'Houses in Motion', Academy Editions, London, 1995, p.21

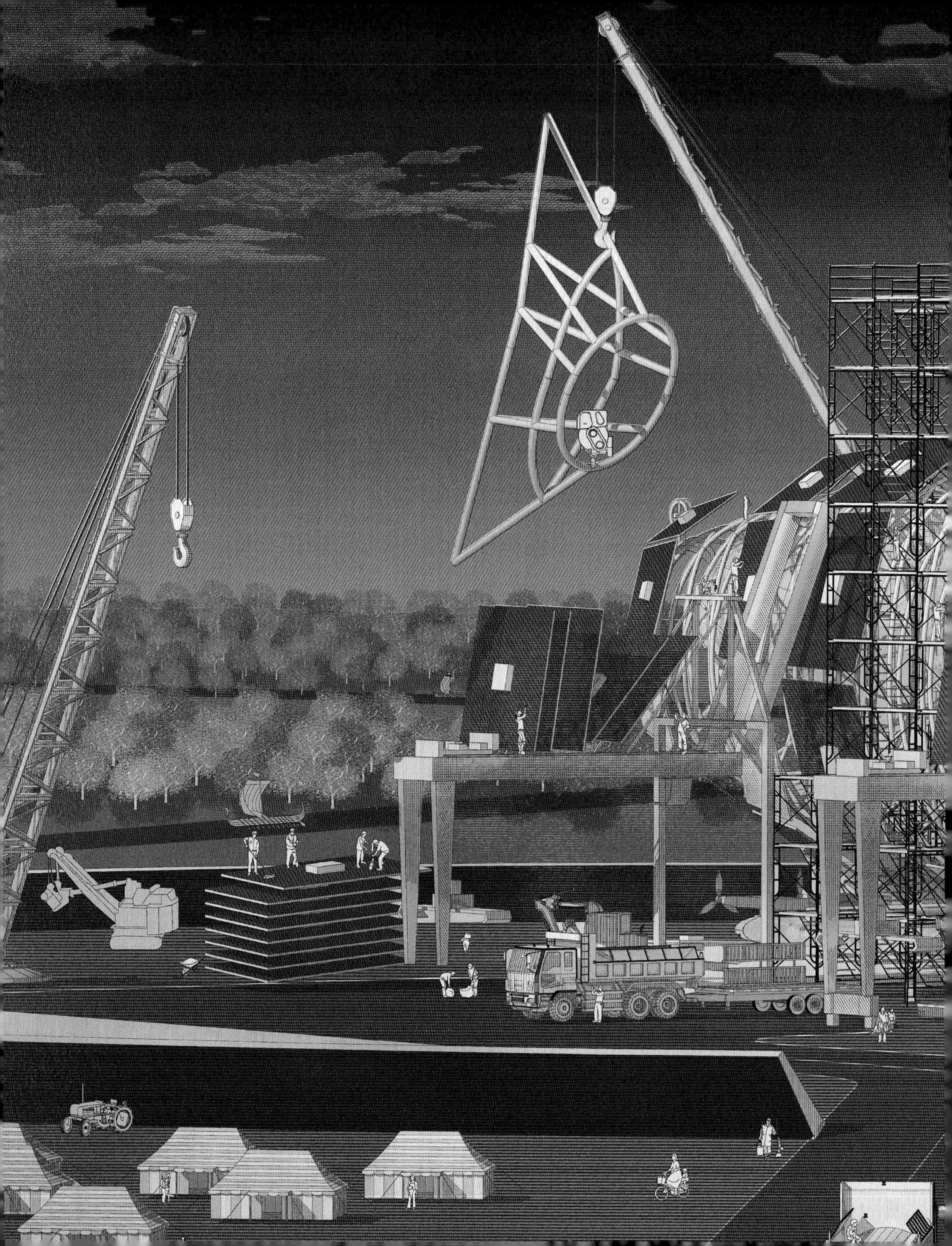

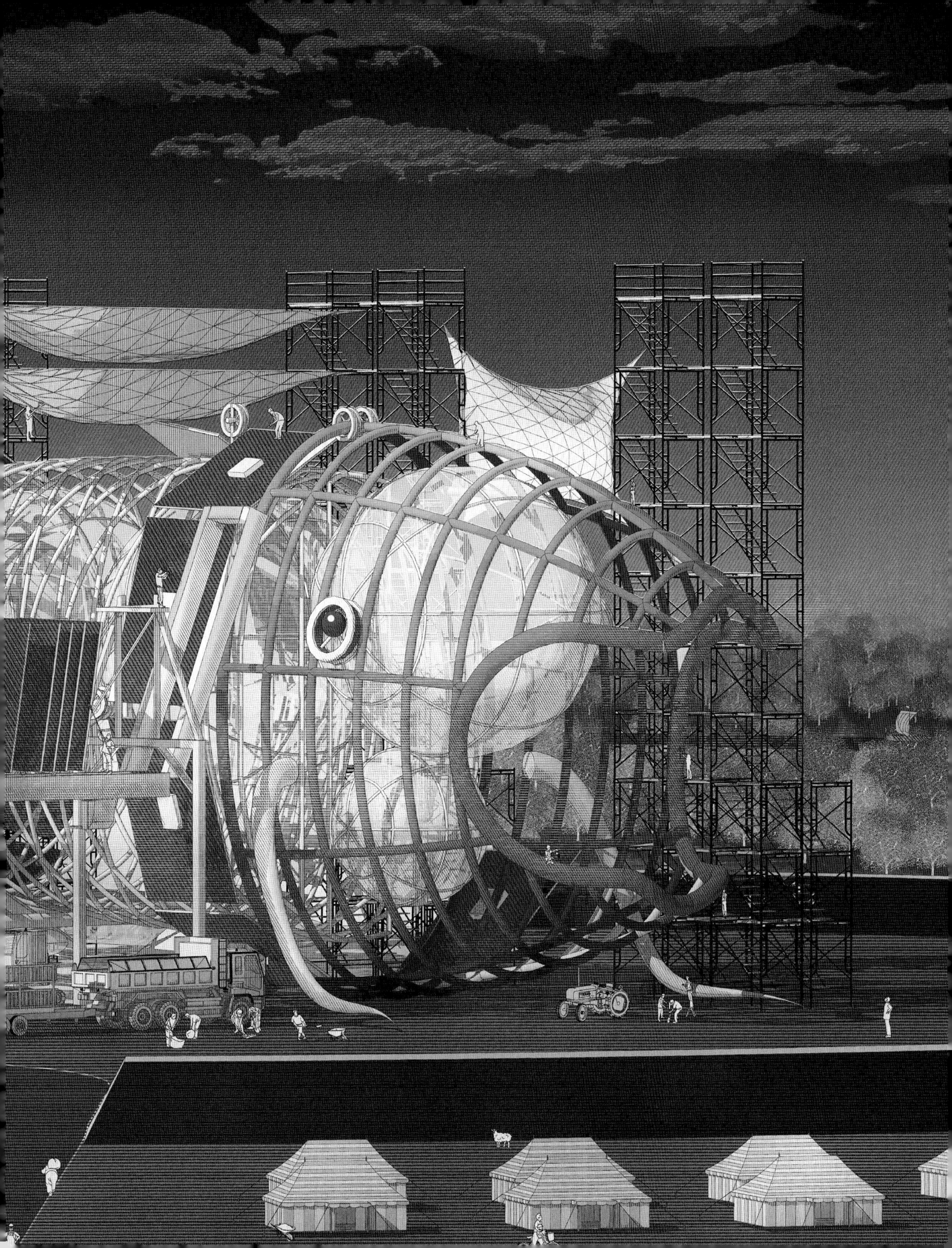

196

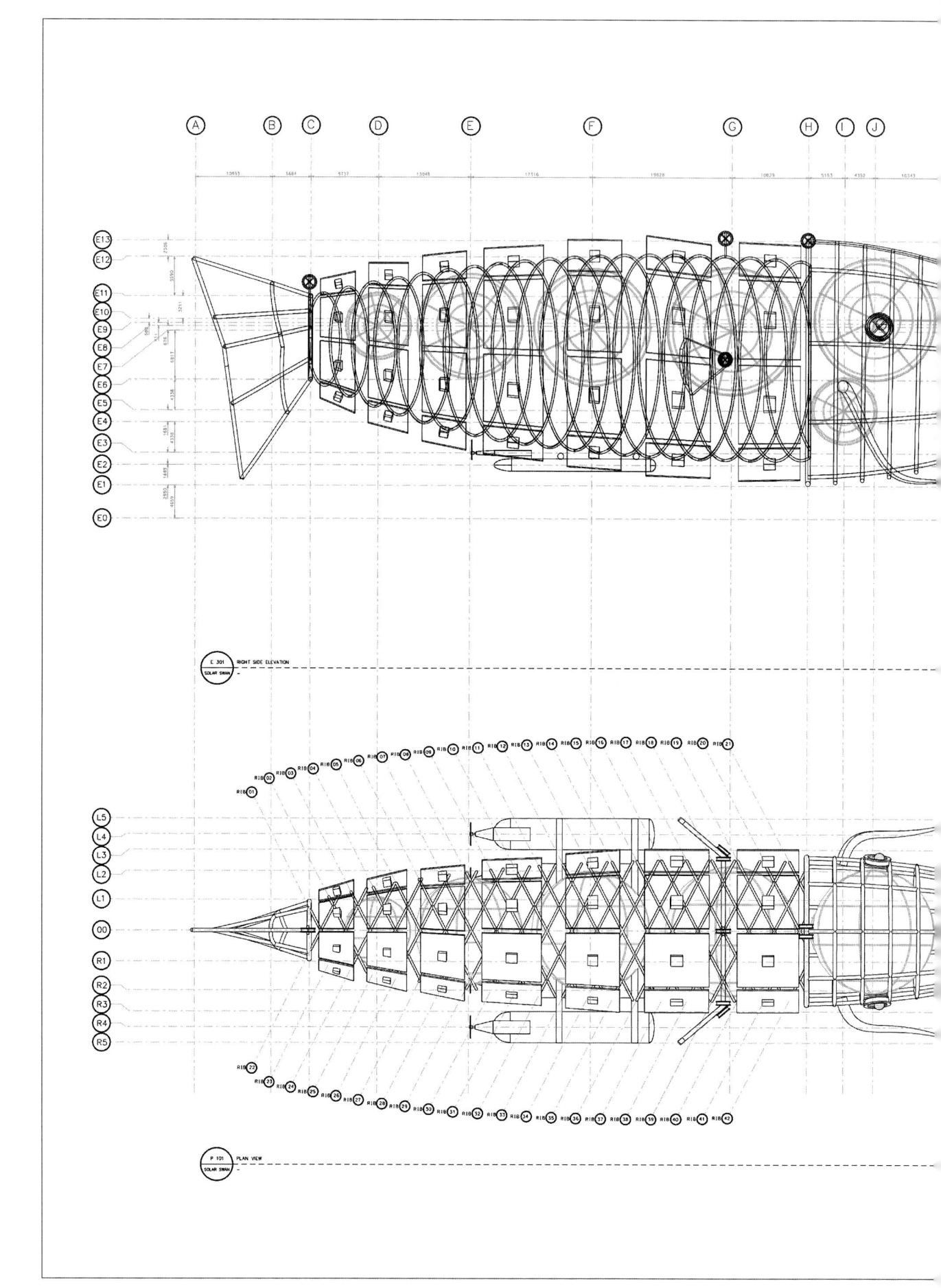

NOTES:

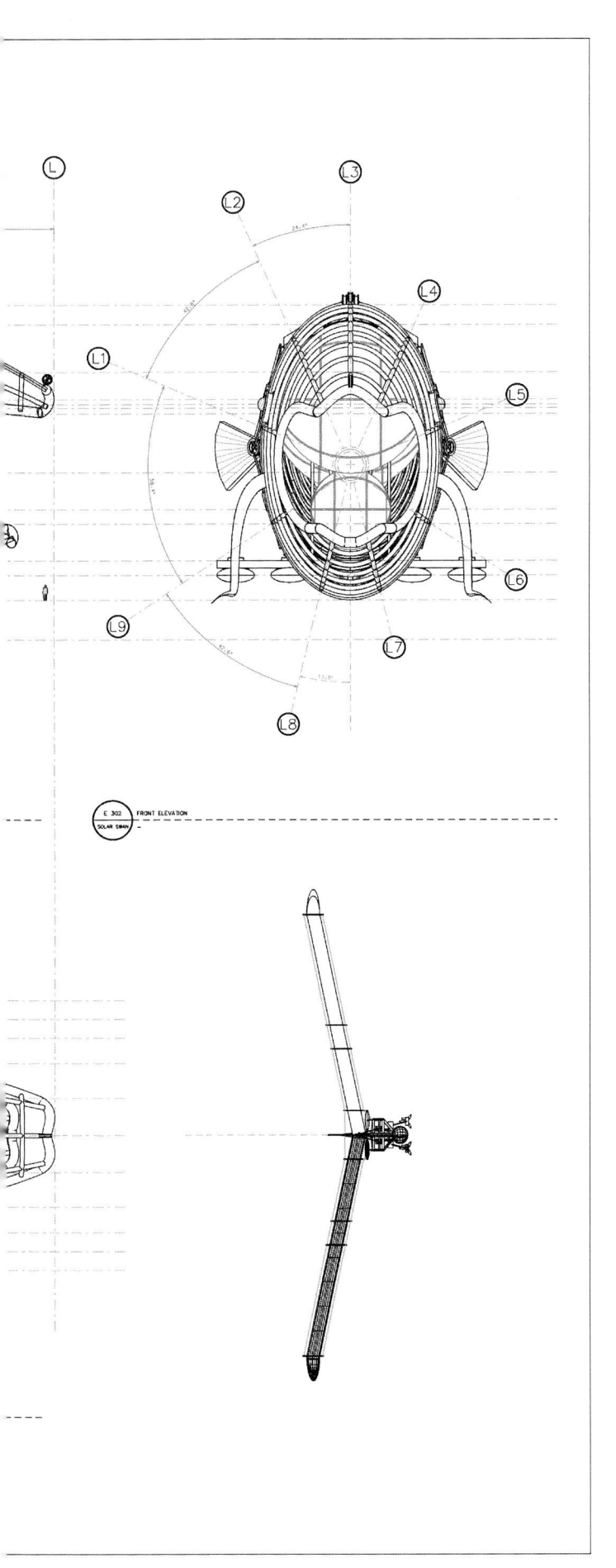

INITIAL FISH TO BE CONSTRUCTED AND SET SAIL FROM THE TRELLEBORG

STATUS

APPROVED

INITIAL PROTOTYPING

PROJECT

SUSTAINABLE FISH INFRASTRUCTURE

SUBJECT

PROTOTYPE ASSEMBLY TECHNICAL

ISSUED BY

SM

CHECKED BY

EW

DATE

14/01/2040

DRAWING No.

5211_SUSTAINABLEFISH_A000_UNIT

E 302 FRONT ELEVATION
SOLAR SWAN

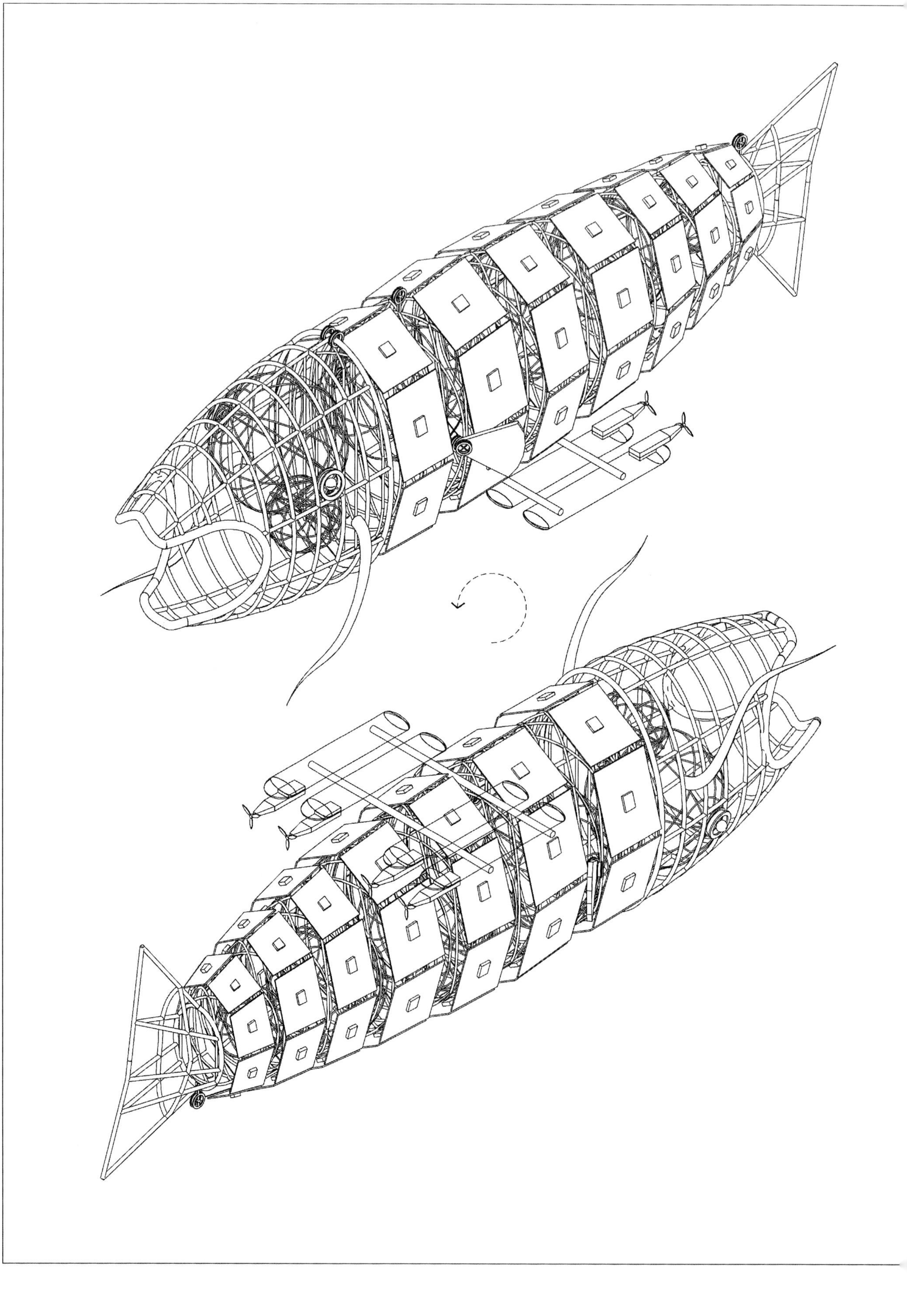

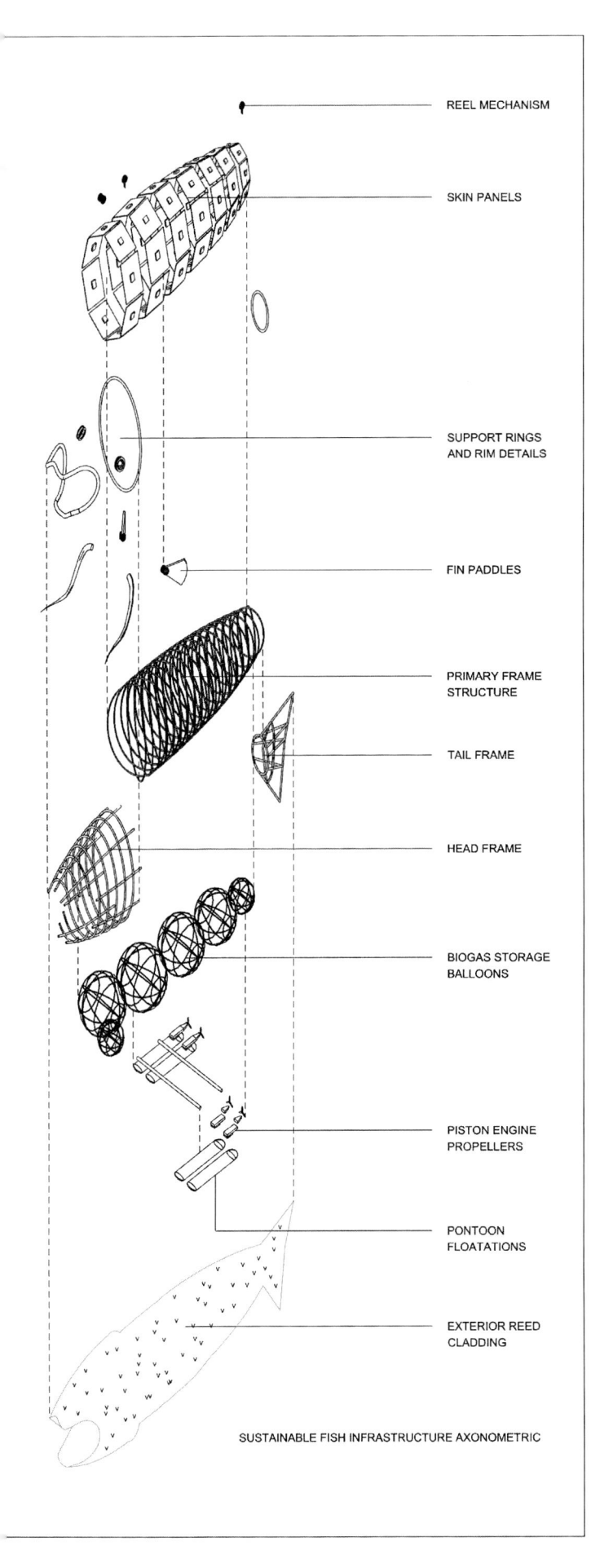

- REEL MECHANISM
- SKIN PANELS
- SUPPORT RINGS AND RIM DETAILS
- FIN PADDLES
- PRIMARY FRAME STRUCTURE
- TAIL FRAME
- HEAD FRAME
- BIOGAS STORAGE BALLOONS
- PISTON ENGINE PROPELLERS
- PONTOON FLOATATIONS
- EXTERIOR REED CLADDING

SUSTAINABLE FISH INFRASTRUCTURE AXONOMETRIC

NOTES:
INITIAL FISH TO BE CONSTRUCTED AND SET SAIL FROM THE TRELLEBORG

STATUS

APPROVED

INITIAL PROTOTYPING

PROJECT
SUSTAINABLE FISH INFRASTRUCTURE

SUBJECT
PROTOTYPE ASSEMBLY TECHNICAL

ISSUED BY
EW

CHECKED BY
SM

DATE
14/01/2040

DRAWING No.
5211_SUSTAINABLEFISH_A000_UNIT

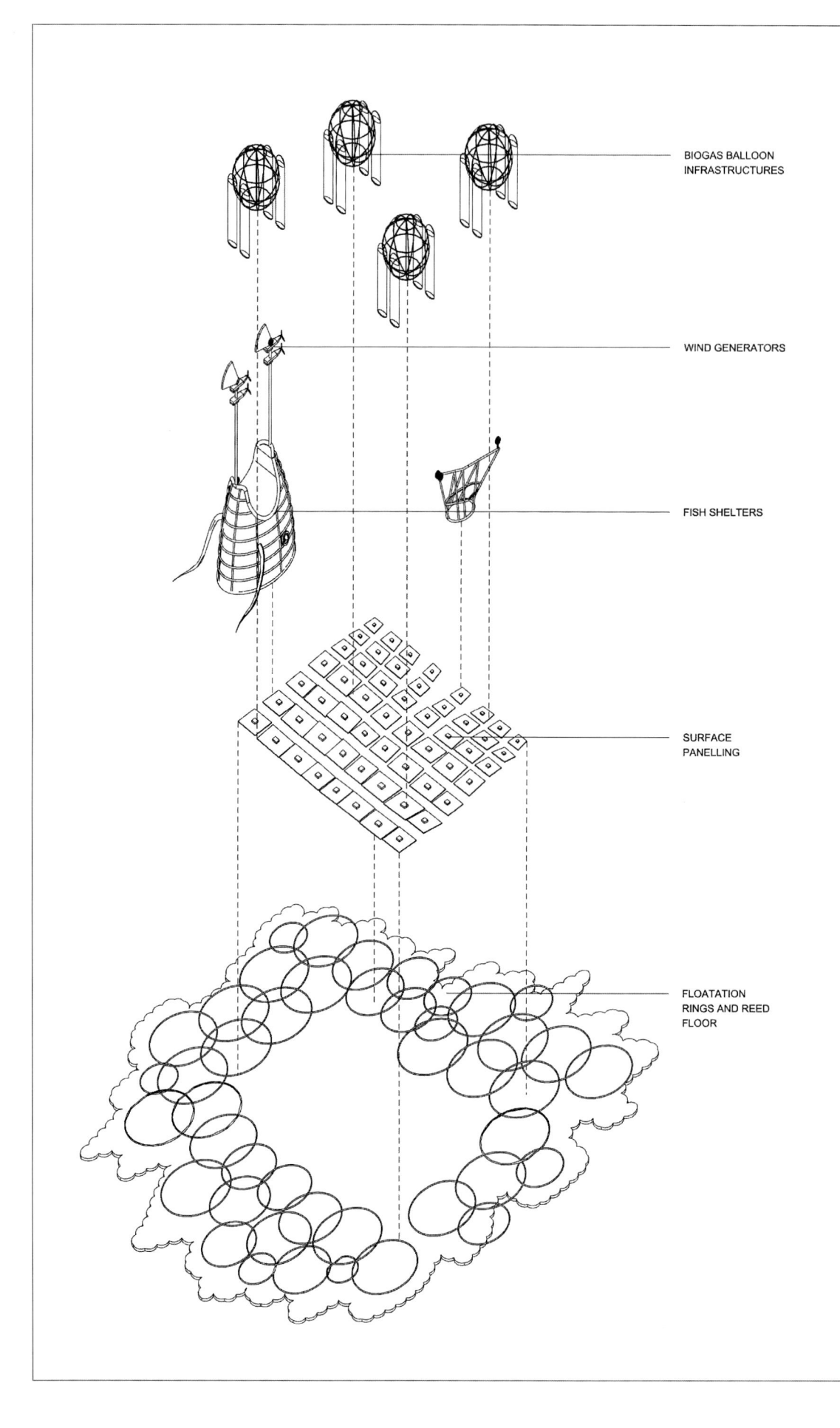

- BIOGAS BALLOON INFRASTRUCTURES
- WIND GENERATORS
- FISH SHELTERS
- SURFACE PANELLING
- FLOATATION RINGS AND REED FLOOR

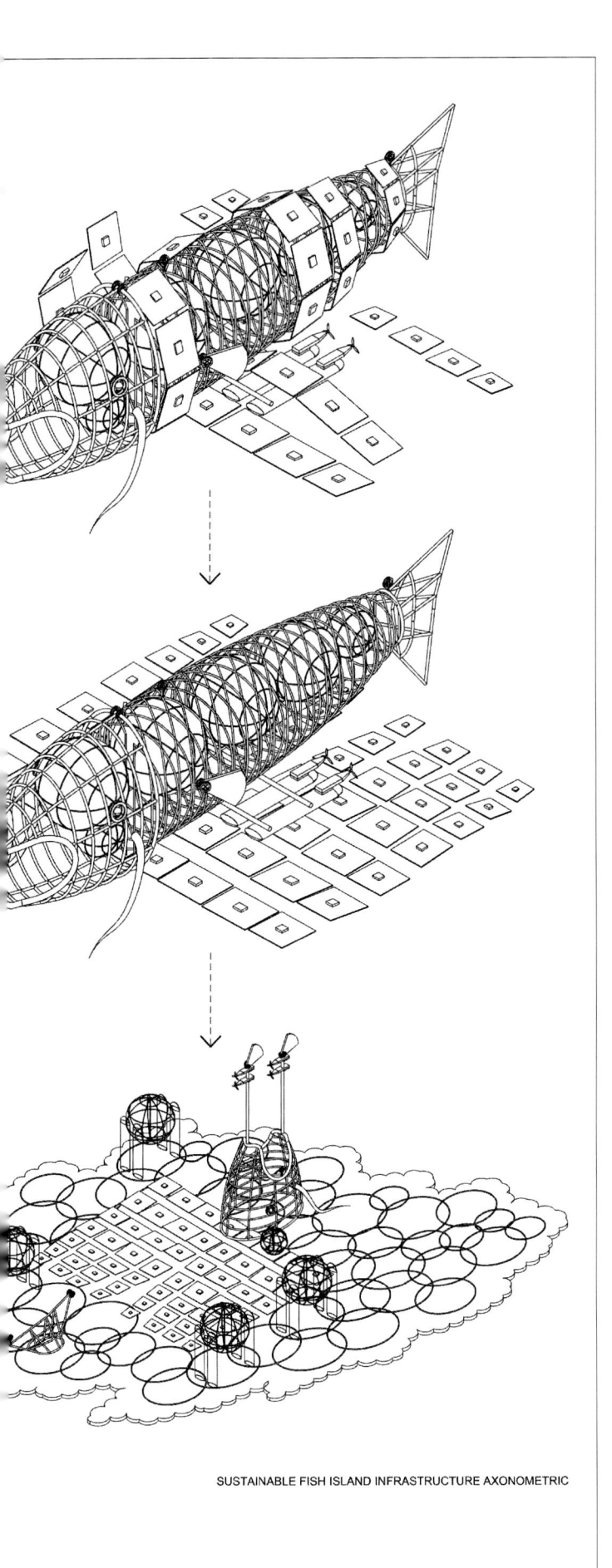

SUSTAINABLE FISH ISLAND INFRASTRUCTURE AXONOMETRIC

NOTES:

FISH UNFOLDING SEQUENCE IN TO SUSTAINABLE ISLAND

STATUS

APPROVED

FISH SEQUENCING TRANSFORMATION

PROJECT

SUSTAINABLE FISH ISLAND INFRASTRUCTURE

SUBJECT

PROTOTYPE ASSEMBLY TECHNICAL

ISSUED BY

EW

CHECKED BY

SM

DATE

14/01/2040

DRAWING No.

5211_SUSTAINABLEFISH_A000_AXONOMETRIC

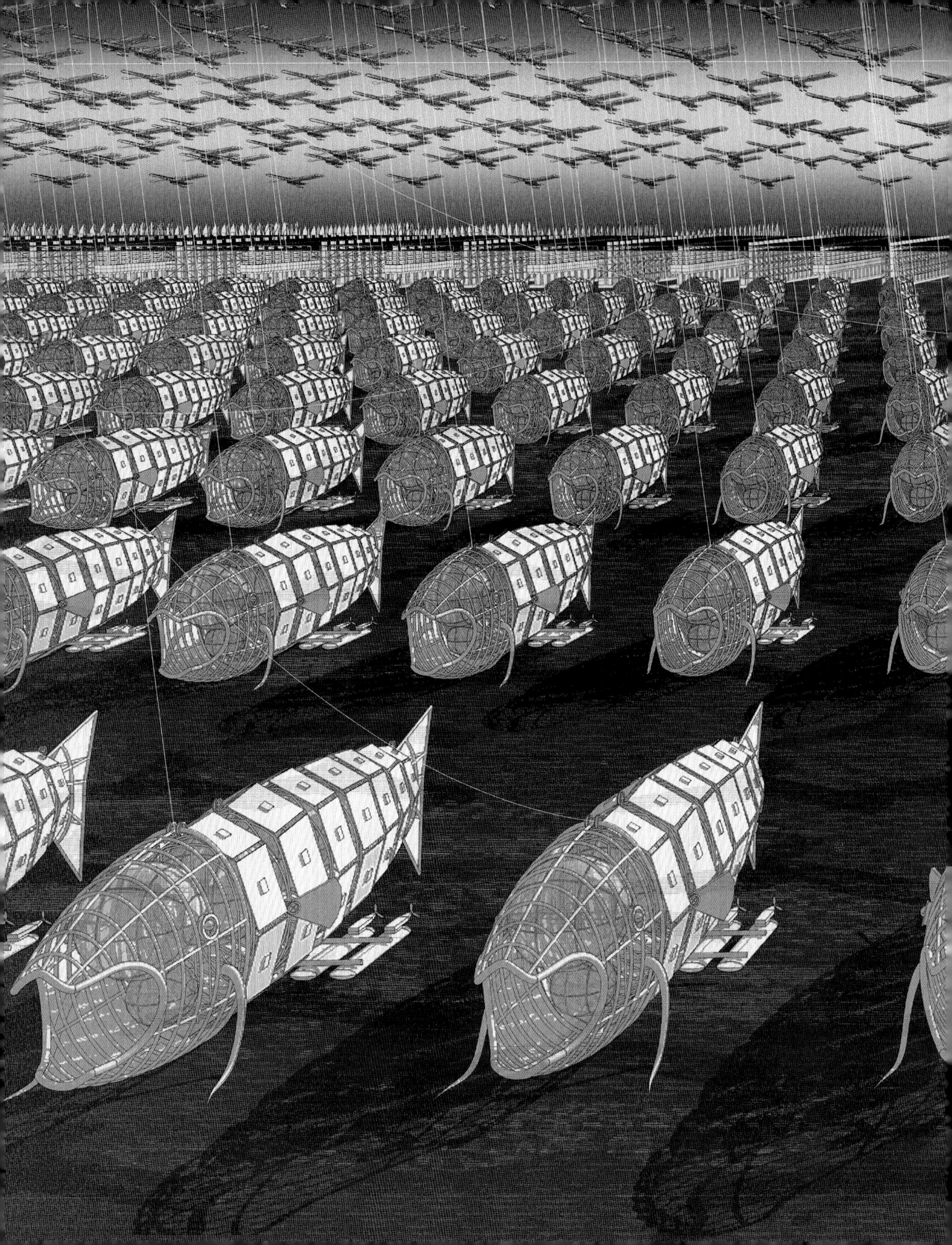

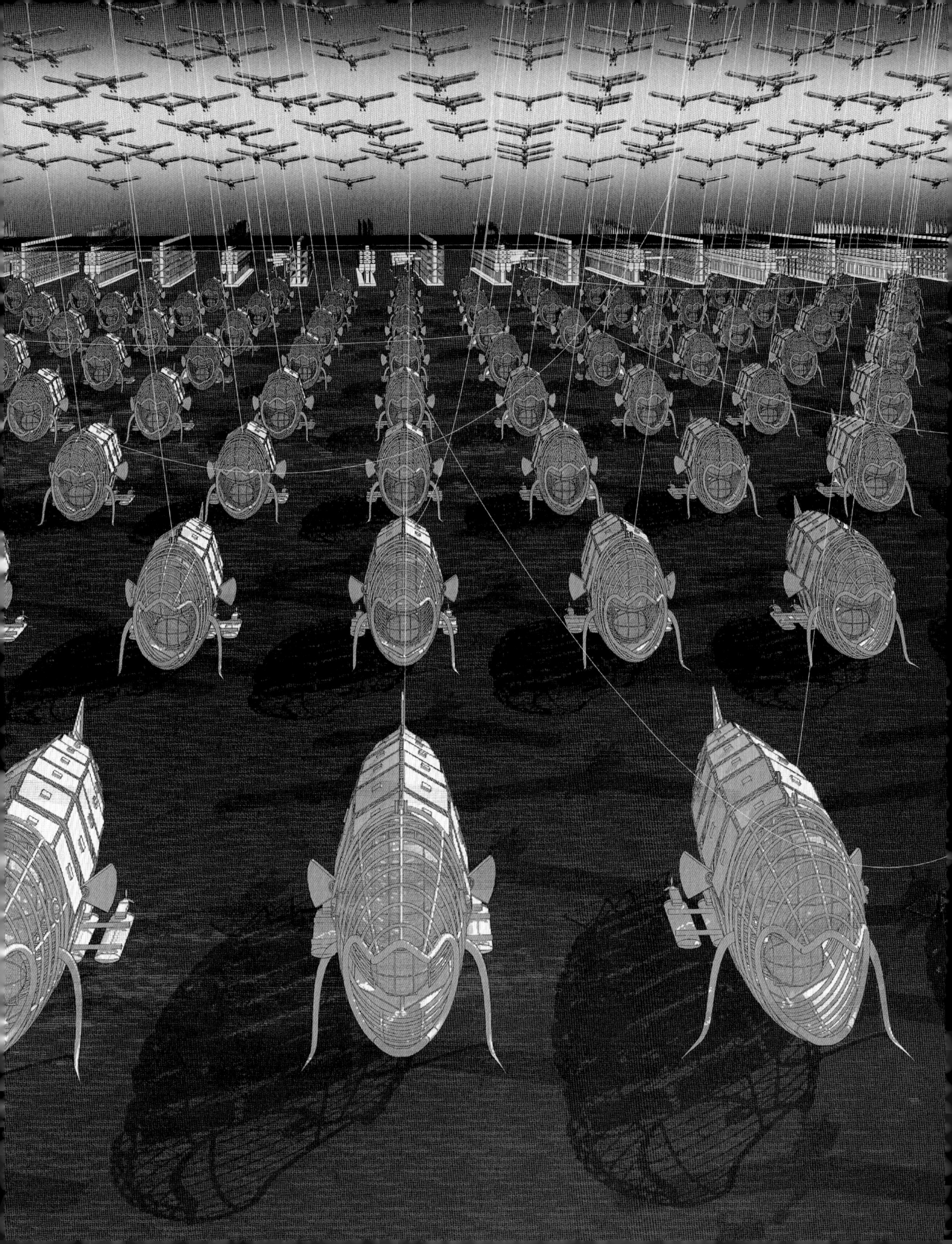

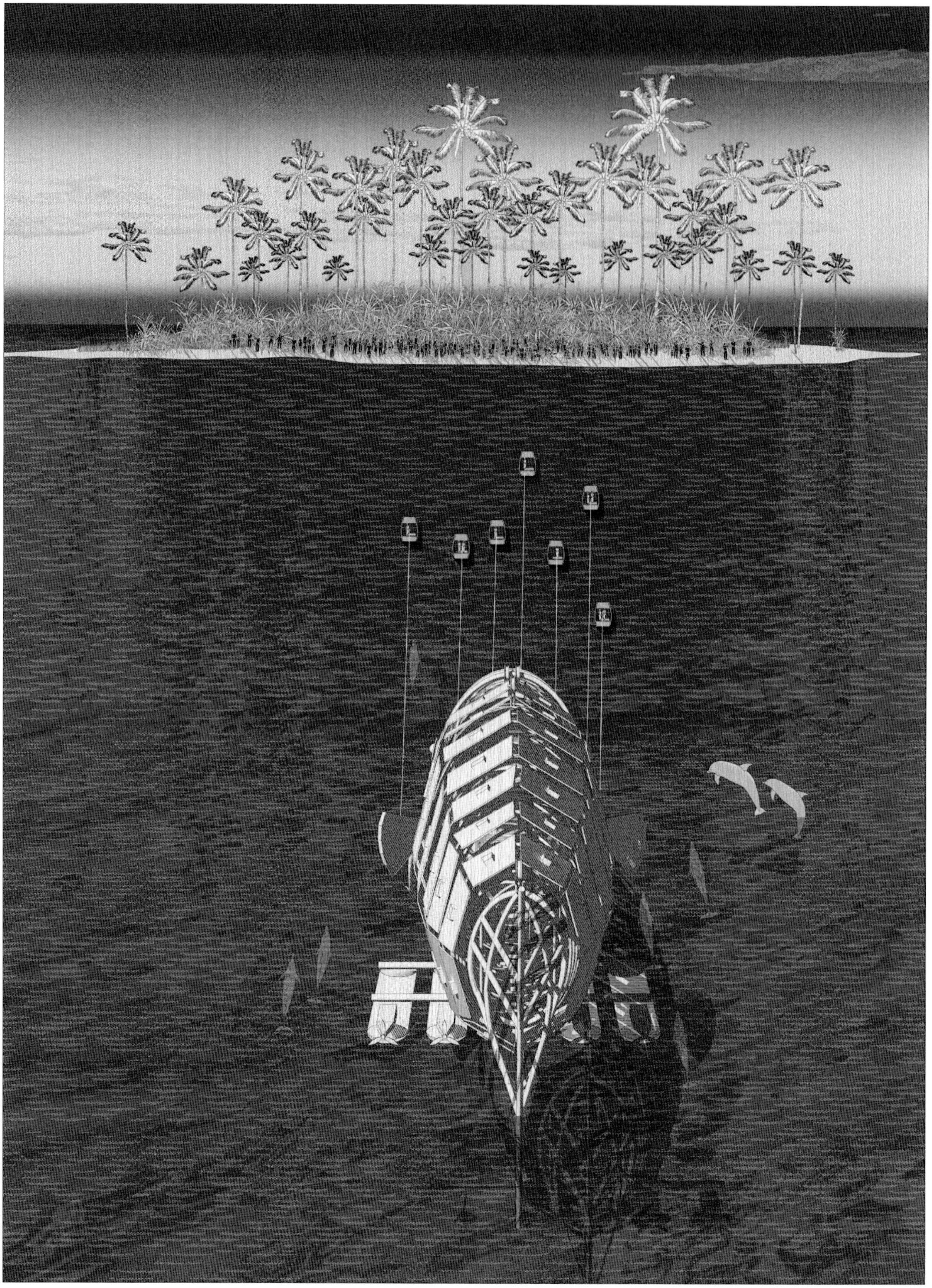

twenty thousand fish above the sea

In more recent times, there is of course the tax haven 'Freedom Ship' – a floating city for 50,000 people to live, work, vacation and enjoy retirement. The proposed portable infrastructure would continuously circle the globe every three years, with the intention to offer residential space, a library, schools, and a first-class hospital in addition to duty-free shopping malls, banks, hotels, restaurants, entertainment facilities, casinos, offices, warehouses, and light manufacturing and assembly enterprises. To ensure first-class accessibility, there is the airport on the ship's top deck to serve private and small commercial aircraft. The community on the sea measures 107 meters in height, with a width of 230 meters, and a length of 1,370 meters, more than four times longer than the RMS Queen Mary.[6]

At the opposite end of scale and luxury, mobile homes, the traveling circus, the Native American Tipi and the Mongolian Yurt have provided the necessary facilities and freedom to migrate. Mongolian nomads historically moved three to four times a year. A yurt is easy to set up and take down; and with a few animals, the entire packed dwelling can be transported from one place to another as seasons change or as pastures become greener elsewhere. In contrast to mankind's migration on land and water, expeditions by air have been rare after the catastrophic disasters that befell the giant airships 'Hindenburg' and 'Macon'. Dirigibles, however, have more recently been used to ingenious effect by French architect Gilles Ebersolt to position living environments on the treetop canopies of tropical rainforests. The 'Radeau des Cimes' (1989) is an inflatable raft that floats on the forest canopy like a boat sailing on the waves. Constructed out of lightweight materials with a large surface area to maximize stability, the raft provides previously unimaginable access to the forest environment.

Migration is not the only response strategy to climate change; it is widely agreed that many displaced people are likely to remain in their communities and seek to adapt to nature's impacts. Correspondingly, rather than 'fighting' climate change, governments together with planners and architects need to envision built environments that embrace the enemy; strengthening community resilience with flexible systems and portable infrastructures that are able to adapt in uncertainty can reduce displacement and relocation – this is both an opportunity and a challenge. Kronenburg singled-out Archigram, Cedric Price, Future Systems and Lebbeus Woods, who have come to influence the design of architecture and infrastructures 'usually in situations where necessity, imaginative thinking and a consummate understanding of the issues have been factors in the generation of the solution'.[7]

In 2008, the then President-elect of the Maldives, Mohammed Nasheed, announced a plan to create a 'sovereign wealth fund' using tourism revenues to buy higher land so that the future descendants of the 300,000 islanders will have somewhere to rebuild their lives as sea level rise threatens. Nasheed told the media that Maldivians do not want to 'trade a paradise for a climate refugee camp'.[8] With future sea levels projected to increase in the range of 10 to 100 centimeters by the year 2100, the entire country of the Maldives, including its capital city Malé, could be submerged. A series of low-lying archipelagos with more territorial sea than land, the islands are the flattest and lowest country in the world.

As an alternative to buying higher land, 'Twenty Thousand Fish Above the Sea'[9] might be the solution for island nations like the Maldives facing the choice of either taking to the water or becoming climate

previous pages: Rather than 'fighting' climate change, governments together with planners and architects need to envision built environments that embrace the enemy.

facing page: The Fish might be the solution for island nations like the Maldives facing the choice of either taking to the water or becoming climate migrants.

6. 'City At Sea', Freedom Ship International [http://freedomship.com], retrieved 3 August 2016

7. R Kronenburg, 'Houses in Motion', Academy Editions, London, 1995, p.133

8. J Vidal, 'Global Warming Could Create 150 Million Climate Refugees by 2050', The Guardian: Climate Change, 3 November 2009

9. The title makes reference to Jules Verne's 'Twenty Thousand Leagues Under the Sea' (1870)

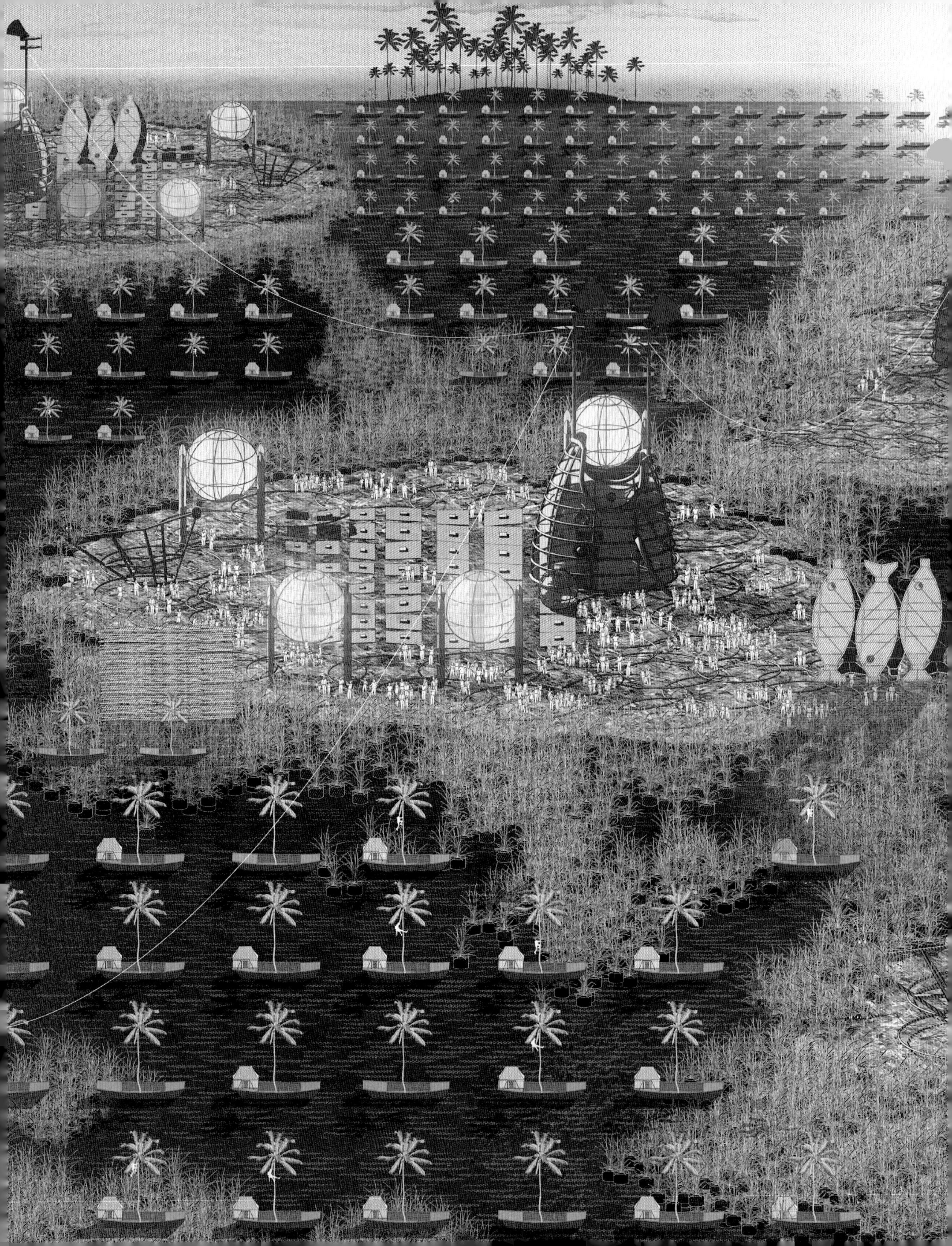

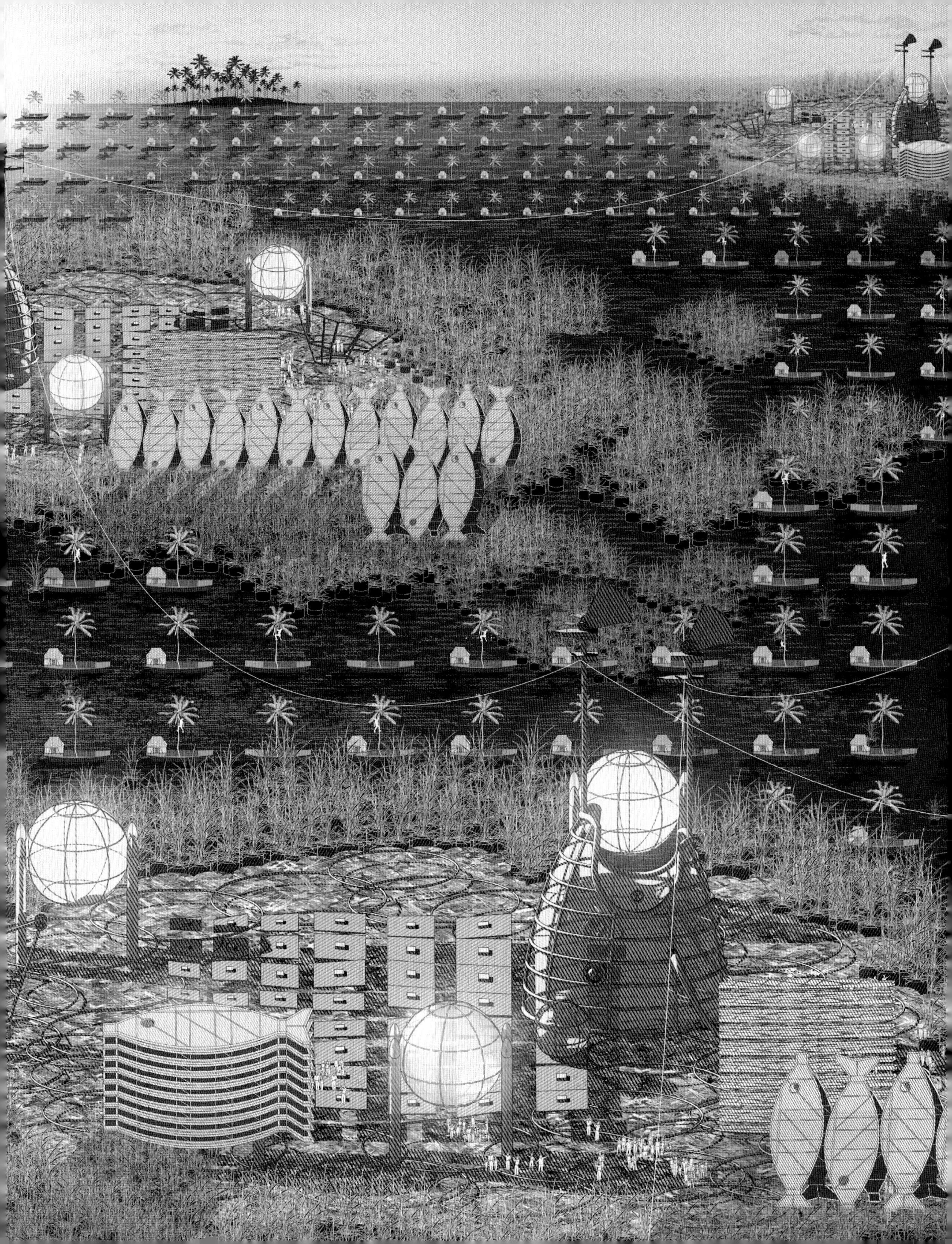

migrants. Portable, lightweight, and sustainable, the Fish is a floating infrastructure that advocates three principles of action: to protect, provide and encourage participation in the anticipation or the aftermath of an environmental disaster. The Fish, in the speculative tradition of Peter Cook/Archigram's 'Instant City' (1971), is a practical reality since at every stage it is based on existing techniques and their application. There is a combination of several different artifacts and systems, which hitherto remained as separate machines, enclosures or experiments.

For many who chose to remain in their community, the alien infrastructure offers an imaginative multi-use adaptation kit. The primary aim is to prevent human casualties by making available immediate protection in a safe environment – each large Fish is big enough to shelter 500 people, and the smaller modules are equipped with pop-up medical surgeries. Collectively, the new typology of humanitarian outpost provides access to the essentials of clean water, sanitation, food, and health care. Lifeboats, from within the main Fish infrastructure, are dispatched to affected communities, in hope of rescuing dislocated individuals and isolated groups as well as heritage artifacts, and native fauna and flora.

From the moment of arrival, the armada of Fish deconstructs – the tail flips into a vertical position to harvest wind and solar energy, while its head has the facility to desalinate and filter seawater. Filtered potable water is stored in the hollow structural framework of the Fish for everyday consumption. Provision of energy is a crucial part of humanitarian response and can contribute substantially to the transformation of the affected environment. Raffaella Bellanca of the International Lifeline Fund in Haiti argues that 'camps can be imagined as ordinary towns that function on the standard economic principles that regulate the exchange of goods and services. These towns need energy to maintain the life they host. The greater the access to energy, the more opportunities there is for a meaningful life, for reintegration into society afterwards, for less dependence on donors and for a chance to live with dignity.'[10] The Safe Access to Fuel and Energy (SAFE) initiative has secured the participation of many UN agencies, peacekeeping forces and NGOs in energy issues and focuses on how best to 'green' procurement.[11]

In view of the shortage of dry or safe ground in affected environments, each Fish carries tools to provide the technology of structural self-replication. The fish scale-like panels form the foundations of the new ground; the portable and buoyant panels are tiled over water to provide an instant emergency floating surface. The kit has a further adaptation opportunity to 'make-your-own-land', akin to the reed-woven floating infrastructures on Lake Titicaca. Local participation in land fabrication can create livelihood opportunities and help manage natural resources in a sustainable manner. Some within the community are responsible for cultivating and harvesting the reed, while others participate in crafting new ingenious woven-ground. The program relies heavily on collaboration of all stakeholders. Finally, the Fish recognize the importance to nurture talents, skills, and aspirations of the displaced; spaces within the infrastructure that encourage multi-use participation including community halls, schools and playgrounds on open platforms and floating terraces. Fin-like antennas connect the armada of fish whilst servicing communication networks between neighboring communities.

Whether communities opt to remain or migrate, the 'Twenty Thousand Fish Above the Sea' offers an allegorical adaptable 'Noah's Ark' to the globally displaced in the context of climate change and sustainability. It may seem like SF, but as rising sea levels threaten low-lying nations around the world, communities like the one in Malé may become more common. An effective and timely humanitarian relief infrastructure has the capacity to save thousands of lives – its adaptability and multi-use is limited only by the imagination.

twenty thousand fish above the sea

previous pages: The Fish presents opportunities for a meaningful life, for reintegration, and for a chance to live with dignity.

left: Humanitarian relief infrastructures have the capacity to save lives; their adaptability and multi-uses are limited only by the imagination.

10+11. R Bellanca, 'Sustainable Energy Provision Amongst Displaced Populations: Policy and practice', The Royal Institute of International Affairs (Chatham House): Energy, Environment and Resources, December 2014, p.42 & p.2 [https://www.chathamhouse.org/sites/files/chathamhouse/field/field_document/20141201EnergyDisplacedPopulationsPolicyPractice Bellanca.pdf], retrieved 11 June 2016

210

urban future
The City of a Thousand Lakes
(v)

'Everything made by man's hands has a form, which must be either beautiful or ugly; beautiful if it is in accord with Nature, and helps her; ugly if it is discordant with Nature, and thwarts her; it cannot be indifferent.'
– William Morris, 'The Lesser Arts', 1877

In the seminal science fiction (SF) novel 'Looking Backward: 2000–1887' (1888) Edward Bellamy writes of a protagonist who wakes into a future where the USA has been transformed into a socialist utopia. As the reader is invited to discover the new world, they learn of all the improvements that had been the reward of an egalitarian, nationalized and urbanized condition. The power of the industrial revolution and mechanized society is celebrated in the heroic image of the city.

The idea did not leave William Morris feeling impressed. In fact, Morris was so incensed by 'Looking Backward' that in addition to a highly severe review of the book, he penned his own SF novel 'News from Nowhere' (1890). He was convinced that the restoration of pastoral life and a dedication to craft would provide an alternative to the heavy-mechanization and sterilization of industry. Morris favored the romantic idyll, his utopia was in the form of libertarian socialism, believing that all work should be incentivized by its very nature as creative and pleasurable – the kind of work presumably available with the rejection of crowded towns and cities, and the adoption of the virtues of his 'arts and crafts' lifestyle.

Nevertheless, Bellamy's book had great influence on the real politics of the late 19th century; the text inspired intellectuals and Marxists, and was successful in its portrayal of urban socialism. 'Looking Backward' influenced Sir Ebenezer Howard when he founded the Garden City Movement in England, though he must also have been sympathetic toward Morris's concerns. The famous 'Three Magnets' diagram which addressed the question 'where will the people go?' seems to demonstrate that having a hybrid territory of 'Town-Country' will cure the ills of 'Town' whilst simultaneously lifting the restrictions of 'Country'. Howard knew that a polemic world-view would be good for discussion and influence, but at the point of application would need to be softened and contextualized.

The medium of the SF novel had allowed Bellamy to make a provocative speculation, which presented the ideas in an all-encompassing vision. However, the act of criticism can also be the encouragement for further enquiry – in 'Equality' (1897) Bellamy expanded on many of the concepts from 'Looking Backward', but his futuristic world is substantially softened. With far less emphatic authoritarian presence, and images of future society shifting away from the urban to the rural, Bellamy changed tack.

facing page: The City of a Thousand Lakes is a place whose physicality, social wellbeing, culture and economy revolve around water and its natural landscape.

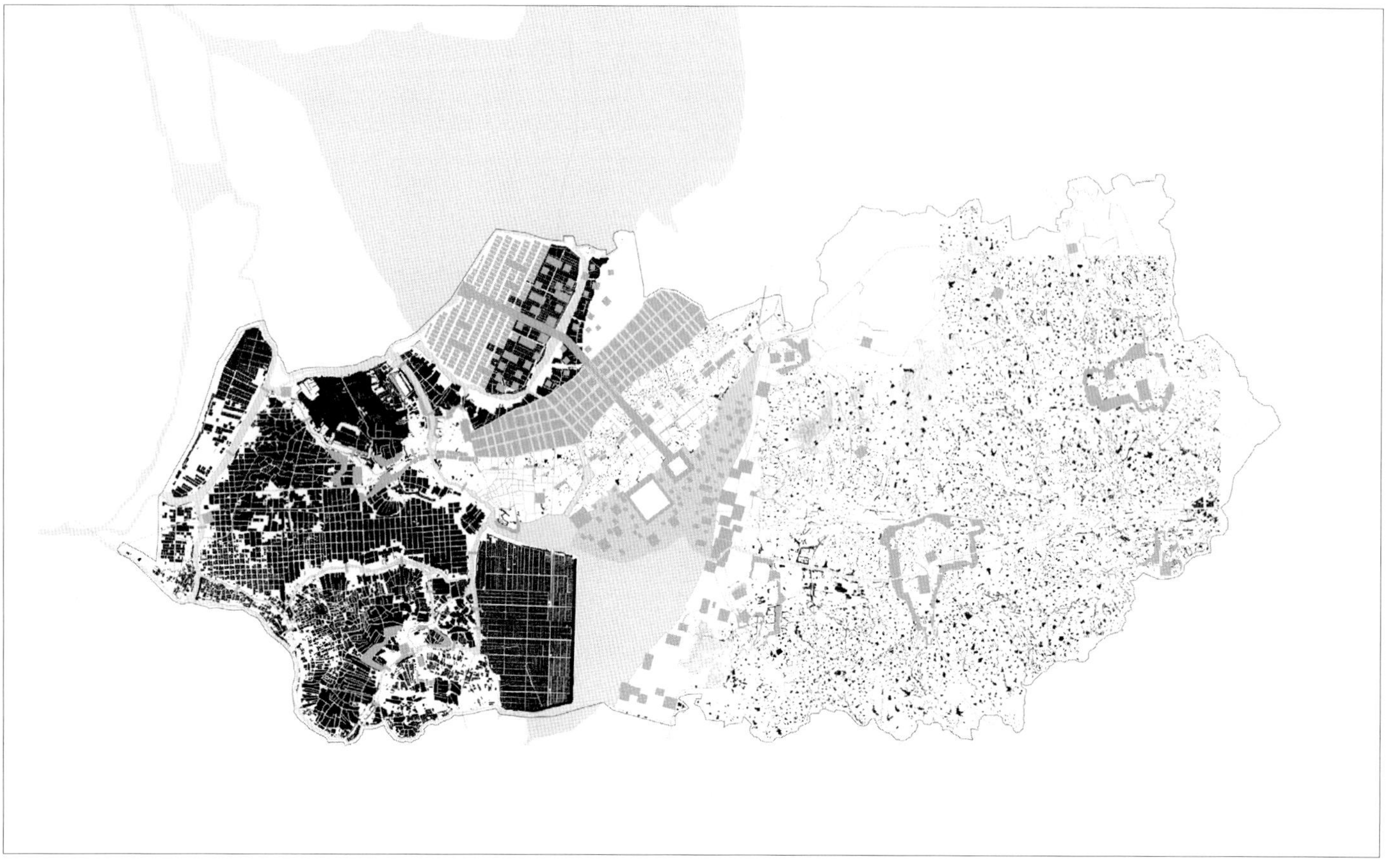

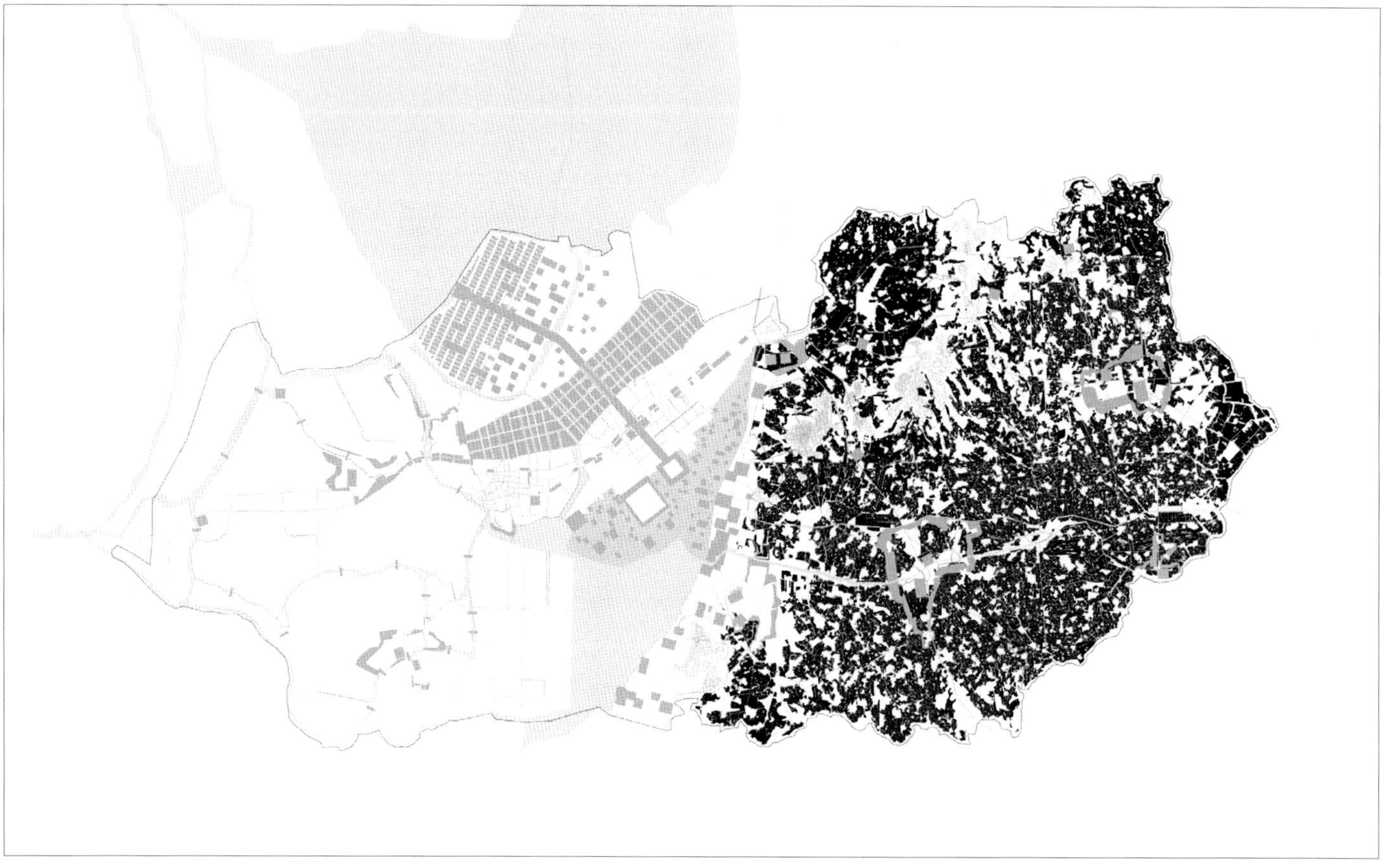

the city of a thousand lakes

Cities, in the 21st century, are becoming ever more densely urbanized and congested. In countries such as China, there are huge migrations of workers from rural areas into the cities, each holding onto the promise that echoes 'Looking Backward', whether it is the opportunity for education, better paid jobs, or healthcare. With any opportunity in the mega-city, inevitably, also come the limitations and challenges of life. It might be worthwhile for the Chinese to consider Bellamy's insights in 'Equality'. According to the 2014 McKinsey & Company 'Rethinking Infrastructure: Voices from the global infrastructure initiative' report, new and adapted infrastructures are key to delivering on the country's economic goals: 'China's people-centred effort emphasizes city clusters as its major component. Urbanization will provide economic integration, growth, and the benefits of an urban lifestyle to populations of 10 million to 50 million people in each cluster.'[1]

The director of the planning department of China's National Development and Reform Commission, Xiaodong Ming, recognizes that '[regarding infrastructure] the next task is to improve the layout patterns of urbanization... the goal is to balance the spatial layout, optimise the scale of cities and towns. It requires promoting urbanization strictly in accordance with plans for managing land, water and ecology.'[2] There is the need for an alternative form of infrastructure for China, instead of the polluted and overflowing cities, one that cultivates sustainable and mutually beneficial links to rural communities and the natural landscape. In 'Equality', Bellamy had considered that, although the most important parameter for the development of a city was its economy, 'given improved technology (i.e. telephone, television, high speed distribution networks), the need to locate in highly dense areas no longer existed'.[3] Now is an opportunity for China to reconsider its urban futures, as the country has widely available communication technologies in its swathes of open countryside.

The rural district of Gaochun in Jiangsu Province is an ecological hinterland of Nanjing, situated between two large lakes – the 196-square-kilometer Lake Shijiu to the north and the 35-square-kilometer Lake Gucheng to the south. The total water surface occupies one-third of the district's physical area and is actively protected by the local government. The region recalls the city of 'Isaura' in Italo Calvino's 'Invisible Cities' (1972): 'the city of a thousand wells' is built over a subterranean lake. Two forms of religion exist in the city, both asserting that the Gods associate themselves with water. Some believe they live in the depths of the subterranean lake, whose traces can be seen as a living green territory above ground; others believe the gods live in the infrastructure of water collection – in buckets, arches of aqueducts, pump handles and windmills to name a few.[4] Likewise, Gaochun is a place whose physicality, social wellbeing, culture and economy revolve around water and its natural landscape – 'The City of a Thousand Lakes'.

Currently, the economic draw of neighboring cities has rendered Gaochun district a surreal environment – the aquaculture villages are almost completely inhabited by the third age and the very young, while those of working age have migrated for job opportunities, only to reappear transitorily in droves at key moments during the crab-catching calendar. The dichotomy of old and young is exaggerated in the built environment of many developing communities. The situation in Gaochun exemplifies a surreal opposite to the dystopic ageist future society of William F Nolan and George Clayton Johnson's 'Logan's Run'

facing page top: The total aquatic surface occupies one-third of the district's physical area and is actively protected by the local government.

facing page bottom: The inhabitable infrastructure is reimagined as soft agriculture landscapes.

1+2. X Ming, 'Rethinking Infrastructure: Voices from the Global Infrastructure Initiative', McKinsey & Company, 2014, p.52

3. JR Mullin, 'Edward Bellamy's Ambivalence: Can Utopia be urban?', Journal of Utopian Studies, vol.11, issue 1, 2000 [http://scholarworks.umass.edu/cgi/viewcontent.cgi?article=1019&context=john_mullin], retrieved 12 August 2016

4. I Calvino, 'Invisible Cities', Vintage Classics, London, 1997, p.17

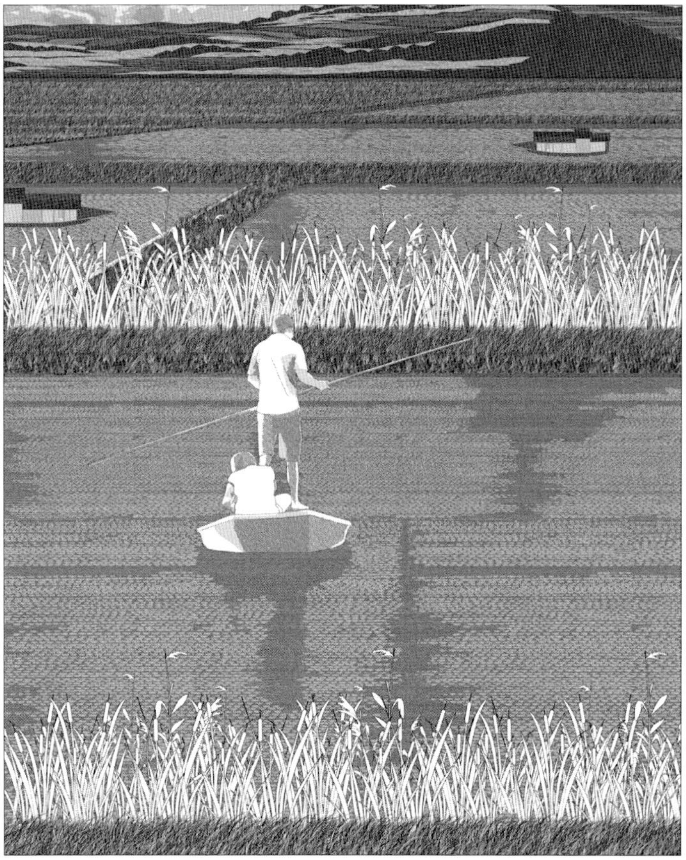
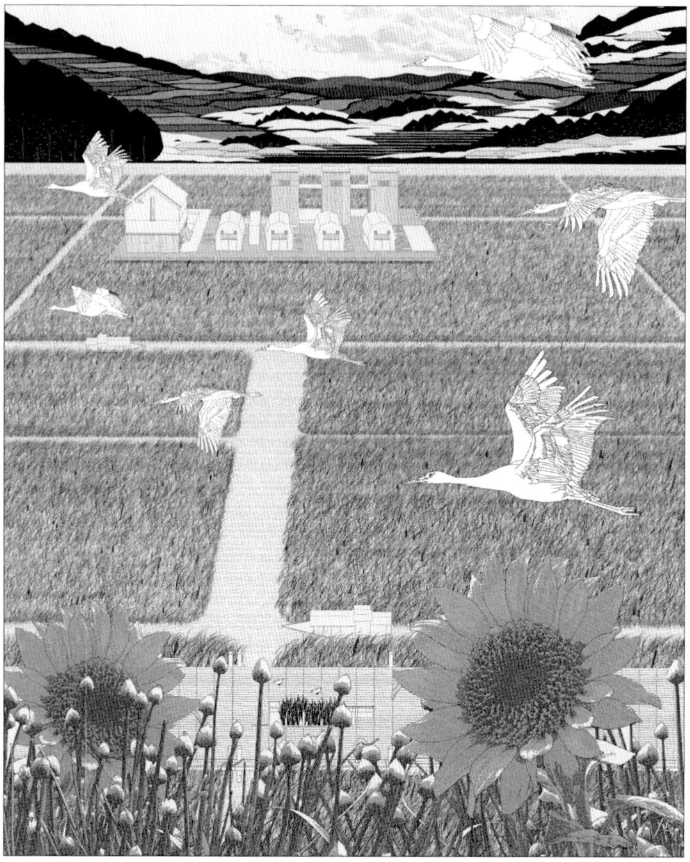
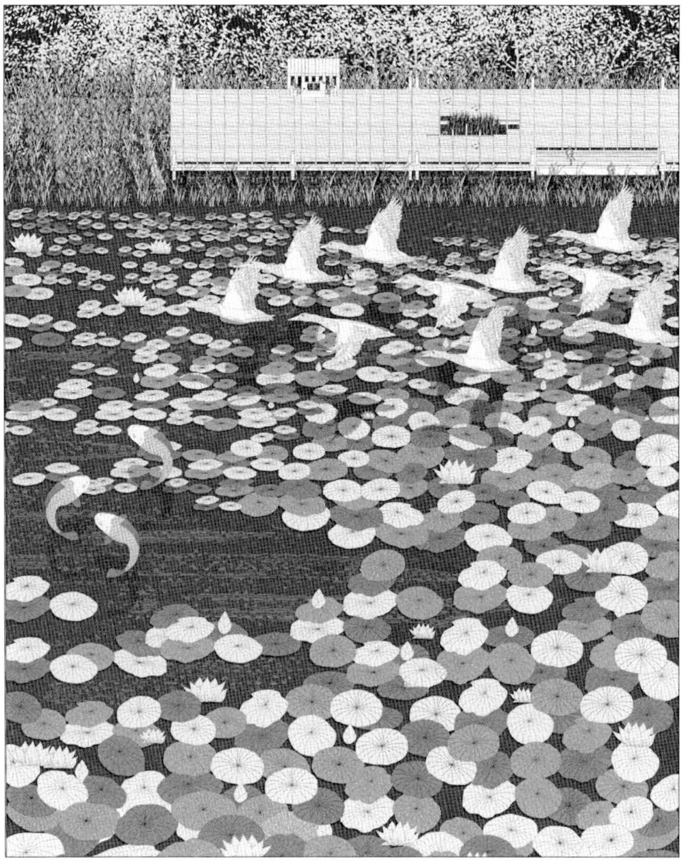
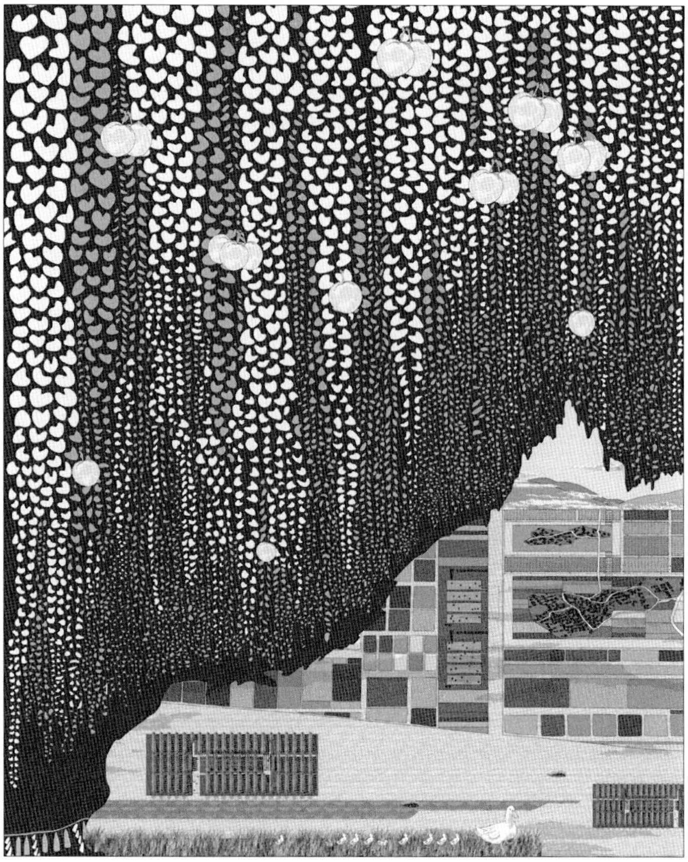

the city of a thousand lakes

facing page: The blue sustainable pension plan adapts aquatic habitats for the district's celebrated crab, fish, ducks and lotus.

left: Tourism forms a large part of the local economy, especially during the Crab Festival in September.

216

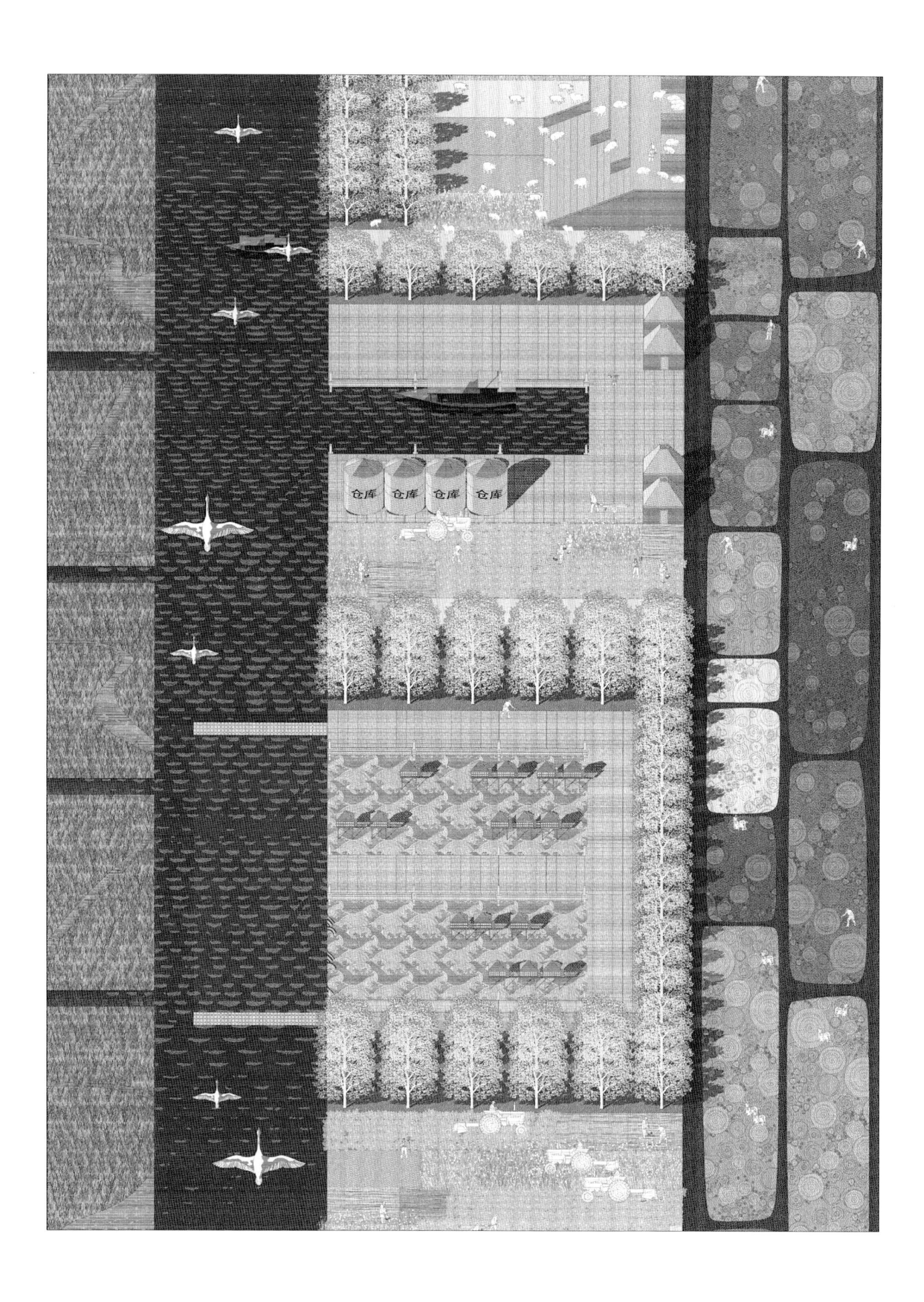

(1967); where the law requires the termination of any persons at the critical age of 30. People are either willingly executed by pleasure inducting gas or, if they try to run, they are hunted down by a 'Sandman' who inflicts a painful death.[5]

With the legacy of a one-child policy introduced in 1979, China joins the list of countries with a rapidly aging population. Theoretically in China, there is a '4-2-1' family – for each four retired grandparents and two aging parents there will be just one grandchild to provide financial or other care. The United Nations, Department of Economic and Social Affairs, Population Division estimates that by 2050, China will have 331 million over 65s, three times as many as reported in 2010, but still with a total population which remains roughly the same at 1.3 billion.[6]

How can nature facilitate equilibrium between younger and older generations and mediate new and old infrastructures for a sustainable community? In the City of a Thousand Lakes, sustainability is defined as development that meets the needs of the present without compromising the ability of future generations to meet their own needs. The 'blue sustainable pension plan' provides the perfect opportunity – people of the third age contribute to local food culture and economy, disseminate their knowledge and manual skills to future generations to tackle an accelerating rural migration epidemic, benefit from mental and physical stimulation, and achieve financial independence while receiving companionship and security.

The vision of Gaochun district has one eye on an urban future and one eye looking warily at the state of unsustainable ghost cities in China. From high-rise apartment complexes to shopping malls, hundreds of grand scale cities in China are largely empty, obsolete before they were ever inhabited. Instead, the blue sustainable pension plan for the City of a Thousand Lakes rests solely on working with nature, and understanding the significance of its ecosystems. The inhabitable infrastructure is reimagined as soft aquaculture landscapes, rather than civil engineering constructs, alluding to the nation's foundation in agricultural practice and the development of Chinese agricultural cities. The community recognizes the benefits from employing gentle yet strategic adaptations of the district's low-lying land and vast complex jigsaw of lakes, ponds and paddies that stretch-out as far as the horizon.

Nature in the City of a Thousand Lakes differs from Morris's – pastoral life is idealized and purposefully constructed versions of nature, more aligned to those in 'Equality'. The aging generation act as mentors within the aquaculture scenario. The blue sustainable pension plan adapts aquatic habitats for the district's celebrated crab, fish, ducks and lotus, and together with bamboo, wild grasses and agriculture soften the clusters of human inhabitation. There are farming outposts scattered on mud embankments to store and distribute animal feed, and to collect duck droppings for fertilizer. The serenity of the infrastructure and its waters are only interrupted at specific times of the year to harvest crab, fish and lotus. The aquaculture has long maintained an empowering poetic presence; there are no vacuous developments, and all sectors of the city are animated and made accessible by water.

Satellite villages are dotted in amongst the multi-use infrastructure of expansive water. Behind a perimeter bamboo forest, each village functions as an energy hub and actively converts biomass and

facing page: The pastoral life is idealized and purposefully constructed versions of nature.

following pages: Behind a perimeter bamboo forest, each village functions as an energy hub and recycles the district's grey water.

5. WF Nolan & GC Johnson, 'Logan's Run', Dial Press, New York, 1967

6. D Bailey, M Ruddy & M Shchukina, 'Ageing China: Changes and challenges', BBC: News Asia, 20 September 2012 [http://www.bbc.co.uk/news/world-asia-19630110], retrieved 9 August 2015

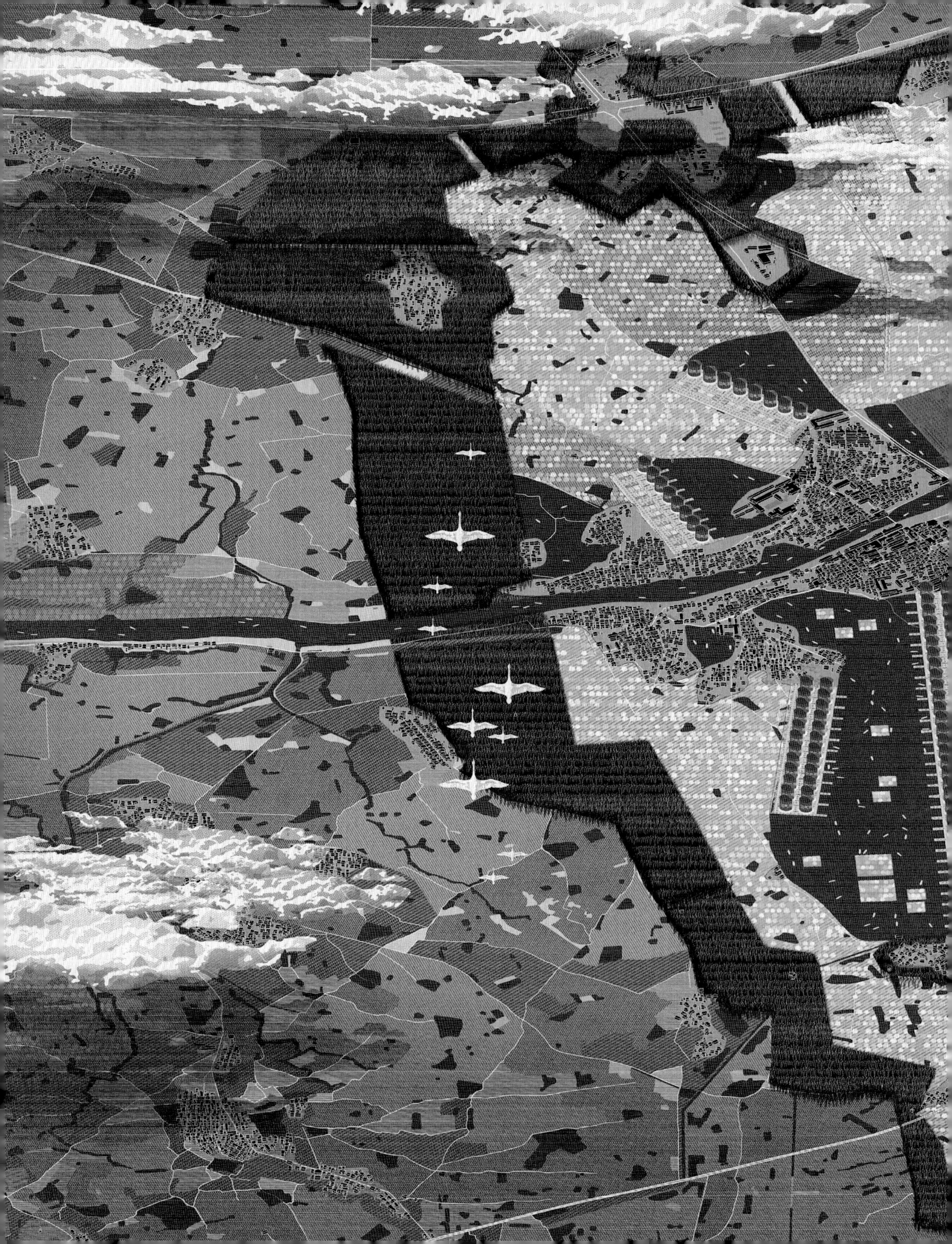

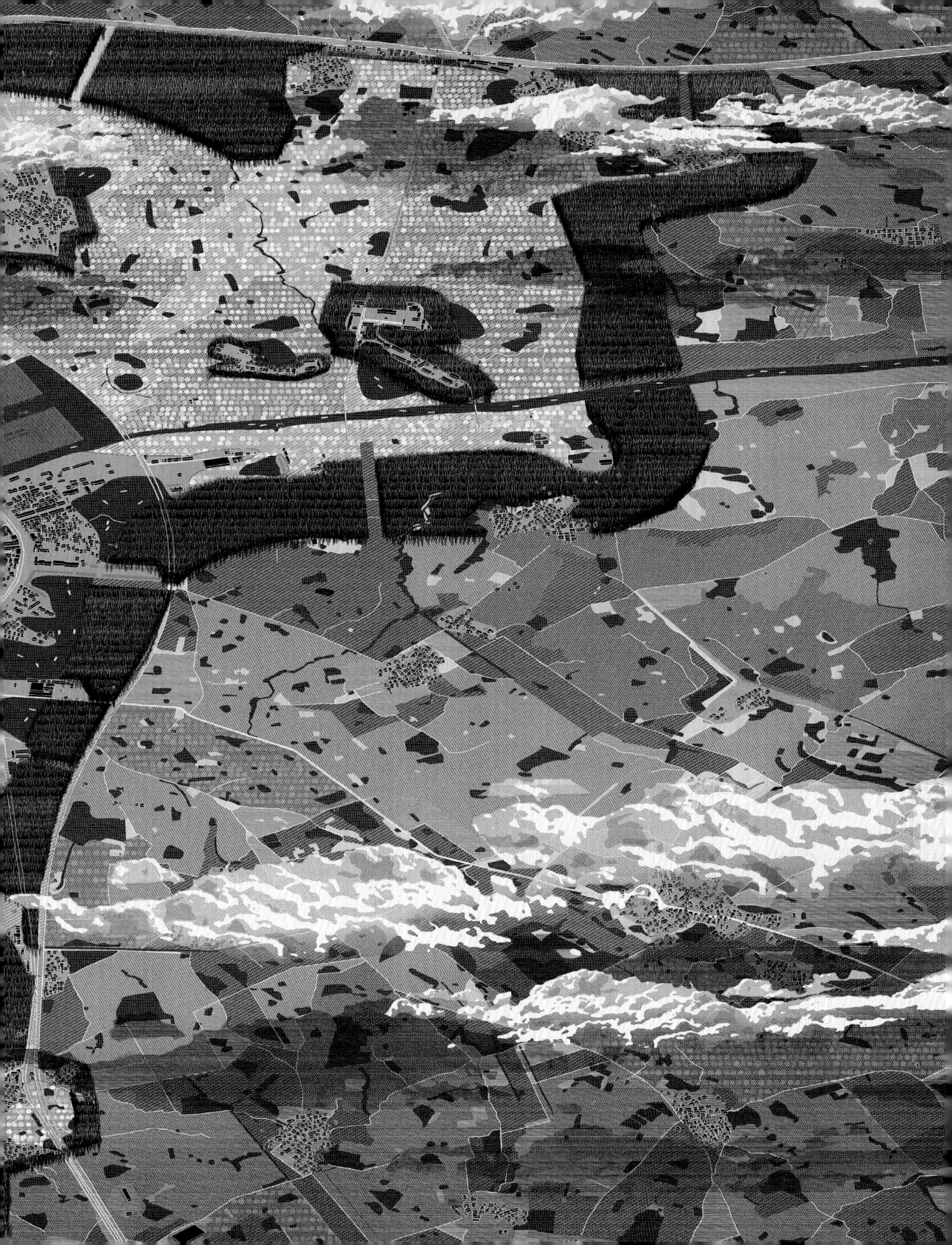

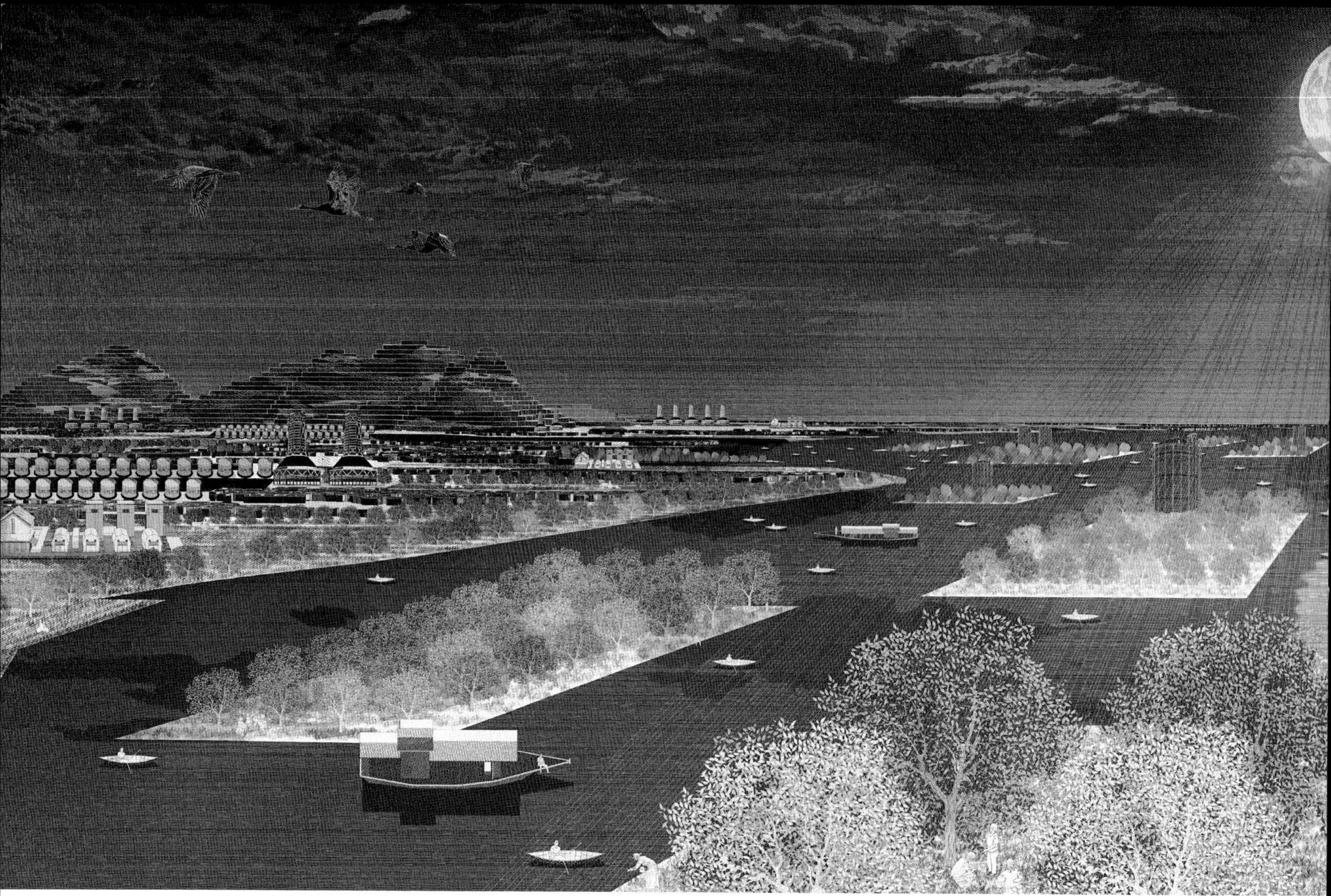

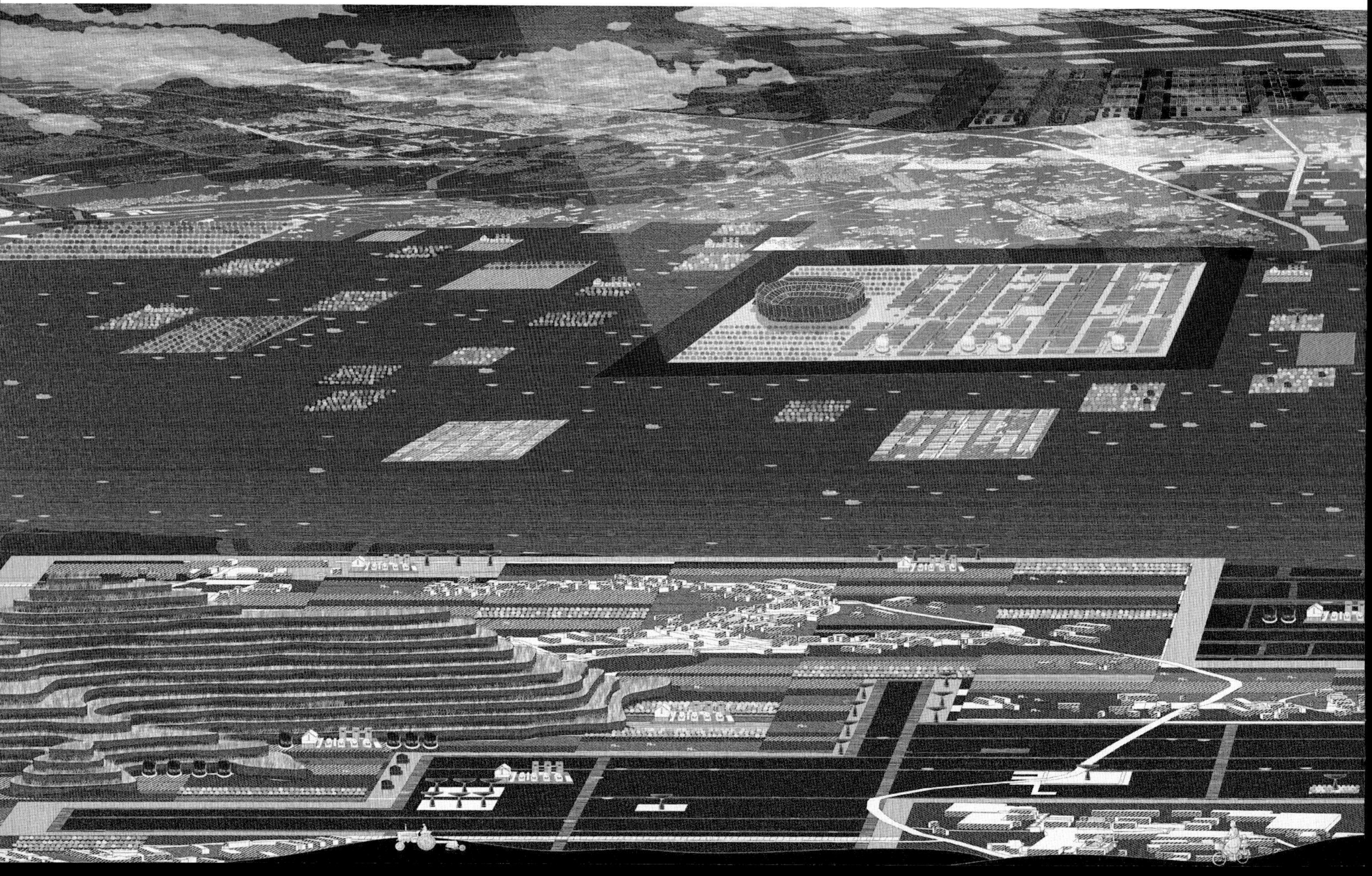

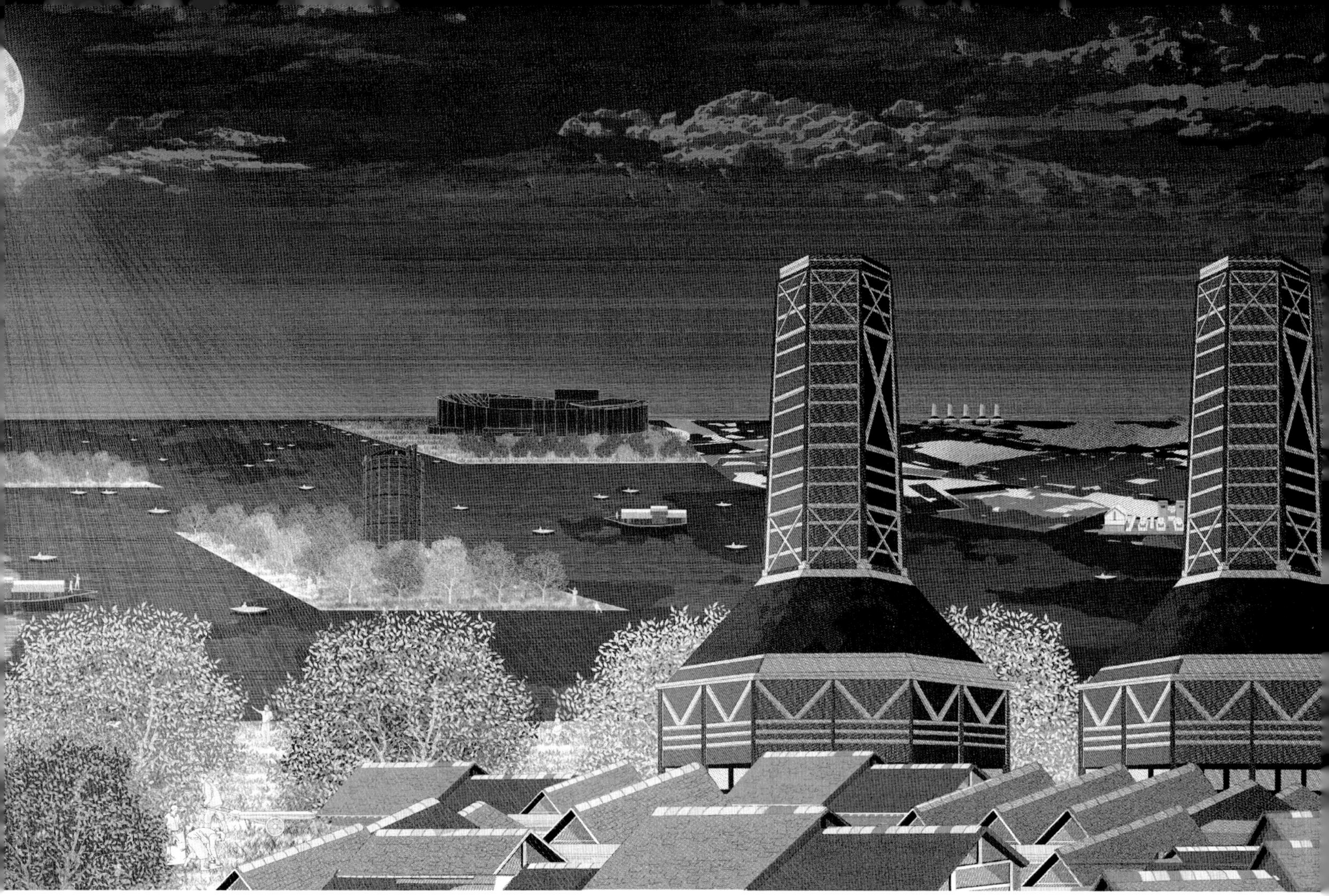

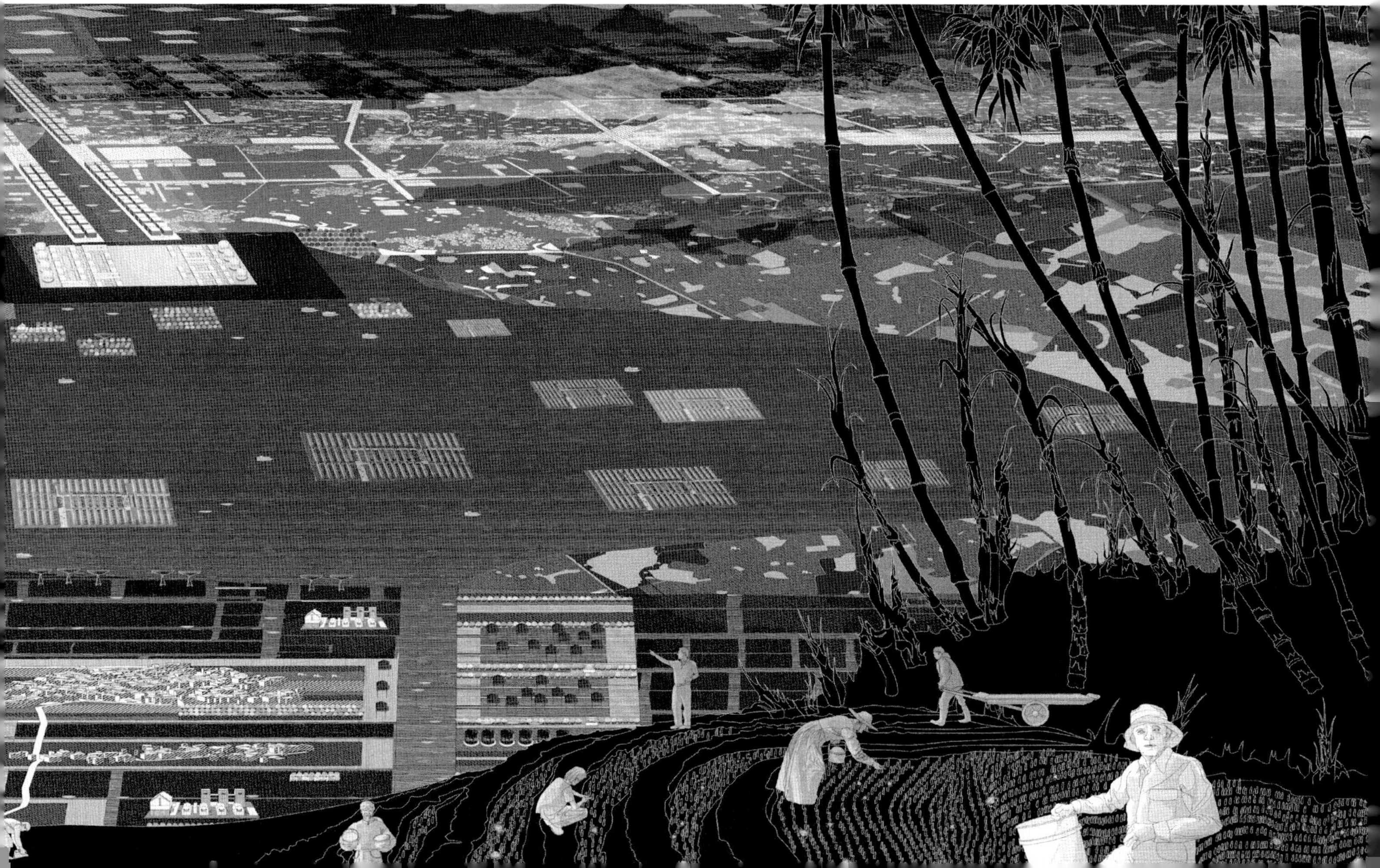

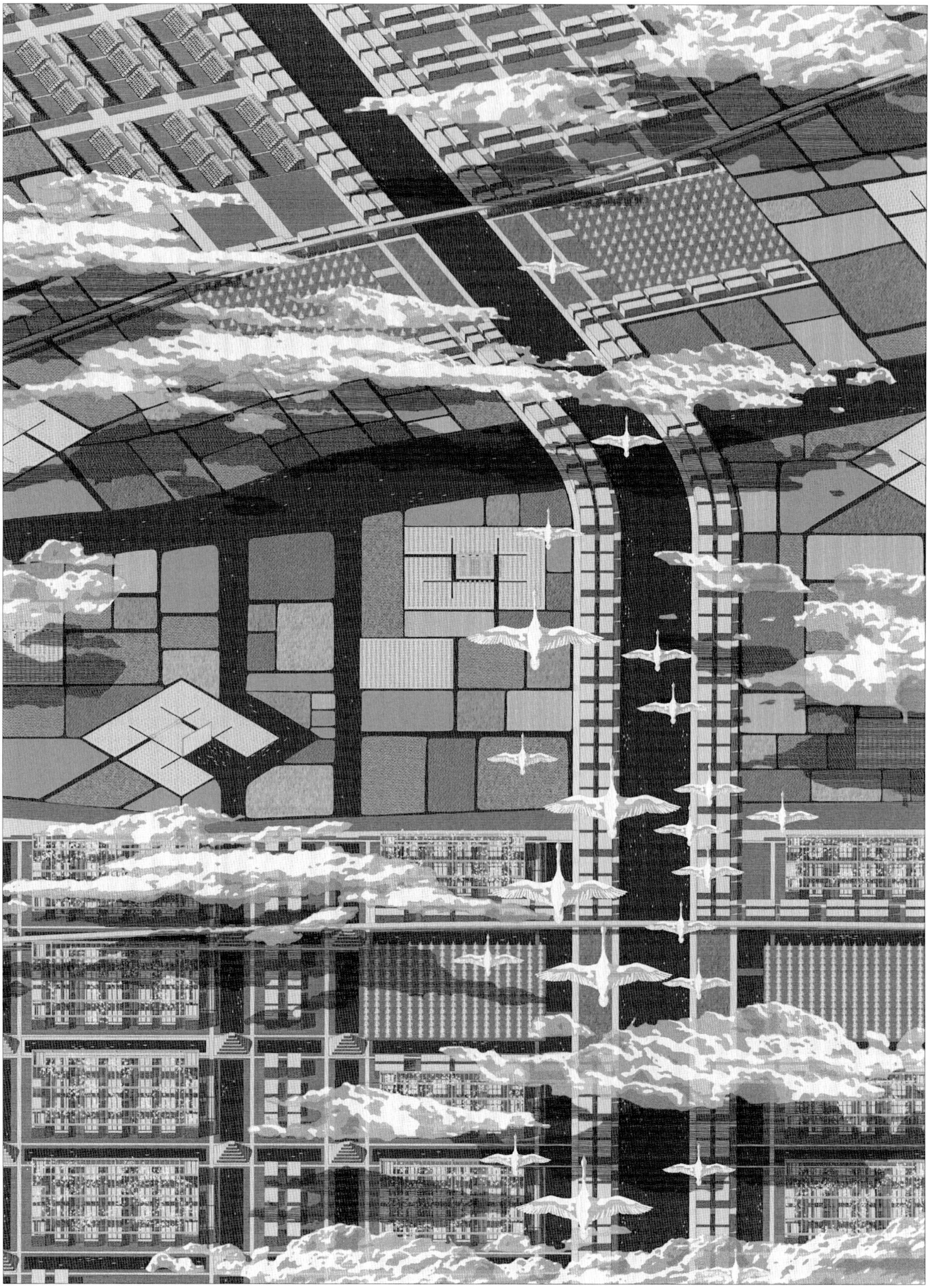

the city of a thousand lakes

human waste into biogas, and recycles the district's grey water. Children keep healthy and play in never-ending water fields, whereas the elderly wander at their leisure through gardens and orchards devoted to specific indigenous fruits. Flora are integrated into the new housing, where a more metabolic or symbiotic relationship with nature can occur. From their dwellings, the inhabitants can contently take in the panoramic views of lakes, ponds and paddies – a celebration of the romantic idyll favored by Morris. In addition, the infrastructure provides job opportunities, mobility and a fairer distribution of wealth, combining lifelong health and wellbeing targets; but just as determined to defend against Lois Lowry's dystopian world where society has eliminated pain, suffering and struggle by imposing the bland equality of 'sameness' described in 'The Giver' (1993).[7]

Shallow dredging is employed to expand the southern lake into a zone of constructed water filtration wetland, which features numerous artificial floating islands. The multi-use islands provide additional space for orchards, bamboo forests, and community activities. On the lakeshores, a new university campus and stadium are positioned at the end of an axis that runs through the city. They are linked to an existing innovation park and continue into the new ecological residential area in the north. The 'high street' axis connects the city's aquaculture developments to commercial activities, prioritizing the services industry. Tourism forms a large part of the local economy, especially during the Crab Festival in September. Rather than the high street being dominated by cars, vessels gliding along at a glacial pace in the broad tree-lined canal replace road traffic.

The subtle aromas of nature arouse a new interpretation of the senses and memories of a traditional Chinese garden. The melancholy shimmer and flatness of the waterlogged infrastructure reflect a peculiar yet poetic and beautiful aspect of the province. The water somehow holds a sense of time, a sense of the sublime in its reflective surface and its inability to be stopped. The City of a Thousand Lakes does not retreat to the 'traditional' nor does it shy away from strategic density – it has achieved multiple interpretations of Bellamy's 'Equality' to allow the region to localize its economy and much of its population. The blue sustainable pension plan provides a mutual, self-sustaining support network that develops socio-economic-environmental relations and contributes to community cohesion. As for Morris, the aquaculture infrastructure serves to remind its inhabitants of their faith and loyalty, and it is nature that unites and provides. In a country as large as China, pockets of self-sustainable communities can question the nation's vision of urban futures and wellbeing.

previous pages + facing page: The panoramic views of lakes, ponds and paddies celebrates the romantic idyll. Flora is integrated to cultivate a symbiotic relationship with nature.

following pages: The high street axis connects the aquaculture developments to commercial and services industries.

7. L Lowry, 'The Giver', Houghton Mifflin, Boston US, 1993

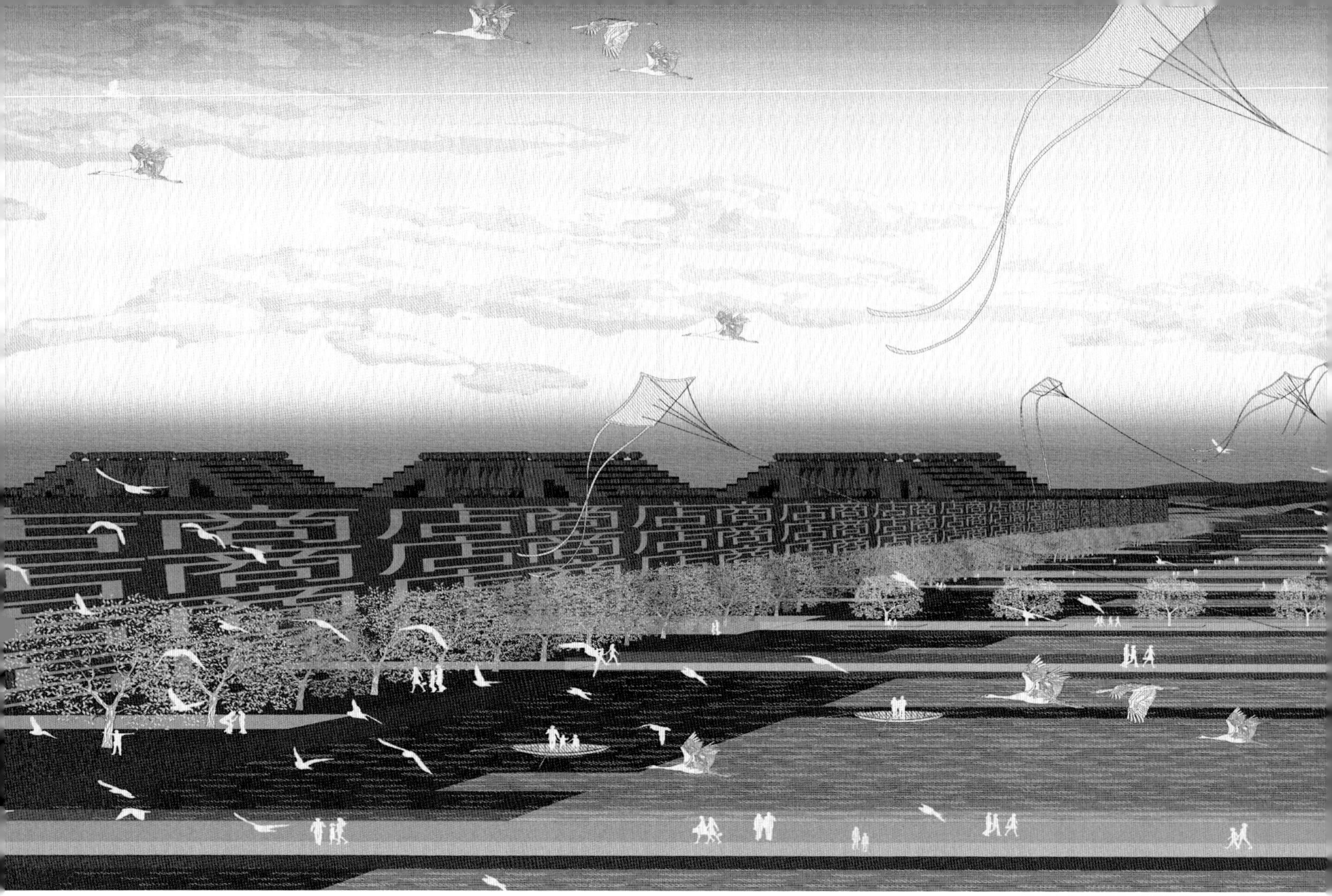

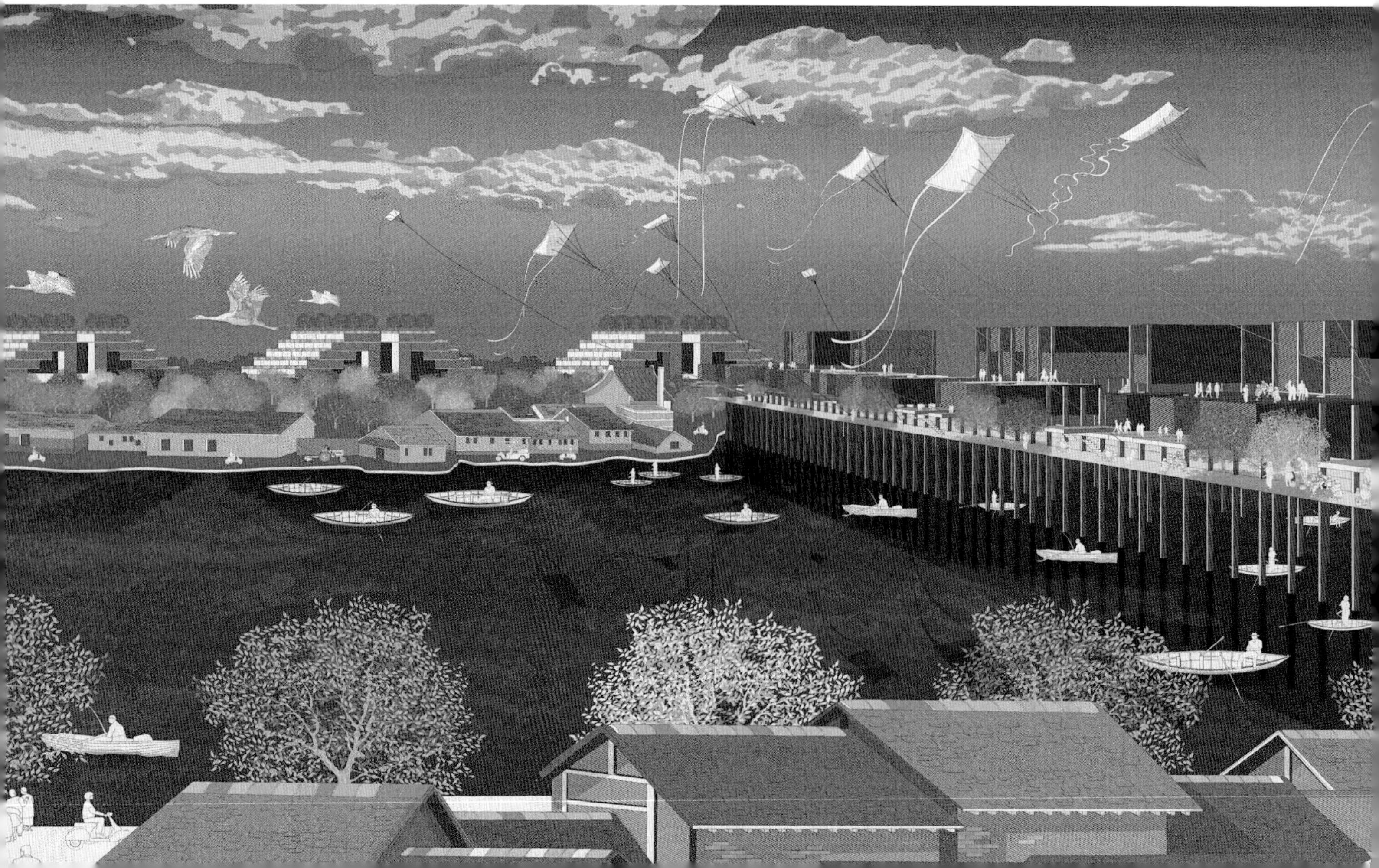

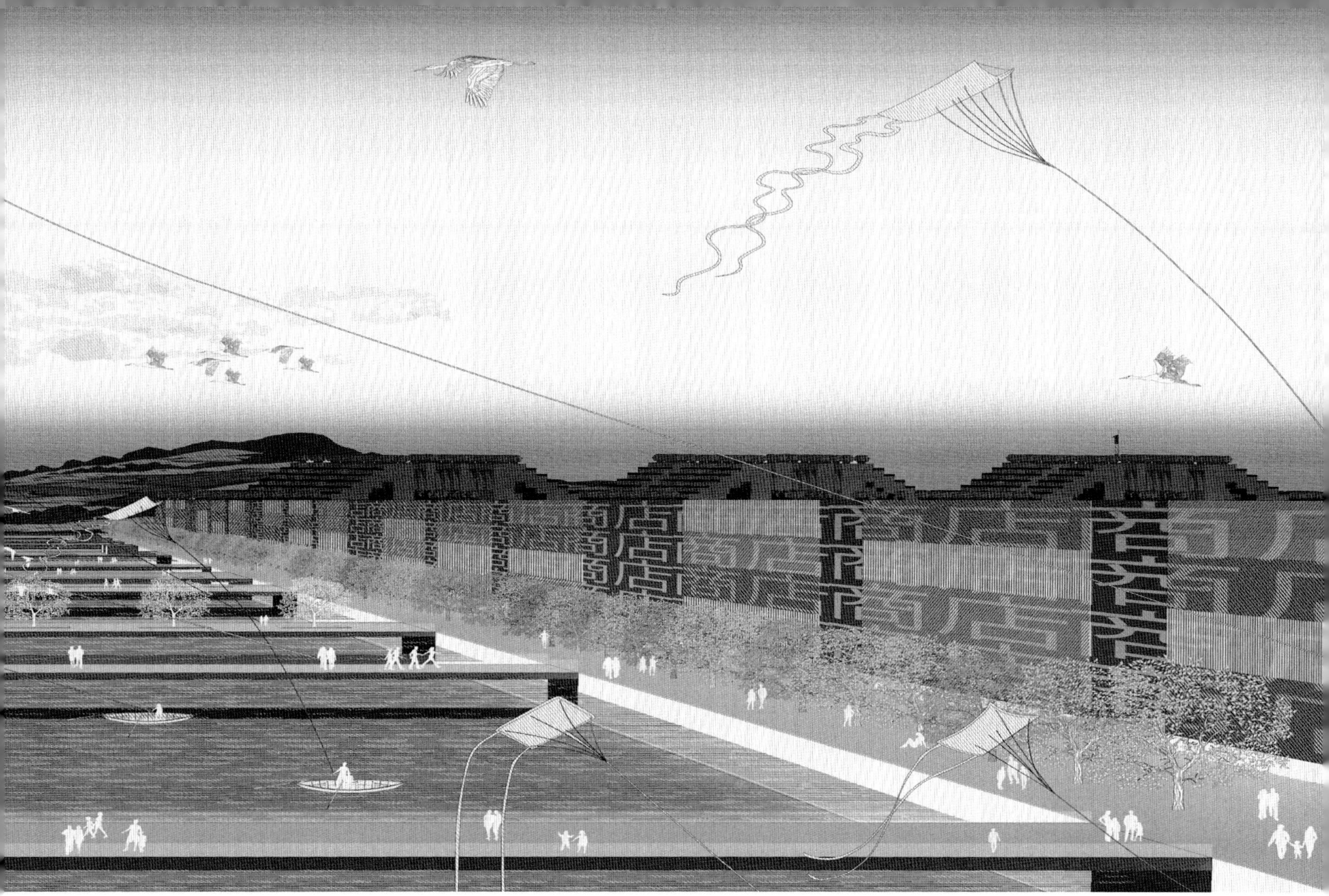
商店
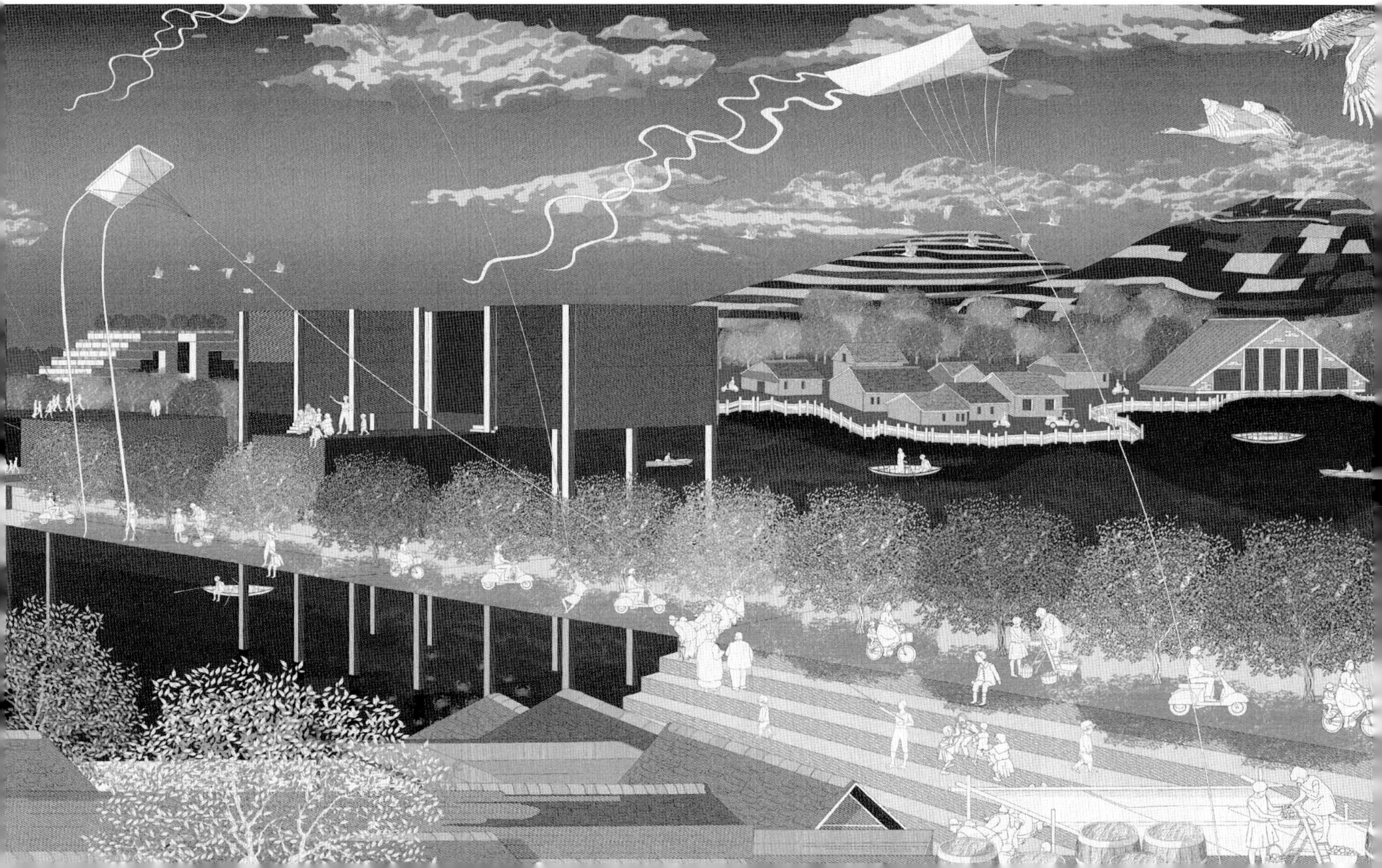

226

urban future

The Forest: An infrastructure for urban resilience

(vi)

'... of the land of Cockaygne, edible food grows wild, cooked animals present themselves for feasting, and houses are built of sugar and the streets are paved with pastry. In Cuccagna, the Italian version of this fantasy of gluttony, there are bridges made of salami, rivers of milk or wine, and mountains covered with cream cheese.'

– Gregory Claeys, 'Searching for Utopia: The history of an idea', 2011

Today, the peripheries of our cities and towns are instead dominated by massive infrastructures of the food industries, caused by the rise of globalization and high-mileage trading of produce. Nicola Twilley, creator of the exhibition 'Perishable: An Exploration of the Refrigerated Landscape of America' (2014) summarized: 'The diet of the average American is almost entirely dependent on the existence of a vast, distributed winter – a seamless network of artificially chilled processing plants, distribution centers, shipping containers, and retail display cases that creates the permanent global summertime of our supermarket aisles.'[1]

'Porkopolis', the million-square-foot slaughterhouse of Smithfield Foods in North Carolina, processes up to 32,000 hogs per day via its heavily automated disassembly line. Dakota City, Nebraska, and Amarillo, Texas, host some of the largest beef packing plants for Tyson Foods, the largest meat company in America.[2] Many large cities have wholesale markets, with sales conducted mostly in the pre-dawn hours. The Philadelphia Wholesale Produce Market has 224 sealed dock doors that surround its perimeter, allowing the market's entire loading dock and sales floor to be kept chilled to 50°F all day.[3] New York City's Hunts Point market, originally built in 1972, is a 60-acre infrastructure with seven buildings and a million square feet of refrigerated space. With a cooperative membership of 52 companies, it is the 'largest of its kind in the world' and is the major distribution hub for the New York City metro area.[4]

The infrastructures that accommodate the average network of chilled warehouses, packing plants, food factories, and supermarkets are most often lacking in identity. The resultant of efficiency, low cost, and mass commercialization of goods sold; the soulless constructs do not attempt to forge relationships with place, people or the produce, at least not as a priority. At the best of times, they are the product of standardized utilitarian structures made in a factory-factory devoted to efficient production of cheap pre-fabricated building components.

Alas, these are not the portrayals of science fiction (SF) environments in 'Metropolis', 'Looking Backward: 2000–1887' or HG Wells' 'The Time Machine', which satirized England some 800,000 years

227

facing page: The Exchange brings its inhabitants back to an absent tradition of hunting and gathering, and adopts food sovereignty policies to address issues of climate change.

following pages: The masterplan of the green infrastructure.

1. AC Madrigal, 'A Journey Into Our Food System's Refrigerated-Warehouse Archipelago', The Atlantic: Technology, 2013 [http://www.theatlantic.com/technology/archive/2013/07/a-journey-into-our-food-systems-refrigerated-warehouse-archipelago/277790], retrieved 28 August 2015

2. N Twilley, 'Refrigerated Nation: The landscape of perishable food in America', The Center for Land Use Interpretation, Lay of the Land Newsletter, Winter 2014 [http://clui.org/newsletter/winter-2014/refrigerated-nation], retrieved 28 August 2015

3. Philadelphia Wholesale Produce Market, 'Facility' [http://www.pwpm.net/about/facility/], retrieved 28 August 2015

4. Hunts Point Cooperative Market, 'The World's Largest Food Distribution Center' [http://huntspointcoopmkt.com], retrieved 28 August 2015

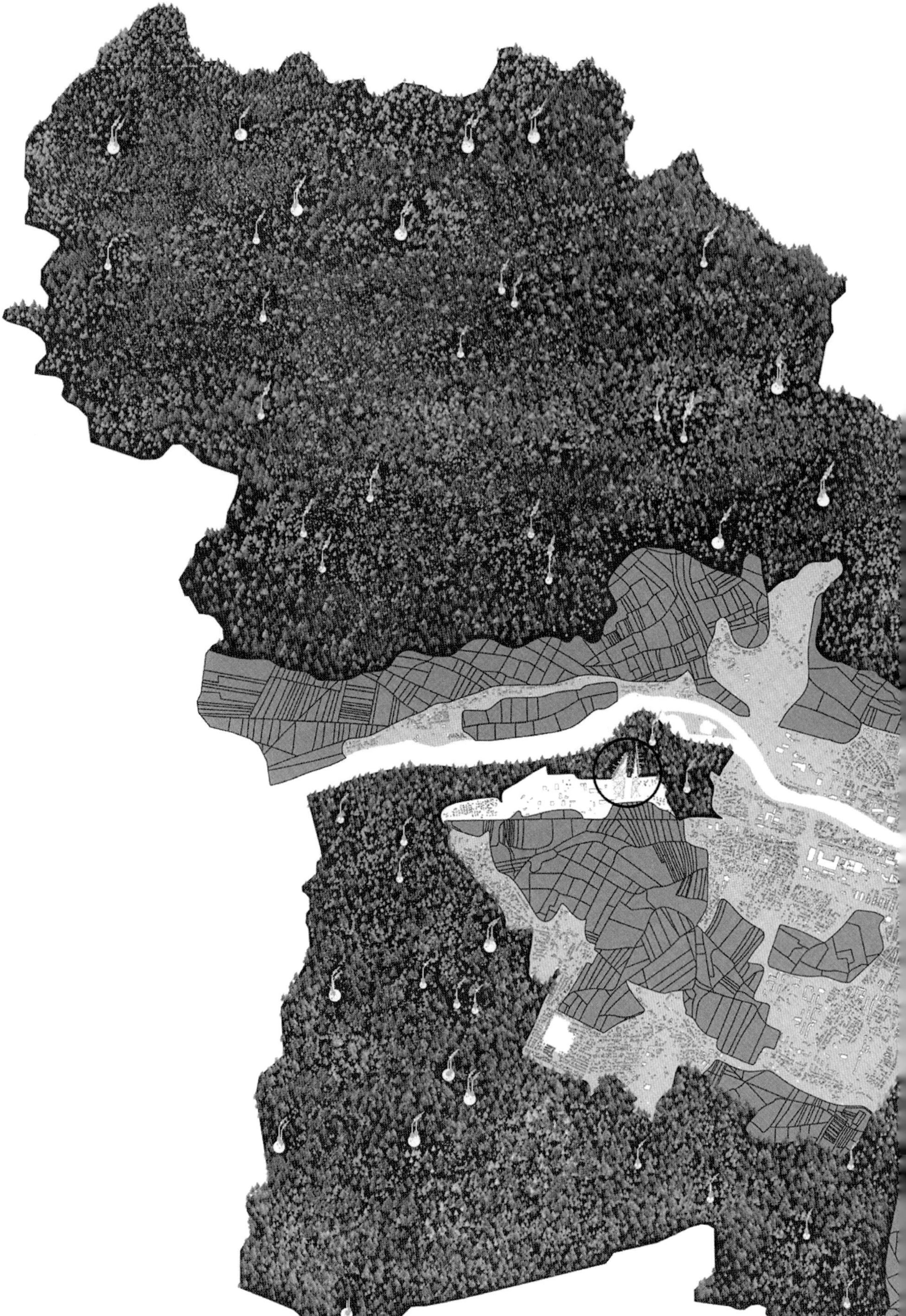

Hunting Exchange Gatehouse

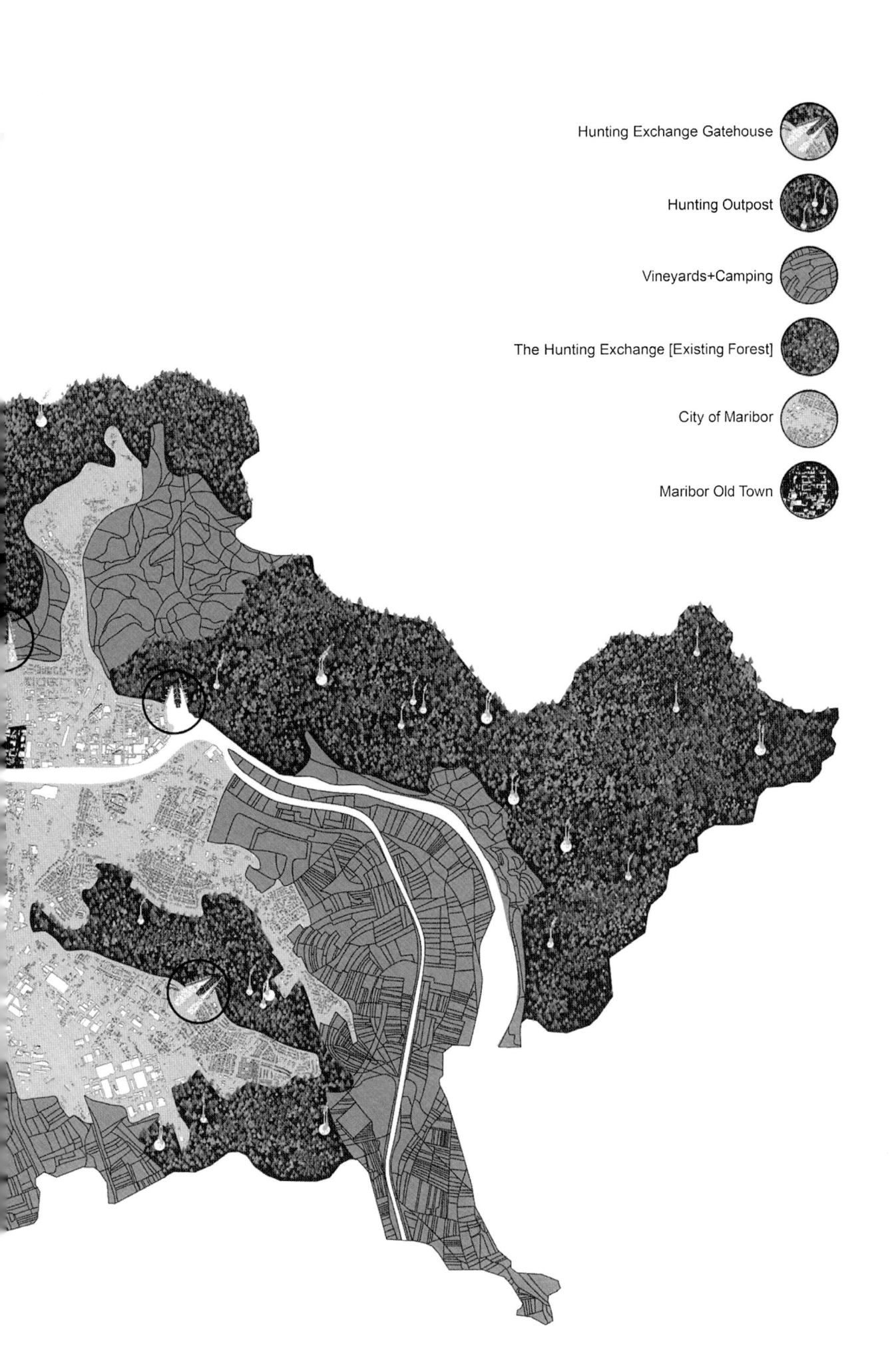

Hunting Outpost

Vineyards+Camping

The Hunting Exchange [Existing Forest]

City of Maribor

Maribor Old Town

229

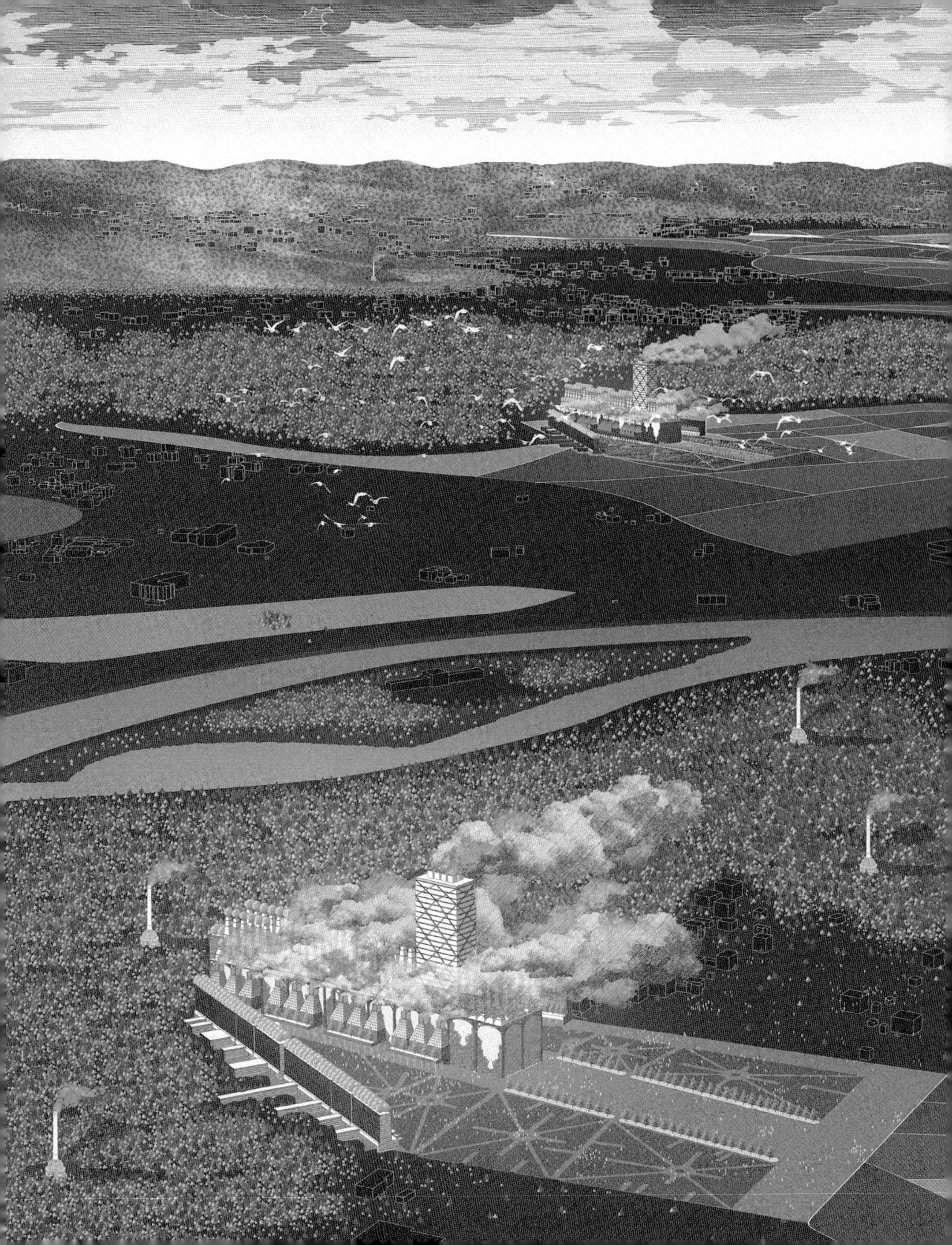

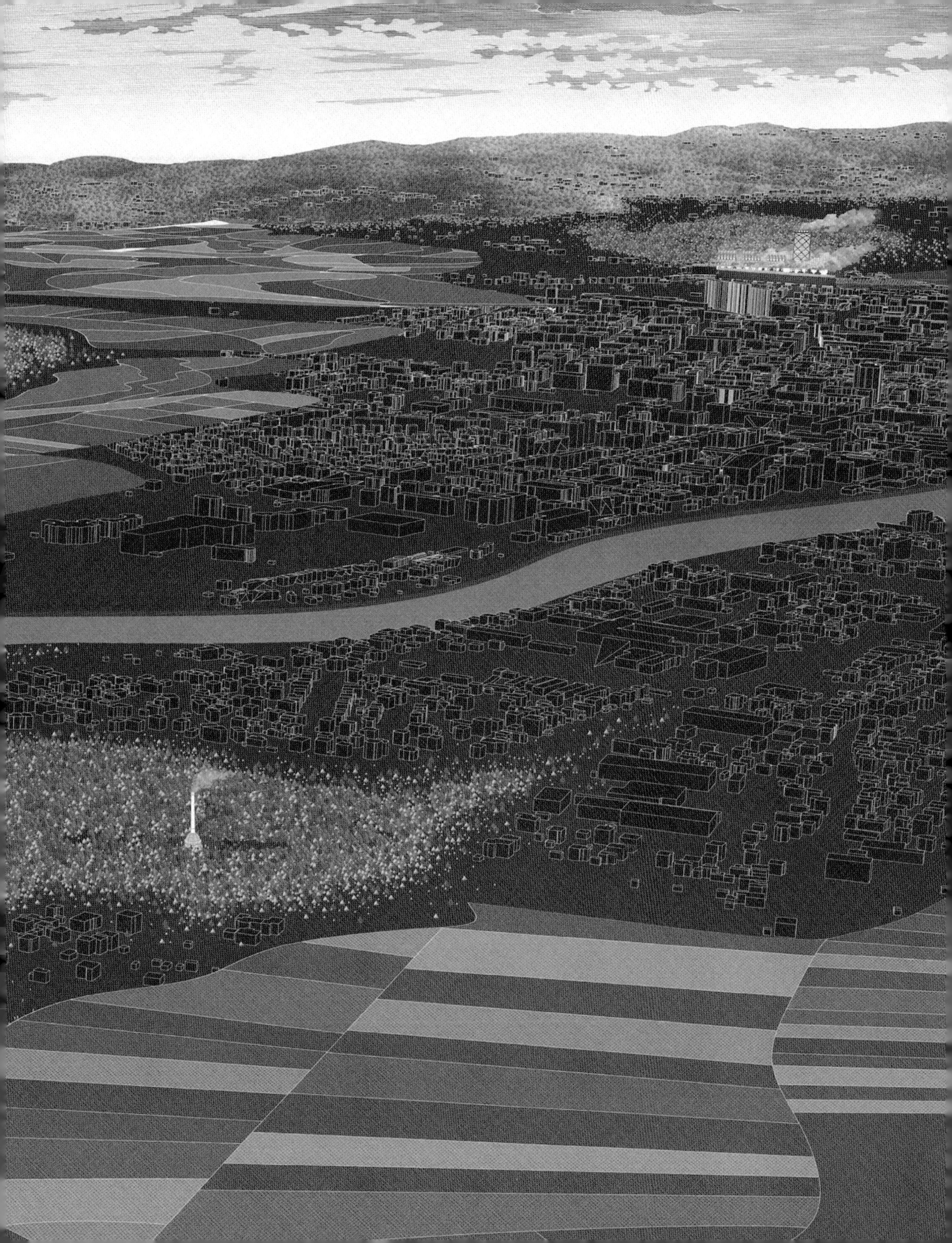

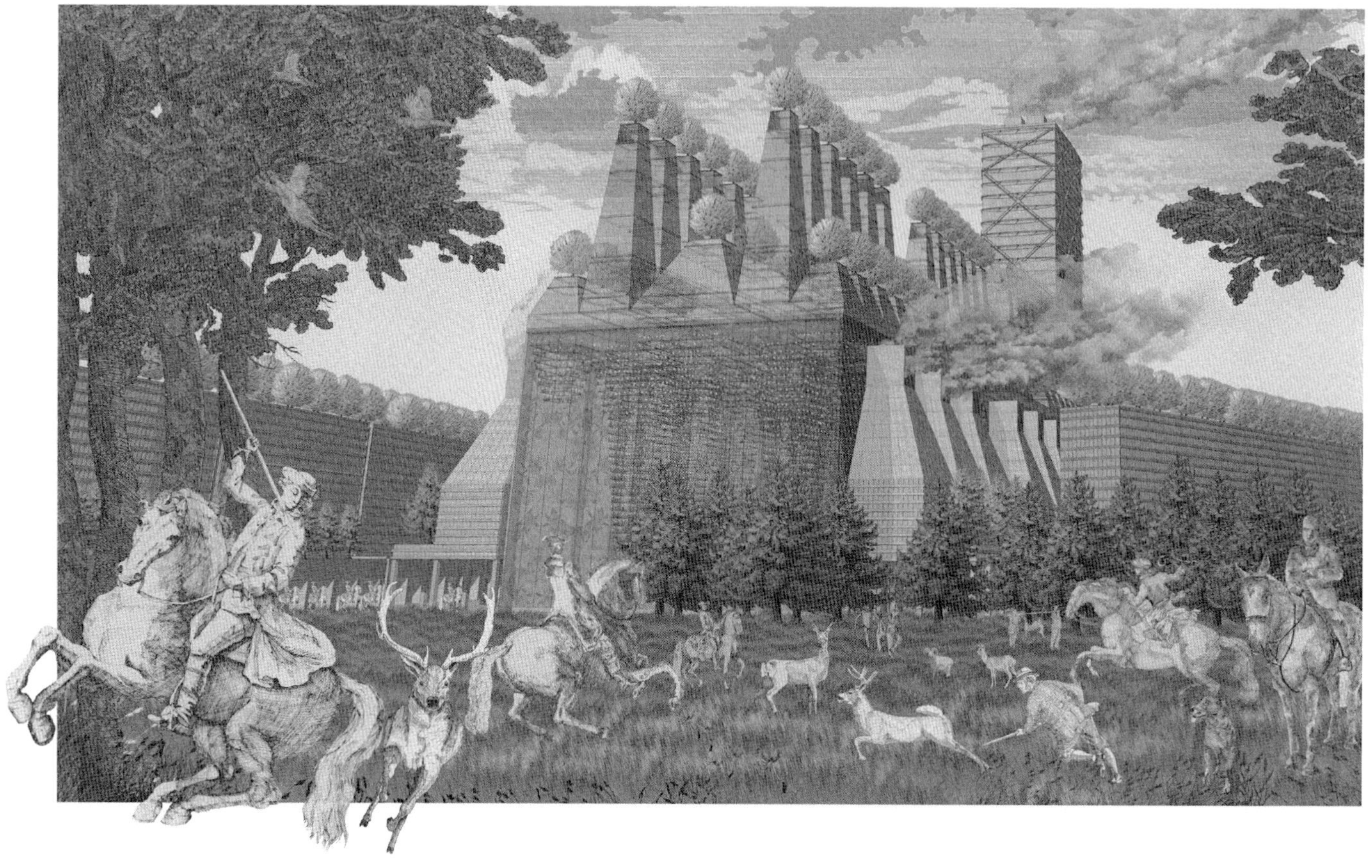

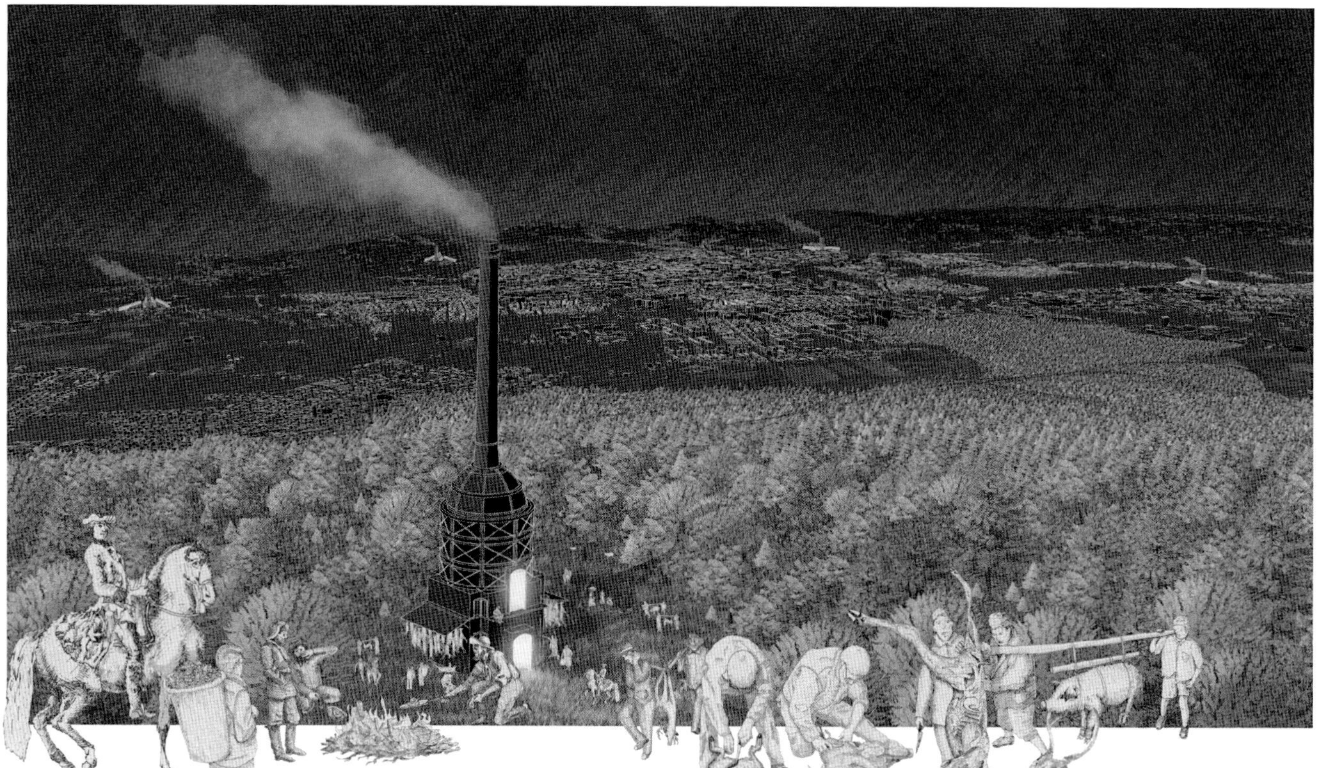

the forest: an infrastructure for urban resilience

on from our own, where its inhabitants toil among the machines of the subterranean tunnels. Even the romanticized images of supermarkets from Edward Burtynsky's film 'Manufactured Landscapes' (2006) cannot disguise our current dystopian built environments – endless perfectly arranged lines of flamboyantly branded products, practically marching off the shelves.

SF has often warned of futures we want to avoid – how can society function differently to prevent them? Food sovereignty proposes community control on the production, distribution and consumption of food, an alternative system to the failed industrialized food model. The movement adheres to food systems working with nature, and respecting the integrity of ecosystems.[5] Concerted action must be taken to challenge conventional understanding of food security, as the foods we choose to eat will have substantial environmental consequences in the coming decades. Agriculture accounts for 14% of total greenhouse gas emissions, with another 17% attributed to changing land-use linked to deforestation.[6] Before the arrival of agriculture, humans were hunter-gatherers until around 10,000 years ago.

Irrespective of their eventual fall, the Garden of Eden provided Adam and Eve with all that they required. According to Genesis 2:9, 'And out of the ground the Lord God made to spring up every tree that is pleasant to the sight and good for food. The tree of life was in the midst of the garden.' With the same belief, 'The Hunter-Gatherers Exchange' in Maribor re-imagines the multifarious forests of Pohorje and its surrounding greens as a 'living supermarket' infrastructure. With over half of Slovenia forested, the Exchange brings its inhabitants back to an absent tradition of hunting and gathering, and adopts food sovereignty policies to address issues of climate change and food sustainability. The intention is that the forest infrastructure gradually extends its footprint; declining and abandoned industrial zones are adapted into wildlife habitats for cultivation of deer and other game.

In Slovenia in years gone by, it was common for the populace to hunt wild boar, chamois, deer, mouflon and other fauna that thrive within the local forests. Despite some ethical issues concerning hunting, many consider regulated and sustainable hunting to be an effective, low-cost green method for maintaining wildlife population. In this context, soft infrastructures of hunting schools and proper gun-control regulations would provide the local stakeholders with the skills and professionalism to act humanely and responsibly. With three different climates – the Alpine, Mediterranean and Pannonian – there is also an abundance of 'non-wood forest products' including walnut, chestnut, forest fruits, medicinal herbs and a wide variety of mushrooms. The EU-funded 'STARTREE' project (2016) identified the huge untapped commercial and nutritional potential of the forest and its non-wood forest products. According to Robert Mavsar from the European Forest Institute, 'the diversification into non-wood products also means that the forestry sector and related business activities are better prepared to deal with economic crises that may hit the commercial value of a particular product'.[7]

The Exchange promotes sustainable management of the forests and innovative solutions to help resolve forest-use conflicts that can arise between rural and urban communities. Dotted within the green infrastructure, outposts allow hunters and gatherers to replenish their supplies, but more essentially, provide a sense of communion and solidarity amongst those living this reinterpreted historical

facing page top: The 80-meter tall meat-smoking chimney, an acknowledgement of the city's ancient farming towers, marks the entrance to each gatehouse.

facing page bottom: Dotted within the green infrastructure, outposts provide a sense of communion and solidarity.

5. 'What is Food Sovereignty?', The Food Sovereignty Movement [http://foodsovereigntynow.org.uk/foodsov/], retrieved 28 August 2015

6. KA Wheeler, 'Building Resilient Food Systems in a World of Climate Uncertainty', The Guardian: Sustainable Food, 21 December 2012 [https://www.theguardian.com/sustainable-business/building-resilient-food-systems-climate], retrieved 28 August 2015

7. Horizon 2020: The EU Framework Programme for Research and Innovation, 'Foraging Untapped Value of Europe's Forests', The European Commission, 9 January 2015 [http://ec.europa.eu/programmes/horizon2020/en/news/foraging-untapped-value-europe's-forests], retrieved 28 August 2015

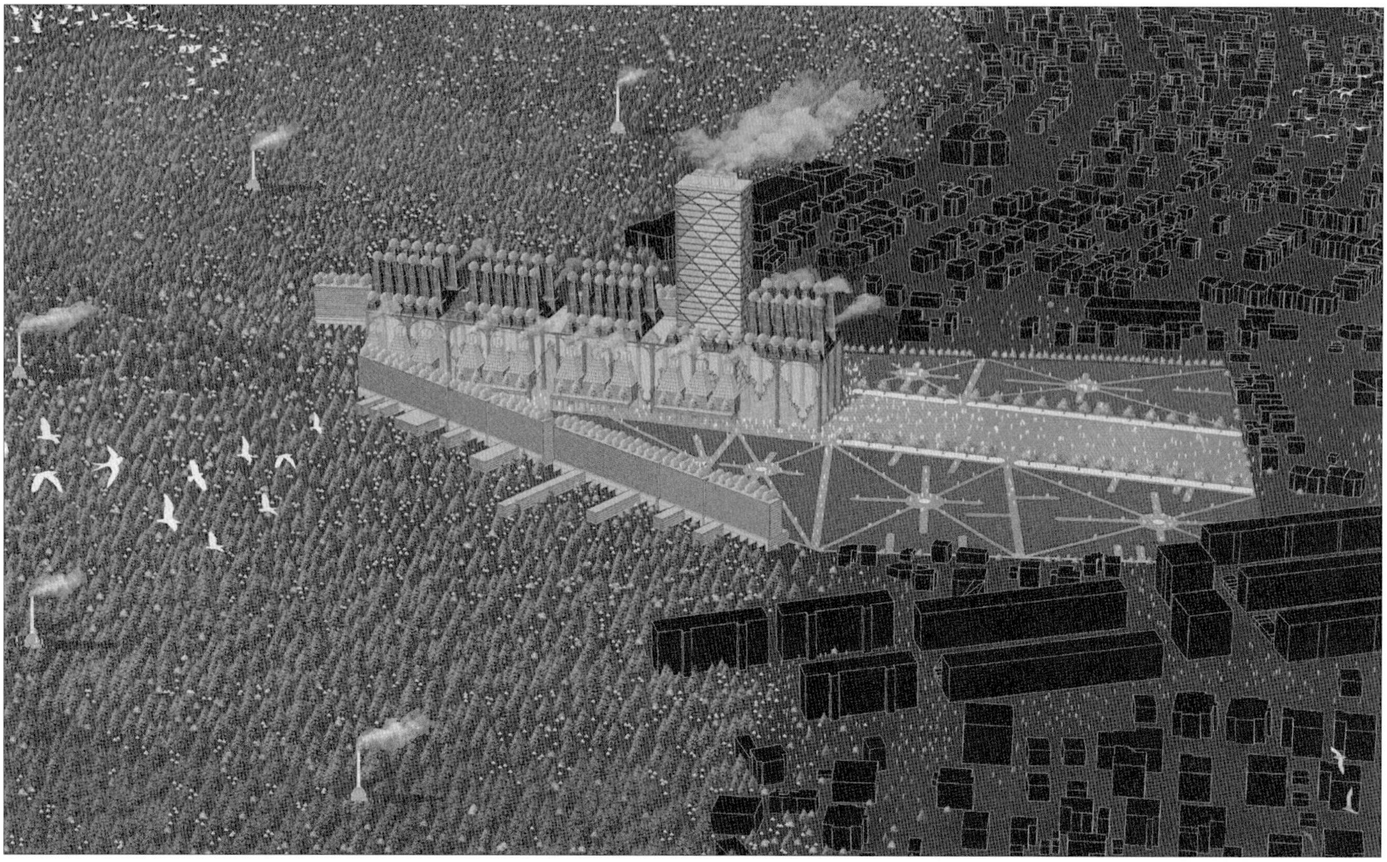

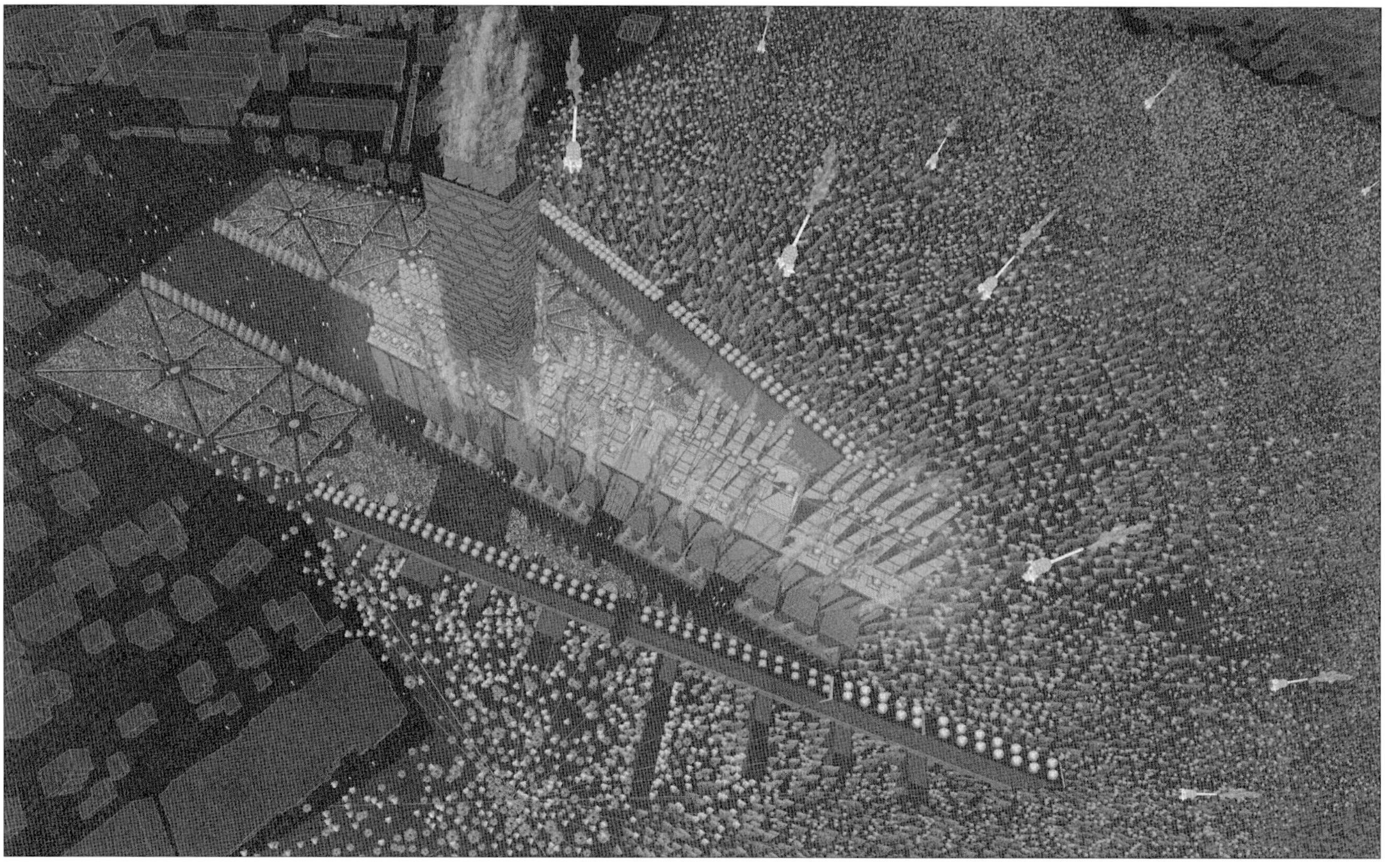

the forest: an infrastructure for urban resilience

lifestyle. Indeed, mushroom- and dandelion-picking have probably been the country's most widespread recreational activity for all age groups and demographics over the past few decades. Dandelions and mushrooms are traditional Slovenian cuisines; the hunter-gatherers' paradigm ensures Slovenian gastronomic heritage lives on in the narratives of their urban futures.

Food trading in a city affects its public space, architectural landscape and consequently the wellbeing of its inhabitants. The four towering gatehouses of the Exchange are the embodiment of community empowerment and food sovereignty brought into practice – the inhabitants not only buy and exchange goods and services, furthermore they come to share municipal news and community gossips, and attend gastronomic seasonal gatherings. Inside, trading spaces line-up alongside facilities for traditional culinary processes and storage, communal kitchens and dinning-halls. At the end of each hunting season, the inhabitants of Maribor garner in the cathedral-esque dining halls to share experiences and knowledge, nurturing social cohesion under the meat-curing chandeliers. The interiors of the halls are lined with hundreds of thousands of glass jars filled with pickled and preserved edible forest products. Filtered light streams through the various openings of the gatehouses only to create multiple rich-colored reflections off the jars. Drying of medicinal herbs perfumes the halls, thus bringing the forest indoors to further animate the infrastructure.

The 80-meter tall meat-smoking chimney, an acknowledgement of the city's ancient farming towers, marks the entrance to each gatehouse. The production line of steaming, curing and preserving meats slowly travels through the height of the chimneys, presenting the community's eco-conscious awareness for food procurement and preparation – and thus bridging the knowledge gap between the consumer and the consumed. As the smoky plumes proudly rise to herald yet another great harvest, Maribor is draped with a distinct aroma.

In the age of abundance and cheap food, more sophisticated palettes of nutritional understanding have to be made readily available. The World Wide Fund for Nature (WWF) focuses on raising awareness about the inherent link between forests and human wellbeing amongst the youth.[8] Similarly, the World Health Organization (WHO) Healthy Cities Programme appeals to cities and their governments to incorporate food policies into their urban futures.[9] Community health and wellbeing, and economic developments in Maribor can only improve if the city considers the resurgence of local sustainable food provision as the principal agent for municipal planning. A diet that revolves around sustainable hunting and foraging will have a reduced toll on the world's resources than one that is solely dependent on agriculture. The Hunter-Gatherers Exchange embodies a very locavore (gathering food as close to home as possible) culture – a reminder that nature's landscapes can be an infrastructure for urban resilience and an adaptation strategy.

facing page top + bottom: The towering gatehouses of the Exchange are the embodiment of community empowerment and food sovereignty brought into practice.

8. WWF Bolivia, 'Cities For Forests', World Wildlife Fund [http://wwf.panda.org/who_we_are/wwf_offices/bolivia/our_work/forest_program/responsible_trade/cities_for_forests/], retrieved 28 August 2015

9. A Robertson, C Tirado et al., 'Food and Health in Europe: A new basis for action', WHO Regional Publications, European Series, no.96, 2004 [http://www.euro.who.int/__data/assets/pdf_file/0005/74417/E82161.pdf], retrieved 28 August 2015

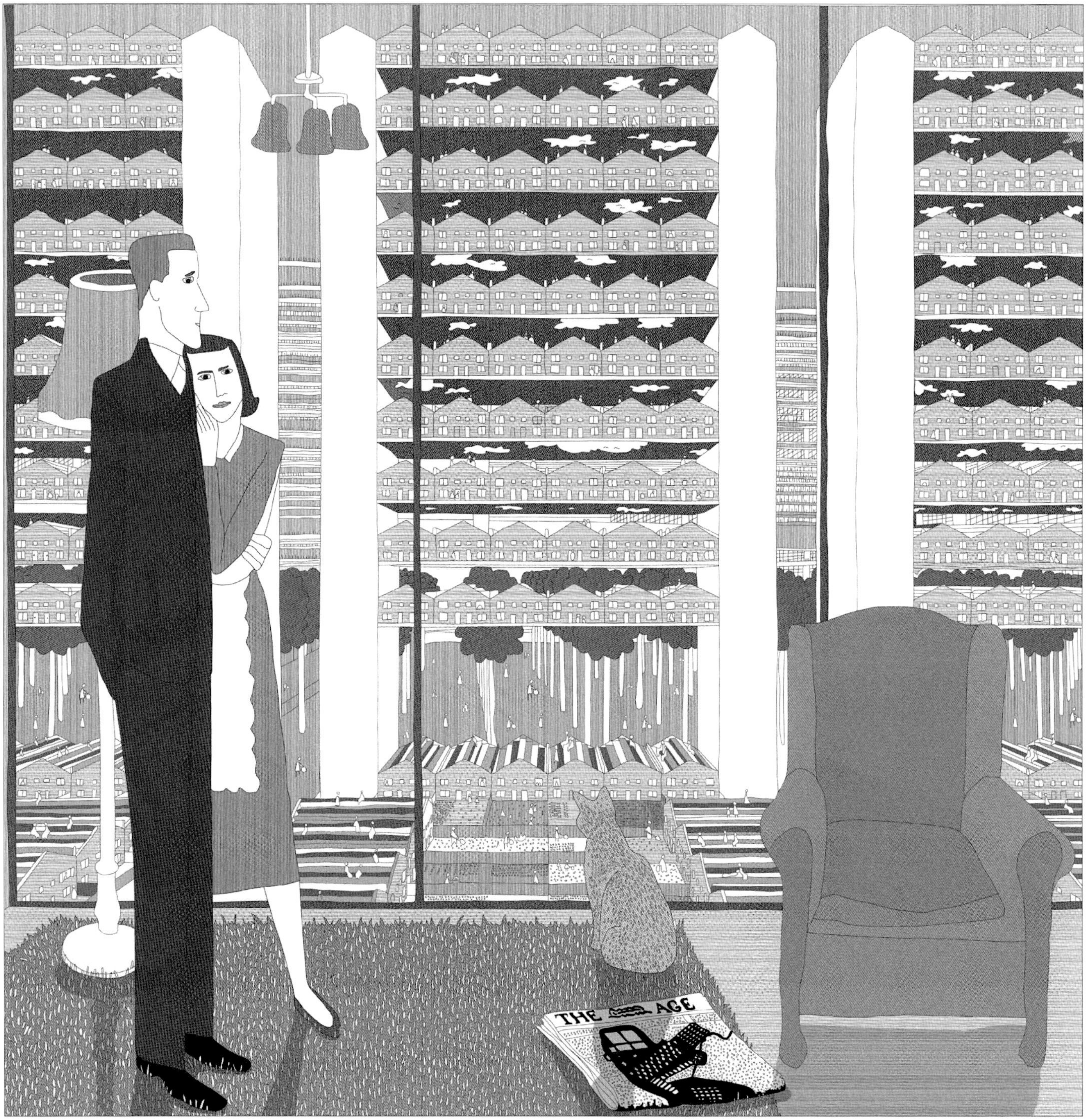
THE AGE

urban future (vii)
Perfection

'Well, he's not homeless, Howard, they just don't say where he lives. – Well, it's a silly question! – Because nobody's homeless in Pleasantville. 'Cause that's just not what it's like.'
– David Wagner/Bud Parker, 'Pleasantville', 1998

Robb McDaniel of 'Film & History' described the town of Pleasantville as the perfect place: 'It never rains, the highs and lows rest at 72 degrees, the fire department exists only to rescue treed cats, and the basketball team never misses the hoop…'[1] Perfection is a fruitless endeavor and it resonates with the work of science fiction (SF). The major themes of Gary Ross' 'Pleasantville' (1998) are that of personal repression, simple-mindedness and political oppression, played out in a perfectly complacent and literally black and white universe. When the film's protagonists find themselves accidently time traveled into a parallel world, their actions spur on the beginning of a domestic scale revolution where each broken rule brings color into life.

There is always the hidden reality behind what is apparent. It is the inner beauty that we search for in Victor Hugo's 'The Hunchback of Notre-Dame' (1831), 'Hitchhiker's Guide to the Galaxy' (1979) reveals that the earth is a super-computer built by Magrathean mice, and the bountiful sexual energy and culinary mastery of 'The Stepford Wives' (1972) are virtues not of women, but of man-made artifices. Sometimes fear may be mistaken for peace or contentedness; even fear itself or other delusions can be propagandized. In 'Nineteen Eighty Four', Orwell describes a world where political motives and sycophants are abjectly sinister, and a never-ending war and mounting 'victories' keep the world poor. In 'Brave New World', Huxley presents a version of a 'perfected' society.[2] But things are not always what they seem.

The pursuit of community perfection is often blamed for social tensions and violence; the sprawling suburbs have been accused of producing intolerance and ghettoization. The vast population growth has huge implications on the infrastructures that are largely responsible for the city; many in global cities worry their high quality of life might be in jeopardy. Anxieties of immigration and overpopulation have risen to the fore in recent works of SF. In 'Elysium' (2013), the rich, having escaped to live in the earth's orbit, violently defend their floating technologically advanced habitat against immigrants. A number of the promotional posters released for 'District 9', a film with numerous references to apartheid, and the cruel treatment of the under-class, feature the all-too-familiar slogan 'You Are Not Welcome Here'. An inward looking or 'village-mentality' is hardly likely to rise up to the challenges of climate change, or compassionately negotiate the tough decisions of globalization.

facing page: Might Perfection be the morality tale of over determined romantic visions of utopia?

following pages: Within the 25-year development plan, the self-sustaining network of infrastructures aims to cultivate socio-economic relations.

1. R McDaniel, 'Pleasantville', Film & History, Center for the Study of Film & History, 2002, vol.32, no.1, p.86 [http://muse.jhu.edu/article/400236/pdf], retrieved 25 June 2016

2. A Huxley, 'Brave New World', Chatto & Windus, London, 1932

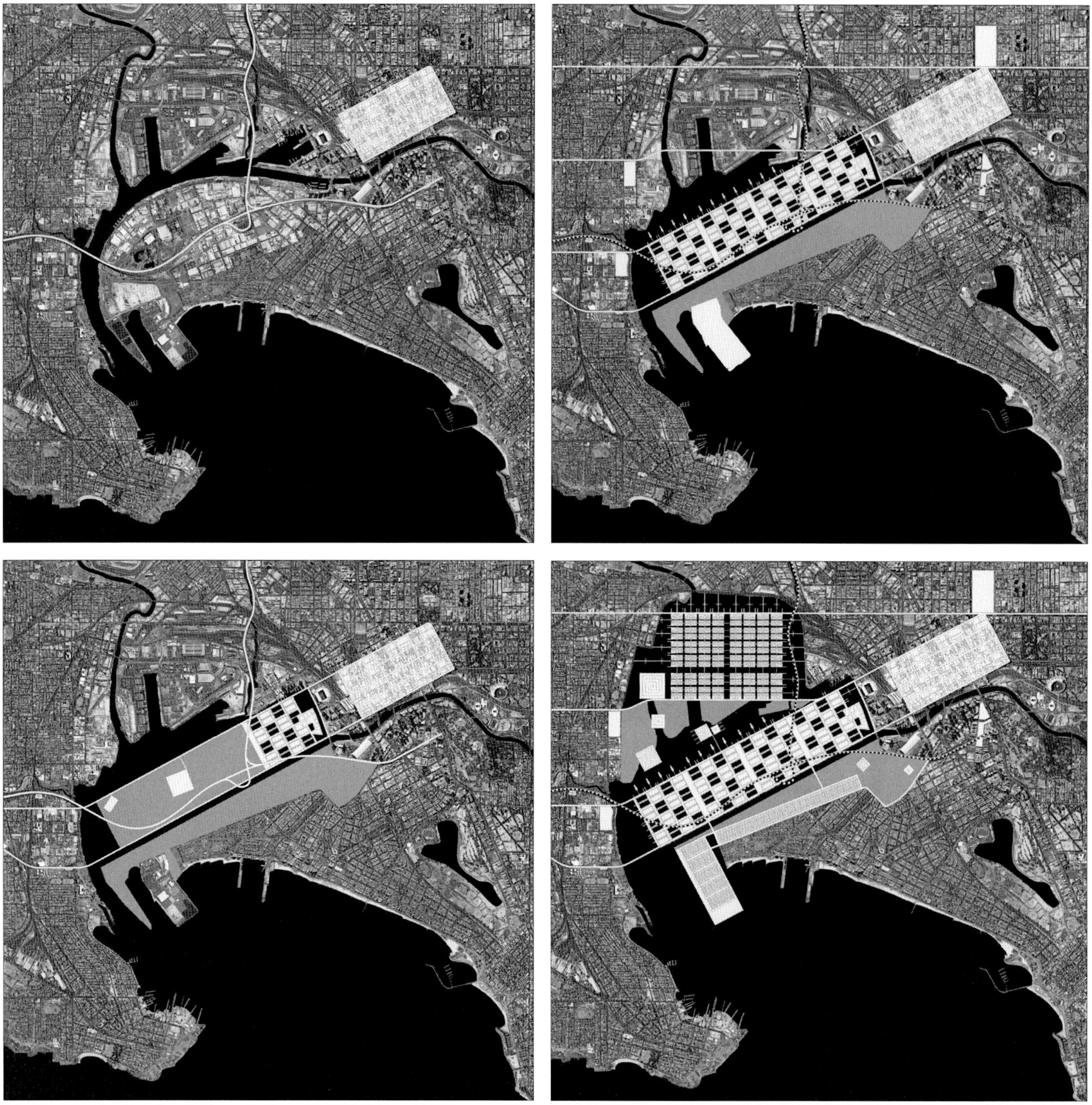

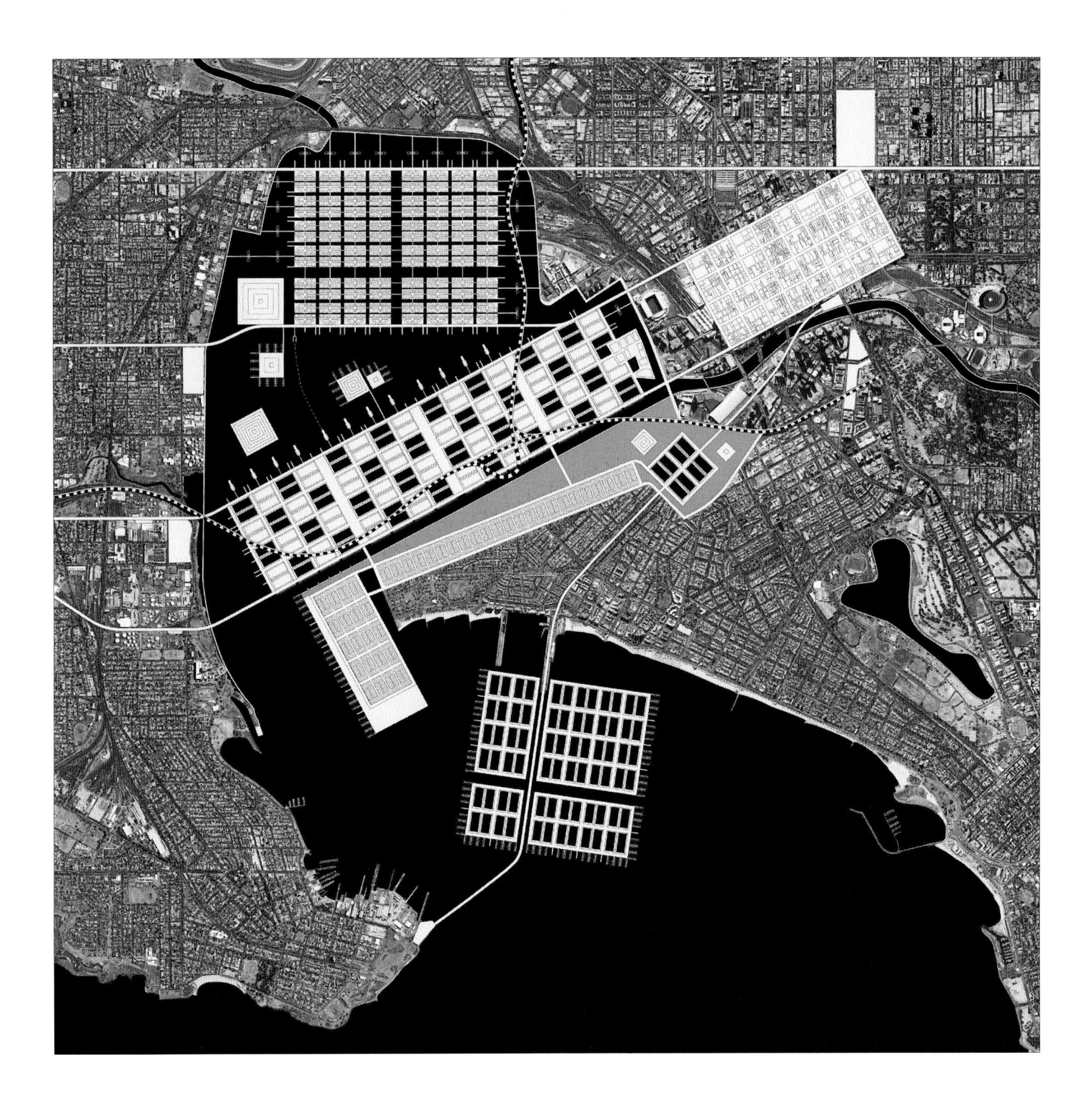

perfection

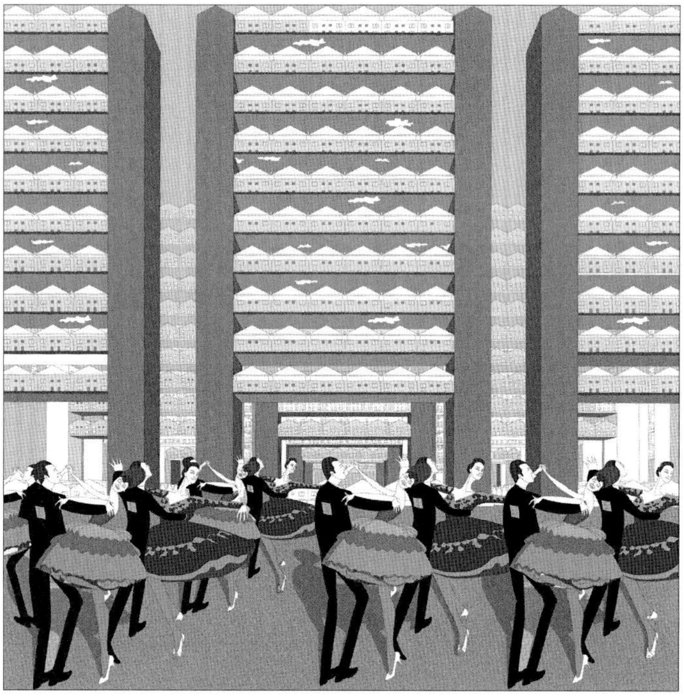

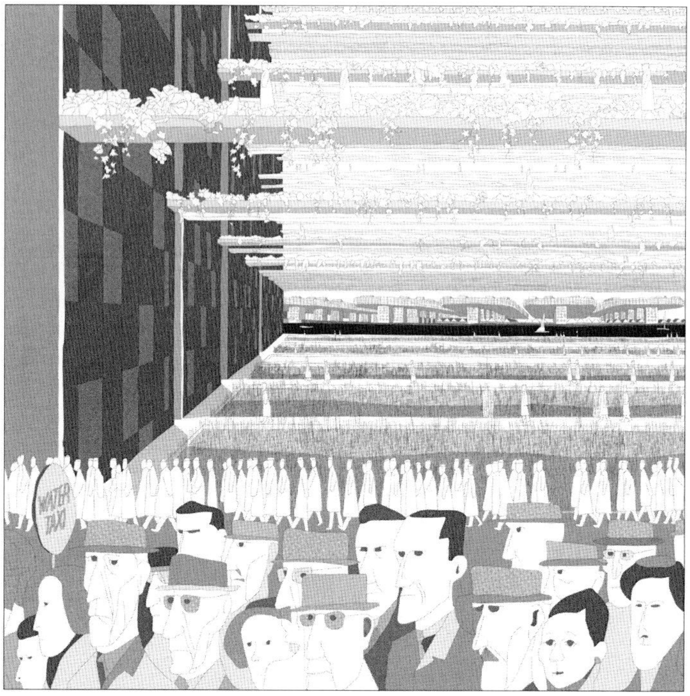
WATER TAXI

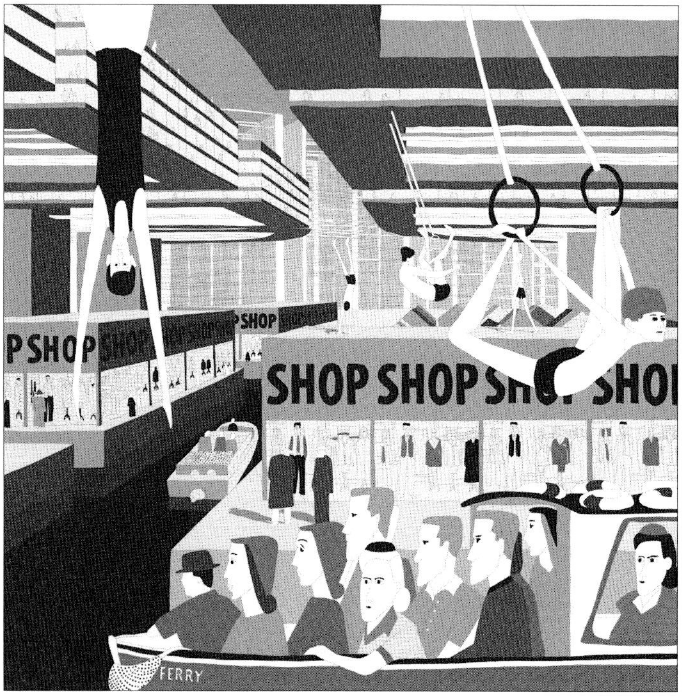
SHOP SHOP
SHOP SHOP SHOP SHOP
FERRY

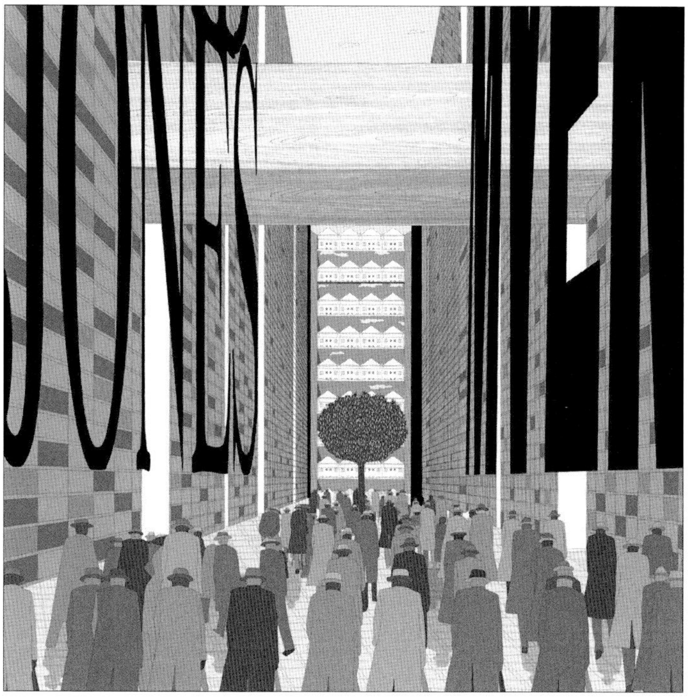

perfection

The city of Melbourne has been hailed as 'The World's Most Liveable City' for many years.[3] Its ubiquitous urban grid distributes services and traffic by an alternation of little and large streets (and they are named as such), and is punctuated by public plazas and green space. There is a regular system of rational coordinated public transport that extends far out into the Victorian suburbs. The cultural quarters with their diverse ethnic and food groups have earned the city its reputation as a friendly metropolis. Melbourne's temperate oceanic climate, whilst occasionally bringing unpredictable weather, is rarely too hot, too cold, too wet or too dry.

A city designed from first principles by European settlers in a vast open countryside bay, Melbourne is marked with trade centers, train stations, civic institutions and places of worship, and is fairly dense but low-rise. The surrounding suburbs maintain an organizational grid of the same scale, resulting in a sprawling mass of small low-rise detached housing with front-and-back gardens, which extends for miles into the open wilderness. The suburbs, until recently a symbol of the perfect habitat, are now the domain of cars and out-of-town shopping centers. The homogenization of the suburban landscape and its relentless rhythm has become a dangerous urban model when faced with predictions of large population increase and global warming.

In 2014, the Victoria state government announced plans to double the size of Melbourne's central city by linking it to 250 hectares of the 'Fishermans Bend Urban Renewal Area'. The aims are to provide an additional 40,000 jobs and 80,000 residential units in the area by 2050.[4]

How can Melbourne's old industrial port, Fishermans Bend, adapt itself to become 'Perfection'? The living infrastructure of Perfection mixes dense human population, water treatment and urban agriculture whilst supporting biodiversity. Located less than seven kilometers from Melbourne's central business district, local qualities such as the big and little streets are referenced into the new water-based dwellings. Redefined typologies of public spaces, schools and commerce can strengthen the 'wealth' of the plan to include physical and social wellbeing, nutrition, mental health, independence and the greening of the city. Green engineering strategies are established with an emphasis on infrastructures to bridge diverse generational demographics – a mutual, self-sustaining support network cultivates socio-economic relations and contributes to community cohesion.

Perfection, with a carefully planned future phasing strategy, starts by securing reservoirs and transport infrastructures. The land released from industrial to autonomous residential, in its infancy, offers a prototype for sustainable and affordable urban dwellings – grids of new housing blocks rolls westwards towards the city's central business district. Later as the city advances, it establishes a marshland zone capable of filtering large amounts of the development's grey water, and the constructed wetlands act as a bio-filter to remove sediments and pollutants such as heavy metals from incoming river water. Vegetation in a wetland provides a substrate upon which microorganisms can grow; they are capable of removing approximately 90% of pollutants and actively break-down organic waste.[5] The backdrop of the wetlands bestows a pastoral quality on Perfection.

facing page: The infrastructures promote community wellbeing.

following page left: Rooftop open-air screenings and floating plug-ins disseminate the ideals of Perfection.

following page right: Perfection has a carefully planned green strategy.

3. 'A Summary of the Liveability Ranking and Overview', The Economist Intelligence Unit, p.1 [http://www.eiu.com/Handlers/WhitepaperHandler.ashx?fi=Liveability-rankings-Promotional-August-2014.pdf&mode=wp&campaignid=Liveability2014], retrieved 10 September 2014

4. 'Fishermans Bend – a new suburb is born', Department of Environment, Land, Water & Planning, Victoria State Government, 29 July 2014 [http://www.dtpli.vic.gov.au/planning/news-and-events/fishermans-bend-a-new-suburb-is-born], retrieved 10 September 2014

5. AK Choudhary, S Kumar & C Sharma, 'Removal of Chlorinated Resin and Fatty Acids From Paper Mill Wastewater Through Constructed Wetland', World Academy of Science, Engineering and Technology, August 2011, p.56 & pp.67–71

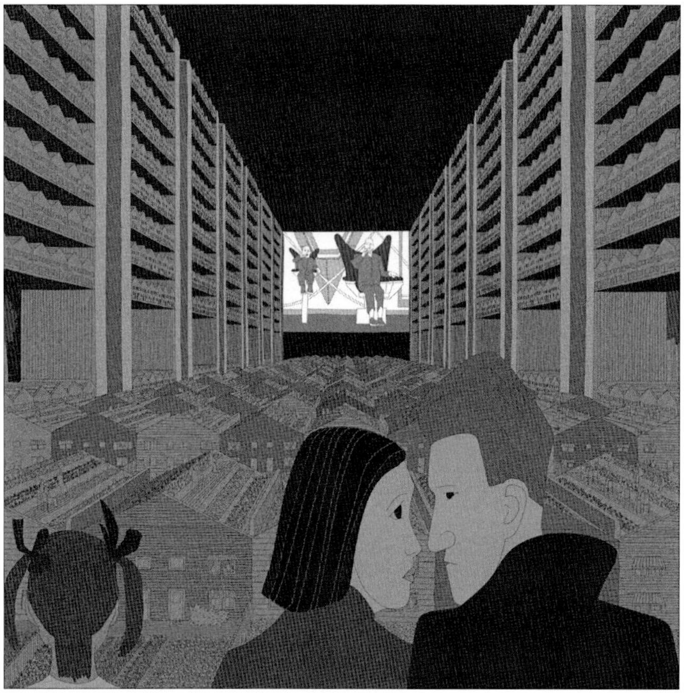

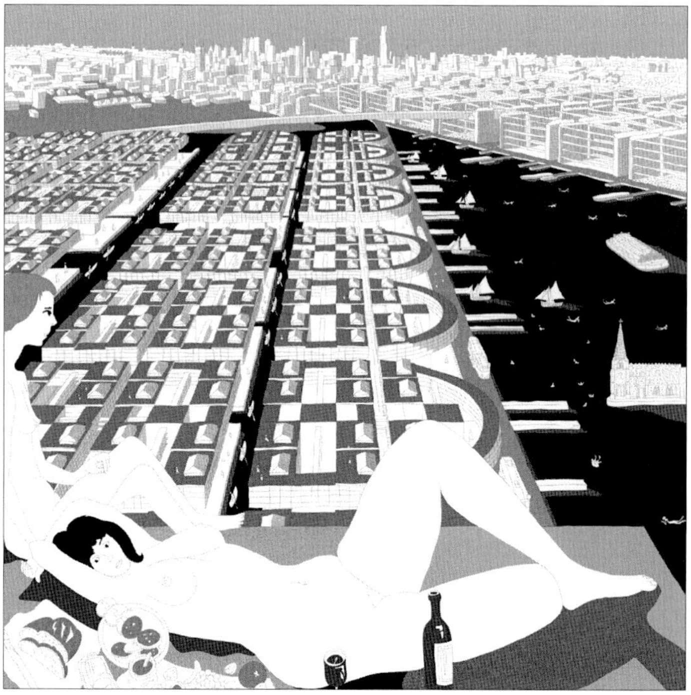

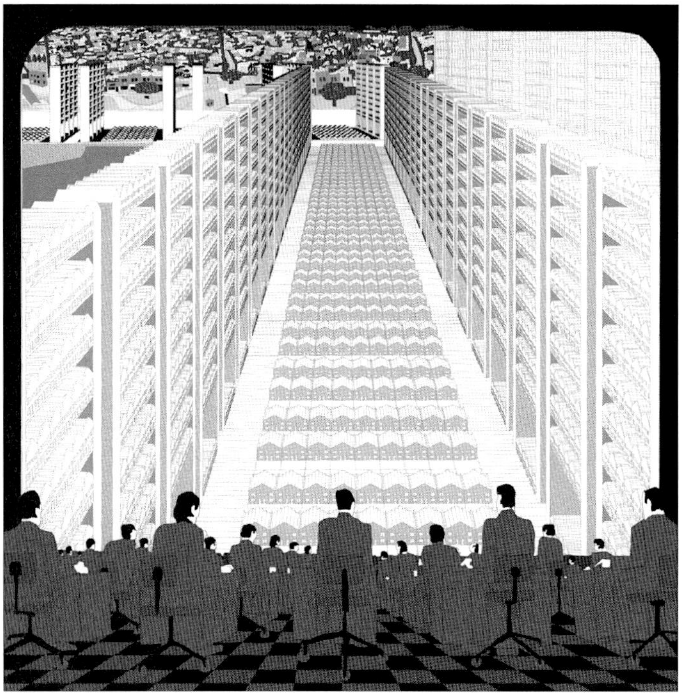

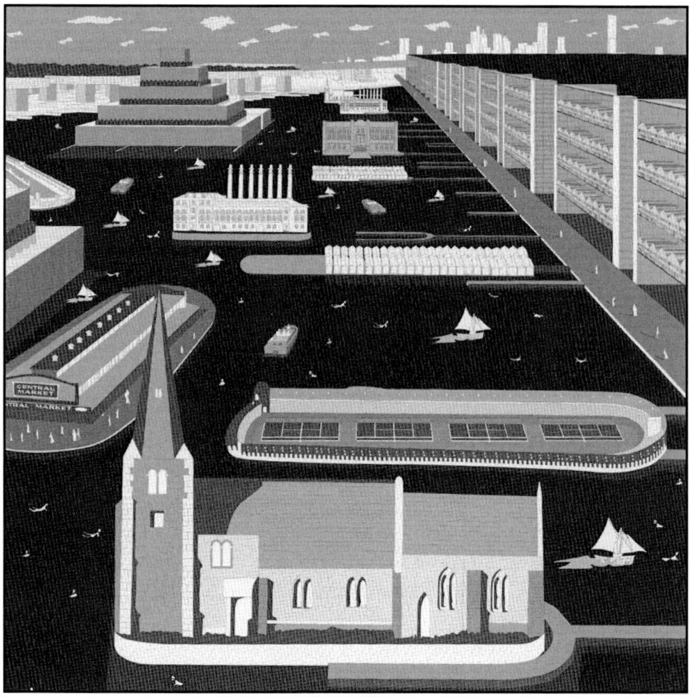

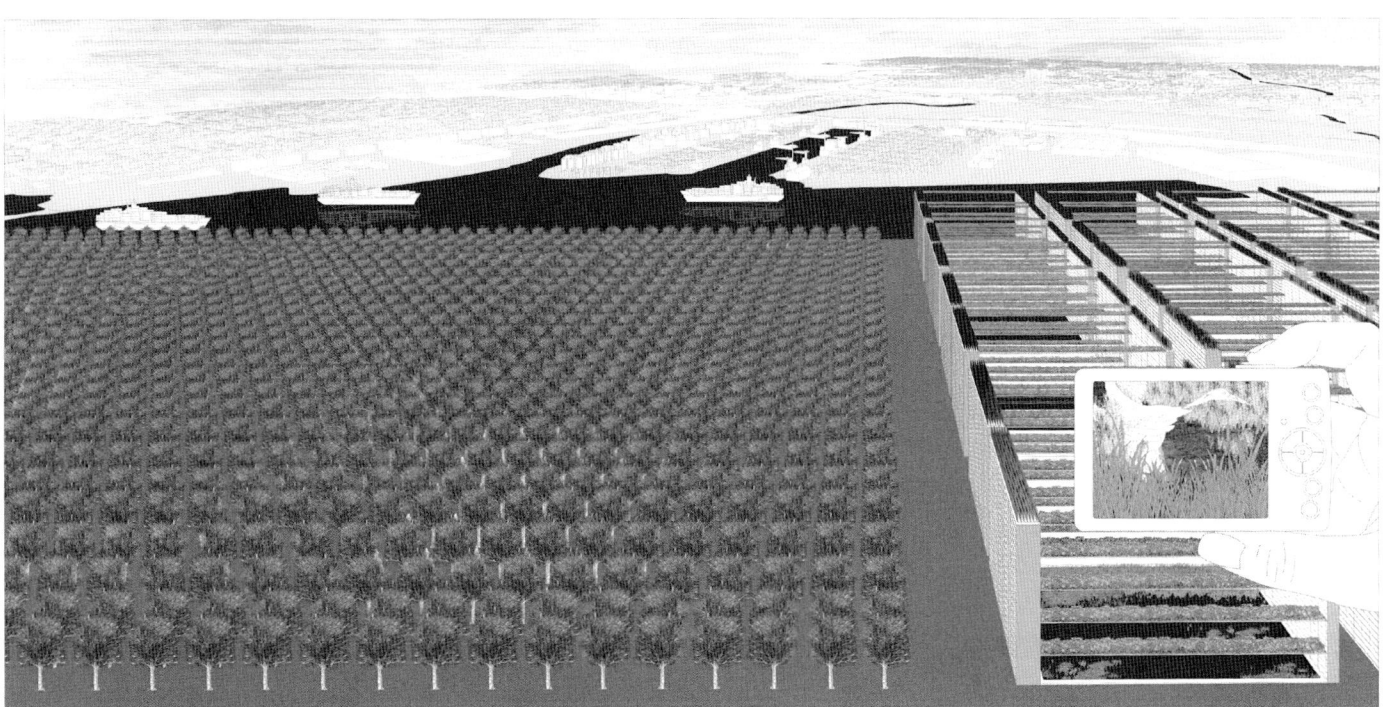

perfection

Phytotechnology:

The term phytotechnology describes the application of science and engineering to study problems and provide solutions involving plants. Phytotechnologies are an emerging set of techniques that use certain trees and other plants to remove organics and metals from soil and groundwater. Potential applications include remediating contaminated sites, as alternative landfill cover systems. Underlying this concept is the use of plants as living technologies to help address environmental challenges.

Phytoremediation is the term that refers to the use of plants for cleaning up contaminants in soil, groundwater, surface water and air. The use of phytoremediation can be a non-polluting and cost effective way to remove or stabilize toxic chemicals that might otherwise be leached out of the soil by rain to contaminate nearby watercourses. It is also a way of concentrating and harvesting valuable metals that are thinly dispersed in the ground, and offers an attractive option for the remediation of brownfield sites. Although phytoremediation has not been used extensively, it has many advantages:

- It is low cost in comparison to current 'mechanical' methods for soil remediation.
- It is passive and solar.
- It is faster than natural attenuation.
- The amount of contaminated material going to landfills can be greatly reduced.
- Energy can be recovered from the controlled combustion of the harvested biomass.
- It is low impact and public acceptance of phytoremediation is expected to be high.

The table below shows different methods of soil remediation and its advantages and disadvantages compared to Phytoremediation.

[Phytotechnologies: A Technical Approach in Environmental Management United Nations Environment Programme]

Treatment Name	Advantages Compared to Phytoremediation	Disadvantages Compared to Phytoremediation
Solidification / Stabilization	Not seasonally dependent; well established; rapid; applicable to most metals and organics; simple to operate during treatment.	Site is not restored to original form; leaching of the contaminant is a risk; can result in a significant volume increase.
Soil Flushing / Soil Washing	Not seasonally dependent, except in cold climates; methods well established for several types of sites and contamination.	Removal of metals using water flushing requires pH change; additional treatment steps and chemical handling add complexity and cost; possible lengthy period of treatment.
Bioremediation	Established and accepted; a bioreactor can be utilized for existing work; may be faster than phytoremediation.	Requires nutrient addition at a much greater level than phytoremediation; applicable to organics only.
Electrokinetics	Not seasonally dependent; can be used in conjunction with phytoremediation to enhance rhizosphere biodegradation.	Useful for soil only, not wetlands; uniformity of soil conditions is required.
Chemical Reduction / Oxidation	Not seasonally dependent; relatively short treatment time frame; usually off site.	Requires excavation; uses chemical additives; fertility of the soil after treatment may be damaged.
Excavation / Disposal	Rapid, immediate solution for site owner.	Transfers contaminants to landfill; does not treat.

A *Casuarina Cunninghamiana*: an evergreen tree with fine greyish green needle-like foliage that grows to a height of 10–35 meters with a spread of about 10 meters. Cones are small, nearly round to elongated and about 10 millimeters across.

B *Isolepis Nodosa*: is native to Australia and grows to between 15–100 centimeters in height. It occurs in sandy coastal areas and near lakes in Western Australia, South Australia, Tasmania, Victoria, New South Wales and Queensland.

C *Allocasuarina Nana*: is a small plant found in eastern Australia. Often seen around one meter tall.

D *Schoenoplectus Validus*: Schoenoplectus validus shows good establishment and growth in constructed wetlands. It is widely distributed in populations across the eastern states, to the south-east corner of South Australia.

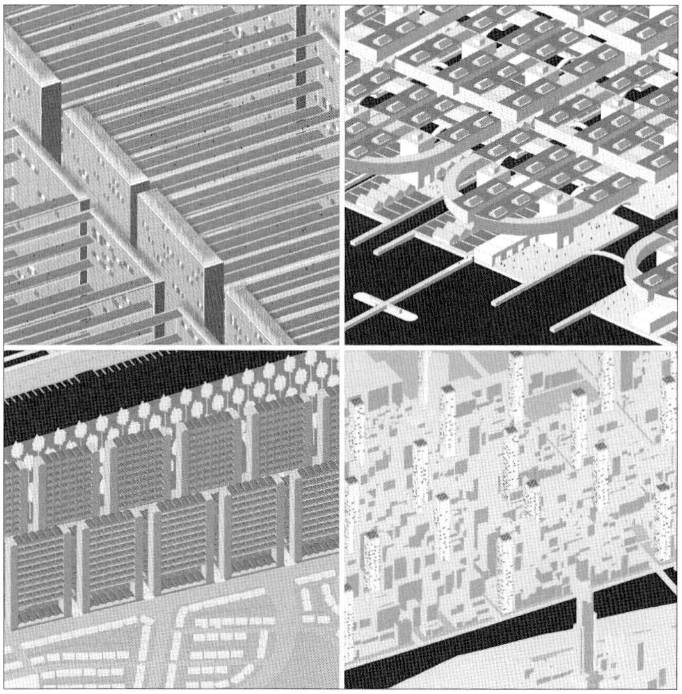

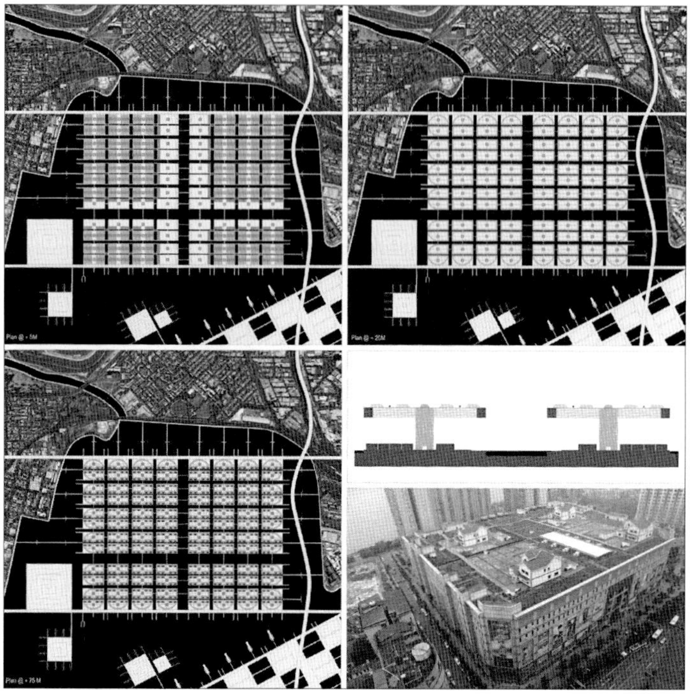

Plan @ ~5M
Plan @ ~20M

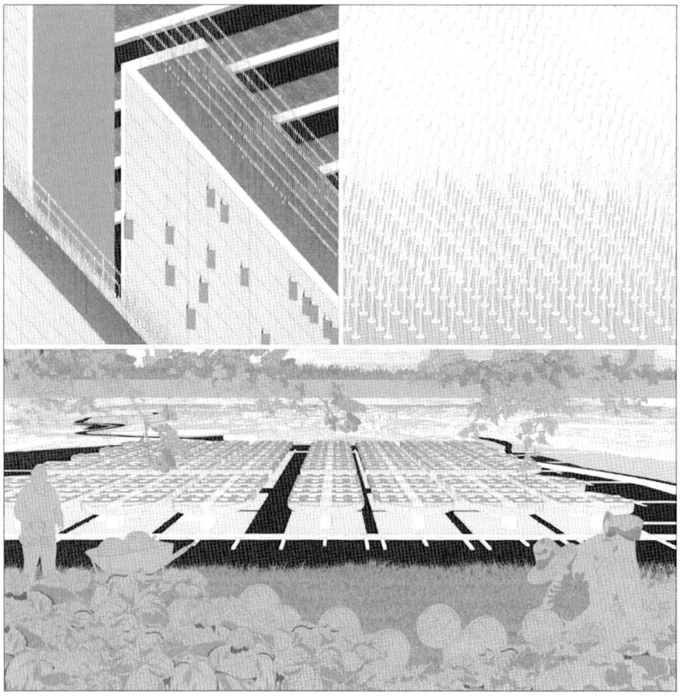

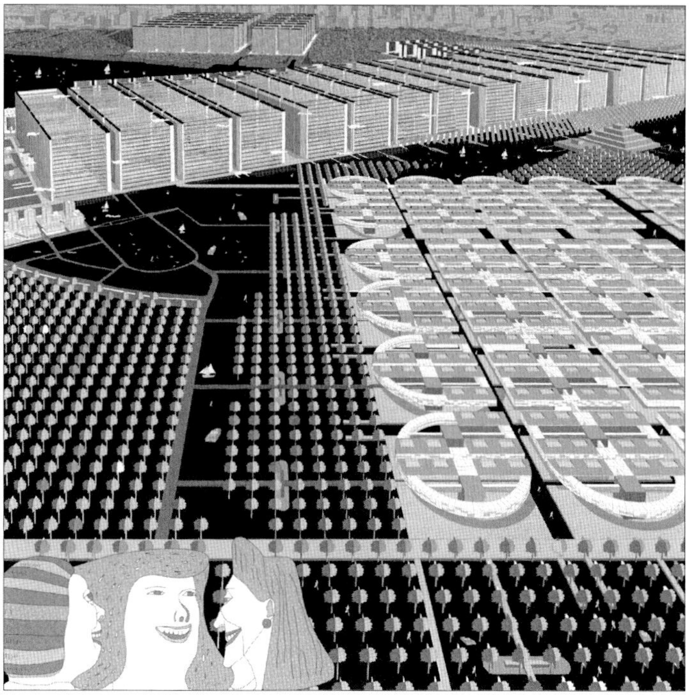

perfection

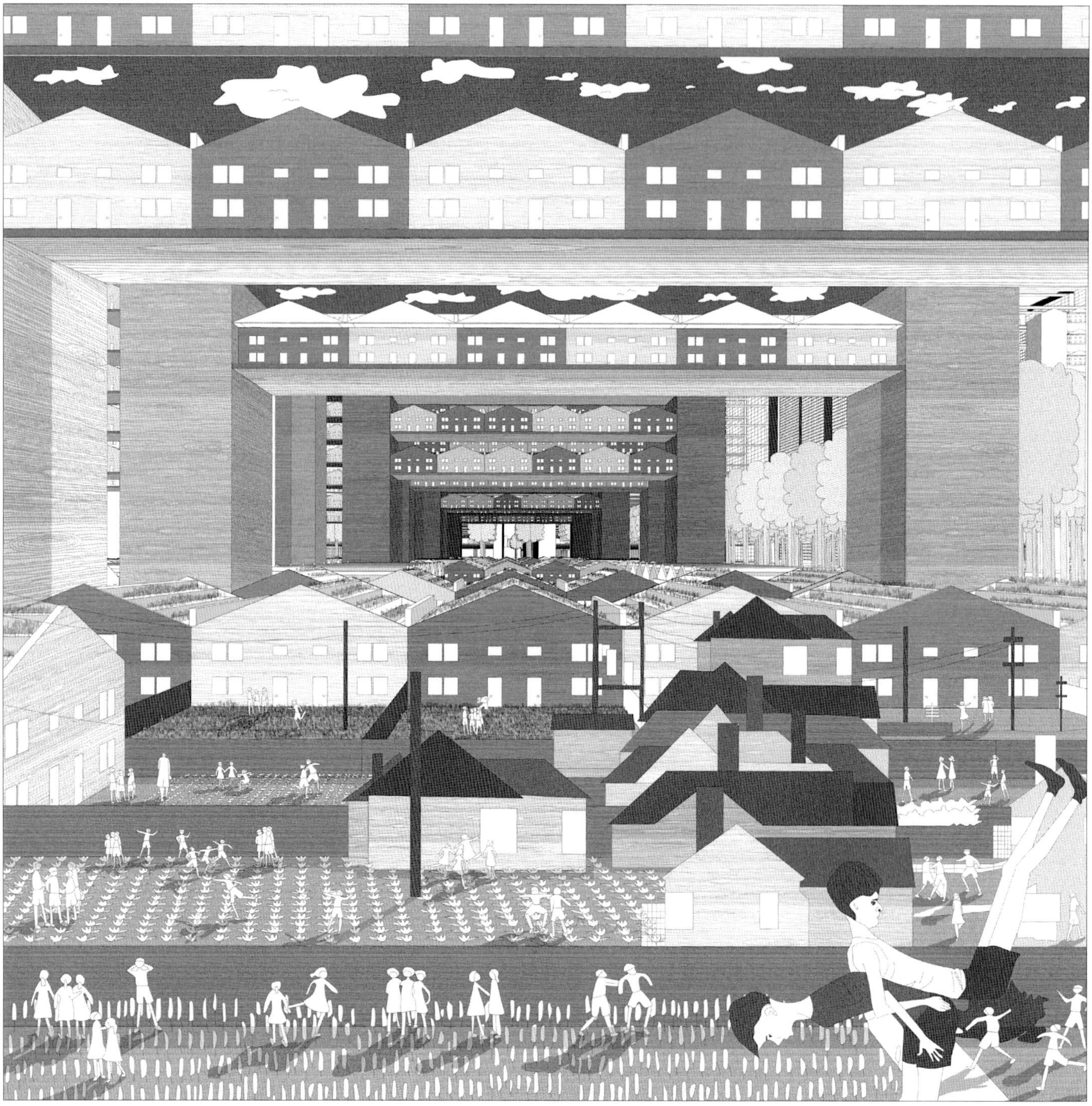

perfection

The wetlands act as floodwater attenuation zones; on a day-to-day basis, the water accommodates the civic, leisure and retail sectors. The earthworks from the wetland constructions are used to manufacture new landmass including uninterrupted pristine ziggurat beaches and islands. An armada of 'plug-ins', including a church, library and other mobile civic and celebratory cultural structures, choreograph the expansion of Melbourne's fluctuating harbors and embankments. These floating plug-ins periodically perform outreach visits to other parts of Victoria state, spreading the ideals of Perfection.

The grids of Perfection are concurrent with that of Melbourne's city center; the new chessboard of housing features the 'Little-and-Large' strategy for urban massing. The common housing block constitutes thin rows of dual aspect apartments with different sizes to accommodate a cross section of the community. Studio apartments to townhouse typologies interweave across a simple grid of suspended urban agriculture walkways. Reeds from the wetlands are used for the cladding and insulation of buildings; similar to thatched roofs, the rustic dry reeds ensure that a building is cool in summer and warm in winter. The roofs of the housing blocks feature reeds of another kind – the mechanical 'spikey hair-do' piezoelectric rods are strategically planted for harvesting wind energy.

The Cloud Housing presides above the shopping islands; it, at once, separates and mixes the idea of urbanity and the private home. The opportunity to live in the cloud, elevated far into the air, affords the inhabitants the vista of Perfection seamlessly merging into Melbourne's already perfect cityscape. For those who yearn for the romance of suburbia, Perfection offers a vertical configuration of Ebenezer Howard's 'Garden City'. The 100-meter towers have 'plug-in' low-rise detached housing with front-and-back gardens; the units also come with a digital ceiling of the perfect spring-blue sky peppered by an occasional 'candyfloss' cloud. Here, the inhabitants religiously mow the lawn, prune the fruit trees and rose hedges, paint their picket fences, and of course, polish the surface of the digital sky.

As Perfection develops, elevated transport connections are made to complement Melbourne's landmark tram routes. These also connect to future speculative sites including the artificial island of housing and recreation out in the bay, and multi-use inhabitable barriers that will hold-off tidal surges and flood risk. Eventually, as horseback riding, cycling, water taxis and trams become the only transport permitted, the gigantic (once-polluted) overpass adapts into a lush, linear elevated public park to 'manufacture' an endless supply of fresh air. Aspirations of modernity are revisited – if perfect weather and clean air can be made available, then so too can a healthy life of romance and 'the body beautiful' be promoted on rooftop open-air film screenings and Olympic quality sport facilities. As the sun goes down, lovers of different ages settle down into deckchairs under the stars, to be spellbound by neon-soaked glamour. Open-air cinemas, with the sound of the city all around, hold a special place in our imaginations.

By echoing Melbourne's successful urban grain and by ensuring the provision of affordable dwellings, cultural facilities, green space and easy connectivity, there is no reason to suppose that its new infrastructure, Perfection, would be any less successful, diverse or contain less variety of nuanced spaces. Nevertheless, just like Pleasantville, Perfection might be a false hope and a morality tale of urban planning concerning the values of over determined romantic visions of utopia.

previous pages: Housing in Perfection features the 'Little-and-Large' massing as well as vertical configurations of Ebenezer Howard's 'Garden City'.

facing page: 'Plug-in' low-rise detached housing units with front-and-back gardens boost digital ceilings of perfect spring-blue sky peppered by 'candyfloss' clouds.

following page left: Urban agriculture allotments are cultivated on elevated housing walkways.

following page right: The gigantic (once-polluted) overpass adapts into a lush, linear public park to 'manufacture' an endless supply of fresh air.

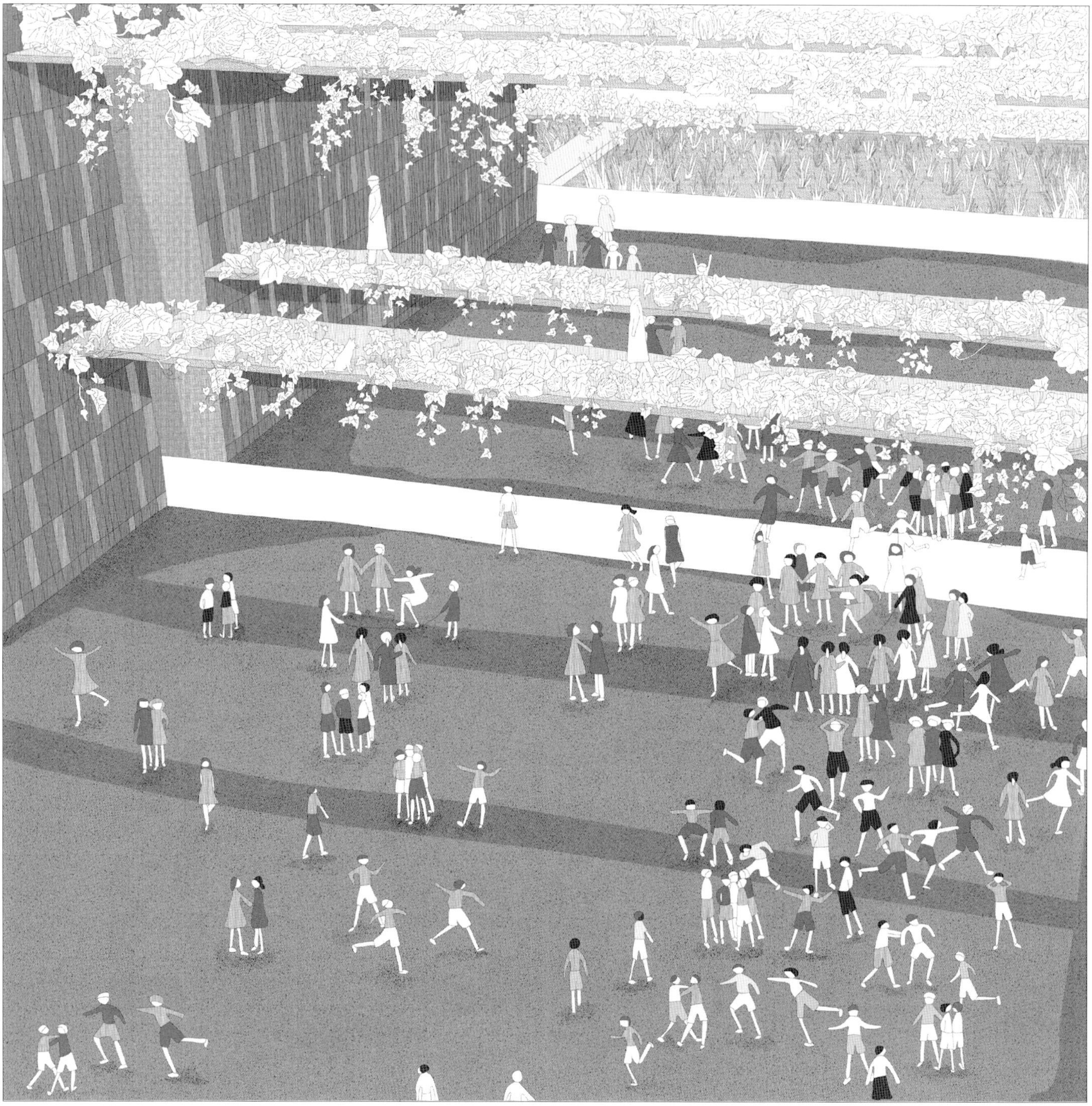

perfection

250

To Participate

'Our infrastructure is on life support. You could go to any major city in America and see roads, and bridges, and infrastructure that need to be fixed today. Public spending on infrastructure has fallen to its lowest level since 1947. Congress doesn't have the political courage to do what it takes. They don't want to spend the money. They don't want to raise the taxes. They don't really have a vision of America the way that other Congresses have had a vision of America.'

– Ray LaHood, 'Falling Apart: America's neglected infrastructure', 60 Minutes, CBS, 2014

The evolution of society and the city must endure to invest and participate in the civic culture and economic development of infrastructures and urban spaces. Collective public convictions are disappearing with the arrival of an increasingly individual 'consumer society'. Inadequate infrastructure is not just an inconvenience for the community but has significant long-term consequences, and associated costs for the city. Economic and social decline occur when there are problems with the quality of the physical environment, poor local and national services and weak social networks in the community.

In the United States, roads and bridges are in need of repairs, the vast majority of airports and seaports are out of date, and high-speed rail does not exist, resulting from decades of under funding and political paralysis in Washington. As of 2014, the infrastructure problem is so severe that one out of every nine of the nearly 70,000 bridges in America is considered to be structurally deficient. The American Society of Civil Engineers estimated that spending of $450 billion per year is required to bring national infrastructure to an adequate level by 2020. The political parties have suggested everything from raising the gas tax to funding infrastructure through corporate tax reform to secure the funding needed. Furthermore, continuing to underfund it will cost American businesses a trillion dollars in lost sales and will cost the economy 3.5 million jobs.[1]

LaHood, a former congressman and the first secretary of transportation in the Obama administration, reiterated that men of vision built the New York State Erie Canal, the Hoover Dam, the Golden Gate Bridge, and the Interstate Highway System, and all these infrastructures have been of tremendous benefit to the economy. President Dwight Eisenhower championed the Interstate Highway System and the establishment of the Federal Highway Trust Fund. President John F. Kennedy encouraged Congress and the imagination of all Americans to participate in an infrastructure of a different kind – to support the space program. Kennedy, in his historic 'Address to Congress on Urgent National Needs' pledged that the space, moon and planets must not be 'governed by a hostile flag of conquest, but by a banner of freedom and peace'. He believed that America 'should commit itself to achieving the goal, before this

facing page: The old cantilever San Francisco–Oakland Bay Bridge, built in 1936, carries about 240,000 vehicles a day on its two decks.

following pages: The amount of concrete used in building the Hoover Dam was enough to pave a road stretching from San Francisco to New York City.

1. S Kroft, 'Falling Apart: America's neglected infrastructure', 60 Minutes, CBS, 23 November 2014 [http://www.cbsnews.com/news/falling-apart-america-neglected-infrastructure], retrieved 3 August 2015

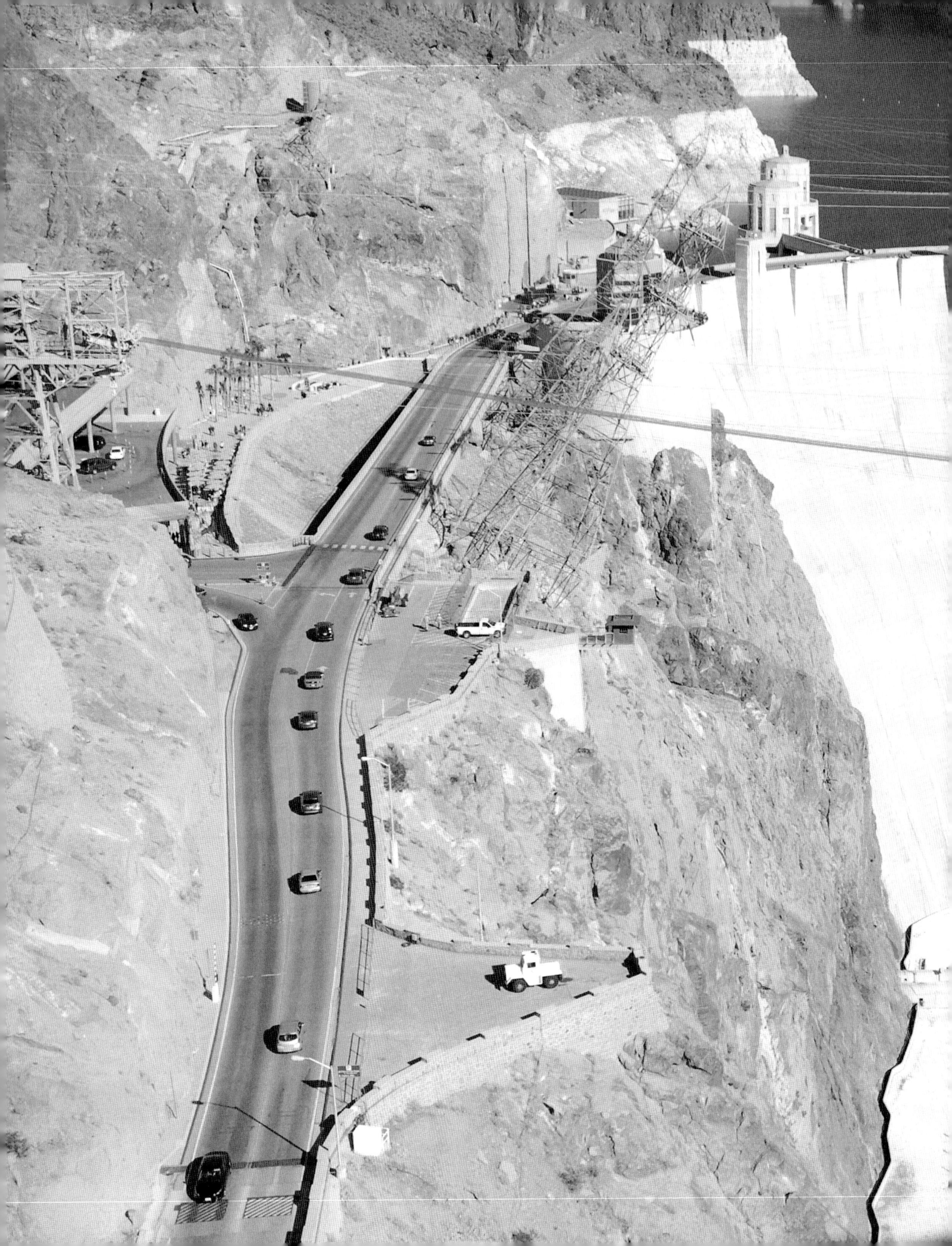

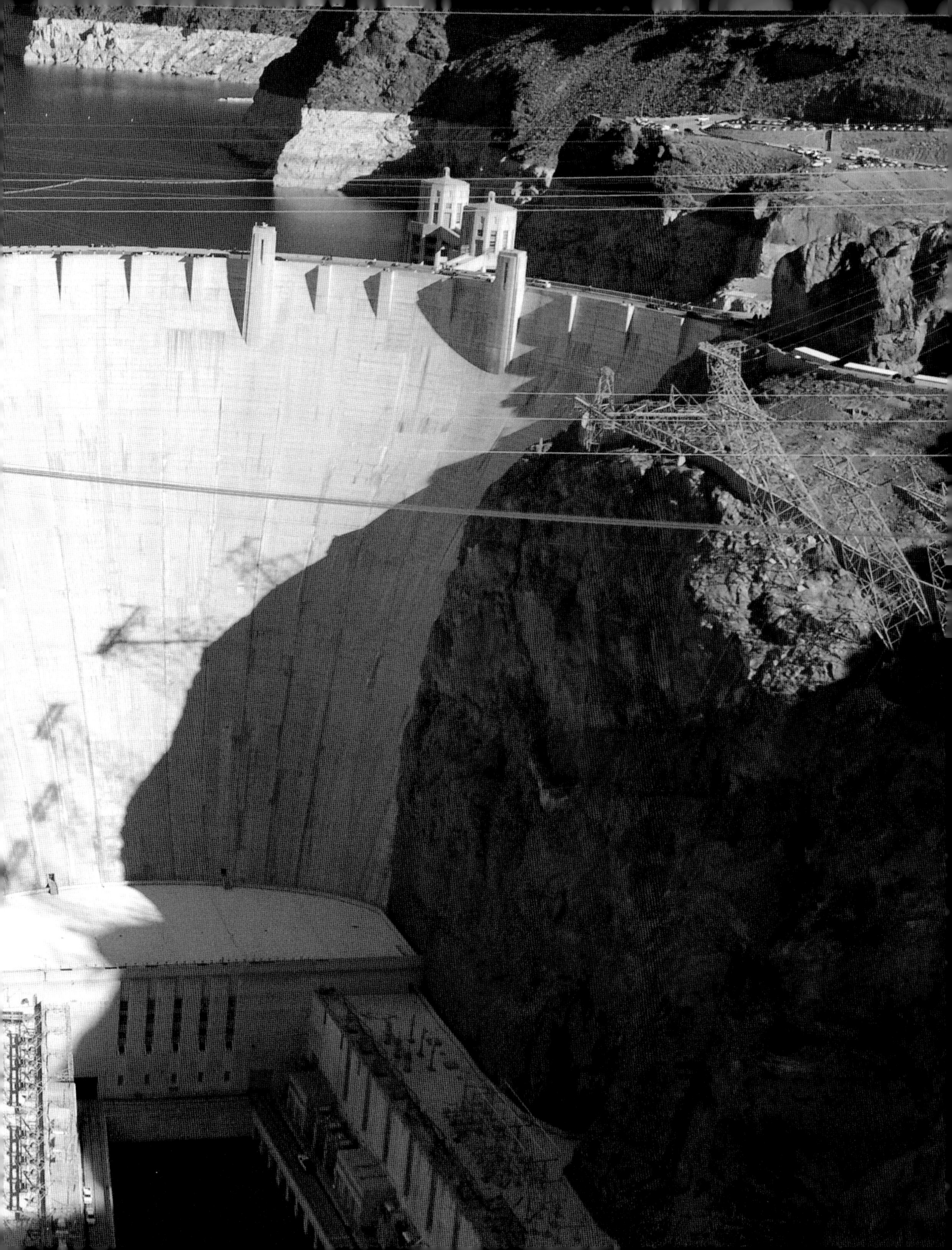

decade is out, of landing a man on the moon and returning him safely to the earth. No single space project in this period will be more impressive to mankind, or more important for the long-range exploration of space.'[2]

That goal was achieved on 20 July 1969 when 'Apollo 11' commander Neil Armstrong made the first step onto the lunar surface and described the event as 'one small step for man, one giant leap for mankind'[3] on live TV, broadcasted to a global audience. The impact of Kennedy's words lingers long after; the speech fundamentally transformed NASA's public profile and created a huge infrastructure that continues to exist today, the John F. Kennedy Space Center (KSC) in Florida. The center has been used to launch every NASA human space flight, and for landing the reusable Space Shuttle orbiters when weather permitted. In 2014, the KSC launched the first unmanned flight test of the 'Orion Multi-Purpose Crew Vehicle', to facilitate human exploration of the Moon, Mars and asteroids.[4] The moon landing was a remarkable achievement for humanity and the country's global status, which had been seriously wounded by several earlier space race defeats to the Soviet Union. Economically, it was a huge boost to American aerospace industry.

Many years earlier, political and economic gains from huge infrastructures had already been demonstrated in the construction of the Hoover Dam at the Nevada-Arizona border. For millions of dispossessed Americans in the 1930s, the Hoover Dam came to symbolize hope and what American industry could achieve in the depths of the Great Depression. President Herbert Hoover feared nurturing public expectations and dependence on the federal government, and was strongly opposed to direct economic relief for business and private citizens. As the unemployment lines increased and the Depression proved to be more than a temporary dip, Hoover realized the dam could be the tool to encourage many individuals within the United States to participate in working out their common financial woes. A brilliantly conceived scheme of uniting public works and private enterprise, the infrastructure put people back to work, improved the quality of life of communities, and simultaneously invested in the American economic growth out West.

Built in less than four years in blistering desert heat, the Hoover Dam remains an icon of American technological ambition, where American humanity tamed nature.[5] For the English novelist JB Priestley upon visiting the Hoover Dam while still under construction, the infrastructure embodied the very image of the science fiction (SF) future predicted by HG Wells. 'It is like the beginning of a new world, and that world we catch a glimpse of in one of the later sequences of Wells' film, "Things to Come", a world of giant machines and titanic communal enterprises. Here in this Western American wilderness, the new man, the man of the future has done something, and what he has done takes your breath away. This is a first glimpse of what chemistry and mathematics and engineering and large-scale organization can accomplish when collective planning unites and inspires them.'[6]

As the Great Depression advanced, those hired to work on the Hoover Dam moved to Boulder City, a tightly controlled Levittown-like company town built six miles away. The 300-acre settlement housed a population of 5,000, and up to 8,000 at the height of construction.[7] Built by the Bureau of Reclamation and run under the auspices of the federal government, construction started with a large water tank in the spring of 1931. Within a short schedule of six months, Boulder City had installed eight 172-man dormitories, one 53-man office dormitory, and 600 of three, two, and one room cottages. Every cottage looked identical, all built with minimal concern to construction quality and aesthetics. Boulder City sprung into being almost overnight and its buildings were never meant to be permanent. At the same time, they completed the mess hall and recreation hall, office buildings, the Boulder City Company Store, a laundry, and a 20-bed hospital, as well as the entire basic infrastructure needed for sewerage, water, electricity and the streets. Access to the dam from the new city was convenient and easily provided by double-decker buses. Determined to transform the dust bowl into a lush oasis, the city brought in a six-mile network of pumps and pipes that carried water from Colorado out of the Black Canyon to the Eldorado Valley at great expense.[8]

The Bureau was authoritarian in its enforcement of the government's control of the city's planning and general conduct of the residents – the city manager was the law. There was absolute prohibition on drinking or gambling (the sale of liquor was finally permitted in 1969, while gambling is still illegal today).[9] In fact, Boulder City was a society under benevolent dictatorship[10] where the physical, moral, and racial purity of the worker was enforced in return for security.[11] It resembled an industrial SF dystopia, a place of bleakness and monotonous struggles against the dehumanizing effects of the machine in the Industrial Age. Yet amongst the dispossessed men, women and children, there was a strong sense of belonging and solidarity in the community, qualities much appreciated during the Depression. Boulder City might be a rough-and-tumble settlement but to them it was paradise and was their home. The city's tremendous growth and purpose grew out of the fellowship of shared hopes and hardships, and participation in a giant collective enterprise that was something new and indefinably special.[12]

The Hoover Dam did everything the president and all its supporters had hoped for, and continues to do so to this day. The National Park Service proudly describes the infrastructure as a modernist spectacle par excellence: 'the Hoover Dam is as tall as a 60-story building. It was the highest dam in the world when it was completed in 1935. Its base is as thick as two football fields are long. Each spillway, designed to let floodwaters pass without harming the dam itself, can handle the volume of water that flows over Niagara Falls. The amount of concrete used in building it was enough to pave a road stretching from San Francisco to New York City.'[13]

By harnessing the notorious and dangerous Colorado River, it protects southern California and Arizona from the disastrous floods, and created Lake Mead, the 110-mile reservoir capable of holding nearly nine trillion gallons of water. Some 25 million residents in Los Angeles, Las Vegas, Phoenix and other rapidly growing cities in the Southwest rely on the water supply and its hydroelectric plant for producing dependable and cheap electricity. In addition, the infrastructure supplies water to irrigate an estimated 1.5 million acres of farmland, sustaining a multi-billion-dollar agriculture industry in California and Arizona.[14] As climate change threatens to reduce the overall amount of water in the Lower Colorado Basin, it is causing tension between cities and the farming communities in the region.

The Democracy of Growing Land
A product of the country's successful battles against the North Sea for centuries, polder infrastructure originated in the Netherlands during the Middle Ages. In 'Hollands Welbehagen' (The Well-being of Holland; 1998), Herman Pleij, professor of Dutch Historical Literature, wrote 'The Netherlands owes its existence to the democracy of dry feet. We need each other literally in order not to drown.'[15] More than a quarter of the country is below sea level and 60% of its people live in flood-risk areas. Land reclamation to protect villages and towns from the sea to enable agricultural and urban expansion has required extraordinary community cooperation and a decisive governing authority. The necessity of close

2+3. 'NASA Moon Landing', John F. Kennedy Presidential Library and Museum [http://www.jfklibrary.org/JFK/JFK-Legacy/NASA-Moon-Landing.aspx], retrieved 9 March 2015

4. 'Kennedy Space Center Story', Kennedy Space Center [http://www.nasa.gov/centers/kennedy/about/history/index.html], retrieved 9 March 2015

5+11. D Rosenberg, 'No One is buried in Hoover Dam' in 'Modernism, Inc: Body, memory, capital', J Scandura & M Hurston (eds.), New York University Press, New York, 2001, p.85 & p.97

6. JB Priestley, 'Arizona Desert: Reflections of a winter visitor', Harper's Magazine, New York, issue 173, March 1937, p.365

7. MG Rodden, 'Boulder City, Nevada', Arcadia Publishing, 2000, Chicago, pp.7–9

8, 10+12. JE Stevens, 'Hoover Dam: An American Adventure', University of Oklahoma Press, Norman, 1988, pp.129–131, p.142 & p.138

9. F McCabe, 'Boulder City: Built by the dam, for the dam', Las Vegas Review-Journal, 2014 [http://www.reviewjournal.com/nevada-150/boulder-city-built-dam-dam], accessed 2 August 2015

13. National Park Service, U.S. Department of the Interior, 'The Greatest Dam in the World: Building Hoover Dam' [http://www.nps.gov/nr/twhp/wwwlps/lessons/140hooverdam/140hoover_dam.htm], retrieved 30 July 2015

14. J Mark, 'Climate Change Treatens to Dry up the Southwest's Future', Earth Island Journal, 16 October 2008 [http://www.alternet.org/story/103366/climate_change_threatens_to_dry_up_the_southwest's_future], retrieved 5 May 2016

15. D Dickson, 'The People's Government: An introduction to democracy', Cambridge University Press, New York, 2014, p.13

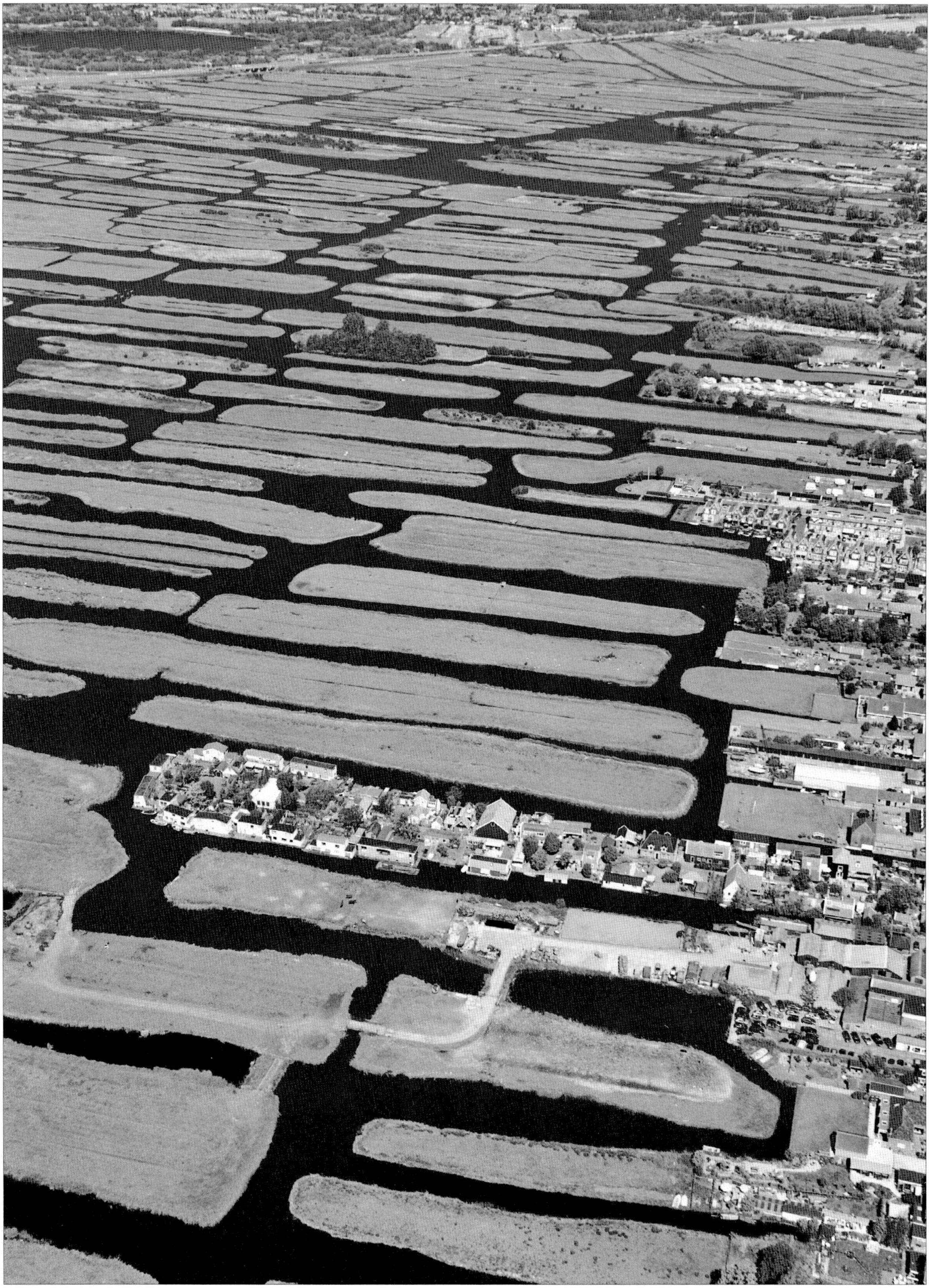

community participation between local residents and elected local water boards, sustained the polder system and led the Dutch to develop an ingrained consensual democratic habit. Dating from the 13th century, the elected local water boards are the oldest democratic institutions in the Netherlands, and are responsible for polder, waterway and sewerage construction and maintenance, and enforce water laws and taxes.[16]

Polders are low-lying tracts of formerly submerged land and are completely enclosed by embankments. Their hydrology is regulated through a network of dikes, canals, and pumps powered by windmills. After drainage, the polders are planted with a succession of plants to create an increasingly fertile soil structure – starting with reeds to assist with the drying of the soil, followed by colza, and eventually grain crops. It can take up to five years to turn the sandy reclaimed polder land into fertile soil, before being leased to farmers or used for construction.[17]

It is the popular axiom that 'God made the world, but the Dutch made the Netherlands'. The Netherlands has an innovative history of flood management and land reclamation. Since around 800 BC, early Dutch built 'terps' or man-made hills to escape rising seawaters. About 2,000 years ago, monks constructed the oldest dike in the Netherlands from piled turf, near the village of Peins in Friesland. The primitive dike lines were floodplains for controlling rivers. In the north, villages combined their dikes and created Westfriese Omringdijk, a vast living area about 126 kilometers long and a couple of meters high.[18]

In the 20th century, new technology advanced the two major land reclamation efforts, the 'Zuiderzee Works' along Amsterdam and the 'Delta Works' in the southwest corner of the Netherlands. Collectively, the American Society of Civil Engineers now considers the infrastructures one of the Seven Wonders of the Modern World. The Zuiderzee Works featured the Afsluitdijk, an enclosing dam measuring over 30 kilometers in length, 90 meters in width and a height of 7.25 meters above sea-level, running northeast to connect the provinces of Noord-Holland and Friesland. The dam separated the Zuiderzee from both the Waddenzee and the North Sea, thus transforming the former salt-water in-land sea into the fresh water lake IJsselmeer and over 1,600 square kilometers of the Zuiderzee into four vast polders by 1968.[19] The desalinated soil on the reclaimed land was made fertile for agriculture and pastures for grazing cattle, and was offered as residential spaces for the inhabitants from the very densely populated cities of Amsterdam, Rotterdam, The Hague and Utrecht. In 1986, three of IJsselmeer's polders, Northeast Polder, Eastern Flevoland, and Southern Flevoland, developed into a single administrative province of Flevoland. Amongst the cities built on these reclaimed areas of land are Lelystad and Almere.

The Delta Works, an ingenious network of dams, sluices and barriers, were installed after the North Sea flooded in 1953 to protect the Rhine-Meuse-Scheldt delta from the sea. Apart from draining the low-lying areas, it regulated the flow of saltwater, providing both potable water and fresh water for irrigation. The inland waterway shipping routes, especially between Antwerp and Rotterdam, and the mobility between various islands and peninsulas were beneficiaries of the infrastructure. The Oosterschelde barrier/Eastern Scheldt storm surge barrier, located between the islands of Schouwen-Duivelend and Noord-Beveland, is the largest of the 13 dams under the Delta Works. The dam was initially built in a

facing page: The Netherlands has more than 3,000 polders, which will continue to transform as a result of conflicting interests from urban and rural factors.

16. D Dickson, 'The People's Government: An introduction to democracy', Cambridge University Press, New York, 2014, p.13

17. W Horobin, 'How It Works: Science & technology', Marshall Cavendish Corporation, New York, vol.6, 2003, p.1208

18. 'The Netherlands: A brief history', The Royal Netherlands Embassy [http://waterandthedutch.com/delta], retrieved 11 August 2015

19. Encyclopaedia Britannica, 'Ijsselmeer Polders, Netherlands' [http://www.britannica.com/place/IJsselmeer-Polders], retrieved 12 August 2015

closed configuration, but later changed into an open dam containing a number of sluices that would only be closed during heavy storms and high water levels; this was due to concerns about the saltwater environment and the fishing industry. The dam structure consists of 62 steel doors, which are 42 meters wide each, to regulate the flow of water. The Maeslant Barrier near Rotterdam acts as the Delta Works' final line of defense against incoming seawater. Two storm surge gates, each almost as long as the Eiffel tower and weighing about four times as much, automatically start to float and move towards each other closing the waterway in the event of storm tides. The computer-operated system is linked to weather and sea level data.[20]

While the Delta Works and the Zuiderzee Works were costly ventures, they provided thousands with employment; especially with the construction of the Afsluitdijk during the Great Depression. These visionary infrastructures, like the Hoover Dam, tamed the forces of nature and they are SF made real.

With rising sea levels induced by climate change, floods remain a major threat to the Netherlands today. The country is now going through a process of 'de-polderization',[21] and implementing instead a future flood-defense strategy of 'soft infrastructure' – employing natural ecological systems, and embracing nature's power to protect its exposed land. The 'Sand Engine' is a prototype of 'Building with Nature', a collaborative participation of Dutch industries, research institutes, and public water agencies looking to incorporate natural systems for next-generation hydraulic engineering. A large amount of sand is deposited in a single operation to avoid repeated disruption of the vulnerable seabed. The waves and ocean currents slowly redistribute the sand to create peninsulas, fortifying the eroding land.[22] Using seed bombing techniques, seeds are scattered from the air to vegetate the new sandy strips.

Cost effective and adaptable natural vegetated buffers, for example a mangrove forest, will grow with sea level rise. At the same time, new infrastructure must minimize environmental impacts by transforming existing dikes into ecologically enhanced habitats for marine organisms. Matthijs Kok, a flood-risk professor at TU Delft, prefers multi-use levees, which combine ecological, recreational, and business functions such as restaurants and hotels with flood control infrastructure. One such example, the seaside resort of Scheveningen, is a new multifunctional inhabitable dike with a widened beach and is concealed beneath an undulating pedestrian and bicycle-friendly esplanade.[23] Jerry Van Eyck, a Dutch landscape architect and principal of !melk, asserted that 'we can't put more dikes, or "hard" infrastructure in place to control against sea level rise. There is no solution to climate change, only combinations of engineered hard and soft protections.'[24]

The Rockefeller Foundation's president, Judith Rodin, defined resilience as 'the capacity to bounce back from a crisis, learn from it, and achieve revitalization'.[25] Communities and cities need awareness, diversity, integration, the capacity for self-regulation, and adaptiveness to be resilient to survive the onslaught of unpredictable environmental conditions.

The Nature of Survival
With all the attributes of SF genre survivalist themes, and tropes such as safe havens, the Aztecs and the Uros have originated poetic yet strategic approaches for 'growing land' by engaging nature and its systems as construction and cultivation resources. The Aztecs, with their technical skills and knowledge of aqua-terra, created an ingenious example of ancient urban agriculture infrastructure – the chinampas 'floating gardens' in the Valley of Mexico. The construction of the 'floating islands' of the Uros community on Lake Titicaca is completely dependent on a single plant, the Totora reeds.

to participate

In about 1300 AD, the nomadic hunter-gatherers the Aztecs wandered into the Valley of Mexico and built the great city of Tenochtitlan on a marshy island in the lake. The city of Tenochtitlan was divided into four districts of neighborhood wards or 'house groups'. Although being fully surrounded by water made it easy to defend from other tribes, it was not a desirable location to farm. The modest landmass of Tenochtitlan was artificially expanded to cover an area of eight square kilometers with the chinampas system, a series of rectangular raised platforms (30 meters by 2.5 meters) built on a strong framework of poles and tree branches fastened firmly to the lakebed.[26] Most farmers owned two or three chinampas, located adjacent to their houses. The farmers would regularly layer the chinampas until it was above the level of the lake with nutrient-rich mud from the bottom of the lake, and decaying organic matter of inconsumable vegetation and human waste from the city itself. The process enabled the city to treat its waste and improved fertilization of its crops, producing three to four harvests a year. Along the edge of the platforms, willows and alder trees would grow through the chinampas to provide further anchorage; they also act as environmental shelters and habitat for birds and insects.[27]

The spaces between the chinampas served as canals; six major canals with many smaller ones criss-crossed the entire city, making it possible to travel virtually anywhere by boat. The surrounding lake water irrigated the chinampas, and aqueducts transported fresh water from surrounding mountain springs for human consumption. Three causeways with drawbridges connected the island with the mainland, and when raised, sealed the city off entirely. While the four districts each had temples dedicated to the principal gods, the Great Temple resides within the central precinct, a city within a city of temples, public buildings, palaces, and plazas enclosed by a defensive bastion.

Abundant amounts of flowers were cultivated together with crops of corn, beans, and squash, making the Aztec city an even more lush and colorful place. After years of layering, each of the chinampas eventually became a small island. At its height, 300,000 people lived in Tenochtitlan, and crops grown on chinampas made up one-half to two-thirds of the food eaten by the people of the city.[28] Today, Mexico City, built on and around the ancient city of Tenochtitlan, is currently planning to reintroduce the chinampas to create a sustainable wastewater treatment system.

The construction of the 'floating islands' on the giant Lake Titicaca, 3,800 meters above sea level between Peru and Bolivia, is completely dependent on the long Totora reeds. The plant is central to the Uros' everyday survival and provides materials for the construction of boats, houses and, most distinctive, the terra firma. The foundation of the man-made floating island is formed from the plant's roots, a peat-moss like substance. It is then layered with dried reeds painstakingly interwoven in a cross-hatch pattern to create a dense base approximately two meters deep – there is a spongy feel to every step.[29] Anchorage is provided by fixing the island to the bottom of the lake with wooden posts and ropes. In the rainy season from November to February, the islands are often found navigating around the lake. The reed layers decompose fairly quickly from the bottom up, releasing natural gasses that essentially cause the island to float. The replacement process occurs about four times a year, but with appropriate maintenance, each island can last up to 30 years.

20. 'The Delta Works: History', Deltawerken [http://www.deltawerken.com/Deltaworks/23.html], retrieved 11 August 2015

21+24. J Green, 'The Netherlands' Evolving Relationship with Water', The Dirt, American Society of Landscape Architects [http://dirt.asla.org/2010/09/10/the-netherlands-changing-relationship-with-water], retrieved 11 August 2015

22. D Carrington, 'Taming the Floods, Dutch-Style', The Guardian: Climate Change, 19 May 2014 [http://www.theguardian.com/environment/2014/may/19/floods-dutch-britain-netherlands-climatechange], retrieved 11 August 2015

23. C Katz, 'To Control Floods, The Dutch Turn to Nature for Inspiration', Yale Environment 360 [http://e360.yale.edu/feature/to_control_floods_the_dutch_turn_to_nature_for_inspiration/2621], retrieved 12 August 2015

25. S Moss, 'Judith Rodin's Warning for the World: Crisis is becoming the new normal', The Guardian: Cities, 27 January 2015 [https://www.theguardian.com/cities/2015/jan/27/judith-rodin-warning-world-crisis-new-normal-rockefeller-foundation], retrieved 16 August 2015

26. V Bulmer-Thomas, J Coatsworth & R Cortes-Conde, 'The Cambridge Economic History of Latin America: The colonial era and the shorten nineteenth century', vol.1, Cambridge University Press, New York, 2006, p.280

27. JN Pretty, 'Regenerating Agriculture: An alternative strategy for growth', Earthscan, New York, 1995, p.127

28. G Sundem & KA Pikiewicz, 'Hands-on History World History Activities', 'Aztec: Floating Gardens', Shell Education, Huntington Beach, 2006, p.7

29. JP LaCount, 'Lake Titicaca's Uros Floating Reed Islands', New Spore, 2010 [http://newspore.com/2010/peru/lake-titicacas-floating-reed-islands/], retrieved 17 August 2015

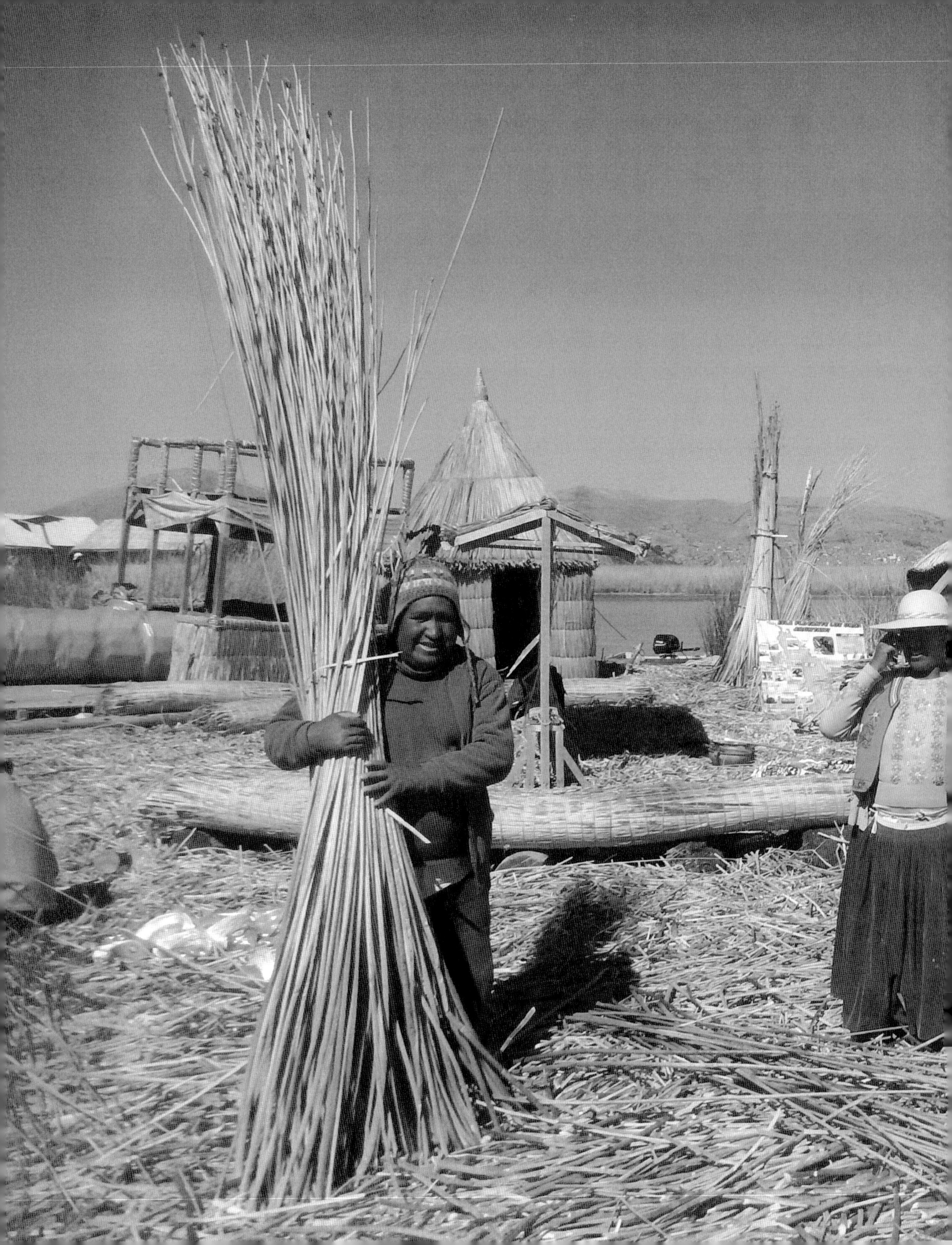

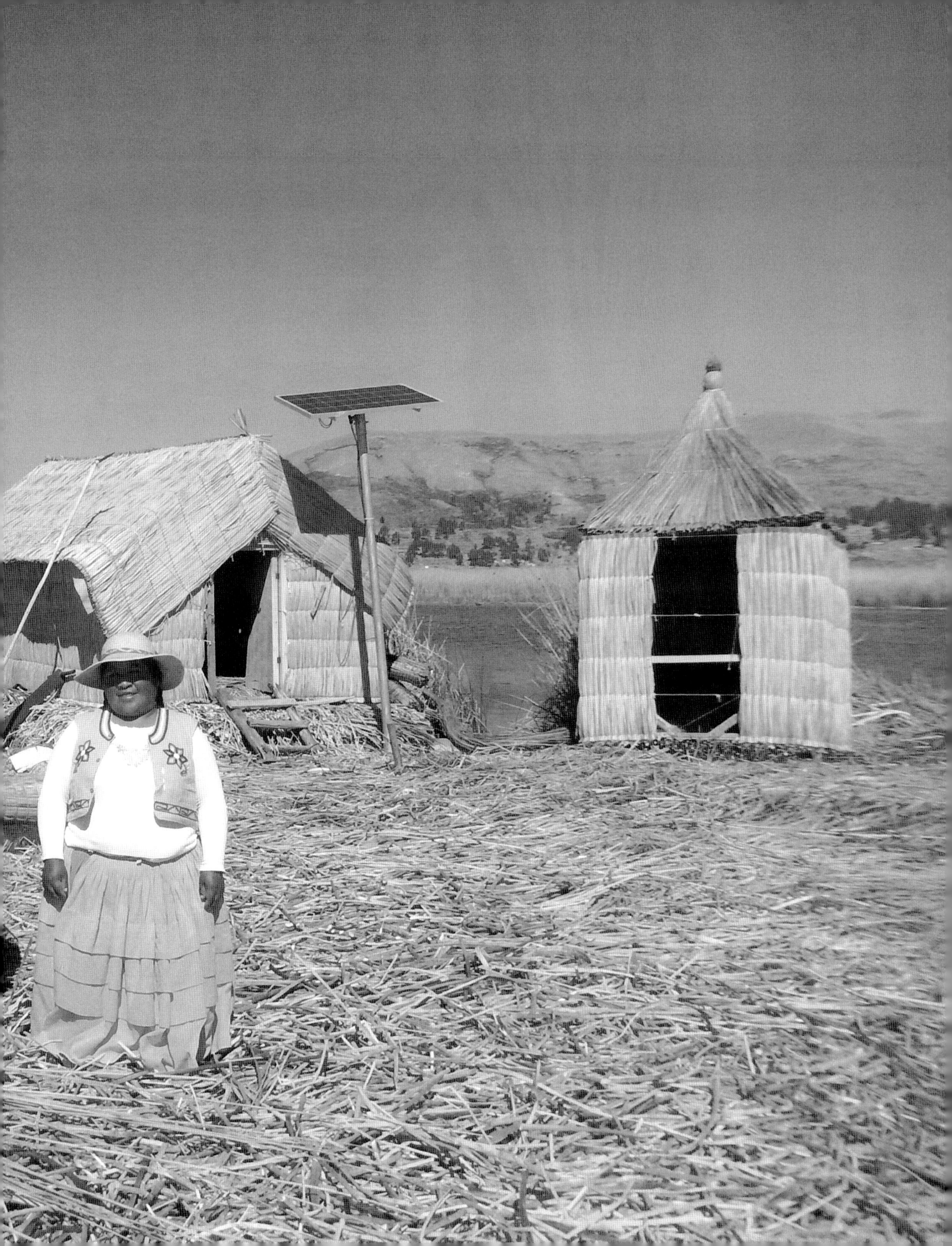

Lake Titicaca, today, is home to about 40 small floating islands of approximately 200 square meters. Most have an elevated watchtower to look over the other islands, while the largest central island acts as the focal point of the tribal community and has a radio station and several schools. Smaller islands to answer calls of nature are built a short distance from the houses. Human waste is dried out in the sun to avoid polluting the lake, from which they get drinking water. The bigger islands house up to 10 families living in woven houses, equipped with solar panels to help run electronic appliances.[30] Although the floating infrastructure was initially created from fear of suppression and for defensive purposes, it is now under threat by modern life. Many of the community have moved to the mainland, leaving only a few hundred inhabitants behind on the miracles of nature and human ingenuity.

Intoxicating Infrastructure – Water Into Wine
In the Biblical story of the Marriage at Cana, Jesus performs his first divine miracle. When the drinks supply of the celebration party ran out, Jesus turned jugs of water into wine.[31] Service infrastructures which are deemed essential have, over the course of the last century, been piped directly into every home and workplace. These include the seemly obvious; potable water, electricity, internet and gas. Whilst those in developing countries may lack this kind of access, there are places where piped infrastructure extends beyond the essentials.

In Leuven, Belgium, thought by some to be the beer capital of the world, the Stella Artois Brewery operates a round-the-clock fully automated manufacturing, ordering and delivery service. It can produce up to 150,000 cans of beer and 200,000 bottles per hour, a feat of modern commercialism. In the same city, copper pipes run directly from the Domus Brewery into neighboring bars. Bruges too is to re-route its beer underground, through three kilometers of polyethylene pipeline capable of carrying 6,000 liters per hour.[32] The five-century-old brewery, De Halve Maan, located in the historic center of Bruges, a UNESCO World Heritage Site, will pump beer direct to a bottling plant in the suburbs. The 'Willy Wonkian' system will replace around 500 tankers on the medieval cobbled streets that were transporting the beer to the plant, reducing traffic pollution in the city and preserving the city's beer brewing heritage. With such inventive intoxication infrastructure, there is little need for miracles in Belgium.

According to 'The Lack of Importance of Religion in Europe' by Gallup Poll (2007–2008),[33] 61% of Belgians felt religion was unimportant, compared to Turkey, where just 9% of people felt it was unimportant, and alcohol consumption is the lowest of any European country. In 2013 the Turkish AKP government brought in regulations to prohibit alcohol retail between 10:00 pm and 6:00 am, ban all alcohol advertising and promotion, and stop new shops and bars from opening within 100 meters of schools and mosques. A bar manager in Istanbul's bustling Beyoglu district bemoaned that 'places like ours do not fit in the AKP's vision of Istanbul. In the future, there will be no room for alternative places like ours. All leftist opposition groups, associations and cultural spaces will be rooted out, and the only place to get a drink will be expensive luxury hotels and restaurants.'[34]

Alcohol related infrastructures could make a large impact on the landscape of countrysides and cities alike, from the hard infrastructure of fields that grow barley or grapes, and the machinery that plough and harvest, to the breweries and distilleries that become prominent engineering or architectural structures. Alcohol is an industry that relates directly to human activities; drinking halls, pubs and clubs form the soft infrastructures that can define territories within cities. Once the nine-to-five relinquishes control, the city's ability to draw-in regenerative energy and money relates directly to how alcohol and nightlife re-configure urban spaces. Peter Rees, head planner for London for almost 30 years, was adamant that the city of London 'is the UK's engine room and it's crucial it's not impeded. London is the best part of the world. People come for the nightlife and then they get the job to pay for it. Clubs, pubs and restaurants attracts the young, highly skilled and mobile people who would otherwise work in New York, Hong Kong or Dubai and go to where the most fun is to be had.'[35]

Rain and Snow Under Burning Desert Sun
An aerial photograph of the city of Dubai reveals numerous man-made islands extending into the bay, adding hundreds of kilometers of private coastline for tourism. The hedonistic infrastructures are probably synonymous with many SF stereotyped images of the future city – segregation between the social classes, opulent built environments masking unpleasantness, and the missing appreciation of civilization. The islands have the hallmarks of the luxurious floating resort of 'Cloud City' from 'Star Wars: The Empire Strikes Back' (1980); and the 'Capital' of 'The Hunger Games' (2008) where its citizens are wealthy, stylish and have a passion for technological excess – each window in the city has a self-selected customized view at a click of the remote.

The islands were developed through dredging millions of cubic meters of sand from the Arabian Gulf and spraying it to form landmasses about 4.5 meters above sea level, all protected from the local currents by a giant breakwater arc.[36] While these creations are true feats of engineering, there have been concerning reports on the ecological and environmental impacts of these artificial islands. Dubai's cluster of manufactured infrastructure by Nakheel, a Dubai Government owned developing company, the 'Palm Trilogy' Islands and 'The World', are 'so substantial that they have changed the ecology in ways that are only going to become clear in decades', according to Peter Sale, a marine ecologist at the United Nations University (UNU) Institute for Water, Environment and Health.[37]

The first of the Palm Trilogy Islands, the Palm Jumeirah, consists of a trunk, a crown with 16 fronds, and a surrounding crescent island that forms an 11-kilometer-long breakwater and has hotel rooms and homes for 65,000 people. A report by the UNU team has highlighted that 'water around the islands remained almost stationary for several weeks, increasing the risk of algal blooms. And although fish have colonized the new environment, they are not all the same species that were there before. The region has already lost 70% of its coral reefs since 2001, with most of the remaining reefs threatened or degraded.' The construction of Dubai's Palm Jebel Ali, an even larger man-made island of the Palm Trilogy, has already destroyed eight square kilometers of natural reef.[38]

'The World', is another fantastical archipelago-infrastructure of 300 artificial islands laid out in the shape of the world map, offering wealthy multinational luxury homes. The developer for the European islands from The World, the Kleindienst Group, has planned to introduce 'rain and snow' under the burning sun. The impossible is allegedly made possible by implementing a system of underground cooling pipes and a 'German-designed' climate control system.[39] In an interview with UAE's 7Days newspaper, CEO Josef Kleindienst explained 'rain comes through a pump system like in a Hollywood movie. It is the same principle with snow. This in turn cools the temperature in areas on the island, thus creating outdoor temperature-controlled areas. It will be collected sub-surface and pumped back in, so the water is in a

previous pages: The floating infrastructures on Lake Titicaca are now under threat by modern life.

30. M Vennard, 'Tough Life of Titicaca Islanders', BBC News, 2005 [http://news.bbc.co.uk/1/hi/4123926.stm], retrieved 17 August 2015

31. 'The First Sign: Jesus Turns Water Into Wine (John 2:1-11)', www.bible.org [https://bible.org/seriespage/5-first-sign-jesus-turns-water-wine-john-21-11], retrieved 14 March 2015

32. C Hooton, 'Bruges to get Underground Beer Pipeline', The Independent, 5 January 2015 [http://www.independent.co.uk/life-style/food-and-drink/news/bruges-to-get-underground-beer-pipeline-9958420.html], retrieved 14 March 2015

33. Gallup Polls, Lack of Importance of Religion in Europe [http://www.gallup.com/poll/1690/religion.aspx], retrieved 14 March 2015

34. C Letsch, 'Turkey Alcohol Laws Could Pull The Plug On Istanbul Nightlife', The Guardian: World, 23 May 2013 [http://www.theguardian.com/world/2013/may/31/turkey-alcohol-laws-istanbul-nightlife], retrieved 14 March 2015

35. H Morris, 'Sex and The City: An interview with Peter Rees', The Planner, June 2014 [http://www.theplanner.co.uk/features/sex-and-the-city-an-interview-with-peter-rees], retrieved 14 March 2015

36. 'How Green Is The World?', The Economist: Green.View, March 2008 [http://www.economist.com/node/10870938], retrieved 18 August 2015

37+38. D Cressey, 'Gulf Ecology Hit By Coastal Development', www.nature.com, 16 November 2011 [http://www.nature.com/news/gulf-ecology-hit-by-coastal-development-1.9374#/b1], retrieved 18 August 2015

264

to participate

cycle. We also cool the floor with a pipe system. Every time the temperature rises above 27C, "Europe" will experience rain coming from vents disguised in decorations 18 meters in the sky. In "Switzerland", the rainwater will be frozen and it will actually snow.'[40] The World might aspire to minimal energy consumption and even to achieve high rating certificates from The Emirates Green Building Council;[41] however, the engineering in this highly commercial environment would require a sophisticated series of technology and plentiful desalinated water to make such an effect possible.

Global sustainability concerns have not prevented further fantastical constructions of environmental irresponsibility that are extremely energy-intensive. The Palazzo Versace Hotel will soon boast a refrigerated 820-square-meter swimming pool, a beach with artificially cooled sand and wind machines for gentle breeze all day long to pamper its guests from the scorching climate of summer temperatures exceeding 50C.[42] Owing to its heavy reliance on air conditioning and desalinated water, the city's continued expansion is adding to its already huge carbon footprint, causing a serious impact on global warming and sea level rise. Consequently, for those select few still in the market for exorbitant luxury, the private low-lying man-made islands might be less than a paradise, as the sea level continues to rise.[43]

Equality on the Beach
Life is a beach. All across the world, and for centuries, the beach has accumulated a vast amount of cultural importance, symbolic meaning, and monetary investment. Major infrastructures are often built or are built as on territorial thresholds; bridges form over rivers, and airports are the entrances into the world of the sky. The beach, 'a pebbly or sandy shore defined especially by the sea between high- and low-water marks'[44] is such a territory; it is made up of layers of sediment deposited by the waves, and has proven to be largely uninhabitable by permanent structures. Reyner Banham argues in 'Los Angeles: The architecture of four ecologies' that the culture of the beach is 'a symbolic rejection of the values of the consumer society. There is a sense in which the beach is the only place in Los Angeles where all men are equal and on common ground.'[45]

The beach is accompanied by all manner of specialist infrastructure, from leisure and tourism, to disaster prevention and wildlife habitat protection. For many cities, it is an infrastructure that has been fundamental to the development of economies and lifestyles. As a key public urban space, the beach with the support from the catering and hotel industries encourages the pursuit of leisure for the masses. In 'Life Between Buildings', Jan Gehl identifies three types of outdoor activities: necessary activities, optional activities and social activities. He argues that 'poor outdoor areas' restrict themselves to only necessary activities, whereas 'good outdoor areas' generate a higher frequency of optional activities, which 'tend to take a longer time', resulting in social interaction. Gehl sees public space and voids in the city as definitive for identity and success of urban design; it is ownership and success of human social activities that allow us to maintain civilized and healthy cities.[46]

In Richard Rogers and Philip Gumuchdjian's 'Cities for a Small Planet', a public space is argued to be essential for political freedom as well as defining a democratic transparency. 'Active citizenship and vibrant urban life are essential components of a good city and of civic identity. To restore these where

facing page: In Dubai, the hedonistic infrastructures are probably synonymous with many science fiction stereotyped images of the future city.

265

39. The Heart of Europe Official Website, 'The Project Overview' [http://www.thoe.com/the-project/the-project-overview], retrieved 20 August 2015

40. J Abdel-Razzag, 'Snow Scheme Revealed for The World Island, Dubai', The Big 5 Hub, 23 December 2014 [https://www.thebig5hub.com/news/2014/december/snow-scheme-revealed-for-the-world-island-dubai/], retrieved 18 August 2015

41. G McDonald, 'Snow Falling on Sand, Dubai's New Winter Wonderland' [http://news.discovery.com/tech/alternative-power-sources/snow-falling-on-sand-dubais-new-winter-wonderland-150102.htm], retrieved 18 August 2015

42. L Hickman, 'Chilling Developments in Dubai', The Guardian: Environment, 18 December 2008

43. 'How Green Is The World?', The Economist: Green.view, March 2008 [http://www.economist.com/node/10870938], retrieved 18 August 2015

44. Oxford Dictionaries Online, 'Beach' [http://www.oxforddictionaries.com/definition/english/beach], retrieved 18 April 2015

45. Reyner Banham, 'Los Angeles: The architecture of four ecologies', Penguin Books, London, 1971, pp.38-39

46. Jan Gehl, 'Life Between Buildings: Using public space', Island Press, London, 2011, p.11

266

they are lacking, citizens must be involved in the evolution of their cities. They must feel that public space is in their communal ownership and responsibility.'⁴⁷

There is a kind of special significance of the seaside public space in the USA and Europe. It may be the novelty of ocean bathing, or playing in sand. There is also a cultural celebration of the holiday, which might be best exemplified by the sexual appeal of bathing suits, wet skin, and sunshine on tanned skin; these are attractors of serious industry from Saint Tropez to Miami. In the UK it is the world of lewd postcards, deckchairs and the vanilla '99 Flake' ice cream.

Reyner Banham further applauded the beaches and that they 'are what other metropolis should envy in Los Angeles, more than any other aspect of the city'.⁴⁸ 'Muscle Beach' in Santa Monica is the spiritual home and birthplace of the American fitness boom and rise of the body-building phenomenon from the 1930s, an idiosyncratic development on the fringe of city and beach. 'Venice Beach', founded as a seaside resort town in the early 1900s, had streets organized around an expensive network of new canals and waterways, populated with gondoliers and other small boats that strictly reflected the American block-suburbia footprint. They were imagined and sold to the public with romanticized Venetian style scenes, painted and photographed by lifestyle magazines. The canals opened in 1905, but by 1929 the majority of the 16 miles of waterway were filled-in following the advent of the 'Age of the Automobile'.⁴⁹ Today, the eccentric development is notorious for a two-and-a-half-mile pedestrian-only circus-like promenade animated by vendors, street performers, fortune-tellers, and artists.

Los Angeles has another key infrastructure – the highways. The images presented in Ed Ruscha's 'Thirtyfour Parking Lots in Los Angeles' (1967) revealed the expansiveness of roads, tarmac and painted lines of vast automobile infrastructure, supplemented by vast compounds and parking spaces. His images of stadia show the expanse of land given to the car, in this case strictly for leisure purposes. Los Angeles has a leisure economy reflected in its infrastructure and architecture of hotels, beaches, casinos, bars and its highways. The film studios and palm tree-lined boulevards are triumphant symbols of a capitalist utopia. According to JG Ballard, 'Ruscha's images are mementos of the human race taken back with them by visitors from another planet'. Ruscha produced the images having hired a helicopter one Sunday morning; the photographs were published as one of the artist's key seminal book projects.⁵⁰

The infamous pollution levels are almost the antithesis of the city of dreams, and come as such a blatant ironic contrast to the glamour of Hollywood. Apart from the carcinogenic products of car engines, there are other threats to beach-goers: 'Climate change could make progress on air quality more difficult as an increasing number of hot, sunny days favor the formation of ozone [which is] generated when pollution bakes in sunlight. Ozone inflames the lungs, aggravates asthma and other respiratory illnesses and is especially harmful to children.'⁵¹ The threat of losing the beach is of serious concern to the culture of the city; the dangerous air quality, car-culture and wide unfriendly sprawling streets qualify as 'poor outdoor areas' by Jan Gehl's criteria. The beach is one of the few remaining infrastructures to offer social equality, a level of public access and liberty.

facing page: Longues-sur-Mer Gun Battery from WW II overlooking the D-Day landing zone on Omaha Beach, Normandy.

47. R Rogers & P Gumuchdjian, 'Cities for a Small Planet', Faber & Faber, London, 1997, p.16

48. R Banham, 'Los Angeles: The architecture of four ecologies', Penguin Books, London, 1971, p.37

49. Westland Network, 'Venice Canals History' [http://www.westland.net/venice/canals.htm], retrieved 9 May 2015

50. M Richards, 'Ed Ruscha's Thirtyfour Parking Lots in Los Angeles', 1967 [http://www.tate.org.uk/context-comment/articles/microtate-13], retrieved 9 May 2015

51. T Barboza, 'L.A., Central Valley have worst air quality, American Lung Association. Says', Los Angeles Times, 2016 [http://www.latimes.com/science/la-me-0430-air-pollution-20140430-story.html], retrieved 9 August 2016

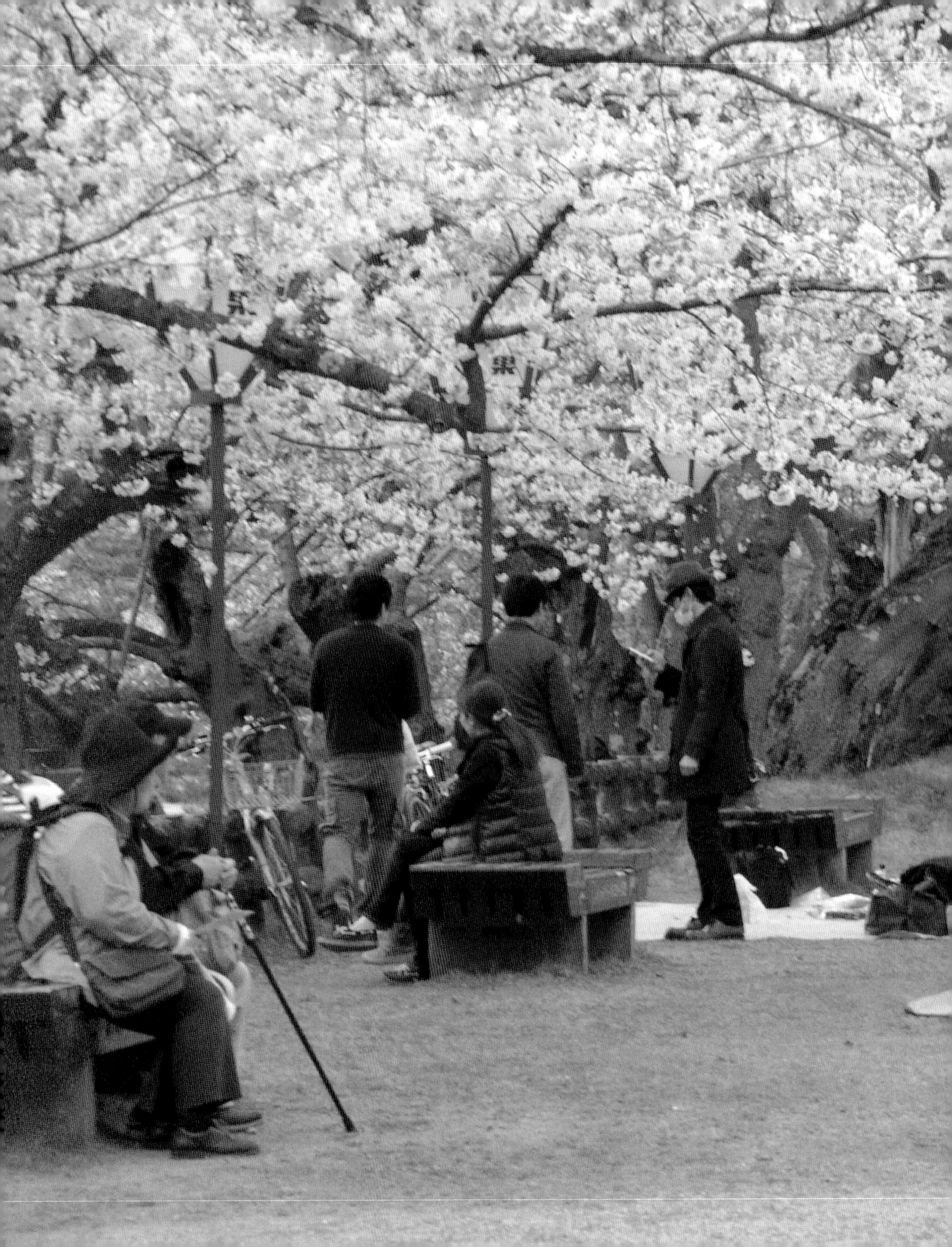

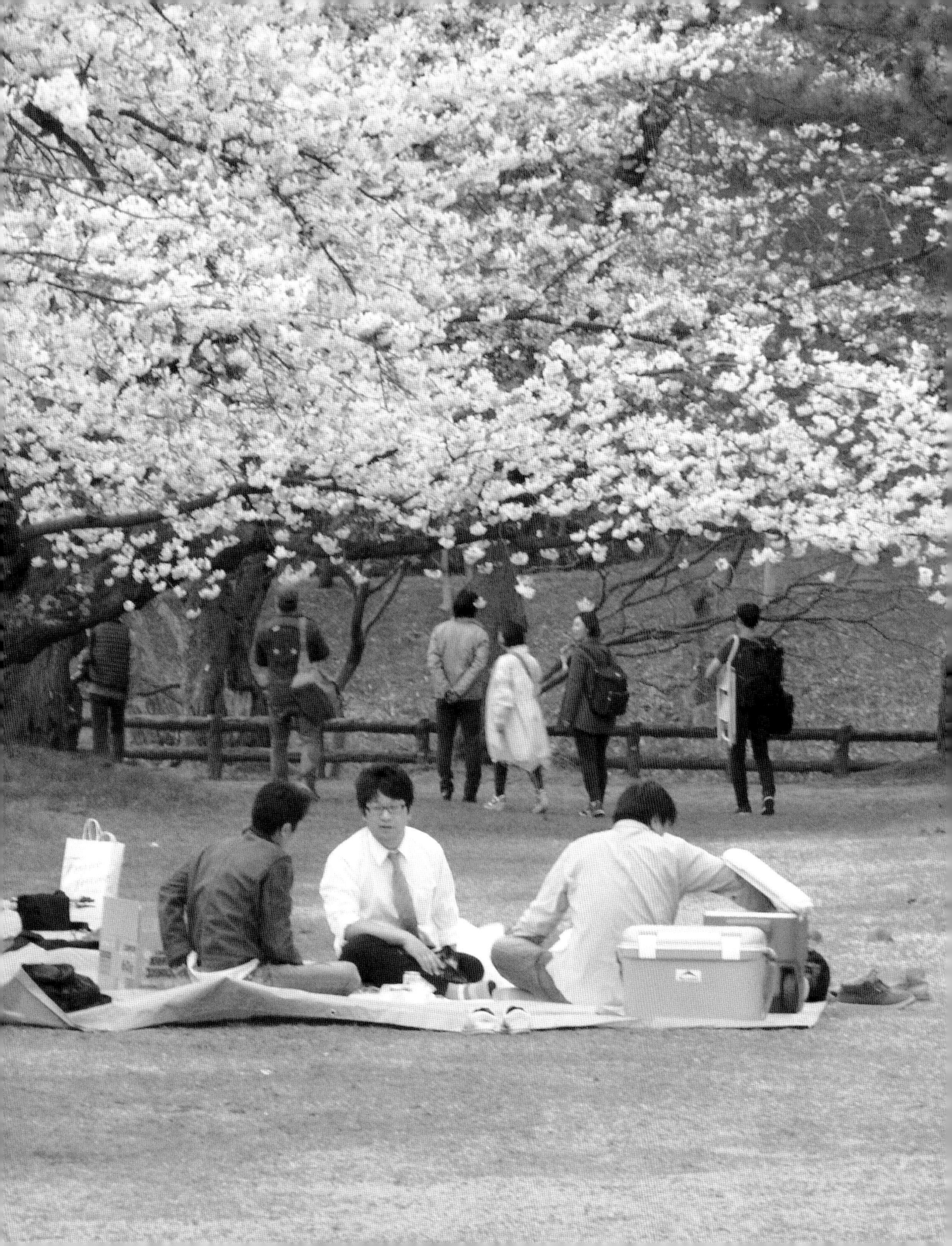

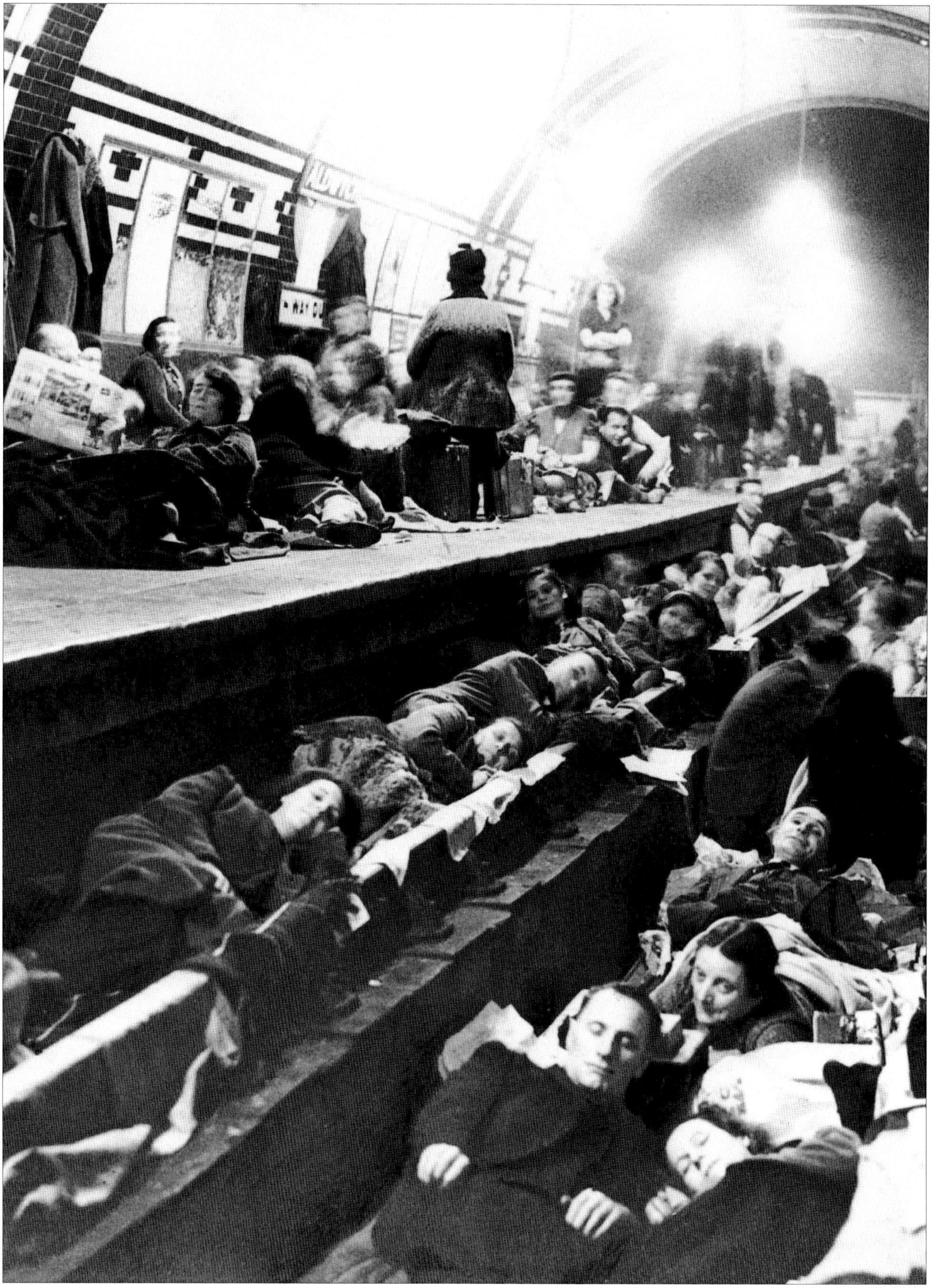

Seasonal Infrastructure

'The public domain is the theatre of urban culture. It is where citizenship is enacted; it is the glue that can bind an urban society', described Richard Rogers.[52] For hundreds of years, millions of Japanese have hosted 'hanami' (lavish picnics and parties) under cherry trees in parks during the blossom festival – the infrastructure of transient beauty only last a week or two. Schools and neighborhoods organize viewings while companies stake out areas in the parks for corporate picnics. A symbol of a fresh new start, the cherry blossom season traditionally coincides with the start of Japan's school and business year.

Hirosaki, located in the northern region of Japan, is one of the country's most celebrated cherry blossom festivals, attracting more than two million visitors each year. The park is about 49.2 hectares, and has more than 2,500 trees. There are over 1,000 trees in Tokyo's crowded Ueno Park, and over 30,000 trees in Nara Prefecture, its historic park and Mount Yoshino. With great anticipation, the exact moment for the arrival of the blossom is the subject of extensive media coverage, and the blossom forecast is announced each year by the weather bureau.[53]

Alas, the beautiful pink infrastructures that blanket the country in soft colorful splendor are under threat from global climate change and local urban heat island effects caused by urbanization. In southern Japan, cherry trees have not flowered after extremely warm winters. Urban, suburban, and rural sites are witnessing differing flowering times; for example, the warmer temperatures in Tokyo had shifted the flowering of cherry trees by eight days earlier than nearby rural or suburban areas.[54] Cherry trees have blossomed an average of 4.2 days earlier than usual during the last 50 years; and with temperatures in Japan predicted to rise, they will bloom a further 14.5 days earlier by the end of this century.[55]

Old court diaries of the Edo era often included the festival dates that allow modern scientists to track the influence of a changing climate on flowering times. The dates of cherry blossom festivals in Japan have emerged as one of the most important sources of information on the impacts of climate change. 'Many trees were "not blossoming as well as they used to" due to the effects of global warming. With the change in temperatures and a more erratic rainy season, I am not sure that we will still have cherry trees in 50 or 100 years', warned Nobuyuki Asada, a member of the Japan Cherry Blossom Association.[56]

Most people in Japan are aware of the impacts not just on their pretty national emblem. The shifting hue of the endangered landscape spectacle acts like a litmus test for the wider environment; with more than 90,000 species of fauna, flora and fungii in an area of 380,000 square kilometers, the islands of Japan are globally important ecological infrastructures.[57]

Tunnels of Desperation

Many kinds of infrastructure facilitate public participation. Historically it was roads that allowed products to be brought from outside of cities into public squares and markets. When trading with other nations the development of ports and harbors was intrinsic to the success of cities; their ability to import and export goods via large-scale transportation infrastructure was the determining factor in their economies

previous pages: The cherry blossom infrastructures that blanket Japan in soft pink splendor are under threat from global climate change.

facing page: Londoners used the Underground Stations as air raid shelters during bomb attacks in WW II.

52. R Rogers & P Gumuchdjian, 'Cities for a Small Planet', Faber & Faber, London, 1997, p.30

53. 'Where To See Cherry Blossoms', Japan National Tourism Organization, 2016 [http://www.seejapan.co.uk/jnto_consumer/experience/outdoor/enjoying-japans-seasons/where-to-see-cherry-blossoms], retrieved 12 May 2016

54. R Primack & H Higuchi, 'Climate Change and Cherry Tree Blossom Festivals in Japan', Arnoldia, Arnold Arboretum of Harvard University, vol.65, no.2, 2007, pp.14-23

55. M Konishi, 'Climate Change Hits Japan's Natural Icons', WWF for a living planet, 26 March 2014

56. D Demetriou, 'Global Warming Hits Japan's Cherry Blossom Season', The Telegraph: Global Warming, 26 March 2009 [ww.telegraph.co.uk/news/earth/environment/globalwarming/5052867/Global-warming-hits-Japans-cherry-blossom-season.html], retrieved 12 May 2016

57. R Hooper, 'Effects Will Become More Obvious as Japan's Climate Changes', The Japan Times: News, 13 July 2013 [http://www.japantimes.co.jp/news/2013/07/13/national/science-health/effects-will-become-more-obvious-as-japans-climate-changes/#.V9EoSRRi6FJ], retrieved 12 May 2016

58. Globalization and World Cities Research Network, 'The World According to GaWC 2012' [http://www.lboro.ac.uk/gawc/world2012t.html], retrieved 27 August 2015

and urban fabric. A great number of large and important trading cities were built either coastally or on the banks of major rivers; examples include Hong Kong, Tokyo, Dubai, New York, and London. These cities are also examples of contemporary economic 'Global Cities'. London and New York are the highest performing global cities according to the criteria of the Globalization and World Cities Research Network (GaWC), achieving 'Alpha++' ranking.[58]

The short distance from France to Great Britain across the English Channel offers easy opportunities for economic and political participation. The history of one of Europe's most ambitious infrastructure projects, the Channel Tunnel, dates back to 1802 when French engineer Albert Mathieu-Favier drew up plans for a tunnel that would allow horse-drawn coaches to cross under the channel. Later, French mining engineer Aimé Thomé de Gamond spent around 30 years of his career on the project, which was approved by Queen Victoria and Napoléon III. Built between 1987 and 1994 for freight and passenger trains and vast vehicle-carrying shuttles, the north–south tunnels and the third service tunnel were opened by Queen Elizabeth II and French President François Mitterrand.[59]

The success of this connection has also been exploited by the very desperate. In the summer of 2015, a crisis developed on the French side of the tunnel where refugees and illegal immigrants smuggled themselves into trucks, cars and freight in the hope of gaining entry into the UK; many lost their lives in the process, being either suffocated or crushed. The situation escalated into riots and the building of illegal refugee camps near Calais. Politicians on both sides of the channel were criticized for indecisive action on the crisis, attempting to balance the lawful migration process with compassionate refugee treatment. In an article in The Guardian newspaper, the executive director of the health charity 'Doctors of the World UK' described the conditions in Calais as a disaster zone and further stated: 'I've visited the wretched refugee camps in Darfur and I've walked around post-earthquake Haiti. But in all my years of working in aid and development, I've never been as shocked as the day I met a group of 10-year-old Syrian boys, riddled with scabies, huddled together in a rain-sodden ditch under scraps of tarpaulin.'[60]

It is not the first of great tunnels to be used by the desperate. Between 1940 and 1941, the Nazi German forces made 71 attacks on London using the Blitzkrieg or 'lightning war' tactic. The Luftwaffe bombed London for 57 consecutive nights, caused massive loss to building stock and infrastructure, and in the terrifying process killed 40,000 of the unevacuated population of the city.[61] For the first two weeks of the Blitz, Londoners pleaded with the authorities for shelter in the London Underground stations; the government were concerned that overcrowding of the lines could cause disruption to the essential services for the war-effort. Eventually the tunnels and underground stations were opened as sanctuaries during the night-time raids. Informal groups such as the Boy Scouts volunteered to participate in mitigating the damage of the Blitz by guiding fire engines, sounding alarms and making sure other civilians were directed into the underground shelters. Although many were killed whilst hiding in the tunnels, as a result of direct bombings, the relative protection and psychological security of the quieter space meant that people could actually get some sleep during the raids, even on the platforms and between the tracks. Henry Moore, the official war-artist, took cover in Belsize Park underground station and became 'fascinated by the sight of people camping out deep underground'. He captured the squalid conditions and the darkness in the infrastructure, as well as the little individuality of the grey and faceless figures in pure abjection.[62]

Bombsite rubble from London and other cities was later used for runway construction at RAF and US Air Force Airbases; recycling of materials was a key strategy to streamline production and use of resources during wartime and post-war years. Many of the bombsites effectively opened up areas of the city and in a way created another important survival infrastructure – the 'Victory Gardens' helped to heal morale amongst civilians while providing fresh food and vegetables to those who had been struggling on meagre rations. The movement was popularized by propaganda posters issued by the British Ministry of Agriculture and featured images of strong men and women. Slogans such as 'Dig For Victory' or 'Beans are Bullets' emphasized that 'every available piece of land must be cultivated', including the Royal Parks.[63]

Today, the length of the London Underground network has 270 stations and measures 402 kilometers.[64] Opened in 1863, the majority of the world's first underground lines were circular tunnels dug through the London clay, which gave rise to its nickname, the Tube. It has been, throughout its life, a multi-use infrastructure carrying passengers, small freight and once even had a separate line for the Royal mail. Complete with smaller versions of the trains for distributing letters and parcels between London sorting offices, the mail-rail was closed down following modernization and digital communication. Significant investment in the infrastructure, including the Jubilee Line and Crossrail developments, has had great economic benefits to London and historically has introduced important architectural interventions to the city. Most evidently, in the case of Leslie Green who was commissioned to design over 50 of London's tube stations, the majority of which re-used the same arch design and oxblood-red tiles externally and green tiles internally. Green's buildings are a cohesive demarcation of an unseen infrastructure; they are esteemed as a pride of London and instantly recognizable.[65]

'Our infrastructure projects should engender national pride, matched by a sense of local ownership, from electricity pylons to flood defences, bridges to road signs.'
– Sadie Morgan, UK National Infrastructure Commissioner

Intelligent and well-designed infrastructure has greatly demonstrable advantages. Protection, provision, and participation are not limited to one of either social issues or commercial value. Cities with contemporary civilized society in recent millennia have all relied on such systems and organizations at an urban infrastructural level for support and coherence. Infrastructure has a manifold identity; it is misguided to see roadways, bridges and harbors as the sole proponents of the term. Markets, parks and squares, cultural hubs and other multi-use infrastructures define the urban fabric and therefore influence the appearance and wellbeing of cities much more than discreet individual buildings ever could.

It is also important to understand how both hard and soft infrastructures can be deployed, encouraged or regulated with special regard to the specificity of local and global context. Sadie Morgan is convinced that investments and intelligent design in infrastructure are key for national economic growth, and that 'imagination needs to be at the heart of our thinking, moving towards a healthier, more compassionate and greener philosophy than before. Dividing and separating the big issues of our day will not conquer them. Successful design is about not just aesthetics but an enjoyable experience of life, and it is this that we must remember and encourage at all times.'[66] 'Re-generation' has been the buzzword for urban politics; national and regional urban re-generation must creatively connect to a collective economic and social infrastructure vision. We need to move away from

---

59. 'The Channel Tunnel: History', Groupe Eurotunnel [http://www.eurotunnelgroup.com/uk/the-channel-tunnel/history/], retrieved 27 August 2015

60. L Daynes, 'Gangrene and Razor Wire: Charity in Calais is no different to a disaster zone', The Guardian: Voluntary Sector Network, 6 August 2015 [http://www.theguardian.com/voluntary-sector-network/2015/aug/06/gangrene-razor-wire-charity-calais-no-different-to-a-disaster-zone], retrieved 26 August 2015

61. BBC History Online, 'The Blitz: September 1940-May 1941' [http://www.bbc.co.uk/history/events/the_blitz], retrieved 26 August 2015

62. H Moore, 'Grey Tube Shelter, 1940', TATE Collection: Art & Artists [http://www.tate.org.uk/art/artworks/moore-grey-tube-shelter-n05706], retrieved 27 August 2015

63. T Way & M Brown, 'Digging for Victory: Gardens and gardening in wartime Britain', Sabrestorm Publishing, Kent, 2010

64. 'Facts & Figures', Transport for London [https://tfl.gov.uk/corporate/about-tfl/what-we-do/london-underground/facts-and-figures], retrieved 27 August 2015

65. J Bull, 'The Man Who Painted London Red', London Reconnections, 1 January 2010 [http://www.londonreconnections.com/2010/the-man-who-painted-london-red/], retrieved 25 August 2015

66. S Morgan, 'UK Infrastructure: Thinking big', Building, 24 February 2016 [http://www.building.co.uk/uk-infrastructure-thinking-big/5080204.article], retrieved 27 February 2016

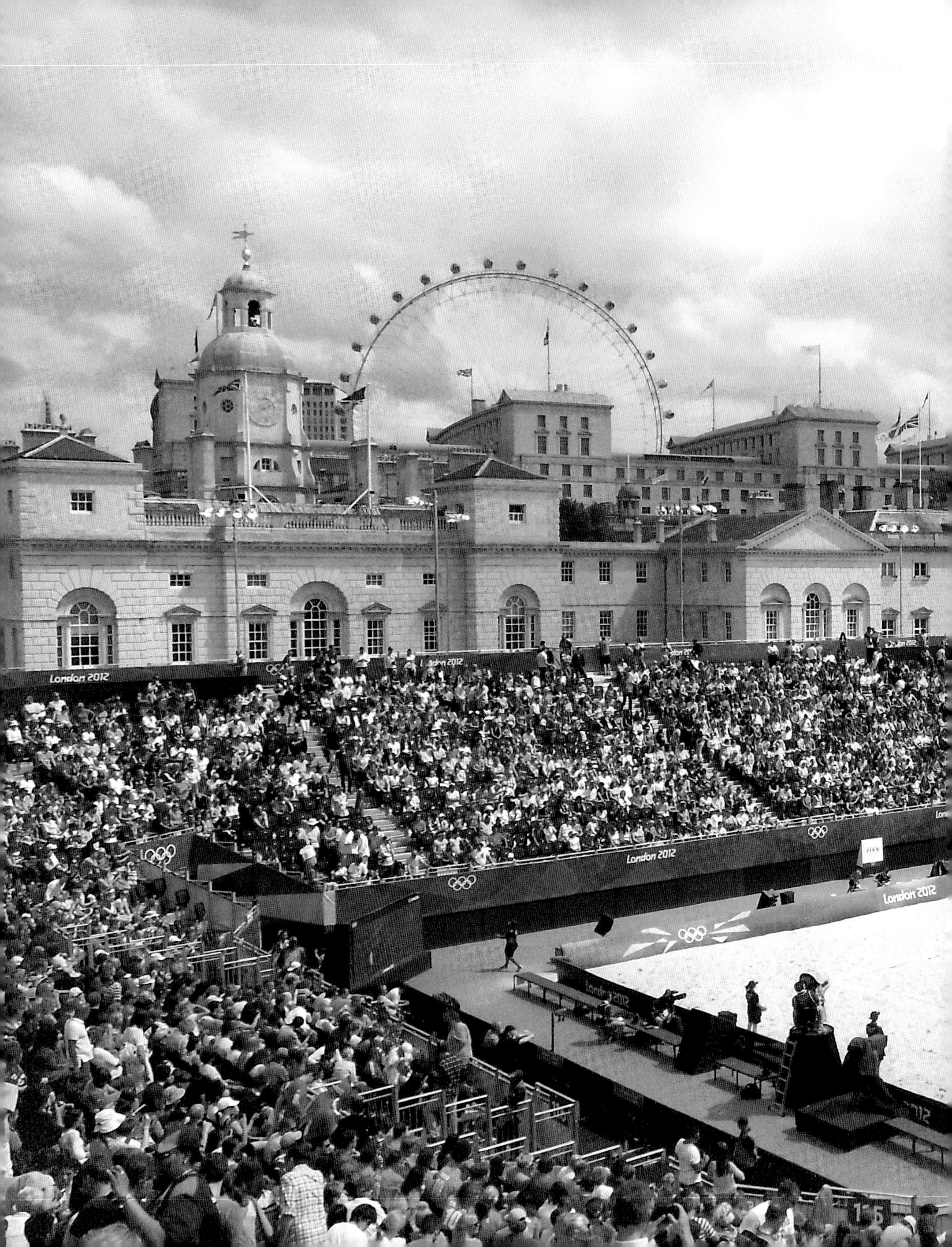

London 2012
London 2012
London 2012
London 2012

London 2012
London 2012
London 2012
London 2012
London 2012

political gestures, and into providing genuine freedom for cities to plan their own future and to future-proof their infrastructure. However, in a great number of cases, governments have misunderstood the requirements of the city and its communities.

Poorly planned transport infrastructure can cause damage to urban grain, as demonstrated in many cities which have been retrofitted with large-scale trainlines and multi-lane highways, since the industrial and post-war revolutions. In Paris, the Boulevard Périphérique was planned along the former site of the Thiers Wall to alleviate traffic congestion, and was completed under the presidency of Georges Pompidou in the early 1970s. Providing a route for a quarter of all Parisian traffic movements, it quickly became the busiest road in France.

The infrastructure became a victim of its own success with widespread congestion, while the dense surrounding urban areas prevented its expansion. The road is now widely regarded as a blight on the city and remains a site of civil unrest, poverty and pollution. Entrance into Paris requires passing through Portes or 'gates' in the road which are foreboding and unfitting the urban finesse. It is important to note that in a city such as Paris, large and perhaps uncompromising grand gestures have driven the character of its wide straight boulevards, splendid cathedrals, vast palaces and extravagant monuments, including Gustav Eiffel's 324-meter tower – the symbol of the city.

Politics and visionary infrastructure have a long relationship in Paris – it was Napoleon III who hired Baron Haussmann, Francois Mitterand who made his 'Grands Projets', and Nicholas Sarkosy who in 2007 declared his intent to create a 'new comprehensive development project for Greater Paris'. In 2008, an international urban design competition for the future development of metropolitan Paris was launched – 10 teams gathering architects, urban planners, geographers, and landscape architects offered their visions for building a Paris metropolis of the 21st century. Richard Rogers led a team that recognized the significant urban opportunity of the five major train lines into Paris which currently appear as boundaries; if they could be bridged or buried then the city's wounds could heal. Referring to the trainlines and the Périphérique, he remarked 'I don't know of any other city where the heart is as detached from its limbs'.[67] Justinien Tribillon, in his article 'Dirty Boulevard: Why Paris's ring road is a major block on the city's grand plans', exposes the infrastructure as a health hazard and a lost opportunity in a city where land is scarce, and 'by cutting across the city, the périphérique's viaduct structure is omnipresent in the working-class neighbourhoods of north-east Paris, but in well-off areas – such as Vincennes in the east, and Boulogne in the west – it discreetly passes underground as a tunnel. In the main, though, a formidable ring of concrete now stands where fortifications once did. London has its green belt, Paris its concrete one.'[68]

The inextricable, powerful bond between prevalent political systems and the creation of infrastructure is absolute. Nothing imagined of such scale could be implemented without either government procurement, or being commissioned by companies for commercial or economic gains. Many of our infrastructures, or at least the DNA of them, had been inherited from decades, hundreds or even thousands of years into the past. Pre-democratic political systems brought us the city-walls, viaducts, roads and canals that we build upon today; our borders are also defined by those that lived before, and that in retrospect may not share a great number of the socio-political ideals that we uphold. Globalization and international free markets are stirring up business traditions of almost every country, and technological development into the digital age accelerates and convolutes the manifestation of these changes.

In the face of population growth, global warming, corruption, and financial meltdown, are we armed with enough imagination and foresight to face the coming challenges of the mid-late 21st century? In the Charter of the United Nations, Chapter I: Purposes and Principles, Article 1, the main political responsibility for its member nations is 'to maintain international peace and security, and to that end: to take effective collective measures for the prevention and removal of threats to the peace, and for the suppression of acts of aggression'.[69] Although not explicitly listed as one of the purposes in the charter, today the United Nations stresses the paramount importance of democratic forms of government through agencies such as the United Nations Democracy Fund (UNDEF). In its first 10 years of existence since 2005, the UNDEF, a soft infrastructure, has supported over 600 projects in over 100 countries. UNDEF supports youth engagement programs, women's empowerment campaigns, and works with them to uphold human rights, tools for education and freedom of information.[70] President Barack Obama of the USA described the organization as 'the shapers of human progress' and the 'conscience of communities'.

With the help of volunteers, it took Joseph Beuys five years to plant his '7,000 Oaks – City Forestation instead of City Administration' at the 'documenta 7' in Kassel, despite facing much political opposition from the conservative German state government in 1982. Every time a tree was planted, the pile of 7,000 corresponding basalt stone markers would shrink. The infrastructure of trees, now an important part of the city's identity, has an ongoing global mission to raise awareness about ecological issues and social change, whilst imparting to its audience and those participating in the project that instant gratification is not necessary. Beuys trusted that 'every human being is an artist, a freedom being, called to participate in transforming and reshaping the conditions, thinking and structures that shape and inform our lives'.

The international space station is a great leap for human achievement; the enduring image of the 20th century must remain the moon landing of 1969. No natives to convert and no land to plough, reaching the moon represents man's speculations at their purest, moving President Nixon to remark that heavens had become part of man's world. By looking back at the history and development of key infrastructures that have allowed citizens of the world to protect, provide, and participate, we begin to understand that it could indeed be that the visions of adaptability and inhabitability have afforded structures and systems to add value to our cities and wellbeing, even after the immediate reason for their creation has lapsed. Inhabitable infrastructures deliver a promise and latent ability to be re-imagined.

'The difference between the man who just cuts lawns and a real gardener is in the touching. The lawn-cutter might just as well not have been there at all; the gardener will be there a lifetime.'
— Ray Bradbury, 'Fahrenheit 451', 1953

---

previous pages: For London Olympics 2012, Horse Guards Parade used over 2,000 tonnes of sand for the creation of a temporary beach at the bottom of The Mall – the main boulevard leading to Buckingham Palace.

67. W Wells, 'Big Plans for Grand Paris', France Today, June 2009, vol.24, issue.6, p.10

68. J Tribillon, 'Dirty Boulevard: Why Paris's ring road is a major block on the city's grand plans', The Guardian: Cities, 26 June 2015 [http://www.theguardian.com/cities/2015/jun/26/ring-road-paris-peripherique-suburbs-banlieue], retrieved 27 August 2015

69. Charter of the United Nations, 'Chapter I: Purposes and Principles, Article 1', The United Nations [http://www.un.org/en/sections/un-charter/chapter-i/], retrieved 25 March 2016

70. The United Nations Democracy Fund, 'About UNDEF', The United Nations [http://www.un.org/democracyfund/about-undef], retrieved 27 February 2016

EQUATOR

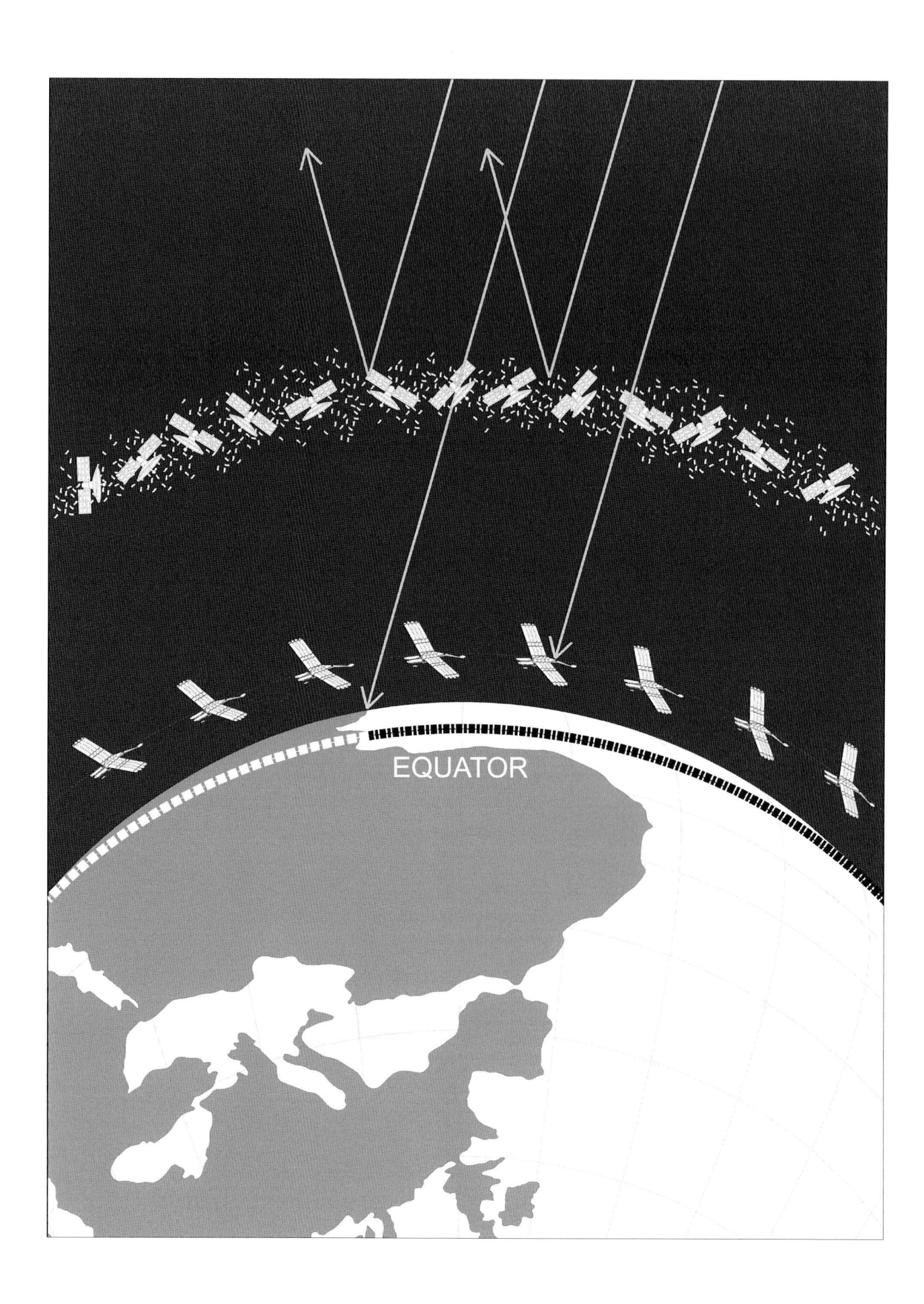

urban future

Corporate Republic: The search for utopia

(viii)

'A map of the world that does not include Utopia is not worth even glancing at, for it leaves out the one country at which Humanity is always landing. And when Humanity lands there, it looks out, and, seeing a better country, sets sail. Progress is the realization of Utopias.'

– Oscar Wilde, 'The Soul of Man Under Socialism', 1891

Imagining 'The Perfect World' is usually the central trait of theological thinking: Elysium is home to gods and heroes, the Garden of Eden is green and plentiful, and the inhabitants of the Gardens of Jannah are clothed in luxury materials residing in palaces built from gold and silver bricks. However, some concepts of religious belief are more concerned with liberation of the soul from torment, rather than paradise of an afterlife. Nirvana is the final release from a cycle of birth, death and re-birth; in Buddhism the religious scripture cannot fully prescribe the journey to that emancipated state, the individual must proceed on their own, in a search.

The search for utopia has been immortalized not only in the temples and pyramids of ancient architecture, but in the great literature of the ages. Often the interesting part of utopia is the search itself – the epic Greek poem 'Argonautica' by Apollonius Rhodius epitomizes the heroic voyage. Jason and his great companions the 'Argonauts' must complete the quest to retrieve the mythical Golden Fleece that would ensure his rightful ascent to the throne of Iolcus. That tradition is passed to the next generation – the seminal period of the science fiction (SF) genre, where Jules Verne sets out on his 'Journey to the Center of the Earth' (1864).

L. Frank Baum gave us 'The Wonderful Wizard of Oz' (1900); the journeys of Dorothy, Toto, Scarecrow, Tin Man and Lion converge along the Yellow Brick Road, with each of the protagonists determined to find their own personal utopias, whether it be wit, courage or an emotion-giving heart. In the end, it was a somewhat perilous journey, and not the destination that had fulfilled their desire – for Dorothy utopia is simply to return home. Evidenced only in works of literature, so we might assume it to be mythical, the golden city of El Dorado has inspired many real-world quests. The search for the legendary gold drew the attention of renowned Spanish conquistador Gonzalo Jimenez de Quesada in 1537, where he and his army of nearly 1,000 men searched throughout Peru and the Andes. Half a century later, the English explorer Sir Walter Raleigh set sail on two separate occasions for Guyana following treasure maps to El Dorado. There was a geo-political aspect to his voyage as he was supposed to establish English colonies in South America to rival the Spanish – however, being unable or unwilling to avoid conflicts with the Spaniards saw Raleigh beheaded upon his return to England.[1] The romantic view of

facing page: The Corporate Republic is located along the equator – the ideal site to exploit the drastic changes in climate, and new global demands and participation.

following page left: The equatorial market is monopolized by the Corporate Republic – a future capitalist community eager to do business with any Equatorialite looking for a higher standard of living.

following page right: The Corporate Republic is a mobile industry that keeps pace with the movement of the sun as a way to comply with international labor laws. Working hours have been surreptitiously extended into one ceaselessly ongoing process – the front of the vessel is always 9:00 am, and the rear, always 5:00 pm.

1. W Drye, 'El Dorado Legend Snared Sir Walter Raleigh', National Geographic [http://science.nationalgeographic.com/science/archaeology/el-dorado/], retrieved 2 August 2016

EMPLOYMENT
BUREAU
CORPORATE
REPUBLIC
ROOMS
4
RENT
PARADISE VIEW
PARADISE VIEW
ROOMS

corporate republic: the search for utopia

SUNSCREEN
BAR
MONSTANTO
Life is Richer
in the Republic
The Equator's Highest Standard of Living
BUY!!! SUNSCREEN
UN STRIP
EMPLOYMENT BUREAU
McMEGA MALL
Cola
CORPORATE REPUBLIC McSHOPS
SUNSCREEN
EQUATOR SUN CREAM
Corporate Republic

corporate republic: the search for utopia

Raleigh's demise would be that he was executed because he failed to find the gold of El Dorado. It is this kind of melancholic impossibility that romantic poet Edgar Allan Poe wrote of in his poem 'Eldorado' (1849), 'Over the mountains of the moon, down the valley of the shadow, ride, boldly ride... if you seek for Eldorado'.[2]

Mention of architectural utopia might at first conjure images of a Retro-Future landscape packed with tall towers, flying vehicles and ground dominated orthogonal infrastructures, as in 'Broadacre City' or the 'Mile High' skyscraper by Frank Lloyd Wright. However, a technocratically perfect and totally egalitarian society might not be the only path or type of utopia. There is the possibility of a glimpse of utopia even in modest-scale constructs such as Wright's signature house 'Fallingwater' (1937). And history would see to it that one of Bruno Taut's smallest buildings would be imbued with the greatest sense of utopia – the 'Glass Pavilion', exhibited at the Cologne Deutscher Werkbund Exhibition in 1914, was a tangible artefact in the transcendental qualities of glass to emerge from the architect's radical search.

The majesty of glass is inseparably linked with utopia in architectural history, whether for its use in depictions of the supernatural, when installed into cathedrals as stained glass windows, or whether it signified the epitome of future technology and engineering when placed in the hands of the builder of 'Crystal Palace', Sir Joseph Paxton. As capitalism gets comfortable in its throne, the dominant religion of our age is worshipped in glass cathedrals, whether it be small chapels such as the 'Fifth Avenue Apple-Store' by Bohlin Cywinski Jackson, Renzo Piano's 'Shard' rising out of south London's skyline with the same imposing presence of medieval 'Notre Dame de Paris', or Skidmore, Owings & Merrill's colossal capitalist temple – the 'Burj Khalifa' in Dubai.

In 1889, Gustav Eiffel positioned his ambition vertically on La Tour de 300mètres (the Eiffel Tower); it was to become the tallest infrastructure in the world for 41 years and an instantly recognizable icon for Paris. Originally constructed as the entrance to the World Fair, the vertical Utopia contained a theatre, restaurants, laboratories and a private apartment for Monsieur Eiffel. The Fair had a long reputation of showcasing advancements in technology; the futuristic inhabitable communications infrastructure was archetypal and sensational, but was also crucially paired with the utopian ideals, artworks and manifestoes of the age. However, 10 years prior, at the Paris Exposition Universelle 1878, Eiffel's plans for an extraordinary 130-meter inhabitable bridge installed above the existing Pont d'Iéna were rejected.[3]

Historically the tradition of utopia is seen not just conquering vertically, but also horizontally. One of the greatest typologies for urban speculation has been the inhabitable bridge. The 'Old London Bridge' (1209) hosted over 200 buildings of up to seven stories high; the ultimate demise of the notorious inhabitable infrastructure followed the Great Fire of 1666, and is immortalized in the nursery rhyme 'London Bridge is Falling Down'.[4] The infrastructural and technocratic nature of a bridge implies industry and grand ambition, and inhabitation under these conditions becomes rather eccentric.

Ponte Vecchio ('Old Bridge') in Florence is a surviving example of the lengths people will go to achieve a dense center to their economically booming but spatially constrained city. The bridge has a route

facing page: The Sun Screen Bar – In the extreme conditions of the equator, sunscreen is a product always heavily in demand and found in abundance in the Corporate Republic's McMega Malls.

2. EA Poe, 'Eldorado (1849)' in 'The Complete Tales & Poems of Edgar Allan Poe', Racepoint, New York, 2011

3. B Lemoine, 'La Tour de 300 mètres', Taschen, Cologne, 2006, p.152

4. S Burgess, 'Famous Past Lives', O-Books, Winchester, 2011, p.130

GOOD MORNING, UK!
CORPORATE REPUBLIC
Here to Serve
YOU
Serve
US
GLOBAL
SURVIVAL
EQUATOR
SUN
CREAM

running through its center and is built up on either side with housing and shops. Paris also witnessed many such structures over the centuries, notably the bridges spanning onto the Île de la Cité, including Pont Neuf, Pont Au Change and Pont Notre Dame. A bridge is a symbol of modernity and a conqueror of nature's obstacles. When faced with the immense issues of the 21st century, the visceral image of great engineering in the inhabitable bridge can catalyse discussion, as the visionaries of the past once did.

The typology of the inhabited bridge has been widely used across the globe and throughout history. Japanese examples can be seen in the artworks of Hiroshige and Hokusai in their depictions of Edo period cities. The Metabolists made several proposals for bridges and bridging structures, which were partially inspired by the historical examples. In the 20th century, there was a renaissance of visionary infrastructures by Konstantin Melnikov, Hugh Ferriss, Kenzo Tange, to Constant Nieuwenhuys' anti-capitalist 'New Babylon' (1959–74) and Yona Friedman's 'Spatial City' in the 1960s. Zaha Hadid, in 1977, designed one of her seminal works around the theme of an inhabitable infrastructure, by applying the Malevich's Tektonik over the Hungerford Bridge on the Thames. Ivan Leonidov proposed his 'Linear City Magnitogorsk' (1930), taking inspiration perhaps from Arturo Soria y Mata's 'Ciudad Lineal, Madrid' (1882); he increased the scale of the infrastructure to intensify the vision of the city, against the notion of sprawl. Alan Boutwell and Mike Mitchell's 'Continuous City for 1,000,000 Human Beings' (1969) is a vast infrastructure elevated on hundred-meter pillars that act to span the multifarious terrain of North America in a straight line.[5] OMA's 'Exodus, or the Voluntary Prisoners of Architecture' and the 'Continuous Monument' by Superstudio exemplified the hard-edged utopias of the 1970s. Both projects dealt with expansive infrastructural cities that are, at times, uncompromising to context and existing city fabric. The radical proposals have portions of matching linear structures that permit the continued existence of certain microcosms of the city.

The USA has a tradition of radical utopianism (and its latent opposite). Over the course of its history, wealthy capitalists were inspired either by utopian politics, profit-motives or spiritual ideologies to construct company towns for their workers. A remake of society in miniature, the neo-feudal model of participation was replicated throughout the country. There were thousands of planned community infrastructures in which the one employer company owns practically all housing, stores, and facilities. In the beginning in the 1820s, there was Lowell in Massachusetts; the textile manufacturing planned community was a demonstration of righteous living and a morally uplifting American capitalist utopia.[6] More symbols of the Pilgrim's ideal 'city on a hill' rapidly followed – Pullman, Illinois, by the railroad-car maker; the lumberjack haven Scotia, California; and Hershey, Pennsylvania, founded by chocolate magnate Milton S Hershey. The quintessential company town is Dearborn, Michigan – the Ford Motor Company owned one-quarter of the city's land including the Fairlane residential estate and Greenfield Village, the Ford Airport, the Henry Ford Museum, and Fairlane Center, a hotel-shopping-campus complex and headquarters of the company.[7]

Companies like Google and Facebook have plans to build all-encompassing infrastructures for their employees' participation. Reported by Newsweek in 2011, 'Google is set to offer on-site employee housing – 120,000 square feet of it, slated for construction on NASA land near Mountain View, California.

facing page: The Vacation Strip – Life for UN citizens living within their designated Equatorial Vacation Strip has become pleasurable, thanks to the Corporate Republic's high level of productivity.

5. S Ley & M Richter, 'Megastructure Reloaded: Visionary architecture and urban planning of the 1960s reflected by contemporary artists', Hatje Cantz, Berlin, 2008, pp.165–168

6. N Partyka, 'The Bosses' Utopia: Dystopia and the American Company Town', The Hampton Institute: A working class think tank, 20 May 2016 [http://www.hamptoninstitution.org/the-bosses-dystopia.html#.V8LK2kv8zfM], retrieved 30 May 2016

7. G Galster, 'Driving Detroit: The quest for respect on the motor city', University of Pennsylvania Press, Philadelphia, 2012, p.55

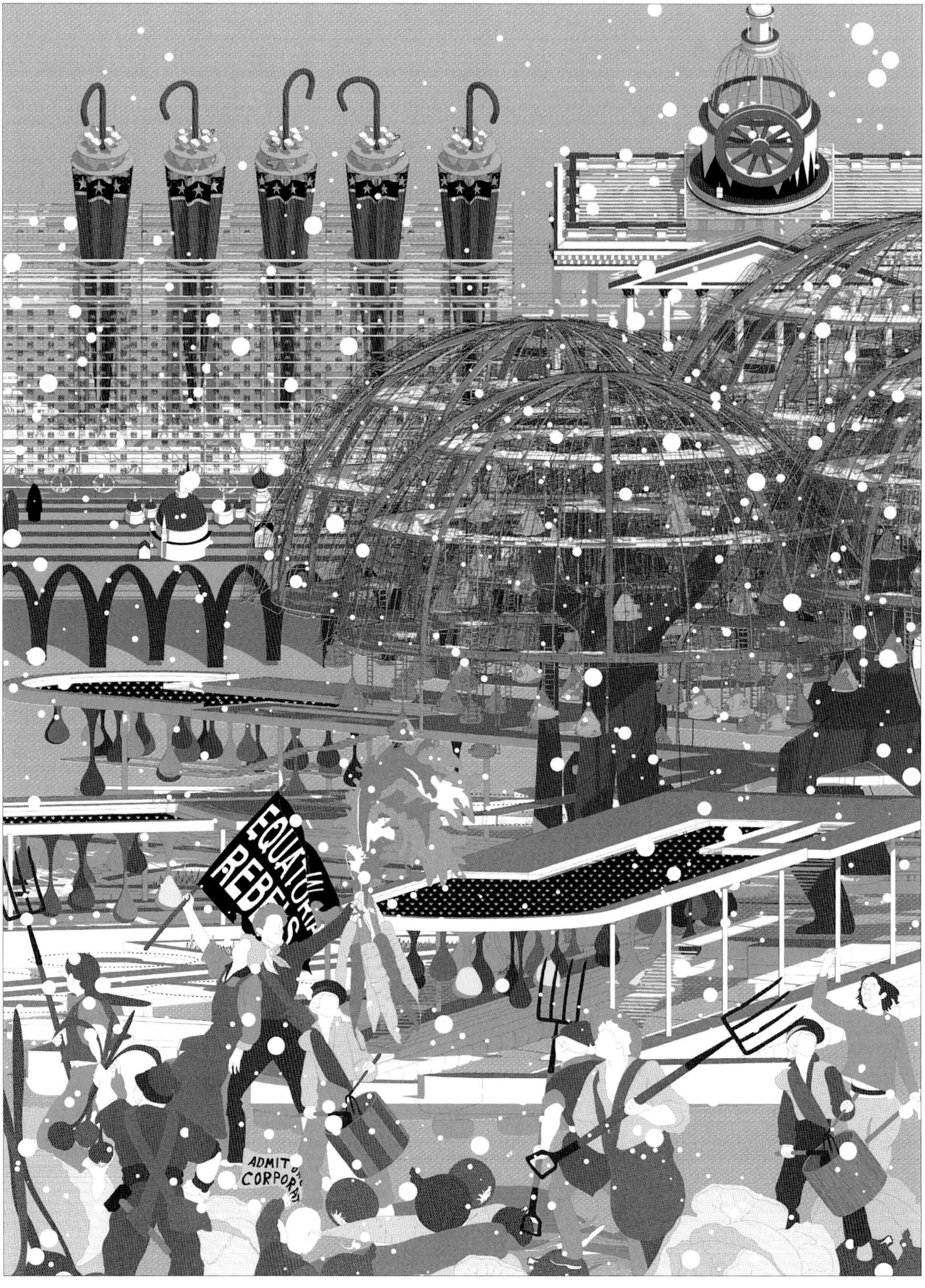
ADMIT

corporate republic: the search for utopia

That's enough for approximately 60 midsize homes, or 400 dorm rooms. Employees enjoy the services of a dry cleaner, hairstylist, massage therapist, and chefs who whip up three meals a day. They commute on company buses, nap in company "pods", and shoot pool in company parlor rooms.' At the forefront of corporate paternalism, Facebook is planning to create a 'small-community feel' for its 79-acre campus.[8]

Company towns will not be the past phenomena as long as we are willing to trade enforced moral codes, lack of independence and uniformity of living standards for employment. Isolated utopias for workers are settings rife for speculative fiction and have all the elements one can find in the works of SF authors, such as Edward Bellamy, George Orwell, Aldous Huxley and more recently in Margaret Atwood's 'The Heart Goes Last' (2015). The latter is a moral tale – those who sign up for a neat suburban house and full employment in the utopian town of Positron/Consilience have no guarantee of a happy ending.

Hadley's Hope (Aliens, 1986), Delta City (Robocop, 1987) and Freya's Prospect (Aliens vs. Predator, 2004) are examples of SF company town infrastructures imagined for the silver screen. Weyland-Yutani Corporation builds a large storm wall to shield Hadley's Hope on LV-426 and directly links it to the Atmosphere Processor via an underground tunnel. Later the Corporation expands onto BG-386 with Freya's Prospect, a vast housing infrastructure with extensive recreational facilities including a small strip club called 'Club Eden' – time has certainly redefined acceptable morality since Lowell! And finally, corporatocracy has fully privatized crime-ridden Detroit, Michigan, into Delta City – the eventual bankruptcy of the Motor City in 2013 was prophesied in the 1987 film.

The reason for the fascination with SF and utopia is about the 'other', it always lies just beyond our consciousness or discoveries – explorers, historically, would voyage to what they thought would be the ends of the earth. In 'Searching for Utopia: The history of an idea' (2011) Gregory Claeys explains that voyages are 'a mixture of fantasy, anticipation and delight in the discovery', which is why utopian thinking gravitates towards moments in time where new explorations are made visible, glamorized and discussed. The search for utopias has extended its interest to space-travel, inspired by the post nuclear age of World War II and the Cold War. Claeys retells 'the period of the first serious exploration and subsequent conquest of the New World… follows the mythic voyage and precedes the age of modern travel. Henceforth the imaginary would fall increasingly by the wayside and the anthropomorphical would come to the fore.'[9] Whether an island can retain its utopian identity after it has been visited or colonized by explorers is another question.

Christopher Columbus, in 1492, described the natives of the New World to be gentle, and without the knowledge or the inclination to kill or to steal. What Columbus was perhaps romanticizing in his 'discovered' civilization was that the uncorrupted innocence of mankind could offer more wisdom than advanced cities and technology. The New World might claim to be 'The Land of the Free, Home of the Brave'; however, if we look critically at the USA today, do we see any remaining traces of that noble wisdom in its advanced capitalism? Or instead do we see a conspiring and convoluted system of big business, political power and mass media that, as political theorist/philosopher Noam Chomsky described, is determined to 'manufacture consent' for their own agendas.

facing page: The stagnant queue for non-United Nations citizens waiting for a UN Visa has developed into a permanent residence. Some have given up on the idea of entering the Corporate Republic and have formed their own rebel societies.

8. T Dokoupil, 'The Last Company Town', Newsweek: World, 2 March 2011 [http://europe.newsweek.com/last-company-town-68763?rm=eu], retrieved 27 May 2016

9. G Claeys, 'Searching for Utopia: The history of an idea', Thames & Hudson, London, 2011, p.71-75

EMPLOYMENT BUREAU
CORPORATE REPUBLIC

corporate republic: the search for utopia

In 'News From Nowhere' (1890) William Morris unveils a paradise-found, a utopian landscape where there are no big cities, private property, money, prisons or class systems. Here, pleasure and wellbeing are both found in nature. Nonetheless the contradictions of urban utopia and societal perfection are explored in Iain Banks' 'The Player of Games' (1988); everything has already been fulfilled, sickness has been overcome and nobody ever dies. The inhabitants of this world never explore anything new – utopia is not searched for hungrily, instead it is the sloth and sluggishness gained from over consumption. 'It is reasonable to suggest that the age of the unrestrained pursuit of happiness, defined in terms of egotistical consumption, has now passed... utopia and dystopia march ever more closely hand in hand.'[10] So we might be prudent to keep checks on those who are striving to build the next utopia or who are insisting that we need to return to it in acts of misleading quasi-nostalgia.

Certain utopia might even be achievable. But like the Eden-esque world full of food and beautiful women to fulfill all desires described in Margaret Atwood's 'The Blind Assassin' (2000), the 'picture is of happiness, the story not. Happiness is a garden walled with glass: there's no way in or out. In Paradise there are no stories, because there are no journeys. It's loss and regret and misery and yearning that drive the story forward, along its twisted road.'[11]

Whether it is grand sea voyages, private islands, or a space exploration program, there is an undeniable relationship between capitalist strength and the search for utopia.

The Linear City at the Equator
The equator is an imaginary plane perpendicular to planet earth's rotational axis. In planetary rotation it also remains more or less the closest area of the planet to the sun, experiencing purely direct overhead sunlight at midday. The sun generates the patterns of weather by heating air, water and the ground; and develops huge convection currents both on land and at sea. Hot air rises strongly at the equator taking with it water as bands of moisture. Clouds form and water falls as precipitation, the currents then form the other half of their cycle; as the air loses its moisture and cools towards the Tropics of Cancer and Capricorn, low level dry air is blown back towards the equator. It is slightly counter-intuitive to think that underneath the colder air would form the world's major deserts, but geographically this is true; the equator lies directly between two colliding halves of a symmetrical weather cycle, and it is the equatorial region that is home to almost all of world's rainforests and its largest rain storms. The clouds and the moisture in the atmosphere block out much of the sun's heat, so that on the surface it feels cooler than it would either to the north or south. The moisture falls, mostly as rain, leaving the land below rich in water and life.

The earth's northern band of desert incudes those of Southern USA and Mexico, the Middle East, Northern China and Mongolia, and the great Sahara. The southern band includes dry areas in South America, Australia, and the Kalahari Desert of southern Africa.

All of the world's major deserts are expanding, and at an alarming rate. Global warming is just one reason in a compounded problem. But there is evidence to suggest that with the advent of climate

---

facing page: Some non-UN citizens managed to obtain a One-Day Working Visa within the Corporate Republic. A candidate must first apply for a vacant position at the Employment Bureau, a rigorous process conducted at a tollbooth at the beginning of the work day.

10. G Claeys, 'Searching for Utopia: The history of an idea', Thames & Hudson, London, 2011, p.207

11. M Atwood, 'The Blind Assassin', First published 2000, Anchor Books, New York, 2001, p.518

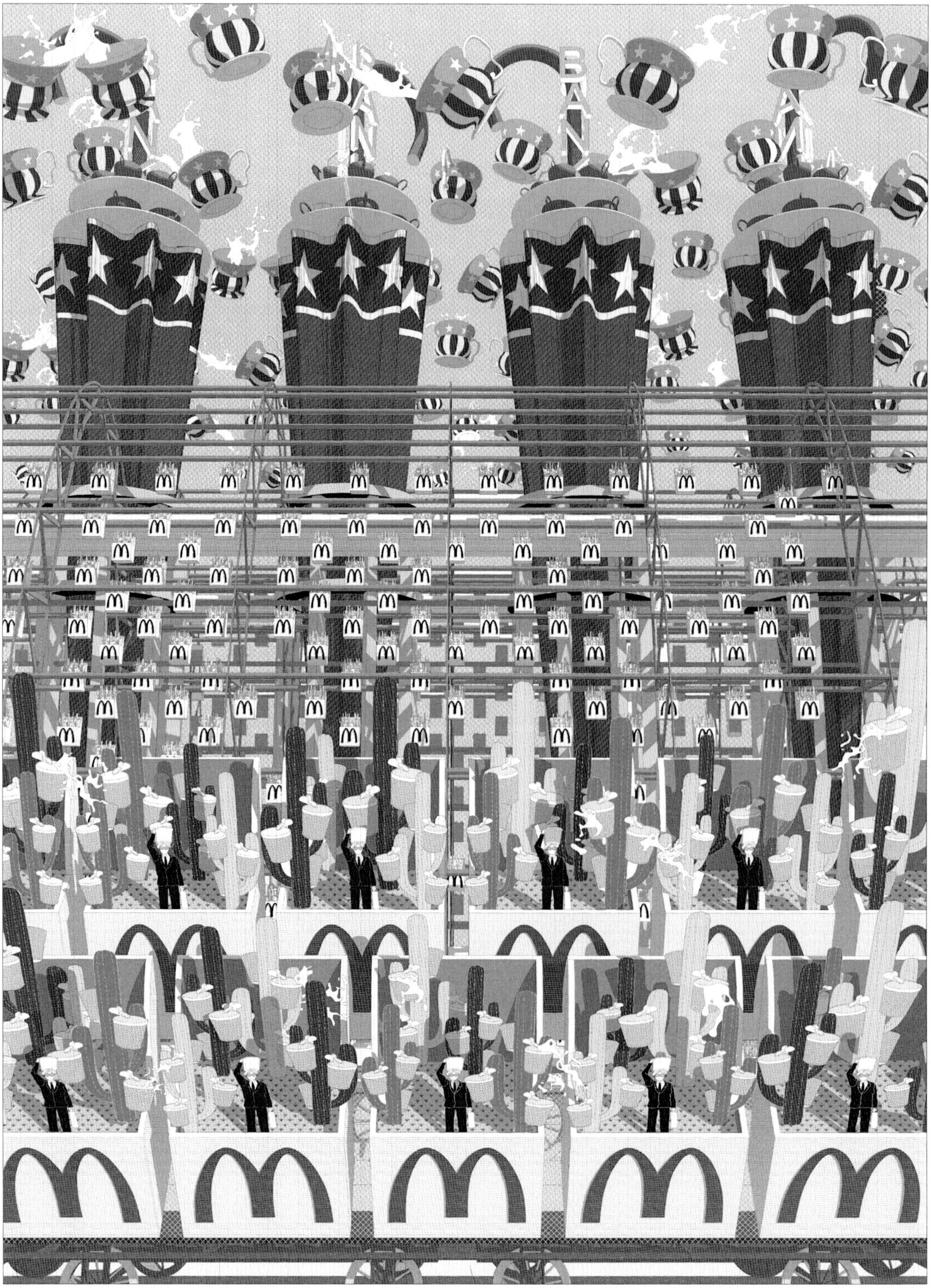

change, the equator itself might actually become an increasingly stormy and rainy environment. Conversely, it might well be that the equator remains the only inhabitable region long into the ecological cataclysm. Revolutionary capitalists are predicted to venture across the seas to seek out the opportunity at the equator. In this scenario, economic enlightenment would require water to become a vital resource and a new form of currency.

Global crisis, fear and uncertainty create market opportunities for products that promise safety or escape. With that in mind, the equator is the ideal site to exploit the drastic changes in priorities and daily habits of global citizens, and to attract private investments and restructure business models that adapt to new demands and participation. What will a business look like in the era of the 'Equatorial Movement'? If today's capitalism flourishes on the thrivalist, what does neo-capitalism look like if it is depended upon for survival? And if capitalism is given full rein, what is its potential?

'The Corporate Republic' defines a form of government where the political structure and all civil workers are replaced with corporate leaders and a capital-driven business. All public sectors, education, healthcare, security, and welfare are privatized. Inspired by SF and company towns such as Boulder City in the USA, Bournville in the UK, and Wolfsburg in Germany, the primary market of the monopoly is its own workers. The conglomerate forms a paternal relationship with its workers by providing all required systems, infrastructure and facilities to increase productivity and fulfill their consumerist hungers.

The Pledge of the Corporate Republic

The Pledge: It is a declaration that compels The Corporate Republic to provide its Workers with a life ample with desire, leisure, and freedom; demonstrates The Corporate Republic's commitment to the Company's way of business. The Pledge stands as a testament of responsibility and respect towards the Workers, and identifies the core values of The Corporate Republic.

Utopia by Desire: Aspiration is the foundation for all that we do, material or otherwise. It includes gluttony, competitiveness, and relentlessness. Building on the values, The Corporate Republic provides members of the Company with a high standard of living. Working in the Company fulfills the promise of equal opportunity to a high standard of living for all Workers of every branch.

Mass Consumption: Commercial exuberance is necessary if all Workers in the Company are to have a high standard of living. What is more important, participation of mass consumption is necessary to support mass production in a corporate economy.

Availability of Employment: Mass consumption cannot exist without mass distribution of purchasing power, which is achieved through mass employment. Employment in the Company is granted to every member that is most fit for the position.

Freedom from Toil: The accumulation of purchasing power grants the Worker the freedom from toil, and engages in activities of leisure and amusement. The difference between efficiency and productivity is the

facing page: Production – Employees work the cacti fields and squeeze cacti for fresh water. The residual pulp is sold as sunscreen to the Equatorialites and the water is stored in the Executives' Umbrella Racks to be later served as tea to the Management.

EMPLOYMENT BUREAU
CORPORATE REPUBLIC
PARADISE VISAS
BANK
LUNCH TIME
MANAGEMENT QUARTERS

corporate republic: the search for utopia

key to accumulation. The Worker is recognized as an individual and is entitled to and compelled to gain personal capital. The secret formula to this happy capitalist state is attributed to the personal gain of the individual Worker and abstaining from idle members in the Company.

Corporate Identity: In a general sense of wellbeing that the Company shares and attributes to the form of capitalism, The Corporate Republic is united, that socialism is the antitheses of the Equatorial way, that it infringes on the pursuit of human freedom and happiness, and that it should be avoided at all costs.

By occupying territory across the entire circumference of the equator, The Corporate Republic can exploit the rotation of the globe and travel against its spin. The world's non-migrant population is fixed to the globe and experiences day and night, restricted by a trend that promotes a reduction in the working hours, due in part to limitations enforced by union laws and federal regulations and in part to traditional notions of day and night. The fixed way of life becomes a hindrance to any attempt to increase production time. Instead The Corporate Republic races around the equator at 1675kph so maintaining a fixed relationship with the sun (as of 2016 the fastest manned air-breathing vehicle was the Lockheed SR-71 Blackbird, with a top speed of over 3,500kph).[12] The Corporate Republic remains perpetually within the hours of nine to five.

The Golden Arches, the 'M', a globally recognized symbol of corporate dominance, gluttony, and excess, is adapted as the new emblem for The Corporate Republic. Its profile is extruded along the equator, spanning the full length of the company's infrastructure for community participation. Its continuity symbolizes the monopolize market and its reluctance to acknowledge the sensitive context that it infiltrates. The 'M' is obtrusive, ubiquitous, and relentless.

Comfort, luxury, and excess are something that The Corporate Republic offers to all those that contribute to its production of a high standard of living. To make the citizens more comfortable during the process of consumption, the M-Mega-Mall has been designed as an automated environment, one capable of efficiently delivering goods and services through various pipelines and conveyor systems. A surreal participation of indulgence of The Corporate Republic is sunscreen, pumped out of barrels and passed over the counters of numerous bars, pubs and off-licences.

The major crops of The Corporate Republic are cacti species and tropical palms; there is a plethora of products derived ranging from oils to aloe. The Corporate Republic primarily cultivates cacti species for healthcare, food, and clean water – the cactus' thick and bulbous forms hold vast volumes of water, and its hairy filaments collect dew from air or fog.[13] With all the stresses and strains of the capitalist life on the equator comes the requirement for decadence, excess and intoxicated escapism. Whilst water remains the most expensive and desired commodity, the citizens who consume the psychoactive plant Peyote cactus and Tequila made from the succulent Blue Agave claim that the products deliver 'deep introspection and insight', an infamous 'Wolf of Wall Street'[14] business model.

facing page: At the end of the day, the Fiscal Barometer determines the level of productivity and reports back to the Management.

following page left: Corporate Living – The Management dispatch the employee appraisals that determine whether an employee is fit for promotion to a higher standard of living, or (which is most likely the case) a demotion to harsher working conditions.

following page right: The Management is located between 12:00 noon and 2:00 pm – that is why they are always out for lunch. The most elite employees fuel the Combustion Chambers with crumbs from their feasting that propels the vessel.

12. Historical Programs, 'Creating The Blackbird', Lockheed Martin Official Website [http://www.lockheedmartin.com/us/100years/stories/blackbird.html], retrieved 10 August 2016

13. T Mace & S Mace, 'Cactus and Succulents', Hamlyn, London, 1998, p.12

14. J Belfort, 'The Wolf of Wall Street', Bantam Books, New York, 2007

294

corporate republic: the search for utopia

295

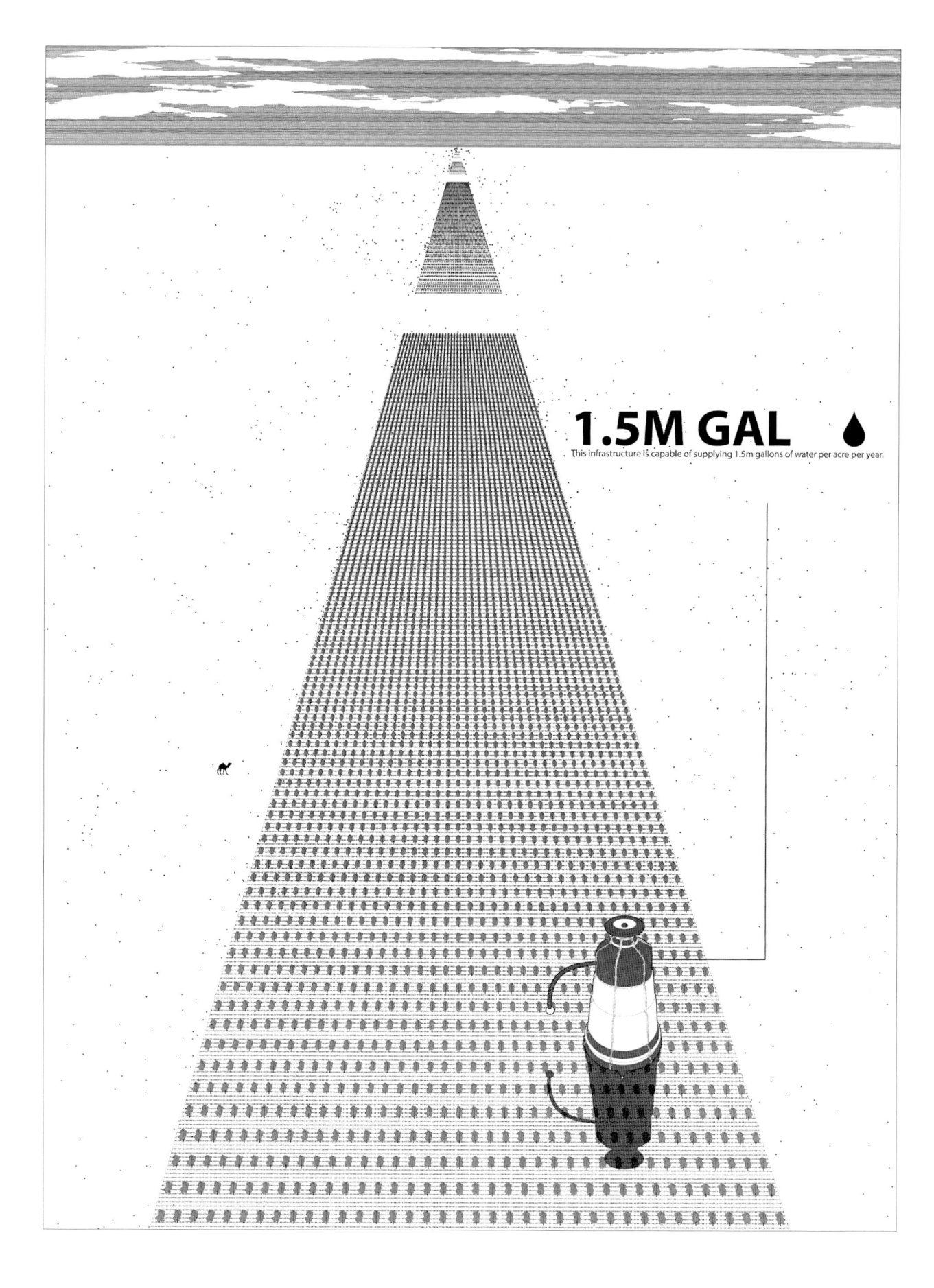

1.5M GAL 💧
This infrastructure is capable of supplying 1.5m gallons of water per acre per year.

corporate republic: the search for utopia

Despite initial perceptions of The Corporate Republic as the capitalist infrastructure of greed, it is important to realize the generosity, albeit commercial, that the enterprise offers. Due to the expanded scale of the construction work, there is a good argument for using recycled and reclaimed materials in the construction of The Corporate Republic's structures. Post-industrial detritus found in contaminated seas is the first to be floated towards the equator for recycling; the Great Pacific Garbage Patch will no longer be an ecological disgrace of the 21st century. Non-recyclable garbage can be cleaned of toxins, and compressed into sustainable and robust building blocks.[15] The seas and natural habitats of non-equatorial regions have a great burden removed, and there is a good opportunity for people living in polluted areas to become entrepreneurs turning trash into cash.

The CEO and the selected Chairmen head the Corporate Republic – there is a division of labor, but everyone seeks promotion in the strictly hierarchical economy. The members are the primary regulators of the 'rate of employment', the 'standard of living', and oversee all production and profit. The importance of their task is represented by the building they inhabit, a replica of the American Capitol Building. Reminiscent of the cloud from Italian cult film 'Fantozzi' (1975); the members consume large quantities of water-currency to create small shading clouds that hover above their building, such that they can enjoy the outdoor environment in comfort. The management division is located between 12:00 noon and 2:00 pm. As a result, they are always out on a business lunch.

As the new linear metropolis begins to establish itself as a dominant global power and the world's cities decant towards The Corporate Republic at the equator, the abandoned planet can breathe a sigh of relief. Climate change will not be reversed and the damage will not be undone, but nature will take over the concrete jungles and its biological systems will begin to reinstate, revive and re-invent themselves. Is it communal-symbiosis, economic-autonomy or the search for utopia that will determine the shape of things to come?

With the same intensity of JG Ballards 'Crash' (1973), The Corporate Republic races along its track; the infrastructural embodiment of utopia is freedom – free from day and night, from geographical history or contexts, and refusing to accept defeat or lose a penny of profit in the face of climate change.

'It was better to live with disappointment and frustration than to live without hope.'
  – Robert A Heinlein, 'Waldo', 1942

facing page: The infrastructure is capable of supplying 1.5 million gallons of water per acre per year.

15. Staff, 'How to Make Eco-Bricks Out of Garbage', Utne Reader, November/December 2012 [http://www.utne.com/environment/eco-bricks-zm0z12ndzlin.aspx], retrieved 10 August 2016

Research Credits

Inhabitable Infrastructures: Science fiction or urban future?
research team (Book): CJ Lim with Steve McCloy

Urban Future Case Studies:

Science Fiction or Urban Future? (2014)
research design team (London): CJ Lim with Eric Wong, Steve McCloy
research design team (Melbourne): CJ Lim and Martyn Hook with Pascal Bronner, Martin Tang, Steve McCloy, Jono Ware, Alan Lau, Caitlyn Parry, Carl Hong, YuLing Cheng, Neha Juddoo, Heather Stevenson, Layla Cluer, Rachel Low, Stephen Sinclair, Vivian Johnny, TengFei Zhu, Zoe Loomes
supported by: Royal Melbourne Institute of Technology (RMIT University); and International Specialised Skills (ISS) Institute Fellowship (Australian Government Initiative)

London is Flooding? (2015)
research design team: CJ Lim with Samson Lau, Yu-Wei Chang, Eric Wong, Jens Kongstad Olesen
supported by: Château d'Oiron, Centre des Monuments Nationaux, and the Ministere de la Culture France; and Fonds Regional d'Art Contemporain du Centre (FRAC) France

Swine Under the Sheltering Skies (2016)
research design team: CJ Lim with Eric Wong, Steve McCloy, Samson Lau, Ryan Hakiaman, Yolanda Leung, Yu-Wei Chang
supported by: Danish Arts Council's Architecture Committee; and the Architecture Research Fund (The Bartlett, UCL)

The City of Frozen Spires (2015)
research design team: CJ Lim with Steve McCloy, Frank Fan, Eric Wong
supported by: Danish Arts Council's Architecture Committee; and the Architecture Research Fund (The Bartlett, UCL)

Twenty Thousand Fish Above the Sea (2016)
research design team: CJ Lim with Eric Wong, Steve McCloy, Jason Lamb
supported by: The Architecture Research Fund (The Bartlett, UCL)

The City of a Thousand Lakes (2015)
research design team (London): CJ Lim with Steve McCloy, Ryan Hakiaman, Jason Lamb, Samson Lau, Woojong Kim, Eric Wong, Yu-Wei Chang, Nick Elias
research design team (Nanjing): Hongyang Wang with Dongfeng Zhu, Yi Chen, Jingjing Li, Wen Yuan, Yan Zhang
supported by: Gaochun District Government and Gaochun Municipal Planning Bureau, China

The Forest: An infrastructure for urban resilience (2014)
research design team: CJ Lim with Franky Chan, Yu-Wei Chang, Samson Lau, Steve McCloy, Ned Scott, Martin Tang
supported by: The Australian Pavilion and Slovenian Pavilion for the Venice Architecture Biennale 2012; and Maribor 2012 European Capital of Culture

Perfection (2016)
research design team (Melbourne): CJ Lim with Pascal Bronner, Martin Tang, Steve McCloy, Jono Ware
research design team (London): CJ Lim with Damien Assini, Freja Bao, Hank Liu, Isabelle Lam, Allen Wen, Michael Quach
supported by: International Specialised Skills (ISS) Institute Fellowship (Australian Government Initiative); and the City of Melbourne

Corporate Republic: The search for utopia (2017)
research design team: CJ Lim with Marcin Chmura, Ashwin Patel, Julia Chen, Lauren Fresle
supported by: The Architecture Research Fund (The Bartlett, UCL)

Reproduction Credits

6, 62+63, 66+67, 68+69, 70 bottom, 72+73, 74 top, 76, 78, 88+89, 92, 98+99, 168+169, 172, 182+183, 186 bottom, 266, 268+269, 274+275 Paul Allen

8 Arco Images GmbH / Alamy

16+17, 66 top left, 74 bottom, 90+91, 166, 178+179, 250, 260+261 CJ Lim

22 AF Archive / Alamy

30 top Moviestore Collection Ltd / Alamy

30 bottom AF Archive / Alamy

32 top AF Archive / Alamy

32 bottom AF Archive / Alamy

44 Granger Historical Picture Archive / Alamy

60 Dereje Belachew / Alamy

70 top Philip Mugridge / Alamy

80 Arco Images GmbH / Alamy

84, 94+95, 104, 176, 188 Thomas R Hilberth

102 David Wall / Alamy

164 Arcaid Images / Alamy

172 bottom imageBROKER / Alamy

184 JRC Inc. / Alamy

186 top BUILT Images / Alamy

252+253 Thomas Hillier

256 Frans Lemmens / Alamy

264 Boaz Rottem / Alamy

270 Trinity Mirror / Mirrorpix / Alamy

18, 38+39, 48+49 images are inspired by original book covers and posters

all other images CJ Lim / Studio 8 Architects

Index

'2001: A Space Odyssey' (Kubrick) 20, 151

Adams, Douglas 26
Adeyemi, Kunlé 24
Afghanistan 173–4
agriculture: controlled burning 103; floating islands 259–62; food and waste management 14; futuristic foods 177; grain elevators and silos 180–1; ice and cold storage 177, 180; irrigation efficiency 190; land reclamation 255–7; terrace farming 178–9; urban, indoor farming 14; windmills in farming 174–5
Alcatraz Prison 102
alchemy 55, 57
alcohol industry 262–3
ancient civilizations: aqueducts and water management 164–5, 167, 170; cisterns for water supply 186, 187; defensive infrastructures 71, 75, 78–9, 81; food storage structures 177, 180; multi-use, communal space 167–70; religious and ritualistic sites 36, 60, 61, 64; rivers, strategic value 85; underground settlements 83, 85; wind powered machinery 174–5
aquaculture, visionary potential 214–15, 217, 220–3
artificial islands: architectural designs 13, 24; depictions in science fiction 23–4; Dubai 263–5; forced migration 24–5; Makoko, Lagos 24; South China Sea 100
Asimov, Isaac 33, 47
atmospheric water harvesting 13, 191
Atwood, Margaret 287, 289
'Avatar' (Cameron) 22

Ballard, J.G.: Ed Ruscha images 267; fear about future 26; fiction subjects 20; 'High-Rise' 21; science fiction's prophetic value 7, 19; 'The Burning World' 57; 'The Drowned World' 107
Banham, Reyner 265, 267
Banks, Iain 289
Banksy 96–7
Battersea Power Station 181
Bazalgette, Joseph William 43
beaches, multi-use environment 265–7
Belgium's beer industry 262
Bellamy, Edward: 'Equality' 211, 212; 'Looking Backward: 2000–1887' 7, 47, 211
Berlin 82, 105
Berman, Marshall 65
Beuys, Joseph 277
'Big Hero 6' 34
'Black Cloud, The' (Hoyle) 34
'Blade Runner' (Scott) 20, 34
Bologna 66
Boutwell, Alan 285
Boyle, Danny 93
Brautigan, Richard 55
'Brazil' (Gilliam) 25
bridges: communal space 68–9; economic legacy 250–1; inhabitable bridges 172, 283, 285
Bruges 64, 262
Buenos Aires 90–1
Burtynsky, Edward 25, 233
Bush, George W. 96

Callebaut, Vincent 13
Calvino, Italo: 'Invisible Cities' 25, 35, 55, 212
Canada: elevated walkway, Calgary 171; Underground City, Montreal 82
Capek, Karel 33
carbon-neutral goals 10, 13
Carroll, Lewis 37, 55
Çatalhöyük, Turkey 79
cave dwellings 83, 85
Channel Tunnel 272
'Children of Men' (Cuarón) 181
China: cave dwellings 83; Dongyi Wan East Waterfront 14–15; dune stabilization (Beijing) 105; Forbidden City, Beijing 42; Great Wall 78; land and sea infrastructure 100–1; population dynamic 217; Shanghai's saltwater issues 11–12; Tiananmen Square 70, 71; urbanization policies 212; wind energy 175
cities: agricultural innovations 14–15; climate change vulnerabilities 9–10, 190–1; CO_2 emissions, energy-related 10; development level 10, 28; earliest 61; fortifications and walls 79–82; infrastructures and city development 61–5, 77, 276; inspirational practicalities 42–3, 45; mitigation options 12, 15; open, public space 67–71, 77; political systems, impact of 276–7; religious foundations 71, 74; slum dwellings, real and fictional 87, 92–3, 96; social tensions 237; strategic importance 71, 75; streets, multi-functional 65–6; urban metabolism indicators 12; water security 11–12, 13, 35, 190, 191, 255
City of a Thousand Lakes (socio-economic sustainability): aquacultural landscape 210, 214–17; community functions and economy 217, 220–5; land-use map 212; satellite villages 217–19
City of Frozen Spires (heritage preservation): city protection 150, 160–3; community sustainability 159; ice protection 154, 155–9; masterplan 152–4
Claeys, Gregory 227, 287
Clarke, Arthur C. 20, 28
climate change: arbitrary causes 7; coastal impacts 10–11, 190–1; comics as information channel 131; displacement risks 9, 193, 205; ecosystems and biodiversity impacts 190; equatorial regions 289, 291; green infrastructure solutions 13–15, 155; natural infrastructure initiatives 103, 105, 258; Pacific nations 25; sea level rises 10, 11–12, 107, 131; security issues 12, 190–1; stakeholder cooperation 12; urban heat island effect 267, 268–9, 271
CO_2 emissions 10, 267
communication infrastructures: 'cloud' computing 29; mobile phone networks 29
company towns, US 285, 287
'Continuous Monument' (Superstudio) 285
Copenhagen: City of Frozen Spires (heritage preservation) 150, 152–63; environmental strategy 10, 155
Corporate Republic (capital-driven society): commercial sustainability 296–7; core values and identity 291, 293; equatorial position 278, 291; management division 294–5, 297; mass employment and consumption 280–2, 284, 286, 288, 291; production 290, 292–3
cryonics 151, 155
cyberspace 26

Dali, Salvador 31
defensive infrastructures: Alexandria and Pharos 71, 75; Berlin Wall 105; bushfire containment 103; fortifications and walls 78–82, 104; gun battery, Normandy 266; invasion sites 173–4; negative re-construction 174; World War I trenches 86–7
Delta Works 257–8
Denmark: City of Frozen Spires (heritage preservation) 150, 152–63; Copenhagen's environmental strategy 10, 155; Elleore's micronation 100; green energy 139, 147; Greenland, protection role 131, 139; pig farming 139, 147; Swine Under the Sweltering Skies (sustainable energy) 130, 132–49; wind energy 175
Despommier, Dickson 14
Devarajan, Sharad 131
Dick, Philip K.: cinematic interpretations 20; 'Do Androids Dream of Electric Sheep?' 20, 33, 34; 'The Penultimate Truth' 82
Disney Company 35
displacement: climate change related 9, 193, 205; economic, political or social factors 24, 193; humanitarian response 208
'District 9' (Blomkamp) 93, 237
Dongyi Wan East Waterfront, China 14–15
'Dream Farm 2' model 14
Dubai: artificial islands, impact of 263–5; Burj Khalifa tower 159, 283
dystopian fiction: cinematic interpretation 25, 31, 181; dark landscapes 20; manga 87; regulated worlds 37, 40, 42, 82, 223

Ebersolt, Gilles 205
Egypt: Alexandria and Pharos 71, 75; grain silos 180; pyramids 36, 60, 64, 74; Suez Canal expansion 173
Eiffel, Gustav 283
Einstein, Albert 29

index

Elleore (Denmark) 100
'Elysium' (Blomkamp) 237
Environment Agency (UK) 103, 117, 123, 127
equator and climate change 289, 291
Ettinger, Robert C.W. 151, 159
'Exodus' (OMA) 285

Ferriss, Hugh 21, 23, 285
'Fifth Element' (Besson) 30
Finney, Tarsha 173
floating islands: Aztec construction 258-9; Lake Titicaca 259-62; Pacific nations 25
flooding issues: beneficial management 14-15; coastal management 258; Copenhagen's strategy 10; Dutch windmills 174; economic factors 117; Mombasa, Kenya 9; sea level rises 9, 10-11, 107, 131; Thames Barrier, London 77, 117; tree planting schemes (UK) 103, 127; Venice 16-17; see also Paranoid City, The
Florence: defensive infrastructures 81; Ponte Vecchio 172, 283, 285
food industry infrastructures 227
food security: agricultural innovations 14; climate change and coastal cities 9; food sovereignty 233, 235; food storage structures 177, 180-1; German civil defense 189-90; global issue 190, 235
Forest: An infrastructure for urban resilience (food sovereignty): hunting exchange and outposts 226, 232-5; masterplan of green infrastructure 228-31
forest management: fire ecology 103; non-wood products 233; tree planting benefits 103, 105, 127; well-being benefits 235, 277
Foster, Norman 35
France: defensive infrastructures 81; Loire's caves 85; Paris, infrastructural developments 64-5, 276
Freedom Ship 205
Friedman, Yona 27, 285
Fuller, Buckminster 26, 151
future, speculation on 47, 55
futurism and machinery 25-6

Gaochun, China: district environment 212, 213; sustainability vision 210, 212, 214-25
garden cities (UK) 7, 211
Gee, Maggie 117
Gehl, Jan 265
Germany: Berlin Wall 105; Beuys's ecological mission 277; civil defense advice 189-90; Wuppertal Suspended Railway 31, 33
Gibraltar 70, 71
Gibson, William 20, 26
glass infrastructures 285
global-mean temperature 11
Greenland 131, 139
Green, Leslie 273
green program investment 11
Grimshaw Architects 13, 151
Gropius, Walter 12-13
Gumuchdjian, Philip 265, 267

Hadid, Zaha 285
Heinlein, Robert A. 171
Herbert, Frank: 'Dune' 13, 191
heterotopia 35, 72-3
Hilbertz, Wolf 24
Ho, Mae-Wan 14
Hong Kong: Central Elevated Walkway System 171; Chungking Mansions 93; Kowloon Walled City 87, 105; street life 66
Hoover Dam and Boulder City 252-5
Hoover, Herbert 254
Howard, Ebenezer 7, 211
Howey, Hugh 82
Hoyle, Fred, Prof. 29, 34
humanity: fears over future 41; sex and reproductive advances 41-2

'Hunger Games' (Collins) 36, 40, 263
Huxley, Aldous: 'Brave New World' 21, 37, 42, 55, 237

ice: futuristic applications 152-63; Persian cold storage 177, 180; polar melt risk and flooding 11, 107, 131; science fiction scenarios 107, 151; US ice trade 180
India: Dharavi, Mumbai slum 93; Ganges' multi-use issues 84-6; Hira Minar Tower 176; Jal Mahal Palace 94-5; Kumbhalgarh Fort, Udaipur 104; Mumbai's skywalk failures 171, 173; stepwells of Gujarat 187-9
infrastructure: hard and soft categories 61; hard/soft functions and city development 61, 64-5
Intergovernmental Panel on Climate Change (IPCC): food and water security 190; greatest threat 7; rising sea levels 10; temperature and precipitation change 11
International Institute of Environment and Development (IIED) 11-12
internet dating 41
Istanbul: Basilica Cistern 186, 187; Blue Mosque 71, 74; Galata Bridge 68-9; religious buildings 71
Italy: defensive infrastructures 80, 81; inhabitable bridges 172, 283, 285; Isola di San Michele Cemetery 88-9; Roman Colosseum 168-9, 170; street life 65, 66; Venetian well 166; Venice and flooding 16-17

Jacobs, Jane 65
Japan: cherry blossom and climate change 268-9, 271; contemporary design 27-8; heritage 77; high-speed trains 31; living walls 103, 105; Metabolist Movement 26-7; Tokyo Station 83
Jones, Diane Wynne 55

Kaufman, Charlie 23
Kennedy, John. F. 251, 254
Koolhaas, Rem 26, 27, 193
Kowloon Walled City 87, 105
Kronenburg, Robert 193, 205
Kuma, Kengo 77

LaHood, Ray 251
Lake Titicaca, floating islands 259-62
Lang, Fritz: 'Metropolis' 21, 37, 171
Las Vegas 72-3
Le Corbusier 25; 'Plan Obus', Algiers 75, 77
Leeds 64
Lee, Stan 131
Le Guin, Ursula 20
Leonard, Andrew 191
Leonidov, Ivan 285
Levin, Ira: 'The Stepford Wives' 33, 237
Lin, Patrick 34
'Logan's Run' (Nolan/Johnson) 213, 217
London: alcohol and service industries 262-3; Battersea Power Station 181; climate change impacts 107; flooding events 107, 117; glass infrastructures 283; infrastructure developments 62-3, 77; London Bridge 283; Olympics 2012 274-5; Oval's gasometer 181, 182-3; public space 71, 77; Thames Barrier 77, 117; 'The Paranoid City', flooding scenario 106, 108-29; Underground's multi-uses 270, 272, 273; World War II survival 270, 272-3
'Looking Backward: 2000-1887' (Bellamy) 7, 47, 211
Los Angeles 265, 267
Lovelock, James 177

'Mad Max' (Miller) 36
Makoko Floating School, Lagos 24
Maldives: islander relocation scheme 205; islands of 8; waste management challenges 11
Maribor, Slovenia: food sovereignty scenario 228-35
marine ecology: destructive artificial islands 263-5; species invasion 173
Marvel comics 131
Masdar City, Abu Dhabi 35
mechanical infrastructures: building forms 25; role in science fiction 25-6

301

Melbourne: Fisherman's Bend renewal program 241; Perfection, utopian community, basis for 236, 238–49; urban development 241
Metabolist Movement 26–7, 285
micronations 97, 100
Miéville, China 20, 55
migration, infrastructure of: Channel Tunnel and Calais camp 272; climate migrants 193; 'Noah's Ark' 23, 32, 127, 193; nomadic tribes 205
Milan 65, 66
Mitchell, Mike 285
mitigation options 12
Mombasa, Kenya 9
Morgan, Sadie 273
Morris, William: 'News From Nowhere' 211, 289
multi-use infrastructures: case study locations 7; cross-disciplinary innovation 12–13; Dongyi Wan East Waterfront 14–15; science fiction, learning from 7; sustainability trade-offs 10

national identity 174
National Marine Data and Information Service (NMDIS) 11
natural infrastructure: dune stabilization 105; tree planting benefits 103, 105, 127; vegetated buffers 258
Netherlands: flood protection 258; land reclamation schemes 257–8; polder infrastructure 255–7; windmills, function and symbolism 174
Newton, Isaac, Sir 57
New York: Croton Water Treatment Plant 13; skyscrapers 75, 76; Times Square 67, 71; water systems 13, 185–7
Niccol, Andrew: 'Gattaca' 42; 'In Time' 57; 'The Truman Show' 21
Nieuwenhuys, Constant 37, 285
'Noah's Ark' 23, 32, 127, 193
nuclear age 29, 31, 37

Obrist, Hans-Ulrich 26, 27
Orwell, George: 'Animal Farm' 55, 139, 181; 'Nineteen Eighty Four' 19, 40, 181, 237; political dystopia 42

Palmanova 80, 81
Paranoid City, The (London underwater): Castle of Economy 123, 128–9; Castle of Knowledge 123; Castle of the Queen 117, 119–21, 123; forested cityscape and hunting 124, 126–7; relics of urban furniture 124–5, 127; safeguard priorities (Queen, economy and knowledge) 108–13; transport system 122–3, 127; vertical living 106, 114–18
Paris: Eiffel Tower 283; infrastructural developments 64–5, 276; inhabitable bridges 285
Perfection (utopian community development): community well-being 240–2, 247; development plan 238–9; green strategies 241, 243–4, 247–9; housing 236, 245–7
Petra, Jordan 83, 85
Piano, Renzo: Kansai airport 24
pigs: 'Animal Farm' (Orwell) 139, 147; biogas for energy, futuristic sources 130, 139, 146, 147–9; Danish farms 139, 147; inflatable notoriety 181
Pink Floyd 181
'Pleasantville' (Ross) 237
polders 255–7
pollution: Ganges' multi-use issues 86; poor air quality, Los Angeles 267
post-war society 37, 40
precipitation changes, global 11
Priestley, J.B. 254
'Prisoner, The' 97
Pullman, Philip 36
pyramids, ritualistic sites 36, 60, 64, 74

Randall, Lisa 41
religious and ritualistic sites: Blue Mosque, Istanbul 71, 74; cathedral cities 71; Christian and Muslim 71; classic civilizations 36; cremations and burials 85–6, 88–9; Eridu (Iraq) 61; Ganges River 84–6; holy wells 187; mosques 71; pyramids, Egypt 36, 60, 64

renewable energy, futuristic sources: biogas from pig farming 139, 147–9; solar swan 132–41
resource management: commodities 35; human survival 41; sustainable cities 35
Rio de Janiero: favelas 92, 94; street life 66
rivers: Ganges' multi-use issues 84–6; strategic importance 85, 271–2
robot ethics 33
Rogers, Richard 27, 265, 267, 271, 276
Roman infrastructure: aqueducts and water management 164–5, 167, 170; multi-use facilities 167–70
Rossi, Aldo 180
Rudofsky, Bernard 83, 180
Ruscha, Ed 267
Rykwert, Joseph 65

San Francisco 34, 170, 250
Sant'Elia, Antonio 20
Sassen, Saskia 33, 77
science fiction (SF): architectural influences 27; artificial islands 22–4; classic publications 18, 38–9, 44, 48–9; corporate infrastructures 287; cryonics 151; currency, religion and ritual 35–7; design inspiration 7, 211; energy of destruction 29, 31; fear and speculation 40–1, 117, 237; futurism and machinery 25–6; infrastructure scales 21, 23, 97; political regimes 25, 40, 42, 93, 181; reproduction 41–2; Retro-Future 37, 40; robots and androids 32, 33–4; speculative visions and innovations 19–20, 43, 45, 47; Steampunk 40; sustainable provision 28–9, 34–5; transport systems 30, 31, 32, 171; Urban Futures, inspired infrastructures 48–59; utopian vision 211, 289
Sealand, Principality of 97, 100
sea level rises: effects and projections 10, 151, 155; flooding issues 9, 10–11, 107, 131; heritage, preservation challenges 155; ice melts, Greenland 131, 139; water security and saltwater 11–12
Self, Will 107, 181
service infrastructures: alcohol related 262–3; beach economy 265, 267; luxury living, Dubai 263, 265
Shanghai 11–12
Shirow, Masamune 87
Situationists 37
skyscrapers 75, 76, 159
slum dwellings, real and fictional 25, 87, 92–3, 96
South Africa: slum redevelopment 25; slums, cinematic view 93
Spain: granaries 180–1; Segovia's aqueduct 164, 165, 167
Spratly Islands 100
St Albans, UK 71
Stapledon, Olaf 28
StarTree project 233
'Star Wars' films 32, 40, 151, 263
Stern Review (2006) 11, 193
streets, multi-functional 65, 66
Stuller, Jennifer K. 40
Swift, Jonathan: 'Gulliver's Travels' 23, 37
Swine Under the Sweltering Skies (sustainable energy): Dynamic Duo of Denmark (DDD) 130, 139; Heliotropic Android Swans (energy/protection) 132–8, 147; Swine Squad and Porktopia 139, 142–6, 147–9

Tange, Kenzo 26, 285
Tanizaki, Junichiro 45
Tao, Rongjia 101, 103
Terasawa, Kazumi 87
territory and boundaries: Afghanistan's land rights 174; China's global infrastructures 100–1; micronations 97, 100; political propositions 103; Vatican City's independence 97–9; West Bank Barrier 96–7
transport systems: 20th Century innovations 31, 33; cable cars, San Francisco 170; Paris Périphérique's congestion 276; Suez Canal expansion 173
Tribillon, Justinien 276
Trumbull, Douglas: 'Silent Running' 23, 27
Trump, Donald 103

index

'Tsotsi' (Hood) 93
Turkey: alcohol regulation 262; Çatalhöyük settlement 79; Istanbul 68-9, 71, 74; underground settlements 83
Twenty Thousand Fish Above The Sea (portable sustainability): Fish, infrastructure construction 192, 194-5; Fish, prototype assembly 196-201; multi-use adaption and integration 206-8; portable infrastructures 202-5
Twilley, Nicola 227

Underground City, Montreal 82
underground constructions: artificial islands, Dubai 263, 265; Bruges' beer industry 262; cave dwellings 83, 85; commercial infrastructures 82; depictions in science fiction 82; sewerage networks 25, 43, 65, 77, 167; transport systems 83, 272; water treatment and supply 13, 167, 185-9
United Kingdom (UK): financial independence 123; suburbia concept 96; tree planting and flood reduction 103, 127; utility infrastructures 181-3, 185; wind energy 177; see also London
United Nations: artificial islands 100; comics as information channel 131; Democracy Fund initiatives 277; ecological damage concerns 173, 263; heritage, preservation challenges 155; UN Habitat 9; West Bank Barrier 96; World Water Development Report 190
United States (US): Afghanistan, invasion impacts 173-4; cable cars, San Francisco 170; Californian droughts, potential solution 191; capitalist vision 287; company towns 285, 287; controversial walls 96, 103; elevated walkway systems 171; food industry infrastructures 227; grain elevators and silos 180; Hoover Dam, visionary infrastructure 251, 252-5; ice trade 180; infrastructure renewal underfunded 251; Kennedy's space program 251, 254; Los Angeles' leisure economy 265, 267; post-war society 37, 40; San Francisco 34, 170, 250; skyscrapers, New York 75, 76; water systems, New York 13, 185-7; wind energy 177; windpump applications 175
Urban Futures: cultural diversity 46; resource management 56, 58-9; science fiction as prophetic guide 50-4, 55, 57
urban metabolism indicators 12
urban planning: Boulder City, utilitarian design 254-5; defensive infrastructures 103, 105; infrastructure legacies 170; inspirational practicalities 43, 45; intelligent design that connects 273, 276; open, public space 67-71, 77, 265, 267; population growth issues 28; see also Perfection (utopian community development)
utility infrastructures: Basilica Cistern, Istanbul 186, 187; Battersea Power Station 181; gasometers, UK 181-3, 185; stepwells in India 187-9; water towers, New York 185-7; water treatment plant 184
utopianism: architectural dismissal 26; El Dorado, explorer's quests 279, 283; garden cities (UK) 7; glass infrastructures 283; human flaws 28; interpretations in science fiction 29, 31, 42, 279; literary visions 279; new world exploration 287; vertical ambitions 285

Vance, Jack: 'Rumfuddle' 28-9
Vatican City 97-9
Vauban, Marquis de 81
Venice: flooding issues 16-17; freshwater wells 166; Isola di San Michele Cemetery 88-9
Verne, Jules 34, 47
'Vertical Farm Project' 14
Vienna 65, 82

walkway systems 170-1, 172, 173
'WALL-E' 28
Walter, Damien 36
'Wandering Turtle' (Brodsky/Utkin) 193
water management: Istanbul's water cisterns 186, 187; New York's systems 13, 185-7; Roman aqueducts and systems 164-5, 167, 170; sewerage networks 25, 43, 65, 77, 167; stepwells in India 187-9
water security: desalination, prohibitive costs 191; German civil defense 189-90; Shanghai's saltwater issues 11-12; United Nations reports 190; water as commodity 35, 191, 255; water treatment plant 184; women and water collecting 189
'Water Tank Project' 185, 187

'Waterworld' 23-4
Wells, H.G.: 'A Modern Utopia' 29; 'The Time Machine' 227, 233; utopian novels 20, 42, 171
Wells, Matthew 75
West Bank Barrier 96-7
Whiteread, Rachel 185
Willis, Connie 20
wind energy: windmills 174-5; windpumps 175; wind turbines 175, 177
Winer, Dave 41
Wong, Kar-wai 93
World Bank 9, 11, 12
World Health Organization 235
world population: displacement risks 9, 11, 193; growth projections 9, 28
World Wide Fund for Nature 235
Wright, Frank Lloyd 159, 283

Zuiderzee Works 257

303